Cases in Marketing Management

Cases in Marketing Management

Kenneth L. Bernhardt
College of Business Administration
Georgia State University

Thomas C. Kinnear
Graduate School of Business Administration
The University of Michigan

Fourth Edition—1988

BUSINESS PUBLICATIONS, INC.
Plano, Texas 75075

© BUSINESS PUBLICATIONS, INC., 1978, 1981, 1985, and 1988

ISBN 0-256-03676-4

Library of Congress Catalog Card No. 87-70723

Printed in the United States of America

234567890K54321098

To Kathy and Karen
To Connie, Maggie, and Jamie

Preface

Marketing is an exciting and dynamic discipline. Unfortunately, much of the excitement is hidden among the definitions and descriptions of concepts that are a necessary part of basic marketing textbooks. We believe that one way to make the study of marketing exciting and dynamic is to use cases. Cases allow the student to work on real marketing problems, to develop an appreciation for the types of problems that exist in the real world of marketing, and to develop the skills of analysis and decision making so necessary for success in marketing and other areas of business. Cases represent as close an approximation of the realities of actually working in marketing as is possible without taking a job in the field.

Your task as a user of this casebook is to work hard to develop well-reasoned solutions to the problems confronting the decision maker in each of the cases. A framework to assist you in developing solutions is presented in Part 1 of this book. Basically, you will be using this, or some other framework suggested by your instructor, to analyze the cases in this book. By applying this framework to each case that you are assigned, you will develop your analytic skills. Like all skills, you will find this difficult at first. However, as you practice, you will get better, until it will become second nature to you. This is exactly the same way one develops athletic or musical skills.

The cases in this book represent a broad range of marketing problems. The book contains consumer and industrial cases, profit and nonprofit cases, social marketing cases, specific marketing area cases, and general cases, plus cases on marketing and public policy. Each case is designed to fit into a specific section of a course in marketing management. The cases are long and complex enough to require good analysis, but not so long and complex to be overly burdensome. Within sections, cases do vary in terms of difficulty and complexity.

Users of the first three editions will note that the fundamental thrust and positioning remains the same in this edition. However, we do note the following changes. First, 16 new cases have been added. Second, a number of cases with greater complexity have been added to allow more in-depth work.

This book contains 42 cases and 2 case-related exercises. Twenty-three of the cases and both exercises were written by the authors of this book. In some instances we had a coauthor, and we have noted the names of the coauthors on the title pages of the cases concerned. We wish to thank these coauthors for their assistance and for allowing us to use the cases: Bruce Bassett, Stephen Becker, Danny N. Bellenger, C. Merle Crawford, Jeanne De Amicis, Sarah Freeman, Tom Ingram, Susan A. Johnstal, Constance M. Kinnear, G. Ludwig Laudisi, Sherri McIntyre, James Novo, Larry M. Robinson, James Scott, Chris S. Thomas, Kevin Tucker, and John S. Wright.

We would like to thank the executives of the organizations who allowed us to develop cases about their situations and who have released these cases for use in this book.

The remaining 19 cases were written by many distinguished marketing casewriters. We appreciate them allowing us to reproduce their cases here. The names of each of these persons are noted on the title page of the cases concerned. They are: Vincent J. Blasko, Christopher Gale, Karl Gustafson, Kenneth G. Hardy, Cleon L. Hartzell, Jr., H. Michael Hayes, Sherri Herman, C. B. Johnston, Jay E. Klompmaker, Fred W. Kniffin, Charles M. Kummel, Aylin Kunt, Zarrel V. Lambert, Michael P. Mokwa, David D. Monieson, Roger More, Rowland T. Moriarty, Jr., James E. Nelson, Charles H. Patti, Douglass G. Norvell, Michael R. Pearce, Don E. Schultz, Anne Senausky, Hirotako Takeuchi, George Taucher, Mark Traxler, Larry Uniac, Carolyn Vose, Martin Warshaw, and William R. Woolridge.

We would also like to thank our colleagues at Georgia State University, the University of Michigan, and the Case Research Association for their helpful comments and their classroom testing of cases.

Kenneth L. Bernhardt
Thomas C. Kinnear

Contents

Part 1

An Orientation to the Case Method

Chapter 1

Note to the Student on the Case Method

The case method is different from other methods of teaching, and it requires that students take an active role rather than a passive one. The case method places the student in a simulated business environment and substitutes the student in the place of the business manager required to make a set of decisions. To define it, a case is:

> typically a record of a business issue which actually has been faced by business executives, together with surrounding facts, opinions, and prejudices upon which the executives had to depend. These real and particularized cases are presented to students for considered analysis, open discussion, and final decision as to the type of action which should be taken.[1]

With the case method the process of arriving at an answer is what is important. The instructor's expectation is that the student will develop an ability to make decisions, to support those decisions with appropriate analysis, and to learn to communicate ideas both orally and in writing. The student is required to determine the problem as well as the solution. This method of teaching thus shifts much of the responsibility to the student, and a great deal of time is required on the part of the student.

The case method often causes a great deal of insecurity on the part of students who are required to make decisions often with very little information and limited time. There is no single right answer to any of the cases in this book, an additional source of insecurity. The goal is not to develop a set of right answers, but to learn to reason well with the data available. This process is truly learning by doing.

Studying under the case method will result in the development of skills in critical thinking. The student will learn how to effectively reason when dealing with specific problems. The development of communication skills is also

---

[1] Charles I. Gragg, "Because Wisdom Can't Be Told," *Harvard Alumni Bulletin*, October 19, 1940.

important, and students will learn to present their analysis in a cogent and convincing manner. They must defend their analysis and plan of action against the criticism of others in the class. In the class discussion, individual students may find that the opinions of other members of the class differ from their own. In some cases this will be because the individual has overlooked certain important points or that some factors have been weighted more heavily compared to the weighting used by other students. The process of presenting and defending conflicting points of view causes individual members of the class to reconsider the views they had of the case before the discussion began. This leads to a clearer perception of problems, a recognition of the many and often conflicting interpretations of the facts and events in the case, and a greater awareness of the complexities with which management decisions are reached.

In preparing for class using the case method, the student should first read the case quickly. The goal is to gain a feel for the type of problem presented in the case, the type of organization involved, and so on. Next, the student should read the case thoroughly to learn all the key facts in the case. The student should not blindly accept all the data presented, as not all information is equally reliable or relevant. As part of the process of mastering the facts, it frequently will be desirable to utilize the numerical data presented in the case to make any possible calculations and comparisons that will help analyze the problems involved in the case. The case will have to be read a number of times before the analysis is completed.

The student must add to the facts by making reasonable assumptions regarding many aspects of the situation. Business decision making is rarely based on perfect information. All of the cases in this book are actual business cases and the student is provided with all the information that the executives involved had at their disposal. Often students cannot believe the low level of information available for decision making, but this is often the case. What is required in those situations is the making of reasonable assumptions and learning to make decisions under uncertainty. There is often a strong reluctance on the part of the student to do this, but the ability to make decisions based on well-reasoned assumptions is a skill that must be developed for a manager to be truly effective.

Once the student has mastered the facts in the case, the next step is to identify and specify the issues and problems toward which the executive involved should be directing his or her attention. Often the issues may be very obscure. Learning to separate problems from symptoms is an important skill to learn. Often there will be a number of subissues involved and it will be necessary to break the problem down into component parts.

The next step in the student's case preparation is to identify alternative courses of action. Usually there are a number of possible solutions to the problems in the case, and the student should be careful not to lock in on only one alternative before several possible alternatives have been thoroughly evaluated.

The next step is to evaluate each of the alternative plans of action. It is at this stage of the analysis that the student is required to marshall and analyze all the facts for each alternative program. The assumptions the student is required to make are very important here, and the student must apply all the analytical skills possible, including both qualitative and quantitative.

After all the alternatives have been thoroughly analyzed, the student must make a decision concerning the specific course of action to take. It should be recognized that several of the alternatives may "work," and that there are a number of different ways of resolving the issues in the case. The important consideration is that the plan of action actually decided upon has been thoroughly analyzed from all angles, is internally consistent, and has a high probability of meeting the manager's objectives.

Once an overall strategy has been determined, it is important that consideration be given to the implementation of that strategy. At this stage, the student must determine who is to do what, when, and how. A professor may start out a class by asking the question, "What should Mr. Jones do tomorrow?" Unless the students have given some thought to the implementation of the strategy decided upon, they will be unprepared for such a question. Improper implementation of an excellent strategy may doom it to failure, so it is important to follow through with appropriate analysis at this stage.

During the class discussion the instructor will act more as a moderator than a lecturer, guiding the discussion and calling on students for their opinions. A significant amount of learning will take place by participating in the discussion. The goal is for the students to integrate all their ideas, relating them to the goals of the company, the strengths and weaknesses of the company and its competition, the way consumers buy, and the resources available. A suggested framework for the integration of these ideas is presented in the next chapter of this book in the Appendix titled "Outline for case analysis."

The student's classroom discussion should avoid the rehashing, without analysis, of case facts. Students should recognize that the professor and all the other students in the class have thoroughly read the case and are familiar with the facts. The objective therefore is to interpret the facts and use them to support the proposed plan of action. The case method obviously requires a great deal of preparation time by the student. The payoff is that after spending this time adequately preparing each of the steps described, the student will have developed the ability to make sound marketing management decisions.

Chapter 2

Introduction to Marketing Decision Making

In Chapter 1, you were introduced to your role in the execution of an effective case course in marketing. In summary, the primary task is to complete a competent analysis of the cases assigned to you. If you have never undertaken the analysis of a marketing case before, you are probably wondering just how you should go about doing this. Is there some framework that is appropriate for this task? Indeed, there are a number of such frameworks. The purpose of this chapter is to present one such framework to you. We think you will find it useful in analyzing the cases in this book.

An Outline for Case Analysis

The Appendix to this chapter is the summary document for the approach we believe that you should use for case analysis. We suggest that you apply the types of questions listed there in your analysis. Figure 2–1 provides an overview of this outline. Basically, we are suggesting that you begin by doing a complete analysis of the *situation* facing the organization in the case. This *situation analysis* includes an assessment of (1) the nature of demand for the product, (2) the extent of demand, (3) the nature of competition, (4) the environmental climate, (5) the stage of the life cycle for the product, (6) the skills of the firm, (7) the financial resources of the firm, and (8) the distribution structure. In some cases legal aspects may also form part of a good situation analysis. The premise here is that one cannot begin to make decisions until a thorough understanding of the situation at hand is obtained.

Once a detailed situation analysis is prepared, one is in a position to summarize the *problems* and *opportunities* that arise out of the situation analysis. These problems and opportunities provide an organized summary of the situation analysis. This in turn should lead to the generation of a set of *alternatives* that are worthy of being considered as solutions to the problems and actualizers of the opportunities.

FIGURE 2-1 Overview of a framework for case analysis

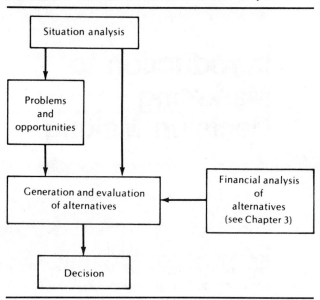

These alternatives are then *evaluated* using arguments generated from (1) the detailed situation analysis, (2) the summary statement of problems and opportunities, and (3) relevant financial analysis (break-even points, market shares, and so on). The use of financial analysis is discussed in Chapter 3. The point here is that we use the situation analysis to generate and evaluate alternative programs. The pros and cons of each alternative are weighed as part of this evaluation and a *decision* is then reached.

A Good Case Analysis

The question naturally arises: In applying the outline in the Appendix to a case, how do I know when I have done a good analysis? The purpose of this section is to raise some points that are often used by instructors to evaluate either an oral or written analysis.

1. Be complete. It is imperative that the case analysis be complete. There are two dimensions to this issue. First is that each area of the situation analysis must be discussed, problems and opportunities must be identified, alternatives must be presented and evaluated using the situation analysis and relevant financial analysis, and a decision must be made. An analysis that omits parts of the situation analysis, or only recognizes one alternative, is not a good analysis. Second, each area above must be covered in good depth and with insight.

2. *Avoid rehashing case facts.* Every case has a lot of factual information. A good analysis uses facts that are relevant to the situation at hand to make summary points of analysis. A poor analysis just restates or rehashes these facts without making relevant summary comments. Consider the use of a set of financial facts that might appear in a case:

Rehash: The current ratio is 1.5:1, cash on hand is $15,000, retained earnings are $50,000.

Analysis: Because of a very weak financial position, as demonstrated by a poor cash position and current ratio, the firm will be constrained in the activities it can undertake to ones requiring little immediate cash outlay.

3. *Make reasonable assumptions.* Every case is incomplete in terms of some piece of information that you would like to have. We would, of course, like to have all the necessary information presented to us in each case. This is not possible for two reasons. First, it would make the cases far too long to be capable of being analyzed in a reasonable period of time. Second, and more important, incomplete information is an accurate reflection of the real world. All marketing decisions are made on the basis of incomplete information. Often, it just costs too much or takes too long to collect the desired information.

A good case analysis must make realistic assumptions to fill in the gaps of information in the case. For example, the case may not describe the purchase decision process for the product of interest. A poor analysis would either omit mentioning this or just state that no information is available. A good analysis would attempt to present this purchase decision process, by classifying the product (a shopping good?), and drawing on the student's real-life experience. Could you not describe the purchase decision process for carpeting, even though you have never read a research report about it?

The reasonableness of your assumptions will be challenged by your fellow students and instructor. This is one of the things that makes case discussions exciting. The point is that it is better to make your assumptions explicit and incorporate them in your analysis than to use them implicitly or not make them at all. If we make explicit assumptions we can later come back and see if our assumptions were correct or not.

4. *Don't confuse symptoms with problems.* In summarizing a firm's problems a poor analysis confuses the symptoms with real problems. For example, one might list two problems as (1) sales are down and (2) sales force turnover is high. This would not be correct. These are symptoms. The real problem is identified by answering the question: Why are sales down or why is sales force turnover high? For example, sales force turnover may be high due to inadequate sales training. But this may not yet be the root problem. You still need to ask: Why is sales training inadequate? It may be that the sales manager has ignored this area through his or her lack of knowledge of how to train people. What you do is keep asking ''why'' until you are satisfied that you have identified the root problem.

5. Don't confuse opportunities with taking action. One can recognize an opportunity, but not take any action related to it. For example, a large market for a product may exist. This is an opportunity. However, a firm may decide not to compete in this market due to lack of resources or skills or the existence of strong competition. Decisions involve the complex trading-off of many problems and opportunities. Thus, don't make statements that direct action—''target to . . . , promote as . . . ,'' and the like—as opportunity statements.

6. Deal with objectives realistically. Most cases present a statement from management about their objectives. For example, it might say they want a sales growth rate of 25 percent per year. Good analysis critically evaluates statements of objectives and revises them if necessary. Then it uses these revised objectives as part of the argument about which alternative to select. Poor analysis either ignores the stated objectives or accepts them at face value.

7. Recognize alternatives. A good analysis explicitly recognizes and discusses alternative action plans. In some cases, these alternatives are stated in the case. In other cases, the student must develop alternatives beyond those stated in the case. A poor analysis explicitly recognizes only one or two alternatives or only takes the ones explicitly stated in the case.

8. Don't be assertive. In some case analyses, the decision that was made is clear to the reader or listener in about the first sentence of the situation analysis. The whole rest of the analysis is then a justification of the desired solution. This type of analysis is very poor. It in effect has asserted an answer before completing a situation analysis. Usually, other alternatives are ignored or treated as all bad, and the desired solution is treated as all good. You must do your situation analysis and recognize alternatives before evaluating them and reaching a decision.

9. Discuss the pros and cons of each alternative. Every alternative always has pros and cons. A good analysis explicitly discusses these. In a poor analysis there is no explicit discussion of the pros and cons of each alternative. Problem and opportunity statements serve as the basis of your pro (opportunities) and con (problems) discussion. Different ones relate to specific alternatives.

10. Make effective use of financial and other quantitative information. Financial data (break-even points and so on) and information derived from other quantitative analyses can add a great deal to a good case analysis. Totally ignoring these aspects or handling them improperly results in a poor case analysis. This analysis should be presented in detail in a written appendix or in class if asked for. However, in the body of a paper or in an oral discussion present only the summary conclusions out of the analysis. Say "The break-even point is 220,000 units," and be prepared to present the detail if asked.

11. Reach a clear decision. You must reach a clear decision. You might like to hedge your bets and say "maybe this, maybe that." However, part of the skill of decision making is to be forced to reach a decision under ambiguous circumstances and then be prepared to defend this decision. This does not mean that you do not recognize limitations of your position or positive aspects of other positions. It just means that despite all that, you have reached a particular decision.

12. Make good use of evidence developed in your situation analysis. In reaching a decision, a good analysis reaches a decision that is logically consistent with the situation analysis that was done. This is the ultimate test of an analysis. Other students may disagree with your situation analysis and thus your resultant conclusion, but they should not be able to fault the logical connection between your situation analysis and decision. If they can, you have a poor case analysis.

The "Outline for case analysis" contained in the Appendix is designed to assist you in doing case analysis. You should keep the points stressed in this section in mind when you apply this outline.

Appendix

Outline for case analysis*

Overview of Analysis Structure

   I. Situation analysis
      A. Nature of demand.
      B. Extent of demand.
      C. Nature of competition.
      D. Environmental climate.
      E. Stage of product life cycle.
      F. Cost structure of the industry.
      G. Skills of the firm.
      H. Financial resources of the firm.
      I. Distribution structure.
  II. Problems and opportunities
      A. Key problem areas.
      B. Key opportunities.
      C. On balance, the situation is.
 III. Generation and evaluation of alternative marketing programs
      A. Objectives defined.
      B. Marketing mix/program decisions.
 IV. Decision

Details of Analysis Structure

I. SITUATION ANALYSIS

    A. Nature of demand

        The purpose of this section is to make *explicit* your beliefs and assumptions regarding the nature of the purchase decision process (consumer or industrial) for the goods or services under investigation. In case analysis we are concerned primarily with developing your *skills* of analysis to identify areas of problems and opportunities and in developing well-supported marketing program recommendations. Conflicting student beliefs and assumptions should lead to interesting and enlightening class discussion regarding the nature of the purchase decision process and its implication for marketing programs. We hope that through this type of class discussion, you will increase your sensitivity to, and understanding of, buyers and

---

* This outline is adapted from an unpublished note by Professor James R. Taylor of the University of Michigan. Used with permission.

their behavior. Again, the value of this type of analysis concerns its application to better *reasoned* and *supported* marketing program decisions. Hopefully, the development of your skills in this area has value in improving your *judgment capabilities* and in increasing your understanding of marketing decision making.

Analysis areas and questions

1. How do buyers (consumer and industrial) currently go about buying existing products or services? Describe the main types of behavior patterns and attitudes.
    a. Number of stores shopped or industrial sources considered.
    b. Degree of overt information seeking.
    c. Degree of brand awareness and loyalty.
    d. Location of product category decision—home or point of sale.
    e. Location of brand decision—home or point of sale.
    f. Sources of product information and current awareness and knowledge levels.
    g. Who makes the purchase decision—male, female, adult, child, purchasing agent, buying committee, so on?
    h. Who influences the decision maker?
    i. Individual or group decision (computers versus candy bar).
    j. Duration of the decision process (repeat, infrequent, or new purchase situation).
    k. Buyer's interest, personal involvement or excitement regarding the purchase (hairpins versus trip to Caribbean).
    l. Risk or uncertainty of negative purchase outcome—high, medium, or low (specialized machinery versus hacksaw blades) (pencil versus hair coloring).
    m. Functional versus psychosocial considerations (electric drill versus new dress).
    n. Time of consumption (gum versus dining room furniture).

    Basically, we are attempting to determine the *who, what, where, when, why,* and *how* of the purchase decision.

    Note: The key to using the above analysis is to ask what are the implications for marketing programs? For example, if the purchase (brand) decision is made in the store and branding is not important to the buyers, what implication does this have for national TV advertising versus in-store display? Do you see how you might *use* this information to support a recommendation for intensive distribution and point-of-purchase promotion and display?

2. Can the market be meaningfully segmented or broken into several homogeneous groups with respect to "what they want" and "how they buy"? Criteria:
    a. Age.

    b. Family life cycle.
    c. Geographic location.
    d. Heavy versus light users.
    e. Nature of the buying process.
    f. Product usage.

Note: For each case situation, you should determine whether a more effective marketing program could be developed for each segment versus having an overall program for all segments. The real issue is whether tailoring your program to a segment will give you a competitive advantage. Of course, there may be negatives to this strategy in terms of volume and cost considerations.

B. Extent of demand

The purpose of this section is to evaluate demand in an aggregate and quantitative sense. We are basically concerned with the actual or potential size of the overall market and developing sound estimates of company sales potential.

Analysis areas and questions
1. What is the size of the market (units and dollars) now and what will the future hold?
2. What are the current market shares and what are the selective demand trends (units and dollars)?
3. Is it best to analyze the market on an aggregate or on a segmented basis?

Note: We are basically concerned with making *explicit* assumptions regarding primary and selective demand trends. These estimates are critical to determining the profit (loss) potential of alternative marketing programs.

C. Nature of competition

The purpose of this section is to evaluate the present and future structure of competition. The key is to understand how the buyer evaluates alternative products or services relative to his or her needs.

Analysis areas and questions
1. What is the present and future structure of competition?
    a. Number of competitors (5 versus 2,000).
    b. Market shares.
    c. Financial resources.
    d. Marketing resources and skills.
    e. Production resources and skills.
2. What are the current marketing programs of established competitors? Why are they successful or unsuccessful?
3. Is there an opportunity for another competitor? Why?

4. What are the anticipated retaliatory moves of competitors? Can they neutralize different marketing programs we might develop?

   Note: Failure to correctly evaluate demand and competition is one common reason for unprofitable marketing programs. Also, Sections A, B, and C are analysis areas particularly important in making decisions concerning "positioning" your product and developing the marketing program to support your positioning strategy.

D. Environmental climate

It's not hard to identify current marketing programs that have been highly disrupted by a changing environmental climate. The energy crisis together with pollution, safety, and consumerism concerns, can bring many such examples to mind. We are sure you can identify firms who have benefited from the energy crisis. The point is that the environment is constantly changing and those organizations which can adapt to change are the ones which enjoy long-run success.

Analysis areas and questions
1. What are the relevant social, political, economic, and technological trends?
2. How do you evaluate these trends? Do they represent opportunities or problems?

E. Stage of product life cycle

The purpose of this section is to make explicit assumptions about where a product is in its life cycle. This is important because the effectiveness of particular marketing variables may vary by stages of the life cycle.

Analysis areas and questions
1. In what stage of the life cycle is the product category?
   a. What is the chronological age of the product category? (Younger more favorable than older?)
   b. What is the state of the consumers' knowledge of the product category? (More complete the knowledge—more unfavorable?)
2. What market characteristics support your stage of life-cycle evaluation?

F. Cost structure of the industry

Here we are concerned with the amount and composition of the marginal or additional cost of supplying increased output. It can be argued that the lower these costs, the easier it may be to cover the costs of developing an effective marketing program (see accompanying table). Basically one is relating the level of fixed cost to variable cost.

	Marginal costs	
	High*	Low†
Selling price per unit	$1.00	$1.00
Variable costs per unit	0.80	0.10
Contribution per unit	$0.20	$0.90

* Such as the garment and auto industries.
† Such as the hotel and telephone industries.

G. Skills of the firm

The purpose of this section is to critically evaluate the organization making the decision. Here, we effectively place limits on what they are capable of accomplishing.

Analysis areas and questions
1. Do we have the skills and experience to perform the functions necessary to be in this business?
    a. Marketing skills.
    b. Production skills.
    c. Management skills.
    d. Financial skills.
    e. R&D skills.
2. How do our skills compare to competitors?
    a. Production fit.
    b. Marketing fit.
    c. Etc.

H. Financial resources of the firm

Analysis areas and questions
1. Do we have the funds to support an effective marketing program?
2. Where are the funds coming from, and when will they be available?

I. Distribution structure

The purpose of this area is to identify and evaluate the availability of channels of distribution.

Analysis areas and questions
1. What channels exist and can we gain access to the channels?
2. Cost versus revenue from different channels?
3. Feasibility of using multiple channels?
4. Nature and degree of within and between channel competition?
5. Trends in channel structure?
6. Requirements of different channels for promotion and margin?
7. Will it be profitable for particular channels to handle my product?

II. PROBLEMS AND OPPORTUNITIES

Here we prepare a definite listing of *key* problems and opportunities identified from the situation analysis which relate to the specific issues or decision questions faced by management.

A. **Key problem areas**

B. **Key opportunities**

C. **On balance, the situation is:**
   1. Very favorable.
   2. Somewhat favorable.
   3. Neutral.
   4. Somewhat unfavorable.
   5. Very unfavorable.

Note: At this point, the critical issue is whether a profitable marketing program can be formulated or whether a current marketing program needs to be changed in order to overcome the problem areas and/or take advantage of opportunities.

III. EVALUATION OF ALTERNATIVE MARKETING PROGRAMS

A marketing program consists of a series of marketing mix decisions which represent an integrated and consistent "action plan" for achieving predetermined goals. Different marketing programs may be required for various target segments. For a given target segment, alternative programs should be formulated and evaluated as to the effectiveness of each in achieving predetermined goals.

A. **Objectives defined**
   1. Target market segments identified.
   2. Volume to be sold (dollars or units).
   3. Profit analysis (contribution analysis, break-even analysis, ROI, etc.).

B. **Marketing mix/program decisions**
   1. Product decisions
      a. Develop new product(s).
      b. Change current product(s).
      c. Add or drop product from line.
      d. Product positioning.
      e. Branding (national, private, secondary).
   2. Distribution decisions
      a. Intensity of distribution (intensive to exclusive).
      b. Multiple channels.
      c. Types of wholesalers and retailers (discounters, so on).
      d. Degree of channel directness.
   3. Promotion decisions
      a. Mix of personal selling, advertising, dealer incentives, and sales promotion.

        b. Branding—family versus individual.
        c. Budget.
        d. Message.
        e. Media.
  4. Price decisions
        a. Price level (above, same or below).
        b. Price variation (discount structure, geographic).
        c. Margins.
        d. Administration of price level.
        e. Price leadership.

Note: The above four decision areas involve specific strategy issues which together form a marketing program.

The key to effective marketing decision making is to evaluate alternative marketing programs using information from the situation analysis. The pros and cons for each alternative should be presented and discussed.

IV. DECISION

The outcome of the evaluation of alternatives is a decision. You must make a decision. Case analysis is designed to develop your skills in making well-supported and reasoned marketing decisions. The quality of your reasoning is much more important than reaching any particular decision. Generally, if your situation analysis is different (you perceive the facts differently and have made different assumptions) from someone else, you should reach different decisions.

Chapter 3

Financial Analysis
for Marketing
Decision Making

In Chapter 2, we laid out an approach to marketing decision making. The "Outline for case analysis" summarized this approach. There is, however, one more important aspect of a competent case analysis that was not presented in that outline. This is the financial analysis of the alternatives presented in a case.

The ultimate goals of all marketing activities are usually expressed in financial terms. The company has a particular return on investment in mind, or growth in earnings per share. Proposed marketing activities must thus be evaluated for their financial implications. Can you imagine asking your boss for $1 million for a new distribution center or an advertising program without having to present the financial implications of such a request? It does not happen in the real marketing world, nor should it happen in a good case analysis.

Financial analysis can be complex. Our purpose here is to present some simple financial calculations that can be useful in case analysis. More sophisticated financial techniques are left to courses in financial management. Basically, the advanced techniques add little to the understanding of the cases in this book, and take too much time and effort for the reader to implement.

It should clearly be understood that financial considerations are only one aspect in the evaluation of marketing alternatives. Marketing alternatives cannot be reduced to a set of numbers. Qualitative aspects derived from the situation analysis are also relevant. Sometimes the qualitative aspects are consistent in terms of pointing to an alternative to select. In other cases, they may point to different alternatives. The task of the student is to formulate both types of arguments for each alternative, and to select an alternative based upon which arguments the student thinks should carry the most weight.

This chapter assumes that the student is familiar with elementary financial accounting concepts. What we will present here are some useful concepts not usually presented in basic accounting courses.

Contribution

Contribution per unit is defined as the difference between the selling price of an item and the variable costs of producing and selling that item. It is in essence the amount of money per unit available to the marketer to cover fixed production costs, corporate overhead and, having done that, to yield a profit. So, if a manufacturer sells an item for $12.00, and the variable costs are $8.40, then

$$\text{Contribution per unit} = \text{Selling price} - \text{Variable costs}$$
$$= \$12.00 \quad\quad - \$8.40$$
$$= \$\ 3.60$$

Each unit this company sells gives it $3.60 to cover fixed costs.

Total contribution is the contribution per unit times the number of units sold. So, if this firm sold 20,000 units:

$$\text{Total contribution} = \text{Contribution per unit} \times \text{Units sold}$$
$$= \$\ 3.60 \times 20,000$$
$$= \$72,000$$

If the total relevant fixed costs of this product were $42,000, the *profit* earned by this product would be:

$$\text{Profit} = \text{Total contribution} - \text{Fixed costs}$$
$$= \$72,000 \quad\quad - \$42,000$$
$$= \$30,000$$

Costs

In determining contributions and profit we used the terms *variable cost* and *fixed cost*. At this point we want to define them more formally. Variable costs are those costs that are fixed *per unit* and therefore, vary in their total amount depending upon the number of units produced and sold. That is, it takes a certain amount of raw materials and labor to produce a unit of product. The more we produce the more total variable costs are.

Fixed costs are costs that remain constant in *total amount* despite changes in the volume of production or sales. These costs would thus vary per unit depending upon the number of units produced or sold.

Sorting out which costs are variable and fixed is important in good case analysis. The rule to apply is: if it varies in *total* as volume changes, it is a variable cost. Thus, labor, raw materials, packaging, salespersons' commissions would be variable costs. Note that all marketing costs except commissions would be considered fixed costs. Don't be fooled if a marketing cost or other fixed cost is presented in a per unit form. It may look like a variable cost, but it is not. It is only that much per unit at one given volume. For example, if we are told that advertising cost per unit will be $1, what this means is that at the end of the year when we divide total sales into advertising expenditures the result is expected to be $1 per unit. What we must be told is at what volume advertising is expected to be $1 per unit. If the expected volume level is 300,000 units, we then know that the firm intends to spend $300,000 ($1 × 300,000 units) on advertising. This $300,000 is a fixed cost. Note that if they sold less than 300,000 units, the cost per unit would exceed $1 and vice versa. So beware of fixed costs that are allocated to units and presented in a per unit form.

Break Even

A solid perspective on many marketing alternatives can often be obtained by determining the unit or dollar sales necessary to cover all relevant fixed costs. This sales level is called the break-even point. We define

1. Break-even point in units $= \dfrac{\text{Total fixed costs}}{\text{Contribution per unit}}$

2. Break-even point in dollars $= \dfrac{\text{Total fixed costs}}{1 - \dfrac{\text{Variable cost per unit}}{\text{Selling price per unit}}}$

or

$$= \begin{matrix}\text{Break-even point} \\ \text{in units}\end{matrix} \times \begin{matrix}\text{Selling price} \\ \text{per unit}\end{matrix}$$

Let's illustrate these definitions. Suppose that (1) direct labor is $7.50 per unit, (2) raw materials are $2 per unit, (3) selling price is $22 per unit, (4) advertising and sales force costs are $400,000, and (5) other relevant fixed costs are $100,000.

$$
\begin{aligned}
\text{Contribution per unit} &= \text{Selling price} - \text{Variable costs} \\
\text{Contribution per unit} &= \$22.00 - (\$7.50 + \$2.00) \\
&= \$22.00 - \$9.50 \\
&= \$12.50
\end{aligned}
$$

$$
\begin{aligned}
\text{Break-even point in units} &= \frac{\text{Total fixed costs}}{\text{Contribution per unit}} \\
&= \frac{\$400,000 + \$100,000}{\$12.50} \\
&= 40,000 \text{ units}
\end{aligned}
$$

$$
\begin{aligned}
\text{Break-even point in dollars} &= \frac{\$500,000}{1 - \dfrac{\$9.50}{\$22.00}} \\
&= \frac{\$500,000}{1 - 0.4318181} = \$880,000
\end{aligned}
$$

Alternatively

$$
\begin{aligned}
\text{Break-even point in dollars} &= 40,000 \times \$22.00 \text{ per unit} \\
&= \$880,000
\end{aligned}
$$

Profit Targets

Breaking even is not as much fun as making a profit. Thus, we often want to incorporate a profit target level into our calculations. Basically, we are answering the question: at what volume do we earn X profits? Covering a profit target is just like covering a fixed cost. So in the previous example, if we set $60,000 as our profit target we would have to sell an additional number of units equal to:

$$\text{Units to cover profit target} = \frac{\text{Profit target}}{\text{Contribution per unit}}$$

$$= \frac{\$60,000}{\$12.50} = 4,800 \text{ units}$$

Total units to reach this target is

$$40,000 + 4,800 = 44,800 \text{ or } \frac{\$500,000 + \$60,000}{\$12.50} = 44,800$$

Break-even analysis is a useful tool for comparing alternative marketing programs. It tells us how many units must be sold, but does not help us with the critical question of how many units will be sold.

Market Share

$$\text{Market share} = \frac{\text{Company sales level}}{\text{Total market sales}}$$

This calculation adds perspective to proposed action plans. Suppose that the total market sales are 290,000 units and our sales level needed to break even is 40,000 units. Thus, the required market share to break even is:

$$\frac{40,000}{290,000} = 13.8\%$$

The question then to ask is whether this market share can be obtained with the proposed marketing program.

Capital Expenditures

Often a particular marketing program proposes expenditures for capital equipment. These would be fixed costs associated with the proposed program. Typically, they should not all be charged to the relevant fixed cost for that proposal. For example, suppose that $5 million are to be expended for equipment that will last 10 years. If we charge all this to the break-even calculation in year one, it will be very high. Further, for years 2 through 10, the break-even point will fall substantially. It is better to allocate this $5 million equally over the 10 years. Thus $500,000 would be a relevant fixed cost in each year associated with the equipment. What one needs to do is to make some reasonable assumption about the useful life of capital assets and divide the total cost over this time period.

Relevant Costs

The issue often arises as to what fixed costs are relevant to a particular proposal. The rule to use is: a fixed cost is relevant if the expenditure varies due to the acceptance of that proposal. Thus, new equipment, new research and development, and so on, are relevant. Last year's advertising or previous research and development dollars, for example, do not vary with the current decision and thus are not a relevant cost of the proposed program. Past expenditures are referred to as *sunk costs*. They should not enter into current decisions. Decisions are future oriented.

Corporate overhead presents a special problem. Generally, it does not vary with a particular decision. We don't fire the president in selecting between marketing programs. However, in some instances, some overhead may be directly attributable to a particular decision. In this instance it would be a relevant cost. We should recognize that to stay in business a firm must cover all its costs in the long run. Also, from a financial accounting point of view all costs are relevant. This type of accounting is concerned with preparing income statements and balance sheets for reporting to investors. In marketing decision making we are interested in managerial, not financial, accounting. Managerial accounting is concerned with providing relevant information for decision making. It, therefore, only presents costs that are relevant to the decision being considered. Such things as allocated overhead or amortized research and development costs only serve to confuse future-oriented decisions.

Margins

Often a case will present us with a retail selling price, when what we really want to know is the manufacturer's selling price. To be able to work back to get the manufacturer's selling price, we must understand how channel margins work.

When firms buy a product at a particular price and attempt to sell it at a higher price, the difference between the cost price and the selling price is called margin or markup or mark-on. Thus,

$$\text{Selling price} = \text{Cost price} + \text{Margin}$$

An example could be:

$$\$1.00 = \$0.80 + \$0.20$$

So a company has bought a product for \$0.80, added on a \$0.20 margin and is charging \$1.00 for the product.

Margins are usually expressed as percentages. This raises the question as to the base on which the margin percentage should be expressed: the cost price or the selling price. Here, if the \$0.20 margin is expressed as a percentage of selling price the margin is \$0.20/\$1.00 = 20 percent. If it were expressed as a percentage of cost price, the margin is \$0.20/\$0.80 = 25 percent. The most common practice in marketing is to express margins as a percentage of selling price. Margins expressed in this fashion are easier to work with, especially in a multilevel channel situation. Unless explicitly stated otherwise, you may assume that all margins in the cases in this book use selling price as the relevant base.

A number of different types of margin-related problems arise. They include:

1. Determining the selling price, given you know the cost price and the percentage margin on selling price. Suppose that a retailer buys an appliance for $15 and wants to obtain a margin on selling price of 40 percent. What selling price must be charged? The answer $21 is not correct because this margin ($6 = $15 × 0.4) would be on cost price. To answer this question we must remember one fundamental relationship. This is that

$$\text{Selling price} = \text{Cost price} + \text{Margin}$$

Here we are taking selling price as the base equal to 100 percent, so we can write

$$100\% = \$15 + 40\%$$

That is, the cost price plus the margin must add to 100 percent. Clearly the $15 must then be 60 percent of the desired selling price. Thus,

$$\text{Derived selling price} = \$15/60\%$$
$$= \$25$$

The dollar margin is then $10 which is $10/$25 = 40 percent of selling price.

The general rule then is to divide one minus the percentage margin expressed as a decimal on selling price, into the cost price. For example, if cost price is $105 and the margin on selling price is 22.5 percent, then the desired selling price is $105/(1 − 0.225) = $105/0.775 = $135.48.

2. Conversion of margin bases. Sometimes a margin is given on a cost price basis, and we wish to convert it to a selling price base or vice versa. How do we make the conversion? Suppose that a product costs $4.50 and sells for $6.00. The margin is $1.50. On a selling price basis the margin is $1.50/$6.00 = 25 percent. On a cost price basis the margin is $1.50/$4.50 = 33.33 percent. The conversion from one percentage margin to the other is easy if we remember that selling price is composed of two parts: margin and cost.

For selling price base.

$$\text{Selling price} = \text{Margin} + \text{Cost}$$
$$\$6.00 = \$1.50 + \$4.50$$

or more important

$$100\% = 25\% + 75\%$$

For cost price base.

$$\text{Selling price} = \text{Margin} + \text{Cost}$$
$$\$6.00 = \$1.50 + \$4.50$$

but here the cost is the 100 percent base, so

$$\$6.00 = \$1.50 + 100\%$$

or

$$133.33\% = 33.33\% + 100\%$$

That is, the selling price should be thought of as 133.33 percent of the cost price. *Conversion from selling price to cost price base.*

$$\text{Selling price} = \text{Margin} + \text{Cost}$$
$$100\% = 25\% + 75\%$$

So if we want to convert the 25 percent margin to a cost price basis, the 75 percent that is the cost becomes the relevant base and

$$\text{Margin as a percentage of cost price} = \frac{25\%}{75\%} = 33.33\%$$

Note that this is exactly the same as dividing $1.50 by $4.50.
    A simple formula for making this conversion is

$$\text{Percentage margin on cost price} = \frac{\text{Percentage margin on selling price}}{100\% - \text{Percentage margin on selling price}}$$

In our example this is

$$\frac{25\%}{100\% - 25\%} = \frac{25\%}{75\%} = 33.33\%$$

Note that the only piece of information that we need to make this conversion is the margin percentage on selling price.
    Conversion from cost price to selling price base.

$$\text{Selling price} = \text{Margin} + \text{Cost}$$
$$133.33\% = 33.33\% + 100\%$$

The margin is 33.33 percent and the relevant selling price base is 133.33 percent, so

$$\text{Margin as a percentage of selling price} = \frac{33.33\%}{133.33\%} = 25\%$$

Note that this is exactly the same as dividing $1.50 by $6.00.
    A simple formula for making this conversion is

$$\text{Percentage margin on selling price} = \frac{\text{Percentage margin on cost price}}{100\% + \text{Percentage margin on cost price}}$$

In our example this is

$$\frac{33.33\%}{100\% + 33.33\%} = \frac{33.33\%}{133.33\%} = 25\%$$

Note that the only piece of information that we need to make this conversion is the margin percentage on cost price.

Multiple Margins

Often a manufacturer gives a suggested retail selling price and suggested retail and wholesale margins. For example, the suggested retail price may be $7.50 with a retail margin of 20 percent and a wholesale margin of 15 percent. To determine the manufacturer's selling price in this situation we simply take the appropriate margins off one at a time. Thus

Retail selling price	$7.50
Less retail margin (20% of $7.50)	1.50
Equals retail cost price or wholesale selling price	6.00
Less wholesale margin (15% of $6.00)	0.90
Equals wholesale cost price or manufacturer's selling price	$5.10

No matter how many levels there are in the channel, the approach is the same. We simply take the margins off one at a time. Note that we cannot just add up the margins and subtract this amount. Here 20% + 15% = 35%, and 35% of $7.50 is $2.63, making the manufacturer's selling price $7.50 − $2.63 = $4.87. This is not correct.

This chapter has outlined some financial concepts that add greatly to our abilities to make sound marketing decisions. These concepts should be applied where needed in the cases in this book.

Chapter 4

A Case with a
Student Analysis

The fundamental premise of this book is that one learns by doing. However, one can also learn from example. The purpose of this chapter is to give an example of a case analysis. The framework of analysis presented in the previous two chapters will be used here in order to clarify how one can use the framework.

The case presented in this chapter, "Crow, Pope, and Land," is a broad issue marketing case that has no textbook or single "correct" answer. A student analysis of the case follows the case presentation, and in the last section of the chapter we present our commentary on the case analysis.

We suggest the following steps in using this chapter:

1. Read and prepare your analysis of "Crow, Pope, and Land." This will give you a better perspective on the case analyses presented in this chapter.
2. Read and evaluate the analysis presented here. You may wish to use the points that constitute a good case analysis as presented in Chapter 2.
3. Read our commentary on the case analysis. Compare our view with yours.

Case

Crow, Pope, and Land Enterprises*

In early August 1973, Mr. Dan Thatcher, vice president of CPL Condominium Enterprises, a subsidiary of Crow, Pope, and Land Enterprises, was planning his strategy for a new condominium project in Jacksonville, Florida. The project was an important one, since it was the company's first attempt to diversify out of the Atlanta area with nonresort condominiums. Earlier in the year, Mr. Thatcher had arranged the purchase of an option on a 40-acre tract just outside the city limits of Jacksonville, and the company had to renew the option in the next week or they would lose their earnest money. Before the senior officers of the firm would approve the final purchase of the land for approximately $700,000, Mr. Thatcher had to prepare a report discussing the proposed marketing strategy for the condominiums to be built there. His report was to include discussions of the target market, the specifications of the units to be built, the price range of the condominiums, and the promotional strategy to be used in marketing the units.

Company Background

Crow, Pope, and Land Enterprises, Inc., is a developer of residential, commercial, and motel/hotel real estate property, with projects located throughout the world. Headquartered in Atlanta, Georgia, the company was incorporated on January 14, 1967, under the name Lincoln Construction Company. Trammell Crow of Dallas, Ewell Pope of Atlanta, and Frank Carter of Atlanta were the shareholders of the company. Mr. Pope and Mr. Carter had been partners in the real estate brokerage firm, Pope and Carter Company, which had acted as the leasing agent for several of Trammell Crow's developments, namely, Chattahoochee Industrial Park and Greenbriar Shopping Center. These two adventures had proved so successful that the three men decided to strengthen their association and form Lincoln Construction Company.

* This case was written by Kenneth L. Bernhardt and John S. Wright, Professor of Marketing, Georgia State University. Copyright © 1975 by Kenneth L. Bernhardt.

In June 1972, Mr. Pope and Mr. Carter decided to establish separate organizations, both of which were formed in association with Mr. Crow. Crow and Carter started Crow, Carter, and Associates, Inc., and Crow and Pope, in association with A. J. Land, Jr., became owners of the continuing company, Crow, Pope, and Land Enterprises, Inc.

The company is organized on a project-management basis, with a managing partner who oversees and is responsible for every phase of the development assigned to each project. The manager of each project acts very much like the president of a small company, with the exception that he has the resources of a much larger corporation to draw upon when it is felt that added expertise would be of assistance. Most of the project managers, including Mr. Thatcher, are young, aggressive MBA graduates from leading schools of business administration.

The projects in which the company is involved range from the development of apartment complexes, condominium complexes, office parks, and shopping centers, to ''total community'' complexes complete with apartments, condominiums, single-family houses, retail outlets, parks, schools, office buildings, and recreational facilities. The firm has recently become active in the development of urban community centers containing a mixture of such features as commercial high-rise office buildings, luxury hotels, retail shopping facilities, and other pedestrian conveniences designed for high architectural impact in downtown environments. Examples of some of the company's projects include the $100 million Atlanta Center project (a large Hilton Hotel together with office buildings and shopping areas in downtown Atlanta), the $40 million Sheraton Hong Kong Hotel and shopping mall complex, and the Cumberland, Fairington, and Northlake total community complexes in Atlanta. Cumberland, a $65 million joint venture development with the Metropolitan Life Insurance Company, will, upon its completion in 1978, include a 1 million-square-foot enclosed shopping center, 750,000 square feet of office space, 1,800 apartments and condominiums situated around a 17-acre lake, an indoor tennis center, and hotel/motel facilities.

Crow, Pope, and Land has built a number of condominium and apartment complexes in Atlanta, and has built more condominiums than any other developer in the area. Among the projects currently being sold in the Atlanta area are projects oriented toward retired couples, young swingers, sports-minded couples and families, and couples who want to own their own residence but cannot afford single-family detached housing. The company also has several resort projects in Florida.

Background on the Jacksonville Project

The original idea for the Jacksonville project came out of a meeting Mr. Thatcher had in early 1973 with Lindsay Freeman, another vice president of CPL Condominium Enterprises. In discussing the future goals and directions for the subsidiary, they decided that a high priority should be placed on reducing their dependence on the Atlanta condominium market where all nine of their projects were located. Since different geographic areas often were at different stages of the business cycle, they felt expansion into new geographical areas would provide a hedge against economic downturns as well as opening up profitable new markets for their products.

The first decision made was that they should concentrate on the Southeast, within a 400-mile radius of Atlanta, allowing greater control from the Atlanta headquarters. Also, projections of housing market demand indicated that this region of the country would experience rapid growth in the coming few years.

A number of cities, including Memphis, Louisville, Chattanooga, Mobile, and Birmingham, were investigated as possible sites for a condominium project. Several criteria were established. The area had to have several condominium projects already in existence since they did not want to be the first project in the area. Their experience had shown that the pioneers had to undertake a large educational effort, which usually took two years and a lot of money. The city should have a population of at least 250,000 so that it would absorb a large number of condominiums if the company decided to add other projects at a later date. Lastly, the area should have a large number of residents in the target market for condominiums—young married couples and "empty nesters," couples whose children are grown and have moved out of the home.

Using census data, information obtained from Chambers of Commerce, and other real estate research sources, Thatcher narrowed the choice to Charlotte, North Carolina, and Jacksonville, Florida. In both places, condominiums had been marketed for two to three years, and a number of developments were being built. In Charlotte, however, the only land that was available for immediate development was not particularly well suited for multifamily building. It had been decided that land that had been zoned for condominium development, with utilities easily accessible, would be favored to avoid the normal two-year period to get undeveloped raw land ready for development. Therefore, it was without reservation that Thatcher made the decision to expand into the Jacksonville market.

Background on the Jacksonville Area

Jacksonville is the most populated city in Florida and ranks second in the Southeast and 23rd in the United States. In October of 1968, the city adopted a new charter which consolidated the city and county governments. All of Duval County is now operated as one government, and the consolidation made the new city of Jacksonville the largest city in the continental United States with 840 square miles (537,664 acres). To put the figures into comparative terms, the city is two thirds the size of the state of Rhode Island.

Recent growth has brought many young people to the Jacksonville area. In 1970, the median age of the population was 26 years, compared to 32.3 years for the state of Florida and 28.3 years for the total United States. Duval County has a large, rapidly growing economy, with a balanced employment profile and a rather diversified economic base. This diversification has produced a stable economy by minimizing its sensitivity to both industrial and national business cycles.

For a distance of approximately 100 miles in all directions, the area surrounding the city is predominantly rural in character. With over 500,000 residents, Jacksonville is the commercial and cultural center of northeast Florida and southeast Georgia. It is one of the principal distribution, insurance, and convention centers in the Southeast.

One of the major impacts on the city's economy is the presence of three large military installations in the area, particularly the Jacksonville Naval Air Station located in the southern part of the county on the St. Johns River just north of the city of Orange Park. This facility is one of the largest naval air bases in the United States. It is supported by a smaller air station, Cecil Field, located in the western part of the county, where several air squadrons operate in preparation for air carrier qualifications. The third facility, the Mayport Carrier Basin east of Jacksonville, has berthing capacity for three of the country's largest aircraft carriers. The military installations employ approximately 34,000 people including some 5,000 civilians, 9,000 shore-based military personnel, and 20,000 mobile/afloat military. Another 5,000 military employees are expected to be transferred to these facilities in the next year or two.

Extensive bedroom areas are forming just outside Duval County, reflecting lower tax rates, lower land prices, an absence of restrictive zoning ordinances, and a preference for suburban living. Also, the city of Jacksonville was busing children to achieve racial integration in the schools, and many residents were moving to Orange Park and other areas of Clay County (just south of Duval County) where there was no busing of students. The impact of all these factors made Clay County, and the Orange Park area in particular, a rapidly growing area.

The city of Orange Park lies adjacent to and south of the Duval County line, and is approximately 15 miles from the central business district of Jacksonville. Exhibit 1 presents a map of the area showing the location of Orange Park in relation to the naval air station, Cecil Field, and the business district of Jacksonville.

After talking with many real estate people in the area, and after reviewing the statistics presented in Exhibit 2, Mr. Thatcher decided to obtain an option on a 40-acre tract of land just west of the city limits of Orange Park. As shown in the exhibit, the residents of Orange Park had an above-average median family income for the area, and were better educated than Duval County residents. Also, over half the population in the area worked outside the county (principally in Duval County). Thatcher thought the higher-income, better-educated people would be receptive to condominiums. Also, he felt that the close proximity to Duval County would be attractive to many potential purchasers.

Access to the site is off Blanding Boulevard (State Road 21 on the map), a heavily traveled two-lane thoroughfare with development, for the most part, consisting of commercial and single-family residential development. Within the

EXHIBIT 1
Map of Jacksonville and Orange Park area

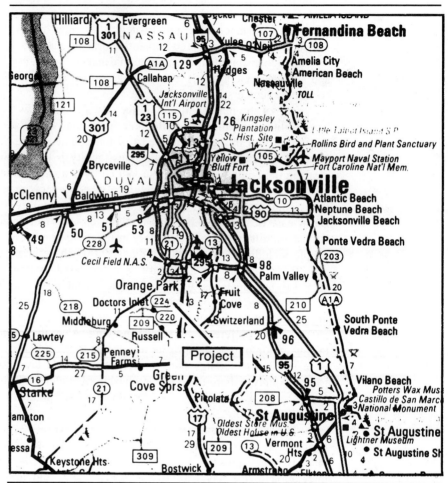

EXHIBIT 2
Selected statistics for Orange Park, Clay County, and Duval County/Jacksonville

	City of Orange Park	Clay County	Duval County/ Jacksonville
Total population, 1970	7,677	32,059	528,865
Median family income, 1970	$10,021	$8,430	$8,671
Median school years completed— 1970, adults	12.5	12.1	12.0
Percent of residents who work outside the county	—	53.5%	2.6%
Percent of residents who have lived in the same area for five years or more, 1970	30.0%	45.6%	67.1%

past year a considerable amount of multifamily development had occurred, but it was mainly concentrated further northeast in the vicinity of U.S. Highway 17.

Within one mile of the site to the north is a minor shopping center with a Winn-Dixie supermarket as the cornerstone tenant. Two and one half miles north, a 1 million-square-foot regional shopping center is being developed and is scheduled to open in 1975. The school system in the area is rated excellent, and several elementary schools as well as junior and senior high schools are in close proximity to the site. Churches of all denominations and hospital and recreation facilities are all well represented in the area.

The current housing market in the Orange Park area is composed substantially of single-family houses, with prices of these units beginning at $32,000. Apartments in the vicinity of the site have achieved 100 percent occupancy, with many of the apartments renting for between $150 and $200 per month. There are a number of condominium projects in the area, as shown in Exhibit 3, although almost all of them are situated much farther north. The price range on these condominium projects typically begins in the low $30,000 range and goes up to almost $60,000.

Marketing Strategy

The first question Thatcher had to resolve concerned the target market for the condominiums. There were three basic strategies he had been considering: (*a*) a specialty type product with a large amenity package oriented toward active, young "swinging" couples; (*b*) a project oriented toward the retiree market; or (*c*) a project oriented toward families who wanted to purchase their residence but could not afford a single-family house. Crow, Pope, and Land had considerable experience in building all three types of condominiums in the Atlanta area, and Thatcher was reluctant to consider other types of condominiums that the company had not had experience with. He reasoned that taking a product that had worked elsewhere would reduce some of the risk of entering a new, relatively unknown market. Also, use of a product that the company had built in Atlanta would save the cost of architect's fees, and he would be in a better position to negotiate with a contractor to build the units because he would know in advance what the costs should be (building costs in the Jacksonville area were virtually the same as costs in Atlanta).

EXHIBIT 3
Condominium projects in the Orange Park area

Project	Rooms	Square feet	Price range
Bay Meadows	2BR,2B –3BR,3B	1,350–2,243	$34,850–$48,300
Solano Grove	1BR,1B –3BR,3B	874–2,006	26,100– 58,200
Regency Woods	2BR,2B –4BR,2½B	1,456–2,102	35,500– 45,900
Sutton Place	2BR,2½B–4BR,2½B	1,366–1,842	31,500– 38,000
Baytree	2BR,1½B–4BR,3½B	1,404–2,214	32,000– 46,750
The Lakes	2BR,2B –3BR,2½B	1,330–2,050	37,500– 59,400
Oxford Forest	2BR,1½B–3BR,2½B	1,282–1,622	28,500– 35,500

Thatcher had located a site along the St. Johns River that would be suitable for the specialty, high-amenity product. There might be some environmental problems with the Army Corps of Engineers, who had jurisdiction over the site, but he thought these could be worked out. The Orange Park site under option would not be suitable for this type of project, which Thatcher thought should be built around a body of water. With the high land cost for an appropriate site, and with the high cost for all the recreational amenities, the company would have to price the condominiums under this strategy at about $40,000 (the same price charged for the comparable Riverbend Condominiums in Atlanta).

The optioned site was also not acceptable for the second alternative, a project oriented toward the retirees' market. Experience in Atlanta had shown that retired couples preferred to purchase condominiums with a golf course on site, and the present site was not suited for development of a golf course. Thatcher had located several possible sites suitable for this alternative several miles south of the property under option. Because of the very large investment involved in building a golf course, he felt that a project oriented toward this market would have to be a large one to support the high fixed cost of the golf course.

If the company decided to purchase the property under option, about 12 units per acre could be constructed, or about 480 in total. As they did with almost all their projects, the units would be built in several phases, with phase I consisting of 50 units. Thatcher had determined that units built in the Fairgrounds project in Atlanta could be built and sold profitably in Orange Park for $24,900 for a 1,040-square-foot, two-bedroom unit, and $29,900 for a 1,265-square-foot, three-bedroom unit. The price per square foot was comparable to the other condominium projects in the area, and the total price was well below most of them because of the smaller size. In addition to the difference in square footage and price, the Fairgrounds models also had different exteriors than the typical ones sold in the Jacksonville area; the Fairgrounds units used brick and aluminum siding, whereas most of the others had a stucco exterior. Although he basically believed that the Jacksonville condominium prospect was very similar to the Atlanta prospect, he wondered whether he should incorporate some stucco treatment into the exterior of the units if he should decide to follow through with this strategy.

Another issue he had not resolved concerned the extent to which the strategy should be oriented toward the large (and growing) military market. If he did define his target market as the military market, what impact would this have on the physical product and on his promotional strategy, which was still to be determined? Close to half of the residents of Orange Park worked at one of the three military installations in the area, and both the naval air station and Cecil Field were within seven miles of the proposed site. He was aware of the large word of mouth influence in the Navy—an apartment project not far from the site which was just beginning to lease new units had gone from 5 percent Navy to 30 percent Navy in less than two months.

Another question which concerned Thatcher was the low sales rate of the other condominiums in the area. He thought the reason was the relatively high prices, which caused them to compete directly against single-family housing. Also, he had shopped all the projects and found the onsite salesmen to be very uninformed and uninterested in selling the condominiums. He felt certain that this was hurting sales, but was still not sure that the consumers in the Jacksonville/Orange Park area would buy condominiums, even in the price range he was proposing.

The senior officers of Crow, Pope, and Land would also expect a detailed promotional strategy as part of his report. In working with budget figures, he had determined that he could afford to spend $22,000 for promotion (1.5 percent of sales) for the first 50 units, which would be about 12 months' projected sales. Brochures, signs, business cards for salesmen, and other miscellaneous items would cost about $2,000 leaving $20,000 for media and production costs.

Crow, Pope, and Land used a small local advertising agency for all their apartment and condominium advertising in Atlanta. Thatcher was uncertain about the role he wanted the agency to play in this project, and was worried that the agency was not attuned to the Jacksonville market. He wondered whether he should try to hire a Jacksonville agency, but was afraid that the account was too small for anyone to pay much attention to it. Also, he felt that the retainer that any decent agency would want to handle the account, about $3,000, could be better spent on media. He had studied advertising and promotion in courses in college, and thought he should consider creating the advertising himself.

There were really only two alternatives for media strategy in the Jacksonville area—radio and newspaper. There were nine AM radio stations and four FM stations. The rates for the four largest stations were all about the same, between $25 and $30 for a one-minute spot during drive time (6–10 A.M. and 3–7 P.M.) and about 20 percent cheaper at other times, assuming 12 spots per week for 13 weeks. There were two daily newspapers in Jacksonville, a morning paper with 210,000 circulation and an evening paper with 148,000 circulation. As a result of common ownership, there was a combination rate available which was only 10 percent higher than the $13.16 per column inch rate for the morning paper alone. The morning paper had a Sunday edition, with a circulation of 182,000 and a cost per column inch of $13.72.

Mr. Thatcher was also concerned about what message to use in his promotional campaign. He was uncertain to what extent they should mention the fact that there was no busing to schools, an important advantage for many potential buyers. He was worried that other people might be upset with the implied racism in such a campaign. He was also concerned with the implications for the advertising creative strategy as a result of the target market decision concerning whether or not to concentrate on the military market. Another advertising issue was the extent to which the copy should promote the fact that Crow, Pope, and Land was a large Atlanta developer, and that this was their first North Florida project.

The one decision Thatcher had made was that there was much opportunity for the company in the Jacksonville market, and, therefore, much opportunity for him personally to expand his responsibilities in the company. As a result, he wanted to make a recommendation that the company definitely enter the market; the only uncertainty was the strategy to be followed. The company had paid $1,000 for the initial option on the Orange Park property. Next week they had to either pay $20,000 to renew the option for 90 days or lose their $1,000 investment. If they decided to renew the option, this would give them time to arrange for the financing of the project and to arrange a production schedule with the contractors. They had to begin this planning immediately since it usually took at least six months to build condominiums, and that meant that they would have to act fast if they wanted to be selling condominiums by the height of the selling season in June. As he sat down to write the report containing his recommendations, Thatcher realized that a decision to renew the option would be a commitment to actually build the units he recommended.

Example Situation Analysis of Crow, Pope, and Land Enterprises (CPL)

CPL Condominium Enterprises, a subsidiary of CPL Enterprises, Inc., a residential housing and commercial builder, had built a number of *condominium* complexes in Atlanta, designed for specific segments such as retired couples, young swingers, families, and low-middle-income couples. In addition, they had several resort projects in Florida.

In order to reduce their dependence on the Atlanta condominium market, a *goal* of expanding into new geographic areas where profitable markets were opening up was developed by two CPL Condominium Enterprises VPs. The *tactics* were to choose a city of at least 250,000 population within a 400-mile radius of Atlanta, since forecasts of the housing market projected rapid growth in this general region in the coming few years. Dan Thatcher was to put together a marketing *strategy* discussing product, price, place, and promotion to pursue in reaching this goal. Since this discussion is centered around Dan Thatcher's review of the Orange Park condominium market, it will be assumed here that the product is *condominiums*. In the larger context of the company, which will be touched on at the end of this paper, the product considered is *housing*.

A. NATURE OF DEMAND

1. How do buyers currently go about buying condos?

In the search for housing, buyers will generally define the neighborhood they are interested in, then select among the alternatives within their price range. The decision to buy a condominium, rather than a single-family detached dwelling, may be influenced by several factors—price, ease of maintenance, amenities, and the like—which are discussed more thoroughly in part 2. The buyer will seek information to a high degree through media, family, friends, co-workers, real estate brokers, and, if available, reports on developers of other condominium projects to ascertain their reputation and workmanship quality. After looking at a number of developments, the decision of which condo to buy will probably be made at home or after a second or third look at the property under consideration. Sources of information about condos in the Jacksonville/ Orange Park area are probably newspapers, some broadcast coverage, and word of mouth. Although condos have existed for more than two years in this area, awareness level seems low due to the slow sales of condos in the area. In 1973, condos were not in vogue, and hence buyer knowledge and acceptability were not particularly well developed. The decision to purchase is made by the adults; if a couple, by a joint decision. This is the most important major purchase decision in most people's lives, thus much time, thought, and effort goes into the decision process. The buyer is highly influenced by the salesperson, the physical plant itself, friends, the real estate broker, and possibly the bank loan officer. This is usually a new purchase situation, evoking high interest, personal involvement, and excitement by the buyer. All of these factors contribute to a high risk associated with a poor purchase decision—it's hard to get rid of a condo that no one else wants either! A number of functional considerations enter into the decision, such as location, utilities, and convenience (more on this in part 2). A number of psychosocial considerations also enter into the decision, such as aesthetics, social contact, safety, prestige, and self-esteem. This being a durable good, the consumption time is long term.

2. Can the market be meaningfully segmented?

Due to CPL Condominium Enterprises' expertise in building condo complexes geared toward specific segments, and since Dan Thatcher desires to use an existing set of plans for the new condo development, it seems best to segment the market into those areas CPL can build for— namely, singles, retired couples, and young (low-middle-income) families. In addition, due to the demographic composition of the area (50 percent employed by the Navy), a Navy/military segment is also relevant. Attributes important to each segment are ranked in Table 1. Table 2 then ranks these attributes together with the housing options in the area, limited here to condos, single-family homes, and rental apartments, since these are the housing types mentioned in the case. Since the median age of Jacksonville is 26, below both the Florida and national medians, we can probably safely assume that there are many young couples and singles associated with the large military labor base, perhaps a growing number of babies and children (helping to lower the median), and that the family life-cycle stage is generally early. Additional data on average household size, the age distribution, and income versus age would be helpful in this analysis. The high turnover rate of Orange Park residents suggests either a very mobile population or a very fast-growing area.

Comparing Tables 1 and 2, there is not a one-to-one correlation

TABLE 1

Attributes	Segments			
	Singles	Retirees	Young families	Navy (families)
Price	+ + + +	+ + + +	+ + + +	+ + + + +
Size	+	+	+ + + +	+ + +
Neighborhood	+ +	+ + +	+ + + +	+ +
Convenience to shopping	+ +	+ + +	+ + +	+
Schools	+	+	+ + + +	+ + +
Social acceptability	+ + + +	+ +	+ +	+ +
Social interaction	+ + + +	+ + +	+ +	+ +
Recreation/amenities	+ + + +	+ + + +	+ + +	+ + +
Safety	+ +	+ + + +	+ + + +	+ +
Low tax base	+	+ +	+ +	+ +
Accessibility to work	+ +	+	+ +	+ + + +
Mass transportation	+ +	+ + +	+ +	+ +
Access to entertainment	+ + +	+ +	+ +	+ +
Maintenance	+ + + +	+ + + +	+ + +	+ + +
Financing convenience*	+ + + +	+ +	+ + +	+ + +
Public works	+	+ + +	+	+
Land availability	+ +	+ +	+ + + +	+ +

* Defined as renting versus down payment/monthly mortgage commitments.

between all the boxed attributes of option: condo and segment. Note, however, that there is a correlation between options: apartment and singles segment.

B. EXTENT OF DEMAND

1. Sufficient demand for more condo housing?

Although there is limited information, one can still make some estimate of the total demand in the Jacksonville market. It is well known that nationally about 20 percent of the population moves each year. We also know from Exhibit 2 in the case that 32.9 percent of the population of Duval County (and a much higher percentage of Clay County) have lived there five years or less. On the basis of this information, we might expect about 5 percent of the households to be looking for a house; and, with an average of about 2.5 children and 4.7 people per family, the number of houses shifting hands may equal about 1 to 1.5 percent of the population or in the neighborhood of 6,000 to 7,000 homes. Even if we recognize that a

TABLE 2

| | Options | | |
| | Our condo | Rental apartment | Single-family home |
Attributes			
Price	+ + + +	+ + + +	+ +
Size	+	+ +	+ + + +
Neighborhood	+ + +	?	?
Convenience to shopping	+ + +	?	?
Schools	+	?	?
Social acceptability	+ +	+	+ + + +
Social interaction	+ + +	+ + +	+
Recreation/amenities	+ +	+ + +?	+
Safety	+ +	+	+ +
Low tax base	+ + +?	+?	+ + +?
Accessibility to work	+ + +?	+ +?	+ +?
Mass transportation	+	+	+
Maintenance	+ + + +	+ + + +	+
Financing convenience*	+	+ + + +	+
Land availability	+ +	+ +	+ + + +
Equity	+ + + +	+	+ + + +

* Defined as renting versus down payment/monthly mortgage commitments.

large proportion of the 20 percent of the population that move in a typical year consists of young people moving from one apartment to another, it would seem that this estimate of 6,000 to 7,000 homes is extremely conservative. Since Jacksonville is a very rapidly growing area full of economic activity, and since the "baby boomers" are just entering the age where they will be buying houses, we might raise this estimate to around 10,000 homes. With projected sales of 50 units the first year, Crow, Pope, and Land is trying to achieve around .5 percent of the market.

What part of this will be condos is the next issue to judge.

2. Current market shares

We have no information to judge this. It appears that single-family home purchases dominate the purchasing mode and that apartment rentals are 100 percent occupied. There may exist excess demand for apartments. This can raise apartment rents (if no new apartments will soon be built), making the price advantage of renting less of a factor over time. Selective demand trends suggest that consumer awareness of condo developments is increasing and, along with that, public acceptance. Since single-family homes start selling at $32,000, it could be that condos are not selling because people can just as easily afford single-family homes. Banks usually like housing to account for only 25 to 30 percent of one's gross income, hence these could be too high priced, even though they are less than the other alternatives. Purchasing the smaller condo at $24,000 would lead to the following results:

a.   12 percent, 20-year mortgage:

$$\frac{\$24,000}{7.469} = \$3,213.28 \text{ or } \$267.77/\text{month} = 32.1 \text{ percent of income.}$$

b.   8 percent, 20-year mortgage:

$$\frac{\$24,000}{9.818} = \$2,444.49 \text{ or } \$203.71/\text{month} = 24.4 \text{ percent of income.}$$

It would be difficult for the average person to finance anything but the lower-priced condo at the lower interest rate. Of course, when Thatcher needs to make his decision, he cannot foresee possible future increases in interest rates.

C. NATURE OF COMPETITION

1. Present and future structure of competition

Seven other condo projects in the general area as well as numerous single-family home developments exist. Market shares are unknown, although we know that rental apartments have 100 percent occupancy. Financial resources of competitors are unknown. Marketing resources and skills of condo competitors, judged by their salespeople, are poor. They lack interest, enthusiasm, and knowledge of the projects they are trying to sell. Production resources and skills of competitors are unknown.

2. Current marketing programs of established competitors

We do not know much but, judging from the slow sales, it might be reasonable to suppose that consumer awareness is low, knowledge of market needs is poor, and the salesperson's role is a very critical part of the competition's marketing program, although it seems to be unsuccessful.

3. Opportunity for another competitor?

The fact that the property Thatcher has an option to buy is *zoned* for condos indicates that the planning body of the county feels that condos will serve as one of the housing mixes for the area. Since the opportunity for CPL to drastically price cut the market exists, there does seem to be opportunity for another competitor. Whether buyer demand exists is another question, however.

4. Retaliatory moves of competitors?

Competitors can probably drop their prices somewhat. The other developments appear to be a few miles away from this one, though, so perhaps another condo development may not greatly affect the competitors.

D. ENVIRONMENTAL CLIMATE

1. Relevant social, political, economic, and technological trends

Since this project is located in the South, busing is a hot issue. People opposed to busing (which is taking place in Jacksonville/Duval County) will want to live in an area with no forced busing. Condominiums are just hitting the market—they are in a young product life-cycle stage, thus social acceptability is currently in the developing stage.

The last lottery for the Vietnam War draft took place in 1973. The war is starting to wind down. In 1975, some military ships were mothballed. Hence the lifeblood of Orange Park, which is over half military, will soon be in a transition stage. Basing a project on military personnel housing demand is probably very risky at this time.

Some of these factors may increase the attractiveness of condos. People will want to live closer to work, but in an area with low land rates and a low tax base due to the ever-increasing squeeze on their pocketbooks. A condo may be easier to keep cool; the accessibility to a pool, which a condo development in Florida is likely to have, may further increase its attractiveness.

E. STAGE OF PRODUCT LIFE CYCLE

The product category, condominiums, is at an early life-cycle point. Some people are aware of their existence, but the concept is not yet so well tested that people are rushing out to buy condos. As the product ages, and as more people begin purchasing condos, its social acceptability will increase. The slow sales of the present condo developments in the area are indicative of this lack of social acceptability due to the product's early life-cycle stage. Of course, other factors that are perhaps more important (price, location, etc.) enter into this, too. The fact that one of CPL's development criteria was that other condo projects should have existed in the area for at least two years supports the argument that an educational and acceptability process must first take place before the product sells well. The more knowledge the consumer has, the more he/she will want to buy this product.

F. COST STRUCTURE OF THE INDUSTRY

Comparing our project to the other projects' $/square feet range, the CPL project is about average in $/square foot price, although lower in total price due to the low square footage of the units. A comparison with competitors is presented in Table 3. The highs and lows are boxed. We know that $22,000 of selling costs equals 1.5 percent of sales. Hence, the first 50 units will bring in an expected revenue of

$$\frac{\$22,000}{.015} = \$1,466,667.$$

For sale of 480 units, total revenues would equal

$$\frac{480}{50} \times \$1,466,667 = \$14,080,003.$$

TABLE 3   Comparison of cost by competitor

Project	Rooms	Sq. ft.	Price range	$/Sq. ft. range
Bay Meadows	2B2B/3B3B	1,350–2,243	$34,850–$48,300	$25.81–$21.53
Solana Grove	1B1B/3B3B	879–2,006	26,100– 58,200	29.86– 29.01
Regency Woods	2B2B/4B2½B	1,456–2,102	35,500– 45,900	24.38– 21.84
Sutton Place	2B2½B/4B2½B	1,366–1,842	31,500– 38,000	23.06– 20.63
Baytree	2B1½B/4B3½B	1,404–2,214	32,000– 46,150	22.79– 21.12
The Lakes	2B2B/3B2½B	1,330–2,050	37,500– 59,400	28.20– 28.98
Oxford Forest	2B1½B/3B2½B	1,282–1,622	28,500– 35,500	22.23– 21.89
CPL	2 Bdr	1,040	$24,900	23.94
	3 Bdr	1,265	$29,900	23.64
Single-family home		Assume 1,400	$32,000	$22.86

Other costs we know of:

Land = $721,000 (include $1,000 + $20,000 in option).
Selling costs = 1.5% = $210,000 ($14 million × .015).

Assume construction is approximately $20/square foot:

1,000 square feet × 480 condos × $20/square foot
= $9,600,000 per condo, approximate.

Sales	$14,080,000	100%
CGS	9,600,000	68%
Gross margin	$ 4,480,000	32%
Sales	210,000	
Land	721,000	8%
Other (guess)	100,000	
Net profit (pretax)	$ 3,449,000	24%

The project looks profitable at this point, if these assumptions are valid. If the company highly leverages the development, this would be a very attractive investment indeed.

G.   SKILLS OF THE FIRM
1.   Marketing

Apparently the firm as a whole has been quite successful, and much of this success for a real estate company must be attributed to marketing. A small Atlanta advertising agency is used for the Atlanta apartment and condominium advertising, but Thatcher is not sure the agency will be able to adequately and successfully come up with a Jacksonville marketing plan. To hire a local Jacksonville agency, about $3,000 would need to be spent on a retainer, which Thatcher thought could be better spent on media.

Since he had studied advertising and promotion in college courses, Thatcher thought he had the skills to create the advertising himself. If CPL commonly has its project managers create the advertising for projects, then

I would question whether the marketing skills of the firm were really very good. I do not think Thatcher is who we want promoting a $14 million condo complex!

We do not know how successful CPL has been with its condo developments, but we can only assume that continued existence and expansion in the business means that it has been successful thus far, and hence its marketing is good.

2. Production

Again, we don't have too much data to access this, but judging from the size of some of the projects, such as the Atlanta Center Project, the Sheraton Hong Kong Hotel, and the Cumberland, Fairington, and Northlake total community complexes, CPL must be able to "produce" buildings or else it wouldn't be undertaking such large efforts. Thatcher says that CPL has experience building the three condominium types in Atlanta (swinging couples, retirees, and young families) and could thus negotiate well with the contractor in Jacksonville since he would have a good idea of what the actual costs would be. He also mentioned that this "product had worked"; therefore he thought it could work again. Also, perhaps the use of brick and aluminum siding exteriors is popular and well liked, thus helping the firm to sell a slightly different product better than the stucco exterior norm in Jacksonville.

3. Management

Apparently, the company has a lot of MBA types and, due to the project-management emphasis, fairly aggressive self-starters. Crow and Pope had a good record of success in the real estate brokerage business prior to their forming CP & L. It looks like we can assume the company has good management skills and talented, although perhaps overly confident, people on staff.

4. Financial

Their financial skills are probably very good, since the owners have over five years of experience in the business and the project managers, similar to Thatcher, have business training backgrounds/education. Due to the size of the projects the parent company is undertaking, we can assume it has a good financial relationship with its bank and must be doing well to continue getting large sums of financing. The subsidiary, CPL Condominiums, is thus backed by a strong parent company. The parent company is probably making nice profits from its hotel operations, as high margins are typically the rule in this area.

5. R&D

R&D in terms of a popular product design appears to be good, since it sounds like a brick and aluminum siding exterior condo is an attractive and long-lasting exterior. Modifying their developments to meet the needs of particular market segments in terms of amenities shows good insight in producing a product to meet the needs of the consumer.

However, the background research Thatcher has performed for judging the Jacksonville condo market is quite limited. He is basing his decision on very limited data. A much better decision could be reached with more research into demographic trends in the area, determining the mobility of the Navy personnel, and finding out how future road work will favorably or adversely affect this proposed condo development. The fact that apartments are 100 percent occupied but condo sales are slow should cause Thatcher to question whether condos are what is needed here. Perhaps apartments would be a better fit to community needs.

As far as comparing CPL's skills to the competitors, we do not know enough about the competitors, except that their marketing seems weak, to make a particularly valid comparison.

H. FINANCIAL RESOURCES OF THE FIRM

As the calculations in part F show, the financial return on this investment looks very attractive. Since CPL Condominium Enterprises has the backing of the parent company, I think it is safe to assume that financing this project will pose no problem.

I. DISTRIBUTION/PROMOTIONAL STRUCTURE AVAILABLE

Classic distribution institutions are not a directly relevant dimension here. However, the existence of an institutional structure for promotion is important.

This is where media advertising comes in: a number of types could be utilized, under the constraint of $20,000 for the first year's promotional activities after spending $2,000 for brochures, wages, and business cards. Advertising on commute time radio could take up most of this budget, if four radio stations are used, with 12 spots a week for 13 weeks (4 stations $\times$ $30/minute $\times$ 12 spots/week $\times$ 13 weeks = $18,700). Advertising in the newspaper only, using the Sunday rate of $13.72/column inch would allow $\frac{\$20,000}{13.72/\text{col. in.}}$ = 1,455 inches over 26 weeks. This is 56 column inches per week, which seems like a lot of newspaper coverage. A combination of these two mixes would probably be good. The Atlanta advertising agency would be able to determine what would be best. In addition, the agency might try to find a Navy newsletter to advertise in because this market, if encouraged to investigate the condo alternative, might through word of mouth be a very helpful advertising method. Also, the use of coupons in the paper to be exchanged for a gift upon coming to look at the development may further increase buying traffic. These media institutions are available for CPL use.

Problems and Opportunities

A. Problems
    1. Dan Thatcher:
        a. His inexperience in the Florida condominium market.
        b. His ambitiousness, possibly causing him to miss opportunities as he sees the "success" of this project promoting his career.

      c. His shortsightedness in only considering condominiums rather than apartments also, which may be more suited to the community needs.

2. Economic dependence of the areas on the three military installations.
3. Availability of close substitutes to condos, namely, similarly priced single-family housing.
4. The instability of the Orange Park housing market, symptomized by the high turnover/mobility.
5. Advertising agency located in Atlanta, with no promotion experience in this Florida, highly military market.
6. High prices of the projects.
7. Low social acceptability, as shown by the low demand.
8. Transportation:
   a. The project under consideration is located on a heavy use corridor. More development will cause traffic problems.
   b. New freeway allowing easy access to the navy base is under construction, thus easy accessibility to work is not yet present.
9. If the young swingers or retirees are the chosen market segment, need more land to put in amenities. Army Corps of Engineers may not approve other option plot if that one is pursued.
10. Need better demographic data to properly evaluate the market, demand, and supply.
11. Public still needs educating about the product itself.

B. Opportunities
1. Very attactive area to build, as there are low taxes, low land rates, and no busing.
2. Military market is large.
3. The aluminum siding and brick exterior condo can provide a new look and style to the Jacksonville condo market.
4. Market for rental housing is excellent, due to low vacancy rates, a large influence of relatively mobile military personnel, and low median age of the area.
5. Good reputation and experience of CPL. They know housing construction and costs. Financial strength of CPL.
6. Market open to new competitor; fast-growing regions are the Southeast and Florida.
7. The plot under option is zoned for condos.

C. On balance, the situation is:
1. Very favorable for *housing*.
2. Neutral for *condo*.

Commentary on the Case Analysis

Table 4 presents our point-by-point summary evaluation of the case analysis. In our view, it is very well done, and our guess is you will agree. We should point out, however, that it is far easier to evaluate an analysis than to do one.

TABLE 4 Summary of the evaluation of the case analysis

Criteria	Analysis
1. Completeness	Very complete on all aspects of situation analysis structure Reasonable depth of analysis
2. Avoids rehash	Good Most points are made with an analysis purpose
3. Makes reasonable assumptions	Excellent
4. Proper problem statements	Excellent; has not confused them with symptoms Somewhat incomplete; e.g., competitors
5. Proper opportunity statements	Good; has not given action statements
6. Deals with objectives realistically	Very good; has questioned this issue Alternatives given and discussed
7. Recognizes alternatives	*
8. Is not assertive	Generally OK Some actions are implied in situation analysis, but not a big problem here
9. Discusses pros and cons of alternatives	*
10. Makes effective use of financial and other quantitative information	Excellent All options are given a good quantitative appraisal
11. Reaches a clear and logical decision	*
12. Makes good use of evidence developed in situation analysis	*
13. Overall appraisal	A very good situation analysis of a tough situation

* Not applicable as only situation analysis is presented.

Part 2

Introduction to Marketing Decision Making

In Part 1 of this book you have studied how marketing decisions should be made. The cases in this section are designed to let you begin to apply this approach in decision making. These cases should be viewed as an opportunity to practice your skills on some broad issue marketing cases before we go to other sections of this book where we study cases that are more specifically tied to product or distribution, and so on.

Case 1

RCA Videodisc Player*

It was December 1981, and it had been nine months since RCA nationally introduced its videodisc player under the SelectaVision label. This introduction was the culmination of $200 million in expenditures, over a decade-long research and development effort to create a videodisc player which RCA felt would become an established consumer good. See Exhibit 1 for introductory promotional materials.

Sales of videodisc players to retailers had been fewer than expected, and sales to consumers were lower still. This slow start coupled with the high stakes involved was cause for concern at RCA. In fact, RCA's entry into this high-risk venture was one of the reasons cited by Standard & Poor's Corporation in June 1981 in lowering the ratings on RCA's commercial paper and preferred stock.[1]

It was unclear which strategy RCA should now pursue, as much of the direction, energy, and momentum behind the introduction of the RCA videodisc player was due to the fact that the videodisc project had been the pet project of RCA Chairman Edgar Griffiths, who retired in June 1981. It was now time, however, to reassess the market and its future, RCA's position in the market, and competitive activity in realigning marketing strategy.

RCA's Videodisc Player Strategy

The unsuccessful introduction by CBS of an electronic video recorder in the 1960s[2] had made RCA actively aware that timing was critical in the introduction of the videodisc player. RCA felt that to be successful, its strategy should simultaneously seek to expand the total videodisc player market, and establish the Capacitance Electronic Disc (CED) technology as the standard in the United States. Equally important to the success of the videodisc player was securing as many rights as possible to software programming. Expansion of the total market could be achieved in part by a heavy $20 million advertising campaign for the introductory months of 1981. While competitive advertising campaigns would also assist in expanding the total market, RCA had to insure itself against the

---

* This case was written by Thomas C. Kinnear and Jeanne De Amicis. Copyright © 1984 by Thomas C. Kinnear.

[1] *Advertising Age,* June 22, 1981.

[2] *Marketing and Media Decisions,* March 1981, p. 62.

EXHIBIT 1 RCA introductory promotional materials

EXHIBIT 1 *(concluded)*

product?

possibility of a competitor with incompatible technology walking off with the largest chunk of the market.

Concurrent with consumer market expansion was the hope to develop new uses and markets for the RCA videodisc player. While RCA had targeted the videodisc player to the mass consumer market, it was learned that the player was of potential interest to educational institutions as a teaching aid; to businesses as a training device; or as a "memory" source on which to store and then easily access large amounts of information. Yet, it was clear that for the time being, the success or failure of the videodisc player depended on its acceptance as a durable consumer entertainment good. It was to this market that RCA management was directing its attention.

Several steps were needed to assure that the Capacitance Electronic Disc technology became the standard in the United States. First, the videodisc player must appeal to the mass market, not just the videophile, and it must be readily available. With this in mind, the RCA SelectaVision (CED) videodisc player *price* was positioned as being the easiest to use (fewer features), being the cheapest ($499 suggested retail), and having better programming than that of competitors.

Second, RCA sought to gain wide distribution through the use of national retailers. By 1980, Sears Roebuck & Co. had agreed to include the RCA videodisc player in its Christmas 1981 catalog. However, the system sold through Sears would carry Sears's brand name rather than the RCA label. While *place* RCA would prefer that its label appear on the product, it was more important that the CED technology gain the broad-based distribution and mass merchandising afforded through the Sears deal than that RCA build brand name recognition. The situation was one of winner takes all, in terms of establishing the dominant technology. J. C. Penney and Montgomery Ward in late 1981 had also agreed to carry the RCA videodisc player. This represented a major victory for RCA as competitors would have to seek distribution through their own retailer system, a system which would be dwarfed by the combined distribution coverage provided by Sears, J. C. Penney, and Montgomery Ward, as well as RCA's regular distribution channels.

promotion Third, the $20 million RCA planned to spend in the introductory advertising blitz was designed to expand the total videodisc player market, and also help to increase the market share of the RCA player, hence its technology, over those of competitors with incompatible technology.

Development of the RCA Videodisc Player

In the mid-1960s, while still concentrating on competing in the color television market, RCA was concerned over its future direction once the saturation level for color television sets had been reached. It was reasoned that once everyone had a color television, the time would be ripe for the introduction of devices that would supplement the normal function of a color television set. Hence, the ideas of the videocassette recorder and the videodisc player were developed.

The videocassette recorder (VCR) is a tape system that is attached to a television set, and can both record programs and play prerecorded programs. The videodisc player is the visual equivalent of a phonograph; it is a playback-only system that uses prerecorded software and has no recording capabilities. It is attached to a television set and plays discs, prerecorded with television signals just as a phonograph plays prerecorded records.

RCA felt that the videodisc player would have wide appeal as it would be less expensive and less complicated a device than videocassette recorders. Consequently resources and energy were expended on developing a videodisc system. This paid off, when by the late 1970s RCA had developed the Capacitance Electronic Disc system (CED). This system is a mechanical one that uses a microscopic diamond-tipped stylus that travels through the grooves of a disc, reproducing signals embedded on the surface. This technology features fast forward, and fast reverse, but does not have stereo sound capabilities. Sanyo and Zenith were expected to market CED technology systems.

Two other incompatible technologies had also been developed by competitors. The laser system had been introduced in the U.S. market by Magnavox, under the name Magnavision in 1978. This laser system is an optical system that uses a small laser to read pits pressed into a disc. It offers stereo sound, fast forward, fast reverse, stop frame, and random access features. Pioneer Electronics also marketed a laser system. See Exhibit 2 for Magnavision and Pioneer ads.

The third incompatible technology, the video high density (VHD) system, has not yet been introduced into the U.S. market (although it has been marketed abroad). In this system, the stylus rides on a grooveless disc, picking up electrical capacitance signals pressed into the disc. The VHD player features freeze frame, random access, slow motion, and stereo sound, as well as the fast forward and fast reverse capabilities. Matsushita Electric with its JVC brand, Victor of Japan, and General Electric were expected to utilize this technology in their products. Each of these incompatible technologies requires different software. Exhibit 3 summarizes the advantages and disadvantages of the three main current competitors.

Software Programming

Securing software programming and making it readily available to consumers was also of critical importance to the success of RCA's venture. The software issue was further complicated by the fact that the different technologies require different discs. So it was reasoned that the company able to tie up the majority of software programming, be it by license agreements or some other means, would have a strong competitive advantage. RCA entered into an agreement with CBS whereby CBS, through its CBS Video Enterprises, would press the RCA-type disc. RCA spent millions of dollars in royalty guarantees and signed licensing agreements with United Artists, Paramount, 20th Century Fox, Avco-

EXHIBIT 2 Magnavision and Pioneer advertisements

EXHIBIT 2 *(concluded)*

Once every generation it seems, something comes along that changes the entire nature of home entertainment. That time has come again.

Pioneer introduces LaserDisc™ a whole new technology that makes your television and stereo do things they've never done before. Now you can watch a movie or hear and *see* a concert as easily as playing a record.

And when you hook up the Laser-Disc player to your TV and hi-fi, for the first time, along with a television picture you get true stereo.

And a television picture that's actually a 40% sharper picture than home videotape.

And because the disc is read by a light beam rather than a needle or video head, nothing touches the

disc. So, with normal use, it doesn't wear out from play. You can enjoy the disc forever.

But Pioneer LaserDisc offers you more than superb fidelity, it's truly the first form of personal entertainment. Your television viewing is no longer limited to what's on television. Because you can see what you want to see when you want to see it. A whole library of Pioneer Artists and MCA/Discovision discs with movies like Jaws, Animal House, The Blues Brothers; concerts like Paul Simon, Liza Minelli, Loretta Lynn, and Abba; sports like NFL football, and title fights.

You can study the standard-play discs in fast motion, slow motion, stop motion. Even create your own instant replay.

But there's something even more remarkable. A micro-computer built

into the Pioneer LaserDisc player lets you access any individual frame on the disc at the touch of a button. You can go right to your favorite scene in a movie, or a song in concert in seconds.

And because you can view the up to 108,000 frames on the disc one frame at a time, it just may be the future of education.

The cost of Pioneer LaserDisc is surprising as well. Just $749* (with $50* more for optional remote control). And a full-length movie on LaserDisc can cost less than taking your family out to the movies.

The only way to even begin to experience the magic of this remarkable LaserDisc system is to see it. And we've arranged for that. Just call at **800-621-5199*** for the store nearest you. **(In Illinois 800-972-5822.)

*Suggested retail price. Actual price set by dealers.

Simulated TV picture from Paul Simon.

Finally, high-fidelity television with stereo sound.

© 1981 U.S. Pioneer Electronics Corp.

LaserDisc

① PIONEER

We bring it back alive.

(handwritten: $BE\$ - VC\# = FC$)

(handwritten: $\# P_r - VC\# = FC$)

(handwritten: $\# = \dfrac{FC}{P_r - VC}$)

EXHIBIT 3 A consumer's guide to videodisc players

Features	Philips-MCA (1978)	RCA (early 1981)	JVC (Matsushita) (late 1981)
Retail price	Disadvantage	Advantage	Advantage
No disc or stylus wear	Advantage	Disadvantage	Disadvantage
Stereo sound	Advantage	Disadvantage	Disadvantage
Two-hour playback	Advantage	Advantage	Advantage
Freeze frame	Advantage *	Disadvantage	Advantage
Automatic stop frame	Advantage *	Advantage	Advantage **
Multiple speeds, forward and reverse	Advantage		Advantage
Random frame access	Advantage	Disadvantage	Advantage **
Softwear variety	Advantage	Advantage	Disadvantage

*Available only with 1-hour discs.
**Option.

▨ = Advantage

▤ = Disadvantage

(handwritten: $\dfrac{1,000,000}{15-2}$ 24.98 $BE\#$ 14.98 $43,516 - 76973$)

Embassy, Rank Film Distributors, and MGM Film Co. (a subsidiary of CBS)
for rights to reproduce 520 films on disc.

The initial RCA disc catalog offered 150 titles including feature movies,
Walt Disney movies, sports and music/variety programs, the Best of Television,
Drama and Performing Arts programs, programs for children, and programs of
special interest. The retail price of the discs ranged from $14.98 to $24.98.
Discs would be available through the retail chains, and distribution channels
that sold the RCA videodisc player, as well as through the regular CBS record
distribution network. Retail margins were about 50 percent. However, complaints had already been received that adequate programming was not available
late in 1981 at the retail level. Fixed costs for a disc were about $1 million,
while variable costs ran about $2 per pressed disc.

A programming area where RCA chose not to enter was that using X-rated
materials. Industry analysis and reports from retail outlets indicated a substantial demand for X-rated programs. RCA felt that any association with X-rated
programming, materials, or promotion would severely hurt their corporate
image, perhaps causing irreparable damage. Clearly RCA would not exploit this
area of programming.

(handwritten: $\# PR + FC = BE$ $BE = FC$ $BE - VC\# = FC$)

The possibility of establishing a studio to produce programming exclusively for CED videodisc players had been considered by RCA, but company officials felt it was too early a stage in the market development of videodisc players to warrant a heavy investment in such a venture. They felt that for the time being there was ample programming available to satisfy the needs of the videodisc player owners.

RCA was also aware that film producers were considering the possibility of licensing their films to more than one type of disc producer. This was of concern to RCA who had gone to great lengths to secure what it hoped would be exclusive rights to the film reproduction. Some competitors had already entered into joint ventures with studios to produce original programming for the consumer and industrial market needs, as well as to secure licenses.

Market Size

Industry analysis in 1980 predicted that videodisc player purchasers would buy an average of eight discs a year. They estimated that by 1990 the videodisc player market, along with the software market, would be a $7.5 billion business at retail, with prerecorded discs constituting a $200 to $250 million annual retail business. Despite this rosy prediction, there was a shortage of disc manufacturers. Consequently, although RCA had the rights to a substantial amount of software programming, the slow hardware sales coupled with the ensuing low volume of software sales dampened many disc manufacturers' plans to enter the disc market. There were many companies preparing to enter the disc manufacturing business, but choosing to wait until the seemingly inevitable industry shakeout occurred, and product standardization ensued.

Another consideration was the possibility of renting discs. RCA felt disc rental or disc swapping might stimulate the use of, and demand for, videodisc players, but it realized that the film studios would frown upon such activities. The recent film industry legal fight with the videocassette recorder producers concerning royalties, ownership, and production rights in taping programs, was indicative of the battle that might await them if they advocated and participated in disc rental activities. (The film industry suffered a setback in the Supreme Court and the battle has now shifted to the U.S. Congress.)

U.S. demographic changes (such as increasing amounts of leisure time and an increasing emphasis on recreational activities) have helped the growth of the entire video field. RCA felt these trends would carry over to videodisc player sales. RCA also felt that the increased dissatisfaction with broadcast television would aid in the expansion of this market. According to RCA, individuals who own color televisions, who watch a substantial amount of television, and are middle to upper income would most likely be the initial purchasers of videodisc players.

The intent of RCA was to eventually gain as high a level of home penetration as had been achieved with color and black-and-white televisions. Anyone who owned a color television was a potential videodisc player purchaser. Analysts predicted that videodisc players would be in 14 percent of the 85 million television homes by 1986 (VCRs are expected to be in 18 percent of the television homes). RCA predicted a 60 percent market share, with Philips having a 30 percent market share, and Matsushita a 10 percent market share. RCA also forecasted that annual videodisc player sales will pass 5 million by 1990. These sales coupled with disc sales of 200–250 million units would total a $7.5 billion annual business at retail by the end of the decade.

Due to delays in the introduction of the SelectaVision videodisc player and slow initial sales, RCA changed its initial 1981 forecast sales figure of 500,000 units to 200,000 units. By early November 1981, with Christmas sales yet to come, RCA had distributed 100,000 videodisc players to retailers and 1.4 million discs had been sold. Retail sales were about 60,000 to 80,000 players.

Competition

The videocassette recorder (VCR) was the major competitive substitute product for the videodisc player. The major differences between the two products were recording capability and price. A stripped down videocassette recorder had a suggested retail price of about $700, while the RCA Videodisc Player retailed at $499.[3] However, the videocassette recorder had recording capabilities where the videodisc player did not. Further confusing the customer was the incompatible laser technology videodisc player which retailed for as high as $750. RCA felt there was a market for a product without recording capabilities, but with a lower price. In fact, price, ease of use, and abundant programming were the distinguishing features of RCA's videodisc player.

Cable television and movie channels were also possible product substitutes for the videodisc player. Consumers could pay as little as $12–$15/ month and see many first-run movies on television while a videodisc player calls for an initial $499 outlay and $15–$25 for each disc. For many it may become a question of how often they view movies a second, third, or fourth time. Assuming a new videodisc player purchaser buys eight discs with the initial videodisc player purchase (ignoring the estimated eight discs purchased yearly thereafter), the average total price of $679 would purchase four years of cable television. RCA recognized pay television as a formidable competitor, but the cable industry was still young too, and videodisc players might be able to move in and gain the upper hand.

Philips' North American subsidiary, Magnavox, had been RCA's primary videodisc competitor to date. They were first to market videodisc players, having introduced their laser optical system in 1978. The introduction was a gradual one, going from test market to test market (Atlanta, Dallas, Seattle) before deciding on a city-by-city rollout. By October 1980, Magnavision was available in 30 markets. RCA was aware of some technical difficulties encoun-

---

[3] Retail margins were about 50 percent. RCA's variable costs were estimated at $150 per player on average over the first 200,000 units.

tered in the Magnavox laser system, problems that were not resolved until the summer of 1980. Prior to this time, there had been a significant reliability problem where between 50 percent and 60 percent of the players had to be returned for servicing. This problem appears to have been resolved and Magnavox has continued to be a strong competitor.

North American Philips had changed its strategy by late summer/early fall 1980, and began positioning its videodisc as being the most technically sophisticated player on the market and on the leading edge of laser technology. Its fall 1980 $5 million ad campaign was designed to appeal to the videophile, the video hobbyist, and the innovative individual. It was precisely those individuals who are the first to try something new that Magnavox wanted to attract. However, with a price of $775 Magnavision was significantly more expensive than RCA's SelectaVision videodisc. The Magnavox videodisc player did offer more features than the RCA product, namely: random access, multiple speeds, forward and reverse, automatic stop, freeze frame, and stereo sound. Another attractive feature of the Magnavox videodisc player was the fact that because the system is optical, there is no stylus that could wear down. The laser beam does not wear down the disc either. But RCA felt that a disc would have to be played hundreds of times before the CED system would wear it out.

By December 1980, anticipating RCA's entry into the market, Magnavox sought to change its strategy to appeal to the mass market. Because of its technical sophistication and higher price (Magnavision's price had now come down to $750), Magnavox sought to differentiate its product as being the gourmet video, yet still having mass appeal.

Despite some feeling that two incompatible videodisc technologies could coexist in the marketplace, the general consensus was that only one technology would be the clear winner. North American Philips was just as interested as RCA in gaining a stronghold and eventually dominating this market. Two moves helped to solidify this goal. First, North American Philips bought the Sylvania and Philco television manufacturing operations from GTE. Secondly, North American Philips had bought Magnavox at the outset in preparation and anticipation of entering the videodisc player market. In purchasing Magnavox, North American Philips gained access to the retail and distribution network already in place at Magnavox as well as the well-known name of Magnavox.

Because a color TV screen is needed to display the videodisc player programs, and because of the tendency of many people not to mix components that are not the same brand name, the purchase of the Sylvania and Philco television manufacturing operations by North American Philips was understandable. The reasoning was that a consumer owning a Sylvania TV would be most likely to purchase a Sylvania videodisc player. Undoubtedly this transaction would assist Magnavox's efforts to sell videodisc players, but perhaps more important, it would eliminate a potential ally for RCA in the technology war.

Just as RCA sought to gain the majority of software programming as part of its initial strategy in entering the videodisc market, Magnavox, early on, signed a joint venture agreement with MCA (Universal Studio's parent company), IBM, and Pioneer Electronics. This joint venture established Disco

Vision Associates which will manufacture the discs. Concurrently, Magnavox, Pioneer, and MCA each put up $1 million to create Optical Program Associates to produce original programs and take advantage of the stereo, freeze frame, and other features unique to the laser videodisc system. The association with MCA would also provide Magnavox with the movies and television programs produced by Universal Studios.

The other major competitor on the verge of entering the U.S. market with yet another incompatible technology was Matsushita. Matsushita had had the option of either licensing the RCA CED technology, North American Philips' laser optical technology, or developing its own proprietary technology. Licensing either RCA's or North American Philips' technology would virtually guarantee that Matsushita must compete on something other than price as both RCA and North American Philips would have lower costs by the time Matsushita entered the market. Hence, Matsushita felt the most viable option was to develop its own technology. Consequently the video high density (VHD) technology was developed and Matsushita felt it could sell these VHD videodisc players in the range between RCA's $500 model and Magnavox's $750, probably closer to $500. Furthermore, the Japanese government wanted manufacturers to agree on a single format before entering the Japanese market. Not surprisingly, Japan's Ministry for International Trade and Industry (MITI) announced that Matsushita's VHD technology was the agreed-upon format. If RCA or any other manufacturer wanted to enter the Japanese market, it would have to be done by licensing the VHD technology from Matsushita.

Matsushita, the world's largest consumer electronics company, sells its products in the United States under the brand names National, Panasonic, and Quasar. Victor Co. of Japan, which sells under the JVC label, is also a subsidiary of Matsushita. Matsushita's anticipated late 1981 entry into the U.S. market did not materialize. However, the company had predicted that 30,000 units would be distributed by the end of calendar year 1982.

Zenith Radio Corporation planned to enter the U.S. videodisc market in 1982 with a CED system. Prior to this time, Zenith had agreed to merely market RCA units under its Zenith label. The intent had been to begin in-house videodisc player equipment manufacturing in two to three years. Zenith had purposely kept a low profile and launched no national advertising campaigns. Instead, it left the advertising battlefield open for RCA and Magnavox (and Matsushita when it enters the market), thus forgoing the expense a national advertising campaign necessitates.

Zenith's second quarter 1981 profits fell 50 percent and RCA felt this might interrupt Zenith's ambitious plans to tap the rapidly expanding video market. It was announced that Zenith had already postponed plans to manufacture its own videodisc player. On the other hand, there was some speculation that Zenith intended to change videodisc manufacturers in 1982, presumably to distinguish itself from RCA and to get out of RCA's shadow.

Both Hitachi and Sanyo were planning entry into the U.S. market with the CED system, the Japanese market with the VHD system, and the European market with the laser optical system. All three technologies must be obtained from the respective technology developers. Hitachi will supply Radio Shack with its video players. Neither Hitachi nor Toshiba intended to advertise heavily as RCA was expected to carry the marketing efforts for the CED format.

Pioneer had already entered the U.S. market (and 14 others) with a laser-stylus system that is compatible with Magnavox's laser system, and priced between $750 and $775. Like RCA, in the fall of 1981, Pioneer offered three free discs with the purchase of its videodisc player.

Toshiba plans to enter the U.S. market with a CED player. Neither Sony nor Kenwood have entered the U.S. market yet, but are ready to enter with either/or the CED and VHD systems. They are waiting for the outcome of the initial struggle between RCA, Magnavox, and Matsushita. Both Gold Star and Thomson-C8F were preparing to introduce the laser system.

The International Videodisc Player Market

The international market for videodisc players was quite different from the U.S. market. Often videodisc players filled a void in countries where color television programming was poor, or where television programs and movies were censored by local officials. N.V. Philips (North American Philips' parent company) was based in the Netherlands and already enjoyed a dominant position in the European market with many of its products. Philips might be able to dominate the European videodisc player market with relative ease and establish its laser technology as the standard. Still, RCA felt that there were opportunities to break into this European market.

MITI's announcement that only VHD videodisc players would be sold in Japan put RCA in the disadvantageous position of having to license the VHD technology from Matsushita if it wanted to enter the lucrative Japanese market. VHD technology was not available to all companies, limiting in effect the number of competitors in the Japanese market, as well as giving a boost to Matsushita and other Japanese companies where the VHD technology is proprietary. RCA felt that the reasoning behind the Japanese government's move was to allow Matsushita to become the major manufacturer of videodisc players in Japan, such that it could rapidly develop production cost advantages and lower the price on its product. Then this lower-priced product could be marketed in the United States. In this manner Matsushita could become price competitive with RCA, and perhaps gain a stronghold in the marketplace, and even come to dominate the U.S. videodisc market.

Other world markets were not sufficiently developed to support a product such as videodisc players. RCA felt it was not necessary to actively pursue these markets.

First Nine Months' Performance

By late 1981, RCA was clearly disappointed in the first nine months of sales. Not only had the sales forecast of 500,000 units been reduced to 200,000 units, but only 100,000 units had been sold to distributors. One analyst estimated that between 60,000 and 80,000 units had been sold to consumers. Christmas season sales failed to help much. Consequently, RCA began offering a $50 manufacturer's rebate and three free discs with the purchase of a videodisc player, and retailers began cutting prices by $100 to $200 per unit. Concurrently, the $20 million advertising blitz was covering broadcast and print media. Yet RCA had already announced the layoff of 400 of its 4,100 workers at its videodisc and color television manufacturing plant in Bloomington, Indiana. Further action might have to be taken if sales did not pick up.

RCA realized from the beginning that the videodisc player venture was both risky and would require substantial amounts of resources and time before the concept was readily accepted. How much should continue to be invested in the videodisc player business? How might this affect RCA's other businesses? What could RCA do to help boost sales? Unfortunately no consumer studies were available to identify why sales were below expectations.

Case 2

Santa Clara Terminals, Inc.*

Ed Zimmer, the president of Santa Clara Terminals (SCT), leaned back in his chair and contemplated the future of his company. He knew that the company was at a crisis point, not for the first time in its history. Sales and orders were down substantially. The future of the marketing organization was in question. Engineering talent was in short supply, and the existing engineering group was stretched to its limits.

The industry in which SCT operated was undergoing major changes and SCT, as a small company, would have trouble keeping up and competing on a general basis. He wondered what was the best direction to take the company—and how to get there. He summarized the situation as follows:

> Our biggest challenge right now is survival. The field has always been extraordinarily competitive, and the last five years it's been impossible. The Koreans are now strongly in the market, along with the Japanese. Everyone else is manufacturing offshore, and I don't want to. I can't compete in the normal CRT market. I compete in a tiny niche characterized by lots of characters on the screen.

The vice president of operations also noted,

> The company is more interested in staying healthy than in growth. Growth is closely controlled in terms of the company's capabilities. We could go to double our current volume in sales without anything except hiring entry-level production people. Beyond that, growth is not planned and would come as a surprise. It would require adjustments.

Company Background and History

General Information

Santa Clara Terminals is a privately held corporation engaged in the manufacture of CRT display terminals for the commercial computer market. The company was formed in 1970 in Santa Clara, California, and has grown to have

---

* This case was written by Sarah Freeman under the supervision of Thomas C. Kinnear. Copyright © 1987 by Thomas C. Kinnear.

50 employees. No outside venture capital has ever been solicited or used; all growth has been from retained earnings.

SCT evolved from a company that would sell anything to anyone in terms of CRT display electronics to a company that manufactures custom versions of a few basic designs and builds exceptionally high-quality terminals. SCT's products were priced higher than its competition's to allow for this greater flexibility and reliability.

When this approach was no longer feasible, given the greater flexibility provided all manufacturers with the use of the microprocessor, SCT struggled to redefine its niche. That niche is now defined as the very high-end CRT terminal for the professional user. Professional users are defined as those who work with CRTs for a living—not the clerical worker who spends a great deal of time in front of a CRT, but professionals such as programmers and engineers, who often see their terminals as extensions of themselves.

1970–1973

SCT was founded by three engineers, all of whom had worked for other California firms in the computer and electronics fields. Each of the founders put up $5,000 of their own funds to start the company, and they took no salary during the start-up phase. Of the three, Ed Zimmer is the only one still active in the company, and he now owns it in its entirety.

The company's original products were printed circuit board sets and display controllers, aimed at the OEM and industrial markets. These consisted of display electronics only, packaged in a sheet metal enclosure in the case of the controllers, and could be considered a CRT terminal without the CRT, or screen. Although the company offered a broad range of "standard" products, varying mainly by display format (from 8 lines of 32 characters to 24 lines of 80 characters) and data interface (serial or parallel), virtually all products were sold customized according to the customer's requirements.

At this time, most marketing was by word of mouth, reflecting the fledgling company's limited resources and confidence in its ability to deliver quality products. However, SCT did score some success with an unusual approach to promotion. For instance, at the National Computer Conference in 1971, the company was unable to afford or obtain an exhibit booth. The National Computer Conference was, and still is, the main annual trade show for the computer industry, and SCT's founders thought its products should be on display there. They got into the show as attendees, trailing a small red wagon that contained their products. Although show management later forced them to leave, they stationed the wagon at the door of the exhibit hall. In addition to attention at the show, the ploy earned Santa Clara Terminals a front page story in *Electronic News's* coverage of the NCC.

During these early days, the company also signed up manufacturers' representatives to sell its products to OEMs and large industrial users. The rep firms carried several related product lines, sometimes including a CRT terminal, and received a commission on all sales within their geographic territories. By 1973, SCT had representatives covering the United States, Canada, and most of Western Europe.

1973–1977

In 1973, SCT introduced its first desktop design, with full CRT display and keyboard. Like other new products, the Design III was designed in response to a customer requirement and then broadened into a standard product line. In this instance, the customer was a West Coast think tank that wanted to display 40 lines of data in order to be able to review more text at one time. The terminal included a monitor and keyboard from other manufacturers, packaged with the display electronics in SCT's case. The desktop design was made to accommodate all SCT board sets, giving the company a full line of desktop terminals.

In 1977, the company was still manufacturing these terminals, in both desktop and controller configurations. All products were essentially "dumb" terminals, with just basic input/output and display capabilities. SCT's sales still consisted largely of customized versions of its standard products, sold to OEMs (both manufacturers and systems houses) and to industrial customers who particularly liked the more rugged controllers.

OEMs were in all fields but had the design and manufacture of computer-based systems in common; systems might be for process control, medical diagnostics, or general-purpose computer systems. Systems houses did not manufacture but rather put together a computer and peripherals from several manufacturers, along with their own specialized applications software, to sell to vertical end-user markets. SCT's customizing could consist of anything from a change of the case color, to the addition of a specialized command or emulation of other manufacturers' code sets, to a complete design to the customer's specifications.

After a brief initial campaign to introduce the Design III, SCT did little or no advertising during this period, but relied on its reputation as a manufacturer of high-quality, reliable products, especially of custom designs. This reputation was passed along mainly by word of mouth, particularly by job-hopping engineers.

The company considered itself largely a service operation. It prided itself on its excellent reliability and display quality, and on its ability to respond quickly and efficiently to special requirements. SCT was set up to handle custom products in low volume at reasonable cost—minor changes were often designed by technicians rather than engineers, and all products were built to order. This makes sense particularly when one notes that "standard" products accounted for only about 20 percent of SCT's sales. Production operated basically as a large job shop, building standard PC boards and then modifying them to the requirements of each order.

During a period in 1973–74, SCT made an attempt at instituting a middle management structure. One of the three founders had left the company, and the remaining two wished to remove themselves from its day-to-day operations.

Managers were recruited from outside the company to be put in charge of engineering, marketing, and production. However, top management found that this approach required more of their attention than anticipated; results were mediocre, and the entire middle management structure was disbanded within nine months.

Around the same time, Ed Zimmer made the decision to pull out of Western Europe and cancel all representation there. SCT would be a domestic company only for the time being. Zimmer had determined that the company was too small to provide the level of support required overseas. However, at least one of the representatives, covering Scandinavia, elected to continue the relationship by buying at a discount and reselling within the area.

1977–1980

Late in 1977, SCT started moving toward vertical integration and more standardized products. The proliferation of the microprocessor was making its terminal designs obsolete and unnecessary for many industrial customers. In addition, functional customization could now be achieved via simple firmware changes (code changes to the memory chip that determined the terminal's functions) rather than the more complex and less reliable wiring changes used in the past.

The Model 400 was introduced at the National Computer Conference of 1977, and shipping started in December of that year. It was a first for SCT in many respects. It used the first monitor of SCT's own design and manufacture, and it was also SCT's first microprocessor-based product. The company designed the keyboard logic into the terminal itself and was able to use a simple switch matrix key array from another manufacturer. Because many fewer components were required, the Model 400 in its new case took up less than half the desk space of earlier terminal designs.

Following the introduction of the Model 400, the company ran into several production and design-related problems. First, SCT quickly discovered that it was not expert at building quality monitors; its reputation for clear display and reliability suffered while the monitor went through many design changes and was reengineered. In addition, production fell behind schedule and deliveries slipped. Finally, the Model 400 was not code compatible with SCT's previous products. This meant that existing customers would have to rewrite their software if they were to switch over to the new product. The older products were still available but considerably more expensive, and were in the process of being phased out.

SCT addressed these problems first by introducing new versions of the older products, using the Model 400 board sets and design. Monitor quality and reliability problems were eventually corrected, although there is little doubt that the sales and irritation levels of existing customers suffered in the meantime. Delivery problems were not finally corrected until the company moved to new manufacturing facilities in the fall of 1979.

With the advent of the Model 400 and its related products, SCT continued its customization approach. Some of the custom products were microprocessor-based versions of previous products. Others were emulations of other companies' terminals, particularly the VT52 from Digital Equipment Corp. (DEC), which was being phased out but was still in great demand. So, although the company used fewer different PC boards in the manufacture of its products, all were still customized to a great extent, and OEMs and systems houses accounted for most of the company's sales.

Marketing continued to rely mainly on word of mouth, with some limited fractional advertising in electronics trade journals, such as *Electronic Products*, or programmers' computer magazines, such as *Mini Micro Systems* or *Computer Decisions*. The company also issued regular press releases on new products and enhancements, which were sent to a customer mailing list as well as to the trade press.

Selling was handled by the manufacturers' reps organization, which still covered the United States and Canada. The field reps were supported by an in-house staff responsible for answering their questions, providing quotations for custom products, and coordinating all rep- and customer-related activity. Sales calls by SCT personnel, with or without the sales reps, were rare and limited to major prospects.

1980–1984

Things began to change drastically when the SCT Ambassador was introduced in 1980. This product used the code set specified by the ANSI (American National Standards Institute) X3.64 standard. The ANSI standard had been developed to cover most of the functions offered by computerized alphanumeric display equipment. It was intended to address problems encountered by users in switching between or adding equipment from different manufacturers.

Acceptance of the ANSI standard code set would mean that the market for customized terminals could all but dry up. Although the standard allowed a great deal of latitude in how commands were actually implemented, it specified the code structure for over 100 possible commands and functions.

The SCT Ambassador was introduced at the National Computer Conference in the spring of 1980, and shipping started late that year. It was the first CRT on the market to implement virtually the entire ANSI X3.64 code set, although other terminals, most notably DEC's VT100 and its emulations, implemented portions of the standard.

The Ambassador was a high-end product, with many editing and form-filling capabilities, as well as programmable function keys. What made the terminal unique, however, was its display capability. The Ambassador could display up to 60 lines of 80 characters—a full typewriter page. Most CRTs on the market were limited to a 24-line display. In addition, display formats could be selected with the terminal's local "zoom" capability, ranging from 18 to 60 lines. No other CRT on the market at the time offered either 60-line display or a selectable number of lines.

Because of its unique capabilities, the Ambassador was immediately popular among users interested in a high-end, versatile terminal with large display formats. These especially included programmers (who wanted to see more of their program at one time) and others whose work required a great deal of text editing.

However, OEMs did not find the terminal as attractive. This was partly because of its high price tag ($1,395 list price, while low-end terminals had just been introduced at under $500), but also because they did not face the same problems of code compatibility as end users did. Many functions and great flexibility offered little to a company that could accomplish these easily in its own software. Price, reliability, and basic functions were more important to this customer set.

During the same time frame in which the Ambassador was introduced, lower-end terminals were beginning to add more features at lower cost. The dumb terminal became a thing of the past as even the lowest-priced units offered a wide range of "smart" features like editing and programmable function keys.

SCT attempted to address some of this low-end challenge with modified versions of its Ambassador. The Genie and Genie + Plus terminals were introduced in 1982, offering ANSI X3.64 compatible code sets with a reduced set of functions. The Genie + Plus had all the features of the Ambassador except the 60-line display capability; it had 60 lines of memory, but could only display up to 30 at once. The Genie had only 30 lines of memory, and also removed some of the editing capability and function keys.

With the introduction of these products, the Ambassador's price was increased to $1,595, with the Genie and Genie + Plus priced at $1,195 and $1,395, respectively. The price increase had almost no effect on sales of the Ambassador, which continued to rise, but the Genies were not very successful and were purchased mainly by customers who had not been using all the features of the Ambassador.

In 1983, several more new products were introduced. One was a stand that could be added to SCT's products, providing tilt and swivel for operator comfort. It was intended to address complaints about the "industrial box" look of SCT's case while allowing more ergonomic placement of the terminal. The company also started offering the Ambassador in a portrait display (vertical tube) configuration, intended for customers who used the terminal primarily in its 60-line mode. The portrait display more closely resembled an $8\frac{1}{2} \times 11$ page than did the normal landscape, or horizontal, version.

Another new product was the Graphics Master. This was an add-on to the Ambassador, providing it with graphics capabilities that were code compatible with some of the more popular graphics devices in the field. A major problem with the Graphics Master was that it would not function with most of the Ambassadors already in the field, requiring several internal changes and making retrofits all but impossible for the end user.

The final product introduced in 1983 was the Guru. This product went beyond the Ambassador to include display formats that could be changed both horizontally and vertically—ranging from 20 to 66 lines and from 32 to 170 characters per line. It also included 15 pages of display memory, usable for editing, printing, and transmission. With the Guru, SCT introduced a product as advanced as an alphanumeric CRT terminal could be at the time.

With these products, SCT decided to confine itself to the very high end of the CRT terminal market, offering lower-end products only for customers who wanted to buy a complete line from the same manufacturer. The company's customer base had changed dramatically over the years, to where they were predominantly end users taking standard products that offered some degree of user customization. The users were mainly people who depended on CRTs for their living—programmers, think tanks, and those who did a great deal of screen editing. SCT's products were particularly well known in the artificial intelligence (AI) community, which, although spread throughout the country in many different companies and universities, communicated regularly with each other and had strong opinions about how computer equipment should function.

With the introduction of the Ambassador, SCT was for the first time attempting to market a product rather than respond to the needs of specific customers. SCT had always marketed more expensive products than its competition, but the criteria for what justified a higher price had changed. SCT moved away from customization to high-end, flexible CRT terminals—essentially, terminals with functions that could be customized by the user. With this move, the nature of its customer base changed.

In 1981, the company started selling Ambassadors through distributors of computer peripherals. In 1982, SCT terminated contracts with all its manufacturers' reps and began to sell direct and through distributors. Direct sales were handled by a field representative, as well as by staff located at the factory. At this point, the company would take any order that came to them, although prospects were referred to a local distributor on initial contact. The general intent was for distributors to handle small-quantity customers, whether they were end users or systems houses, while SCT would handle larger accounts.

At this time, SCT also started advertising more heavily, as it felt that it needed to establish its own name and an awareness of its individual products, particularly the Ambassador. Full-page ads were placed in end user, systems house, and programmer publications. Regular mailings of press releases to customer and prospect lists continued as well.

The CRT Terminal Industry

Industry Structure

According to a 1981 article in *Computerworld*, there were nearly 200 manufacturers, including computer makers and independents, selling CRT terminals in the United States at that time. However, in a 1985 research study, Datapro found only 100 manufacturers to survey. Although there has been substantial dropout of CRT manufacturers during this time, new producers have continued to enter the market, particularly offshore facilities that may have originally manufactured under contract for U.S. companies.

The Datapro research study lists 91 manufacturers with a total of 361 models of CRT terminals. These terminals cover the range from dumb teletype replacements to sophisticated cluster configurations and editing terminals. However, most are in the middle range. Prices for stand-alone alphanumeric configurations ranged from $325 to $4,600, but most independents (i.e., non-computer manufacturers) have terminals priced in the $600–$800 range for basic alphanumerics, with editing, highlighting, and programmable function keys. Graphics and color capabilities add considerably to the price. A bewildering variety of options and standard features are also available, further complicating the user's choices.

According to a November 1984 article in *Computerworld*, the IBM 3270 and compatible market accounts for approximately one quarter of the installed base of CRT terminals; non-IBM-compatible editing terminals account for an additional 15.5 percent of the base, while conversational CRTs make up 23 percent. The remainder is split between a variety of cluster configurations, graphics terminals, and other special-protocol products.

An International Data Corporation study on the CRT terminal market found the following market segments and breakdown, based on 1983 shipments:

IBM 3270-type	30%
Low-end ASCII	24
Full-editing ASCII	21
IBM GSD-type	13
Cluster processing	7
Non-IBM synchronous (Honeywell, Sperry, etc.)	5

According to the same study, the market share leaders in the low-end ASCII segment were Digital Equipment (DEC) with 28.1 percent, ADDS with 14.9 percent, IBM with 8.6 percent, Lear Siegler with 7.2 percent, C. Itoh with 6.3 percent, and Hewlett-Packard with 5.5 percent.

In the full-editing segment, where Santa Clara Terminals' products belong, eight vendors accounted for more than 60 percent of total shipments. They were Televideo with 20 percent, Hewlett-Packard with 8.7 percent, Esprit Systems with 6.5 percent, Lear Siegler with 5.4 percent, Micro-Term and Liberty Electronics with 5.3 percent each, and Wyse and Visual Technology with 4.6 percent each. A total of nearly 380,000 full-editing ASCII terminals were shipped in 1983.

Market Size and Growth

According to Datapro, there were approximately 10 million CRT terminals of all types installed in the United States as of the end of 1984. In the IDC study cited above, it was found that a total of 1.78 million CRT terminals were shipped in 1983, for a total of $3 billion in sales. This represents an 18 percent increase over 1982 unit volume.

The increase was not even across all segments. Low-end ASCII terminal shipments increased by only 10 percent over 1982, while full-editing ASCII shipments grew by 30 percent. Through 1988, *Mini Micro Systems* predicts annual growth of editing terminals to run at 27 percent, while conversational (low-end) terminal shipments will increase by only 9 percent per year. The continual price cutting is reflected in its forecasts for dollar volume growth—18 percent for editing units, and -0.7 percent for conversational CRTs.

Evidence of Shakeout

There is some evidence of a shakeout within the CRT terminal industry beyond simply noting the estimated number of manufacturers in various years. Several of the major players within the industry have undergone substantial changes in recent years.

In 1982, Applied Digital Data Systems (ADDS), the largest OEM supplier of CRT terminals, was acquired by its main customer, NCR. Since then, ADDS has continued to operate independently, but NCR takes an increasing share of its production.

Three manufacturers have filed for Chapter 11 bankruptcy protection within the last two years. General Terminal is one of these. The other two, Beehive International and Soroc Technology, were in the top five by market share as late as 1979. Hazeltine, which held the number two position among independents in the late 70s, elected to exit the CRT terminal market and sold this business to its managers in 1983; this is now Esprit Systems.

Several CRT terminal manufacturers have attempted to enter the personal computer or small systems markets, but there have been no notable successes. Televideo holds the leading share of ASCII terminals among the independents, but is said to be losing money largely because of its unsuccessful venture into microcomputers. Other terminal manufacturers have attempted mergers, but without bringing them off. Many are rumored to be in financial difficulty.

Other Changes in the Industry

Technological changes and continual feature enhancements have blurred the distinctions between dumb and smart terminals, smart and intelligent terminals, and intelligent terminals and workstations. The introduction and popularity of the personal computer has further confused definitions, particularly when it can be used in local area networks. The ease of adding features with the microprocessor, along with dropping hardware and memory costs, have contributed to the trend for manufacturers to add advanced features to even their low-end products.

Some experts predicted that readily available and inexpensive microcomputers would mean the end of CRT terminals. This has not happened, although microcomputers have made some inroads in the intelligent and high-end segments. Microcomputers can be used in place of CRT terminals to provide more local processing power, but they can still be connected to a host computer. At the present time, CRT terminals are still more cost effective than personal computers for most applications. However, this depends on how much local processing is desired.

Another major change is the number of CRT terminals that, like other electronics, are now being manufactured offshore, primarily in Asia. U.S. manufacturers started moving their production in the late 70s to take advantage of lower labor costs and to try to match falling hardware prices. Most used contract manufacturing, although some have their own overseas manufacturing subsidiaries. Now all the major U.S. companies do at least some portion of their manufacturing offshore.

In some ways, this strategy came back to haunt them when the contractors in Taiwan and Korea began to produce their own brands and market them in the United States. Televideo, the number one independent in ASCII terminals, started by manufacturing monitors for Atari. Liberty Electronics began by manufacturing for Hazeltine.

The price cutting and feature enhancing that have gone on for several years show no signs of abating. CRT vendors are each struggling for their share of the market, accepting lower margins to do so. It was not uncommon for CRT manufacturers to have gross margins as high as 40 percent in 1980; now 10 percent margins are common in the more crowded segments.

Finally, ergonomic features have become a requirement rather than a market advantage. When terminals began to include more function at lower prices, some manufacturers used human engineering (ergonomics) to distinguish themselves from their competitors and create a differential advantage. Features such as tilt and swivel screen, low-profile keyboards, nonglare screens and keytops, and different screen colors were touted for their enhancement of operator comfort. More terminal makers incorporated these features into their designs, so that virtually all now have some aspects that are considered user friendly or ergonomic.

Santa Clara Terminals' Primary Competition

SCT considered just a few companies to be its direct competition, and these it watched more closely than others. The following section contains a brief description of each of these key competitors.

Digital Equipment Corporation

DEC was considered a main competitor, not because its CRT terminals competed head on in the same range as SCT's, but because the majority of SCT customers had DEC computers and were therefore likely to consider and possibly buy DEC terminals.

DEC had been influential in defining and later establishing the ANSI

X3.64 standard in the CRT industry. Its VT100 had been "the" ANSI standard terminal for many years. Introduced in 1978, it was estimated that over 500,000 had been shipped as of the end of 1983. In November 1983, DEC introduced its replacement for the VT100—the VT200 line of CRT terminals. These products included ergonomic advances, along with some more functionality, over the VT100.

With the VT200 series, DEC also corrected some mistakes it had made with the introduction of the VT100. When the VT100 was announced, DEC had not anticipated the extent of demand and was unable to produce enough terminals for the first couple of years of production. Consequently, the door was opened to independent manufacturers, many of which came out with VT100 emulations. Generally, the emulations were more readily available and often included more features at a lower price than the DEC unit. However, DEC was able to gear up manufacturing more quickly on the VT200; Dataquest estimates that it shipped between 50,000 and 60,000 of these units in the second quarter of 1984 and predicts that it will be able to retain at least 60 percent of the VT200-compatible market segment.

There are three main models in the VT200 line, with list prices ranging from $1,395 for the basic alphanumeric terminal to $3,195 for a unit with color graphics capabilities. Display formats on the alpha terminals were always 24 lines, but could switch between 80 and 132 characters per line.

CIE Terminals

CIE Terminals was a wholly owned subsidiary of C. Itoh Electronics, a large Japanese company, and was formed when C. Itoh bought its exclusive distributor in early 1983. C. Itoh had established itself in the U.S. terminal market with an emulation of DEC's VT100. It was one of the first manufacturers to develop a copycat of this popular unit, and emulated it almost completely. In fact, its CIT-100 was so close to DEC's product that DEC sued C. Itoh for copying its case and design.

SCT considered CIE a closer competitor than other companies because it was one of the few that produced a full-page display. The CIT-500 displayed 66 lines of 80 characters, which were not selectable, displayed on a vertical tube. Overall, it has less function than SCT's Ambassador—for instance, it had no form-filling capability. The single-quantity price for the CIT-500 was $2,150. However, in late 1984 there was a rumor that CIE would be discontinuing it and was dumping its stock at $1,200.

Micro-Term, Inc.

Micro-Term was a small, privately held manufacturer founded in St. Louis in 1976. As of 1982, it reported $7 million in sales, with 80 employees. Micro-Term sold through distributors and direct field sales. It was believed that the company would give its distributor price to any bona fide reseller, without requiring stocking or minimum quantities. In 1983, it moved production off-shore, contracting with Sampo Electronics.

The Datapro report of 1985 lists five models from Micro-Term, priced from $399 to $1,595. The one that most interested SCT was the Twist, Micro-Term's top of the line. This unit was actually private-labeled from Facit, a Swedish company. Micro-Term had exclusive distribution rights for the Twist in the United States. The Twist could display a 72-line page in a vertical screen format, or it could be turned 90 degrees to display the more common 24 lines on a horizontal screen.

Micro-Term had made an unsuccessful earlier attempt at marketing its own full-page display terminal, the ERGO 4000. Although the company advertised the product largely on its ergonomic features, it was also pushed as a word processing unit. After introducing the ERGO 4000 at $1,695, Micro-Term dropped the price to $1,195 six months later and finally withdrew it from the market after a little over a year.

Human Designed Systems

HDS was another small, privately held company that was started in Philadelphia in 1975. Its Concept line of CRT terminals was fairly sophisticated and high end in terms of advanced editing capabilities, form-filling, and multiple pages of memory. The 1985 Datapro report lists three basic models, with list prices ranging from $1,295 to $1,895. All were available with extra memory for $150 additional.

Although HDS did not produce a full-page display terminal, SCT considered the company a key competitor because of its reputation within the AI community. Its products were targeted at the high end of the market, and it was known to produce high quality. HDS reported 1982 sales of $7 million, with 35 employees.

SCT's customer service manager had the following to say about its competition and the advantages offered by SCT's products:

> People might buy any one of our competitors' products. DEC, obviously, because it's DEC and the systems and software are known. Others they buy on price and because SCT has too many features they may not need. They buy us because of the flexibility—for instance, the zoom for selectable display formats. People may be using 24-line software today, but they too are thinking ahead to future needs. SCT makes products they can grow into, while using them all along.

The vice president of operations further defined why companies would purchase SCT's products by saying:

> Needs don't necessarily dictate what product you buy—money does. Anyone can have high-end needs. A company will allocate more money to an engineer's terminal than to a clerk's. It's a cost-benefit trade-off for the customer. . . . Loosening up the money to buy it determines the sale more than the functionality of the terminal. But it's in terms of *who* you're making more

productive. Like company cars—you buy a stripped-down van for the delivery person, and a Mercedes for the salesperson.

Santa Clara Terminals Today

Marketing Approach

In general, SCT continues to target the high-end, sophisticated user of CRT terminals. Its products push the limits of CRT terminal technology; some have hardware that could be used to provide full workstation functions, although there is currently no software to support it. The vice president of operations explained:

> Our basic marketing approach is to provide high-end products not sold on price. They must be sold on a feature level and on a need level—why it's worth the extra money. It's not a commodity sale, like a $500 terminal. We need people who are trained and understand the product, because no one will know it by themselves. . . . We've been reasonably lucky in that the people we sell to aren't shy. They have their own customer network, and it's developed into an underground marketing approach.

Current marketing is limited. An in-house customer service and support staff fields phone calls and requests for information, as well as answers questions about terminal function and operations. The same people provide after-the-sale support over the phone and interface with the company's engineering, production, and service departments to resolve customer complaints. They also provide support to SCT regional sales representatives and distributors. (See Exhibit 1 for SCT organization chart.)

Paid advertising at this time is limited to new product introductions. The company places a block of ads to run for one to two months in trade publications. The last of these ran in March–April of 1985 to introduce the new XL product line. SCT continues to send out mailings of press and product releases to trade publications and a customer/prospect mailing list. It also exhibits at the computer industry's major trade shows.

The marketing director explained some problems with SCT's marketing:

> A small company takes on the owner's personality—and we're engineering, not marketing, oriented. There's reasonable resistance to marketing here. It's owned by one person, who doesn't have a "big" or "growth" mentality. We're constrained by the current survival mode.

Product

As stated above, SCT's products are at the very high end of the ASCII editing terminal market (see Exhibit 2). It recently introduced the XL series of CRT terminals. These units have the same basic functions as the earlier Ambassador,

EXHIBIT 1 Organization chart—January 1, 1985

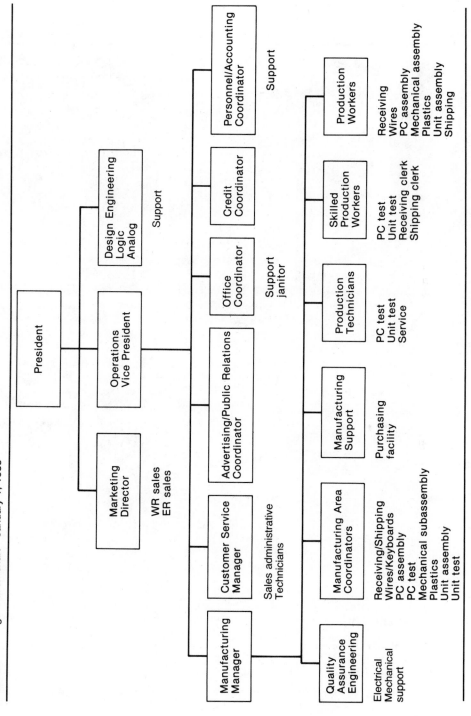

EXHIBIT 2

**THE
XL SERIES:**

**A DISPLAY OF
EXCELLENCE IN
FORM & FUNCTION**

Product excellence doesn't happen overnight. we've been designing quality terminals for professionals for over 15 years. We've innovated many of the time- and eye-saving features you now take for granted. And many you don't, if you're not already a user. Now we're unveiling another masterpiece: Our XL Series of ANSI-Standard Terminals.

Designed with you in mind.
The real beauty of the XL Series is its focus on your comfort. Its fully programmable keyboard saves you typing time and effort. Its dynamically selectable display lets you zoom more data onto the screen when you want more context, and less data when you just want bigger characters. With 15-inch or 17-inch portrait or landscape screens, offered in a full spectrum of phosphors, Ann Arbor is easy on your eyes.

Within the XL Series you'll find displays up to 170 characters per line and up to 66 lines per screen.

With plain English setup lines that give you a free hand in feature selection. And a whole palette of diagnostics and data-line monitoring aids to complete the picture.

There's an XL for every application.
Start with the Genie+Plus XL to meet your basic terminal needs. Move to the Ambassador XL when you want a full-page display.

When words alone no longer tell the story, switch to the GXL and add vector graphics. Finally, when you need even more memory and display than any other terminal provides, move all the way to the Guru® XL.

Take a closer look.
Study the specs. View the ergonomic design. See for yourself what it is that makes the XL Series the state-of-the-art display terminal you've been looking for

EXHIBIT 2 *(concluded)*

The XL Series
Features and Capabilities

Industry Standard Interface
☐ ANSI X3.64 Standard Controls
☐ DEC Software Compatibility
☐ EIA RS232 Interface (110-19.2K Baud)
☐ Tektronix 4010/4014 Compatibility

Advanced Video Features
☐ 15-inch Screen, Portrait or Landscape
☐ Slow Scroll
☐ Double-Size Characters
☐ User-Selectable Display Formats
☐ Vertical/Horizontal Keyboard Zoom
☐ Up to 28K Memory
☐ Paging/Windowing
☐ Split Screen Format
☐ Pause Key

Enhanced Functional Capabilities
☐ Fully Programmable Keyboard
☐ 8-Bit Data Mode (Meta Mode)
☐ Efficient Forms-Filling Mode
☐ Programmable ENQ and DA Responses
☐ Fast Editing with Local Move
☐ Independent Cursors
☐ RS232 Printer Port with Local and Remote Print and Copy Functions

Ergonomic Design
☐ Low-Profile Detached Keyboard
☐ Non-Glare Screen
☐ Mouse Interface (GXL)
☐ Tilt/Swivel Base
☐ Small Footprint
☐ Amber, Green, White Phosphors
☐ On/Off and Contrast Controls in Front
☐ Operator Convenience Modes
☐ English Setup Identifiers

High-Resolution Graphics (GXL)
☐ Vector Drawing Speeds of 9600 Baud
☐ 11 Line Types (3 User-Defined)
☐ Polygon Draw and Fill with 16 Patterns
☐ Selective Erase of Vectors, Points, Characters and Windows
☐ Alphagraphic Characters with User-Settable Angle, Size and Spacing
☐ Viewport Mapping from Drawing Window
☐ Print Spooling Mode

Reliability
☐ State-of-the-Art Technology in Design, Manufacturing, and Quality Control
☐ Internal Test Diagnostics
☐ Data-Line Monitor Mode
☐ Transparent Test Mode

Maintainability
☐ More-than-Fair Exchange Program
☐ Economical Factory Service
☐ Field Support Program
Note: Not all features are available on all models. Refer to product data sheets for exact specifications.

XL Product Summary
☐ The GENIE+PLUS XL is a high performance editing/form-filling terminal with a 30-line display and 60-line memory.
☐ AMBASSADOR XL adds a 60-line display capability is available in either a portrait (vertical) or landscape (horizontal) screen orientation.
☐ AMBASSADOR GXL adds a vector graphics capability to the standard Ambassador.
☐ The GURU XL adds more memory (up to 28K) and more display (up to 66 lines of up to 170 columns), for the most demanding word-processing and text-editing applications.

The portrait display, with the CRT housed vertically, gives the appearance of an 8½" x 11" page, making it appropriate for word-processing applications that involve editing lengthy documents.

The landscape screen display, with the CRT housed horizontally, is well suited to applications involving accounting spreadsheets or vector graphics.

Physical Dimensions
☐ XL Terminals—width: 15"; height: 12 3/8"; depth: 13 3/8"
☐ XL Stand—footprint: 8 1/2" x 10"; height: 3 3/8"
☐ XL Keyboard—length: 16 7/8"; width: 7 3/8"; depth: 1 3/4"
☐ 360 degrees of rotation
☐ 12 degrees of tilt

Genie + Plus, and Guru products, which they replaced. However, they have been repackaged in an updated, more ergonomic case, which features tilt/swivel stand and low-profile keyboard with coiled cable. SCT is also offering the GXL, which is the Ambassador packaged with the Graphics Master introduced earlier as an add-on. This unit is a full graphics display, with resolution of 768 x 600 dots; it can be used with many popular graphics software packages.

SCT has considered bringing out a bit-mapped terminal, which provides much higher-quality display than the dot matrix technique, or a full workstation, but feels it does not have the engineering resources available at this time.

The next new product, the VXL, is scheduled to be introduced in July 1985 at the National Computer Conference. This product goes beyond the current Guru design to provide capabilities for connecting to several host computers at one time, along with multiple windows. This will allow the user to view or edit several files or programs at once, without waiting for the host to complete processing on each one. The VXL will not have local processing abilities.

The marketing director expressed his concerns regarding SCT's product line, saying,

> The product line is too limited, though that depends on the company's objectives. It's all full-page, high-priced—that's a limited market. We need a good, lower-priced terminal, and we could get more business.
>
> Around here you have to prove yourself with increasing sales before you can get the products you want. That doesn't make sense. On the good side, we've addressed some problems. The looks [of the product] were the most important, and we've taken care of that with the XL series. But we could double sales if we had a low-cost, 132-column display.

Distribution

There are currently two regional sales managers, one located on each U.S. coast. They report to the marketing director and are responsible for selling direct to OEMs and large end users, as well as for supporting the distributors in their half of the United States.

There is a network of eight U.S. distributor firms with 25 offices, plus another firm in Canada. The distributors are to sell to smaller-volume (under 100 units) accounts. However, at the current time, SCT will take sales of any volume direct. The company instituted this policy when it was felt that distributors were providing little value-added to the distribution channel. SCT suspected that some distributors were not stocking the products and felt that most were not making the effort to actually sell SCT equipment. In taking orders direct, SCT will discount without a firm volume commitment, more in line with the prices distributors offer to end users.

Previously, SCT had made a greater effort to push products through distribution, except in the case of large-volume and contract orders. Distributors were expected to stock equipment, and all leads were referred to them. The company offered some support in the way of training on SCT's products.

Pricing

SCT's pricing reflects its high-end products. List prices are as follows on the standard product line:

Genie XL	$1,395
Ambassador XL	1,595
Guru XL	2,395
GXL (graphics)	3,590

As noted previously, SCT sells at discounts off these prices, as required. It prefers to sell under an OEM or volume contract, but will give one-time discounts if necessary to get the business, although these are not given out lightly. Distributors' discounts range from 25 to 38 percent off list price.

Service

SCT services all equipment sold by the company, including equipment several generations old, at its facilities in Santa Clara. Recognizing, however, that field service was becoming more important to many end users, the company developed an innovative approach to this problem.

SCT realized that its resources did not make field service outside its own immediate area feasible. At the same time, the specialized nature of its products, along with a relatively small installed base, would make it difficult to attract the attention of a third-party service organization.

To counter these problems, SCT offers the More-Than-Fair-Exchange program for users who require better than normal factory service. For a $25 per unit initial registration fee, the company will ship a replacement unit within 24 hours of being notified of a failure. Returned units are repaired and put back into the replacement pool, with actual repair charges billed to the customer. This approach is much faster than factory service, yet is much less expensive for the customer than full-scale field service.

Engineering

SCT is an engineering-driven company, and a steady flow of new products is vital to its long-term health. Basic research and development engineering is handled by a three-person design group located in Portland, Oregon. This group is responsible for keeping up with the latest computer and display technology

EXHIBIT 3
SANTA CLARA TERMINALS, INC., AND SUBSIDIARIES
Consolidated Balance Sheet
As of June 30, 1984, and June 25, 1983

	1984	1983
Assets		
Current assets:		
Cash and cash equivalents	$1,273,643	$1,137,856
Accounts receivable		
Less: Allowance		
for uncollectible accounts of $50,000	1,140,539	973,794
Inventories—at lower of cost		
(first in, first out) or market	611,202	593,714
Refundable income taxes	—	288,000
Prepaid expenses	296,363	284,440
Total current assets	$3,321,747	$3,277,804
Investments:		
Rental property		
Land	161,600	161,600
Buildings	1,000,186	1,000,186
	1,161,786	1,161,786
Less: Accumulated depreciation	205,000	138,322
Total rental at depreciated cost	956,786	1,023,464
Marketable securities	809,536	636,874
Total investments	$1,766,322	$1,660,338
Property and equipment:		
Land	200,283	200,283
Buildings	938,363	938,363
Machinery and equipment	711,789	726,219
Office furniture	125,974	125,974
	$1,976,409	$1,990,839
Less: Accumulated depreciation	903,918	781,110
Total property and equipment		
at depreciated cost	$1,072,491	$1,209,729
Total assets	$6,160,560	$6,147,871

and for seeking ways to apply it to SCT's products, both in hardware and software.

Analog (monitor) engineering, as well as manufacturing and product engineering, are located at the Santa Clara factory. These groups "productize" designs. They may be adding refinements requested by the customer, fixing "bugs" that have been found in the firmware, or cleaning up the basic design to get a product to the final production stage.

Finding engineers with experience and high-level capabilities can be a problem for the company. Because of the very sophisticated, state-of-the-art nature of its products, it needs engineers who are not just well abreast of the latest technology but are also able to apply that technology in creative ways to SCT's products.

The customer service manager expressed her concern about the possibilities for growth as follows:

EXHIBIT 3 *(concluded)*

	1984	1983
Liabilities and Stockholders' Equity		
Current liabilities:		
Current maturity of long-term debt	$ 9,606	$ 8,531
Accounts payable	637,654	370,485
Employees' deductions for withheld taxes	8,835	8,949
Accrued expenses		
Salaries, wages, and commissions	232,568	712,430
Taxes, other than income	81,042	152,389
Other	17,600	17,600
Pension plan	—	480,000
Deferred income tax	70,400	—
Total current liabilities	$1,057,705	$1,750,357
Long-term debt:		
Land contract payable		
Less: Current maturity	890,962	901,387
Stockholders' equity:		
Common stock, $0.01 par value, 5,000,000 shares authorized; issued and outstanding 504,000 shares	8,064	8,064
Capital paid in excess of par value	2,354,568	2,354,568
Retained earnings	1,849,261	1,133,494
Total stockholders' equity	$4,211,893	$3,496,126
Total liabilities and stockholders' equity	$6,160,560	$6,147,870

Note: All figures are disguised.

> We need to plan a reorganization if we want to grow. We can handle what we do now, but the current structure isn't viable for heavy growth. . . . We currently have a sales staff, but no marketing staff—no one's in charge of marketing. From an engineering standpoint, we should be telling the engineers what to do and what to build, as opposed to putting the stamp of approval on what they've decided is neat to build.

As Ed Zimmer thought about the future of the company, he had several thoughts:

> Our current marketing approach won't work, but I don't know what will. I see SCT as the only real manufacturer of a full-page terminal. I *know* there's a market out there for it, but I don't know how to reach it.

At the same time, he thought of totally new directions the company could go. For instance, he thought of the printing business and how changes in technology and hardware prices might open it up for creative competitors. He wondered if SCT should be looking at opportunities there or in other segments of the computer industry. Perhaps SCT should get out of manufacturing altogether, or maybe look for another company to acquire it.

EXHIBIT 4
SANTA CLARA TERMINALS, INC., AND SUBSIDIARIES
Consolidated Statement of Income
for the Years Ended June 30, 1984, and June 25, 1983

	1984	Percent of Net sales	1983	Percent of Net sales
Net sales	$7,959,242	100.0%	$6,821,744	100.0%
Cost of goods sold:				
Inventories,				
beginning of year	593,714		376,483	
Purchases	1,823,819		1,534,394	
Direct labor	519,827		516,454	
Manufacturing expenses	1,595,339		1,689,573	
	4,532,699		4,116,904	
Less: Inventories, end of year	611,202		593,714	
Cost of sales	3,921,497	49.3	3,523,190	51.7
Gross profit on sales	4,037,745	50.7	3,298,554	48.3
Operating expenses:				
Research and development	1,761,747	22.1	765,685	11.2
Selling	682,400	8.6	698,765	10.2
General and administrative	828,429	10.4	1,565,763	23.0
Total operating expenses	3,272,576	41.1	3,030,213	44.4
Income before other income				
or (expense) and income tax	765,169	9.6	268,341	3.9
Other income or (expense):				
Loss from rental operations	(86,082)		(78,051)	
Interest and sundry income	107,080		154,797	
Total other income				
or (expense)	20,998	.3	76,746	1.1
Income before income taxes	786,167	9.9	345,087	5.0
Income Tax—deferred	70,400	.9	—	—
Net income	$ 715,767	9.0%	$ 345,087	5.0%

Note: All figures are disguised.

EXHIBIT 5
SANTA CLARA TERMINALS, INC., AND SUBSIDIARIES
Consolidated Statement of Changes in Financial Position
for the Years Ended June 30, 1984, and June 25, 1983

	1984	1983
Sources of working capital:		
Net income	$ 715,767	$ 345,087
Add: Charge or (credit) to net income not affecting working capital		
Depreciation	207,178	225,186
Gain on sale of vehicle	(6,880)	—
Total provided from operations	916,065	570,273
Transfer of working capital on corporate reorganization	—	1,248,640
Proceeds from sale of vehicle	6,880	—
Total sources of working capital	$ 922,945	$1,818,913
Applications of working capital:		
Increase in investments	172,662	248,018
Acquisition of property and equipment	3,261	34,216
Decrease in long-term debt	10,426	9,232
Total applications of working capital	186,349	291,466
Increase in working capital	$ 736,595	$1,527,447
Changes in working capital:		
Increase or (decrease) in current assets		
Cash and cash equivalents	$ 135,787	$1,137,856
Accounts receivable	166,746	973,794
Inventories	17,488	593,714
Refundable income taxes	(288,000)	288,000
Prepaid expenses	11,923	284,440
Total	43,944	3,277,804
Increase or (decrease) in current liabilities:		
Current maturity of long-term debt	1,075	8,531
Accounts payable	267,197	370,458
Employees' deductions for withheld taxes	(114)	8,949
Accrued expenses	(1,031,210)	1,362,419
Deferred income tax	70,400	—
Total	(692,652)	1,750,357
Increase in working capital	$ 736,596	$1,527,447

Case 3

Huron Valley
Girl Scout Council

> On my Honor, I will try:
> To serve God,
> My Country and Mankind,
> and to live by the Girl Scout Law.

This promise is recited by Girl Scouts around the world to reaffirm their beliefs in the movement. Traditionally, Scouts say the promise at the start of every meeting and when they become a full member. The number of girls who can say it, though, is a matter of concern for the directors of Huron Valley Girl Scout Council. They are noticing a decline in membership, especially as girls reach the sixth and seventh grades, when they tend to drop out of Scouting. To remedy this problem, Wendy Mellenthin, director of field services, wants to develop a new strategy aimed at this age group. Her recommendations must remain consistent with the traditional Girl Scout program.

History of Girl Scouts

On March 12, 1912, Juliette Low founded the Girl Scouts of America. The goal of the organization, as stated in its constitution, is to provide a program that so inspires "girls with the highest ideals of character, conduct, patriotism, and service that they become happy and resourceful citizens." Leadership skills can be developed in an atmosphere free of competition with boys. Four program emphases were established to help a girl: (1) deepen her awareness of herself as a unique person of worth, (2) develop values to give meaning and direction to her life, (3) contribute to her society through her own talents and in cooperative effort with others, and (4) relate to others with increasing skill, maturity, and satisfaction. These emphases are to be used as guidelines for all planned activities. In its earlier days, Girl Scouts was mostly a camping group. Since then, it has evolved into a group that encompasses many diverse activities.

The Girl Scout movement is divided into four program levels based on

This case was prepared by Leo Burnett Fellow Sherri Herman under the direction of Professor Martin R. Warshaw, Graduate School of Business Administration, The University of Michigan. Copyright © 1985 by Martin R. Warshaw. Used with permission.

age: the familiar Brownies (grades 1–3), Juniors (grades 4–6), Cadettes (grades 7–8), and Seniors (for high-school-age girls). The basic programming unit is the troop, consisting of up to 25 girls at the same level and 1 or 2 adult leaders. Troops generally function independently, but there are programs offered on the council and national levels (discussed later).

The Program

Although every troop operates under the guidelines established in the constitution, the focus differs among the age groups. At the Brownie level, emphasis is on making new friends, learning to work together, and discovering the world about them. As a troop, and with the volunteer troop leader, girls decide and plan activities of their choosing, such as arts and crafts, field trips, cookouts, and community service days.

Junior Girl Scouts can earn individual badges that demonstrate knowledge in a particular area. Upon completion of the requirements (see Exhibit 1), the girl will receive a special patch. By earning these badges, they develop skills in sports, art, music, drama, camping, sewing, traveling, and so forth. As a troop, the Scouts can plan any activity, work on a troop badge, go camping, or develop special interests.

Cadette Scouts continue to earn interest badges, and they can also work toward patches, which are more group oriented. Cadettes focus on a Scout's awareness of herself, her interests, and her future. She learns skills that will develop her own potential and works with her troop to explore new opportunities. It is up to the Cadette and her fellow troop members to plan their activities, based on common and new interests.

Senior Girl Scouts concentrate on the same interest programs as Cadettes and begin to explore career interests. Attention is focused on leadership, community service, and individual accomplishments. The troop supports the girl as she faces the uncertainties of the present and plans for her future.

Cadette and Senior Scouts are also eligible for special leadership awards and can participate in "Wider Opportunities." These are special events sponsored by councils across the country that provide the opportunity to travel to new places and take part in a new experience. For example, Tip of Texas Girl Scout Council, Weslaco, Texas, is sponsoring a "Fiesta in Mexico," a two-week trip to Mexico. Beaver-Castle Girl Scout Council, Beaver, Pennsylvania, is sponsoring a Canadian canoe trip. Within Huron Valley Council, Cadette and Senior troops can plan intertroop events and attend the Fall Ball or Spring Fling. These are councilwide weekend camping trips for all Cadette and Senior Scouts.

Girl Scout Traditions

All Girl Scouts participate in the annual cookie sale. Besides teaching Scouts how to take and deliver orders, handle money, and meet their obligations, the

EXHIBIT 1

Huron Valley Girl Scout Council
Marketing Badge

Purpose: To learn the process of marketing by developing skills used during the cookie sale: planning, promotion, sales, and evaluation.

Complete the following requirements:

1. Find out how the cookies you are selling are produced. Who bakes your cookies? Where are they made? What varieties are you selling? How are they different? How do the cookies get from the baker to you?

2. Find out what the cookies cost. How much profit does your troop receive? How much profit does your council receive? How does the council use its profits? How will your troop use its profit? Estimate the profit you wish to make to meet your goal and how many boxes of cookies you will need to sell to achieve your goal.

3. Find the meaning of the words *profit*, *overhead*, *margin*, and *net*. Visit a business, discuss these concepts with the manager, and observe the various jobs and departments in the business.

4. What makes a good salesperson? Get as many ideas as you can from salespeople and customers. Make a list of the do's and don'ts in selling.

5. Prepare a sales speech which promotes cookies and Girl Scouting to use with your customers. Present your speech to your troop.

6. What is advertising? Why is it important? Find various kinds of ads that appeal to you. Discuss why you like some ads better than others. Design your own advertisements to place in stores, school, etc.

7. Develop a 10-day plan to sell your cookies. Who will you go to see in person? Who can you telephone?

8. Plan an efficient way to deliver your cookies to customers. Can you save time? Can you save gasoline? Do you need someone to help you make the deliveries?

9. Keep accurate records on all customers' orders. Give your troop cookie chairperson an exact record of all cookies sold with the exact amount of cash.

10. Review what you have learned about marketing. Evaluate your personal sale. Evaluate your troop's sale. Were both goals met? Did the council meet its goal? Make a list of suggestions for improving your troop's next cookie sale.

My Signature

Leader's Signature   Date Badge Completed cookie sale is a valuable form of public relations for Girl Scouting in general. Also, the proceeds are a major source of revenue for the council, and supplement dues for each troop. Dues usually range between 25 and 50 cents per week for each girl. The amount, and how to spend it, is decided by the troop and the troop leader. In addition, every member pays a $3 annual registration fee to the national organization.

The uniform, another tradition of the Girl Scout organization, is designed specifically for Girl Scouts and is available at local department stores. Each level has a different uniform, as indicated by the following:

Level	Uniform
Brownies	Brown jumper or slacks
	Brownie blouse
	Tie
	Beanie
Juniors	Green jumper or slacks
	Girl Scout blouse
	Tie
	Cap
Cadettes	Green vest
	White blouse

Area troop leaders try to arrange uniform exchanges to alleviate the expenses involved in purchasing a new uniform. For instance, a Junior uniform costs about $34 for the jumper, blouse, hat, tie, and sash. Members are encouraged to purchase the Girl Scout handbook (Brownie/Junior—$3.50; Cadette/Senior—$3.00). It gives the history of Girl Scouts, discusses camping and other common activities, and explains the badges. The girls frequently consult their handbooks when planning activities.

Recruitment

Membership recruitment is organized and overseen by the council. Generally, it operates within the structure of the school system. If allowed by the elementary school, prospective Brownies and Juniors are given flyers and information packets in their classrooms (see Exhibit 2). Cliques among junior high girls make it more difficult to contact girls through the school. Therefore, one-to-one contact is usually the solution to this problem. Pamphlets have been left in high school guidance and physical education offices, but this recruitment method has not been effective. Initial contact is also made through community centers and public posters.

After interest is established, girls are placed in an existing troop, or a new one can be formed (provided there is sufficient interest and an available leader). If girls and/or parents require more information before joining, they are invited to view a film that highlights the Girl Scout program.

EXHIBIT 2

GIRL SCOUTING
Is NOT
"Just for Kids"!

Today's young woman has greater freedom and more opportunities than ever before. But with that freedom comes more responsibilities, more decisions, and more pressures...GIRL SCOUTING can help you meet these daily challenges.

In Cadette and Senior Girl Scouting you'll meet young women, who, like yourself, have a lot of ideas to share. You'll find friends in the adults you work with, and you'll get to know the people in your community.

Camping, hiking, trips, career exploration, and fun-filled activities will be part of the program that you help plan.

So get in touch with yourself...and others... Give Girl Scouts a try!

_____ I am interested in becoming a Cadette Girl Scout. (ages 12, 13, 14)

_____ I am interested in becoming a Senior Girl Scout. (ages 15, 16, 17)

Name _____ Fall grade _____

Address _____ City _____

Zip code _____ Phone _____ Birthdate _____

Parent's Signature _____

Parents: Please check where you'd be willing to help - Mothers AND Fathers!

____ Leader or Senior Advisor   ____ Assistant Leader   ____ Troop Committe

____ Driver   ____ Other   ____ Would like more information

GIRL SCOUTS

Huron Valley Girl Scout Council
P.O. Box 539
19 North Hamilton
Ypsilanti, Michigan   48197
483-2370

EXHIBIT 2 (concluded)

GIRL SCOUTS

G I R L   S C O U T I N G

O F F E R S   M A N Y

W O R L D S   T O   E X P L O R E !

THE WORLD OF WELL-BEING
THE WORLD OF PEOPLE
THE WORLD OF TODAY AND TOMORROW
THE WORLD OF THE ARTS
THE WORLD OF THE OUT-OF-DOORS

Brownie Girl Scouting is for 1st, 2nd, and 3rd grade girls. They make friends, meet in groups and have fun together while learning to "Be a Discoverer", "Be a Friend-Maker" and "Be a Ready-Helper."

Junior Girl Scouting is for 4th, 5th, and 6th grade girls. They make friends, meet in groups and have fun together while camping, hiking and earning badges.

The fall membership lists for Brownie and Junior Girl Scout troops at your school are being made up now. Parents, if your daughter is interested in being a Brownie or Junior Girl Scout, her troop will need your support.

PLEASE FILL OUT THIS FORM AND RETURN IT TO YOUR TEACHER. DON'T PUT THIS NOTICE IN A DRAWER!

Thank you! Any questions? Call:
Huron Valley Girl Scout Council
19 N. Hamilton, P.O. Box 539
Ypsilanti, MI 48197 (313) 483-2370

CHILD'S NAME _____ PHONE _____ AGE ____ FALL GRADE ____

ADDRESS _____ SCHOOL _____ BIRTHDATE _____

ESY track _____ Previous Troop Number _____

I could help my daughter's troop in the following ways:

(Troop Organizer)
___ LEADER; ___; ___ ASST. LEADER; ___ Troop Committee; ___ Troop Services Director

___ Phoning; ___; ___ Driving; _ Music; ___ Crafts; ___ Shopping; ___ Camping;

___ With Badges; ___ Providing Refreshments; ___ Attending an occasional meeting;

___ Cooking with a small group; ___ Babysitting for the leader; ___ Sharing a hobby

___ Other ways. (Please specify hobby, skill or "Other" on back of page)

PARENT'S SIGNATURE _____

Current Scouts also help with the recruitment process. Make New Friends is a program designed to add new members to a troop by sharing the Scouting experience with more girls. Brownies work on this project as a troop, while the other levels can do it individually or as a troop. Cadette–Senior Go-Getter is designed to help and encourage Scouts to recruit their friends to join Girl Scouting. If the new girl joins, the recruiter and the recruitee each receive half a patch; the two pieces fit together like a puzzle.

Organization Structure

There are 336 Girl Scout councils in the United States. Councils are formed on the basis of geographical areas, usually clustered around a large city. In the western regions, though, a council can span several states. A council is directed by a volunteer board of directors from the community, elected by older Scouts and adult volunteers. Directors have varied backgrounds and serve a three-year term.

Depending on its size, each council is assigned to one of three field centers. The Dallas field center oversees councils with less than 4,000 members; Chicago oversees the 4,000–10,000-member councils; and New York oversees the largest councils. Field centers provide consulting in finance, marketing, and camping. They also organize training for executives and volunteers. However, they have little jurisdiction over a council's operations.

The National Girl Scout organization has no direct supervision over councils. Its roles are as a policymaker for the entire movement and as a long-run planner.

Huron Valley Council Structure

The council is divided into seven geographic area associations (see Exhibit 3). All Girl Scouts aged 14 and over and all adult volunteers are members of an area association, which serves as the line of communication between the board of directors and volunteers. AAs meet at least three times a year to provide input into goals, objectives, and policies of the board. Area associations may also plan special activities such as fairs, family events, and recognition dinners. The majority of the leaders do not participate in the area association. Those that do participate have usually been a volunteer for two or more years.

The everyday operations are carried out by paid staff members and the many adult volunteers. The staff positions, their duties, and the personnel are described below.

Executive Director

Gail Slusser has held this position for three years but has been involved with the council for eight years. Previously, she was a volunteer. Gail has a BA degree in home economics. Her responsibilities include:

EXHIBIT 3 Huron Valley Girl Scout Council and Neighboring Girl Scout councils

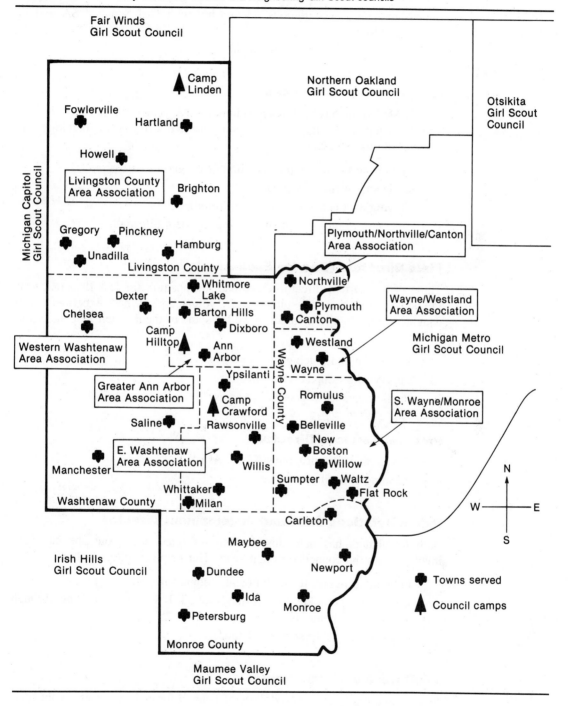

Overall fiscal management.

Maintaining a continuous relationship with Girl Scouts USA and the community.

Advising on budget development.

Director of Field Services

Wendy Mellenthin has held this position for three years. She has been involved with the council for eight years. Wendy has a BA degree in sociology. Her responsibilities include:

Administering the implementation of program to areas.

Collecting membership data.

Serving as a general membership resource.

Selecting, training, and supervising the field directors.

Field Directors (One for Each Area)

Three of the current directors have had the position for less than one year. Previously, the directors either were volunteers or had experience with daughters. This is a first career move for some of them. Their responsibilities include:

Recruiting and placing girls in troops.

Supervising troop service directors.

Public relations in geographic areas.

Program Services Director

Developing new programs (i.e., SAFE).

Planning councilwide events.

Public Relations and Fund Development Director

Barb Radabaugh has held this position for three years, but she has been involved with the council for eight years. Her responsibilities include:

Publicity program for recruitment, cookie sale, etc.

Coordinating cookie sale, Friends of Girl Scouting, funding through grants and bequests.

Investigating other sources of funds.

Adult Development Director

Joyce Smith has been involved with the council for eight years as a volunteer. Her primary responsibility is the recruitment and training of adult volunteers.

In addition, the council employs a Camp Ranger at Camp Linden and a six-person business staff.

Volunteers

The adult volunteers are an invaluable resource for the functioning of the Girl Scout program. They participate in all phases, from planning to implementing, with assistance from the staff members. The volunteer's most viable role is at the grass roots level. Every troop has at least one troop leader and, preferably, an assistant troop leader also. Her or his responsibility is to ensure that the girls experience a well-rounded and beneficial program. The quality of the troop leader is an important factor in determining a girl's evaluation of Girl Scouts. Therefore, the council provides training for all volunteers so they can serve their troop to the best of their abilities. An added benefit for the volunteers is that the training sessions are approved as a continuing education service through Washtenaw Community College.

Being a troop leader is not an easy job. One leader believes that to ensure good programming, she has to devote approximately 20 hours a week to the job. Because of the time commitment required, it is difficult to recruit leaders. Membership growth is restricted without enough leaders. A troop leader in Dexter said that more girls want to join but they cannot, due to a lack of leaders. This trend will most likely continue as more mothers enter the work force.

Other volunteer positions at the troop level include troop cookie chairman, troop badge assistant, and troop badge consultant. These jobs are not as time-consuming as troop leader but nonetheless are important. Parental support is needed in all areas, ranging from encouraging their daughters to remain active, driving to and from meetings, donating a talent, or supplying materials. The responses to the troop leader questionnaire (see Exhibit 4) indicated that, overall, parents do lend their support. They believe in the Girl Scout program and so encourage their daughters to participate. However, because they are working and have other children to care for, they cannot make very many time commitments. This is an obstacle that troop leaders face when attempting to do an excellent job.

Moving beyond the troop level, the next volunteer position is troop services director. She or he is assigned one or two schools and is in charge of establishing and maintaining troops in this area by recruiting adults and girls. Area projects and the cookie sale are coordinated by separate volunteer chairmen.

Council Services and Programs

Huron Valley Girl Scout Council owns and operates three campgrounds in the area. Camp Linden, located in Livingston County, has over 400 acres of land, with swimming and boating facilities. Winterized lodges, platform tent units, and primitive sites are available for troop camping trips. Camp Hilltop is also available year-round. It is located in Ann Arbor on 7½ acres of land. Camp

EXHIBIT 4 Troop leader questionnaire

Number of girls in troop _____

How often does troop meet? _____

On the average, how many attend each meeting? _____

Besides yourself, how many mothers help the troop? _____

Fathers? _____ What is their function?

_____

_____

Do you have trouble getting parents to cooperate? _____

_____

Why do you think this is? Lack of interest _____

Don't have time because they're working _____

Don't have time because of other children _____

Other _____

Overall, do most parents encourage their daughters to join and participate in activities? Why or why not?

_____

_____

Additional comments:

Crawford's facilities include a year-round lodge and primitive sites with shelters. It is located in Milan. The campsites are available for troop use at any time, either for daytime outings or overnight camp-outs. Fees range from $5/night to $40/weekend.

The council has developed several programs, and troops are encouraged to take advantage of them. SAFE (Social Awareness For Everyone) deals with sexual abuse and substance abuse with a nonthreatening presentation. Trained facilitators present a film and lead discussions. This program is available to all age levels, with a modification for Brownies and Juniors.

Latch Key, geared for 6–12-year-olds, gives safety information about staying home alone. Planning for Success teaches job-hunting skills, career development, and so forth to Cadette and Senior Scouts. A Stop Shoplifting program is currently being developed, but funds are still needed. Huron Valley Council has developed a reputation among other councils as being a maverick. This is because it tackles programs (i.e., SAFE) that other councils are not ready to handle.

Financial Situation

Exhibit 5 lists the estimated 1984 revenue sources. The largest source of funds is the cookie sale, followed by United Way funds. Although in the current year United Way will contribute 32 percent of the council's funds, in 1975 it contributed 50 percent. Unfortunately, the situation will not improve. United Way ranks the programs it assists, and as more social services require its funds, Girl Scouts is losing its priority status. Therefore, the council is investigating other possible funding sources and evaluating the possibility of becoming self-sufficient.

Environmental Issues

Changing demographics and social trends will affect the future of the Girl Scout program. A report published by Girl Scouts of the USA discusses many environmental issues and their implications for Scouting. Within the next

EXHIBIT 5 1984 proposed budget

Support and revenue	
Friends of Girl Scouting (annual giving)	$ 20,000
Unsolicited gifts	2,500
Cookie sale	348,345
United Way	219,670
Detroit United Foundation	
Plymouth	
Washtenaw	
Chelsea	
Manchester	
Livingston County	
Monroe County	
Equipment rental fees	500
Troop camp fees	6,000
Investment income	10,000
Badge and insignia sales	6,500
Subtotal—operating budget	613,515
Resident camp fees	78,000
Grand total	$691,515

decade, the number of children under 14 years is expected to increase. Initially, the 5–13-year age group will decrease from 31 million to 30 million, but by 1995 its size will increase to 34 million. In general, the population is older; parents are, on the average, older than in the past.

Financially, Girl Scouts may be able to benefit from an increase in corporate gifts that favor social welfare and educational services. Currently, almost half of American adults engage in some form of volunteer activity. The newer college population, which is older and more female, provides an additional resource for volunteers. The growing population of foreign students has knowledge and interests that Girl Scouts can use. The informal education that Scouting offers should increase in value as the nation becomes more concerned about its education system.

Competition

Girl Scouts competes with a host of other activities for girls' membership. Participation in sports is increasing among girls, and schools offer a variety of interest clubs. Music lessons, art classes, and dance classes offered by private businesses or the YMCA also appeal to many girls. Choices have to be made, and are often restricted by parents' willingness to pay.

Two organizations very similar to Girl Scouts are Campfire Girls and Explorer Scouts. Campfire Girls considers itself unique with its philosophy of a small club. Sparks, the kindergarten level, has no more than 6 girls per 2 adults, while the older levels have no more than 12 girls per 2 adults. Program emphases are on skill building, social development, and self-development. These are accomplished through crafts, service projects, songs and games, and camping. Recruitment consists of handing out flyers at school about a meeting and introducing the program to adults to get leaders. Some leaders are mother/father teams. Weekly dues of 25 to 50 cents go into a club treasury. Fund raising is not encouraged; each club is allowed only one fund-raising event a year. The council relies on an annual product sale and donations for its funds. It is not a United Way program.

Washtenaw Council membership is:

Sparks (kindergarten)	10 clubs
Bluebirds (grades 1–3)	13 clubs
Adventure (grades 4–6)	5 clubs
Discovery	1 club

The program is open to boys and girls, but membership is predominantly girls.

Explorer Scouts, available to boys and girls ages 14–20, provides hands-on learning of careers; businesses are visited, and there are lectures by the business people. Posts are chartered by a company, which provides the lead-

EXHIBIT 6 Monthly membership analysis, September 1983

	Troops						Girls					
Areas	Br.	Jr.	Cdt.	Sr.	Total Trps.	1982	Br.	Jr.	Cdt.	Sr.	Total Girls	1982
2. Plymouth/Northville/Canton	61	49	7	1	118	112	1,019	817	109	17	1,962	1,965
Nontroop											25	5
3. Wayne/Westland	41	21	4	1	67	69	642	397	36	9	1,084	1,228
Nontroop											53	4
4. South Wayne/Monroe	51	44	15	4	114	127	778	742	133	29	1,682	1,685
Nontroop											13	5
5. East Washtenaw	38	24	6	3	71	67	635	443	65	29	1,172	1,167
Nontroop											29	24
6. Greater Ann Arbor	50	37	6	2	95	87	780	635	113	15	1,543	1,529
Nontroop											61	14
7. West Washtenaw	20	16	5	5	46	39	277	237	57	14	585	583
Nontroop											14	4
8. Livingston County	50	29	9	3	91	98	749	483	94	11	1,337	1,420
Nontroop											46	30
Nontroop											241	86
Total 1983 registration	311	220	52	19	602		4,880	3,754	607	124	9,606	
Total 1982 registration	310	211	43	14	579		4,871	3,960	586	136	9,656	

ership and a meeting place. Posts are organized when a company invites parents and the teenagers to a meeting. There are posts for many professions including medical, fire service, law, secretarial, computer, and engineering. Membership in Monroe, Livingston, and Washtenaw counties totals 1,350 boys and girls.

The Current Situation

Despite a 70-year tradition and a strong program to back it, the Girl Scouts are experiencing membership difficulties. Exhibit 6, a membership summary for the seven areas comprising the council, compares September 1983 with the 1982 statistics. Although total membership has declined only slightly, the 200-girl decrease at the Junior level is very significant. Penetration rates by program level give a clearer indication of the membership decline at the sixth and seventh grades (Exhibit 7).

EXHIBIT 7 Comparative penetration rates by program level, 1981–1983

	School year		
Program level	1980–1981	1981–1982	1982–1983
Brownie (grades 1–3)	37.2%	34.6%	36.7%
Junior (grades 4–6)	27.1	25.1	25.6
Cadette (grades 7–8)	4.1	3.6	3.9
Senior (high school)	1.1	.9	.9
Overall	17.2%	15.8%	16.5%

EXHIBIT 8 Girl Scout questionnaire

Dear Girl Scout:

Please answer the following questions as best as you can. Answer every question. You can also write more comments if you would like. Your answers will help us make Girl Scouts even better than it is now!

1. What school do you attend? _____

2. What grades are there? _____ 3. Your grade _____

4. How many years have you been a Girl Scout? _____

Number of years

5. Brownie   _____

6. Junior   _____

7. Cadette   _____

8. Why did you join Girl Scouts for the first time? (Check box)
   - ☐ 1. My older sister was a Girl Scout
   - ☐ 2. My parents wanted me to join
   - ☐ 3. My friends were joining
   - ☐ 4. I heard about it in school
   - ☐ 5. I like the activities
   - ☐ 6. Any other reason? _____

9. Why did you join this year?
   - ☐ 1. My parents wanted me to join
   - ☐ 2. My friends were joining
   - ☐ 3. It is fun being a Girl Scout
   - ☐ 4. Any other reason? _____

10. What do you like best about being a Girl Scout? (Check 3)
    - ☐ 1. Being with my friends and making new friends
    - ☐ 2. Going on camping trips
    - ☐ 3. Selling cookies
    - ☐ 4. Working on badges
    - ☐ 5. Special activities planned by my troop (field trips, arts and crafts, parties)
    - ☐ 6. Wearing my uniform
    - ☐ 7. Anything else? _____

    Cadettes only
    - ☐ 8. Attending programs with Girl Scouts from other troops all over the state and country

Wendy asked the casewriter to conduct a survey to find out what could be causing this membership decline. A questionnaire was developed and distributed to seven Junior troops and seven Cadette troops, one from each area of the council (see Exhibit 8). The questions are aimed at determining what girls

EXHIBIT 8 *(concluded)*

11. Is there anything you do not like about being a Girl Scout?
    - [ ] 1. Going on camping trips
    - [ ] 2. Selling cookies
    - [ ] 3. Working on badges
    - [ ] 4. Activities planned by my troop   Which ones?
    - [ ] 5. Wearing my uniform
    - [ ] 6. Anything else? _____

    12. Do you have friends that are not Girl Scouts?   Yes _____
        No _____
        What do they think about the Girl Scouts?
        13. 1. They want to be a Girl Scout _____
        14. 2. They think it is OK _____
        15. 3. They do not like the Girl Scouts _____

16. What other activities do you do? (for example, art classes, dance classes, clubs at school, religious school)

    _____

    _____

17. If you could only do one of these (including the Girl Scouts), which would you choose? _____

    Why? _____

like/dislike about Scouting, the competition Scouting faces, and how Scouting compares to these activities.

The responses are summarized in Exhibit 9. Frequency tabulations were calculated for each troop level, as well as an overall count. Some of the key findings are:

> Most girls become Girl Scouts because of the nature of the program.
>
> The strongest dislike is having to wear the uniform.
>
> Girls enjoy camping the most. They also enjoy the other troop activities.
>
> A high percentage of the girls participate in sports and dance classes.
>
> If girls had to choose between Girl Scouts and their other activities, 50 percent of the Juniors would choose Girl Scouts. However, only 39 percent of the Cadettes would choose it.
>
> Friends' and parents' influence on girls is greater for Cadettes than Juniors.
>
> Girls may join and/or rejoin because of the troop leader.

Several of the girls commented that they prefer their other activity because they

EXHIBIT 9 Summary of questionnaire responses

	All (percent)	Juniors (percent)	Cadettes (percent)
Q3. Your grade			
4	32.5	43.0	—
5	28.1	37.2	—
6	14.9	19.8	—
7	12.3	—	50.0
8	5.3	—	21.4
9	7.0	—	28.6
Q4. Years a Girl Scout			
1	13.2	16.3	3.6
2	9.6	11.6	3.6
3	25.4	30.2	10.7
4	19.3	23.3	7.1
5	18.4	18.6	17.9
6	.9	—	3.6
7	5.3	—	21.4
8	6.1	—	25.0
9	1.8	—	7.1
Q5. Years a Brownie			
0	19.3	20.9	14.3
1	18.4	17.4	21.4
2	30.0	30.2	28.6
3	32.5	31.4	35.7
Q6. Years a Junior			
0	2.6	—	10.7
1	42.1	54.7	3.6
2	31.6	36.0	17.9
3	23.7	9.3	67.9
Q7. Years Cadette			
0	75.4		—
1	14.0		57.1
2	4.4		17.9
3	6.1		25.0
Q8. Why did you join Girl Scouts for the first time?*			
Older sister	3.8	5.3	—
Parents wanted	11.3	9.7	15.9
Friends join	15.0	12.3	20.4
Heard in school	24.4	25.4	22.7
Like activities	44.4	47.4	38.6
Meet new people	1.3	—	2.3
Q9. Why did you join this year?*			
Parents wanted	9.7	5.6	13.6
Friends joining	11.3	10.0	11.4
Fun being a Girl Scout	77.4	83.3	50.0
Work with people	1.6	1.1	2.3
Q10. What do you like best about being a Girl Scout?*			
Being with/making friends	19.1	18.1	22.7
Camping	26.5	25.0	31.8
Selling cookies	16.5	19.0	10.2
Working on badges	11.2	11.3	11.4
Troop activities	23.2	24.6	20.5
Wearing uniform	2.4	2.0	—
Cadette programs	1.2	—	3.4

EXHIBIT 9 *(concluded)*

	All (percent)	Juniors (percent)	Cadettes (percent)
Q11. Anything you do not like about being a Girl Scout?*			
Camping	4.3	4.8	—
Selling cookies	8.0	7.7	9.4
Working on badges	11.6	13.5	6.3
Troop activities	2.2	2.9	—
Wearing uniform	44.2	42.3	50.0
Nothing	30.0	28.8	34.0
Q12. Friends that are not Girl Scouts?			
Yes	98.2	97.7	100.0
No	1.8	2.3	—
What do they think about Girl Scouts?			
Q13. Like? Yes	21.3	22.5	21.4
No	78.7	77.5	78.6
Q14. OK? Yes	58.3	61.3	46.4
No	41.7	38.8	53.6
Q15. Do not like? Yes	31.8	26.3	46.4
No	68.2	73.8	53.6
Q13. What other activities do you do?*			
Art class	6.2	6.8	4.4
Band/chorus	11.7	10.2	15.6
Bowling	3.1	3.4	2.2
Clubs at school	8.6	8.5	8.9
Dance class	11.1	8.5	17.8
Drama	1.2	.8	2.2
4H	1.9	2.5	—
Junior Achievement/Business Organization	1.2	—	4.4
Music lessons	12.3	15.3	6.7
Religious school	15.4	15.3	17.8
Soccer	2.5	2.5	2.2
Swimming	8.0	10.2	2.2
Softball	1.9	1.7	2.2
Other sports	13.6	13.6	13.3
Hobbies	1.2	.8	—
Q14. If you could only do one, which would you choose?			
Art class	5.9	6.6	3.8
Band/chorus	6.9	3.9	15.4
Bowling	2.0	2.6	—
Clubs at school	2.9	1.3	7.7
Dance class	12.7	11.8	15.4
Drama	—	1.3	3.8
4H	2.0	2.6	—
JA/Business Organization	—	—	—
Music lessons	5.9	6.6	3.8
Religious school	2.0	1.3	3.8
Soccer	2.9	2.6	3.8
Swimming	2.9	2.6	3.8
Softball	—	—	—
Other sports	4.9	6.6	—
Hobbies	—	—	—
Girl Scouts	47.1	50.0	38.5

* Three responses allowed.
All: N = 114.
Juniors: N = 86.
Cadettes: N = 28.

want to get good at playing the musical instrument, or be on a sports team, or learn to dance. They recognize an opportunity to develop a skill and excel in a specific area. From their point of view, Girl Scouts does not offer this skill development. They do not see the long-run benefits from Scouting, but they do see them in other activities. They have fun being a Girl Scout, but it is not something they can do forever.

The troop leaders were also asked to comment on their perceptions of the membership situation. Responses included the following:

> Help is needed while girls are still in the Junior level to have them be interested in Cadettes.

> Time, teasing, embarrassment, unfriendly troop members, friends not involved, too much work to Scouting.

> By the time girls reach sixth grade, they're just plain tired of Scouting . . . nothing "new" to do.

The responses form a telephone survey of recent Girl Scout drop-outs confirmed these results. The main reasons for quitting Girl Scouts are boredom with the program and a lack of time due to homework and other activities. When it came time to choose between Girl Scouts and another activity, the girls were ready for a change.

Now that Wendy has more information about what is causing the decline in membership, she is ready to develop a new marketing strategy. She hopes to have the plan ready in time for next year's recruiting effort.

Case 4

Edgewater Marina*

In early January Captain Nathan Rutledge, proprietor of Edgewater Marina, looked out over the mostly empty docks and remarked to John Burnhart, a graduate student at The Citadel, ''I'm starting my second year in this business and I've still got half a mile of empty slips. All I've heard about from Charleston boat owners is that there's a lack of marina space around here, but most of my docks are still empty. I just can't figure out what is wrong with my operation. Any ideas you have, John, would be greatly appreciated.''

Background of the Marina

Edgewater Marina, the newest in the Charleston, South Carolina, area, opened for business the previous February (see Exhibits 1 and 2). The proprietor, Nathan Rutledge, was a retired Navy captain who had spent the last six years of his Navy career in the Charleston area. As he was a sailing enthusiast who had spent the greater part of his adult life near ships and the sea, a marina seemed the ideal business to challenge his managerial talents and provide him the less structured lifestyle he was seeking. The apparent lack of marina space in Charleston (the local Municipal Marina had a long waiting list for slips and the others appeared to be always full) plus his love for the Charleston area provided the incentive for him to construct and operate the Edgewater Marina.

To begin the operation, Rutledge purchased a 10-acre plot of land on the Stono River (see Exhibit 3) with 1,200-foot frontage on the river and began construction in January a year ago. The site seemed ideal for a marina as it provided sheltered deep water and was only a quarter mile off the Intracoastal Waterway. The marina is located just off a major two-lane road and is five miles from downtown Charleston. Transit to the ocean could be achieved by either following the Stono River south to its mouth (8 nautical miles) or by following the Intracoastal Waterway to Charleston Harbor and exiting there (13 nautical miles). The Stono River inlet was generally used only by knowledgeable local boaters, as the entrance channel was bordered by shifting sandbars. As a result, marker buoys were always being relocated.

---

* This case was prepared by Cleon L. Hartzell, Jr., under the supervision of Professor Douglass G. Norvell of The Citadel as a basis for class discussion rather than to illustrate either effective or ineffective handling of an administrative situation. Used with permission.

EXHIBIT 1 Map of the Charleston area

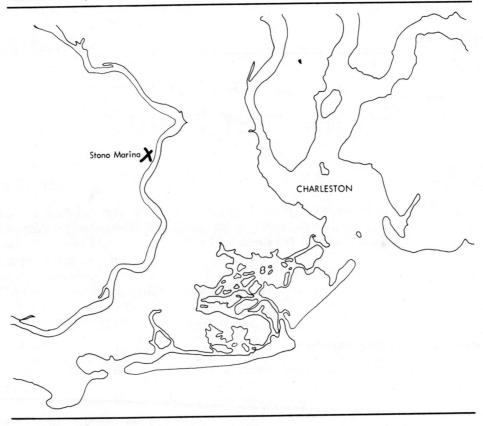

EXHIBIT 2 Charleston area marinas

	Breach Inlet	Mt. Pleasant	Charleston Municipal	Ashley	Ria Scott	Edgewater
Total number berths	6	60	308	92	80*	120
Usually available to transients	0	10	30	12	0	24
Per foot overnight	—	.25	.25	.20	—	.25
Per foot monthly	1.50	1.50	†	2.00	‡	1.75
Gasoline	X	X	X	—	X	—
Diesel	—	X	X	—	—	—
Water	X	X	X	X	X	X
Electricity	X	X	X	X	—	X
Showers	—	—	X	—	—	—
Laundry	—	—	X	—	—	—
Groceries	X	—	X	—	—	—
Restaurant	—	—	X	X	X	—
Snack bar	X	X	X	—	—	X
Ice	X	X	X	X	X	X
Bait	X	X	—	—	—	—
Boat landing	X	X	X	—	—	—

* Dry stack berths limited to boats under 24 feet.

† Monthly charge averaged $35 per month per berth.

‡ Monthly charge of $50 and one-year lease required.

EXHIBIT 3 Depths of the river near the marina

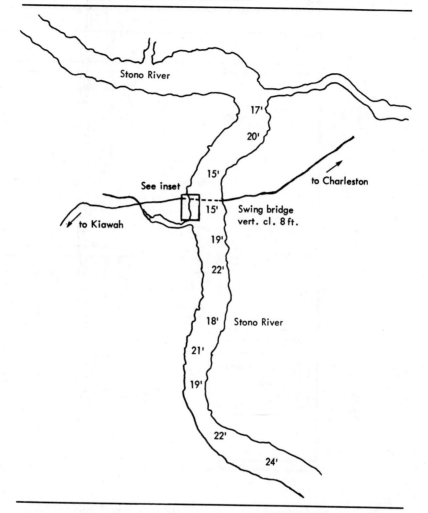

The marina was composed of three 660-foot floating docks connected to the shore by a floating access dock and fixed wharf (see Exhibit 4). Utilities provided on the docks included water (marina well), electricity (110/220), and telephone service (hook-up jacks). A public phone was available at the head of the wharf. The docks were lighted at night, and a dockmaster or assistant dockmaster was always present. The one building constructed at the marina served by partitioning as storage area, toilet facility, and vending machine location. Only one sink and toilet were provided in this building, but facility improvement plans called for the construction of a separate toilet/shower. Captain Rutledge was having problems with the local board of health on this issue and extensive sewage disposal facilities would be required before the

EXHIBIT 4 Docks and facilities at the marina

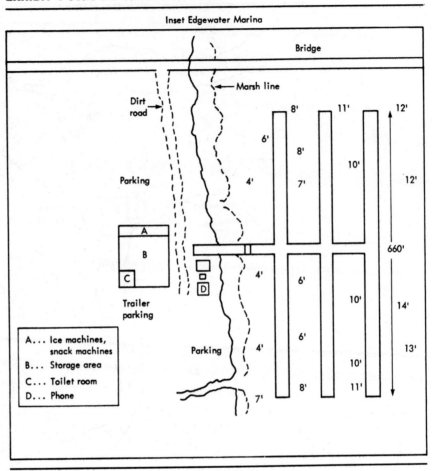

Inset Edgewater Marina

Bridge

Marsh line

Dirt road

Parking

A... Ice machines, snack machines
B... Storage area
C... Toilet room
D... Phone

Trailer parking

Parking

additional toilet/shower building could be constructed. Because of the large capital investment required (estimated at $5,000), this project had been indefinitely delayed. The access road was unpaved but well drained. Parking for about 30 cars was provided on an unpaved surface with trees scattered through it. About one fourth of the parking area was unusable after a heavy rain because of the muddy conditions, but this was to be corrected by paving the parking areas within the year. Exhibit 5 shows the financial development plan projected for the marina's first year.

Captain Rutledge hoped that the marina would be a family business. His eldest son was to act as dockmaster and live aboard a houseboat at the marina. Also, a second son and a daughter acted as assistants during the peak boating season. All were to be paid wages for their services, and these were deducted from operating revenue as expenses. Because of his independent retirement

EXHIBIT 5

EDGEWATER MARINA

Financial Development Plan

Pro Forma Statement of Sources and Application of Funds

For the Year Ending December 31

Sources of net working capital:

Net income[1]	$ 24,583	
Depreciation	200	
Issuance of long-term debt	100,000	
Owner input	50,000	
Total sources		$174,783

Applications of net working capital:

Procurement of land	81,950	
Land clearing	1,500	
Installation of electricity	1,550	
Storage/toilet building	2,000	
Auto parking area	4,600	
Septic tank	1,180	
Well and pump	300	
Construction of wharf	1,789	
Construction of docks	43,827	
Installation of pilings	18,000	
Installation of water main	1,000	
Toilet/shower building	2,000	
Fuel pumps and storage tanks	7,000	
Total applications		166,696
Increase in net working capital		$ 8,087

Notes:

[1] Owner agreed to not remove any of the net income from the business during the first year of operation.

income from the Navy, Captain Rutledge was to leave the first operating year's income from the marina in the business to build up the net working capital. The dock rental rate structure was based on the prevailing rates at the other local marinas. Charges were $1.75 per month per foot of the boat length plus 10 percent of the boat's length for maneuvering room. Rents were due monthly in advance and no leases were required. The rate for transient boats was set at 25 cents per foot per day with no surcharge for utilities (except telephone). Exhibits 6, 7, and 8 show the projected financial statements of the Edgewater Marina for the first year.

The First Operating Year

By May all dock construction was complete and utilities installed. Costs for materials and labor used in building the docks ended up being 26 percent higher than was originally planned. As occupancy rate for dock space was only 15 percent, the marina was experiencing a severe cash flow problem. Captain Rutledge contacted an old friend from his Navy days, Captain Alan Jones, and convinced him to invest in the marina. The details of this arrangement are

EXHIBIT 6

EDGEWATER MARINA

Pro Forma Cash Budget—First Year

	January	February	March	April
Cash receipts:				
Collection of dock rents[1]	$ 0	$ 1,848	$ 3,696	$ 5,544
Boat care service	0	0	0	0
Fuel, oil, and parts	0	0	0	0
Total cash receipts	0	1,848	3,696	5,544
Cash disbursements:				
Procurement of land	80,000	0	0	0
Administrative services	2,000	50	75	100
Supplies	100	50	50	50
Utilities	50	110	120	170
Loan payments	0	1,170	1,170	1,170
Land improvements	2,100	600	600	0
Facilities				
Wharfs and docks[2]	1,200	35,026	14,195	14,195
Building/equipment	3,830	0	0	0
Insurance	800	0	0	0
Wages[3]	0	0	0	0
Taxes	0	0	0	0
Miscellaneous	0	100	100	100
Total cash disbursements ...	90,080	37,106	16,310	15,785
Net cash gain (loss)	($ 90,080)	($ 35,258)	($ 12,614)	($ 10,241)
Cumulative net cash flow	(90,080)	(125,338)	(137,952)	(148,193)
Analysis of cash flow				
Beginning cash balance[4]	150,000	59,920	24,662	12,048
Net cash gain (loss)	(90,080)	(35,258)	(12,614)	(10,241)
Ending cash balance	59,920	24,662	12,048	1,807

Notes:

[1] Dock rent based on $1.75/foot of dock space at 80 percent usage rate.

[2] Total of 3,960 linear feet of dock space available by April 30.

[3] Wages are for the assistants to owner/manager. Initially these positions are not filled.

[4] Initial cash provided by owner's investment and bank loans.

EXHIBIT 6 (continued)
EDGEWATER MARINA
Pro Forma Cash Budget—First Year

	May	June	July	August
Cash receipts:				
Collection of dock rents	$ 5,544	$ 5,544	$ 5,544	$ 5,544
Boat care service	700	700	700	700
Fuel, oil, and parts	0	0	0	0
Total cash receipts	6,244	6,244	6,244	6,244
Cash disbursements:				
Administrative services ....:.....	100	150	150	150
Supplies	50	50	100	100
Utilities	270	380	430	430
Taxes	150	150	200	200
Insurance	150	200	200	200
Wages	1,000	1,000	1,000	1,000
Facilities				
Buildings[5]	2,000	0	0	0
Equipment[6]	0	0	2,700	900
Payment on loans	1,170	1,170	1,170	1,170
Fuel	0	0	0	4,000
Land improvements[7]	0	0	0	1,400
Miscellaneous	200	200	200	200
Total cash disbursements ...	5,090	3,300	6,150	9,950
Net cash gain (loss)	$ 1,154	$ 2,944	$ 94	($ 3,706)
Cumulative net cash flow	(147,039)	(144,095)	(144,001)	(147,607)
Analysis of cash flow				
Beginning cash balance	1,807	2,961	5,905	5,999
Net cash gain (loss)	1,154	2,944	94	(3,706)
Ending cash balance	2,961	5,905	5,999	2,293

Notes:

[5] Additional toilet building to be built in May.

[6] Fuel pumps and storage tanks installed starting in July and ending in November.

[7] Improvements to automobile parking area.

EXHIBIT 6 *(concluded)*
EDGEWATER MARINA
Pro Forma Cash Budget—First Year

	September	October	November	December
Cash receipts:				
Collection of dock rents	$ 5,544	$ 5,544	$ 5,544	$ 5,544
Boat care service	700	700	700	700
Fuel, oil, and parts	300	300	400	450
Total cash receipts	6,544	6,544	6,644	6,694
Cash disbursements:				
Administrative services	150	150	150	150
Supplies	100	100	100	100
Utilities	455	455	530	530
Taxes	200	200	250	250
Insurance	200	200	300	300
Wages	1,500	1,500	1,800	1,800
Facilities				
Buildings	0	0	0	0
Equipment	1,500	1,500	500	0
Payment on loans	1,170	1,170	1,170	1,170
Fuel	0	0	0	4,000
Land improvements	700	700	0	0
Repairs	0	100	100	350
Income tax	0	0	0	200
Miscellaneous	200	200	300	300
Total cash disbursements ...	6,175	6,275	5,200	9,150
Net cash gain (loss)	$ 369	$ 269	$ 1,444	($ 2,456)
Cumulative net cash flow	(147,238)	(146,969)	(145,525)	(147,981)
Analysis of cash flow				
Beginning cash balance	2,393	2,762	3,031	4,475
Net cash gain (loss)	369	269	1,444	(2,456)
Ending cash balance	2,762	3,031	4,475	2,019

EXHIBIT 7

EDGEWATER MARINA

Pro Forma Income Statement—First Year

	Actual	Pro forma
Revenues:		
Dock rent	$18,480	$55,440
Boat care service	3,800	5,600
Sales of fuel, oil, and parts	0	1,450
Total revenue	22,280	62,490
Expenses:		
Administrative	1,200	1,425
Utilities	3,100	3,930
Wages	5,000	10,800
Interest	5,534	5,534
Sales tax	600	1,600
Cost of goods sold	0	1,368
Depreciation	200	200
Repairs	400	550
Miscellaneous	1,000	2,100
Insurance	2,550	2,550
Supplies	850	950
Total expenses	20,434	31,007
Earnings before income taxes	1,846	31,483
Income taxes	0	7,100
Net earnings	$ 1,846	$24,383

why is dep. 200 here and 2130 on the next page?

EXHIBIT 8

EDGEWATER MARINA

Pro Forma Balance Sheet—End of First Year

		Actual		Pro forma
Assets				
Current assets:				
Cash		$ 6,885		$ 2,019
Accounts receivable		1,200		0
Fuel/supplies		700		6,632
Prepaid expenses		315		0
Total current assets		9,100		8,651
Fixed assets:				
Land		84,400		88,050
Buildings	$ 3,830		$ 5,830	
Equipment	0		7,000	
Wharfs and docks	81,400		64,616	
Less: Accumulated depreciation	2,130[1]		200	
Net buildings/equipment/wharfs and docks		83,100		77,246
Total fixed assets		167,500		165,296
Other assets:				
Intangible assets		300		300
Total assets		$176,900		$174,247
Liabilities and Net Worth				
Current liabilities:				
Accounts payable		$ 1,390		$ 0
Accrued taxes		0		7,100
Expenses payable		1,000		0
Total current liabilities		2,390		7,100
Long-term liabilities:				
Notes payable		92,664		92,664
Total liabilities		95,054		99,764
Net worth:				
Rutledge, capital		40,923		74,483
Jones, capital[2]		40,923		0
Total capital		81,846		74,483
Total capital and net worth		$176,900		$174,247

Notes:

[1] Depreciation calculated on straight-line basis over 40-year period.

[2] In May Edgewater Marina was changed from a sole proprietorship to a partnership between Captain Nathan Rutledge and Captain Alan Jones. The owners' equity in the marina was recapitalized as follows:

Rutledge, capital $40,000
Jones, capital $40,000

Captain Jones is to be a silent partner. All profits will be equally divided between Captain Rutledge and Captain Jones. As of January 1 Captain Rutledge will receive a salary of $15,000 per year for managing the marina.

shown in note 2 to Exhibit 8. This provided a fresh infusion of $40,000 into the business and figuratively allowed Rutledge to keep his head above water. All additional facility improvements were deferred until revenues picked up, and costs were closely monitored to conserve cash.

It was obvious by July that the marina would not come close to the 80 percent occupancy rate that had been envisioned. While the docks were now half full, many of the boat owners indicated that they would be either moving their boats to warmer climates in the fall or removing them from the water altogether. Up until this time Captain Rutledge had relied on word-of-mouth advertising to make the public aware of his marina. The Mid-Atlantic edition of the Waterway Guide made no mention of the Edgewater Marina and only hinted that a marina might be constructed soon along the Stono River. The swing bridge just north of the marina blocked its view from the Intracoastal Waterway, and the few transients that managed to find it were usually boats that had been turned away from the full Municipal Marina. Exhibit 9 shows the breakdown of the boats at the Edgewater Marina in July.

The rest of the first year showed no improvement, and many boat owners left the marina that fall. The occupancy rate averaged out to 27 percent the first year instead of the hoped for 80 percent. No additional facility improvements were accomplished, and this left the marina without a toilet/shower building, paved parking, or fueling equipment. One bright spot had been the demand for boat care service (hull painting, minor mechanical repairs) that had come from the boats that had utilized the marina. If the same demand percentage had occurred from an 80 percent full marina, income from this source would have been twice that predicted. With the start of the boating season only two months away Captain Rutledge was indeed anxious for any ideas to improve marina operations and occupancy rate.

EXHIBIT 9 Edgewater Marina list of boats present (July)

Trailer boats	
14 feet–20 feet	4
20 feet–28 feet	11
Sailboats	
20 feet–30 feet	12
30 feet	5
Pleasure cruisers	
26 feet–34 feet	10
34 feet–44 feet	4
Sport fishermen	
20 feet–30 feet	6
30 feet	3
Yachts	
45 feet	1
Houseboats	3
Total	59

The Market

John Burnhart's interest in boating and a course he was presently taking in marketing at The Citadel motivated him to undertake an analysis of the market for marinas in the Charleston area. He first talked to some of the boat owners who were still present at the marina and asked them how they had come to choose the Edgewater Marina. All were local boat owners and 30 percent indicated lack of space at other marinas caused them to pick Edgewater. Another 40 percent chose Edgewater because it was the most convenient for their needs. The remaining 30 percent were either dissatisfied with something at other marinas (long leases, lack of dredging, lack of personal service) or said they just like the friendly relaxed atmosphere at Edgewater. Many indicated that the lack of fueling facilities was a bother and could cause them to switch marinas at a later date. While this told Burnhart why the present occupants of Edgewater Marina were there, it didn't explain all those empty spots.

A survey of the other area marinas revealed that all of their occupancy rates were at least 75 percent and that the 308-slip Municipal Marina was completely full. A comparison of marinas (see Exhibit 2) showed that Edgewater offered fewer facilities than most other marinas its size. Data from the boating registrations office showed 27,244 powered boats registered in the Charleston area. While most of these boats were not candidates for marina berths, they did use marine supplies. The number of boat registrations had been growing at an average rate of 8 percent over the past five years, and it was anticipated that this trend would continue.

While Burnhart knew that transient boat traffic on the Intracoastal Waterway was seasonal, he learned that both the boating season and the total number of boats traveling was on the increase. In an attempt to gauge this traffic, he examined the records of a bridge across the Waterway near Charleston which had a low vertical clearance. The bridge operator was required to record the name, type, and state of registration of all boats for which the bridge was opened. Results of this examination are shown in Exhibit 10. If the seven busiest months are averaged (April–October) and it is assumed that the bridge acts as a gate for 80 percent of the traffic, then approximately 565 transient boats pass through Charleston per month during the boating season. This does not take into account any boats not using the Intracoastal Waterway by making the outside passage (assumed less than 5 percent). The only marinas presently catering to these boaters were the Charleston Municipal and the Ashley. Only the Charleston Municipal offered showers, laundry facilities, and marine supplies. In the peak months many transients were rafted against one another or were turned away completely at the Municipal Marina because of lack of space.

Advertising by the local marinas was almost nonexistent. Of the local marinas only the Municipal and the Ashley had paid advertisements in the Waterway Guide. Edgewater was now running a daily ad in the classified section of the local paper, and Mt. Pleasant Marina had its fishing supply store advertised in a small local distribution fishing magazine. The Municipal re-

EXHIBIT 10 John F. Limehouse swing bridge
(vertical elevation 12 feet)

Bridge openings for the year. Bridge operator records
name of boat, type, and state of registry.

	Yachts	Sailboats	Monthly total
January	45	32	77
February	24	14	38
March	116	42	158
April	309	167	476
May	511	185	696
June	230	74	304
July	141	66	207
August	244	81	325
September	498	192	690
October	312	152	464
November	101	51	152
December	32	20	52

Note: It is estimated that 80 percent of all transient boats
passing under the bridge require its opening.

ceived indirect advertising through yacht brokers and repair facilities who were
located near it. No organization existed to represent the interests of Charleston
area marinas although there had been talk of organizing one when the city
proposed the building of a new city supported marina. The proposed marina
would have 400 slips and be located at a naval museum across the harbor from
downtown Charleston. Local private marina operators expressed concern that
this constituted unfair competition in that the proposed marina would be
subsidized by the city. No action had been taken since the proposal was made,
and if such an undertaking was authorized, it would not go into operation for at
least three years.

The Analysis

It was now early February and John Burnhart knew Captain Rutledge was
eagerly looking forward to his comments and recommendations. As John
looked through the data collected (including Exhibit 11) he realized the problems the Edgewater Marina was experiencing could only be solved by a
complete marketing analysis and program. Who were the Marina's intended
customers, how numerous were they, and what products and services were they
seeking? How do you reach and influence this market segment? What would the
boating population want in the future and should preparations be made now to
meet these needs? These were just a few of the questions that required answering.

EXHIBIT 11 Boating registrations in Charleston County

Boat length	Number of boats	Open	Cabin	House	Other	Outboard	Inboard	In/out	Auxiliary	Other
Less than 14 feet	4,920	4,651	0	0	269	4,127	12	0	13	768
14 feet to less than 18 feet	10,887	10,435	62	1	389	9,601	211	327	35	813
18 feet to less than 22 feet	882	656	179	4	43	506	84	206	29	57
22 feet to less than 26 feet	414	179	200	13	22	141	123	114	7	30
Greater than 26 feet	338	111	173	29	25	21	246	52	10	9
Total	17,441	16,032	614	47	748	14,396	676	699	94	1,677

Exercise on Financial Analysis for Marketing Decision Making*

An important part of the analysis of alternatives facing marketing decision makers is the financial analysis of these alternatives. This exercise is designed to give students experience in handling the types of financial calculations that arise in marketing cases. If you can do the calculations in this exercise, you should be able to handle the financial calculations necessary to properly do the cases in this book.

1. You have just been appointed the product manager for the "Flexo" brand of electric razors in a large consumer products company. As part of your new job, you want to develop an understanding of the financial situation for your product. Your brand assistant has provided you with the following facts:

a.	Retail selling price	$40 per unit
b.	Retailer's margin	20%
c.	Jobber's margin	20%
d.	Wholesaler's* margin	15%
e.	Direct factory labor	$2 per unit
f.	Raw materials	$1 per unit
g.	All factory and administrative overheads	$2 per unit (at a 100,000 unit volume level)
h.	Salesperson's commissions	10% of manufacturer's selling price
i.	Sales force travel costs	$200,000
j.	Advertising	$800,000
k.	Total market for razors	1 million units
l.	Current yearly sales of Flexo	290,000 units

* An agent who sells to the jobbers, who in turn sell to the retailers.

* Copyright © 1987 by Thomas C. Kinnear.

Questions
1. What is the contribution per unit for the Flexo brand?
2. What is the break-even volume in units and in dollars?
3. What market share does the Flexo brand need to break even?
4. What is the current total contribution?
5. What is the current before-tax profit of the Flexo brand?
6. What market share must Flexo obtain to contribute a before-tax profit of $4 million?

2. One of the first decisions you have to make as the brand manager for Flexo is whether or not to add a new line of razors, the "Super Flexo" line. This line would be marketed in addition to the original Flexo line. Your brand assistant has provided you with the following facts:

a. Retail selling price	$60 per unit
b. All margins the same as before	
c. Direct factory labor	$ 3 per unit
d. Raw materials	$ 5 per unit
e. Additional factory and administrative overheads	$ 3 per unit (at a 50,000 unit volume level)
f. Salesperson's commissions the same percent as before	
g. Incremental sales force travel cost	$ 50,000
h. Advertising for Super Flexo	$600,000
i. New equipment needed	$900,000 (to be depreciated over 10 years)
j. Research and development spent up to now	$200,000
k. Research and development to be spent this year to commercialize the product	$500,000 (to be amortized over five years)

Questions
1. What is the contribution per unit for the Super Flexo brand?
2. What is the break-even volume in units and in dollars?
3. What is the sales volume in units necessary for Super Flexo to yield, in the first year, a 20 percent return on the equipment to be invested in the project?

3. The $60 per unit selling price for Super Flexo seems high to you. You thought you might lower the price to $50 per unit and raise retail margin to 25 percent.

Question
What is the break-even volume in units?

Part 3

Marketing Research and Forecasting

The need for good information is pervasive of all marketing decision making. Most cases in this book present some information provided by marketing research. However, they also leave many points of uncertainty. The skill of marketing decision making is the use of the information that is available, along with explicit assumptions about uncertain points to make good decisions. The suggestion that we do marketing research has usually not been allowed in other parts of this text. In this section we turn to the undertaking of marketing research activity.

First, let us define marketing research. It is the systematic gathering, recording, and analyzing of data about problems relating to the marketing of goods and services. There are three kinds of marketing research: (1) exploratory, (2) conclusive, and (3) performance monitoring. Exploratory research is useful for identifying situations calling for a decision and for identifying alternative courses of action. Conclusive research is useful for evaluating alternative courses of action and selecting a course of action. Performance monitoring research is designed to provide the control function over marketing programs.

The marketing research process may be thought of as being composed of the following steps:

1. Establish the need for information.
2. Specify the research objectives and information needs.
3. Determine the sources of data.
4. Develop data collection forms.

5. Design a sample.
6. Collect the data.
7. Process the data.
8. Analyze the data.
9. Present research findings.

The responsibility for the execution of these stages is shared by the marketing manager and the marketing researcher. They both must be sure that the problem has been defined properly, that the objectives make sense, and so on. The researcher holds primary responsibility for the technical details of the study. However, he or she must always be prepared to explain these aspects to the manager in nontechnical terms.

Marketing research costs money. Before it is undertaken, it must be ascertained that the value of the information provided justifies the cost. Also, before research is undertaken, the use to which that research will be made should be clearly understood. A specific decision should be the target of the research and the way the new information will be used in helping make the decision should be clearly understood.

This note and the cases in this section focus on the managerial aspects of marketing research. The technical details are mostly left for more advanced texts.

Case 6

Bay-Madison, Inc.*

In January 1987, Mr. George Roberts, research director of Bay-Madison, Inc., a large advertising agency, was faced with the problem of how best to conduct a study on Rill, a product of the Ellis Company, one of the agency's clients.

Rill, a powdered cleanser, was first introduced by the Ellis Company in 1966. Its original use was as a heavy-duty cleansing agent for removing dirt and stains from porcelain, metal, and ceramic tile surfaces. A unique bleaching property of the product eliminated the necessity for scrubbing and it contained no abrasive material. In 1976, the company's research department developed and added to the product an ingredient which imparted a light, fluffy texture to textile products washed in a mild solution of Rill. Recognizing the problem of keeping such articles as baby clothes, towels, and blankets soft through repeated washings, the company had promoted Rill both as a cleanser and as a laundry wash water additive since 1977. Over the years, about 50 percent of the company's advertising had featured the product solely as a cleanser, 30 percent as a laundry additive, and 20 percent as a dual-purpose product.

Rill was nationally distributed in a concentrated form in three can sizes— 4 ounces, 8 ounces, and 1 pound. Six other nationally distributed cleansers and two nationally distributed laundry additives posed formidable competition.

The product had sold well during the earlier years, but during the past five years unit sales had declined considerably apparently because of competition, although dollar volume over this period had remained fairly constant.

Company and agency personnel were in basic disagreement as to whether the product should be promoted as a cleanser, a laundry additive, or a dual-purpose product. In order to formulate marketing and advertising strategy for the coming year, the agency personnel believed it was necessary to supplement the quantitative information they had on unit sales, outlets, margins, and distribution with information of a more qualitative nature on consumer attitudes toward the product, usage patterns, and opinions on different product characteristics such as strength or concentration, odor, and package size.

In November 1986, Mr. Roberts and his staff had drawn up a research proposal which they had forwarded to six marketing research firms for detailed information regarding the following:

---

* This case was written by C. B. Johnston, Dean and Professor of Marketing, University of Western Ontario. Used with permission.

1. An appraisal of the proposal and suggestions for any changes.
2. A price quotation on the project (*a*) as outlined and (*b*) including any suggested changes.
3. A brief description of the staff who would handle the project.
4. Time required for preparation, implementation, tabulation, and final presentation.
5. Pilot testing suggested.
6. Detailed explanation of suggested sample size.
7. Information on the firm's executive personnel, interviewing staff, and the projects handled over the preceding two years.

The research proposal contained a description of the product's marketing problems, the objectives of the proposed research, broad suggestions regarding research methodology, and a proposed questionnaire.

In his proposal, Mr. Roberts outlined the major marketing problems as follows:

1. We really want to know how many people would buy Rill because (*a*) it is a cleanser, (*b*) it is a laundry additive, or (*c*) it is a dual-purpose product.
2. How do people buy products like Rill? Is it better to have a strong product or a weaker one? What size package should we have? Should it smell like soap or like perfume? At what price should it be retailing?
3. Do people see Rill as being a good, average, or poor product? What do they like about it? What don't they like about it?
4. Do people want a one-use product or a multi-use product?

By early in January, Mr. Roberts had received the submissions of all six marketing research firms requested to bid on the job.

Three of these firms were eliminated after preliminary consideration of their submissions revealed either inadequate staffs, superficial recommendations, or excessively high costs.

In considering the three remaining firms, Mr. Roberts felt he was hampered by his lack of knowledge of the techniques proposed by two of the firms and his inability to decide whether it was reasonable to expect that a detailed plan could be drawn up from the information he had provided in his proposal.

Two of the firms under consideration, National Research Associates and The Progressive Research Group, had outlined quite comprehensive plans for the research. The third, H. J. Clifford Research, had merely stated that they would not attempt to formulate any research plans from what they considered inadequate information. They believed the only way a detailed plan could be formulated was "through a continuing cooperation, based on mutual confidence, between the research firm, the advertising agency, and the client."

Mr. Roberts knew that many marketing research executives considered the third firm to be the outstanding marketing research company in the country and because of this, he did not believe they could be overlooked.

SUBMISSION OF NATIONAL
RESEARCH ASSOCIATES

Introduction

The present research proposal is based upon the assumption that it is crucial to obtain answers to the following marketing problems:

1. Is it advisable to continue to promote Rill as a multipurpose product?
2. If it is, should its various uses be promoted simultaneously or separately and what are the promotional approaches which would be most effective?
3. If it is not advisable to continue its promotion as a multipurpose product, for what uses could Rill be most successfully promoted?
4. What would be the most effective promotional approaches for the uses decided upon?
5. Would it be advisable to launch another product, or possibly the same product under a different name, for either of its uses?
6. What are the ways in which Rill distribution, packaging, pricing, and merchandising could be improved?

Research Objectives

To be able to plan a sound and effective marketing policy for Rill it will be essential to know:

1. The present market position of Rill in relation to its competitors in each of the fields in which it is used.
2. The reasons why Rill is in its present position in each of these markets.

I. Consumer Habits and Practices

The study will provide as complete a description as possible of the cleanser and laundry additive markets. Data will be provided in regard to (1) users and nonusers, (2) brand usage, (3) purchasing habits, and (4) usage habits.

This information will be cross-analyzed by age, socioeconomic status, community size, and level of education of the respondent.

II. Consumer Attitudes, Opinions, and Motivations

The study will thoroughly explore the underlying reasons for the market strengths and weaknesses of Rill in each of the usage categories as completely as possible under the broad headings of:

1. The underlying attractions or resistances to using any product for each of the purposes with which Rill is concerned.
2. The comparative strength of attractions to using Rill and to using competing brands for each of these purposes.
3. The comparative strength of resistances to using Rill relative to competing brands.

Some of the specific topics which will be investigated under these general headings are discussed below:

1. The perceived uses of Rill and its major competitors.
2. Factors affecting the perception of Rill; i.e., confusion regarding usage, incompatibility of uses, one use more efficient than the other, and where the attitudes toward the product originated.
3. Attributes of the most desirable product for each of the uses.
4. Common knowledge of the attributes of various brands now on the market.
5. Associations evoked by the brand name Rill and the brand names of competing products.

III. Consumer Knowledge of, and Attitudes toward, Relevant Advertising

1. How far the terms and phrases currently used in promoting Rill and competing brands are seen as (a) meaningful, and (b) appropriate to the product and its uses?
2. What copy points and adjectives might be most effective for the promotion of each use?

IV. An Evaluation of the Advertising Themes and Approaches Used by Rill

The research will attempt to determine whether the themes and approaches used in past and present Rill advertising are likely to operate toward overcoming resistances to Rill and capitalizing on sources of attraction.

V. An Assessment of the Rill Packages

The Rill package will be tested to determine:

1. Its visual effectiveness as evidenced by its attention-getting ability, its legibility, its memorability, its apparent size.
2. Its psychological effect on the consumer's perception of the brand.

Methodology

Market survey. Face-to-face interviews will be conducted with 2,275 homemakers who will be asked to give factual information about the products they use for each purpose. This survey will show the competitive position of Rill, but will not attempt to provide "reasons why."

Intensive interview study. The "reasons why" Rill is in its present position will be explored in 200 one-and-one-half to two-hour depth interviews which will attempt to discover attitudes, perceptions, and feelings toward the product and its uses.

The depth interview is designed to prompt the revelation of true attitudes and reasons for them by employing projective techniques which, instead of emphasizing personal behavior, invite comment on the behavior of others.

In-depth interviewing takes place in a relaxed, informal atmosphere. Interviews are usually conducted in the respondent's home and her verbatim responses to questions are noted.

The interview schedule contains a large number of open-ended and close-ended queries.

In addition, it employs a variety of techniques, most of which are taken from, or patterned after, standard psychological tests. A description of some of these techniques is given below.

1. The Personification Test. This is essentially an extension of the projective technique employed in psychological testing. It involves an attempt on the part of the respondent to describe certain products in human terms. Such an approach provides an opportunity for the expression of attitudes and opinions not otherwise easily obtainable.

2. The Thematic Apperception Test (TAT). Like the Personification Test, this test is similar to the TAT in psychological projective testing. It consists of presenting to the respondent an unstructured drawing of a particular situation and asking him to "make up a story" of what is happening.

3. Word Association Tests. Respondents are asked to relate what comes to mind when a given word or phrase is read to them. This technique aids in throwing light on areas which may warrant fuller investigation.

4. The Semantic Differential Test. This method, developed by us, has been designed to provide insights and information in regard to the perception of company and product attributes.

Fundamentally, the test consists of having the respondent rate a series of products on specially designed scales. The scales are so designed as to provide an extremely sensitive measure in regard to many dimensions as applied to the various products.

The manner in which these data (along with the data obtained through the use of other techniques) are analyzed makes it possible to determine:

A. The extent to which a given product's image is correlated with the perceived "ideal" product.
B. The desirable direction of change in the perceived product attributes, if such change is found necessary.

Other techniques which may be employed include: (*a*) rank-ordering tests, (*b*) sentence completion tests, (*c*) forced choice tests, (*d*) paired comparison tests, and (*e*) true-false tests.

Laboratory study. Our visual laboratory is equipped to evaluate the relative effectiveness of various merchandising and advertising stimuli. By means of specially designed instruments it will be possible to evaluate the relative effectiveness of the Rill package and label in comparison with those of major competitors.

The various tests which will be conducted include:

1. Attention-getting tests.
2. Product recognition tests.
3. Brand identification tests.
4. Visibility and legibility tests.
5. Memorability tests.
6. Apparent size tests.
7. Color preference and association tests.

Sample

Market survey. For the purposes of economy it is suggested that a quota-controlled, weighted, national sample of 2,275 homemakers be employed. The accom-

| | Rural | | | | Urban | | Total | |
| | Farm | | Nonfarm | | | | | |
	Unweighted	Weighted	Unweighted	Weighted	Unweighted	Weighted	Unweighted	Weighted
Southeast	44	44	76	76	132	132	252	252
Northeast	101	101	110	110	614	614	825	825
Midwest	126	63	139	70	837	436	1,102	569
West	179	90	107	53	324	162	610	305
South Central	22	22	60	60	242	242	324	324
Total	472	320	492	369	2,149	1,586	3,113	2,275

panying table presents an unweighted sample in proportion to household figures and the proposed weighted sample.

The unweighted sample exceeds the number of interviews necessary to ensure reasonable reliability.

However, to allow for a cross analysis of white and black and urban and rural respondents, a total of 3,113 interviews would be required. The weighted sample cuts by 50 percent the number of interviews in the Midwest and the West. The data from these areas will be mathematically converted to representative proportions in the final tabulation.

Intensive study. Quota-controlled samples of 450 white and 150 black homemakers will be used.

Laboratory study. The number of respondents varies from test to test, but the samples will be designed to ensure statistical reliability.

Field Staff

Market survey. Our field staff of 455 interviewers located across the country will conduct the interviews and will be specially briefed and trained for this survey.

Intensive study. Our staff of 88 university-trained depth interviewers will conduct an average of seven interviews each.

Brief Description of Firm

National Research Associates has conducted almost 400 separate and varied research projects since its establishment in 1964. The success of the organization is portrayed by its rapid growth from a small unknown company to a recognized leader in the field in the United States. Further attestation has been the establishment of "continuing relationships" with many clients. The company is an "official training ground" for graduate students in the Department of Social Psychology at a prominent university.

The following individuals will be involved in this project:

> *R. J. Morrison, PhD,* research coordinator and major client and agency contact; academic training—BSc, MSc, and PhD, 1964 to 1969, major universities; research experience—wide experience in research as study director, consultant and research associate in four U.S. universities from 1964 to 1976; teaching experience—seven years of lecturing in psychology at two American universities.
>
> *A. Milton,* study director; graduate in economics with 10 years' experience in the research field including 3 years with a prominent United Kingdom research firm and a number of years with other English companies.
>
> *H. W. Rolland,* associate study director; senior staff psychologist who will coordinate the intensive study phases of the research. MSc working on PhD.
>
> *R. W. Brown,* associate study director; university graduate in sociology and statistics—10 years' experience in research—will handle tabulation and statistical analysis.
>
> (Four additional staff members were listed, all of whom were university graduates.)

Time and Cost Estimates

The research can be completed in 12 weeks after finalization of the research design. The cost is estimated at $130,000, 50 percent payable upon initiation of the study and 50 percent upon completion.

SUBMISSION OF THE PROGRESSIVE RESEARCH GROUP

Nature of the Problem

It is possible that the two major uses of Rill may, in combination, affect the market negatively. Women may think of it primarily in one sense or the other and those who regard it as a cleanser may not be willing to use it as a laundry additive, or vice versa.

In addition to this possible overall problem, there are certain marketing specifics which may also be important.

1. Is the product right?
2. What about its physical characteristics (strength or concentration, odor, physical form)?
3. What about its psychological connotations?
4. What about the packaging (size of package, nature of package, labeling, and package)?

We propose a consumer study covering the major areas of behavior and attitude including:

1. Brand personality and image for each of several cleansers (including Rill).
2. Brand personality and image for each of several laundry additive products (including Rill).
3. Habit pattern on home cleaning (including products used).
4. Habit pattern on laundry additives (including products used).

Scope of the Study

We see this as a national study as it is entirely possible that varying areas may display differing habits and attitudes.

The section of this proposal dealing with the sample will show the reasons underlying our recommendations. We suggest a total of 750 interviews in this consumer study and the sample will be of a "tight" nature.

The Sample

Type of sample. The sample will be of such a nature that it properly represents the homemaker population in terms of region, socioeconomic group, urban-rural, and the like.

The sample design will be a known probability sample. Primary sampling units will be selected proportionately across the country, and randomly selected starting points will be chosen from which a predetermined path of interviewing will be followed.

Size of sample. We recommend a total sample of 750 homemakers.

There are several reasons. The first concerns our belief that no subsample on which results are based should have fewer than 150 cases.

The other reason concerns overall accuracy with a sample of 750 cases. Better than 9 times out of 10, results based on this total sample should be accurate within some 2.4 percent; this level of sampling accuracy on an overall basis seems highly acceptable for the purposes of this particular study.

Numerical distribution of interviews is indicated in the accompanying table.

	Natural proportional distribution of sample	Proposed sample distribution	Weighting factor	Weighted cases
Southeast	77	125	2	250
Northeast	211	211	3	633
Midwest	265	177	5	885
West	130	130	3	390
South Central	67	107	2	214
	750	750		2,372

Fieldwork

Our field staff is of highest quality. It has been built over a 10-year period, and we spend a sizable amount of money each year on maintenance and development of this staff.

The field staff totals 723 workers, and all states and community sizes are represented.

Supervision

We maintain a staff of 20 salaried regional supervisors across the country. With the exception of a few small remote areas, this means that every interviewer works under the direct control of a regional supervisor.

Qualifications of Interviewers

The average interviewer on our staff has been working for the firm for approximately four years. For our consumer work, we make use of women who, on the average, have the following characteristics: (1) they fall between the upper middle and lower middle socioeconomic group, (2) they have completed some or all of high school, (3) they are extroverted, and (4) they are above the average in intelligence.

The Questionnaire

It is difficult to evaluate your questionnaire without considerable field testing. In the present case, there has been no effort at all to do so. We would save our "criticism" for (a) detailed discussion with the agency, and (b) considerable field testing.

We have conducted a group interview with the subject matter pretty much in its present sequence, though the questions asked were more of an open-minded variety than contained in the questionnaire draft submitted with your specifications.

We do know that the sequence of questions will work. We also know that women can and will answer these questions, despite their nature, if the right approach is used. We further know that while the questionnaire form is quite lengthy, it is still feasible in terms of its length. So it is not as if we know nothing about feasibility of the instrument.

Field Testing

As a result of the group interview, it will be possible—though we have not taken the time to utilize it in such a manner—to study the consumer response to the interview so carefully as to make sure that the phrasings used in the questionnaire follow the words and phrases used in the consumer's actual thinking. The group interview thus means that we are that much further ahead in the phrasings of this questionnaire, even though it so far has not been utilized for such a purpose.

We plan a field test—or perhaps several—with a total of 100 homemakers distributed among people of varying socioeconomic groups, largely concentrated (for efficiency of handling) in the Chicago Metropolitan Area to make sure that the sequence and phrasing are of such a nature as to be understandable, to get cooperation, and to obtain unbiased replies.

Description of the Firm

The Progressive Research Group began operations in 1958 and, as such, is one of the oldest marketing research companies. Over the years the company has handled a large number of projects and has among its clients many of the largest consumer goods manufacturers.

The company possesses the most advanced computer equipment in the country and constant improvements are being adopted to speed up and make more economical, complete, and detailed client reports.

The following persons will direct the project:

- *A. W. Willis,* BA, overall project coordinator; president of The Progressive Research Group and a graduate in economics from a large university.
- *B. K. Walker,* MBA, project director and client contact; vice president and a graduate in business administration from a major university.
- *R. C. Moffatt,* PhD, project adviser; major in sociology—five years' research experience as project director with large U.S. advertising agency before joining The Progressive Research Group in 1967. Three years spent as lecturer and consultant at two large American universities.

Time and Cost

Our report should be available 12 weeks after the finalizing of the project details. Our estimate of the cost of this project is $90,000 plus or minus 10 percent. It is our practice to bill one half of the estimated cost at the time of authorization with the final half billed on delivery of the report.

In discussing these proposals with his assistant, Mr. Jacks, Mr. Roberts wondered whether his own staff could not answer some of the questions if a thorough study of past Consumer Panel reports were conducted. For some 10 years Bay-Madison had received full reports from an independent research company which ran a consumer panel, but these had only been used for day-to-day planning. Never, for instance, had a long-term, thorough study of the trends in Rill sales been compared with the various advertising and promotional campaigns the company had used or to the various price levels that had existed from time to time. Mr. Jacks was particularly enthusiastic about the idea as he had long maintained that the agency was not getting full value from the panel data. He said that he would personally like to work on such a project.

Mr. Roberts, in considering the idea further, estimated that such an analysis could be done for approximately $25,000. He had checked with the research company and found that all past reports were kept on automatic data processing cards. The company was most interested in the idea as an experiment and estimated that all the data required by the agency could be compiled for about $6,500. Mr. Roberts thought he could release Mr. Jacks from his other duties for a period of two months and that the cost of Mr. Jacks' salary, statistical and secretarial help, and other expenses would not exceed $12,000.

It was at this point that Mr. Roberts found himself in January 1987. He knew a decision had to be made quickly as the client was very anxious to get the Rill situation straightened away.

Case 7

The Atlanta Journal and Constitution (A)*

Mr. Ferguson Rood, research and marketing director for *The Atlanta Journal* and the *Atlanta Constitution,* was still perspiring from the three-block walk in the hot August sun back to his office from the meeting he had just been to at Rich's Department Store. At the meeting, he had been told that Rich's, the newspaper's largest advertiser, wanted to test the effectiveness of TV and radio advertising versus newspaper advertising for its upcoming Harvest Sale. He had promised to make his suggestions for the research plan in 48 hours, and felt he had much work to do in that short time. He wondered what recommendations he should make for the study, and was concerned that the research design and questionnaire be developed so that the study would represent fairly the effectiveness of *The Atlanta Journal* and the *Atlanta Constitution.* As he began to review his notes from the meeting, he picked up the phone to call his wife and tell her he would be home very late that evening.

Background

The Atlanta Journal and the *Atlanta Constitution* are a union of two of the largest circulation newspapers in the South. The *Atlanta Constitution,* winner of four Pulitzer Prizes for its efforts in the area of social reform, was founded June 16, 1868. *The Atlanta Journal,* founded February 24, 1883, became the largest daily newspaper in Georgia by 1889. Also a winner of the Pulitzer Prize, *The Journal* is the Southeast's largest afternoon newspaper.

In 1950, *The Atlanta Journal* and the *Atlanta Constitution* were combined into Atlanta Newspapers, Inc., a privately held company. The two newspapers maintained independent editorial staffs, and there was very little overlap of readers. Exhibits 1 through 4 present data concerning the adult readership of the newspapers, the gross reader impressions, reach and frequency, and readership over five weekdays and four Sundays.

To provide the advertisers and potential advertisers with information necessary to help them make their advertising media decisions, the newspaper does a considerable amount of research, often approaching $25,000 in a year.

---

* This case was written by Kenneth L. Bernhardt. Copyright © 1987 by Kenneth L. Bernhardt.

EXHIBIT 1 Gross readership impressions, reach, and frequency of *The Atlanta Journal and Constitution*

Gross reader impressions

The Atlanta Journal and *Constitution* in 15-county metro Atlanta:

During any five weekdays, 864,500 adults read *The Atlanta Journal* or *Constitution* an average of 3.5 times for a total of 3,025,800 weekday gross reader impressions.

During any four Sundays, 907,600 adults read *The Atlanta Journal* and *Constitution* for an average of 3.4 times for a total of 3,085,800 Sunday gross reader impressions.

These newspapers deliver 3,933,400 adult gross reader impressions when one Sunday is added to five weekdays.

Reach and frequency of newspaper reading

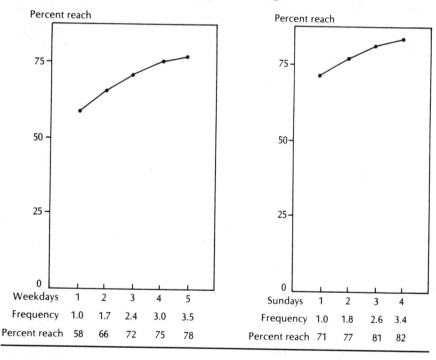

Weekdays	1	2	3	4	5
Frequency	1.0	1.7	2.4	3.0	3.5
Percent reach	58	66	72	75	78

Sundays	1	2	3	4
Frequency	1.0	1.8	2.6	3.4
Percent reach	71	77	81	82

EXHIBIT 2 *The Atlanta Journal* and *Constitution* readership information

78 percent of all daily circulation and 66 percent of all Sunday circulation is within 15-county metro Atlanta.

Of all metro Atlanta adults, 644,400 read *The Atlanta Journal* or *Constitution* on the average weekday. Of this total, 412,700 read *The Journal* and 366,100 read the *Constitution*. 134,400 adults read both. On the average Sunday 782,200 metro Atlanta adults read *The Atlanta Journal* and *Constitution*.

15-county metro Atlanta

Adult readers of *The Atlanta Journal* and *Constitution* in 15-county metro Atlanta

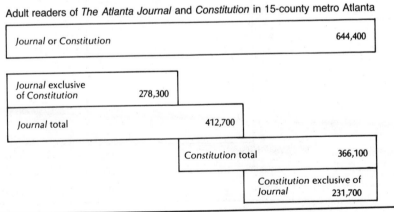

Journal or Constitution	644,400
Journal exclusive of Constitution	278,300
Journal total	412,700
Constitution total	366,100
Constitution exclusive of Journal	231,700

EXHIBIT 3 Readership of *The Atlanta Journal* and *Constitution* over five weekdays

644,400, or 58 percent, of all metro Atlanta adults read *The Atlanta Journal* or *Constitution* on the average weekday. Over five weekdays these newspapers deliver 864,900, or 78 percent, of all metro-area adults with an average frequency of 3.5 days.

	Total metro area adults	Average 1-day readership		Cumulative 5-weekday readership		Frequency
		Number	Percent	Number	Percent	
Total adults	1,105,500	644,400	58	864,900	78	3.5
Sex						
Female	588,500	331,700	56	447,600	76	3.5
Male	517,000	312,700	61	416,800	81	3.5
Household income						
$25,000 and over	104,200	85,900	82	102,700	99	4.2
$15,000–24,999	195,300	146,400	75	181,900	93	4.0
$10,000–14,999	241,900	152,800	63	203,900	84	3.7
$5,000–9,999	334,200	170,600	51	241,800	72	3.5
Under $5,000	229,900	88,500	39	133,000	58	3.3
Age						
18–34	470,500	234,500	50	345,200	73	3.4
35–49	305,600	197,200	65	250,300	82	3.9
50–64	211,900	145,800	69	184,600	87	3.9
65 and over	116,500	66,700	57	84,700	73	3.9
Race						
White	872,800	528,800	61	685,100	78	3.9
Nonwhite	232,700	115,600	50	180,100	77	3.2
Education						
College graduate	173,500	138,000	80	172,600	99	4.0
Part college	194,700	137,600	71	174,100	89	4.0
High school graduate	360,500	225,000	62	302,900	84	3.7
Part high school or less	365,600	137,000	38	202,200	55	3.4

Most of the research is designed to be used in selling advertising to a wide range of advertisers, and includes data on retail trading areas, shopping patterns, product usage, and newspaper coverage patterns. In addition to Mr. Rood, the research department had two other trained market researchers and one secretary.

Although there are nine daily newspapers in the Atlanta trading area, all but *The Journal* and the *Constitution* have very small circulations. The principal competition for large advertisers is with radio and TV stations. Exhibit 5 presents information on the circulation of the print media in the Atlanta area. Exhibit 6 contains information on the broadcast media in Atlanta. Although there were 40 radio stations, 28 AM and 12 FM, and 6 TV stations, WSB Radio and TV dominated the market. WSB Radio, for example, was consistently rated among the top six stations in the nation, and had a greater Atlanta audience than the next four stations combined. WSB-TV and WSB Radio, both affiliated with the NBC Network, were owned by Cox Broadcasting Corporation, which also

EXHIBIT 4 Readership of *The Atlanta Journal* and *Constitution* over four Sundays

782,200, or 71 percent, of all metro Atlanta adults read *The Atlanta Journal* and *Constitution* on the average Sunday. Over four Sundays these newspapers deliver 907,300, or 82 percent, of all metro-area adults with an average frequency of 3.4 Sundays.

	Total metro area adults	Average 1-Sunday readership	Cumulative 4-Sunday readership	Number of Sundays frequency
Total adults	1,105,500	782,200	907,300	3.4
Sex				
Female	588,500	418,800	477,800	3.5
Male	517,000	363,400	429,500	3.4
Household income				
$25,000 and over	104,200	89,100	97,200	3.7
$15,000–24,999	195,300	168,800	180,700	3.7
$10,000–14,999	241,900	190,100	216,400	3.5
$5,000–9,999	334,400	215,600	267,300	3.2
Under $5,000	229,900	118,500	145,600	3.3
Age				
18–34	470,500	313,000	390,000	3.2
35–49	305,600	221,300	248,500	3.6
50–64	211,900	167,000	179,900	3.7
65 and over	116,500	80,600	88,500	3.6
Race				
White	872,800	633,100	727,900	3.5
Nonwhite	232,700	149,100	179,100	3.3
Education				
College graduate	173,500	150,200	163,700	3.7
Part college	194,700	157,300	180,200	3.5
High school graduate	360,500	273,900	313,500	3.5
Part high school or less	365,600	192,300	240,000	3.2

owns television stations in Charlotte, Dayton, Pittsburgh, and San Francisco and radio stations in Charlotte, Dayton, and Miami. Cox Broadcasting and WSB-TV and Radio stations shared corporate headquarters in Atlanta.

WSB Radio was founded in 1922 by *The Atlanta Journal* newspaper. In 1939, former Democratic presidential nominee and Governor of Ohio James M. Cox acquired the newspaper-radio combine. In 1948, WSB-TV was founded, and two years later the newspapers and broadcast media were separated when Atlanta Newspapers, Inc., was established. Today, there is no relationship between the newspapers and WSB Radio and TV.

Rich's Department Store was the largest advertiser for *The Journal* and the *Constitution,* accounting for almost 5 percent of their advertising revenue, and was WSB's largest local advertiser. Founded in 1867, Rich's by 1970 had grown to a company with seven stores distributed throughout Atlanta as shown in Exhibit 7. Sales were approximately $200 million per year with earnings after taxes of almost 5 percent of sales. The company was classified as a general merchandise retailer, and carried a very wide line of products including clothing, furniture, appliances, housewares, and items for the home. Rich's dominated the Atlanta market, with close to 40 percent of department store sales

EXHIBIT 5 Circulation of print media in Atlanta

Metro Atlanta newspapers	Edition	Total circulation
Dailies		
Atlanta Constitution	Morning	216,624
Atlanta Journal	Evening	259,721
Journal-Constitution	Sunday	585,532
Gwinnett Daily News	Evening (except Sat.)	10,111
Gwinnett Daily News	Sunday	10,100
Marietta Daily Journal	Evening (except Sat.)	24,750
Marietta Daily Journal	Sunday	25,456
Fulton County Daily Report	Evening (Mon.–Fri.)	1,600
Atlanta Daily World	Morning	19,000
Atlanta Daily World	Sunday	22,000
Wall Street Journal	Morning (Mon.–Fri.)	16,180
Jonesboro News Daily	Evening (Mon.–Fri.)	9,100
North Fulton Today	Evening (Mon.–Fri.)	2,300
South Cobb Today	Evening (Mon.–Fri.)	2,400
New York Times	Morning (Mon.–Sat.)	500
New York Times	Sunday	3,100
Weekly newspapers		
Atlanta Inquirer		30,000
Atlanta Voice		37,500
DeKalb New Era		16,400
Atlanta's Suburban Reporter		3,900
Lithonia Observer		2,765
Northside News		8,000
Georgia Business News		4,900
Southern Israelite		4,300
Decatur-DeKalb News		73,000
Southside Sun (East Point)		37,700
Tucker Star		10,000
Alpharetta, Roswell Neighbor		6,800
Austell, Mableton, Powder Springs Neighbor		12,123
Acworth, Kennesaw-Woodstock Neighbor		3,242
Northside, Sandy Springs, Vinings Neighbor		20,836
Smyrna Neighbor		6,872
College Park, East Point, Hapeville, South Side, West End Neighbor		18,813
Chamblee, Doraville, Dunwoody, North Atlanta Neighbor		14,963
Clarkston, Stone Mountain, Tucker Neighbor		15,074
The Journal of Labor (Atlanta)		17,500
Austell Enterprise		1,911
The Cherokee Tribune (Canton)		7,100
Rockdale Citizen		6,031
The Covington News		6,000
The Forsyth County News		4,800
Dallas New Era		4,075
Douglas County Sentinel		7,350
South Fulton Recorder (Fairburn)		4,000
Fayette County News		4,500
Jackson Progress Argus		2,635
The Weekly Advertiser (McDonough)		5,650
The Walton Tribune (Monroe)		5,102
Lilburn Recorder		5,000
Lawrenceville Home Weekly		2,000
The Great Speckled Bird (Atlanta)		7,925
The Georgia Bulletin		14,000
The Covington News (Tues. & Thurs.)		6,200
Creative Loafing in Atlanta		30,000

EXHIBIT 5 *(concluded)*

Metro Atlanta newspapers	Edition	Total circulation
Atlanta area newspapers*		
Cobb		28,000
North Fulton		36,000
North DeKalb-Gwinnett		45,000
South DeKalb		44,000
South Fulton-Clayton		53,000
Major magazines in Georgia		
American Home		70,485
Better Homes and Gardens		145,962
Good Housekeeping		114,045
McCall's		139,728
Ladies' Home Journal		128,331
Family Circle		106,245
Woman's Day		100,566
Redbook		86,354
National Geographic		103,941
Reader's Digest		331,240
Newsweek		41,070
Time		60,438
U.S. News & World Report		40,417
TV Guide		345,871
Playboy		98,389
Sports Illustrated		38,263
Outdoor Life		25,918
True		18,244
Southern Living		95,000
Progressive Farmer		70,000
Cosmopolitan		25,075
Calendar Atlanta		50,000

* These are supplements to *The Atlanta Journal,* and circulation is to *The Atlanta Journal* subscribers only.
Source: WSB Research Department.

and approximately 25 percent of all the sales of general merchandise. The merchandising highlight of the year was the annual Harvest Sale, first held in October 1925. The sale typically ran for two weeks, and had become a yearly tradition at Rich's.

Background on the Media Effectiveness Study

Before preparing his proposal to Rich's for the media effectiveness study, Mr. Rood reflected upon the events of the past 24 hours. The day before, he had received a phone call from the vice president and sales promotion director from Rich's, inviting him to the meeting at Rich's the next day. Having been told that Rich's research director and the research director of WSB-TV and Radio would also be there, Mr. Rood had been a little apprehensive before going. At the start of the meeting he was asked if the Atlanta newspapers would be interested in

EXHIBIT 6 Broadcast media in Atlanta

Location	Station/network	Established	Frequency	Power	Channel	Network
Metro Atlanta AM radio stations						
Atlanta	WSB (NBC)	1922	750 khz	50 kw		
	WAOK	1954	1380 khz	5 kw		
	WGKA (ABC)	1955	1190 khz	1 kw day		
	WGST (ABC-E)	1922	920 khz	5 kw day 1 kw night		
	WIGO (ABC-C)	1946	1340 khz	1 kw day 250 w night		
	WIIN (MBS)	1949	970 khz	5 kw day		
	WPLO	1937	590 khz	5 kw		
	WQXI	1948	790 khz	5 kw day 1 kw night		
	WXAP	1948	860 khz	1 kw		
	WYZE (MBS)	1956	1480 khz	5 kw day		
Decatur	WAVO	1958	1420 khz	1 kw day		
	WGUN	1947	1010 khz	50 kw day		
	WQAK	1964	1310 khz	500 w		
N. Atlanta	WRNG (CBS)	1967	680 khz	25 kw day		
Morrow	WSSA	1959	1570 khz	1 kw day		
East Point	WTJH	1949	1260 khz	5 kw day		
Smyrna	WYNX	1962	1550 khz	10 kw day		
Buford	WDYX	1956	1460 khz	5 kw day		
Austell	WACX	1968	1600 khz	1 kw		
Lawrenceville	WLAW	1959	1360 khz	1 kw		
Marietta	WCOB	1955	1080 khz	10 kw day		
	WFOM	1946	1230 khz	1 kw day 250 w night		
Canton	WCHK (GA)	1957	1290 khz	1 kw day		
Covington	WGFS	1953	1430 khz	1 kw day		
Cumming	WSNE	1961	1170 khz	1 kw		
Douglasville	WDGL	1964	1527 khz	1 kw		
Jackson	WJGA	1967	1540 khz	1 kw day		
Monroe	WMRE	1954	1490 khz	1 kw		
Metro Atlanta FM radio stations						
	WSB-FM	1934	98.5 mhz	100 kw		
	WPLO-FM	1948	103.3 mhz	50 kw		
	WZGC-FM	1955	92.9 mhz	100 kw		
	WKLS-FM	1960	96.1 mhz	100 kw		
	WQXI-FM	1962	94.1 mhz	100 kw		
	WBIE-FM	1959	101.5 mhz	100 kw		
	WLTA-FM	1963	99.7 mhz	100 kw		
	WJGA-FM	1968	92.1 mhz	3 kw		
	WCHK-FM	1964	105.5 mhz	3 kw		
	WGCO-FM	1969	102.3 mhz	100 kw		
	WABE-FM	1948	90.0 mhz	10.5 kw		
	WREK-FM	1968	91.1 mhz	40 kw		
Metro Atlanta television stations						
	WSB-TV	9/29/48			2	NBC
	WAGA-TV	3/8/49			5	CBS
	WXIA-TV	9/30/51			11	ABC
	WTCG-TV	9/1/67			17	IND
	WETV	1958			30	NET
	WGTV	1960			8	NET

Source: WSB Research Department.

EXHIBIT 7 Map of Atlanta and seven Rich's stores

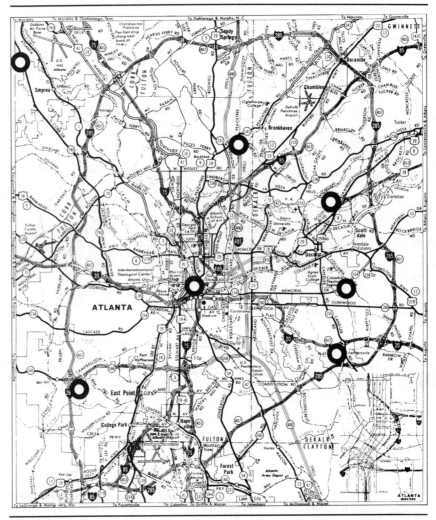

participating in a cooperative research study aimed at measuring the effectiveness of various advertising media during Rich's September Harvest Sale, their largest annual sales event. It became immediately apparent that the research director from WSB, Jim Landon, had met with the Rich's people the week before, and was undoubtedly the source of the idea to conduct the study. A document was then passed out that had been prepared by WSB and was entitled "Suggestions for Rich's Media Research." This document is included in the Appendix, and outlines the objectives of the study, a suggested methodology, together with a questionnaire.

The suggested objectives for the project were: (1) to measure the ability of

TV, radio, and newspapers to sell specific items of merchandise in Rich's seven Atlanta stores; (2) to determine how each advertising medium complements the others in terms of additional units sold to various segments of the customer population (age, sex, charge account ownership, and so on); (3) to determine what each advertising medium contributed in regard to additional store traffic. Mr. Rood's broadcasting counterpart stated at the meeting that "If Rich's is interested in conducting research to measure the effectiveness of various advertising media, WSB-TV and WSB Radio will be happy to assist." Rood had no choice, so he volunteered the support of the newspapers to the study.

The Rich's research manager then asked if the media would participate financially in the study. Mr. Rood suggested that each of the three media participate equally and committed the newspapers to $500 for a study that he figured should cost between $2,500 and $3,000 for interviewing. Mr. Landon indicated that Cox Broadcasting would be willing to put in $500 each for TV and radio.

They then discussed how the research could be conducted. The WSB proposal suggested in-store surveys, with a separate survey conducted for each item of merchandise tested. The survey would be conducted by Rich's employees working overtime in appropriate store locations during the peak shopping hours. The tabulation of the results could be handled by the broadcast station's computer. Care was to be taken to ensure that the TV, radio, or newspaper advertising for the individual items not be "stacked" in favor of one particular medium. The questions in the proposed questionnaire (see the Appendix) included questions on how the respondents happened to buy the merchandise at Rich's, if they recalled seeing TV, newspaper or radio advertising, and if they bought anything else. Questions were also asked concerning age and ownership of a Rich's charge account.

Mr. Landon stated that WSB was not trying to take business away from the newspapers, and that Rood had nothing to fear. His recommendation was that Rich's not take anything away from the newspaper advertising budget. He suggested that the amount of space purchased in the newspapers be the same as the previous year, with additional monies being committed to the broadcast media. The Rich's sales promotion director then discussed some of his thoughts concerning the study. He indicated that Rich's had been sending 400,000 direct mail pieces to announce the Harvest Sale; this year they would send 200,000, diverting the other money to broadcast. This would make $7,600 available for broadcast, and another $12,000 to $15,000 would be made available to purchase broadcast time.

The Harvest Sale was to open with courtesy days on Monday and Tuesday, September 21–22, with the sale beginning the evening of the 22nd and running for 13 days. While decisions concerning which sales items were to be included in the study and the media schedules to be used were not yet available, some progress had been made. Approximately 10 items were to be researched, and the newspaper ads on Sunday, September 20, would include all or most of the 10 items. Newspaper ads for the items would be repeated Monday and

Tuesday with emphasis on *The Journal*. The interviews were to be conducted Monday through Wednesday.

On Sunday and Monday, with a possible spillover to Tuesday due to availability, Rich's would run 120, 30-second TV commercials on all commercial stations except Channel 17. During the same time they would run 120 radio 30-second commercials on a list of stations which had not yet been determined. With both TV and radio, WSB was to get the lion's share if availability could be arranged. Mr. Rood felt certain in view of the client and the research that WSB would manage to come up with several prime-time commercial openings even if it meant bumping some high-paying national advertisers.

Eleven items were mentioned as possible subjects for the research. The 10 final items selected would come mostly from this list, although 1 or 2 other items might be chosen. The items mentioned included (1) color TV console at $499; (2) custom-made draperies; (3) Sterns & Foster mattress at $44; (4) carpeting at $6.99 per square yard; (5) Gant shirts at $5; (6) Van Heusen shirts and Arrow shirts at two for $11; (7) women's handbags at $9.99; (8) Johannsen's shoes; (9) pants suits; (10) Hoover upright vacuum cleaner; and (11) GE refrigerator.

Mr. Rood, who had not said very much at the meeting, then asked for 48 hours to review the proposal. Everyone agreed to this, and Mr. Rood promised to present a counterproposal at that time.

Even though it had been rather obvious who initiated the idea for the study and that he at first felt that newspapers were being ''set up'' by WSB, it had been basically a friendly and relaxed meeting among friends. Mr. Landon and Mr. Rood had worked together in the Atlanta Chapter of the American Marketing Association and had a great deal of mutual respect. Mr. Rood thought Landon was a tough competitor, and understood that he had been successful using awareness-type studies in Cox Broadcastings' other markets to gain additional advertising for broadcast.

When he returned to his office, Rood pulled out some of his files on Rich's. He noticed that the amount of advertising had been fairly constant, approximately 40 pages over the two-week period, during the past three Harvest Sales, and that basically the same products had been promoted. A typical Harvest Sale ad is included in Exhibit 8. He also pulled from the files rate schedules for *The Atlanta Journal* and *Constitution* and WSB (see Exhibits 9 and 10), even though he realized that the exact media schedule would be developed by Rich's advertising agency. Approximately $100,000 would be spent promoting the Harvest Sale, with perhaps a third of this amount being devoted to the sale items.

Mr. Rood decided that he would have to assume confidence in the effectiveness of the newspapers. He felt if the study were done right he would get his share of media exposure and influence. The other decision he quickly made was that in preparing his comments on the proposed research, he would take Rich's point of view rather than that of *The Atlanta Journal* and *Constitution*. He then began to review the events of the day and the WSB proposal in

EXHIBIT 8 Typical Rich's Harvest ad

EXHIBIT 9 The *Atlanta Journal* and the *Atlanta Constitution* retail display rates

Open rate per column inch:*

Constitution	$8.15
Journal	$11.27
Combination	$14.83
Sunday	$15.56

Yearly bulk space rates:

Inches per year	Cost per inch			
	Constitution	Journal	Combined	Sunday
100	$6.21	$8.43	$11.09	$11.65
250	6.16	8.35	11.00	11.55
500	6.10	8.28	10.90	11.45
1,000	6.05	8.21	10.81	11.35
2,500	5.99	8.13	10.70	11.24
5,000	5.93	8.05	10.59	11.12
7,500	5.90	8.01	10.54	11.07
10,000	5.87	7.97	10.48	11.01
12,500	5.85	7.93	10.43	10.96
15,000	5.82	7.89	10.38	10.90
25,000	5.70	7.73	10.17	10.68
50,000	5.61	7.69	10.05	10.61
75,000	5.51	7.65	9.93	10.53
100,000	5.41	7.61	9.81	10.46
150,000	5.21	7.51	9.56	10.31
200,000	5.01	7.41	9.32	10.15
250,000	4.81	7.31	9.08	9.99

* There are 8 columns by 21 inches or 168 column inches on a full page.

EXHIBIT 10 WSB radio and TV advertising rates

	One minute	20/30 seconds	10 seconds
WSB-AM radio: Spot announcements— package plans*			
12 per week	$40.00	$34.00	$24.00
18 per week	38.00	30.00	21.00
24 per week	32.00	26.00	19.00
30 per week	28.00	24.00	17.00
48 per week	26.00	20.00	15.00
WSB-FM radio: Package plan—52 weeks†	16.00	14.00	

WSB-TV
  Daytime rates
    60 seconds $ 75–235 depending on program
    30 seconds   40–140 depending on program
  Prime-time rates
    60 seconds‡ $540–660 depending on program
    30 seconds   390–725 depending on program

* Available 5:00–6:00 A.M., 10:00 A.M.–3:30 P.M., and 7:30 P.M.–midnight, Monday–Saturday; and 5:00 A.M.–midnight, Sunday. Best available positions in applicable times—no guaranteed placement.

† Quantity discounts available. For example, 18 times per week for 52 weeks is one half the above rates.

‡ Very few available.

light of what he felt Rich's needed to know. He also knew that whatever he proposed would have to be acceptable to Mr. Landon. Noting the lateness in the day, he began work on the counterproposal.

Appendix   Suggestions for Rich's Media Research

Objectives

If Rich's is interested in conducting research to measure the effectiveness of various advertising media, WSB-TV and WSB-Radio will be happy to assist. As a basis for discussion, here are suggested objectives for this project:

1. Measure the ability of TV, radio, and newspapers to sell specific items of merchandise in Rich's seven Atlanta metro stores.
2. Determine how each advertising medium complements the others in terms of additional units sold to various segments of the customer population (age, sex, charge account ownership, etc.).
3. Determine what each advertising medium contributes in regard to additional store traffic.

How the Research Could Be Conducted

The project could consist of a series of in-store surveys. A separate survey would be conducted for each item of merchandise tested. The more items tested, the more reliable the results of the overall research project.

If possible, all seven Rich's stores in the Atlanta metro area should participate in the research.

Each survey could be conducted by placing interviewers (Rich's personnel working overtime) in appropriate store locations during "peak" shopping hours with instructions to complete *brief* questionnaires with customers purchasing the item being tested. (See accompanying questionnaire.)

The interview could cover how the customer got the idea to buy the item, other planned purchases in the store during the same visit, charge account ownership, and any other pertinent data. Each interview would last less than a minute and would not bother the customers.

The sample size would vary, depending upon the number of stores participating, the type of merchandise and the sales volume. Interviewers would strive to include all customers purchasing the items during peak hours. Tabulation of the results could be handled by the WSB computer.

Careful Attention to Items and Media Schedules

In order to make the research valid and meaningful, the items to be tested must be selected carefully. In addition, care should be taken to ensure that the TV, radio, or newspaper advertising for these items is not "stacked" in favor of one particular medium. Close attention to the items being tested and the media schedule for each is necessary.

Questionnaire

The proposed questionnaire follows:

(All customers purchasing the item advertised are interviewed.)

1. *How* did you happen to buy this merchandise at Rich's?

Saw on TV	( )
Heard on radio	( )
Saw in newspaper	( )
TV and radio	( )
TV and newspaper	( )
TV, radio, and newspaper	( )
Saw on display	( )
Other: _____	( )

   ASKED OF CUSTOMERS NOT MENTIONING A MEDIUM: (2, 3, 4)

2. Do you recall seeing this merchandise advertised on the TV?
   Yes   ( )
   No   ( )

3. Do you recall seeing this merchandise advertised in the newspaper?
   Yes   ( )
   No   ( )

4. Do you recall hearing this merchandise advertised on the radio?
   Yes   ( )
   No   ( )

5. Are you buying *anything* else at Rich's today?
   Yes   ( )
   No   ( )
   Maybe   ( )
   Don't know   ( )

6. Do you have a charge account at *Rich's*?
   Yes   ( )
   No   ( )

7. In which group does your age fall?
   Under 25   ( )
   25–34   ( )
   35–49   ( )
   50 and over   ( )

Store _____

Time of Interview _____

Case 8

Wyler Unsweetened Soft Drink Mixes*

As Kenneth Otte sat in his office in Northbrook, Illinois, in early October 1977, he felt a bit like Jack in the children's story "Jack and the Beanstalk." He was facing a major challenge against a dominant foe, General Foods' Kool-Aid powdered soft drink mix, the giant of the unsweetened drink mix category.

The question Otte was considering was whether or not to recommend a major national introduction of Wyler's Unsweetened Soft Drink Mix against Kool-Aid in 1978. He knew RJR Foods' Hawaiian Punch was considering such a move and because of Kool-Aid's dominant position in the market, a 92 percent share and virtually unchallenged in its 50-year existence, he questioned whether there was room for more than one additional brand in the market. If he waited another year, it might be too late. If, however, he introduced in 1978 and Hawaiian Punch did, too, perhaps neither would achieve their goals. The question was more complex than just whether or not to introduce the product. Wyler's Unsweetened Soft Drink Mix had just completed the second year of testing under Otte's direction with somewhat mixed results. There was certainly time to make changes and adjustments to the program, but the question was, what changes should he investigate or recommend prior to a January meeting with the Wyler sales and broker force?

Management had requested a review of the situation and Otte's recommendations by November 1, 1977. Since a national introduction in 1978 would require substantial investment spending, Otte had several questions facing him. Should he recommend a national program for 1978? If not, what recommendation should be made? More test markets or fine-tuning of his present program?

If he did recommend a national program, what, if any, changes should be made in the recently completed test program? He wondered about such questions as advertising, promotion, distribution, and others. He still had time to investigate and test new ideas, but exactly what did the results of the test markets mean? As Otte prepared to develop his recommendation, he reviewed the entire situation of the category, the product, competition, and test market results. Did he have enough ammunition to challenge the Kool-Aid giant?

* This case was prepared by Professor Don E. Schultz and Mark Traxler of Northwestern University. Reproduced by permission.

Company History

Wyler Foods is a Chicago-based company manufacturing several products. Their line includes instant soups, boullion powders and cubes, and powdered soft drink mixes. The original company was organized in the late 1920s and in 1930 introduced Cold Kup soft drink, a presweetened mix in a pouch. It was available in four flavors. About the same time, Peskin Company introduced Kool-Aid, an unsweetened soft drink mix. Peskin was later acquired by General Foods and Wyler was purchased by Borden. Wyler continued to concentrate on the presweetened soft drink mix market. In 1954, a powdered lemonade mix was introduced very successfully. By 1977, lemonade flavor accounted for approximately 40 percent of all Wyler soft drink mix sales.

Wyler and Kool-Aid continue to battle in the soft drink mix market with Wyler dominant in the presweetened market and Kool-Aid in the unsweetened area. In the early 1960s, Kool-Aid entered the presweetened market with an artificially sweetened product using cyclamates. This sweetener was banned by the federal government in 1969 and Wyler, with its sugar sweetening, rapidly gained ground in the mix market. As a result of the ban Wyler moved up to a 20 percent share of the presweetened market. In 1972, Wyler introduced an industry "first" by packaging presweetened soft drink mixes in cannisters of 10 to 15 quarts. With this innovation, Wyler's share of the presweetened market increased to over 40 percent. Shares have declined slightly from this level as increased competitive pressures have segmented the market. Wyler did not have an unsweetened entry until initiating a test in 1976.

Soft Drink Market

The liquid refreshment market, composed of hot, cold, and alcoholic beverages, is limited in growth by the "Share of Belly" concept which suggests that human beings can consume just so much liquid in a given year. All entries in the soft drink mix market are competing with all other potable refreshments for some space in an unexpandable belly. The level of per capita liquid consumption, under this concept, is tied to the U.S. population growth rate and changing consumer preferences.

In 1977, soft drink mix quart sales increased 9 percent over the previous year. During that same period, single-strength drinks remained unchanged while carbonated beverage sales increased 7 percent. Otte predicts that soft drink mix tonnage will increase by 5 percent in 1978. Carbonated soft drinks will continue to grow, but less dramatically; canned fruit drinks will decline by 10 to 15 percent; and iced tea mixes will grow between 5 and 7 percent.

Powdered Soft Drink Mixes

The soft drink mix business, the 12th largest dry grocery product category, accounts for about 10 percent of all soft drink sales. It has increased in both quart and dollar sales each year since 1970. This growth is due to a greater demand for more product convenience, a wider assortment of flavors, and a more economical cold beverage alternative to carbonated drinks and single-strength canned drinks. In 1977 the segment is expected to produce sales of $503 million. Otte predicts that with a 5 percent growth in 1978, soft drink mixes will generate $565 million in sales.

The division of the powdered drink mix market is somewhat confusing. In terms of quart equivalent tonnage, the market is divided into 52.4 percent presweetened and 47.6 percent unsweetened. In terms of dollar sales, the split is 74.6 percent presweetened and 25.4 percent unsweetened. The major difference is the cost per quart of the sweetened product versus the unsweetened. More families purchase presweetened soft drink mixes than unsweetened; however, the unsweetened buyer appears to be a much heavier consumer (or purchaser at least). The presweetened buyer purchases the product an average of every 56.5 days compared to the more frequent purchase pattern of the unsweetened buyer who purchases every 46.7 days. Consumer panel data shows that both unsweetened and presweetened purchasers pick up an average of six pouches on each shopping occasion.

In comparison with other beverage categories, soft drink mixes are inexpensive, with unsweetened drink mixes the least expensive of all. Mixes are less than half the cost of carbonated beverages and single-strength canned drinks. Unsweetened mixes are least expensive due to the economy of adding one's own sugar. Exhibit 1 compares beverage costs per 4-ounce serving.

The buyer profile for powdered soft drink mix users shows that about two thirds of all U.S. households purchase the product. The primary buyer is the female homemaker between the ages of 18 and 44, with the heaviest concentration in the 25 to 34 age range. She is unemployed and has a high school education. Husband's occupation is blue collar, clerk, or salesman with an annual household income between $10,000 and $20,000. The typical family has three or more individuals including children under age 18. Users who consume at least five glasses per day are concentrated in the north central and southern United States (Exhibit 2).

Soft drink mix sales are highly seasonal. Sales peak during the summer months and drop off entirely during the winter. Many grocers, particularly in

EXHIBIT 1 Beverage cost per 4-ounce serving

Beverage	Price
Unsweetened powdered mix	3.0¢
Presweetened powdered mix	4.7
Iced tea mix	5.0
Frozen orange juice	10.2
Single-strength drinks	10.4
Carbonated soft drinks	11.7
Chilled orange juice	11.7

Source: *A. C. Nielsen Food Index*, May 1977.

EXHIBIT 2 Soft drink mix usage by area

	All users				Heavy users			
Area	Number of people who use product (000)	Percentage of users in each area	Percentage of people in each area who are users	Relative index	Number of people who use product (000)	Percentage of users in each area	Percentage of people in each area who are users	Relative index
Northeast	5976	18.8	40.5	81	2206	21.7	15.0	94
North central	10484	33.0	59.5	119	3220	31.7	18.3	114
South	10128	31.9	49.4	99	3353	33.0	16.3	102
West	5209	16.4	48.0	96	1393	13.7	12.8	80
Total	31797	100.1			10172	100.1		

Source: Target Group Index, 1977.

the northern climates, do not stock powdered soft drink mixes during the winter months after the summer inventory is sold. An attempt to overcome this extreme seasonality was initiated in 1976 by Wyler's. Their "second season" promotion strategy, which promotes to both the consumer and the trade, was designed to encourage year-round product usage.

Unsweetened Powdered Soft Drink Mixes

The basic ingredients of a powdered soft drink mix consist of citric acid, artificial flavors, ascorbic acid (vitamin C), artificial color, and, depending on whether sweetened or unsweetened, some sugar. Kool-Aid and Wyler's are packaged in 2-quart foil pouches. Hawaiian Punch is expected to follow that format. Directions for mixing a single package are as follows: Empty contents into a large plastic or glass pitcher. Add one cup of sugar and quantity of ice water to make 2 quarts. Stir.

A comparison of the available and most popular flavors shows that the "red" flavors and grape are by far the fastest selling. Exhibit 3 lists the available flavors for Wyler's and, in the case of Kool-Aid, the 6 out of 16 flavors that constitute 73 percent of their unsweetened volume. The flavors

EXHIBIT 3 Unsweetened mix flavors

Kool-Aid	Wyler's	Hawaiian Punch
Strawberry	Strawberry	Strawberry
Cherry	Cherry	Cherry
Fruit Punch	Fruit Punch	Red Punch
Grape	Grape	Grape
Orange	Orange	Orange
Lemonade	Lemonade	Lemonade
		Raspberry

listed for Hawaiian Punch are those that they have offered in their presweetened line. The unsweetened market is dominated by Kool-Aid with a 92 percent share, 4 percent is private label (A&P Cheri-Aid and Kroger's Flavor Aid), and 4 percent goes to others including Wyler's test market.

The unit cost to the retailer for the major competitors is 9.4 cents per pouch. The wholesale selling price for Wyler's and Kool-Aid is $26.95 per case. Although the store price per pouch ranges from 10 to 13 cents, suggested retail is 12 cents. This provides a 21.7 percent profit margin. The following figures show the retail profit margin for the common out-of-store prices.

Price	Retail profit margin
10 cents	6.0 percent
11	14.5
12	21.7
13	27.7

In the grocery aisle, the unsweetened category is normally placed next to the presweetened powdered soft drink mix section. The product is displayed on trays containing 72 pouches with three shelf facings. Wyler's and Kool-Aid cases contain four 72-pouch trays. Hawaiian Punch has announced that they will offer trays containing 36 pouches with two shelf facings, two trays per case.

Wyler's has instructed their food broker salespeople to position Wyler's unsweetened next to the same Kool-Aid flavor, to stack no more than two trays high, and to avoid stacking one flavor on top of another. Floor display racks are offered by both Wyler's and Kool-Aid to increase brand awareness and stimulate trial. The Wyler's rack holds 15 cases and provides secondary distribution. However, store managers are reluctant to use racks because the aisles are becoming too cluttered.

Introducing Wyler's Unsweetened

In 1977, Wyler's Unsweetened was introduced into 33 broker areas representing 28 percent of the U.S. population and 40 percent of total unsweetened category sales. Only 25 of the 33 areas had achieved adequate distribution by mid-1977. The successful 25 areas comprised 17.2 percent of the U.S. population and 33.7 percent of the total unsweetened category volume. The unsweetened case volume achieved a 6 percent share during the peak months of June and July 1977 and declined to 5 percent in October. Projected for the whole nation, the share was 3.2 percent in the peak and 2.5 percent on a continuing basis.

According to 1977 Target Group Index figures, Kool-Aid's strongest concentration both presweetened and unsweetened was in the south and north central regions. Wyler's strength, primarily based on presweetened sales, was centered in the north central region. Possible reasons for this difference are that powdered soft drink mixes started and have remained popular in the north central region and that Kool-Aid has many more users in each region than Wyler's, with only 33 measured broker areas. Exhibit 4 shows the regional concentration.

The target market selected for Wyler's introduction differed slightly from the one selected by Kool-Aid. The notable differences were household head's occupation and the market size. Exhibit 5 summarizes Wyler's target market demographics. The prime users were children 2 to 12 who were thought to have little influence on the purchase decision. The female homemaker bought the products she thought best for her family. Hence, most Wyler's advertising was directed at mothers.

Wyler's entered the market with two main advertising copy themes. "Double Economy" stressed Wyler's as an unsweetened drink for the entire family which was economical because you add your own sugar and the entire family enjoyed. The second advertising theme claimed that Wyler's unique flavor boosters (salt and other flavor enhancers) made Wyler's taste better. Both executions emphasized the red flavors and vitamin C content and soft-pedaled lemonade. While the two campaigns were used in the test, they were both considered interim efforts. On the basis of the test, a new claim based even more on flavors was being considered. This involved the use of Roy Clark, the television personality, as spokesperson, who would stress the good taste of Wyler's. Spot television was the major medium used in the market tests but was backed by print as coupon carriers.

Kool-Aid's advertising came in three varieties with separate messages for general brand awareness, economy of use, and children. The general brand awareness execution was a nostalgia appeal to mothers which said, "You loved it as a kid. You trust it as a mother." The economy of use execution showed children's preferences for Kool-Aid's flavor over single-strength beverages and the economy of adding one's own sugar. The execution with children showed the Kool-Aid "Smiling Pitcher" saving the day by foiling some dastardly deeds. Most advertising was placed in television; 70 percent network and 30 percent spot, evenly divided between day and night. It is anticipated that Hawaiian Punch would take advantage of their character "Punchy" to intro-

EXHIBIT 4 Kool-Aid soft drink mix usage by area

	All users				Heavy users			
Area	Number of people who use product (000)	Percentage of users in each area	Percentage of people in each area who are users	Relative index	Number of people who use product (000)	Percentage of users in each area	Percentage of people in each area who are users	Relative index
Northeast	4109	17.0	27.8	73	2441	23.2	16.5	100
North central	7660	31.6	43.4	114	4298	40.9	24.4	148
South	8372	34.6	40.8	107	2490	23.7	12.1	74
West	4073	16.8	37.5	99	1288	12.2	11.9	72
Total	24214	100.0			10517	100.0		

EXHIBIT 5 Wyler's target market demographics

Demographic variable	Wyler's	Kool-Aid
Income	$15,000–$19,999	$15,000–$19,999
Household size	3 or more	3 or more
Age of female head	Under 45	Under 45
Age of children	12 and under	Any under 18
Occupation of household head	White collar	Blue collar
Market size	500,000–2,500,000	Non-SMSA

duce the new unsweetened powdered mix since he has been used extensively before.

For the 1977 test, Wyler had divided the media budget into a peak and second season push. A total of $1,010,000 was to be invested in spot television in the 33 broker areas that made up the test. From mid-April to mid-August, Wyler had purchased spot TV in prime, day, and early fringe time. For the second season, the schedule was to be composed of day, early, and late fringe time from September until Christmas and from late January into late March. Otte had received a suggestion from the agency that if the tests were continued in 1978, media weight tests should probably be undertaken since a level pattern had been used in the 1977 test markets.

Compared to Wyler's test program, Kool-Aid was spending approximately $18 million in measured media in 1977. Six million dollars were being spent for presweetened, $6 million for unsweetened, and $6 million for the Kool-Aid brand. Two thirds of the network budget was being used for weekdays and was directed toward women. The remainder was being spent on a Saturday/Sunday rotation directed at kids. Spot TV funds were being allocated almost evenly between day (36%), night/late night (34%), and early fringe (30%). During the peak season, Kool-Aid planned on spending $13,405,000 divided into $6.580 million in the second quarter and $6.825 million in the third quarter. The second season expenditure was $4.59 million divided into $2.57 million in the first quarter and $2.025 million in the fourth quarter. It was expected that Kool-Aid would probably spend about $20 million in 1978 for consumer advertising.

Otte anticipates that Hawaiian Punch, if they introduce, would spend $4.7 million in a 1978 introduction. Two thirds would probably be used in network (33.5% each for day and prime) and 33 percent for spot. Advance information indicated that this budget would break down to $3.2 million for network ($1.6 million in prime and daytime) and $1.5 million for spot.

In addition to the heavy consumer advertising, Wyler's spent $827,670 on consumer promotions during the tests to generate trial and awareness. These included samples and various coupon drops. Several print media were being used to deliver both coupons and samples, such as Sunday supplements and best food day newspaper sections. It was still too early to determine the results of these promotions for 1977.

Trade promotions in 1977 were budgeted at $292,330. All were in case allowances to encourage retailers to stock Wyler's unsweetened. No matter how much money Wyler's spent on consumer advertising and promotion it appeared from tests the trade would not stock another powdered soft drink mix without sizable case allowances to sweeten the deal since most of the powdered drink mix inventory traditionally had been sold to retailers on trade deals. Whether entering additional tests or going national in 1978, Otte felt to ensure successful distribution a case allowance of $3.60 between the end of February and the end of April 1978 would be needed if Wyler's continued the test market or went national. The case allowance would be the highest ever offered in the unsweetened drink mix category.

Otte had conducted research testing consumer reactions to both the product and the advertising. In terms of product quality, the difference between Kool-Aid and Wyler's unsweetened was essentially parity. However, in-depth taste tests revealed that the grape and strawberry flavors of Kool-Aid rated higher than Wyler's. This was a matter of substantial concern since these two flavors were the two most popular in the unsweetened category.

Wyler's "Double Economy" commercial was evaluated by Burke Research in 1977 and by the McCollum/Spielman research organization in July–August 1977. By Burke norms, Wyler's did very well. For the target market of women 25 to 34, 35 percent recalled the commercial in "day after" testing. The norm was 27 percent. The McCollum/Spielman study indicated strong awareness of the brand name, but specific recall of Wyler's unsweetened was low.

The situation, as Otte sees it, is that heavy advertising and consumer promotion are necessary to combat the consumer's neutral attitude toward unsweetened powdered soft drink mixes. Awareness of unsweetened brands is much lower than that of presweetened mixes. However, Kool-Aid has extremely high brand awareness. Otte feels that the Wyler's name is associated with powdered soft drink mixes in the consumer's mind, though there is no consumer research to back this up. Also heavy trade promotion is necessary to get the product on the shelves.

If he decided on another test plan in 1978, Otte estimated that he would need a minimum investment of $4 million for Wyler's unsweetened. The plan would involve $2.2 million in media advertising and $1.8 million in consumer promotions. If he decided to introduce nationally, he would need a substantially larger budget than that. What to do? Should he risk another test and perhaps lose the opportunity to go national to Hawaiian Punch or should he develop a plan to invade Kool-Aid's territory in 1978 on a national basis? The risks and the rewards were great either way.

Case 9

Modern Plastics (A)*

Institutional sales manager Jim Clayton had spent most of Monday morning planning for the rest of the month. It was early July and Jim knew that an extremely busy time was coming with the preparation of the following year's sales plan.

Since starting his current job less than a month ago, Jim had been involved in learning the requirements of the job and making his initial territory visits. Now that he was getting settled, Jim was trying to plan his activities according to priorities. The need for planning had been instilled in him during his college days. As a result of his three years' field sales experience and development of time management skills, he felt prepared for the challenge of the sales manager's job.

While sitting at his desk, Jim recalled a conversation that he had a week ago with Bill Hanson, the former manager, who had been promoted to another division. Bill told him that the sales forecast (annual and monthly) for plastic trash bags in the Southeast region would be due soon as an initial step toward developing the sales plan for the next year. Bill had laughed as he told Jim, "Boy, you ought to have a ball doing the forecast being a rookie sales manager!"

When Jim had asked what Bill meant, he explained by saying that the forecast was often "winged" because the headquarters in New York already knew what they wanted and would change the forecast to meet their figures, particularly if the forecast was for an increase of less than 10 percent. The experienced sales manager could throw numbers together in a short time that would pass as a serious forecast and ultimately be adjusted to fit the plans of headquarters. However, an inexperienced manager would have a difficult time "winging" a credible forecast.

Bill had also told Jim that the other alternative meant gathering mountains of data and putting together a forecast that could be sold to the various levels of Modern Plastics management. This alternative would prove to be time-consuming and could still be changed anywhere along the chain of command before final approval.

Clayton started reviewing pricing and sales volume history (see Exhibit

* This case was written by Kenneth L. Bernhardt, Professor Tom Ingram, University of Kentucky, and Professor Danny N. Bellenger, Texas Tech University. Copyright © 1982 the authors.

EXHIBIT 1 Plastic trashbags—sales and pricing history, 1983–1985

	Pricing dollars per case			Sales volume in cases			Sales volume in dollars		
	1983	1984	1985	1983	1984	1985	1983	1984	1985
January	$6.88	$ 7.70	$15.40	33,000	46,500	36,500	$ 227,000	$ 358,000	$ 562,000
February	6.82	7.70	14.30	32,500	52,500	23,000	221,500	404,000	329,000
March	6.90	8.39	13.48	32,000	42,000	22,000	221,000	353,000	296,500
April	6.88	10.18	12.24	45,500	42,500	46,500	313,000	432,500	569,000
May	6.85	12.38	11.58	49,000	41,500	45,500	335,500	514,000	527,000
June	6.85	12.65	10.31	47,500	47,000	42,000	325,500	594,500	433,000
July	7.42	13.48	9.90*	40,000	43,500	47,500*	297,000	586,500	470,000*
August	6.90	13.48	10.18	48,500	63,500	43,500	334,500	856,000	443,000
September	7.70	14.30	10.31	43,000	49,000	47,500	331,000	700,500	489,500
October	7.56	15.12	10.31	52,500	50,000	51,000	397,000	756,000	526,000
November	7.15	15.68	10.72	62,000	61,500	47,500	443,500	964,500	509,000
December	7.42	15.43	10.59	49,000	29,000	51,000	363,500	447,500	540,000
Total	$7.13	$12.25	$11.30	534,500	568,500	503,500	$3,810,000	$6,967,000	$5,694,000

* July–December 1985 figures are forecast of sales manager J. A. Clayton and other data comes from historical sales information.

1). He also looked at the key account performance for the past two and a half years (see Exhibit 2). During the past month Clayton had visited many of the key accounts, and on the average they had indicated that their purchases from Modern would probably increase about 15–20 percent in the coming year.

Schedule for Preparing the Forecast

Jim had received a memo recently from Robert Baxter, the regional marketing manager, detailing the plans for completing the 1986 forecast. The key dates in the memo began in only three weeks:

August 1	Presentation of forecast to regional marketing manager.
August 10	Joint presentation with marketing manager to regional general manager.
September 1	Regional general manager presents forecast to division vice president.
September 1–September 30	Review of forecast by staff of division vice president.
October 1	Review forecast with corporate staff.
October 1–October 15	Revision as necessary.
October 15	Final forecast forwarded to division vice president from regional general manager.

Company Background

The plastics division of Modern Chemical Company was founded in 1965 when Modern Chemical purchased Cordco, a small plastics manufacturer with national sales of $15 million. At that time the key products of the plastics division

EXHIBIT 2 1985 key account sales history (in cases)

Customer	1983	1984	First six months 1985	1983 monthly average	1984 monthly average	First half 1985 monthly average	First quarter 1985 monthly average
Transco Paper Company	125,774	134,217	44,970	10,481	11,185	7,495	5,823
Callaway Paper	44,509	46,049	12,114	3,709	3,837	2,019	472
Florida Janitorial Supply	34,746	36,609	20,076	2,896	3,051	3,346	2,359
Jefferson	30,698	34,692	25,044	2,558	2,891	4,174	1,919
Cobb Paper	13,259	23,343	6,414	1,105	1,945	1,069	611
Miami Paper	10,779	22,287	10,938	900	1,857	1,823	745
Milne Surgical Company	23,399	21,930	—	1,950	1,828	—	—
Graham	8,792	15,331	1,691	733	1,278	281	267
Crawford Paper	7,776	14,132	6,102	648	1,178	1,017	1,322
John Steele	8,634	13,277	6,663	720	1,106	1,110	1,517
Henderson Paper	9,185	8,850	2,574	765	738	429	275
Durant Surgical	—	7,766	4,356	—	647	726	953
Master Paper	4,221	5,634	600	352	470	100	—
D.T.A.	—	—	2,895	—	—	482	—
Crane Paper	4,520	5,524	3,400	377	460	566	565
Janitorial Service	3,292	5,361	2,722	274	447	453	117
Georgia Paper	5,466	5,053	2,917	456	421	486	297
Paper Supplies, Inc.	5,117	5,119	1,509	426	427	251	97
Southern Supply	1,649	3,932	531	137	328	88	78
Horizon Hospital Supply	4,181	4,101	618	348	342	103	206
Total cases	346,007	413,217	156,134	28,835	34,436	26,018	17,623

were sandwich bags, plastic tablecloths, trash cans, and plastic-coated clothesline.

Since 1965 the plastics division has grown to a sales level exceeding $200 million with five regional profit centers covering the United States. Each regional center has manufacturing facilities and a regional sales force. There are four product groups in each region:

1. Food packaging: Styrofoam meat and produce trays; plastic bags for various food products.
2. Egg cartons: Styrofoam egg cartons sold to egg packers and supermarket chains.
3. Institutional: Plastic trash bags and disposable tableware (plates, bowls, and so on).
4. Industrial: Plastic packaging for the laundry and dry cleaning market; plastic film for use in pallet overwrap systems.

Each product group is supervised jointly by a product manager and a district sales manager, both of whom report to the regional marketing manager. The sales representatives report directly to the district sales manager but also work closely with the product manager on matters concerning pricing and product specifications.

The five regional general managers report to J. R. Hughes, vice president of the plastics division. Hughes is located in New York. Although Modern

Chemical is owned by a multinational oil company, the plastics division has been able to operate in a virtually independent manner since its establishment in 1965. The reasons for this include:

1. Limited knowledge of the plastic industry on the part of the oil company management.
2. Excellent growth by the plastics division has been possible without management supervision from the oil company.
3. Profitability of the plastics division has consistently been higher than that of other divisions of the chemical company.

The Institutional Trash Bag Market

The institutional trash bag is a polyethylene bag used to collect and transfer refuse to its final disposition point. There are different sizes and colors available to fit the various uses of the bag. For example, a small bag for desk wastebaskets is available as well as a heavier bag for large containers such as a 55-gallon drum. There are 25 sizes in the Modern line with 13 of those sizes being available in 3 colors—white, buff, and clear. Customers typically buy several different items on an order to cover all their needs.

The institutional trash bag is a separate product from the consumer grade trash bag, which is typically sold to homeowners through retail outlets. The institutional trash bag is sold primarily through paper wholesalers, hospital supply companies, and janitorial supply companies to a variety of end users. Since trash bags are used on such a wide scale, the list of end users could include almost any business or institution. The segments include hospitals, hotels, schools, office buildings, transportation facilities, and restaurants.

Based on historical data and a current survey of key wholesalers and end users in the Southeast, the annual market of institutional trash bags in the region was estimated to be 55 million pounds. Translated into cases, the market potential was close to 2 million cases. During the past five years, the market for trash bags has grown at an average rate of 8.9 percent per year. Now a mature product, future market growth is expected to parallel overall growth in the economy. The 1986 real growth in GNP is forecast to be 4.5 percent.

General Market Conditions

The current market is characterized by a distressing trend. The market is in a position of oversupply with approximately 20 manufacturers competing for the business in the Southeast. Prices have been on the decline for several months but are expected to level out during the last six months of the year.

This problem arose after a record year in 1984 for Modern Plastics. During 1984, supply was very tight due to raw material shortages. Unlike many of its competitors, Modern had only minor problems securing adequate raw material supplies. As a result the competitors were few in 1984, and all who remained in business were prosperous. By early 1985 raw materials were plentiful, and prices began to drop as new competitors tried to buy their way into the market. During the first quarter of 1985 Modern Plastics learned the hard way that a competitive price was a necessity in the current market. Volume fell off drastically in February and March as customers shifted orders to new suppliers when Modern chose to maintain a slightly higher than market price on trash bags.

With the market becoming extremely price competitive and profits declining, the overall quality has dropped to a point of minimum standard. Most suppliers now make a bag "barely good enough to get the job done." This quality level is acceptable to most buyers who do not demand high quality for this type of product.

Modern Plastics versus Competition

A recent study of Modern versus competition had been conducted by an outside consultant to see how well Modern measured up in several key areas. Each area was weighted according to its importance in the purchase decision, and Modern was compared to its key competitors in each area and on an overall basis. The key factors and their weights are shown below:

		Weight
1.	Pricing	.50
2.	Quality	.15
3.	Breadth of line	.10
4.	Sales coverage	.10
5.	Packaging	.05
6.	Service	.10
	Total	1.00

As shown in Exhibit 3, Modern compared favorably with its key competitors on an overall basis. None of the other suppliers were as strong as Modern in breadth of line nor did any competitor offer as good sales coverage as that provided by Modern. Clayton knew that sales coverage would be even better next year since the Florida and North Carolina territories had grown enough to add two salespeople to the institutional group by January 1, 1986.

Pricing, quality, and packaging seemed to be neither an advantage nor a disadvantage. However, service was a problem area. The main cause for this, Clayton was told, was temporary out-of-stock situations which occurred occasionally primarily due to the wide variety of trash bags offered by Modern.

During the past two years, Modern Plastics had maintained its market share at approximately 27 percent of the market. Some new competitors had entered the market since 1983 while others had left the market (see Exhibit 4). The previous district sales manager, Bill Hanson, had left Clayton some comments regarding the major competitors. These are reproduced in Exhibit 5.

EXHIBIT 3 Competitive factors ratings (by competitor*)

Weight	Factor	Modern	National Film	Bonanza	South-eastern	PBI	BAGCO	South-west Bag	Sun Plastics	East Coast Bag Co.
.50	Price	2	3	2	2	2	2	2	2	3
.15	Quality	3	2	3	4	3	2	3	3	4
.10	Breadth	1	2	2	3	3	3	3	3	3
.10	Sales coverage	1	3	3	3	4	3	3	4	3
.05	Packaging	3	3	2	3	3	1	3	3	3
.10	Service	4	3	3	2	2	2	3	4	3

Overall weighted ranking†

1.	BAGCO	2.15	6. Southeastern	2.55
2.	Modern	2.20	7. Florida Plastics	2.60
3.	Bonanza	2.25	8. National Film	2.65
4.	Southwest Bag (Tie)	2.50	9. East Coast Bag Co.	3.15
5.	PBI (Tie)	2.50		

* Ratings on a 1-to-5 scale with 1 being the best rating and 5 the worst.

† The weighted ranking is the sum of each rank times its weight. The lower the number, the better the overall rating.

EXHIBIT 4 Market share by supplier, 1983 and 1985

Supplier	Percent of market 1983	Percent of market 1985
National Film	11	12
Bertram	16	0*
Bonanza	11	12
Southeastern	5	6
Bay	9	0*
Johnson Graham	8	0*
PBI	2	5
Lewis	2	0*
BAGCO	—	6
Southwest Bag	—	2
Florida Plastics	—	4
East Coast Bag Co.	—	4
Miscellaneous and unknown	8	22
Modern	28	27
	100	100

* Out of business in 1985.

Source: This information was developed from a field survey conducted by Modern Plastics.

EXHIBIT 5 Characteristics of competitors

National Film	Broadest product line in the industry. Quality a definite advantage. Good service. Sales coverage adequate, but not an advantage. Not as aggressive as most suppliers on price. Strong competitor.
Bonanza	Well-established tough competitor. Very aggressive on pricing. Good packaging, quality okay.
Southeastern	Extremely price competitive in southern Florida. Dominates Miami market. Limited product line. Not a threat outside of Florida.
PBI	Extremely aggressive on price. Have made inroads into Transco Paper Company. Good service but poor sales coverage.
BAGCO	New competitor. Very impressive with a high-quality product, excellent service, and strong sales coverage. A real threat, particularly in Florida.
Southwest Bag	A factor in Louisiana and Mississippi. Their strategy is simple—an acceptable product at a rock bottom price.
Sun Plastics	Active when market is at a profitable level with price cutting. When market declines to a low profit range, Sun manufactures other types of plastic packaging and stays out of the trash bag market. Poor reputation as a reliable supplier, but can still "spot-sell" at low prices.
East Coast Bag Co.	Most of their business is from a state bid which began in January 1984 for a two-year period. Not much of a threat to Modern's business in the Southeast as most of their volume is north of Washington, D.C.

EXHIBIT 6 1986 Real growth projections by segment

Total industry	+5.0%
Commercial	+5.4%
Restaurant	+6.8%
Hotel/motel	+2.0%
Transportation	+1.9%
Office users	+5.0%
Other	+4.2%
Noncommercial	+4.1%
Hospitals	+3.9%
Nursing homes	+4.8%
Colleges/universities	+2.4%
Schools	+7.8%
Employee feeding	+4.3%
Other	+3.9%

Source: Developed from several trade journals.

Developing the Sales Forecast

After a careful study of trade journals, government statistics, and surveys conducted by Modern marketing research personnel, projections for growth potential were formulated by segment and are shown in Exhibit 6. This data was compiled by Bill Hanson just before he had been promoted.

Jim looked back at Baxter's memo giving the time schedule for the forecast and knew he had to get started. As he left the office at 7:15, he wrote himself a large note and pinned it on his wall—''Get Started on the Sales Forecast!''

Part 4

Product and Brand Management Decisions

The six cases concerned with product strategy decisions in this section involve a number of different kinds of decisions. Many marketers believe that product decisions are the most critical of the marketing mix variables because of their importance to consumers in their decision-making process, and because product decisions, once made, are not quickly or easily reversed or changed. Promotion and pricing changes, for example, can be made much more quickly and with greater ease. Furthermore, most product changes usually require changes in the rest of the marketing strategy—changes in promotion, pricing, and sometimes distribution.

Before examining the various issues in the product strategy area, the concept of what a product is should first be understood. A product is "anything that can be offered to a market for attention, acquisition, or consumption; it includes physical objects, services, personalities, places, organizations, and ideas."[1] A product is thus much more than its physical properties and is everything a consumer buys when he or she makes a purchase. It is a set of want-satisfying attributes. It is important to understand this definition because what the consumer is buying is not necessarily what the company thought it was marketing. So marketers must be aware of consumer attitudes, values, needs, and wants with respect to their products.

The major decisions related to product strategy are:

---

[1] Philip Kotler, *Marketing Management: Analysis, Planning and Control*, 3rd ed. (Englewood Cliffs, N.J.: Prentice-Hall, 1976), p. 183.

1. What new products should be developed?
2. What changes are needed in current products?
3. What products should be added or dropped?
4. What positioning should the product occupy?
5. What should the branding strategy be?

A brief discussion of some of the concepts related to each of these decisions follows.

New Product Development

The sales and profits of a product category tend to change over time. The pattern a product category typically follows is called the product life cycle. It is defined to have the introductory, growth, maturity, and decline stages. Because most products reach the maturity and decline stages eventually, a marketer must continually seek out new products which can go through the introductory and growth stages in order to maintain and increase the total profits of the firm. But what new products should be introduced?

To answer this question, a marketer must consider the objectives of the firm, the resources available, the target markets the firm is trying to satisfy, and how the new product would fit in with other products offered by the company and the competition.

To successfully develop new products, the organization will have to set up formalized strategies for generating new product ideas, means for screening these ideas, product and market testing procedures, and finally commercialization. The objective is to obtain products which are differentiated from those of its competitors and which meet the needs of a large enough segment of the market to be profitable.

Changes in Current Products

The needs, wants, attitudes, and behavior of consumers change over time, and a company must change its products also or risk losing these consumers to a competitor who more quickly responds to these changes in the marketplace.

Should new features be added to the product? Should the warranty be extended? Should the packaging be changed? Should new services be offered? The marketer must continually monitor its target market and the competition to be able to answer such questions.

What Products Should Be Added or Dropped

A marketer must make decisions concerning the product mix or composite of products the firm will offer for sale. This requires decisions concerning the width and depth of products. Width refers to the number of product lines marketed by the firm. For example, General Electric has many lines while

Kellogg's has concentrated on breakfast foods. The depth of the product mix is the number of items offered for sale within each product line. Kellogg's, for example, would have a very deep product line with many different alternatives offered for sale.

Whether a product line should be extended or reduced depends on a number of factors, including financial criteria, market factors, production considerations, and organizational factors. The marketer in making these decisions must examine the potential profit contributions, return on investment, impact on market share, fit with consumers' needs, fit with the needs of the channels of distribution, and the expected reactions of competitors. The production and organizational considerations include impact on capacity for other products, and on the goals and objectives of the firm, both in the short and long run.

Product Positioning

Product positioning is defined as that idea that is put into the consumers' minds by telling them how our product differs from its competitors. The position we strive to occupy will depend on the different market segments available, the attributes of our product compared to the needs of each segment, and the positions occupied by our competitors against each market segment.

Branding Strategy

The basic decisions here are whether or not to put brand names on the organization's products, whether the brands should be manufacturers' or distributors' brands, and whether individual or family brands should be used.

These decisions depend on the company's resources, objectives, the competition, and consumer choice behavior. For example, a small firm with little resources and much competition in a product category where consumers perceived small differences in the brands available would probably choose to market its product using private distributors' brands. Family brands such as General Electric and Campbell's are used when the marketer wants the consumer to generalize to the new products all those attributes he associates with the family brand name. The time and money required to establish the brand's name is much lower with this strategy but it does not allow the marketer to establish a separate image for the new product.

Case 10

Amtrak*

In late 1975, the management of Amtrak faced a number of major decisions concerning their Detroit–Chicago route. They were considering purchasing a number of new Amfleet trains to put on this run. There were also questions about what services to offer on these trains if they were purchased.

History of Amtrak

Amtrak was established through federal legislation on April 30, 1971, as a last-ditch attempt to revitalize intercity rail service in the United States. Railroads, during the previous 10 years, had found it difficult to compete with other modes of transportation—in particular, the private automobile (and the new interstate highway system it used), and the jet aircraft in domestic service. Travel by rail in the United States had declined from 70 percent of all intercity travel in 1947, to less than 5 percent in 1971.

Amtrak, a single nationwide passenger rail system, was designed to lure travelers back to the rails. In an era of increasing awareness of energy limitations, and of ever-growing numbers of people utilizing modes of transport other than the auto, revitalization of American rail service was viewed as a necessity. Amtrak's goal was increased ridership through refurbished equipment, modernization of terminal facilities, speed increases, and greater overall convenience.

At the time of the Amtrak takeover, no intercity passenger rail cars had been built in 10 years, and no passenger technology existed in the country to design and build modern cars. Stations were antiquated and without modern facilities of any kind in many cases. Equipment was in an almost constant state of malfunction, and was seldom cleaned. Connections were often impossible, or highly inconvenient. Rail service held little attraction for anyone except fearful flyers and train buffs. The National Railroad Passenger Corporation (Amtrak's official name) had its hands full.

For the purpose of service development, the various railroad lines and routes were divided into two categories: long-haul services and short- and medium-distance corridors. Long hauls were generally those routes of 700 or more miles, serviced by overnight or two day trains (e.g., The Broadway Limited, 900 miles, 17 hours, overnight between Chicago and New York).

* This case was written by Thomas C. Kinnear and G. Ludwig Laudisi. Copyright © 1978 Thomas C. Kinnear.

Corridors were lines over which several trains a day in each direction were operated. In particular, the corridors of less than 300 miles were thought to be ideally suited for high-quality, high-speed service, which could compete with the airlines. This style service if implemented, it was reasoned, could attract business travelers and others for whom travel time was of great importance. Amtrak had a good reason to believe this would work too: the New York–Washington corridor had offered such service since 1969—the Metroliners—and was very successful.

The Detroit-Chicago Corridor

In the case of the Detroit–Chicago corridor (279 miles), Amtrak saw an opportunity to duplicate the fine operation between New York and Washington. As late as the early 1960s, the New York Central Railroad (which originally operated Amtrak's Detroit–Chicago line) had offered high-quality rail service on the route. Running times between the two cities were as fast as four and a half hours, and luxurious meal and parlor car service was offered. With the completion of Interstate 94 through to Detroit from Chicago, and the introduction of the 727 jet on "short-hop" flights, much of the market for this type of service disappeared. The train was no longer fast enough. As travel volume dwindled, services were cut.

First the parlor cars (first-class service aimed toward business travelers) came off, then the diners with their sitdown meal service. Coaches and snack bars remained. When Penn Central was formed in 1967 (via the merger of the Pennsylvania and New York Central Railroads), high losses were viewed as reason to further cut service quality. Car cleaning was minimized; maintenance became irregular. In 1969, running times were lengthened to five and a half hours. The Penn Central in its annual report served notice it wanted as few passenger trains as possible. Just prior to Amtrak's takeover of the route, Penn Central offered three trains in each direction a day over the route, one without food service at all, the other two with limited snack service. On-time performance was poor. Rats were once reported in the coaches. The service offered was as poor as it could possibly be.

On May 1, 1971, Amtrak took over this corridor. And as with many routes throughout the country, its first major step was to cut the frequency of service. Thereafter, two trains a day in each direction operated between the two cities. It was, according to Amtrak, a temporary economy move to limit the deficit. Further, said Amtrak in newspaper advertising, the remaining trains would be vastly improved.

Improvement was first accomplished by running the trains (the *Wolverine* and the *Saint Clair*) with cars from the C&O Railroad. Its equipment was in far better shape than the Penn Central's, which was immediately withdrawn from service to be rebuilt. The replacement equipment was more comfortable and better maintained, but meal service was still very limited. The schedule remained five and a half hours from endpoint to endpoint. Amtrak also began an advertising program in Detroit, basically just to tell people that the trains were there (many had forgotten or didn't know rail service existed to Chicago). As with other areas of the country, Amtrak promised refurbished cars within a year. The result was a stop in the decline of ridership, and a gradual turnaround by the end of the first year of operation. Unlike the original plans, refurbished cars began to arrive piecemeal—a car here or there, mixed in with older, untouched equipment. But this nonetheless showed good intentions. Schedules were better adhered to as well, and connections at Chicago were improved. This was aided by Amtrak's consolidation of all operations to one Chicago terminal—Union Station—and the elimination of across-town transfers.

But there were many problems with the initial effort as well. Amtrak operated its trains by contractual arrangement with the railroads—in this case, Penn Central. Because of this, they had only indirect control over on-board staff, and the dispatching and running of trains. Problems en route were handled by the railroad in the old manner—which often meant not handling them at all. Amtrak couldn't instruct attendants as to the way to deal with passengers, because the attendants still worked for the railroads. Amtrak, because of the situation, could say little about service quality or uniformity.

Equipment was also maintained by the railroad. Often, after individual cars had been rebuilt (at very high cost), they fell into disrepair because of continued poor maintenance. The age of the equipment was also a problem. The average car was 20 years old. While pleasant inside and comfortable to travel in, they were too old to be completely reliable. Air-conditioning failed or heating gave out while trains were en route. Since no passenger railroad cars had been built in the United States for almost 10 years, no technology was immediately available to construct new equipment.

Stations along the route presented many problems. Without exception, they were run-down, dirty, and without modern facilities. The Detroit station, once a busy rail center, was a decaying edifice, vast and frightening. Serving only four trains a day when Amtrak first took over, it was far too large for its task. Located on the west side of Detroit, it was inconvenient for persons from the east and north suburbs to get to it. The Niles, Michigan, station had no heat, and in Battle Creek the main body of the station had been closed for several years. Conditions were so bad, several of Amtrak's advisory board recommended that three of the stations be ripped down rather than trying to fix them up, and new ones be built in their place.

The Energy Crisis

In 1973, after two years of operation, refurbished equipment ran on the corridor exclusively, stations were painted at last, and on-time operation (on the same slow schedule) became a reality. Then, in the fall of that year, the energy crunch descended on the nation. Gasoline prices and air fares went up substantially, and millions of Americans were forced onto public transportation. Suddenly, Amtrak had its hands full. Trains that were never more than half full *no count of tickets!*

were carrying three times their normal load. Overcrowding became commonplace. On the corridor, trains were unreserved (meaning that there was no limit on the number of tickets sold per train). Trains that could comfortably seat 300 people were carrying about 600. Food would run out almost before the trains left their originating stations. Passengers, due to the crowding, sometimes stood for four or five hours, or sat on suitcases in the aisles. Personnel became rude and discourteous. Fistfights broke out on occasion between conductors and irate passengers. The refurbished equipment in many cases couldn't take the abuse and wear it received from carrying this many people. The interiors became damaged and weren't repaired. Heating and air-conditioning were as erratic as ever. Malfunctioning equipment was allowed out on the line for the first time in Amtrak history, so that more cars were available to seat more people.

Amtrak received a ghastly black eye during the energy crunch. It was not able to adequately meet the hordes of people who suddenly came back to the rails. The Detroit–Chicago corridor in particular fared dismally in terms of service, with equipment, food service, and personnel getting more complaints than almost anywhere else in the system. But in two areas, things were positive. On-time performance remained good despite the crowds (which often slowed things down elsewhere) and ridership remained high into the summer of 1974.

The Turboliners

Based on these final two factors, Amtrak made a firm commitment to upgrade service on the route. In late 1973, the corporation leased two French Turboliner trains for experimental use on the St. Louis–Chicago corridor. Since no modern passenger equipment was yet available in the United States, Amtrak went to Europe where new trains could be acquired almost immediately. The Turbos' better schedules, improved food service, and high on-time reliability resulted in greatly improved ridership to and from St. Louis. Amtrak decided to purchase these two and four more sets of Turbo equipment, and to place some of them in service between Detroit and Chicago. In April of 1975, the Detroit–Chicago corridor became all turbo. As part of the service improvement program, an additional midday train was added, bringing the number of trains on the route to six daily; that is, in each direction, a morning, noon, and evening train. The new equipment was extremely sleek and modern. Its exterior was reminiscent of the Japanese "Bullet" train, and its interiors were plush, quiet, and featured giant windows and automatic sliding glass doors between each car. Food service was provided cafeteria-style, with an area adjacent to the galley for eating and lounging, and fold-down trays available at each coach seat.

Because of the new technology that the equipment utilized, it was maintained at a special service facility in Chicago constructed specifically for this purpose. Service personnel were specially trained to work on board the new trains and thus the quality level of individual service was vastly improved. The introduction of the new service was accompanied by an innovative and clever advertising campaign on Detroit and Chicago television stations, and on local radio stations along the route. Perhaps because of the new trains themselves, or the extensive advertising, or the added service, or the coordination of the entire promotion, ridership on the corridor increased 72 percent the first month, and over 150 percent within three months. The trains ran regularly at their 300-passenger capacity. They were so successful, in fact, that a whole new set of problems arose.

Foremost among them was a problem related to their new technology. Because the equipment was foreign, it was constructed in a manner quite different from traditional American railway design. Hence, the maintenance people "out on the line" (that is, anywhere but at the service facility) didn't know how to work on the new trains. The troubleshooting manuals on board each train were no help to them either—they were in French. As a result, if air-conditioning failed on a trip, it probably remained broken until the train returned to its Chicago maintenance facility. Sometimes that meant several trips if loads were heavy, and 300 . . . , 600 . . . , 900 uncomfortable passengers. More than once public address announcements were made asking anyone who could read French to come to the cockpit and translate the manual for the English-only maintenance personnel.

The popularity of these trains led to another problem—overcrowding. Unlike conventional American equipment, cars couldn't be added or removed from the Turbos. They had a fixed number (five) and a standard carrying capacity of 300 people. They ran as unreserved trains, however, meaning that Amtrak would sell tickets to as many people as wanted to ride, and often that was over 300. On weekends, some passengers stood for five and a half hours, all the way to Detroit, or Chicago. Even when there were no technical or capacity difficulties, the sleek, new Turbos still serviced stations in Michigan that were at least 50 years old, and which for the most part hadn't been renovated. Ann Arbor was the single exception, but its refurbished station was far too small for the growing number of passengers using the facility. These difficulties marred the generally good impression the turbotrains gave in advertising, and on the many good trips they made. The public failure resulted in a somewhat negative reputation. This was by no means pervasive though, and the trains continued to do well on the route. On subsequent routes where Turbos were assigned, ridership increased as well, seemingly justifying the argument that if modern services were provided, the American public would travel by rail.

The success of this equipment also occurred, it should be pointed out, without great schedule improvement. Due to track conditions, the high-speed capabilities of the new trains could not initially be used, so it was the trains themselves, rather than their speed, that accounted for their popularity. With track improvement, it was reasoned, they would be even more attractive to intercity travelers.

Research data indicated that the average age of Detroit–Chicago train riders was 35 years old, with about 65 percent traveling on vacations, 25 percent on business, and 10 percent for other reasons.

The Decisions to Be Made

In late 1975, the management of Amtrak faced a number of decisions with respect to the Detroit–Chicago route.

1. The first decision concerned the possibility of purchasing a number of Amfleet trains for the route. These trains were being built by the Budd Company of Philadelphia for use on a number of Amtrak routes. Amfleet trains combined the modern aspects of the European Turboliners (speed, new interiors, standardized seating and food service) with the flexibility of old-style conventional equipment. On an Amfleet train, cars could be added or removed as load factors changed. Since they were American built, the difficulty of foreign technology was eliminated. In addition, Amfleet trains offered the possibility of first-class, daytime accommodations featuring reserved seats and at-seat meal service.

In order to run three trains a day in each direction, Amtrak would have to purchase four locomotives and 24 Amfleet cars. The average Amfleet train on this run was thus expected to have one locomotive and six cars. Each locomotive would cost about $540,000. The price of cars varied depending on whether the car was a coach, first-class, parlor, dinette, and so on. On average the cars would cost Amtrak $425,000 each. A car would hold up to 84 passengers, with 60 in some cars. The useful life of this equipment was expected to be 20 years.

2. The second decision related to whether or not first-class accommodations should be available on the Detroit–Chicago Amfleet trains, if these trains were purchased. This service would include reserved seating and meal service at that seat. Reserved seats were spaced two together and a seat by itself, giving three seats across the car. About 10 percent of the seating capacity of an average six-car train could be available for first-class service. The incremental cost of meals and personnel to Amtrak of each first-class seat sold was estimated to be about $5.

3. A related decision here concerned the price of a first-class ticket, if such service were made available. The price of a coach ticket was $17.50 one way. This compared to $19.50 for the five-hour bus ride, and $39 for a coach seat, and $58 for a first-class seat for the one-hour plane ride.

4. At first, the Amfleet trains would continue to take five and a half hours to travel from downtown Detroit to downtown Chicago. They were capable of traveling much faster, but track conditions would not allow this. Amtrak was considering spending $3 million on track and signal improvements in the next year. This money and a great deal more to be put up by Conrail (the regional freight railway of the northeast) could improve the tracks such that travel could be cut to under four hours within a few years. The Amtrak-funded improve-

ments were expected to have about a 10-year useful life. The management of Amtrak was wondering whether or not they should spend this money, and aim for shorter run times.

5. There were five major stations on the Detroit–Chicago run. Amtrak was considering upgrading them. The cost to Amtrak would be $150,000 per station. The rest of the cost would be covered by the state of Michigan, and local cities. A 20-year useful life was expected on each improved station.

6. Amtrak's advertising agency was Needham, Harper, and Steers. They had developed an advertising campaign for the Amfleet trains in general, and the Detroit–Chicago corridor more specifically. They planned to use a mix of television, radio, and newspapers. The media costs to Amtrak for the Detroit–Chicago run were proposed to be $300,000 per year.

The management of Amtrak wondered what decisions should be made with respect to the Detroit–Chicago corridor.

Case 11

VideoShop—Mark-Tele, Inc. (II)*

Cable television began to spread rapidly across the United States during the late 1970s. It was promoted to subscribers predominantly as an entertainment media that would provide an expanded choice of high-quality television programming.

Some advertising and marketing experts perceived cable television differently. They saw it as opening a revolution in commercial communications. As telecommunication technology improved, cable television could become a direct threat to conventional shopping systems. Most experts, however, forecasted that significant changes in consumer shopping patterns were at least a decade or two away. Mr. Richard Johnson disagreed. He was the managing director of Mark-Tele, Inc., one of the most innovative and aggressive cable television companies.

During the fall of 1981, Mr. Johnson began to prepare a proposal for presentation to his board of directors. The proposal would suggest that Mark-Tele develop several new television channels. Most cable channels involved either an entertainment, educational, or public information format. The proposed new channels would involve innovative commercial formats using telecommunications technology that would allow organizations to market and sell directly to consumers in their own homes. Mr. Johnson named this concept "VideoShop."

The New Venture

Several months earlier, Mr. Johnson had created a new ventures task force to generate and study novel programming formats that could be developed into new cable channels in the near term, and possibly into new networks in the long run. These channels would be used by Mark-Tele to generate additional revenues, to increase its subscription base, and to allocate operating costs more effectively.

---

* This is an abridged version of a case prepared by Professor Michael P. Mokwa and Mr. Karl Gustafson, MBA 1981, of the Arizona State University, as a basis for class discussion. It is not intended to illustrate either effective or ineffective handling of a managerial situation.

The current capacity of the Mark-Tele cable system was 52 channels. But only 31 were in use. When Mark-Tele began operations, they had only 12 channels but had grown steadily. Costs had been relatively constant regardless of the number of channels that Mark-Tele operated. Thus, Mr. Johnson perceived Mark-Tele's cost structure as highly fixed, and he foresaw the development of new channels as a means of distributing these costs. Mr. Johnson expected that new channels would draw new subscribers, that subscription rates could be raised as more channels were added, and that subscription revenue could grow faster than corresponding operating costs.

The new ventures task force included the operations and sales managers from Mark-Tele, two product development specialists from Mark-Tele's parent company, and a consultant from the communications industry. An excerpt of their report is presented in the Appendix. The task force recommended that Mark-Tele develop several new cable channels using the television as the primary medium for shopping.

Mr. Johnson was thrilled with the new venture idea and the task force report. He wanted to develop and implement the new concept quickly. He selected a distinctive name for the venture, identifying it as VideoShop. He met informally with some prospective salespeople, distributors, and retailers from different product and service fields, and sensed strong but very cautious interest and support from prospective suppliers.

Mr. Johnson felt that a number of proposed channels were feasible, but he wanted to focus his efforts on those products and services (a) that appeared to be easiest and most profitable to implement in the near term, and (b) that appeared to have the strongest interest among the prospective suppliers with whom he had met. He selected five prospects for development:

1. Catalog sales by regional and national retailers.
2. Ticket reservations for concerts, plays, and sporting events, as well as reservations at local restaurants.
3. Airline ticket reservations and vacation planning.
4. A multiple-listing service for real estate companies to display homes and commercial property that were for sale in the area or possibly from areas across the country.
5. Grocery products.

Mr. Johnson expected that he could find outstanding firms from each product or service field to participate in the VideoShop venture under terms that Mark-Tele would set forth.

Mark-Tele's Background

Mark-Tele was founded in 1977, as a wholly owned subsidiary of Intertronics, Inc., a large corporation based in New York City. Intertronics was founded in 1973 as a joint venture among three well-respected, multinational firms. One firm was primarily in the information processing industry. Another was a publishing and broadcasting conglomerate, and the third was a high-technology producer in electronics. The mission of Intertronics was to design, develop, and implement innovative, applied telecommunications systems for domestic consumer markets. Intertronics received financial support and full technological cooperation from its parent companies, but was operated as an autonomous venture. Intertronics managed each of its subsidiaries using the same orientation.

During 1978, Mark-Tele bid to install cable television systems in several large metropolitan areas in the United States. Late that year, Mark-Tele was granted the right to install a cable television system in a large, growing southwestern metropolitan area. The area had more than a sufficient number of households to profitably support a cable television company according to industry standards. More important, the population was growing rapidly. Corporations were locating headquarters or building large manufacturing facilities in the area. Growth was projected to continue for at least the next 15 years, thus representing a very attractive cable market for Mark-Tele.

Intertronics would use Mark-Tele's location as the test site for a new type of cable television technology. The traditional type of cable used in cable television systems was a "one-way" cable—a signal could be directed only from the cable television company *to* the individual households attached to the service. Recently, Intertronics had developed a "two-way" cable that was capable of transmitting and receiving signals both from the cable television company and from individual households connected to the system. The cost of the new two-way cable was nearly four times the cost of one-way cable. Because Mark-Tele was a test site, they and their subscribers received the cable system at a substantially reduced cost.

To implement the two-way cable, Mark-Tele installed an interactive device to the television set of each of its subscribers. The interactive devices were expensive to install, but Intertronics absorbed most of the installation cost. The subscription charge for basic cable services from Mark-Tele was $11 per month. The comparable rate for one-way cable would be $8.50 per month.

Mark-Tele's first year of operations concluded with 5,000 subscribers and a small negative net operating profit. In the following year, Mark-Tele subscriptions increased to 38,000, generating a net profit of almost $1.4 million. In 1980, Mark-Tele continued to aggressively attract more subscribers, reaching 50,000 total. Net profit increased to exceed $2 million. Financial statements for 1979 and 1980 are presented in Exhibit 1.

Research by Mark-Tele suggested that the potential number of homes for the cable network in their market area exceeded 400,000 over the next five years. In 10 years, the market potential was forecasted to be nearly 750,000 homes. A demographic profile of current subscribers is presented in Exhibit 2.

Mark-Tele offered a wide variety of programming for virtually any type of viewer. Several of the channels were "pay television." For these, a household would pay an additional charge beyond the basic monthly rate. The revenue from pay services nearly matched basic subscription revenue for Mark-Tele in 1980. A schedule for the allocation of Mark-Tele's 52-channel capacity is presented in Exhibit 3. Both current and prospective channels are listed.

EXHIBIT 1
MARK-TELE, INC.
Income Statement
Fiscal Years Ending
December 31, 1979, and 1980

	1979*	1980†
Revenues:		
Subscription revenue	$4,560,000	$ 6,600,000
Pay service revenue	4,104,000	5,400,000
Total revenue	$8,664,000	$12,000,000
Expenses:		
Operation expense (includes salaries)	$3,852,000	$ 5,248,000
Sales expense	1,913,400	2,610,300
Interest expense	136,200	136,200
Depreciation expense	74,800	74,800
Rent expense	46,000	46,000
Equipment maintenance expense	32,500	34,700
Total expense	$6,054,900	$ 8,150,000
Gross profit	$2,609,100	$ 3,850,000
Taxes @ 47%	$1,226,277	$ 1,848,000
Net profit	$1,382,823	$ 2,002,000

* Based on subscriptions of 38,000 homes with a subscription rate of $10 per month per home, and average home "pay service" of $9 per month per home.
† Based on total subscriptions of 50,000 homes with a subscription rate of $11 per month per home, and average home "pay service" of $9 per month per home.

Cable Television Technology

The Mark-Tele cable television system was controlled by a sophisticated configuration of computers with high-speed communications between each processor. Three computers, each used for a different task, insured that viewers would have access to the cable network at all times. The main computer transmitted cable signals to each individual home using the two-way cable lines. The second computer's function was to back up the main computer in the event that a system failure occurred. The second computer would be a vital element of the VideoShop system because it could be used as an update system for suppliers to amend information regarding their products or services. This computer also could be used to transmit the orders or reservations placed by "shopping" subscribers directly to prospective suppliers. The third computer functioned as another backup, if system failures would occur simultaneously to the main computers. A very sophisticated software application integrating the communication network and operating system had been developed to assure 99 percent uptime for the cable system. A diagram sketching the Mark-Tele cable system is presented in Exhibit 4.

The cable system incorporated two different types of storage devices. The first type of storage disk (a magnetic disk) was used to store data, such as billing information about a particular subscriber. The second type of disk involved an innovative technology that could be used extensively by the VideoShop suppliers. Images of products and services could be stored on these disks so that

EXHIBIT 2 1980 Demographic analysis of Mark-Tele subscribers*

Family size	Percent	Family income	Percent	Number of hours home television active per week	Percent	Age of paying subscriber	Percent	Residency	Percent	Number of years of education of paying subscribers	Percent
1	17.6%	$ 0 –$ 8K	1.3%	0– 7	2.5%	18–25	22.4%	Homeowners	71.6%	0– 8	1.4%
2	22.8	$ 9K–$18K	15.7	8–14	15.1	26–35	19.2	Renters	28.4	9–11	22.5
3	10.8	$19K–$28K	18.3	15–21	17.2	36–45	19.6			12–	21.8
4	19.3	$29K–$35K	17.5	22–28	40.7	46–55	17.7			13–15	26.3
5	15.1	$36K–$45K	19.6	29–35	20.8	56–65	7.1			16 +	28.0
6	5.8	$46K–$59K	12.7	36 +	3.7	66–75	8.3				
7+	8.6	$60,000 +	14.9			76 +	5.7				

* Based on 50,000 subscribers.

EXHIBIT 3 Channel allocation schedule

Cable channel number	Designated programming service
1	Mark-Tele Channel Listing*
2	Program Guide*
3	Local Transit Schedule*
4	Classified Ads and Yard Sales*
5	Weather Radar and Time*
6	Dow Jones Cable News*
7	Reserved for future use
8†	Home Box Office*
9†	Showtime*
10†	The Movie Channel*
11†	Golden Oldies Channel*
12	Reserved for future use
13	Reserved for future use
14	Cable News Network*
15	Reserved for future use
16	UPI News Scan*
17	Government Access*
18	Music Television*
19†	Stereo Rock Concert*
20	Educational Access*
21	Educational Access: New York University*
22	Proposed educational access
23	Proposed interactive channel for lease
24	Proposed interactive channel for lease
25	Proposed interactive channel for lease
26	VideoShop: *Retail Sales Channel*
27	VideoShop: *Entertainment Tickets and Restaurants*
28	VideoShop: *Grocery Products*
29	VideoShop: Reserved
30	VideoShop: Reserved
31	USA Network*
32	WTBS, Atlanta, channel 17*
33	WOR, New York, channel 9*
34	K/ / /, local ABC affiliate
35	Christian Broadcasting Network*
36	ESPN (Sports) Network*
37	K/ / /, Local station, channel 15*
38	K/ / /, local NBC affiliate, channel 8*
39	K/ / /, local CBS affiliate, channel 11*
40	Proposed channel for lease
41	Concert Connection*
42	WGN, Chicago, channel 9*
43	Public Access: Cultural Bulletin Board*
44†	Proposed games channel
45	Public Access: Library Information*
46	Proposed public access
47	Public Broadcasting System
48	Reserved for future banking transactions
49	VideoShop: *Airline Tickets and Travel*
50	VideoShop: *Real Estate Showcase*
51	Reserved for future use
52	Reserved for future use*

* Active channel.
† Optional pay service.

EXHIBIT 4   VideoShop—Mark-Tele, Inc.: Mark-Tele two-way cable system

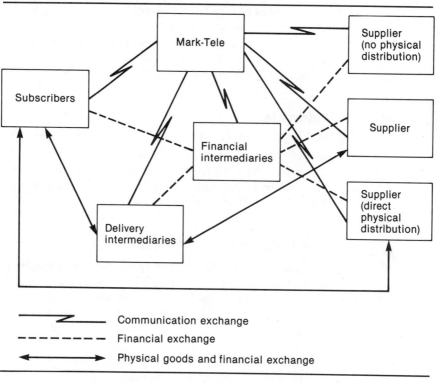

subscribers to the cable system could access the images at any time. Only through the use of the new two-way cable developed by Intertronics would it be possible to incorporate the video disk units (VDU) into a cable network. The two-way cable allowed signals to travel from the main computer to an individual television, and from the television back to the main computer.

Two-way communication was possible through the use of an interactive indexing device attached to each subscriber's television. This indexing device contained special electronics allowing the device to transmit data back to the main computer. On top of the indexing device were 12 keys, simply called the keypad. An individual subscriber could use the keypad to call up "menus," sort through a menu, and send data back to the main computer. A *menu* is a computer term used to describe listings of general categories from which additional information can be drawn.

Using a prospective VideoShop example, a menu for a channel containing airline information could first indicate to a viewer the different airlines from which to choose. The viewer could then push the key on the keypad that corresponds to the airline that he or she was interested in using. The next menu could show all the different cities to which the chosen airline flies. The viewer then could push the key on the keypad that corresponds to the city to which he or she wishes to travel. The following screen could provide the flight numbers and times during which flights are available. From the information on that screen, the user could make a reservation, which would be transmitted to the airline's computer through the Mark-Tele computer. Finally, the reservation would be logged, confirmed, and ticket(s) mailed to the viewer.

VideoShop Channels

Mr. Johnson felt that the five shopping channels that he had selected from the list generated by the task force would work well. He prepared a brief description for each of the prospective shopping channels. He would use these to build his presentation for the forthcoming board meeting and to develop a prospectus to sell the VideoShop concept to suppliers.

The Catalog Sales Channel(s)

National and regional retailers could use the VideoShop system to sell and promote their entire merchandise lines including their most current items and prices. Shoppers would have the opportunity to view merchandise on the television screen in their own home, avoiding the inconvenience of a shopping trip or the boredom of thumbing through a catalog book. Information about products and prices could be presented in a format similar to catalog books, or innovative action formats could be developed to simulate a store environment or create some novel context. Retailers would be responsible for developing appropriate video disk units and keeping information current. Mark-Tele could provide a consulting service to help suppliers produce effective video disks. Mark-Tele could also reserve the right to reject any material that was felt to be inappropriate.

A shopper could use the interactive indexing device to direct and control an entire shopping experience. This could involve viewing information about product features and prices from one retailer, and then quickly switching to another retailer's presentation for comparative information. In addition, a shopper desiring more extensive information could access a brief demonstration or informative advertisement about a product. After selecting a product, the interactive device could transmit the order through Mark-Tele's computing system directly to the retailer's processing system. The retailer could present alternative payment programs and specific delivery schedules or instructions. The shopper could charge purchases using national or store credit cards and could pick up the merchandise directly or have it delivered.

Mark-Tele could charge each retailer a service fee based on a fixed percentage of shoppers' invoice values (before taxes). Individual retailers could be billed monthly, and various payment programs could be formulated. The new ventures task force estimated that an average home would purchase a minimum of $300 worth of retail merchandise annually through VideoShop.

They proposed a service charge rate of 2 percent. Mark-Tele could also generate revenue by selling video consulting services to the suppliers.

Ticket Sales and Restaurant Reservation Channel

VideoShop could provide detailed information concerning local entertainment alternatives to subscribers. Entertainment organizations could present exciting promotional spots using the video disk technology and sell tickets directly to VideoShop subscribers. Another dimension of this channel could be a restaurant promotion and reservation feature. Restaurant menus and promotional spots could be made accessible for diners. Once diners have chosen a particular restaurant using the memo and spots, they could make a reservation and even select a specific table (if the restaurant developed, as part of its VideoShop system, a seating arrangement routine similar to that of the entertainment organizations).

All VideoShop ticket purchases and reservations could be transmitted directly from the shopper's home through Mark-Tele computers to the restaurant or ticket outlet. Most restaurants and small entertainment organizations would have to purchase or lease a small "intelligence" computing terminal to receive reservations or ticket orders and to keep information updated. Intertronics could supply these.

The task force felt that this channel could generate at least $150,000 revenue per year given the current subscriber base. They recommended a $25 per month minimum charge to restaurants and a 50-cent service fee per ticket reservation. They were unsure of a fee schedule for entertainment organizations that would only promote events and would not be selling tickets directly through VideoShop. However, they thought that rates similar to commercial advertising rates would be appropriate.

Airline Ticket Sales and Travel Accommodations Channel

Discussions with the task force concluded that an airline ticket sales channel could be the easiest for Mark-Tele to implement and operate in the short run, and also could be the most lucrative financially. Projected revenue for the first year of operating this channel was $400,000 based on a very conservative usage rate and an extremely competitive pricing policy. This channel could allow subscribers to make airline reservations, purchase their tickets, and select travel accommodations using the same fundamental interactive shopping procedures as other VideoShop channels.

Perhaps the most important characteristic of this channel could be the potential ease of implementation, once cooperation was secured from the airlines. The format and basic system used within the airlines industry to transmit, display, and process schedules, fares, and ticket information appeared to be compatible with the Mark-Tele system. VideoShop could be used to link shoppers directly with airline ticket reservation systems, bypassing reservationists and travel agents. Subscribers could select itineraries, then secure reservations and pay, using major credit cards. Tickets could be mailed or picked up at airport ticket counters or other service locations.

Mark-Tele could record each ticket purchase and charge the appropriate airline a fixed fee of $4 per ticket. This rate was approximately half of the average rate charged by most travel agents. The task force believed that a minimum average of two tickets would be purchased by each subscribing household per year. Revenue estimates were not made for the travel accommodations feature of this channel.

Multiple-Listing Service Channel

A few local realtors expressed strong interest in the VideoShop concept. Traditional promotional tools used to stimulate buyers' interest and assist them in making decisions about what properties to see in person included classified newspaper ads, newspaper supplements, brochures, "for sale" signs, the multiple-listing catalog, and photographs of properties posted on an agency's wall. Most realtors and buyers found these boring. More important, these simply did not present most properties effectively. A frequent complaint among realtors and buyers was the high cost in time and dollars wasted traveling to and viewing personally properties that were not represented well in a promotion or informational item. VideoShop could provide an exciting and effective method for presenting realty.

A specific issue regarding this channel was whether to limit access to realty agencies and others willing to pay an additional fee for it or to open it for public access. The task force recommended open access and suggested that a minimum of 30 realty agencies would need to participate. Each could be charged a monthly fee of $100 for producing and maintaining high-quality video disks with accurate and updated information. Mark-Tele could provide technical assistance and would monitor this channel carefully.

Grocery Products Channel

One of the most exciting prospects for VideoShop could be a grocery products channel. It was the most interesting but difficult channel for which to design a format.

A VideoShop grocery channel could provide consumers with convenience, comfort, low shopping risks, and potential savings. For suppliers, it could generate increased control over operations and costs, and higher profits. However, this VideoShop channel would directly attack an expensive, firmly established distribution network and basic, traditional patterns of shopping. Strong resistance from many consumers could be anticipated, and suppliers not involved in the venture could be expected to retaliate competitively. Also, there could be critical barriers to providing shoppers a total assortment of grocery products including frozen and "fresh" items and to implementing a cost-effective delivery service or pickup procedure. Undoubtedly, these ''bugs'' could be worked out.

Conclusion—A Time for Reflection and . . . or Action

One more time, Mr. Johnson reviewed the task force report and his brief descriptions of prospective VideoShop channels. He felt excitement, enthusiasm, and some frustration. He and the task force had worked hard and creatively to formulate the idea of VideoShop. They thought that most technological barriers could be overcome, and they projected a very favorable cost structure. Definitely, VideoShop was a concept whose time had arrived! But, Mark-Tele is a small company with only a few people and tight resources. It is a high-investment and high-risk experimental venture receiving considerable financial support and subsidy from Intertronics. Would Intertronics feel that VideoShop is an extension of the Mark-Tele experiment, or a contamination of it?

Appendix New Venture Task Force Report Proposing a Telecommunications Shopping System for Mark-Tele

We recommend that Mark-Tele design and implement a telecommunication shopping (TCS) system immediately. This proposed new venture appears to be a natural extension of Mark-Tele's experimental mission and an excellent application of Mark-Tele's distinctive technological capabilities in the telecommunications field.

A TCS system would allow a Mark-Tele subscriber to become an active shopper and buyer in the privacy of the home using only the television. Facilitated by Mark-Tele's sophisticated communications and computing technologies, a TCS system subscriber would be able to view and buy a large variety of products and services that conventionally would have required the shopper to leave the home and travel to view and purchase. A TCS system would also serve the suppliers of many different products and services with an opportunity to break away from costly traditional market channels and to inexpensively expand their market coverage and increase sales substantially.

For Mark-Tele, a TCS system would increase revenues, diversify its revenue base, and distribute its high fixed costs efficiently. A TCS system could be used as a promotional tool to build and maintain Mark-Tele's local subscription base. Current subscription rates could be raised with the addition of the TCS system, or an additional fee could be charged to subscribers who desire to participate in the TCS system. Suppliers and shopping subscribers would also be charged for services that Mark-Tele would provide in the development and operation of the TCS system. In the longer run, Mark-Tele could potentially develop TCS networks that could be sold to other cable systems. Clearly, early entry into the TCS field would be lucrative financially for Mark-Tele.

The Environment of TCS

Economic, technological, legal and regulatory, and social trends are emerging in support of a TCS system. Increased consumer spending is predicted to continue, but gains for retailers will be restricted by inflationary pressures. There will be a slower pace of store expansion during the 1980s. Many of the major metropolitan areas are overbuilt with retail space, and developers often are experiencing difficulty obtaining sites and financing. Retailers similarly are experiencing rising rents. Sales growth at many shopping centers has fallen due to slow growth of suburban communities and shrinking distances that consumers are willing to travel to shop.

Retailers are attempting to boost productivity, consolidate store space, and cut costs to improve returns. Inflation has increased operating costs more rapidly than sales during the last 10 years. Many retailers have been attracted to discount pricing policies. The catalog showroom has become one of the fastest growing segments of discount merchandising, featuring national brand products at discount prices.

Considering sociocultural trends, women are continuing to enter the work force, thus have less time to engage in shopping. Greater emphasis on recreational activities continues, and individuals are reluctant to sacrifice leisure time to shop in stores. Convenience is emerging as a high priority.

Consumers are emphasizing their self-identity. As such, consumers are demanding more individuality in goods and services, often desiring distinctive products that individual stores may not be able to afford to inventory and display. Definitely, there has been more intense consumer preference for specialty items and services difficult to find in the Mark-Tele market area.

An increase in the number of single-parent and single-person households has led to increased in-home shopping. Nonstore innovations such as pay-by-phone, specialty mail-order catalogs, and toll-free phone ordering have become increasingly popular. Catalog shopping currently offers a full line of merchandise together with prices and features that permit a consumer to comparison shop at home without having to spend time inefficiently searching for products in crowded stores, waiting for sales help, or at times being annoyed by overzealous clerks. In addition, the increasing age of the population, proliferation of retirement communities, and declining mobility of individuals in their later years make catalog shopping very attractive.

There are significant technological advances that will influence the TCS system. In the past, alphanumerics and graphics but not still or moving "pictures" could be retrieved from a data bank and displayed on a television screen; however, Intertronics' innovative technologics have advanced moving picture capabilities. This new technology has permitted the consumer to control the timing, sequence, and content of information through the use of the keypad.

Development of videodiscs and videocassettes, which to date have been used by viewers to record television programs, have significant promise for advertising and catalog media. Potential exists for suppliers to mail lower-cost video catalogs on a complimentary basis or in lieu of printed direct-mail offerings.

Consumers are being exposed to, and are accepting, complex, technical items such as videotape recorders, home computers, and debit cards for use with automatic teller machines. Home computers and the development of *videotex,* the generic term for home information-retrieval systems, will provide functions compatible with those of the TCS system.

The political-legal context is confusing. The Federal Communications Commission has decided that cable franchising is mainly the province of local jurisdictions. All cable companies must interact with local governments to obtain and maintain authority to operate. While Mark-Tele has secured exclusive rights in their metropolitan area, changes in federal and local policy must be monitored.

The TCS venture raises questions concerning supplier and financial contractual arrangements. The antitrust implications of arrangements with some large institutions should be studied in more detail on a case-by-case basis. Moreover, movement into the retail sector by Mark-Tele through the TCS system will mean closer scrutiny by federal and local consumer protection agencies such as the Federal Trade Commission and the Consumer Product Safety Commission. Finally, Mark-Tele will need to carefully consider protection of the privacy of personal, financial, and transactional data about subscribers of the TCS system. Controls must be established to prevent unauthorized access to information in the system data banks and to guard against unauthorized purchasing.

The General Competitive Context

Industry observers clearly are divided when projecting the evolution of electronic shopping and its acceptance by both consumers and the industry. However, all forms of nonstore retailing currently are growing rapidly, and continued growth is forecasted. Major developments in nonstore retailing will be reviewed.

Mail-Order Catalogs

General department store merchandisers, catalog showrooms, and specialty houses periodically mail catalogs to targeted groups of consumers. An average mail-order house distributes from 6 to 20 catalog issues yearly at a cost often approaching $2 each. Circulations range from about 100,000 to over 1 million for each mailing. The results have been outstanding. Over $26 billion was spent by consumers on mail-order items in 1978—an increase of $12 billion in three years. By comparison, in-store retailing sales grew at a rate less than half of the mail-order rate. Specialty-oriented catalogs are accounting for 75 percent of total mail-order sales, and mail-order catalogs currently contribute 15 percent of the total volume of Christmas season sales. Telephone- and mail-generated orders received by traditional store retailers such as Bloomingdales, J.C. Penney, and Sears are increasing three to five times faster than in-store sales. In-flight shopping catalogs used by major airlines are additional evidence of the increasing popularity of nonstore shopping. Master Card, American Express, and Visa have increased their direct-mail offerings to their credit card holders and are expanding their assortments of merchandise.

The Catalog Showrooms

The catalog showroom is one of the fastest growing fields of retailing. Catalogs are used to promote and feature jewelry, housewares, appliances, sporting goods, and toys at discount prices. Customers visit the showroom to inspect merchandise and to make purchases. Sales for 1980 are estimated to be $7.8 billion, an increase of 11 percent from 1979. Forecasts for 1981 suggest a 20 percent gain in sales revenue. The number of showrooms across the country is nearly 2,000.

Noninteractive Shopping Using the Cable

Comp-U-Card, of Stamford, Connecticut, is a seven-year-old telephone merchandising firm. For an annual fee of $18, it offers members a discount on a broad line of durable goods. Members shop around, familiarizing themselves with products and prices. Then, they call Comp-U-Card toll free for specific information about an item's availability and price. If a purchase decision is made, the consumer provides membership and credit card numbers to an operator, and the merchandise is prepared for delivery. An experimental project has been proposed in which Comp-U-Card would use cable systems and satellite transmission to present product and price information to its subscribers. A transmitted schedule would alert subscribers to the time when particular product information would be presented. Subscribers would continue to use the telephone when ordering.

Telephone purchasing systems using cable presentations are currently operating in Europe. In March 1979, the British Post Office, which runs Britain's telephone system, opened a "viewdata" service called Prestel. Viewers are presented listings of games, restaurants, and consumer product evaluations. Products and services can be purchased on credit by phone. France launched a similar service, called Antiope, in 1979.

A few U.S. companies are testing similar systems. Viewdata Corp., a subsidiary of the Knight-Ridder newspaper chain, proposes to install a permanent system in southern Florida by 1983. First Bank System of Minneapolis will be testing a videotex system in North Dakota similar to the Antiope system of France.

Interactive Cable Systems and Videotex

Since December 1977, Warner Communications and American Express have been involved with a $70 million joint venture testing the QUBE two-way system of Warner Amex Cable in Columbus, Ohio. Currently, the system serves 30,000 of the 105,000 homes in its service area. American Express and Warner Communications propose to build other QUBE systems in such metropolitan areas as Houston, Pittsburgh, and Cincinnati. Both Sears and J.C. Penney currently are testing the QUBE system.

In May 1981, American Telephone & Telegraph Co. (AT&T) endorsed a videotex concept in which a home computer terminal must be purchased. AT&T has set out to develop its own system. AT&T would be a formidable opponent to anyone in the market, considering the firm's capabilities and financial strength. Thus, there are a number of legal actions being undertaken to prevent AT&T's direct entry into the videotex market, fearing it could become a monopoly power. However, strong deregulation sentiments may overcome the opposition and facilitate AT&T's entry into the market.

Over $100 million already has been invested by U.S. firms to design and test various TCS systems, and at least 83 experimental projects are being conducted around the world. As a result, Mark-Tele must be prepared to match formidable competition, and we feel confident that Mark-Tele can.

Target Market Considerations

There are two different markets that must be considered when developing this venture: (1) the suppliers and (2) the shoppers. We propose that the TCS system be "targeted" to the ultimate *user*—the subscribing shopper. A TCS system that is designed well should sell itself to suppliers. Suppliers, therefore, should be considered as a dimension of the total product that will be offered to target shoppers. This approach will allow Mark-Tele to retain maximum control and autonomy in the design and implementation of this venture.

The Target Market—Shoppers

A review of the size and characteristics of the current and potential Mark-Tele subscription base indicates substantial market potential and buying power. However, critical analysis of shopping and buying behavior is necessary to isolate the most lucrative prospective customer segments and to understand their prospective TCS behavior. Three buying factors appear to be very important: (1) risk perceptions, (2) convenience orientations, and (3) buyer satisfaction.

Buying is a complex experience filled with uncertainty and related risks of unfavorable consequences. Fundamentally, consumers confront the uncertainty of achieving their buying goals and risks such as embarrassment or wasting time, money, or effort in a disappointing buying or shopping experience. A consumer must have a satisfying experience each time that the TCS system is used. Otherwise, it is very likely that the consumer will not use TCS again and may discuss the bad experience with other shoppers and discourage their future use of the system.

Supplier Market Implications

After selecting general product and service categories and designing a general format for each TCS channel, Mark-Tele should direct attention to the supplier market. Mark-Tele should evaluate prospective suppliers regarding the relevance of their product or service assortment, their delivery and financial capabilities, and quality of their promotional strategies, and their desire to enter into this unconventional market. We feel that Mark-Tele's technical competence and captive subscription base will provide substantial leverage in all negotiations with suppliers. The actual marketing effort should involve personal selling programs, custom designed for each prospective target supplier.

Prospective Products and Services

Preliminary research has uncovered a number of product and service lines that are appropriate for our target market and appear to be financially and technically feasible. As this innovative approach to shopping evolves and consumer acceptance and involvement grows, many other products and services could be incorporated. However, the most feasible products and services currently are:

Standard catalog items.

Grocery items.

Gifts and specialty items.

Appliances, home entertainment, and personal computer equipment.

Toys, electronic games and equipment, basic sporting goods.

Banking and financial services.

Classified ads.

Multiple-listing service of local properties.

Ticket, restaurant, and accommodations reservations.

Educational and recreational classes.

Automobiles.

We cannot stress too strongly that TCS will involve a high degree of risk perceived by consumers. This must be reduced by offering products and services with which consumers are familiar and comfortable and which involve a minimum number of basic shopping decisions for consumers.

The consumer must *learn* to use the TCS system. Mark-Tele must guide this learning experience and make sure that consumers have consistent, positive shopping experiences that become reinforcing. The following services/features should be incorporated into the TCS system to reduce shopping risks and facilitate consumer satisfaction:

Easy-to-use indexing devices.

Top-quality visual and audio representation.

Professional promotions.

Up-to-date information on specials.

Competitive pricing policies and convenient payment methods.

TCS availability 24 hours per day, seven days per week.

Maintenance service availability 24 hours per day, seven days per week.

Accurate order taking and fulfilling.

Prompt delivery or pickup services.

Quick and equitable handling and resolution of customer complaints.

Exceptional reliability.

Eventually, the TCS product and service assortment could be broadened and channel features changed. However, the products and service lines outlined in this report appear to involve minimal consumer risks, high potential for competitive advantage and target consumer satisfaction, and substantial returns for Mark-Tele.

The Competitive Advantage

A competitive advantage over conventional suppliers can be achieved by Mark-Tele if the TCS system is designed to serve the needs and expectations of the identified target market by actively considering their prepurchase deliberations, by guiding their purchase activities, and by reinforcing their postpurchase satisfaction. This must be complemented with accurate and reliable order processing and with prompt, efficient logistical support. Above all, Mark-Tele must communicate and promote its distinctive capabilities. We believe that the following distinctive features of the TCS system should be emphasized:

The extensive variety and depth of product and service assortments.

The vast amount of relevant information that is easily accessible and allows consumers to make better choices.

The excitement, involvement, convenience, and satisfaction of shopping in the privacy of one's home, using space-age technology and the simplicity of the television.

The insignificant, negligible, and indirect costs to consumers, particularly when compared to the opportunities and benefits.

The recommendation of our committee is that Mark-Tele design and implement the proposed new venture concept. We have identified the target customers and viable products and services to satisfy their needs and Mark-Tele's objectives. Development of the supplier market and control over suppliers also has been discussed. We recommend immediate action.

Case 12

The Gillette Company*

In July 1978, Mike Edwards, brand manager for TRAC II®,[1] is beginning to prepare his marketing plans for the following year. In preparing for the marketing plan approval process, he has to wrestle with some major funding questions. The most recent sales figures show that TRAC II has continued to maintain its share of the blade and razor market. This has occurred even though the Safety Razor Division (SRD) has introduced a new product to its line, Atra. The company believes that Atra will be the shaving system of the future and, therefore, is devoting increasing amounts of marketing support to this brand. Atra was launched in 1977 with a $7 million advertising campaign and over 50 million $2 rebate coupons. In less than a year, the brand achieved a 7 percent share of the blade market and about one third of the dollar-razor market. Thus, the company will be spending heavily on Atra, possibly at the expense of TRAC II, still the number one shaving system in America.

Edwards is faced with a difficult situation, for he believes that TRAC II still can make substantial profits for the division if the company continues to support it. In preparing for 1979, the division is faced with two major issues:

1. What are TRAC II's and Atra's future potentials?
2. Most important, can the SRD afford to heavily support two brands? Even if they can, is it sound marketing policy to do so?

Company Background

The Gillette Company was founded in 1903 by King C. Gillette, a 40-year-old inventor, utopian writer, and bottle-cap salesman in Boston, Massachusetts. Since marketing its first safety razor and blades, the Gillette Company, the parent of the Safety Razor Division, has been the leader in the shaving industry. The Gillette safety razor was the first system to provide a disposable blade that could be replaced at low cost and that provided a good inexpensive shave. The early ads focused on a shave-yourself theme: "If the time, money, energy, and brainpower which are wasted (shaving) in the barbershops of America were applied in direct effort, the Panama Canal could be dug in four hours."

---

*This case was written by Charles M. Kummel under the direction of Professor Jay E. Klompmaker of the University of North Carolina. Copyright © 1982 by Jay E. Klompmaker, reproduced by permission.

[1] TRAC II® is a registered trademark of The Gillette Company.

The Pre-World War Years

With the benefit of a 17-year patent, Gillette was in a very advantageous position. However, it was not until the First World War that the safety razor began to gain wide consumer acceptance. One day in 1917 King Gillette came into the office with a visionary idea: to present a Gillette razor to every soldier, sailor, and marine. Other executives modified this idea so that the government would do the presenting. In this way, millions just entering the shaving age would give the nation the self-shaving habit. In World War I, the government bought 4,180,000 Gillette razors as well as smaller quantities of competitive models.

Daily Shaving Development

Although World War I gave impetus to self-shaving, World War II popularized frequent shaving—12 million American servicemen shaved daily. This produced two results: (1) Gillette was able to gain consumer acceptance of personal shaving and (2) the company was able to develop an important market to build for the future.

Postwar Years

After 1948, the company began to diversify through the acquisition of three companies which gave Gillette entry into new markets. In 1948, the acquisition of the Toni Company extended the company into the women's grooming aid market. Paper Mate, a leading maker of writing instruments, was bought in 1954, and the Sterilon Corporation, a manufacturer of disposable supplies for hospitals, was acquired in 1962.

Diversification also occurred through internal product development propelled by a detailed marketing survey conducted in the late 1950s. The survey found that the public associated the company as much or more with personal grooming as with cutlery and related products. Gillette's response was to broaden its personal care line. As a result, Gillette now markets such well-known brands as Adorn hair spray, Tame cream rinse, Right Guard antiperspirant, Dry Look hair spray for men, Foamy shaving cream, Earth Borne and Ultra Max shampoos, Cricket lighter, Pro Max hair dryers as well as Paper Mate, Eraser Mate, and Flair pens.

Gillette Today

Gillette is divided into four principal operating groups (North America, International, Braun AG, Diversified Companies) and five product lines. As Exhibit 1 indicates, the importance of blades and razors to company profits is immense. In nearly all the 200 countries in which its blades and razors are sold, Gillette remains the industry leader.

EXHIBIT 1 Gillette sales and contributions to profits by business segments

Year	Blades and razors Net sales	Contributions to profits	Toiletries and grooming aids Net sales	Contributions to profits	Writing instruments Net sales	Contributions to profits	Braun electric razors Net sales	Contributions to profits	Other Net sales	Contributions to profits
1977	31%	75%	26%	13%	8%	6%	23%	13%	12%	(7)%
1976	29	71	28	15	7	6	21	10	15	(2)
1975	30	73	30	15	7	5	20	8	13	(1)
1974	30	69	31	17	7	6	20	5	12	3
1973	31	64	32	20	7	5	22	10	8	1

Source: *Gillette Annual Report for 1977*, p. 28.

In 1977, Gillette reported increased worldwide sales of $1,587.2 million with income after taxes of $79.7 million (see Exhibit 2). Of total sales, $720.9 million were domestic and $866.3 million were international, with profit contributions of $109 million and $105.6 million, respectively. The company employs 31,700 people worldwide with 8,600 employees in the United States.

Statement of Corporate Objectives and Goals

At a recent stockholders' meeting, the chairman of the board outlined the company's strategy for the future:

> The goal of The Gillette Company is sustained growth. To achieve this, the company concentrates on two major objectives: to maintain the strength of existing product lines and to develop at least two new significant businesses or product

EXHIBIT 2 The Gillette Company annual income statements, 1963–1977 ($000)

Year	Net sales	Gross profit	Profit from operations	Income before taxes	Federal and foreign income taxes	Net income
1977	$1,587,209	$834,786	$202,911	$158,820	$79,100	$79,720
1976	1,491,506	782,510	190,939	149,257	71,700	77,557
1975	1,406,906	737,310	184,368	146,954	67,000	79,954
1974	1,246,422	667,395	171,179	147,295	62,300	84,995
1973	1,064,427	600,805	155,949	154,365	63,300	91,065
1972	870,532	505,297	140,283	134,618	59,600	75,018
1971	729,687	436,756	121,532	110,699	48,300	62,399
1970	672,669	417,575	120,966	117,475	51,400	66,075
1969	609,557	390,858	122,416	119,632	54,100	65,532
1968	553,174	358,322	126,016	124,478	62,200	62,278
1967	428,357	291,916	101,153	103,815	47,200	56,615
1966	396,190	264,674	90,967	91,666	41,800	49,866
1965	339,064	224,995	75,010	75,330	33,000	42,330
1964	298,956	205,884	72,594	73,173	35,500	37,673
1963	295,700	207,552	85,316	85,945	44,400	41,545

lines that can make important contributions to the growth of the company in the early 1980s.

In existing product lines, the company broadens its opportunities for growth by utilizing corporate technology to create new products. In other areas, growth is accomplished through either internal development or the acquisition of new businesses.

The company uses a number of guidelines to evaluate growth opportunities. Potential products or services must fulfill a useful function and provide value for the price paid; offer distinct advantages easily perceived by consumers; be based on technology available within, or readily accessible outside the company; meet established quality and safety standards; and offer an acceptable level of profitability and attractive growth potential.

The Safety Razor Division

The Safety Razor Division has long been regarded as the leader in shaving technology. Building on King Gillette's principle of using razors as a vehicle for blade sales and of associating the name "Gillette" with premium shaving, the division has been able to maintain its number one position in the U.S. market.

Share of Market

Market share is important in the shaving industry. The standard is that each share point is equivalent to approximately $1 million in pretax profits. Over recent history, Gillette has held approximately 60 percent of the total dollar market. However, the division has put more emphasis on increasing its share from its static level.

Product Line

During the course of its existence, Gillette has introduced many new blades and razors. In the last 15 years, the shaving market has evolved from a double-edged emphasis to twin-bladed systems (see Exhibit 3). Besides Atra and TRAC II, Gillette markets Good News! disposables, Daisy for women, double-edge, injector, carbon, and Techmatic band systems (see Exhibit 4). Within their individual markets, Gillette sells 65 percent of all premium double-edged blades, 12 percent of injector sales, and almost all of the carbon and band sales.

Marketing Approach and Past Traditions

During 1977, the Gillette Company spent $207.9 million to promote all its products throughout the world, of which $133.1 million was spent for advertising, including couponing and sampling, and $74.8 million for sales promotion. In terms of the domestic operation, the Safety Razor Division uses an eight-cycle promotional schedule whereby every six weeks a new program is initiated. During any one cycle, some but not all the products and their packages are

EXHIBIT 3 Gillette percentage of U.S. blade sales (estimated market share)

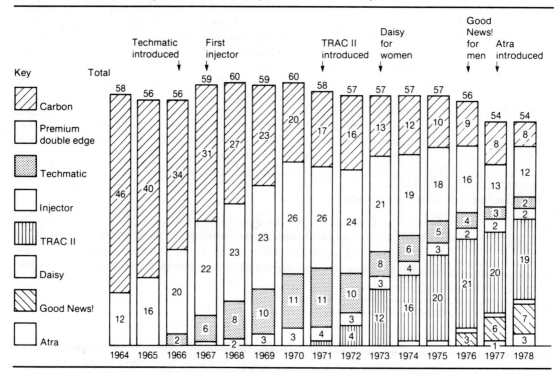

sold on promotion. Usually one of the TRAC II packages is sold on promotion during each of these cycles.

Gillette advertising is designed to provide information to consumers and motivate them to buy the company's products. Sales promotion ensures that these products are readily available, well located, and attractively displayed in retail stores. Special promotion at the point of purchase offers consumers an extra incentive to buy Gillette products.[2]

In the past the company has concentrated its advertising and promotion on its newest shaving product, reducing support for its other established lines. The theory is that growth must come at the expense of other brands. When TRAC II was introduced, for example, the advertising budget for other brands was cut, with the double-edged portion being decreased from 47 percent in 1971 to 11 percent in 1972 and TRAC II receiving 61 percent of the division budget (see Exhibit 5).

A long-standing tradition has been that razors are used as a means for

---

[2] *1977 Gillette Company Annual Report*, p. 14.

EXHIBIT 4 Safety Razor Division product line, June 1978

Product line	Package sizes	Manufacturer's suggested retail price
Blades:		
TRAC II	5,9,14,Adjustable 4	$1.60, 2.80, 3.89, 1.50
Atra	5,10	$1.70, 3.40
Good News!	2	$.60
Daisy	2	$1.00
Techmatic	5,10,15	$1.50, 2.80, 3.50
Double-edged		
Platinum Plus	5,10,15	$1.40, 2.69, 3.50
Super-Stainless	5,10,15	$1.20, 2.30, 3.10
Carbon:		
Super Blue	10,15	$1.50, 2.15
Regular Blue	5,10	$.70, 1.25
Injector:		
Regular	7,11	$1.95, 2.60
Twin Injector	5,8	$1.40, 2.20
Razors:		
TRAC II	Regular	$3.50
	Lady	$3.50
	Adjustable	$3.50
	Deluxe	$3.50
Atra		$4.95
Double-edged:		
Super Adjustable		$3.50
Lady Gillette		$3.50
Super Speed		$1.95
Twin Injector		$2.95
Techmatic	Regular	$3.50
	Deluxe	$3.95
Three-Piece		$4.50
Knack		$1.95
Cricket Lighters	Regular	$1.49
	Super	$1.98
	Keeper	$4.49

selling blades. Thus, with razors, the emphasis is on inducing the consumer to try the product by offering coupon discounts, mail samples, and heavy informational advertising. Blade strategy has been to emphasize a variety of sales devices—such as discounts, displays, and sweepstakes at pharmacies, convenience stores, and supermarkets—to encourage point-of-purchase sales. In spite of this tradition, razor sales are a very significant portion of division sales and profits.

At the center of this marketing strategy has been the company's identification with sports. The Gillette "Cavalcade of Sports" began with Gillette's radio sponsorship of the 1939 World Series and continues today with sponsorship of the World Series, Super Bowl, professional and NCAA basketball, as well as boxing. During the 1950s and 1960s, Gillette spent 60 percent of its ad dollars on sports programming. Influenced by research showing that prime-time entertainment offered superior audience potential, the company switched to a prime-

EXHIBIT 5 Gillette advertising expenditures, 1965–1978 (percentage of total market)

| Total market ($ millions) | 20.5 | 21.4 | 21.0 | 23.6 | 20.5 | 21.7 | 24.8 | 20.5 | 23.7 | 26.5 | 24.0 | 24.3 | 29.8 | 33.0 |

Legend:
- Double-edge
- Bands
- Injector
- TRAC II
- Other
- Daisy
- Atra
- Good News!

Years: 1965, 1966, 1967, 1968, 1969, 1970, 1971, 1972, 1973, 1974, 1975, 1976, 1977, 1978 (estimate)

Bar totals: 43, 53, 54, 46, 50, 53, 38, 44, 43, 39, 46, 44, 38, 41

time emphasis in the early 1970s. However, Gillette has recently returned in the last two years to its sports formula.

Marketing Research

Research has been a cornerstone to the success of the company, for it has been its means of remaining superior to its competitors. For example, Gillette was faced in 1917 with the expiration of its basic patents and the eventual flood of competitive models. Six months before the impending expiration, the company came out with new razor models including one for a dollar. As a result, the company made more money than ever before. In fact, throughout the history of shaving, Gillette has introduced most of the improvements in shaving technology. The major exceptions are the injector, which was introduced by Schick, and the stainless-steel double-edged blade introduced by Wilkinson.

The company spends $37 million annually on research and development for new products, product improvements, and consumer testing. In addition to Atra, a recent development is a new sharpening process called "Micro-smooth" which improves the closeness of the shave and the consistency of the blade. This improvement was to be introduced on all of the company's twin blades by early 1979. Mike Edwards believes that this will help to ensure TRAC II's retention of its market.

At the time of Atra's introduction, Gillette research found that users would come from users of TRAC II and nontwin-blade systems. This projected loss was estimated to be 60 percent of TRAC II users. Recent research indicates that with heavy marketing support in 1978, TRAC II's loss will be held to 40 percent.

The Shaving Market

The shaving market is divided into two segments: wet and electric shavers. Today, the wet shavers account for 75 percent of the market. In the United States alone, 1.9 billion blades and 23 million razors are sold annually. Gillette participates in the electric market through sales of electric razors by its Braun subsidiary.

Market Factors

There are a number of factors at work within the market: (1) the adult shaving population has increased in the past 15 years to 74.6 million men and 68.2 million women, (2) technological improvements have improved the quality of the shave as well as increased the life of the razor blade, and (3) the volume of blades and razors has begun to level off after a period of declining and then increasing sales (see Exhibit 6). Although the shaving market has increased slightly, there are more competitors. Yet Gillette has been able to maintain its share of the market—approximately two thirds of the dollar-razor market and a little over half of the dollar-blade market.

Market Categories

The market is segmented into seven components: new systems, disposables, injector, premium double-edged, carbon double-edged, continuous bands, and single-edged systems. In the early 1900s the shaving market consisted primarily of straight-edges. During the past 70 years, the market has evolved away from its single- and then double-edged emphasis to the present market of 60 percent bonded systems (all systems in which the blade is encased in plastic). Exhibit 7 shows the recent trends within the market categories.

Competitors

Gillette's major competitors are Warner-Lambert's Schick, Colgate-Palmolive's Wilkinson, American Safety Razor's Personna, and BIC. Each has its own

EXHIBIT 6 Razor and blade sales volume, 1963–1979

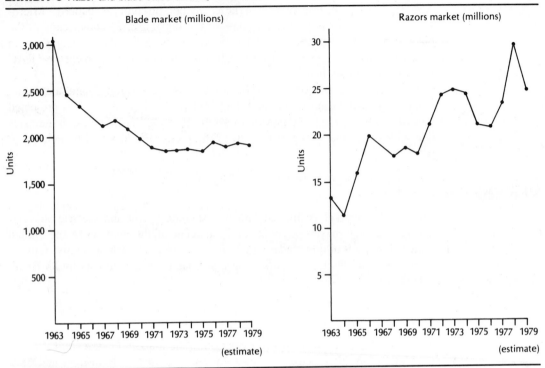

EXHIBIT 7 Recent share trends (percent)

Volume	1972	1973	1974	1975	1976	1977	1978, 1st half
Units:							
New systems	8.8%	20.6%	28.8%	36.2%	39.9%	40.8%	43.8%
Injector	20.2	17.6	17.1	16.3	15.7	14.2	12.8
Double-edged:							
Premium	39.4	34.9	30.8	27.4	24.5	21.1	19.0
Carbon	12.0	10.6	9.4	8.1	7.3	7.6	6.6
Bands	13.1	10.3	8.0	6.4	4.7	3.7	2.7
Disposables	—	—	—	—	2.5	6.9	9.7
Single-edged	6.5	6.0	5.9	5.6	5.4	5.7	5.4
Total market	100.0%	100.0%	100.0%	100.0%	100.0%	100.0%	100.0%
Dollars:							
New systems	11.8%	26.9%	36.9%	46.0%	50.1%	50.1%	52.1%
Injector	21.8	18.6	17.8	16.4	15.0	13.8	12.5
Double-edged:							
Premium	41.5	34.2	28.7	24.0	20.8	18.1	16.1
Carbon	6.1	5.4	4.7	4.2	4.0	4.1	3.5
Bands	15.4	11.8	8.7	6.5	4.8	3.6	2.8
Disposables	—	—	—	—	2.8	7.5	10.5
Single-edged	3.4	3.1	3.2	2.9	2.5	2.8	2.5
Total market	100.0%	100.0%	100.0%	100.0%	100.0%	100.0%	100.0%

strongholds. Schick, which introduced the injector system, now controls 80 percent of that market. ASR's Personna sells almost all of the single-edged blades on the market. Wilkinson's strength is its bonded system which appeals to an older, wealthier market. BIC has developed a strong product in its inexpensive disposable system.

Competitive pricing structure is comparable to Gillette within the different system categories. Although all the companies have similar suggested retail prices, the differences found on the racks in the market are a function of the companies' off-invoice rates to the trade and their promotional allowances. It is not much of a factor at this time; private labels cover the range of systems and continue to grow.

Market Segmentation

The success of Gillette's technological innovation can be seen in its effect on the total shaving market. Although there are other factors at play in the market, new product introductions have contributed significantly to market expansion as Exhibit 8 indicates.

Twin-Blade Market

Research played a key role in the development of twin blades. Gillette had two variations—the current type in which the blades are in tandem; the other type in which the blades' edges faced each other and required an up-and-down scrubbing motion. From a marketing standpoint, and because the Atra swivel system had problems in testing development, TRAC II was launched first. The research department played a major role in the positioning of the product when it discovered hysteresis, the phenomenon of whiskers being lifted out and after a time receding into the follicle. Thus, the TRAC II effect was that the second blade cut the whisker before it receded.

Since its introduction in 1971, the twin-blade market has grown to account for almost 60 percent of all blade sales. The twin-blade market is defined as all

EXHIBIT 8 New product introductions and their effects on the market, 1959–1977

Year	Product segment	Sales blade/razor market ($ millions)	Change (percent)
1959	Carbon	122.4	Base
1960	Super blue	144.1	+ 17.7 over 1959
1963	Stainless	189.3	+ 31.3 over 1960
1965	Super stainless	201.2	+ 6.3 over 1963
1966	Banded system	212.1	+ 5.4 over 1965
1969	Injector	246.8	+ 16.3 over 1966
1972	Twin blades	326.5	+ 32.2 over 1969
1975	Disposable	384.0	+ 17.6 over 1972
1977	Pivoting head	444.9	+ 15.9 over 1975

EXHIBIT 9 The twin–blade market,1972–1978 ($ millions)

	1972	1973	1974	1975	1976	1977	1978, estimate	1979, estimate
Razors	$ 29.5	$ 32.1	$ 31.4	$ 31.3	$ 31.5	$ 39.7	$ 53.8	
Disposables	—	—	—	—	14.5	41.5	64.9	
Blades	31.6	72.0	105.7	147.5	176.3	183.7	209.2	
Total twin	61.1	104.1	137.1	176.2	222.3	264.9	327.9	
Total market	$326.5	$332.6	$342.5	$384.0	$422.2	$444.9	$491.0	$500.0

bonded razors and blades (e.g., new systems: Atra and TRAC II; disposables: Good News! and BIC). Exhibit 9 shows the trends in the twin-blade market.

During this period many products have been introduced. These include the Sure Touch in 1971, the Deluxe TRAC II and Schick Super II in 1972, the Lady TRAC II, Personna Double II, and Wilkinson Bonded in 1973, the Personna Flicker, Good News!, and BIC Disposable in 1974, the Personna Lady Double II in 1975, and the Adjustable TRAC II and Schick Super II in 1976.

Advertising

In the race for market share, the role of advertising is extremely important in the shaving industry. Of all the media expenditures, television is the primary vehicle in the twin-blade market. For Gillette, this means an emphasis on maximum exposure and sponsorship of sports events. The company's policy for the use of television is based on the concept that TV is essentially a family medium and programs should therefore be suitable for family viewing. Gillette tries to avoid programs that unduly emphasize sex or violence.

As the industry leader, TRAC II receives a great deal of competitive pressure in the form of aggressive advertising from competitors and other Gillette twin-blade brands (see Exhibit 10). For example, the theme of recent

EXHIBIT 10 Estimated media expenditures ($000)

	1976	1977, 1st half	1977, 2nd half	Total 1977	1978, 1st half	Total 1978 estimate
Companies:						
Gillette	$10,800	$ 4,800	$ 6,400	$11,200	$ 8,100	$13,800
Schick	7,600	3,700	4,300	8,000	4,300	8,900
Wilkinson	2,700	1,400	2,200	3,600	1,400	2,200
ASR	2,600	700	200	900	200	800
BIC	600*	4,300	1,800	6,100	4,000	7,300
Total market	$24,300	$14,900	$14,900	$29,800	$18,000	$33,000
Brands:						
TRAC II	$ 6,000	$ 3,300	$ 1,700	$ 5,000	$ 2,400	$ 4,000
Atra	—	—	4,000	4,000	4,500	7,500
Good News!	1,900	1,200	600	1,800	700	1,600
Super II	2,600	1,400	2,600	4,000	3,000	4,600

* Product introduction.

Schick commercials was the "Schick challenge," and BIC emphasized its lower cost and cleaner shave in relation to those of other twin-blade brands. However, competitive media expenditures are such that their cost per share point is substantially higher than TRAC II's.

Despite competitive pressures, TRAC II is aggressively advertised too. As a premium product, it does not respond directly to competitive challenges or shifts in its own media; rather, the advertising follows a standard principle of emphasizing TRAC II's strengths. As Exhibits 11 and 12 indicate, the TRAC II media plan emphasizes diversity with a heavy emphasis on advertising on prime-time television and on sports programs. In addition, TRAC II is continually promoted to retain its market share.

For 1978, the division budgeted $18 million for advertising, with Atra and TRAC II receiving the major portion of the budget (see Exhibit 13). The traditional Gillette approach is for the newest brand to receive the bulk of the advertising dollars (see Exhibit 5). Therefore, it is certain that Atra will receive a substantial increase in advertising for 1979. Whether the division will increase or decrease TRAC II's budget as well as whether it will increase the total ad budget for 1979 is unknown at this time.

TRAC II

The 1971 introduction of TRAC II was the largest in shaving history. Influenced by the discovery of the hysteresis process, by the development of a clog-free dual-blade cartridge, and by consumer-testing data which showed a nine to one preference for TRAC II over the panelists' current razors, Gillette raced to get the product to market. Because the introduction involved so many people

EXHIBIT 11 TRAC II media plan, 1976, 1977 ($000)

	Quarter				
	1	2	3	4	Total
1976					
Prime	935	575	1,200	550	3,160
Sports	545	305	450	1,040	2,440
Network total	1,480	880	1,650	1,590	5,650
Other	80	85	70	165	400
Total	1,560	965	1,720	1,755	6,000
1977					
Prime	1,300	900	300	—	2,500
Sports	500	400	400	400	1,700
Network total	1,800	1,300	700	400	4,200
Print	—	—	200	200	400
Black	75	75	75	75	300
Military, miscellaneous	25	25	25	25	100
Total	1,900	1,400	1,000	700	5,000

EXHIBIT 12 TRAC II media plan, 1978

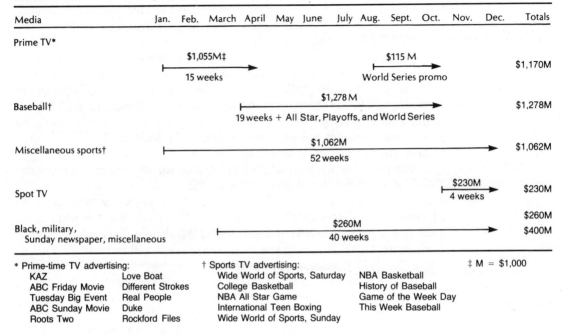

Media	Jan.	Feb.	March	April	May	June	July	Aug.	Sept.	Oct.	Nov.	Dec.	Totals
Prime TV*			$1,055M‡ → 15 weeks					$115 M → World Series promo					$1,170M
Baseball†					$1,278 M → 19 weeks + All Star, Playoffs, and World Series								$1,278M
Miscellaneous sports†			$1,062M → 52 weeks										$1,062M
Spot TV											$230M → 4 weeks		$230M
Black, military, Sunday newspaper, miscellaneous					$260M → 40 weeks								$260M / $400M

* Prime-time TV advertising:		† Sports TV advertising:		‡ M = $1,000
KAZ	Love Boat	Wide World of Sports, Saturday	NBA Basketball	
ABC Friday Movie	Different Strokes	College Basketball	History of Baseball	
Tuesday Big Event	Real People	NBA All Star Game	Game of the Week Day	
ABC Sunday Movie	Duke	International Teen Boxing	This Week Baseball	
Roots Two	Rockford Files	Wide World of Sports, Sunday		

and was so critical to reversing a leveling of corporate profits (see Exhibit 2), the division president personally assumed the role of product development manager and lived with the project day and night through its development and introduction.[3]

Launched during the 1971 World Series promotion, TRAC II was the most frequently advertised shaving system in America during its introductory period. Supported by $10 million in advertising and promotion, TRAC II results were impressive: 1.7 million razors and 5 million cartridges were sold in October; and during the first year, the introductory campaign made 2 billion impressions and reached 80 percent of all homes an average of 4.7 times a week. In addition, a multimillion-unit sampling campaign was implemented in 1972 which was the largest of its kind.

For five years TRAC II was clearly the fastest growing product on the market, and it helped to shape the switch to twin blades. Its users are predominantly young, college-educated, metropolitan, suburban, and upper-income men. The brand reached its peak in 1976 when it sold 485 million blades and 7 million razors. In comparison, projected TRAC II sales for 1978 are 433 million

---

[3] For an excellent account of the TRAC II introduction, by the president of Gillette North America, see William G. Salatich, ''Gillette's TRAC II: The Steps to Success,'' *Market Communications*, January 1972.

EXHIBIT 13 Razor Division marketing budget, 1978

	Atra line	TRAC II line	Good News!	Double-edged blades	Double-edged razors	Techmatic line	Daisy	Injector line	Twin injector	Total blade/razor
Marketing expenses:										
Promotion*	42.3	69.4	65.2	92.2	75.4	52.7	58.4	77.5	48.3	60.7
Advertising†	55.6	28.8	31.2	4.6	—	—	39.0	—	26.3	36.5
Other	2.1	1.8	3.6	3.2	24.6	47.3	2.6	22.5	25.4	2.8
Total marketing	100.0	100.0	100.0	100.0	100.0	100.0	100.0	100.0	100.0	100.0
Percentage line/total direct marketing	34.1	38.4	14.9	7.6	.4	.3	3.4	.2	.7	100.0
Percentage line/total full revenue sales	20.5	41.8	13.4	16.8	1.4	2.1	2.2	.6	1.2	100.0

* Defined as off-invoice allowances, wholesale push money, cooperative advertising, excess cost, premiums, contests, and prizes.
† Defined as media, sampling, couponing, production, and costs.

blades and 4.2 million razors. During this period, TRAC II brand contribution decreased 10 percent (see Exhibit 14). Competitors' responsive strategies seem to be effective. The growth of Super II during the last two years is attributed to certain advantages it has over TRAC II. Super II has higher trade allowances (20% versus 15%), improved distribution, an increased media expenditure, and generally lower everyday prices.

In preparing the 1979 marketing plans, the objective for TRAC II was to retain its consumer franchise despite strong competitive challenges through consumer-oriented promotions and to market the brand aggressively year round. Specifically, TRAC II was

1. To obtain a 20 percent share of the cartridge and razor market.
2. To deliver 43 percent of the division's profit.

EXHIBIT 14 TRAC II line income statement, 1972–1978

	1972*	1973	1974	1975	Base 1976	1977	Estimated 1978
Full revenue sales (FRS):							
Promotional	28	41	71	100	100	110	112
Nonpromotional	38	91	89	83	100	80	65
Total	32	60	78	93	100	99	95
Direct cost of sales:							
Manufacturing	63	77	93	111	100	88	83
Freight	51	80	91	106	100	82	80
Total	62	77	93	111	100	88	83
Standard profit contribution	26	56	75	89	100	101	97
Marketing expenses							
Promotional expenses:							
Lost revenue	26	39	72	100	100	114	126
Wholesale push money	455	631	572	565	100	562	331
Cooperative advertising	27	36	58	71	100	115	133
Excess cost	25	50	59	83	100	63	92
Premiums	3	29	16	28	100	78	217
Contests and prizes	7	21	110	115	100	215	109
Total	26	40	67	90	100	112	129
Advertising:							
Media	90	83	110	119	100	96	75
Production	96	128	130	104	100	196	162
Couponing and sampling	470	344	177	112	100	166	131
Other	19	120	68	78	100	54	54
Total	124	110	108	117	100	96	78
Other marketing expenses	108	120	847	617	100	242	86
Market research	122	65	47	34	100	134	91
Total assignable marketing expenses	67	69	87	102	100	106	108
Net contribution:	14	53	81	85	100	100	94
Percentage of promotional FRS/total FRS	56	43	58	76	63	70	74
Percentage of promotional expenses/promo FRS	15	16	16	15	11	17	20
Percentage of promotional expenses/total FRS	9	7	9	10	11	12	15
Percentage of advertising expenses/total FRS	28	13	10	9	7	7	6
Percentage of Media expenses/total FRS	17	8	8	8	6	6	5

* Each year's data are shown as a percentage of 1976's line item. For example, 1972 sales were 32 percent of 1976 sales.

3. To retain its valuable pegboard space at the checkout counters in convenience, food, and drug stores as well as supermarkets.

In 1978, Mike Edwards launched a new economy-size blade package (14 blades) and a heavy spending campaign to retain TRAC II's market share. He employed strong trade and consumer promotion incentives supported by (1) new improved product claims of a "microsmooth" shave, (2) new graphics, and (3) a revised version of the highly successful "Sold Out" advertising campaign (see Exhibit 15). Midyear results indicated that TRAC II's performance had exceeded division expectations as it retained 21.6 percent of the blade market and its contribution exceeded the budget by $2 million.

Atra (Automatic Tracking Razor Action)

Origin

Research for the product began in Gillette's United Kingdom Research and Development Laboratory in 1970. The purpose was to improve the high standards of performance of twin-blade shaving and, specifically, to enhance the TRAC II effect. The company's scientists discovered that a better shave could be produced if, instead of the shaver moving the hand and face to produce the best shaving angle for the blade, the razor head could pivot in such a way as to maintain the most effective twin-blade shaving angle. Once the pivoting head was shown to produce a better shave, test after test, research continued in the Boston headquarters on product design, redesigning, and consumer testing.

The name "Atra" came from two years of intensive consumer testing of the various names which could be identified with this advanced razor. The choice was based on how easy it was to remember the name, how well it communicated the technology, its uniqueness, and the feeling of the future it conveyed. Atra stands for *Automatic Tracking Razor Action.*

Introduction

Atra was first introduced in mid-1977. The introduction stressed the new shaving system supplemented by heavy advertising coupled with $2 razor rebate coupons to induce trial and 50-cent coupons toward Atra blades to induce brand loyalty. An example of Atra advertising is shown in Exhibit 16. During its first year on the national market, Atra was expected to sell 9 million razors although 85 percent of all sales were sold on a discount basis. Early results showed that Atra sold at a faster level than Gillette's previously most successful product, TRAC II. The Atra razor retails for $4.95. Blades are sold in packages of 5 and 10. TRAC II and Atra blades are not interchangeable. Because of Gillette's excellent distribution system, it has not had much problem gaining valuable pegboard space.

EXHIBIT 15

Gillette **TRAC II**

THE GILLETTE COMPANY
SAFETY RAZOR DIVISION

LENGTH: 30 SECONDS

"SOLD OUT"
(MICROSMOOTH-GIRL) SUPER II

BBDO

COMM'L NO.: GSRD 8033

IRVING: Sold out again!???
(SFX: DING!)

CUSTOMER 1: The new improved
Gillette TRAC II, please.

IRVING: Er . . . say . . . who needs
improved when these twin blades'll do.

CUSTOMER 1: TRAC II has micro-
smooth edges . . . makes the blades
smoother than ever.

IRVING: Shave better than these?

CUSTOMER 1: Better, safer, smoother
. . . and comfortable.

IRVING: Comfort . . . schmomfort . . .
you don't have . . . But . . . but . . . b-b . . .

CUSTOMER 2: Do you have the new
improved Gillette TRAC II?

IRVING: Improved TRAC II??
(INNOCENTLY) Improved TRAC II?

ANNCR: The new improved Gillette
TRAC II. Micro-smooth edges make
it a better shave.

EXHIBIT 16

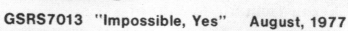

:30 second commercial GSRS7013 "Impossible, Yes" August, 1977

ANNCR (VO): Could Gillette make a razor that does the impossible?

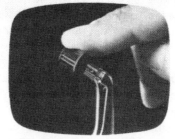

Yes.

Could it shave closer with even more comfort?

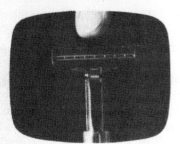

Yes.

Gillette introduces Atra . . .

the first razor with a pivoting head . . .

that safely follows every contour of your face.

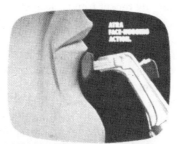

This Atra face-hugging action keeps the twin-blades at the perfect angle.

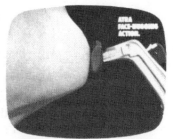

You've never shaved this close with this much comfort.

MAN: Impossible!

*ANNCR: The New Gillette Atra Razor.

Yes, it's the impossible shave.

Current Trends and Competitive Responses in the Twin-Blade Market

There was quite a bit of activity in the shaving market during the first half of 1978. Atra had increased the total Gillette share in the razor and blade market. During the June period, Atra razors continued to exceed TRAC II as the leading selling razor whereas Atra blades share was approximately 8 percent, accounting for most of Gillette's 4 percent share growth since June 1977. Thus, the growth of Atra has put more competitive pressure on TRAC II. In addition, the disposable segment due to BIC and Good News! has increased by five share points to a hefty 12 percent dollar share of the blade market. Combined with TRAC II's resiliency in maintaining share, competitive brands have lost share: Schick Super II, ASR, and Wilkinson were all down two points since June 1977.

In response to these recent trends, the TRAC II team expected competition to institute some changes. In an effort to recover its sagging share, Edwards expected the Schick Muscular Dystrophy promotion in October 1977 to help bolster Super II with its special offer. The pressure may already be appearing with Schick's highly successful introduction of Personal Touch for women in this year, currently about 10 percent of the razor market, which has to draw TRAC II female shavers. In addition, it appears inevitable that Schick will bring out an Atra-type razor. This will remove Atra's competitive advantage but increase pressure on TRAC II with the addition of a second pivoting head competitor.

Continuing its recent trends, it appears that the disposable segment of the market will continue to expand. The first sign of this is the BIC ads offering 12 BIC disposables for $1. Good News! received additional advertising support in the latter half of the year as well as the introduction of a new package size. One of Edwards's major objectives is to emphasize the importance of TRAC II to upper management. Besides the introduction of the microsmooth concept, a price increase on TRAC II products will be implemented soon. It is unclear whether the price change will have an adverse effect on brand sales.

In preparing the 1979 TRAC II marketing plan, Edwards realized that Atra would be given a larger share of the advertising dollars following a strong year, and the disposable market would continue to grow. TRAC II share remained questionable, depending on the level of marketing support it received. Whether TRAC II will be able to continue its heavy spending program and generate large revenues for the division remains to be seen. These factors, as well as the company's support of Atra, made 1979 a potentially tough year for Mike Edwards and TRAC II.

1979 Marketing Plan Preparation

Edwards recently received the following memorandum from the vice president of marketing:

Memo to: Brand Group

From: P. Meyers

Date: July 7, 1978

Subject: 1979 Marketing Plans

In preparation for the marketing plan approval process and in developing the division strategy for 1979, I would like a preliminary plan from each brand group by the end of the month. Please submit statements of objective, corresponding strategy and levels of dollar support requested for the following:

1. Overall brand strategy[4]—target market.
2. Blade and razor volume and share goals.
3. Sales promotion.
4. Advertising.
5. Couponing and sampling.
6. Miscellaneous—new packaging, additional marketing research, marketing cost saving ideas, etc.

See you at the weekly meeting on Wednesday.

In developing the TRAC II marketing plan, Edwards had to wrestle with some strategy decisions. To get significant funding, how should he position TRAC II in relation to Atra and the disposables? Also, how does he convince the vice president that dollars spent for TRAC II are more effective than expenditures on Good News! or Gillette's electric razors?

---

[4] Brand strategy means positioning the brand in such a way that it appeals to a distinguishable target market.

Case 13

Machine Vision International*

> Our industry is very much like a newly found gold mine. Each vein in the mine is a different market opportunity. We're entering the main mine shaft, digging first in the directions our research shows will contain the largest ore deposits, those in the automotive and electronics industries. We'll use the knowledge we gain in those shafts of the mine to tunnel to other veins, finding gold deposits in other markets. This is our approach.
>
> Richard P. Eidswick
> Chairman and CEO, MVI

As 1985 came to a close, Machine Vision International (MVI) was completing its third year of operations. Only two years earlier, MVI had only had 37 employees. By the end of 1985, MVI had expanded greatly. The company now had three sales divisions and was selling products for very diverse applications in many varied industries. However, the financial results for 1985 showed that MVI was not yet making a profit. The question being asked was whether MVI had expanded into too many markets too quickly for a company in a fast-growing, quickly changing industry.

The Machine Vision Industry—A Definition

A machine vision product is a high-technology, computer-based image processing system enabling a machine or other device to "see." The use of this technology permits automation of industrial tasks involving the interpretation of the work scene or the controlling of work activity.

Machine vision may be understood by way of analogy to human vision. A human eye captures an image, which is then transmitted to the brain via the optic nerve. The brain processes those parts of the image most important to the situation; it ignores parts of the image which are irrelevant. The brain then tells other parts of the body what actions to take. In machine vision, the camera (eye) captures an image and transmits it to the controller (brain) via a coaxial cable (optic nerve).

---

* This case was prepared by Constance M. Kinnear, Research Associate, with the assistance of Thomas C. Kinnear, Professor of Marketing, both at the Graduate School of Business Administration, The University of Michigan. Copyright © 1986 by the authors.

The controller sorts relevant from irrelevant data and instructs the machine tool, conveyor, or robot what actions to take.

MVI's Prospectus
September 18, 1985

There are many potential application areas for machine vision in the industrial workplace. Data received by a computer from television cameras viewing an assembly area can be almost instantaneously analyzed so that task performance guidance commands can be sent to a robot. Vision systems can be used in quality control processes to check work in process against required product parameters, which are stored in the system's computer. A vision system can therefore check during production for the proper dimensions and shape of the product, for the presence of all features or parts, and for its general condition including surface flaws. Deviations from acceptable parameters can be brought to the attention of supervisory staff before they cause a substandard product to be produced. Because vision systems can recognize different shapes or identifying markings, production parts can be sorted, facilitating the movement, processing, or assembly of parts. The goals in the use of vision systems are to increase product quality, increase production rates and industrial efficiency, and provide labor savings.

The Market for Machine Vision Products

The machine vision industry did not exist in 1980. In 1981, total industry sales were $7 million. Between 1981 and 1984, sales more than doubled each year, so that by 1984 industry sales totaled $80 million. A compound average growth rate of 60 percent per year has been estimated for the industry as a whole for the period from 1984 to 1990. Estimated sales for 1985 were $125 million. For 1990, the total market was estimated to reach between $750 and $800 million. Machine vision was the fastest growing segment of the factory automation market in the mid-1980s.

Despite all the optimistic estimates for growth in the market, not one competitor in machine vision had consistently made a profit by 1985, though some privately owned companies claimed to have shown a profit in some quarters that year. Between 70 and 100 competitors were vying for the industry's total sales of $125 million in that year, in literally thousands of different applications. The bulk of this revenue was shared among 20 companies. The major competitors in the industry and their sales for the period 1983–85 are shown in Exhibit 1. In 1984, none of these competitors made a profit in this industry. Automatix had a loss of $14.2 million on its sales of $17.3 million. Robotic Vision Systems, Inc. (RVSI), had a loss of $.78 million on sales of $5.1 million in 1984 and a loss of $1.8 million on sales of $9.7 million in 1985. International Robomation/Intelligence (IRI) had a loss of $4.1 million on its sales of $2.3 million in 1984, but announced in late 1985 that it had been profitable during the first half of 1985.

EXHIBIT 1   Competitive sales figures ($ millions)—1983, 1984, 1985

Company	1983 Sales	1984 Sales	Expected 1985 Sales	Type of Financing
Applied Intelligent Systems, Inc. (1976)	$ 0.4	$ 1.4	$ 5.0	Private
Automatix	6.3	17.3	27.0	Public
Cognex Corp.	2.0	5.0	6.0	Private
Diffracto Ltd. (1973)	3.7	5.1	7.3	Private
International Robomation/Intelligence	1.0	2.3	8.0	Public
Itran Corp. (1982)	0.2	1.1	2.2	Private
Machine Vision International	0.5	4.0	10.0	Public
Perceptron, Inc. (1981)	1.0	5.5	15.0	Private
Robotic Vision Systems, Inc. (1977)	1.0	5.1	10.0	Public
View Engineering (1976)	7.5	15.0	19.0	Private
All others	11.4	18.2	15.5	
Total market	$35.0	$80.0	$125.0	

Analysts of the machine vision industry were hard pressed to pick which companies would survive the early growth years.

The industry is very fragmented. There are no clear leaders. Although perhaps only 20 companies or so represent the vast bulk of machine vision revenue . . . there are well over 70 companies that call themselves vision systems companies. One only has to go as far down as company number 5 or so in order to be looking at annual revenues of $5 million or less. The revenue gap between the current leaders and those companies really new to the industry is extremely thin. The obvious conclusion seems, then, to be that the industry is entirely up for grabs. Company number 70 or beyond could still easily overtake company number 1 since there is not much that separates them in terms of sales dollars.

Prudential-Bache Securities
CIM Newsletter, February 6, 1985

Industry analysts do point to some industry conditions which will bear on these conclusions. The first, and possibly the most important, of these arises from the newness and difficulty of the technologies involved in making machine vision really work in an industrial environment. The technologies are not yet perfected. The market is often uneducated or unrealistic about the true capabilities of machine vision. Competitors are finding it very difficult to determine all the variables that have to be satisfied and solved to make the products work in a true, operating, industrial environment.

Experience may represent the single most effective barrier to entry. The vision industry has a lot of companies in it. It is difficult enough to win an order. There are few "easy" wins in the industry. But once you get the order, then the really hard part begins. The winning vendor actually has to deliver a system that works. More often than not, as all the leading companies have undoubtedly discovered, it is simply harder to make the actual system work properly in the real world. There is no substitute for experience, at least not yet. There may be very few ways for a new entrant to take a shortcut in order to circumvent the pack and leapfrog to the top.

Prudential-Bache Securities
CIM Newsletter, February 6, 1985

Though some large companies, most notably General Electric, Eastman Kodak, 3M, and Owens-Illinois, are competitors in the machine vision industry, none has established itself as an industry leader. There are many technologies applicable to vision applications, and these technologies are still very much in the developmental stage. Possible applications of machine vision can be found in almost any industrial setting where part inspection, part identification, or automated assembly processes are used. This ambiguity in the market is often harder for large companies to deal with than for small ones. Large companies commonly only put resources into areas where large dollar revenues or high profits can be quite reasonably predicted. These usually come from large volume sales of repeatably manufacturable products. At the present, machine vision does not offer these possibilities.

Another development that may have far-reaching impact on the machine vision industry is the involvement of General Motors. GM has become very interested in production automation. This interest was spurred by the results of several automobile industry studies. These studies found that the Japanese had a sizable cost advantage, ranging between $1,500 and $1,800 per car, over U.S. producers in 1985. Also, it was estimated that it took approximately three times as many labor-hours for U.S. automobile manufacturers to produce a car than it did their Japanese competitors. Studies predicted that U.S. car manufacturers would have to reduce their costs by about 25 percent between 1985 and 1990 to remain competitive in the industry. GM's internal studies showed that a lot of the gap between U.S. and Japanese production costs could be corrected with increased automation. Of possible automation alternatives, it was determined that the use of robotics and machine vision were key strategies to use to solve the problem. Forty-four thousand machine vision applications were identified within GM alone by GM analysts.

Taking action on these findings, GM has entered into a joint venture with Fanuc Ltd. of Japan, forming GMF, a highly respected robotics firm. To back its belief that vision was also key to automation, GM invested in five machine vision companies in 1983 and 1984. These were Applied Intelligent Systems (AIS), Automatix, Diffracto Ltd., Robotic Vision Systems (RVS), and View Engineering. The full impact of these investments on the machine vision industry is yet unknown. These investments by GM did give higher credibility and visibility to the entire machine vision industry. They helped the machine vision industry gain awareness among potential users in the marketplace. Within GM, the investments came in conjunction with the identification of GM's needs for vision and brought potential users within GM to search for solutions to those needs. GM's goal became that of filling its 44,000 vision needs by 1990. No five companies within the vision industry would be capable of solving all these applications. Thus, the identification of GM's vision needs opened the door to all vision companies—not just the five GM invested in, although they had an advantage over the others if they could do the application.

The Customers for Machine Vision Products

Though the machine vision market is very fragmented and very new, some information about who the buyers of these products will be has been provided by a report entitled *Vision Systems Survey of End Users,* conducted by Prudential-Bache Securities and published on February 6, 1985.

The report showed several interesting characteristics of present and potential machine vision customers. Sixty-seven percent of the companies surveyed achieved annual gross revenues of greater than $1 billion. Eighty-four percent of the companies had annual gross revenues of greater than $100 million. Fifty-seven percent of the companies interested in vision were located in the Midwest. Another 19 percent were located in the Northeast, with 9 percent on the West Coast. The end users surveyed were in the following industries:

Industry	Percentage of study
Automotive	35%
Electrical/electronics	35
Aerospace	12
Construction	3
Pharmaceutical	1
Other*	14

* Ranges from paper products to metal fabricators.

Ninety-seven percent of the end users surveyed indicated that vision was an important factor in the overall manufacturing process. Sixty-four percent had an actual capital budget for vision system purchases.

Decision makers in the purchasing of vision systems were located in many different levels of the companies surveyed. Sixteen percent responded that the purchase decision was made at the corporate level only, while 29 percent said that the decision was made at the division level. Another 37 percent responded that vision system purchase decisions were made at the department level, with the remaining 17 percent of those surveyed answering that the decision involved more than one level within the company.

The length of present and anticipated future buying cycles for vision systems were as follows:

Buying cycles	Present	Future
Less than 3 months	13%	31%
6–9 months	47	41
9–12 months	23	18
Over a year	9	6

Many customers believed that machine vision systems would not only be installed for production work applications but also for internal development work on automation processes. Nineteen percent of respondents had installed vision systems for development work only, while 54 percent said that they had or planned to install vision systems for both production work and development work.

Fifty-nine percent of survey respondents purchased their vision systems through the direct sales forces of the suppliers. Twenty percent used only OEMs, while 8 percent purchased through distributors. The remaining 13 percent used more than one channel for their purchases.

Vision companies most often mentioned as possible suppliers making the "short list" were: Automatix, View Engineering, Machine Vision International, and Perceptron. The factors most important to purchasers of vision systems, in their order of importance, were: technology, service and support, applications engineering, user friendliness, reputation of vendor, expandability, and price. The companies mentioned as most technically advanced were: Automatix, Machine Vision International, Perceptron, View Engineering, and Diffracto. The companies listed as most user friendly were: Automatix, View Engineering, Itran, Perceptron, and Machine Vision International. The vendors listed as providing the best support/service capabilities were: Automatix, Perceptron, View Engineering, Diffracto, Itran, and Machine Vision International.

The end users were also asked to list areas of application of vision systems in both the present and the future. The responses were:

Applications	Present	Future
Inspection	84%	93%
Gaging	44	60
Sorting	21	35
Process control	37	63
Robot guidance	40	45

The Technologies Employed in Machine Vision

At present, there are four main technologies employed in machine vision systems. These are signal processing, mathematical morphology, statistical pattern recognition, and artificial intelligence. These four and the significant characteristics of each are displayed in Exhibit 2.

The dimensions of the graphic used in Exhibit 2 answer the questions "What is being processed?" on the horizontal axis and "How is this processing done?" on the vertical axis. The "What is being processed?" dimension ranges from images on the left to objects on the right. If images are being processed, the computer converts what the camera sees into an array of different sizes and colors of dots and analyzes the placement of these dots. If an object is being analyzed, then the computer compares measurements of what the camera sees to descriptions of what should be in the camera's view. On the vertical dimension,

EXHIBIT 2 Vision systems technologies and their characteristics

	Image Based	Object Based	

How Is the Processing Done?	Signal Processing
	
	High speed
	Simple discrimination
	Requires special
	  hardware
		Statistical Pattern Recognition
		
		Low speed
		Simple discrimination
		No special hardware
		  required
			Arithmetic
			Computations

	Mathematical Morphology
	
	High speed
	Complex discrimination
	High hardware
	  requirements
		Artificial Intelligence
		
		Low speed
		Very complex
		  discrimination
		Can require special
		  hardware
			Logical
			Computations

What Is Being Processed?

the image or object can be processed either using arithmetic, linear analysis in the top two quadrants of the matrix, or using logical, nonlinear analysis in the bottom two quadrants. Arithmetic functions deal with quantities; that is, numbers and equations regarding dimensions or sizes of the image or object are manipulated and analyzed. In logical analysis, binary values that are either true or false are used to determine relationships between what the camera sees and what has been programmed as appropriate.

As shown in Exhibit 2, image processing allows for high-speed analysis but requires extensive hardware to perform its tasks. Object analysis can only take place at slower speeds but does not require as much expenditure in hardware. Arithmetic analysis can only perform simple discrimination, thus it cannot find subtle differences between what is being examined and what is expected. Logical analysis allows for complex discrimination; thus these technologies are capable of handling more difficult or precise problems, and can analyze these with less lighting and placement requirements. The use of statistical pattern recognition produces numerical, quantitative answers, such as "How many parts are present?" or "How big is the part?" The use of artificial intelligence produces qualitative responses, such as "Yes, that is a good part" or "No, that is not properly assembled."

To more fully understand these technologies, it is useful to see what each one is used for in a given application. MVI has a 3-D robot guidance product in which vision is used to direct the robot's placement of windshields in a car moving along an assembly line at the pace of 60 cars per hour. All four technologies are employed in this application. Lighting is used to produce a very sharp, mirrorlike image of the car as it comes into the work area. The bouncing of the light off the car surface to produce this image employs signal processing, a technology developed from radar technology. However, this lighting reflects off more than just the edge of the car body needed to be seen to perform the window insertion task. Mathematical morphology allows the computer control to extract from the image reflected only the part of the image needed for the task, and eliminates the rest from consideration. That is done through complex computer programs that direct the computer to search the image for the exact shape needed for analysis. Statistical pattern recognition is used to take measurements of window position and orientation, since the actual opening size and the position of the car body on the assembly line may vary slightly from car to car. Thus, this technology makes use of another set of computer algorithms to take statistical measurements of the pertinent areas of the problem in question. Artificial intelligence software is used to answer such questions as ''Is the window opening the right shape for the windshield that is here?'' and ''Can the robot reach the opening from its present position?'' These questions can all be answered logically; they are either true or false. If corrections are necessary, the computer controls can command the robot to move and change position before actual insertion commands are given.

Exhibit 3 takes the example given above one step further, showing which technologies are necessary to perform the most common applications of vision systems currently on the market. Many applications require the use of only one of the technologies available, while others require multiple technologies. Thus, gauging or fixtured part measurement require only the use of signal processing. Part identification or part positioning require only statistical pattern recognition. Finished surface inspection can be performed with mathematical morphology only, and assembly verification can be done with artificial intelligence alone. On the other extreme, tasks such as 3-D robot guidance and part defect detection require the employment of all four technologies to achieve proper performance. It has been estimated that between 50 percent and 60 percent of the applications in the market in 1985 applied signal processing. Between 20 percent and 30 percent of applications made use of statistical pattern recognition. The remaining 15 percent of applications relied on mathematical morphology to perform the desired task.

Exhibit 4 shows how many of the current competitors in the vision systems market are positioned along technology lines. Most competitors use only one technology. MVI is currently alone in the employment of all four technologies. MVI began as a mathematical morphology company. MVI has consciously developed the use of the other three technologies in order to be able to better handle more difficult industrial problems and to give itself a technology edge over its competition. This was explained in the company's prospectus as follows:

EXHIBIT 3 Technologies used in machine vision applications

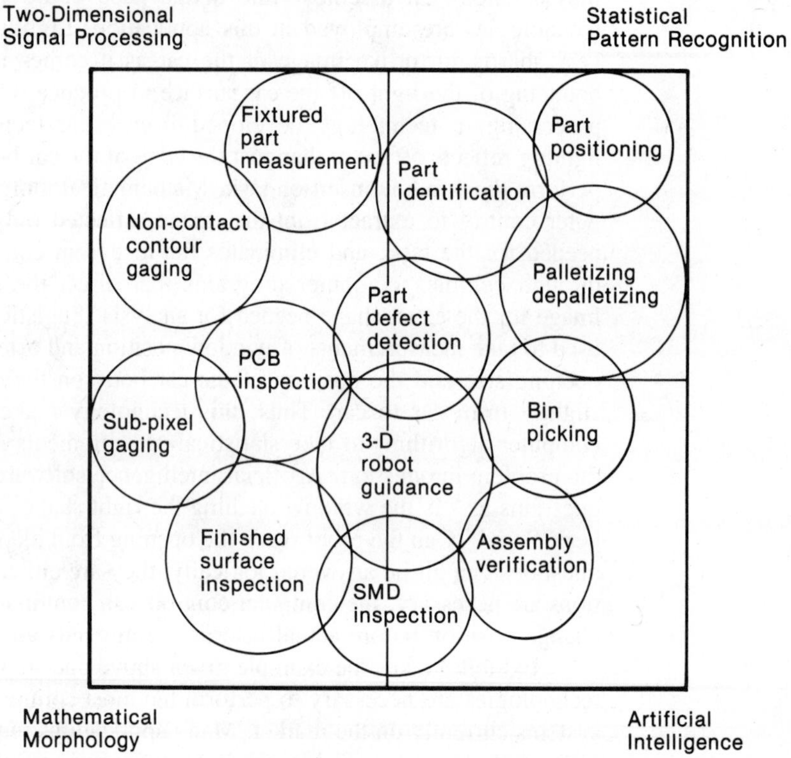

Two-Dimensional
Signal Processing

Statistical
Pattern Recognition

Fixtured part measurement

Part identification

Part positioning

Non-contact contour gaging

Palletizing depalletizing

Part defect detection

PCB inspection

Sub-pixel gaging

Bin picking

3-D robot guidance

Finished surface inspection

SMD inspection

Assembly verification

Mathematical
Morphology

Artificial
Intelligence

The Company specializes in mathematical morphology which it believes is the most suitable technology for application in machine vision. The Company believes that it has advanced the practice of mathematical morphology . . . such that its utilization in the Company's systems enables application of machine vision to widely varied guidance and inspection tasks in the factory environment. Moreover, the Company is complementing its capabilities in mathematical morphology by establishing capabilities in pattern recognition, signal processing, and artificial intelligence, and believes that the combination of these technologies will enhance the applications of the Company's systems. It is the advanced application of mathematical morphology and the move toward a combination of technologies to complement mathematical morphology that the Company believes differentiates it significantly from its competitors.

Dr. Sternberg explained why it is important to use all the available technologies. He said:

You can force a solution using just one tool, but you end up working 10 times harder than if you use the right tool for the right part of the job. You can find a way to change the spark plugs on your car with just a hammer, but it will take you a lot longer to do it this way than if you had all the right tools for the job.

EXHIBIT 4 Industry competitors' technology positions

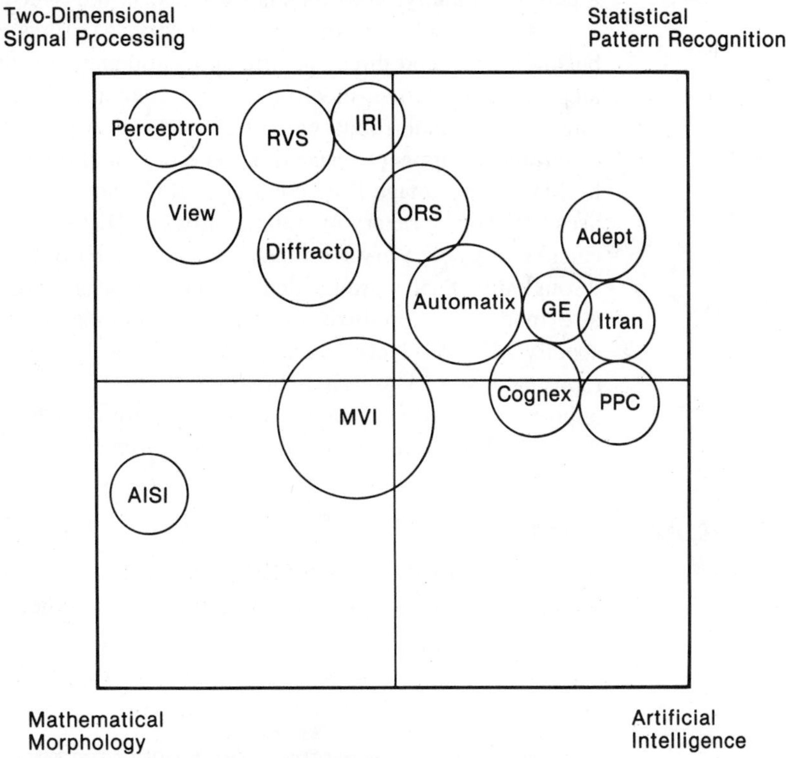

Two-Dimensional   Statistical
Signal Processing   Pattern Recognition

Mathematical   Artificial
Morphology   Intelligence

Machine Vision International—History

MVI was founded as Cyto-Systems Corporation in June 1981 by Dr. Stanley R. Sternberg. Dr. Sternberg had previously worked at the Environmental Research Institute of Michigan, where he was instrumental in the development of the technology of mathematical morphology. Dr. Sternberg's idea was to develop products based on this technology that could be used for measurement, inspection, and control in manufacturing processes. In the fall of 1982, Dr. Sternberg joined with Richard P. Eidswick to develop a plan and strategy to bring this technology to market. Prior to joining MVI, Mr. Eidswick was senior vice president and director of Comshare, Inc., an international computer services company. In May 1983, the company's name was changed to Machine Vision International.

To fund the company, nearly $9.5 million of equity capital was raised through private offerings of MVI securities. Approximately $5 million of these funds were raised through the sale of common stock to Safeguard Scientifics, Inc. In connection with this investment, Safeguard obtained an agreement to make a rights offering of MVI stock to Safeguard's shareholders. This rights offering was completed in November 1985. As of November 5, 1985, MVI was a public company, with its shares traded in the over-the-counter market.

As its strategy in the vision industry, MVI has chosen to focus on three business areas and three specific applications of machine vision. The business areas are automotive, electronics, and general industrial. The applications are three-dimensional robot guidance, surface inspection, and surface-mounted electronic component inspection. The principal component of all systems sold by MVI is the image flow computer (IFC), an image processing computer that uses MVI's proprietary operating software, BLIX, to perform the mathematical calculations necessary for image analysis. MVI markets its products primarily through direct sales groups dedicated to end users in the three business areas. It also markets its products to original equipment manufacturers (OEMs) who specify MVI products in their systems, and through certain specialized sales representatives. Through September 1985, MVI had manufactured and sold approximately 100 machine vision systems for an aggregate sales price of nearly $12 million. Financial statements for MVI are presented in Exhibit 5.

Market Approach

An organizational chart for MVI is shown in Exhibit 6. As the chart indicates, the activities of Mr. Eidswick as chairman and chief executive officer and the

EXHIBIT 5
MACHINE VISION INTERNATIONAL CORPORATION
Statements of Operations

	Period from inception (June 25, 1981) to December 31, 1983	Year ended December 31, 1984	Six months ended June 30, 1984	Six months ended June 30, 1985 (unaudited)
Net sales	$ 541,058	$ 4,011,730	$ 760,807	$ 4,481,476
Cost of sales	338,921	2,536,398	555,891	2,021,068
Gross profit	$ 202,137	$ 1,475,332	$ 204,916	$ 2,460,408
Operating expenses:				
Product development	$ 318,961	$ 1,733,667	$ 610,836	$ 1,354,943
Selling	360,601	1,979,102	652,364	2,011,329
General and administrative	542,101	904,272	420,356	365,184
Total operating expenses	$ 1,221,663	$ 4,617,041	$ 1,683,556	$ 3,731,456
Loss from operations	$(1,019,526)	$(3,141,709)	$(1,478,640)	$(1,271,048)
Other income (expense):				
Interest expense	$ (5,076)	$ (105,089)	$ (15,697)	$ (116,207)
Other	23,342	67,895	64,858	19,410
Total other income (expense)	$ 18,266	$ (37,194)	$ 49,161	$ (96,797)
Net loss	$(1,001,260)	$(3,178,903)	$(1,429,479)	$(1,367,845)
Loss per share	$(.41)	$(.56)	$(.28)	$(.18)
Weighted average number of shares	2,458,495	5,714,391	5,164,775	7,457,460

EXHIBIT 5 *(concluded)*
MACHINE VISION INTERNATIONAL CORPORATION
Balance Sheets

	December 31,		June 30, 1985 (unaudited)
	1983	1984	
Assets			
Current assets:			
Cash and cash equivalents	$ 104,117	$ 191,361	$ 151,601
Receivables—			
Trade, net of allowance for doubtful accounts of zero in 1983, $15,000 in 1984 and 1985	272,945	2,095,875	3,255,081
Inventories	238,772	1,964,951	3,749,191
Prepaid expenses and deposits	8,689	34,961	34,228
Total current assets	$ 624,523	$ 4,287,148	$ 7,190,101
Property and equipment			
Computer and other equipment	$ 221,274	$ 972,614	$ 1,213,574
Office furniture and equipment	91,436	171,737	249,738
Leasehold improvements	6,520	91,665	102,232
	$ 319,230	$ 1,236,016	$ 1,565,544
Less: Accumulated depreciation and amortization	31,154	275,087	470,087
Net property and equipment	$ 288,076	$ 960,929	$ 1,095,457
	$ 912,599	$ 5,248,077	$ 8,285,558
Liabilities and Shareholders' Equity			
Current liabilities:			
Current portion of long-term debt	$ 42,500	$ 74,823	$ 118,000
Note payable	—	675,000	500,000
Accounts payable	246,058	993,292	1,887,677
Accrued liabilities	80,312	155,876	277,417
Accrued payroll	24,228	110,088	262,125
Customer advances	—	141,878	94,167
Total current liabilities	$ 393,098	$ 2,150,957	$ 3,139,386
Long-term debt, less current portion above	$ 118,365	$ 1,671,775	$ 1,205,073
Commitments			
Shareholders' equity			
Preferred stock, no par value, stated value $.001, 10,000,000 shares authorized, no shares issued and outstanding at 1983, 1984, and 1985, respectively	$ —	$ —	$ —
Common stock, no par value, stated value $.001, 30,000,000 shares authorized, 4,017,500, 6,508,620, and 8,213,620 shares issued and outstanding at 1983, 1984, and 1985, respectively	4,018	6,509	8,214
Paid-in capital	1,398,378	5,598,999	9,480,893
Accumulated deficit	(1,001,260)	(4,180,163)	(5,548,008)
Total shareholders' equity	$ 401,136	$ 1,425,345	$ 3,941,099
	$ 912,599	$ 5,248,077	$ 8,285,558

tasks performed by the finance and administration, development and marketing, and product engineering areas impact all functional areas of the company.

The sales function within MVI is divided along market segment lines. The three current sales divisions—automated systems, electronic systems, and manufacturing technology—mirror those markets pointed out by the Prudential-Bache survey as the major customers interested in machine vision products.

EXHIBIT 6 Corporate organizational chart

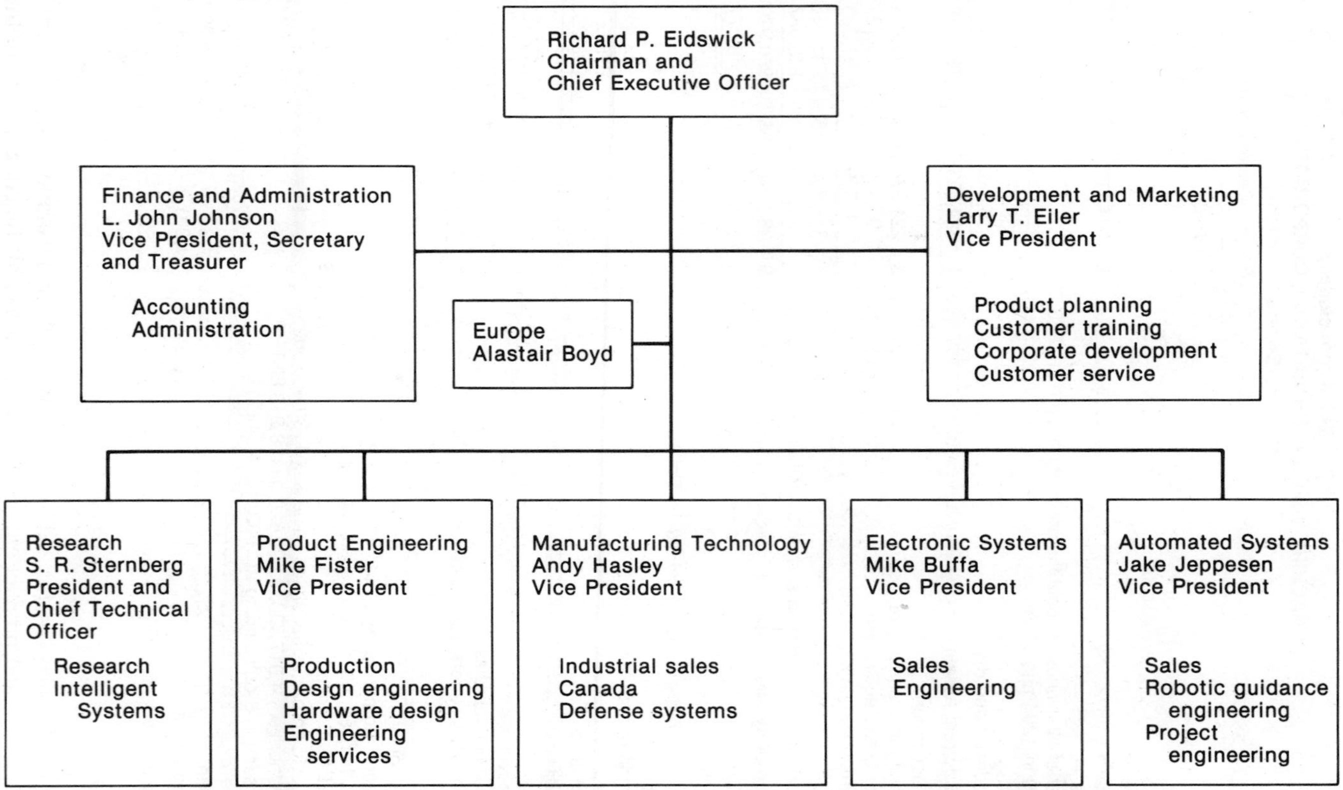

Richard P. Eidswick
Chairman and
Chief Executive Officer

Finance and Administration
L. John Johnson
Vice President, Secretary
and Treasurer

Accounting
Administration

Development and Marketing
Larry T. Eiler
Vice President

Product planning
Customer training
Corporate development
Customer service

Europe
Alastair Boyd

Research
S. R. Sternberg
President and
Chief Technical
Officer

Research
Intelligent
Systems

Product Engineering
Mike Fister
Vice President

Production
Design engineering
Hardware design
Engineering
services

Manufacturing Technology
Andy Hasley
Vice President

Industrial sales
Canada
Defense systems

Electronic Systems
Mike Buffa
Vice President

Sales
Engineering

Automated Systems
Jake Jeppesen
Vice President

Sales
Robotic guidance
engineering
Project
engineering

The Automated Systems Division (ASD)

At its inception, MVI was a company with a technology searching for applications. MVI was looking initially for any project that a customer would give them to prove what could be done with the technology at their disposal. MVI began this search in the automotive industry, where executives were already talking about putting resources into finding vision solutions to solve automation problems. Mr. Jake Jeppesen, who joined MVI in June 1983 to head the Automated Systems Division, found a group at GM that had been talking for two years to various vision companies about the possibility of using vision to automate auto glass insertion. The other companies had failed to develop a product that worked. Mr. Jeppesen convinced them to try again with the different technology that MVI offered with its mathematical morphology. The first order for the window insertion product was received by MVI in December 1983. A prototype was working in a GM lab in March 1984, and the first plant installation was made in June 1984. See Exhibit 7 for a representation of how this product works.

Even though the first vision applications taken on by MVI have shown themselves to be successfully working projects within the automotive industry, the sales process for ASD remains a very complicated one. The division maintains an ongoing educational sales effort, selling everyone from the executive level to the manufacturing staff to the manufacturing research people to plant production people on who MVI is and what the company and machine vision are capable of doing. Since this sales effort is so educational in nature, the decision was made to approach the market on a direct basis; MVI did not want to entrust this type of basic technology and company image selling to any third party. Automotive executives and manufacturing research staff personnel

EXHIBIT 7 Representation of MVI's window insertion system

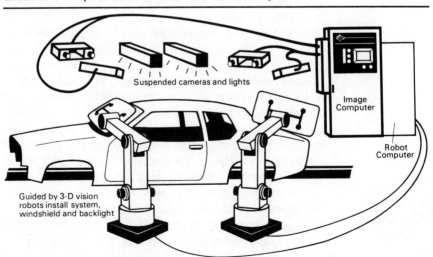

are interested in the technology involved and its advantages over present or alternative assembly automation techniques. However, manufacturing staffpeople are interested in finding ways in which higher-quality cars can be built better, cheaper, and faster. Plant production staff are interested generally in improvements in product quality, but are mainly concerned with production speed so that their quotas can be met. To this group, a product's reliability on the assembly line is of the utmost importance. Since orders within automotive companies come most often from the manufacturing staff or the plant production people, it is the goal of the sales process to give these people confidence that MVI's product "will do what we say it's going to do forever, first time, every time, and never fail," as Mr. Jeppesen put it. These groups are not interested in machine vision for its technology. They want their task performed in the most reliable, fastest way possible. Because of this, Mr. Jeppesen does not describe himself as being in the vision business. He says, "I am in the surface inspection business and I'm in the automatic assembly business. I use vision to accomplish those very difficult tasks."

The ASD is currently selling products for two applications in the automotive industry. These are 3-D robot guidance for window insertion and other applications and surface paint inspection. The window insertion product has a selling price of approximately $450,000 per installation. It is only a part of an entire window insertion system that includes robots, body handling equipment, material handling equipment, and controls supplied by other vendors. This total system costs in the neighborhood of $5 million. The surface paint inspection product is currently only used to inspect finished paint surfaces and sells for approximately $500,000 per system. MVI has received seven orders for window insertion systems and one for a paint inspection system.

Though relatively few orders for these products have been received to date, the markets for these products are very large. Mr. Jeppesen sees many application areas for both MVI's 3-D robot guidance and paint surface inspection products beyond those currently being marketed. 3-D robot guidance can also be employed to automate such tasks as automobile wheel and cockpit loading, for the application of paint stripes, and to control many fluid fill operations. Although paint inspection systems are currently only used for finished product inspection, the market could be expanded to inspection of bare metal after frameup, phosphate coating before priming, primer coats, and other checkpoints during automobile production. In total, Mr. Jeppesen currently foresees 10 application possibilities for 3-D robot guidance and 6 application areas for surface inspection in each automobile plant. In 1985, there were 73 automobile assembly plants operating in the United States, and many of these operated with more than one assembly line per plant.

Currently, no other vision company even claims to be able to supply a product that can perform surface inspection. Mr. Jeppesen lists three companies as major competitors in the 3-D robotics business: GMF Robotics, ASEA Robotics, and Automatix. In this area, Mr. Jeppesen said that many companies claim to be able to perform this task, but they really do not have the necessary capabilities. The result of this is a great amount of confusion in the marketplace. There is much misinformation and confusion regarding the cost of a system that really can accomplish what its people say it will do. But Mr. Jeppesen believes that this confusion will soon be dispelled as competitors try to supply the market and fail. He stated it this way:

> There's just enormous confusion out there. Who can do what? Which companies oversell their capabilities? Which don't? The competitors who fail are beginning to get weeded out. All you have to do is tell GM you can do something and fail, and they throw you out pretty quickly.

Electronics Sales Division (ESD)

The electronics market is very different from the automotive area. Therefore, the sales strategy and marketing positioning employed in the electronics market is unique to it. The sales process for the ESD began with marketing research to find out the vision needs in the electronics industry and has been combined with a concerted effort to get to know the decision makers within that industry. In this effort, MVI marketing personnel attend electronics industry meetings, where they get to know the technology leaders within the industry. They gain firsthand knowledge of the industry's technology trends as well as of what the strategies of the major electronics firms will be. The goal of all this is to put the insight MVI gains from firsthand knowledge of plans and trends into the capabilities of MVI's product to produce a better match between that product and its market.

The U.S. electronics industry is currently undergoing a great change in production procedures. In 1985, 90 percent of electronics assembly was being done on lead-through boards. However, overseas, and especially in Japan, nearly 95 percent of electronics assembly was being done on higher-quality, more reliable surface-mounted boards. It is believed that U.S. production will shift to surface-mounted boards very rapidly. This type of production will be highly compatible with automated assembly techniques since the components on surface-mounted boards are much smaller and require greater production sensitivity than lead-through boards.[1]

The total market for surface-mounted inspection systems has been divided into three segments by MVI's market researchers. These segments are: (1) low speed (less than 6,000 parts per hour), high-precision inspection of a broad range of components; (2) high-volume (up to 20,000 parts per hour), low-precision inspection of a limited range of components; and (3) ultra-high-volume (over 20,000 parts per hour), high- and low-precision inspection of a

---

[1] Surface mount technology (SMT) is an electronic manufacturing method in which miniaturized, prepackaged components are assembled on the top (hence surface) of a circuit. In lead-through assembly, the components have conductors or leads that are inserted through holes that are drilled or punched through the board. These leads are folded or clinched on the back of the board to provide mechanical component attachment. In SMT manufacturing, the components are placed on the board by an automatic mechanism and then soldered in place.

broad range of components. MVI believes its product can be very successful in the first two market segments. For these areas, MVI has made the following total market size projections.

Year	Segment 1 Total no. of vision systems	Segment 1 Total dollar market (in millions)	Segment 2 Total no. of vision systems	Segment 2 Total dollar market (in millions)
1984	30	$ 3.6	7	$ 1.05
1985	65	7.8	20	3.0
1986	90	10.8	130	19.5
1987	125	15.0	340	51.0
1988	350	42.0	525	78.75

MVI has spent two years developing a product that can use vision to control the assembly process and provide inspection for this automated production. MVI believes that the contrast and complexity of the components used in this process require the capabilities of the company's mathematical morphology technology. An effective product for this market must be able to perform three tasks. These are: (1) determine if the correct component (chip, diode, resistor, or capacitor) is present; (2) determine if each part is in the correct position relative to the other components; and (3) check the solder used to attach parts to the board for voids and excess solder material. MVI's vision technology is capable of solving the first two tasks. The third task requires a low-level X-ray capability, which MVI does not currently have but is working to achieve. MVI hopes to eventually be able to market a product that can perform all three tasks required by its users.

Unlike the ASD sales, ESD sales are technology sales. ESD's personnel talk to technical processing engineers, not the traditional purchasing departments within the electronics firms. MVI people talk to these technical people to determine their automation needs and to educate them as to the capabilities of MVI's product. The goal is to get to know the people who will use the system and get their support before there is a quotation request made on the part of the electronics firm.

By the end of the third quarter of 1985, MVI had three working surface-mounted inspection systems in the field. The company expected to make deliveries on 9 or 10 more orders before the end of the year. Prices on these systems ranged from $80,000 to $200,000. The hardware used in these systems is priced to closely match the prices of MVI's competition. The software used is specific to each application, and as such is priced to be the profit margin producer for the company.

Competitors in this market are View Engineering, International Robomation/Intelligence (IRI), and Automatix. IRI was mentioned as an aggressive price competitor. IRI's developmental system is priced at between $22,000 and $26,000. This product is sold for applications in which a firm's engineers want to develop automated processes internally. IRI has been said to sell this development system to get a customer interested in vision, with the hope that the customer will return to IRI for more equipment when they are ready to solve their vision needs. IRI's price for an application system competitive with MVI's system would range from $75,000 to $125,000. Automatix' product is really an assembly guidance system, not an inspection system.

The Manufacturing Technology Division (MTD)

MVI's Manufacturing Technology Division is comprised of two sales groups, the Industrial Sales Group (ISG) and the Aerospace Sales Group (ASG). This division has as its goal that of finding new markets for the products developed by the other sales divisions. Manufacturing technology sales groups are to take on applications that require extensions of existing technology or new combinations of what has already been developed by MVI's R&D and engineering personnel. The MTD is headed by Mr. Andrew Hasley.

Industrial Sales Group. MVI receives between 250 and 300 inquiries each month through its marketing work, its presence in several vision shows, and through the references of its present customers arising from the company's reputation as a successful vision system supplier. Many of these inquiries do not come from people within the automotive or electronics industries. Leads from these other nonspecialized industries are turned over to the Industrial Sales Group, which is under the direction of Mr. John Kufchock.

Mr. Kufchock uses three initial criteria to determine whether MVI will pursue these inquiries. The lead must come from a Fortune 500 company; thus, the company must have considerable funds to spend on capital investments. The application being pursued must involve the use of technology already developed by MVI; thus, sales of the ISG are meant to produce a multiplier effect on sales for MVI. Furthermore, the inquiry must come from a company that has an established engineering group capable of understanding both the technology involved and the advantages MVI's technology has over competitors.

The ISG has made sales in many industries, all of surface inspection products that perform very diversified tasks. In the food industry, surface inspection is used to identify foreign objects in produce coming from the fields as well as produce of less than acceptable grade so that these can be eliminated from further processing. In the lumber industry, surface inspection is used to check plywood as it is produced so that its grade and sales quality can be determined. In the rubber industry, tires are checked for flaws and for whether the white-wall rubber has been applied properly. MVI surface inspection systems have also been used to inspect the edges of machine tool inserts and to determine if packages have been correctly sealed. By the end of 1985, the ISG had placed more than 20 systems in industrial workplaces. Mr. Kufchock expects to have nearly 50 more systems on the market in the first six months of 1986. He predicts that ISG can sell over 100 systems per year from a total of only 20 different customer corporations.

The sales process for the ISG usually begins with an inquiry from a prospective customer. Qualified leads are turned over to one of Mr. Kufchock's two sales-oriented application engineers. Through talking with and visiting the prospect, the application engineer studies the customer's vision needs to determine whether MVI's technology can meet the requirements of the task. The application engineer also finds the right people to deal with in the customer's organization. These include those who will understand the technology, those who will use the product, and those who will actually make the purchase decision. All those involved in the decision process must be "put on the team" if the sales process is to be successful. When this has been completed, a test of MVI's product on the prospect's material will be made at ISG's own lab. When the test is successful, the application engineer contacts the customer, asking that they send people to see the test results. Then, a trip is made to the customer's business to determine the actual conditions under which the system must perform and to talk to all the decision makers involved, getting their input on a preliminary sales proposal. After this proposal has had the input of the customer, a final proposal is drawn up and sent to the purchasing department of the customer. This entire selling process takes between three and nine months.

The ISG not only sells through its direct sales force of applications engineers, but also uses distributors in certain industries. These distributors are established machinery and other capital expenditure products suppliers in their industries. MVI uses this type of distribution channel in those industries where customers are geographically distant from the MVI offices and where it is unlikely that there are people within these firms who will understand or need to understand the technologies involved in the system.

The ISG also sells its products to other firms that need vision to make their large automation systems work for their customers. MVI calls these firms strategic partners because often significant development work has been done by MVI's engineering staff to make the vision products work successfully for this partner. These strategic partners have market knowledge that MVI does not possess. Often, the vision portion of the systems sold by these partners composes less than 20 percent of the entire system's selling price.

Prices on vision systems sold through the ISG range from $45,000 to $75,000 each. These prices include the hardware and software necessary for the application plus a training course held in Ann Arbor for the personnel using the system. Fees for engineering services at the customer's plant to get the system up and running are charged separately at an established per diem rate. In the first applications, it was common for MVI to find this engineering support taking more time than expected. This resulted in profit margins less than what was predicted. However, Mr. Kufchock points out that the experience gained from the first applications has made estimating engineering costs on present projects easier.

Aerospace Sales Group (ASG). The Aerospace Sales Group was established in mid-1985. It was spun off from the ISG when it was believed that there was enough business in this area alone to support a dedicated sales effort. The first sales made in the aerospace industry were made by the ISG group.

This group is selling products for many different applications and involving the different technologies developed by the ASD and ESD. These include 3-D robot guidance systems, small parts inspection systems, surface inspection products, and combinations of small parts inspection and 3-D robot guidance in which the system will recognize, inspect, and control the handling of parts. Current applications include turbine blade inspection, surface-coating inspection on space shuttle booster rockets, and 3-D robot guidance used for finding connectors for the assembling of wiring harnesses in aircraft and in the maintenance inspections of existing Air Force fighter planes.

The defense supply industry has different requirements for vision products than do the other industries MVI sells to. Here speed is of less concern than it is in other industrial environments. What is important here is the complexity of the parts to be inspected or assembled. In this area, many different parts must be inspected, as opposed to many of the same part in other industries. As a result, the systems sold by the ASG are complicated and average in price from $400,000 to $500,000.

The impetus for modernizing and automating production in the defense supply industry is coming from the Department of Defense. The government is providing military suppliers with incentives to improve their capital equipment through such programs as the Industrial Modernization Incentive Program (IMIP). The sales process for the ASG begins with contacts within the armed services to find out which firms are actively working on these programs and to learn the names of the IMIP project managers within each company. To help in finding these contacts, MVI has hired Mr. Jack Lousma, a former astronaut, to work as a consultant on a part-time basis. Once these contacts are found, Mr. Bill Wood, the sales manager of the ASG, calls on these project engineers to make initial presentations on the capabilities of the products MVI can offer. Mr. Hasley, director of the MTD, believes that the success of the ASG's first sales will provide new leads within the industry. Other avenues for sales come from contacts with robot manufacturers who need vision to make their robots work.

The defense market includes a wide variety of firms. There are several large military suppliers, such as General Dynamics, Hughes Aircraft, Lockheed, Boeing, Grumman, and Martin Marietta. There are also engine makers, such as TRW, Rohr, General Electric (GE), and GM, to be approached. Many smaller companies are parts suppliers for the military. Another market to be approached includes the repair and maintenance facilities of the armed services themselves. The Air Force alone has seven major repair facilities.

As major competitors, Mr. Hasley mentioned Robotic Vision Systems, Inc. (RVSI), IRI, and View Engineering. As in the automotive industry, no other competitor even claims to be able to perform surface inspection. Mr. Hasley believes there to be little competition in the area of parts inspection. In discussing the competitive environment, Mr. Hasley said,

> In a lot of cases, we don't find we're competing directly with anybody. We still make a lot of cold calls. Selling here is a market development problem really. It's just getting the application defined. Can you do this? Can you do that? It involves a lot of education on what vision can do.

Commonalities of Sales Approach

Though each of MVI's three sales divisions sells to different markets and to different groups of people within customer firms, each application's real bottom line sales approach is similar. What MVI is really selling is improved return on investment (ROI). In some sales, MVI's salespeople may be showing how their product can reduce warranty claim costs. This is especially true in automobile paint inspection since paint flaws are the industry's fourth largest warranty claim cost. Thus, improving paint finish quality is a paramount goal for these firms. In others, it may be improved product quality and customer perception of quality that results from the use of vision equipment. For yet other applications, the main purpose of the vision equipment may be to reduce the costs of inspection, while also providing 100 percent inspection with 100 percent accuracy. In others, the product may reduce direct labor costs because inspection or assembly personnel can be eliminated. For example, Mr. Kufchock pointed out that the plywood inspection system replaced the use of eight inspectors—each earning $21 per hour—in one facility alone. The use of vision equipment may actually increase the production rate of the business, thus improving productivity. All of these benefits impact ROI. Mr. Eiler said that MVI has found that through the improved ROI benefits of its products the company is getting the attention of many of its customers. He said,

> If the customer can get a 15-, 18-, or even 20-month payback on a paint system, for example, you go right to the head of the list for getting their attention. If you've got a three- or four-year payback, they are not really interested and your product just goes into the pile of other investments with long payback periods. Then you've lost.

Development and Marketing

The development and marketing area serves four distinct functions within MVI. These are product planning, customer training, corporate development, and customer service. These services are under the direction of Mr. Larry Eiler.

The product-planning group is charged with determining the characteristics that will transform a project developed through opportunities discovered by one of the sales divisions into a standard product salable to a defined market. In performing this task, the product-planning group uses market research to analyze a potential market's size, growth rate, opportunities for a given application, and needs of the buyers to be found there. Product ideas are tested in the market so that they can be further specified. The goal is to determine the exact characteristics of a product for that market and then direct engineering to develop that product. Cost and ROI analysis are also done to determine pricing levels. A copy of MVI's product development cycle is shown in Exhibit 8.

The customer-training group provides MVI's customers with courses on the use of MVI's program language, BLIX, and with application-specific

EXHIBIT 8   MVI product development cycle

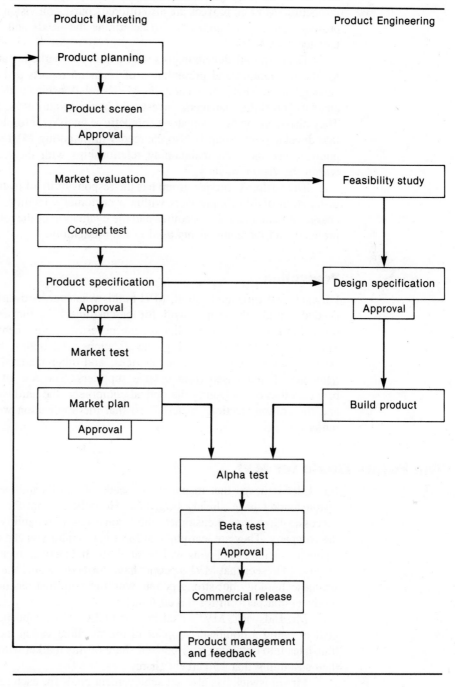

courses in the areas of 3-D guidance, paint inspection, and surface mount inspection. MVI employees are also offered courses on vision technologies and presentations on research done to determine the needs and characteristics of targeted customers.

The corporate development group within the marketing area is responsible for the preparation and presentation of financial reports and for all corporate news releases. This group maintains MVI's relationships with industry security analysts, portfolio managers, investment bankers, attorneys, and accountants. They also develop the company's competitive analysis information. The corporate development group is also charged with handling MVI's public relations publications and with maintaining relationships with the technology leaders within the vision industry.

The customer service group has the responsibility of overseeing the actual installation of MVI's products within a customer's facility. They also are in charge of maintenance procedures and the evaluation of the reliability of MVI's products and the components used in their assembly.

Production

For each first-time application, MVI builds whatever hardware and software is needed to make the project work for the customer. For further similar applications, MVI looks for a supplier for the necessary components of the system. Thus, for all of MVI's multiple applications, the optics, hardware, circuit boards, cables, communications devices, and other material handling equipment are all purchased from outside suppliers. The role of production then becomes that of packaging the optical equipment, the hardware, the software, and the communications materials so that the application works for the customer.

The Future Goals for MVI

Mr. Eiler believes that many of the seeds of MVI's ultimate success in the vision market have already been laid. He believes that the company's early successes have shown customers the "consistency, reliability, and strength of the company. They are learning that MVI is a vendor you can count on; not just a bunch of scientists playing with technology, but businessmen who will be here to stay." He sees that MVI's people have formed a team, and that it is not just strong technology but strong people working with that technology that makes products that perform for the customer.

Mr. Eidswick, MVI's chairman and CEO, has established the company's goal of being a dominant supplier in the machine vision industry. This goal translates into obtaining a 15 percent share of this market within five years and then sustaining that 15 percent share.

Mr. Eidswick has also set achievement goals for each sales division. The ASD and the ESD are to be specialized divisions and, as such, be technology and market share leaders within their industries. Here, there will be a continuing effort to take on new projects that have a strategic purpose. The groups within the Manufacturing Technology Division are to have multiplier strategies; their sales are to come from extensions of products developed by the ASD and ESD. The MTD groups are also to seek out strategic partners, finding companies who need vision in their products and who already have market knowledge and a strong customer base. For this type of customer, MVI would sell its products at a discount from the prices quoted to direct end users since the strategic partners would take over much of the selling process for MVI.

Mr. Eidswick has prepared sales expense breakdowns for the company's two types of sales, those direct to end users and those made through strategic partners, as MVI would like to see them. These expense breakdowns, expressed as percentages of sales revenue, are shown below. The third column shows the breakdown of expenses as percentages of sales for MVI's sales for the first half of 1985.

	End user	Strategic partner	First six months 1985
Revenue	100%	100%	100%
Cost of goods sold	35	55	45
Gross margin	65%	45%	55%
Selling expense	25%	9%	45%
R&D and engineering	10	10	30
Corporate expenses	10	6	8
Total expenses	45%	25%	83%
Profit before taxes	20%	20%	(28%)

These figures tell an interesting story. MVI has not made a profit to date; however, no competitor in the vision industry has been consistently profitable. MVI has bid each project, even the first one for each of its applications, at a price that the company thought would be profitable. However, the number of engineering, selling, and application development hours that these early applications have taken to achieve systems capable of working in real industrial environments and to educate customers on the use of the products has been hard to estimate. These problems have led to the higher than desired selling, R&D, and engineering expenses to date. Mr. Eidswick is most concerned about the high selling expense figure. He is not so concerned about the R&D and engineering expense since this is to be expected in a new, high-technology industry. MVI must, as Mr. Eidswick sees it, find ways to reduce its selling expense.

The Question of Focus

I think the central question right now is, what are we going to be when we grow up? It is not a simple question because the markets right now are small and fragmented. We must be very alert to be successful in the right markets.

Mr. Eidswick

Some vision companies have chosen to be very specialized. They believe that an emerging company cannot afford to spread itself too thin. It must establish a market niche, exploit that niche, make some money, and then go out and spread itself. Others say that this is a new market. No one understands it. What may be a niche one day might just disappear. Some competitors are very specialized. Others are all over the place. Some of each have failed. Why? For the specialized firms, perhaps the market never appeared or the task they chose proved too difficult. For those who were in all markets, each project was different and they had no repeat sales.

Dr. Sternberg

Multiple orders of the same kind of things, that's the kind of result we want to have. We want more repeat orders for the same product, the same application . . . less customization. That way we don't have to keep reinventing the wheel, inventing new technology and engineering new software for every order that we get.

Mr. Eiler

Mr. Eidswick believes that the fact that MVI has "so much going on, in so many markets, with so many different applications" is the company's biggest problem right now. But he explains that "we have to do this if we want to find the applications that will provide repeat business, applications that will establish us as an industry leader."

MVI has consciously moved its technology position within the industry from a company that employed only mathematical morphology to one that could successfully use all four technologies in its products. Mr. Eiler says this was done as a purposeful marketing strategy because many vision problems cannot be solved by one technology alone. They require capabilities of various technologies. Mr. Eiler also points out that the company has purposefully chosen only very difficult applications, a strategic approach he calls "a tough jobs positioning." That product positioning along with what Mr. Kufchock calls the company's credo that "There is no unhappy customer" have been designed to build a strong company image for MVI as "the company that makes products that work," as Mr. Eiler put it.

However, this strategic "tough jobs" approach can lead to another set of problems. Because its applications are so difficult, MVI's products are all very highly priced. This may pose a risk in this new industry where there are so many competitors and where each market is undeveloped. As Mr. Eiler said,

In high tech, everything is too new and the market is too volatile. There are too many factors, too many things driving the marketplace. There are new people coming into this business all the time who think they can make vision systems work. You can lose a job to a low-end, low-price competitor who gets thrown out in three months because his system doesn't work. When others can't do the job, then we all suffer because vision's credibility is questioned.

MVI has not found that it is easy to get a vision application job even after another competitor has failed to provide a product that works. Often customers who have spent thousands and thousands of dollars on vision equipment want to protect that investment by giving their supplier another chance to succeed. Other customers have turned away from vision after initial system failures, waiting for the technology to mature and for the market winners to appear rather than give another company a chance at this time.

The prospectus published by MVI at the time of its stock offering to Safeguard Scientifics, Inc. shareholders states that MVI focuses on three applications. These are three-dimensional robot guidance, surface inspection, and surface-mounted electronic component inspection. Dr. Sternberg believes that, in looking at the company, one should be careful not to confuse its technological diversity with its market position. He said, "MVI is focused; we are working toward three standardized products."

Case 14

K mart Corporation*

> Rising in the early 1960s from a mundane variety store chain, K mart set the retail industry on its ear by stamping out enough prototype stores, like so many apple pies, to become the largest discount store chain. It elbowed J. C. Penney aside as the nation's number two, nonfoods retailer. In the first transformation year of 1962, the former S.S. Kresge Co. had sales of $450.5 million and net profits of $9 million. By 1984's end, those numbers had mushroomed to $21 billion in sales . . . and profits rolled in at $499 million.
>
> *Marketing & Media Decisions*
> Spring 1985 Special Edition

The story of K mart Corporation's rise is one of the truly great success stories in the retailing business. The first K mart was opened in 1962. By 1973, there were 745 K mart stores in 47 states. Total sales in that year were $4.6 billion, with $138 million in net income. Stores were added to the chain at a very rapid rate through the 1970s. One hundred and ninety-three new K marts were opened both in 1979 and 1980, with 171 new stores added in 1981. By 1984, there were 2,041 K mart stores throughout the country. The chain enjoyed a compound growth rate in sales of 16.6 percent from 1974 to 1984. Its share of the total mass merchandising market in the United States grew from 1.8 percent in 1972 to 3.7 percent in 1982.

In the company's 1974 annual report, Mr. Robert E. Dewar, chairman of the board and chief executive officer, defined K mart's market position as that of a mass merchandise retailer. He said,

> As mass merchants, we emphasize basic merchandise rather than discretionary purchases and stress value over fashion. . . . Our most important competitive strategy is to use discount pricing. Our store buildings and fixtures are designed and built, our merchandise assortments are selected, and our distribution systems are developed in order to offer a broad range of general merchandise at the lowest possible prices.

K marts offered everything from clothing to housewares, from delicatessen foods to hardware, from sporting goods to stationery and toys. The product line also included such products as tires, batteries, building materials, and garden supplies not commonly carried by conventional department stores.

---

* This case was written from public sources by Constance M. Kinnear with the assistance of Thomas C. Kinnear. Copyright © 1987 by the authors.

In the first K marts, national brands composed approximately 50 percent of the merchandise mix, with the remainder being private K mart brands, sold at prices approximately 20 percent lower than national brands. K mart priced its goods with a margin of 25 to 26 percent over cost as opposed to regular retailers that priced at 38 to 40 percent over cost. K mart was not alone in the discount merchandising business. Its competitors included several small regional discount operations such as Mammoth Mart, Unishops, Giant stores, and Arlans. The competition also included new discount chains started by previously regular-only retailing firms. These included Federated's Gold Circle stores, Dayton-Hudson's Target stores, May Company's Venture stores, and Woolworth's Woolco stores. These stores offered little customer service, had a low-overhead, warehouse look, and made their profits through high-volume sales, with inventory turnover rates between six and eight times per year. When these stores were opened, their primary customers were blue-collar families with average to below-average incomes. The discounter's primary goal during this period of quick expansion was to convince its customers that it was safe and smart to save money. To this end, K mart offered only first-quality merchandise and a satisfaction-guaranteed return policy. Using low prices, K mart sought to accustom shoppers to a self-service, low-overhead store. Stores' location decisions were carefully made to make shopping K mart convenient for its customers. By 1984, not only were K marts present in over 80 percent of the standard metropolitan shopping areas of the country, but K mart surveys showed that 52 percent of the people in the country shopped at K mart at least once a month.

The K mart story was not one of totally untroubled success, however. Though sales increased annually, net income growth slowed in 1979 and actually decreased in 1980, 1981, and 1982. In 1982, sales growth itself was flat. Average sales per square foot of sales area were also falling. In 1981, K mart sold an average of $146 per square foot. In 1982, that figure dropped to $132 per square foot. In 1983, K mart average sales per square foot were up to $155, but this figure compared poorly to Target stores' figure of $172 per square foot that year. K mart also faced a falling inventory turnover figure. In 1981, inventory turned over only three and one half times, a sizable drop from the company's six times per year goal. Many factors within the retailing industry were affecting K mart's performance, factors which led K mart management to rethink its chain's position within that industry.

Changes in the Retailing Industry

The area of change in the retailing industry that had the most impact on K mart's performance had to do with an increasing demand on the part of consumers for quality in the products they bought. Mr. Fauber described the change in a speech to the New York Society of Security Analysts in 1983 by saying,

> Today's consumer is much more experienced and wiser than in the 60s. Rising levels of education and consumerism and the impact of the media, particularly television, have resulted in a customer who knows how to determine good value

for the money to a much greater extent than in the past. The more informed shopper has become a better shopper—not just for price, but also for value. Our research indicates that many more customers today would rather buy a better-quality product with the knowledge that it will provide a more useful economic life. But they still want these products at a good price.

Several different layers of customer wants, desires, and purchase preferences began to appear in the American retail scene. It was impossible for any one store to accommodate all these needs within one building. Many new retailers began to appear on the scene, zeroing in on changing lifestyles and tastes. These new store types were either upscale discounters or off-price specialty retailers, presenting customers with a new ambience and offering brand and designer merchandise priced some 20 to 70 percent below regular retail levels. Consumer loyalty to particular stores and convenient locations began to disappear as buyers shopped around for the best deals. This, in turn, increased competition among retailers to new heights. Retailers cut prices to boost store traffic and build store loyalties, but, in effect, they even further conditioned consumers to shop for value and price. The effects on K mart were expressed in an article in Fortune, which said,

> Regional discounters with more attractive stores and more fashionable products began to chip away at K mart's share of the market. New kinds of discounters picked off pieces of the company's domain: specialty stores began selling sports equipment, drugs and beauty products, books, apparel, and shoes. Catalog show-room houses moved in on small appliances and jewelry. . . . In this tough new market, K mart's style and quality did not keep pace with the public's taste.

The success of off-price retailers in the early 1980s rivaled that of K mart itself in the 1960s and 1970s. The total sales of off-price retailers were just $3 billion in 1979, but by 1982 sales totaled $7 billion, or nearly 6 percent of total industry sales in that year. Industry observers believed that this type of retail outlet would continue to grow by 30 to 35 percent annually through the end of the decade. This figure compared with a 10 percent expansion expected for the retail industry as a whole. As a result, it was estimated that off-price retailers could capture as much as 20 to 25 percent of total industry sales by 1987. Within the off-price group, growth rates were expected to be the highest for those retailers who were able to best capitalize on such demographic and economic trends as the new baby "boomlet," increasing numbers of households (especially one-person households), increasing numbers of elderly Americans, and a decline in the teenage population. In 1979, there were only a few hundred off-price retailers in the country. By 1984, it was estimated that there were between 4,000 and 5,000 such outlets operating in the United States. One industry analyst suggested why growth in this area would continue when he said, "I believe that every kind, every conceivable type of 'niche' retailing is going to be tested. More and more people are looking for the successful niche." In general, off-price retailers served value-oriented middle- and upper-class consumers seeking upscale merchandise at discounted prices. Industry reports profiled the typical off-price shopper as "the suburban female in her 30s with a family income of $35,000."

Most discount retailers made changes that they hoped would appeal to the shoppers moving away from them to off-price stores. "Upscaling" by everyone became the name of the game. For many discounters, upscaling meant changing the selling environment of their stores with improved ambience, comfort, and convenience for shoppers. For most, it meant providing customers with a more appealing product mix with increased value in the products offered. To directly compete with the off-price and specialty discount operations, many discount chains began treating departments that were being chipped away by specialty stores or that fit defined demographic interests as "stores-within-a-store." Special attention was given to the layouts of these departments, giving them a newer, brighter, more separate appearance within the store. Also, the product mix within these departments was made deeper and broader than in departments that faced less competition from new types of retailers.

The goal of upscaling was to enhance competitive positions and attract a broader customer base. Upscaling was not meant to alienate customers who were already shopping discount stores, but instead was intended to make the stores also appeal to customers from higher economic levels. For example, apparel departments in discount stores began carrying an upgraded fashion mix, which included designer and brand name merchandise as well as improved private brands. In hard goods areas, inventories were being weighted more heavily toward branded goods, which provided increased product quality and customer satisfaction. This trend was summarized in the Standard & Poor's Retailing Industry Survey of July 4, 1985, as follows:

> In contrast to their off-price and department store counterparts, discounters have traditionally geared their mix to less affluent, less fashion-conscious shoppers, and stressed price over quality. More recently, however, leading chains have been "upscaling," both to accommodate the higher income level and shopping savvy of today's prototypical discount store shopper and to attract middle-income customers. Upscaling strategies generally entail adjusting the merchandise mix to include more name brands, lacing existing lines with higher-quality, pricier items, and reformatting and sprucing up the stores themselves.

The result of these upscaling activities was that everyone was copying everybody else, and all the stores began to resemble each other. They were all fighting for the same customers. As one president of a discount chain put it, "We are all selling things that can be purchased elsewhere."

All of these changes in retailing were taking place in conjunction with a long-term drop in per capita spending on general merchandise by U.S. consumers. Per capita spending on general merchandise had dropped 24 percent since the mid-1970s. Industry analysts, looking at this trend, pointed to the failure of several marginal retailing organizations and the subpar profitability of many others as proof that the retailing industry as a whole was "overstored."

The growing similarity of merchandise mix within discount stores, the desire to reach the same consumer groups, and the excess retailing space in the country led to a sharp increase in promotional competition within the retailing industry. Discount retailers began lowering prices on already-discounted products to gain customer traffic and maintain market share in dollar sales. This only encouraged consumers to search further for the best value for their dollar, forcing discounters to continue price promotions in order to maintain position within the industry.

K mart's Image

With the arrival of off-price and discount specialty stores, discount stores in general lost ground in the fight for consumer dollars. The situation was summarized by Fred Wintzer of Lehman Brothers' Kuhn Loeb in 1983 when he said,

> Consumers believed the merchandise carried by discounters was of less than high quality and that the stores were too often out of stock. When items were in stock, shoppers found them difficult to locate. Finally, discount stores were perceived as cluttered, as lacking the neatness of other general merchandise outlets. And K mart was the "king" of the discounters.

Though all discounters were in a fight to maintain sales and market share, K mart, as the largest discounter, had the most to lose and perhaps had to make the most changes if it was to maintain its leadership position. Mr. Norman G. Milley, K mart's executive vice president of merchandising and subsidiaries, assessed the company's position in the early 1980s when he said,

> We recognized a need to reanalyze the K mart position in the consumer's eyes. We took a great number of surveys and were able to determine that we had the price image but did not have the quality image. We had excellent locations, good traffic and customer acceptance, but we were not selling enough merchandise to many of our customers.
>
> We had narrowly defined the K mart customer and were not accepting the fact that these customers were going elsewhere to buy merchandise that we were not offering. We determined that we could sell those coming to K mart more kinds of products than we were carrying. Why could we not sell much higher-ticket merchandise if we presented it properly?

Low prices had always been K mart's strength. Now the image the company had tried to develop for itself when the chain first began was becoming a liability. Now shoppers were looking for value; yes, they were still looking for good prices, but for quality products at a good price. K mart had a very weak quality reputation among consumers. K mart had to take action in several areas to overcome this low-quality image.

K mart's Changes

K mart's consumer research showed that, although sales were leveling off and net income was falling in the early 1980s, the chain's customer count was not decreasing. Over half the people in the country still shopped a K mart at least once a month. People were still coming to K mart for basic needs, but they were not shopping in the store's more "ego-centered" departments like apparel or household furnishings. For these products, K mart shoppers were going elsewhere. The task for K mart was to convince customers to buy more products while in a K mart. The company decided to fight its long-standing image of a low-income, blue-collar store. The goal was to increase sales to the customer group composed of family members aged 25 to 44 with children by offering products that this group wanted. As Mr. Fauber explained it, K mart wanted to increase its interest to its more affluent customers, those who regularly popped into a K mart for the regular price advantage they found for such items as toothpaste or tennis balls. By updating K mart, it was hoped that these customers would stay in the store longer and spend more money on a wider mix of goods.

As a first attempt to reach these goals, K mart's executives felt that all that was needed was an updating of the appearance of the stores and improved stocking methods. It was obvious to them that the stores were dull, and they believed that dull interiors reflected on the quality of the products in the store. Improving the appearance of the stores would improve the impression the stores gave the merchandise. This action was taken first since K mart executives believed that the major advantage regional discounters had over K mart were their clean, bright, modern interiors.

To improve appearance, continuous bands of poppy red, gold, and white were placed in the floor tiles to delineate department areas but yet to encourage shoppers to browse from area to area. Each department was located using the wall signs that continued the color theme used in the floor tile. Individual merchandise signs were standardized and displayed sparingly. Taller, graduated counters were installed. These made better use of vertical space and eliminated visual clutter. They promoted a sweeping view of K mart's merchandise variety. The goal was to present a "complete store" message. With a new simplified, low-key atmosphere, the aim was to let the merchandise speak for itself.

K mart management soon found that the decor changes were very unsuccessful. They soon came to the conclusion that the problem did not lie with the way in which the merchandise was displayed, but rather in the merchandise offered in the stores. Mr. Ed Willer, vice president of E. F. Hutton, described K mart's slowness at realizing the true problem when he said, "For a long time the mousetrap worked so well that it didn't even cross the minds of K mart management to change it. K mart didn't feel it was necessary to fundamentally change what they offered the American consumer." Mr. Fauber himself admitted that the company may have become so engrossed with adding square footage that it neglected a more vital ingredient of success, the stores' contents.

K mart's next changes were based on extensive studies of their customers. The management wanted to learn what K mart's customers wanted and what they were likely to want in the future. The first idea to come from these consumer studies was a belief that young homeowners were concerned with maintaining or improving the condition of their homes, as well as getting the best value possible in that work. The result of this was the development of the Homecare Center, a department that was given the status of a ''specialty'' shop and encompassed 15,000 square feet of space within a K mart store. The Homecare Center consolidated many former departments, including building materials, hardware, power tools, electrical equipment, and lighting, into one area with everything the home do-it-yourselfer would need for fix-up or repair projects. This department was given a distinctive blue-and-white sign to signify its store-within-a-store importance.

The Homecare Center was a great success. Its acceptance encouraged K mart to try other new product mixes. K mart buyers were told to experiment with product purchases and to buy what they thought could be sold. Several different product mix formulations were tried out in prototype stores in different parts of the country. Twenty-five such stores were called ''lead stores.'' In these, new product mixes featured a total selection of name brand products and designer apparel, with the elimination of all private label merchandise. Lead stores were located in higher-income neighborhoods. Other prototype stores, called ''future'' stores, offered ''better-priced'' merchandise made by some of the finest manufacturers in the country, but sold under labels other than those normally sold in department stores. The positive responses these trial stores received convinced K mart's management that K mart had not previously carried the products customers wanted on its shelves. The decision was made to stock the K mart chain with a combination of the two trial mixes. K marts would carry more name brand, more designer, and more high-quality private label goods. Although K mart management knew that there was great diversity among the economic status of the neighborhoods their stores served, they were committed to the idea that K mart was a national chain and that the vast majority of the goods carried by one K mart should be in all K marts. Consumers, they believed, should be presented with a national image of the K mart chain, knowing that products they expected in K mart would be found in all stores in the chain. Eighty percent of K mart's merchandise was standardized on a national basis. Store managers were left free to fine-tune 10 to 20 percent of the product mix in their stores in an effort to appeal directly to local markets, be they rural or urban, black or Hispanic, high or low income.

As higher-quality, higher-priced products were added to the K mart line, the traditional products and their low price points were retained. This policy was explained by Mr. Larry Parkin, chairman and CEO of K mart apparel. He said,

> The tactic is to add on at the top of the line, not to abandon the low end. People who bought in the middle of the range, the thinking goes, will step up. K mart will always have the lower price points because if we didn't have the $9 sweater, lots of people would have no sweater at all.

Items that traditional K mart customers expected to find in the store were still there. The new products were added to appeal to customers who wanted higher quality and who had gone elsewhere to find these products in the past.

More national brands began to appear in K marts. It became common to find such products as Armstrong Solarian no-wax tiles, Corelle dinnerware, Rogers stainless flatware, Libbey glassware, Sharp microwaves, and General Electric food processors in K mart stores. Seiko watches were now carried in the jewelry department along with the familiar K mart line of Timex watches. Casio and Sharp calculators could now be found in the electronics departments. Minolta 35-mm cameras were added to the familiar Kodak lines in the camera departments. Now 14k gold jewelry could be found at the jewelry counter near K mart's less expensive merchandise. More fashionable, brand name clothing was added to each apparel department. Brand names with higher price points became the rule and not the exception at K marts.

In order to make room for this line extension program, K mart began to make use of higher display fixtures, which allowed for additional cubic space usage. For example, in apparel departments, "pipe run" displays, which allowed only the shoulders of garments to be readily visible to customers, were replaced with open, circular racks. Using these racks, the entire front of a garment was plainly visible to the shopper. Other new types of fixtures, called "waterfall" displays, were trilevel and allowed the showing of coordinating slacks, blouses, and jackets on one display.

Other specialty departments began to appear and receive a store-within-a-store status. Housewares became The Kitchen Korner. This department now carried more than just low-cost kitchen utensils. Now the shopper could find cookware by such names as Farberware, Revere Ware, and Club Aluminum. Small kitchen appliances carried such brand names as General Electric, Sunbeam, Oster, and Norelco. Mixing bowls and utensils were now Pyrex. The belief was that the more knowledgeable consumer would know these brands and recognize the value that also came with the K mart price.

The linen department was now called the Bed and Bath Shop. This department was greatly expanded, using new display fixtures to better show off the improved variety and quality of the store's selection of sheets, blankets, towels, bathroom rugs, pillows, and bedspreads. Brand names made available included Pepperill and Springmaid.

Totally new product lines were also introduced. The new Home Electronics department carried name brand computer equipment priced below $500. Also carried were nationally advertised computer software, as well as national brand and private label TVs, VCRs, and a wide range of other video and audio equipment. Where it was believed that demand would be great enough, K mart introduced, expanded, or upgraded other departments, such as nutrition and health food centers, wicker shops, unpainted furniture, hard- and softcover book assortments, and stationery and greeting card departments. These were designed to take advantage of demographic trends. An expansion of the number of K mart pharmacies and automotive service departments was also begun.

Changes for K mart Corporation were not limited to adjustments within the company's discount store chain. The corporation began diversifying into other businesses designed to improve the company's profit performance. K mart Corporation purchased two cafeteria-style restaurant chains, Furr's Cafeteria and Bishop's Buffet, and began expanding the number of these outlets. This move was taken because K mart management believed that eating away from the home would continue to be a growing aspect of American life. Furthermore, these restaurant chains offered low-priced, homestyle cooking, something K mart management thought fit well with K mart's image. Following the lead of Sears, K mart introduced K mart Insurance Services to several stores in the South. The corporation was also moving into new forms of retailing to compete directly with the new off-price outlets. In 1982, K mart began opening off-price women's apparel stores, called Designer Depots, which offered only national brand clothing at discount prices. The company was also developing new discount gift shops, called Accents. These stores offered top-of-the-line home fashions and accessories, such as Limoge china and Oneida silver, at discount prices. K mart also entered into a joint venture with Hechinger Company of Washington, D.C., to develop large, free-standing warehouse-style discount home centers, to be called Builders Square.

Changes were also made in the message delivered by K mart's $580 million advertising budget. K mart advertising had long focused on telling customers of special low prices on specific items within the store. The goods advertised were often special loss-leader items designed to bring buyers into the stores, hoping that they would purchase other items while there as well as those products specially priced. In its change in advertising message, K mart began to advertise whole categories of goods or entire departments within the store. Especially featured in the ads were higher-ticketed, upscale merchandise. K mart wanted its customers to know that the chain now carried better-quality merchandise in departments that offered shoppers a wider range of goods to choose from than ever before.

K mart's Concerns

While trying to better attract those customers with higher incomes and an interest in purchasing products of higher price and value, K mart had to be careful not to alienate its traditional customers who came to its stores for low prices. K mart executives were concerned that the firm might have the same problems that W. T. Grant and Sears had when they upgraded the products in their stores. W. T. Grant's image with consumers became confused. Shoppers were not certain whether the chain was still in the discount business or was becoming a regular department store. W. T. Grant went out of business. When Sears increased the quality and price points on its merchandise, lower-income customers left Sears for discount stores. To win these shoppers back, Sears promoted bargains aggressively, but found its traditional shoppers returned to buy the bargains but little else. K mart did not want to confuse or alienate its traditional customer base. K mart's management was strong in its assertion that the chain was not "Upscaling" as these competitors had done. It was not trying to bring in new shoppers, but just to provide the merchandise its present customers wanted. As explained by Mr. Fauber in late 1985,

Many people studying K mart failed to understand the difference between "trading up," offering a higher-priced product at a higher margin, and K mart's approach of "updating," which was selling a higher-priced product, yes, but at our normal markup, and in the process giving the consumer a better value even than before.

K mart management was also concerned that a low-price, low-fashion, low-quality image could not be easily erased, especially during a period of high competitiveness within the industry. It was a difficult problem to balance the need to let consumers know that the stores had new merchandise of higher quality to offer while not stressing this message to the point where it alienated the company's traditional customer base. K mart needed to convince both the customers who had always relied on K mart for price and those that it was trying to attract more spending from that K mart had become a "smarter place to shop." This message would take time to get across to consumers.

The process of establishing a new image for K mart was made even more difficult by the time it took to make the physical changes in store layout, merchandise display, and merchandise purchasing for a chain of over 2,000 stores. One hundred and twenty-six crews were employed to transform the stores. In 1983, 715 Home Electronic Centers were in place, with another 750 planned for that year. In 1984, 650 Kitchen Korners, 125 Homecare Centers, and several hundred Bed and Bath departments were scheduled for completion. The entire changeover of the chain would take more than five years. The cost of refurbishing a store ran between $80,000 and $500,000. Three hundred million dollars was planned for this program in 1983 alone. The total cost of store renovations would be in excess of $1.25 billion for the period 1981 to 1986. Even spending at this pace, the length of time it took to complete the in-store changes delayed K mart's ability to present a new, chainwide image to the public. It would only confuse consumers to see brand name products in K mart ads if these products were not yet in their local store.

The question also remained as to how far K mart could go toward upgrading the quality and price of the products it sold. By 1984, the specialty departments within K marts were achieving and often surpassing management's goal of sales of $200 per square foot of sales space. Could the merchandise mix be even further raised, resulting in even better sales results? By continued merchandise mix trials, K mart management soon realized that there were limits to what consumers were willing to buy in a K mart store. For example, they found customers unwilling to purchase such items as down pillows or $50 blankets in K mart Bed and Bath departments. Shoppers who purchased items like these bought them in regular department stores or in linen specialty shops. K mart shoppers looked for synthetic-filled pillows and blankets with a top price range of $25. K mart management believed that the stores had to carry predominantly common merchandise mixes across the country. This meant that products that were carried in K marts were carried in all 2,000 stores, and therefore were purchased in massive volumes. There was little room to take gambles on the merchandise to be purchased for the chain. Before an order for a certain product was placed, K mart management wanted to be sure the item would sell.

Opinions of K mart's Success

Opinions expressed in national retailing and business magazines and reports by executives in the retailing industry and industry analysts about what success K mart could expect from all the changes the company had made were as varied as the number of types of retail organizations that existed to serve the American consumer. Excerpts from some of these publications and reports are given below to show some of the controversy that existed regarding K mart's future.

> The hopeful view is that Fauber's moves will yield a resumption of K mart's swift growth and ample profitability. . . . The counterview is that K mart in 1983 is simply grasping for straws. Fauber seems to recognize that the old strategy of forced-draft expansion no longer works. But so far he's replaced it with assorted remedies, not with a well-defined growth strategy. Not with the kind of game plan that made K mart the retailing phenomenon of the 1960s and early 1970s.
>
> Stephen Taub
> *Financial World*
> March 31, 1983

> Other retailers have a stronger position, better profitability, know what they are doing, and have a game plan that's working.
>
> Jeffrey Edelman
> Smith Barney

> Will there be enough off-price merchandise available to meet K mart's huge needs? Will makers of quality-name clothes want to have their merchandise associated with the K mart image? Will the new, more label-conscious customers K mart hopes to attract respond to its bait?
>
> David Taylor
> Prudential-Bache

> The success of private labels hinges on the store's reputation for quality.
>
> Standard & Poor's Industry Surveys
> *Retailing Industry*
> July 4, 1985

> The demographic trends are not going K mart's way. To retailing analysts, the most attractive customer group in the near future will be the fast-growing population of 25- to 44-year-old college graduates living in suburbia and making $20,000 to $35,000 a year from professional and managerial jobs. The typical K mart customer is a blue-collar high school graduate in the $15,000 to $25,000 income bracket. K mart is at the wrong place at the wrong time.
>
> Fred Wintzer, Jr.
> Lehman Brothers' Kuhn Loeb

> On competition, I've seen a definite move toward upgrading. We're not doing that. We're trying to maintain our niche, while several competitors are going after

more of the middle- and maybe slightly higher-than-middle-income customer. Hopefully, they will leave more customers on the lower end for us. What we are doing is emphasizing customer treatment, obviously making our store a nicer place to shop in. That's an important factor.

> President of Wal-Mart Stores
> *Discount Merchandiser*
> September 1985

Asked where the blue-collar people will go for their apparel, K mart replies: "We are still going to maintain those price points that K mart is famous for. They may be on the back of the rack, but they are going to be there. We are not going to avoid them."

> *Discount Merchandiser*
> July 1984

K mart sales per square foot improved 9 percent in 1983 to $155, following a 3 percent decline in 1982. A more upward movement is indicated by the 5.5 percent increase in comparable store sales for the first quarter of 1984. In the case of some remodeled stores, sales have been running 40 percent better than a year ago. How much of the improvement is due to remodeling and how much is due to a change in merchandise is a fine point, and not entirely relevant so long as productivity climbs.

> *Chain Store Age Executive*
> August 1984

People usually think of the K mart customer as a blue-collar worker whose wife works and has a household income of about $22,000 a year. But the K mart customer is the customer who works and lives near the store.

> Mr. Samuel G. Leftwich
> President of K mart Corporation

Our stores are changing faster than ever before. We're not doing Saks or Lord & Taylor or an upscale department store. We're upgrading, but keeping within our customers' price point.

> Larry Parkin
> Chairman and CEO of K mart Apparel

K mart feels that it has gained new and better-heeled customers. Citing Simmons' research, the company says that 23.3 percent of K mart customers in 1980 had family incomes from $25,000 to $40,000, but by the end of 1984, the new program and advertising had pushed that customer income figure up to 28.1 percent. Also, in 1980 only 8.3 percent of K mart's customers had annual incomes of $40,000 or more. Now, that share has risen to 18.9 percent, according to the company.

> *Chain Store Age Executive*
> August 1984

The notion of quality is, by no means, an easy one to nail down. As Fauber says, it is a concept influenced in a number of ways through "convenience, store ambience, advertising, availability of product, service, and employee attitude."

> *Discount Merchandiser*
> September 1985

The difficulty of K mart's task in presenting a new image to America can be shown by the round of applause and laughter the following jokes received when they were included in Johnny Carson's monologue in February 1986:

You know, K mart has made a lot of changes. They now offer valet parking at the front door for your pickup. Inside, I see that they have gotten rid of the used underwear bin. They've made a lot of new room by getting rid of the checkout where you could exchange livestock for household appliances. You notice the change right away—as soon as you walk in, you hear over the loudspeaker, "Pardonez moi, K mart shoppers. . . ."

Case 15

Nigerian Hoechst Limited*

Introduction

In June 1982, Mr. Otto Revier, marketing manager for Nigerian Hoechst Limited (NHL), was preparing his marketing plan presentation for a new pharmaceutical product for the Nigerian market. Before he could proceed with the new product introduction, Mr. Revier had several superiors to satisfy, including Mr. Heinz-Hermann Helms, deputy regional manager (Africa, Central and Latin America) for Hoechst A. G. (HAG), the parent company, which was headquartered in Frankfurt, West Germany. As Mr. Revier looked over his preliminary ideas for the new analgesic product code-named Product H, he decided to review all the data he had on Daga, the product which had been NHL's first venture into the over-the-counter (OTC) market in Nigeria. Daga had been a wonderful success for NHL with first-year sales of ₦1.75 million.[1] Mr. Revier was well aware that not only would Product H's results be compared to Daga's, but also Product H must not unduly cannibalize Daga's sales. Mr. Revier was expected to submit his plans for approval as soon as possible. With this in mind, he began to review all the information he had on the Nigerian market, Daga, and Product H.

---

[1] Currency: The naira is the official currency of Nigeria, signified by an ₦. One naira equals 100 kobo. Coins are ½ (note there were hardly any ½-kobo coins), 1, 5, 10, and 20 kobo. Notes are 50 kobo, 1, 5, 10, and 20 naira. During the time of most of the case events, the ₦ floated with the U.S. dollar, ranging from $1.83 in 1980, $1.63 in 1981, to $1.47 in 1982. The deutsche mark (DM) was used in most of HAG Group records. The average rate of exchange in 1980 was 1 ₦ = DM3.20, DM3.30 in 1981, and DM3.50 in 1982. Management forecasted an exchange rate of DM3.40 in 1983. Because of uncertainty, NHL company officials typically used a 3-to-1 ratio of DM to ₦ in most of their planning for NHL. Because of the volatile currency situation, naira values have been shown throughout the case.

Hoechst A. G.

Hoechst A.G. was founded in 1863 by two German chemists and two German businessmen in the small city of Hoechst on the banks of the Main River near Frankfurt, West Germany. They began with dyes and colouring agents, entering pharmaceuticals in 1883 with new products to combat fever and headaches. By 1982, the Hoechst Group was involved in a very wide variety of product lines including pharmaceuticals, crop protection chemicals, printing plates, waste water purification methods, disease diagnostic systems, plant and animal nutrition, roof covering and paints for buildings, packaging films, fibres, plastics, facsimile copiers, electronics chemicals, and industrial gases. The Hoechst Group operated in 140 countries, employing 182,154 people in 1982.

In 1981, sales of the entire HAG Group were DM34,435 million and net profit after taxes was DM426 million. Approximately 65 percent of sales were from outside the Federal Republic of Germany. Pharmaceutical sales were very nearly DM6,000 million, representing 17 percent of total Group sales in 1981.

Nigerian Hoechst Limited

HAG started its activities in Nigeria in the mid-1950s using a local importer and distributor called Major & Co. to handle its pharmaceutical products. A representative of HAG was stationed in Nigeria to promote Hoechst products, but soon after local pharmacists were hired to intensify this effort. NHL Limited was formed on December 18, 1963, under the name of Hoechst Products Nigeria Limited (HPN). This company was jointly owned by Hoechst and Major & Co. HPN Ltd. sold the entire HAG product range except pharmaceuticals. The name was changed to Nigerian Hoechst Limited in 1973 to reflect the transfer of Major & Co.'s shares to a local company called Chief Ashamu Holdings. This change was in accordance with Nigerian government indigenization policies, that is, local ownership of companies. Indigenization had been promoted strongly since 1972, with the 1977 decree the strictest yet of three major policy positions on the matter. According to Nigerian law, NHL was classified a "Schedule II local manufacturer and own importer." Foreign equity was restricted to 40 percent. NHL could undertake both local manufacture and import activities and thus could be relatively flexible and coordinate all their activities. There was no pressure on NHL to manufacture or repack all its product range within the country.

Until 1981, the NHL pharmaceutical (pharma) business involved ethical and semi-ethical products such as Novalgin, Baralgin, small spectrum antibiotics, Berenil, Lasix, Reverin, Daonil, and Claforan. NHL pharma business in Nigeria prior to 1974 was handled by an agency, Major & Co., who also handled other pharmaceutical companies. NHL pharmaceutical business up to 1974 did not develop as rapidly in Nigeria as expected. Management of HAG believed the major difficulties had been the agency distribution arrangement, with problems such as conflict with other principals regarding the assortment,

TABLE 1 NHL pharma sales and profit summary (in ₦ million and percent)

Year	Sales (including agencies)	Growth (percent)	Hoechst pharma sales	Growth (percent)	Hoechst Consolidated profit
1976	4.9	64%	4.2	54%	(.313)
1977	8.4	72	6.1	45	(1.306)
1978	8.6	3	5.6	(8)	(1.572)
1979	12.2	41	8.6	54	330
1980	17.0	41	11.3	31	2.581
1981	23.0	35	15.5	39	4.217

shortage of stocks, and delays in payments of accounts receivable. The relative lack of attention Hoechst was receiving prompted HAG management to place the pharma business under the same roof as other HAG divisions in NHL. NHL not only looked after HAG products and subsidiaries (such as Optrex) but also represented three other pharmaceutical companies (Roussel, Schering, and Nattermann) in importing, warehousing, and physical distribution. These companies had their own marketing and sales people in Nigeria. NHL management, as they moved from agency distribution to their own direct distribution, realized that they needed sales branches throughout the country, a qualified sales and promotion force, and their own distribution system.

Establishing its own infrastructure became a clear priority for NHL because of the chaotic market infrastructure in Nigeria. As of 1973, NHL was headquartered at Ikeja, just outside Lagos. Industrial chemicals were produced at Ikeja, and pharmaceutical production began at Otta in 1982. There were five pharma branches—Lagos, Ibadan, Benin, Aba, and Kano—in 1981. Branches were planned for Jos in 1982 and Kaduna and Maiduguri in 1983. NHL staff levels had increased steadily during the 1980s. In 1980, there were 40 field force members and 104 additional staff. By 1982, the field force had grown to 55 and the additional staff had increased to 126.

From 1974 to 1980, NHL pharma sales increased tenfold. NHL was divided into two major divisions, industrial and pharmaceutical. With a 41 percent increase in sales from 1979 to 1980 (partly due to a 25 percent price increase), pharma division with ₦17 million sales[2] (DM51 million) accounted for one third of NHL sales in 1980. Pharma division profits of ₦2.7 million (DM8.1 million) were 65 percent of total NHL profits that same year. Total NHL sales were ₦41.8 million for 1981, and total profit for the same year was ₦4.0 million. This moved NHL pharma sales from 22nd in the Hoechst group worldwide rankings in 1979 to 11th largest pharma operation in 1981. Further data are shown in Table 1.

In 1980 dipyrone products (Novalgin and Baralgin) accounted for 48 percent of Hoechst pharma sales. However, there were several concerns being expressed about dipyrone by various international groups, which led NHL

---

[2] Figures include agency operations for Roussel, Schering, Nattermann, and Optrex.

management to believe they should not be so dependent on products containing this substance. Further, Novalgin constituted a substantial proportion of NHL's government business. Government customers had become serious accounts receivable problems—in 1981–82, government outstandings were about 10 months' sales, leading NHL management to believe that reliance on government business had to be reduced.

The Hoechst product line had been predominantly ethical, but this kept NHL out of at least one third of the Nigerian market, that is, the OTC market. Further, new ethical products showed promise only over the mid to long term. Introduction of new ethical products in Nigeria was a slow process because of the substantial conservatism of Nigerian prescribers and dispensers. Further, management believed that the pharmaceutical market would not grow appreciably in the ethical area until there were significantly more doctors in Nigeria. This analysis led management to examine the OTC market.

Nigeria

The Federal Republic of Nigeria in 1982 was the most populous African country, although only the 12th largest geographically. With 923,768 square kilometres in area, Nigeria was about the same size as France, West Germany, and the United Kingdom combined or 50 percent larger than Texas of the United States. Many sources estimated that Nigeria was one of the world's 10 most populous nations and that one in five Africans was Nigerian, although these statements were difficult to confirm. Nigerian population figures were very imprecise because most estimates were still based on the only reliable source, the 1963 census; however, NHL management believed population was growing at an annual rate of 2.7 to 3.5 percent. Using NHL figures, population was 88.2 million in 1980 (the UN estimate was 77.1 million), rising to 94.5 million in 1982.

Half the population was thought to be under 15 years of age. Using the 1963 census applied to the estimated 1982 population, the age structure was as follows:

Age group	Percent
0–4	17.2%
5–9	15.2
10–14	10.7
15–19	9.4
20–24	12.4
25–29	10.0
30–34	7.8
35–39	4.5
40–44	4.3
45–49	2.1
50–54	2.2
55–59	0.8
60–64	1.4
65–69	0.5

There was a very wide range of ethnic, linguistic, cultural, and religious groupings in Nigeria despite efforts of the federal government to create a single national identity. There were some 400 ethnic groups, of which three predominated: the Hausa-Fulani in the north, the Ibo in the southeast, and the Yoruba in the southwest. The north was mainly Islamic and suspicious of westernization (modernization, Christianity, etc.). The north contained 79 percent of the country's area and, in terms of the 1963 census, 54 percent of the population. The western region (which included Lagos) had 8 percent of the land and 17 percent of the population. The eastern region (which had the oil) had 8 percent of the land and 22 percent of the population. The midwest had 4 percent of the land and only 4.5 percent of the population. Often, observers divided the country into north and south. In this sense, the south included the western, eastern, and midwest regions. The south was westernized and moving decades ahead of the north in development. The north was more rural, less industrialized, lower income, about 67 percent in farming, accounted for about 35 percent of national income, and had an illiteracy rate approaching 85 percent. The south was more urban, more industrialized, had higher incomes, had about 45 percent in farming, accounted for 65 percent of national income, and had a lower illiteracy rate. Approximately 34 percent of the adult population were thought to be literate by 1980. The official language was English. Hausa, Ibo, and Yoruba were the principal languages spoken in the north, east, and west, respectively. Exhibit 1 shows a map of Nigeria.

Nigeria has had a great deal of difficulty because of tribalism, which has

EXHIBIT 1   Map of Nigeria

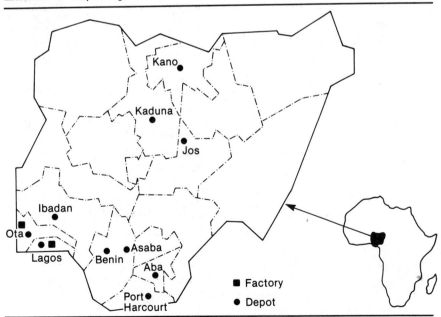

caused much disagreement about political leaders, territorial divisions, etc., and has often resulted in violence and civil war. Nigeria became independent in 1960. There was a bloody civil war from 1967 to 1970. There have been several coups; of its first four heads of state, three were killed in office and the fourth was deposed and exiled. Nigeria was under military rule for 13 years until 1979.

There were 19 Nigerian states as of February 1982 (24 were proposed by the government in late 1981) and five political parties. The system was patterned after that of the United States, requiring five sets of elections. A general election was coming in August 1983. These would be the first elections organized by civilian as opposed to military authorities. It was the general expectation that the government would be reelected and that its main priorities would be overcoming current economic problems, the shift of the capital to Abuja (a new federal capital territory), and the creation of further states to facilitate better government.

The rate of drift of population from rural to urban was more pronounced than in almost any other developing nation. Exact populations of cities also were unknown. Here is an estimate as of 1982:

City	Estimated population
Lagos	4.5 million
Ibadan	2.3 million
Kano	750,000
Illorin	600,000
Port Harcourt	450,000
Kaduna	420,000
Maiduguri	420,000
Ogbomosho	370,000
Oshogbo	265,000
Benin City	265,000
Enugu	265,000
Abeokuta	245,000
Sokoto	185,000
Jos	185,000
Owerri	185,000

Nigeria was a member of OPEC and in 1981 was the world's ninth largest producer of oil. Agriculture used to be the mainstay of the Nigerian economy; but after the development of oil, agriculture dropped to about 20 percent of gross domestic product (GDP) by 1981, even though it still employed about two thirds to three fourths of the working population. GDP at current prices was estimated at ₦39,939 million in 1979, ₦43,280 in 1980, and ₦43,450 in 1981. Adjusted for inflation, 1981 was down by 2 percent. GDP real growth averaged approximately 8 percent throughout the 1970s.

Nigeria had become very dependent on oil income (about 90 percent of the country's foreign exchange earnings and 80 percent of government revenues) and experienced a dramatic decline in this between 1980 and 1981. The trade deficit in 1980 was close to U.S. $5,000 million, which, combined with an outflow of service payments, meant a current deficit of over $7,500 million in 1981. For this reason, the government attempted to cut imports by one third in 1982 and to place greater emphasis on developing Nigerian import replacement industries. However, despite the decline in oil income, Nigeria was regarded as the richest country in Sub-Saharan Africa. Roughly 55 percent of revenues went to the federal government, 35 percent to the states, and 10 percent to local governments.

Gross national income was estimated by NHL management to be ₦50,599 million in 1980, ₦60,000 million in 1981, dropping to ₦57,000 million in 1982. Income per capita was estimated to be ₦574 in 1980 and ₦603 in 1982. Estimates of GDP varied remarkably. Nigerian sources estimated 1981 GDP at ₦54,000 million.

The rate of inflation was high. NHL management estimated it to be 20 percent in 1980, 15 percent in 1981, and 12 percent in 1982. *Business International* ranked Lagos as the world's most expensive city in 1981. Using 1975 equals 100, a composite consumer price index combining urban and rural centres showed all items at 189.2 in 1979, 219.5 in 1980, 257.5 in 1981, and 275.7 at the end of 1982.

Nigerians were on balance extremely poor (approximately one car per 1,000 population), had high malnutrition and disease caused by dietary deficiencies, suffered inadequate standards of environmental hygiene and a shortage of medical facilities, and had a life expectancy at birth of 48 years.

The Nigerian Market for Pharmaceuticals

The pharmaceutical market in Nigeria depended on the disease patterns in the country, the health care system, and the activities of the pharmaceutical companies. The health problems of the country were attributed to the poor quality of public works and education. As of 1979, the prevalent illnesses and causes of death were quite different from those in developed countries. According to a *Business International* 1979 report on Nigeria:

Most prevalent illnesses	*Leading causes of death*
Malaria	Pneumonia
Dysentery	Malaria
Gonorrhea	Cerebrospinal meningitis
Pneumonia	Tetanus
Measles	Infectious hepatitis
Tuberculosis	Tuberculosis

Malaria remained the most commonly reported of notifiable diseases in Nigeria, with its incidence in 1981 at 1,694 cases per 100,000 population. The difficulty with any Nigerian health statistic was that less than a third of the population had access to conventional health facilities, so statistics overemphasized disease patterns in the urban areas. Nonetheless, this pattern of disease meant that the medical needs in Nigeria were for antibiotics, analgesics, vitamins, and tonics. Pharmaceutical usage was quite different from the German market HAG served. For example, various sources compared the market structures in 1981 as follows:

Nigeria	Percent	Germany	Percent
Analgesics	16%	Antirheumatics	6%
Antibiotics	16	Vasodilators	5
Vitamins/tonics	12	Cough and cold	5
Antimalarials	8	Anti-infectives	4
Cough and cold	4	Psychotropics	4
Psychotropics	2	Analgesics	4
Antirheumatics	2	Vasoprotectors	4
Cardiovascular	2	Cardiac-glycosides	3
Antispasmodics	1	Antihypertonics	3

Mr. Jeffrey Ford, marketing manager for the Pharma Division of NHL from February 1980 to March 1982, explained the thinking behind offering a pain and fever remedy in Nigeria as follows:

> Analgesics are a very important product for Nigerians because of the way they live. The Nigerian lives in a climate that contributes to all sorts of exotic tropical diseases. For example, the average Nigerian is stricken with a case of malaria perhaps once a month, diarrhea probably twice a month, and a headache probably once or twice a week. Sanitation is hopelessly substandard, resulting in impure water, proliferation of parasites, and other problems. Further, the average Nigerian has a diet very different from our standards. Instead of a balance of protein, carbohydrates, and minerals, his diet is about 90 percent carbohydrates, which means his body does not get what it should, and malfunction results. Add these factors to the environment of heat, humidity, and dirt and you can see why analgesic consumption is so much higher than in Europe and North America.

Enormous expenditures were planned in public health care in the Nigerian 1975–80 Plan. For example, the plan called for an increase in doctors per million inhabitants from 45 in 1972 to 71 in 1980. Although the Nigerian population was estimated to be nearing 100 million people, only 12 to 20 million Nigerians were thought to have access to the Nigerian governmental medical facilities.

There were free public health care facilities provided at three levels: federal, state, and local. The federal government concentrated much of its expenditure in teaching hospitals at the expense of expanding primary health care. The federal Ministry of Health accounted for roughly half of the total state expenditure on health. The most important federal program for pharmaceutical manufacturers was the Basic Health Service Scheme, which was to initially establish 256 health centres across the country for primary health care. Ultimately, the plan called for about 4,000 health care units and to have the whole population within five kilometres of a dispensary or primary clinic. This program ran into many problems, not the least of which was disagreement among tribal leaders as to where initial units would be located.

The state governments were generally responsible for their own health care outside the teaching hospitals. On the whole, each state was autonomous in health care. There were many malpractices evident to pharmaceutical companies dealing with state health care officials. Some products purchased by institutions were subsequently sold on the private market.

Local governments focused almost completely on prenatal, postnatal, and pediatric activities.

By the end of 1979, Nigeria had a total of 69,670 hospital beds and was expected to have around 82,000 in mid-1982. Facilities as of 1979:

	Hospitals	Health centres	Clinics
North	189	288	4,521
West	196	53	1,850
East	255	197	1,030
Midwest	75	58	611
Total	715	596	8,012

Government hospitals and clinics were chronically short of funds and staff, resulting in less than adequate service levels in the opinion of many. Consequently, private health care facilities were being developed in the major urban areas and particularly in Lagos. Companies in particular were investing in this development.

Undercapitalization of the governmental health care system led to drug shortages and slower than expected development of the institutional market by pharmaceutical companies and led to a substantial growth in the self-medication OTC market. According to *Business International*, there were two principal segments of the Nigerian pharmaceutical market. The urban population, about 10 percent of the total, already provided a considerable and rapidly growing market. As it expands in size and wealth, it was expected to take a larger share of the total market. The public sector, comprising the federal and state governments and public corporations, was also growing fast and would provide more and more opportunities for the drug companies. On the other hand, the purchasing power of the masses was expected to develop more slowly, with deep-rooted traditions, beliefs, and tastes posing major challenges to consumer goods marketers. For the foreseeable future, according to *Business International,* Nigeria was primarily a market for infrastructure (roads, telecommunications equipment, port installations, schools, hospitals, clinics, hotels, etc.) all over the country. And alongside these capital purchases there would be a market for the supplies used—medicines, hospital and school equipment, books, cables, and so on.

It was very difficult to estimate the size of the market. Not only were population and medical statistics inaccurate and unreliable, but there were problems of definition, such as which products were pharmaceuticals and at what level to examine the market. Perhaps most difficult was the lack of consistency as to what price level to use in calculations. The term *market at wholesale prices* is used very loosely in Nigeria and can refer to market size at price to prime distributor or at price to pharmacy level. Most pharmaceutical companies considered prices to wholesalers/prime distributors to form the best basis for determining total market size regardless of product origin (locally manufactured or imported). See Table 2.

TABLE 2 Estimate of total Nigerian pharma market (in ₦ million)

1978	1979	1980	1981	1982 (est.)
160	200	250	350	370

The pharmaceutical market in Nigeria had grown dramatically with the increase in money available due to the oil boom. Analysts predicted that the overall annual rate of growth for pharmaceuticals in Nigeria would average 20 percent until 1985, then drop to 15–18 percent thereafter. Further, the private market was expected to account for 80 percent of total sales by 1985, and local manufacture to account for 50 percent of supply by 1987–88.

Generally speaking, there had been four phases of development in the Nigerian market for pharmaceuticals over the period 1974–81:

1. *1974–1977—Frantic growth.* Growth in private sector was more than matched by demand from institutional sources. Many institutional purchases were delayed, lost, or stolen. The boom in demand encouraged many major suppliers to establish their own importation and primary distribution companies. The retail market was undersupplied.
2. *1978–1979—Austerity.* Easing of port congestion and cutback in institutional purchases led to dramatic increases in inventories at all levels. The indigenization program of 1977 changed many distribution arrangements.
3. *1980—Sharp recovery.* Rapidly rising oil revenues allowed many governmental authorities to increase purchases dramatically.
4. *1981–1982—Economic reversal.* Decline in oil revenues, tighter import restrictions, and lower demand reduced pharmaceutical sales growth.

Analgesics

Analgesics accounted for 16 percent of pharmaceutical sales in Nigeria in 1981. Within the analgesics segment, management estimated that 20 percent of sales were ethical products, including injectable analgesics, narcotics, and Novalgin. Novalgin, the third highest-selling analgesic in Nigeria after Phensic and Panadol, was considered by NHL management to be a premium-priced analgesic targeted at the ethical market. Aspirin and paracetamol could not be injected and were not as effective as Novalgin in the case of severe pains. Direct distribution to the public of OTC analgesics such as aspirin, paracetamol, caffeine, and combinations thereof was permitted. De facto, though not allowed, Novalgin tablets were retailed via OTC channels as well.

Analgesics were estimated to account for ₦56 million in sales in 1981. Acetylsalicylic acid-based analgesics made up around 47 percent of the OTC analgesic market, and plain paracetamol preparations accounted for approximately a further 25 percent. NHL estimates of OTC analgesic market shares by product as of the end of 1981 are shown in Table 3.

Marketing Pharmaceuticals in Nigeria

Reliable market research on the Nigerian market for pharmaceuticals was not readily available. Usually, if a firm wanted in-depth sectoral research, management had to do its own. Even then, management usually found statistical information highly questionable. Consequently, most marketing decisions in Nigeria tended to be made more subjectively than in many other markets. Nonetheless, management believed that the total Nigerian pharmaceutical market could be divided roughly into three equally important customer segments:

1. *Private sector.* Private hospitals, medical doctors, and retail pharmacists purchased directly or via wholesalers approximately an equal value of ethical and OTC products.
2. *Governments.* Federal and state governments purchased almost exclusively on a tender basis primarily ethical products.
3. *Public at large.* Public at large purchased almost exclusively self-medication OTC products via retail patent medicine stores, retail pharmacies, and street vendors.

Traditionally, NHL had been strong through the first two segments; Daga was intended to be NHL's lead product into the third segment.

TABLE 3 OTC analgesic market shares in 1981

Product	Company	Active ingredients*	Share (percent)
Phensic	Beecham	A, Ca	17%
Panadol	Sterling-Winthrop	Pa	14
Cafenol	Sterling-Winthrop	A, Ca	10
Pengo	Christlieb	A, Ca	8
Daga	Hoechst	A, Pa, Ca	4
P.R. Tabs	Boots	A, Pa, Ca	4
Dispirin	R-C	A	3
Aspirin	Boots	A	1
Febrilix	Boots	Pa	1
Top Tabs	Seward	A, Ca	1
Paracetamol	Glaxo	Pa	1
Others			36
Total	50+ products		100

* A = Aspirin; Pa = Paracetamol; Ca = Caffein. Aspirin and paracetamol provided pain and fever relief, while caffeine provided a lift, like a tonic.

Local Manufacturing and Importing

Most of the local formulation industry was based on the repackaging of finished pharmaceutical preparations imported in bulk. The reason was that it was far more profitable, except for low-value/high-volume products, to import rather than attempt to manufacture in Nigeria due to the difficult operating conditions there. Nonetheless, the value of local manufacture had been growing rapidly.

The major sources of pharmaceuticals for Nigeria in 1981 were as follows: United Kingdom (48.3 percent), West Germany (17.3 percent), Switzerland (10.2 percent), and France (4.6 percent). U.S. companies traded mostly through European regional centres.

As a direct consequence of dwindling currency reserves and declining oil export levels, the Nigerian government implemented a series of import restrictions of increasing severity with the aim of halving imports. Thus far, Nigeria had adopted a laissez-faire approach to the pharmaceutical industry, but close observers expected this to change in the mid-1980s. As of early 1982, finished pharmaceuticals could still be imported easily, but import licenses were required for some raw materials, auxiliary chemicals, and virtually all packing materials.

The Nigerian Customs and Excise Tariff used the Brussels Tariff Nomenclature (BTN). A single-column, nonpreferential import tariff schedule applied equally to all countries. Duties were either specific or *ad valorem* depending on the commodity. Duties were computed on the cost and freight c&f value, and all imported goods had to be insured by an indigenous insurance company. All import duties were payable on entry in Nigerian currency. Tariff rates by African standards were moderate. These advance payments were made to the importer's bank before a letter of credit was opened. The funds were then placed in a noninterest account with the Central Bank of Nigeria.

However, even tougher measures were to take effect in April 1982. This new procedure would do the following:

1. Increase the level of import duties on many products including pharmaceuticals, i.e., up 5 percent points from 10 percent to 15 percent on cost, insurance, freight (c.i.f. value).
2. Instruct all state authorities to purchase locally produced products unless a certificate of nonavailability is issued.
3. Introduce a 50 percent deposit requirement. This meant that importers must deposit 50 percent of the value of goods on application and then pay the full amount of the consignment before attempting to recover the deposit. This would force many smaller importers out of the market and perhaps affect the level of parallel importation, which was becoming a growing concern.

Distribution

Wholesaling and retailing of all types were an extremely important component of the Nigerian economy, second only to oil in terms of share of gross domestic product. In general, the Nigerian distributive trades performed the same tasks and were structured similarly to the distributive trades in other countries. However, the infrastructural problems of Nigeria resulted in major physical distribution difficulties and resulted in a very complex, multilevel trade system for most products.

Pharmaceuticals were available to the public from a wide variety of sources in addition to government hospitals: dispensing doctors and private clinics, registered pharmacies, patent medicine stores, other stores with a patent medicine license, and itinerant and market traders. NHL executives estimated there were from 30,000 to 50,000 retail outlets and 1 to 2 million street traders selling pharmaceuticals in Nigeria. Exhibit 2 is an attempt to show diagramatically the distribution system for pharmaceuticals in Nigeria.

A central characteristic of the pharmaceutical distribution system was the relative lack of controlled distribution via registered pharmacists. This was caused by the shortage of doctors and pharmacists in Nigeria. With approximately one pharmacist in private practice per 85,000 Nigerians, doctors tended to dispense their own pharmaceuticals. Further, the shortage of official channels for ethical preparations in particular prompted illegal channels and a lot of self-medication. For example, although a patent medicine store had OTC products legally, often it also had ethical products under the counter, which would be sold without prescription. For example, a man with gonorrhea might go to such a store and get an injection of antibiotic through the trousers. Sometimes, these ethical products had been stolen from shipments to government hospitals. Such products were impossible to identify because there was no marking on the packages to distinguish government sales, etc., so tracing could not be done.

A registered pharmacy employed a registered pharmacist selling both ethical and OTC products typically from behind a counter in an outlet no bigger than 25 square metres. This was the upscale end of the pharmaceutical market. There were about 500 outlets throughout Nigeria, of which about 80 percent were in the major cities.

A patent medicine store (sometimes called a chemist) was a store specializing in OTC products. Such stores may or may not be licensed. These outlets were very small but very popular for the high-volume OTC products, such as analgesics, tonics, and glucose preparations. There were an estimated 13,000 patent medicine licenses as of 1982. Some of these licenses were used to establish patent medicine stores, while some were used to enable other types of stores to add OTC products to their assortment of other goods. Again, there were many thousands of outlets that sold OTC products without a license.

The supermarket had not yet really arrived, in part because of the strength of the street traders. As of 1982, there were only a few supermarkets, and these were not important channels for pharmaceuticals. However, there was an enormous market called Onitsha near Asaba on the banks of the Niger River. This one market accounted for about one fifth of all pharmaceuticals sold in Nigeria.

A major component of pharmaceutical distribution was the grey market of itinerant and market street traders. There were three types of street traders:

EXHIBIT 2   NHL distribution flowchart

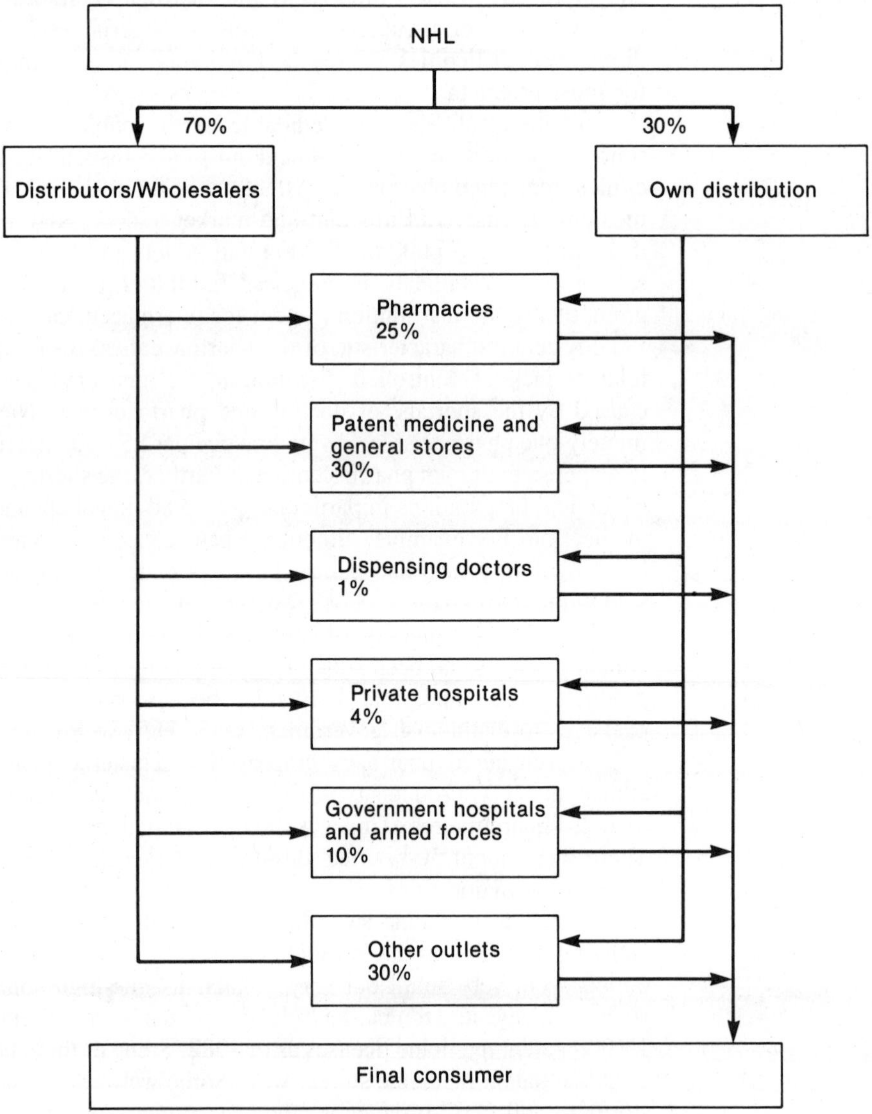

1.   Those with a fixed place of business, usually a very small kiosk (usually one metre square), frequently specializing in a particular type of product.
2.   Sedentary traders who spread their wares out beside them on the ground and usually dealt in goods such as cigarettes and sundries.
3.   Hawkers, a large number of whom carried their wares around in the slow-moving traffic of the cities, especially Lagos, selling quite a variety of products.

EXHIBIT 3 Nigerian mammy stalls

Pharma companies called the stationary traders "mammy stalls." For an example, see Exhibit 3. These traders obtained their goods either by treating other retailers as wholesalers (that is, going to a patent medicine store and carrying purchased product back to the stall) or by salespeople who went up and down the streets looking for them. Mammies operated from their stalls in high-traffic areas and moved around the surrounding area with a circular tray on their heads, selling cigarettes, or condensed milk, or analgesics, or whatever. Many of their sales were one cigarette at a time or two analgesic tablets at a time. Often they had subhawkers working for them, too.

In the view of many observers, the Nigerian wholesale distribution system for pharmaceuticals had changed dramatically since the mid-1970s. Prior to that time, the trade was dominated by a relatively small number of specialist and multidivisional importation-distribution groups, such as Major & Co. They generally had infrastructural and depot networks covering the various regions and were able to meet the needs of the foreign pharmaceutical companies. Then the market grew so rapidly that several companies began to consider the economics and marketing advantages of their own importation-distribution. Further, the Nigerian indigenization decrees affected the independent importer-distributors dramatically. Because they were importing, these companies had to reduce their foreign shareholding to 40 percent. Relatively few of the major pharma companies continued to use the services of the independent importer-distributor companies. The initial impact of this change was to weaken the whole pharmaceutical distribution system as the new entrants sought to build systems as good as the original importer-distributors had established. However, despite this change, a great deal of the wholesaling function continued to be performed unofficially by retailers selling to one another.

Pricing

Price controls were introduced in 1977 by the Nigerian federal government on both locally produced and imported goods. These were not uniformly or completely monitored and enforced. Pharmaceutical products were exempt from official price and markup controls. In general, the industry experienced price increases in small installments twice a year. In general, pharmaceutical companies had great difficulty ensuring uniform prices throughout the country.

Wholesale prices of accepted brands in Nigeria tended to be at least 40 percent higher than those same brands in Germany. Retail prices in turn tended to be high in Nigeria due to the substantial distribution costs and markup requirements that arose out of the multilevel distribution system. Generally speaking, the margin structure meant that the price to pharmacy level was about twice c.i.f. levels for locally manufactured products and three times c.i.f. for imported products. Sales to street traders were typically at chemist prices and for cash only. Invoicing was regarded to be out of the question. Very few outlets resold items at fixed prices; most items were bargained for.

Not only were several suppliers faced by increased competition from other products, but many also had difficulties with illegal parallel imports. This problem could not be solved so long as local manufacture meant higher prices and smuggling remained unchecked. Observers believed parallel importation would become more profitable because Nigerian inflation was higher than inflation in other industrialized countries and there was little indication that local manufacturers were going to reduce their margins and prices.

The Nigerian government used three methods for procurement: open competition, negotiated contract, and selective tender. Selective tender was the most prevalent. All bids were required to be sealed in wax and submitted before the deadline. Contracts had been lost because the wax was omitted. According to NHL officials, it was very difficult to get state tenders in particular. These governments tended to purchase from local wholesalers and often provided little or no notice to companies of opportunities to bid. Goods for tender awards could be supplied duty free. The official commission payable to suppliers in respect to state tenders was 10 percent, although exceptions existed.

One major problem for all suppliers had been the increasingly slow payment by customers, but retailers and governments. Some marketers were less interested in government business for this reason.

Advertising

As of 1982, Nigeria had one of the most developed media systems in developing Africa. There were 14 major daily newspapers, approximately 20 weekly newspapers, and about 25 magazines published in Nigeria. All the dailies were published in English, as were most of the weeklies and magazines. Still, circulation of the newspapers reached very few Nigerians—somewhere in the 2 million range.

Radio was regarded as the best way to reach the Nigerian public. According to a 1979 estimate, there were just over 5 million radios; however, a 1982 estimate said 18 to 20 million radios. There were five federal regional services broadcasting in English and appropriate regional languages, and each of the 19 states had an autonomous radio station. Radio stations accepted commercial advertising.

Each state capital had its own TV station broadcasting in its local language plus the federal station broadcasting in English, making a total of 20 stations. According to a 1980 estimate, there were 450,000 televisions, essentially limited to the urban elite. The number of television sets was growing rapidly and expected to top 2 million in 1983. For transmission purposes, the country was divided into six zones. Commercial television advertisisng was accepted.

There were few guidelines available concerning how to advertise in Nigeria. Most firms were finding their own way. A *Business International* report on Nigeria in 1979 stated:

> The do-you-good theme exerts strong advertising appeal to a people whose diet has always been short of essential nutrients. A local detergent claims its use has a "tonic" effect. A market survey on smoking motivation shows that some Hausas of the north smoke cigarettes because of their cooling effect during the hot season and their warmth on the chilly days of the harmattan. Responses like these give Western advertising experts new vistas for creative action.
>
> The marketing success scored in Nigeria by Guinness stout is another example. Stout is a heavy, warming beverage seemingly ill-suited to the steamy climate of West Africa, yet it has swept the market for some years on the platform of "power." Guinness marketing men discovered that power has many subtle interpretations for the Nigerian. The "Guinness gives you power" formula has struck the fancy of the Nigerian consumer and appeals to his more urgent desires. Primarily, it is seen as a body-building aphrodisiac to be taken just before leaving the bar for home. It is also thought to relieve some pains and blood disorders,

strengthen the lungs, sharpen the brain, add stature to the puny, and make men more dynamic.

Advertising expenditures for analgesics in 1981, excluding point-of-sale promotion and discounts, were estimated at ₦1,715,000, of which NHL's Daga accounted for roughly one quarter.

Personal Selling

The personal sales force was very important to marketing pharmaceuticals in Nigeria. Detailmen visited doctors, pharmacies, patent medicine stores, and, in some instances, street traders. The sales task involved selling, sampling, debt collection, encouragement of wholesaling, and efforts to learn about opportunities for bidding on state contracts. On average, a detailman could make at least six quality calls per day. In 1982, NHL had 28 OTC salesmen, in comparison with Bayer's 10 and Pfizer's 14.

Pharmaceutical Competitors

The leading local pharmaceutical manufacturers in Nigeria in 1981 in order of size were: Sterling Products Nigeria Limited, Pfizer Products Ltd., Glaxo Nigeria Limited, Embechem Ltd., Beecham Ltd., and Wellcome Nigeria Ltd. (Note: If Glaxo's Glucose D was added to its production figure, it would be largest.)

The OTC emphasis in the Nigerian market was reflected in Sterling's Panadol (largest-selling paracetamol preparation) and Cafenol (third largest-selling analgesic on the OTC market). Panadol was promoted as a pain reliever—it did not relieve fever. Cafenol was a combination of aspirin and caffeine. Both of these products had been available in Nigeria for over 10 years. Sterling-Winthrop was the largest manufacturer of analgesics in Nigeria.

Pfizer concentrated most of its efforts on ethical preparations. Glaxo Nigeria Ltd., on the other hand, concentrated primarily on OTC preparations, such as multivitamins, cough preparations, glucose, and baby foods. Approximately 68 percent of its Nigerian sales were OTC; Glucose D accounted for 37 percent of total company sales. Most of its ethical products were imported.

Beecham concentrated on Beecham's consumer toiletry and food preparations. It established a local plant in 1973 and began to produce locally the Phensic analgesic and Macleans toothpaste. Phensic was not a large contributor to Beecham even though it was probably the largest OTC analgesic preparation sold on the Nigerian market and the oldest available in Nigeria. Phensic was promoted for fever relief.

Boots Company (Nigeria) Limited opened a plant in 1981 to produce PR Tabs and blood tonic products.

NHL management estimates of overall competitive results for 1981 were as follows:

Company	Sales (₦ million)	Market share (percent)
Glaxo	₦19.0	5.6%
Beecham Group	18.7	5.5
Hoechst	15.7	4.6
Sterling-Winthrop	14.6	4.3
Wellcome	14.0	4.1
Pfizer	12.8	3.7
Roche	10.0	2.9
Merck Sharp & Dohme	9.0	2.6
E. Merck	8.5	2.5
Bayer	6.2	1.8

The period 1982–85 was very important for local manufacture because several firms were bringing local plants on-stream. By 1985, at least 17 of the major multinational pharmaceutical firms were expected to have their own local formulation plants operating in Nigeria, meaning about 50 percent of pharmaceuticals sold in Nigeria would be manufactured locally. The major reason for this was that companies had been unable to guarantee enough supply to their sales force due to difficulties getting product into Nigeria. Analgesics in particular were well suited to local manufacture because they were low value, high volume, and relatively simple to formulate and tablet.

According to NHL management, as of the beginning of the 1980s, the main differences between the marketing programs of competing analgesics firms and NHL's Daga were mostly in terms of advertising and promotion and the aggressiveness of the sales force. NHL also had an advantage by virtue of having the most elaborate branch distribution system, which enabled it to provide better service to customers.

Doing Business in Nigeria

Doing business in Nigeria was difficult for many reasons. According to the U.S. Department of Commerce:

> The Nigerian market requires a strong commitment over the long term; it cannot be developed from afar. The business environment stresses personal relationships in both direct sales and major products . . . seriously consider appointing an agent or stationing a company official in Nigeria to stay abreast of current developments and to maintain contacts with government officials and the local business community. . . . Companies, however, should not underestimate the cost of maintaining a representative in Lagos, which for the first year could reach close to U.S. $300.000.

HAG had discovered over the years that it was necessary to pay special attention to physical distribution problems at ports of entry. For example, in its budgeting, HAG allowed about an extra 10 percent, for that was required to get imported goods unloaded and out of the port. NHL had its own facilitator team that was absolutely essential in management's view.

The difficult living conditions in Nigeria and the prevailing customs of the country had a substantial impact on the way business was conducted. Management knew that in every deal, and there were innumerable deals, there were extra payments being made, often back to employees and representatives. As one senior Hoechst executive put it:

> I know that many local people have their fingers in the pie. We don't want the moon from our business there. As long as the overall profit level at the end of the year is OK, we're happy. If our people get a little extra, OK, let them have it. They live under very difficult conditions. It's not like working here in Europe. We know what we expect, and if results are less than that, then we look more closely at what happened and ask questions.

The Daga Story

The decision to introduce an OTC analgesic in the Nigerian market was considered by both NHL and HAG management during 1978–79. NHL's reliance on Novalgin (50 percent of volume and 80 percent of profit) and the ethical market worried senior management. Further, the opportunities in OTC analgesics appeared exciting. The key managers involved in Daga were Mr. A. Woerpel, divisional manager pharma of NHL from mid-1979 (and who had been involved in OTC marketing in Asia), and Mr. H. H. Helms of HAG. See Exhibit 4 for an abbreviated organization chart.

Mr. Ford recalled the circumstances when Daga was introduced:

> I first got involved in Nigeria in February 1980, having come from ethical marketing for Hoechst in the United States. I was in Nigeria for a little over two years and had two major products to introduce. The first was an ethical antibiotic aimed at the gonorrhea problem and the other was Daga. Most of my time and that of the rest of the pharma management was directed at Daga.
>
> In terms of marketing activity, the analgesic market had been quite dormant—the lion's share was held by products that in terms of image, packaging, composition, and advertising and promotion were relatively antiquated and quiet.

However, it proved difficult to convince top HAG management that NHL should be allowed to enter the OTC analgesic market. According to Mr. Helms:

> The American approach to pharmaceutical marketing is very different from the German approach. The traditional German method is to spend a lot of money on research and development to pull out a molecule that has medical benefits, and then think, because of its benefits, it will sell itself in the pharmaceutical market. You'd probably call it a research-driven approach. This means that a shift for us to OTC products with all the attendant marketing skills required is a major strategic change. In fact, we got into other OTC markets by acquisition of OTC companies. The soul of our business has remained ethical.
>
> So, when we began to consider OTC analgesics in Nigeria we had two problems. First, prior to 1978, we had really no market data. We knew there was a big market for analgesics, vitamins, and tonics, but we had no figures. Second,

EXHIBIT 4   Partial HAG and NHL organization chart, 1982

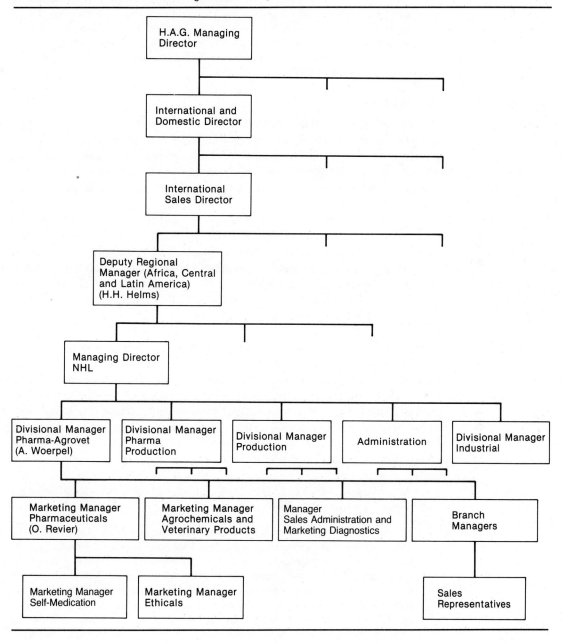

and more important, all our senior Hoechst management think in ethical terms. To go to them and say why don't we sell a tonic or an analgesic with a very simple product composition and use modern mass marketing techniques was a risky proposition. They viewed it as being street hawking, not ethical at all. So, our proposal was a significant strategic decision for senior management. We got permission to proceed by mid-1979.

The Product

After receiving approval to put together a detailed plan for the introduction of an analgesic in Nigeria, NHL executives wanted to get into the OTC market as quickly as possible, which argued for using known ingredients. Candidate products and/or ingredients could be sourced within the Hoechst group. The major effort to develop a marketing approach did not begin, however, until the arrival of Mr. Ford.

Pure acetylsalacylic acid products were the least expensive products to offer. NHL management decided they did not want to enter the lowest-price segment ASA market nor to cannibalize their higher-priced segment captured by Novalgin. This left the middle segment of combination products of ASA and paracetamol and/or caffeine. Within the Hoechst group, there already was a product in Afghanistan and Thailand that had the approximate composition NHL executives thought would be appropriate.

Using a product that had already been marketed elsewhere saved a lot of time. Management wanted a product that had proven galenical properties.

Daga was a triple-formulation product. A Daga tablet contained three active ingredients: aspirin (ASA), 225 mg; paracetamol, 250 mg; and caffeine, 30 mg. By comparison, Tylenol was a single-formulation product using paracetamol. Anacin was a dual formulation of aspirin and caffeine. The Daga triple formulation offered advantages to the user: the lower dosage of two analgesic drugs combined gave synergistic analgesic results with reduced side effects from either analgesic. Daga was the second triple formulation on the Nigerian market.

According to Mr. Ford, Daga was introduced as a two-tablet standard dose because of tradition in the market:

> The standard dose is two tablets at a time. We considered this carefully, but the history of Beecham's Phensic was pivotal. That product has been on the market for 25 years in a two-tablet dose form. We decided we had to continue with a two-tablet format because the consumer was so accustomed to it. So, we formulated the product accordingly. We made it cream coloured to differentiate it from all other tablets, which were white. Many Nigerians used analgesics as tonics and as preventative medicine for headaches by taking a morning dose regularly. In addition, after a stressful day they would take analgesics to help sleep, to ward off headaches, before going drinking to prevent hangovers, and, in general, "to strengthen the body."

Pharma management knew that HAG executives would not favour manufacturing Daga in Frankfurt nor would it be possible to manufacture originally in Nigeria. Registration of Daga in Nigeria would be relatively easy, leaving the question of source of supply. Mr. Woerpel had worked in Asia and knew that Thailand could produce what NHL management wanted, so Thailand was chosen as the initial source of supply for Daga. This continued until the Nigerian factory was ready in 1982.

NHL management had been considering a factory in Nigeria since the latter part of the 1970s but had been waiting for a clearer indication of the future development of the Nigerian market and some way to reduce dependence on the analgesic Novalgin product. The decision to build a factory to produce a high volume of tablets was made in late 1980. This plant was intended to produce Novalgin, Baralgin, Lasix, and Daonil tablets along with the new Daga product; the major justification for the plant was the anticipated volume of Daga product. The foundation stone of the new factory was laid in May 1981, and the factory and central warehouse in Otta were to be officially dedicated in November 1982. The factory was designed to enable liquids production at a later stage with minimal conversion costs.

From the outset, pharma management had conceived line extensions for Daga. The first such product was Daga-Syrup, to be launched in 1982. The Nigerian market was a significant liquid market because of the age distribution of the population. Parents liked liquids to give to children. And although the product was a pure pain and fever medication, parents gave it to their children as a tonic, too. The Daga tablet could also be easily broken in half to give to children. Six to 12 months later, management planned to introduce Daga-Co, which was a Daga and codeine cocktail, to capture a further share in the ethical market since OTC sale of codeine was forbidden. In 1983, the final line extensions would be Daga-Quine—a Daga plus chloroquine combination for malaria relief—and Kiddy-Daga, which was to be a low-dose analgesic for children.

The Name

In March 1980, using personal interviews, 50 Nigerians (half male and half female) were given a choice of three alternative product names, including Daga. Approximately 96 percent chose the Daga name. The attractiveness of the name was apparently due to its simplicity, memorability, and its connotation of force and struggle in Hausa, a major tribal language of the north, and its connotation of violence in the south. The connotation of killing pain and fever with Daga appeared to be very strong.

The Logo and Packaging

Shortly after the product name research, using the same research method, 30 people were asked which of five logos appealed the most. Females were almost unanimous in choosing one logo, so management opted for it because of their significance as customers and traders. Further questioning of consumers revealed that green, yellow, and black packaging was a particularly attractive and appealing combination to Nigerians, who as a group love colour. Management believed that the logo—a black dagger—was related to the concept of killing pain and fever.

Two package sizes were introduced in January 1981. One contained five aluminum foil cards of four tablets each, making it a pack of 20. This package was aimed at the individual user market, while a 200-tablet pack (50 foils of 4 tablets) was aimed at larger-scale institutional markets. The four-tablet foil could be easily divided into two by tearing it down the middle to allow retailers to sell fewer tablets at a time at a greater profit per tablet. The 200-tablet package was the largest on the market. A 50-tablet package was introduced in late 1981 consisting of 25 × 2 foils to facilitate street trading.

Objectives of the Introductory Campaign

Daga was launched January 5, 1981. The main objectives for the introduction were as follows:

1. To establish a large and profitable participation in the self-medication market sector, to reduce outstandings, and to improve liquidity via cash sales.
2. To create a high-unit-volume tablet demand to more optimally utilize production capacity when local production is undertaken.
3. To lessen dependency on products containing dipyrone.
4. To sell 25 million tablets for ₦650,000, contributing 4 percent to overall Hoechst pharma sales.

Introductory Advertising and Promotion

One of the very first tasks assigned to Mr. Ford was "Go see an advertising agency about Daga" because, from the outset, management was determined to advertise and promote Daga heavily. The objective was as follows:

> To allocate a substantial promotional budget to fund a multimedia advertising campaign as the highlight in a multifaceted promotional mix to rapidly establish awareness, appeal, and usage at all levels of the population.

The total advertising and promotional budget established for 1981 was as follows:

Television	₦170,000
Radio	115,000
Press	35,000
Billboards	30,000
Samples	10,000
Giveaways	235,000
Promotion production	70,000
Total	₦665,000

According to pharma management, while materialism was a very powerful social force and a parameter of status in Nigeria, income levels prevented 90 percent of the population from purchasing desired goods. In addition, imported goods were very expensive. Merchandising and promotional gimmicks were thought to be strong contributors to a marketing effort. As a result, promotion was a very important expenditure and consisted of virtually everything management could think of. About two months prior to the launch date, salesmen began delivering a Daga announcement letter to wholesalers and retailers. There were a wide variety of giveaway items for the sales force to use. About 200,000 rectangular Daga car stickers were distributed and attached, with preference to taxis and public transport vehicles. Each of the pharma branches was given large Daga van stickers to put on its vehicles and to put on wholesaler trucks. Approximately 200,000 plastic Daga shopping bags were distributed to retail and wholesale customers. The salesmen also used 10,000 Daga key rings. Advertising space was purchased on 7.2 million match boxes, which were distributed by the match box manufacturer to supermarkets and other retail outlets. The NHL company football team was renamed The Daga Boys and outfitted with equipment bearing the Daga name. There were also a variety of promotional items tied to stipulated sales levels. These items included 10,000 large Daga umbrellas, 20,000 Daga caps, and 10,000 Daga T-shirts. For example, the umbrellas were offered in the third quarter, which was the rainy season, to the wholesalers as a bonus gift item in quantities pegged to packs of Daga purchased. The umbrella became a marketplace status symbol. Twenty-five thousand Daga carton cutters, 5,000 Daga cigarette lighters, 10,000 Daga signs for retailers, and a large quantity of wall calendars, small diaries, lampshades, waving hands for car windows, and point-of-purchase display stands were designed and ordered for the 1982 promotional effort.

Advertising was done using all major media. Television in particular was a major departure for competitive practice for pharmaceuticals in Nigeria. The initial 45-second commercial showed a Nigerian husband in bed, complaining of fever and not being able to sleep. His wife, concerned, turns on the light and from a drawer next to the bed pulls out some Daga. The husband takes two tablets and falls asleep. Next morning, the husband wakes up refreshed to greet a happy wife. This commercial, however, did cause some Nigerians to believe that Daga was a sleeping tablet, and before the first year of introduction was over, NHL was asked to stop that commercial. The television campaign began the same day the product was launched because management, the sales force, and several distributors wished to indicate to their customers that NHL was strongly backing the new product and would encourage both selling in and selling through. Both the television and radio audio finished with a haunting echo effect of "Daga . . . Daga . . . Daga," which was later mimicked by street hawkers when selling the product.

Table 4 shows the introductory year media mix for Daga.

Distribution and Selling Activities

Prior to the introduction of Daga, Hoechst had only developed ethical channels using medical representatives. These 13 medical representatives were used in

TABLE 4 Media mix

Medium	Quarter 1	Quarter 2	Quarter 3	Quarter 4
Television:				
National network news at 9 P.M.; in English; 45 seconds each	45 spots	45 spots	45 spots	45 spots
Radio:				
8 regional stations; local dialect; 30 seconds each		8 × 75 spots	8 × 75 spots	8 × 75 spots
Outdoor:				
16-sheet size; in English	110 sites	110 sites	110 sites	110 sites
Press (all English):				
Daily press—3 papers, full page	24	12	12	12
Sunday press—1, ⅛-page strips	0	12	12	12
Monthly Health Journal—1, full page, 2 columns	0	3	3	3

part to distribute Daga to dispensing doctors, hospitals, and pharmacies. For example, the representatives provided doctors and pharmacies with four-tablet Daga sample packs and distributed samples to all the medical meetings throughout Nigeria.

However, in order to reach the mass Nigerian market, NHL recruited 50 OTC wholesalers and hired 15 new van driver/salesmen, who were provided with vans. Each van cost about ₦8,500. These van salesmen were assigned to branch warehouses. The van sales force called on patent medicine stores, street traders—in fact, anyone who would be interested in reselling Daga. These salesmen provided Daga and other products from the van and collected cash on the spot. They also detailed OTC wholesalers and pharmacies. This sales force was paid salary, with a bonus and a chance to compete for one of six places on a two-week trip to Germany sponsored by the company. In addition, other NHL staff were given the opportunity to buy Daga from the company at wholesale prices in order to resell it in their own communities in their spare time.

The launch manual provided to the sales force said the following about customers other than wholesalers:

> Ensure that all other outlets purchase some quantity of Daga, however small, either from us or from our wholesalers. A fully horizontal spread of Daga must be achieved. Like an oil film on water, it only needs to be thin. Later it can be thickened.

More specifically, NHL distribution objectives were as follows:

1. To achieve cash van sales to all major and large OTC retail outlets.
2. To sell one large pack to 15 different retailers per day from January 5 to February 13, using the special introductory offer.
3. To abundantly stock all OTC wholesalers with both pack sizes.
4. To urge OTC wholesalers to push Daga out into their retail outlet networks.

Pricing

The pricing for Daga was established so that the retail price for one tablet was five kobo, roughly the same price as Panadol. NHL sold Daga with the following suggested price schedule:

Pack size	Wholesale	Patent medicine	Retail
20 tablets	₦0.56	₦0.67	₦1.00
200 tablets	5.10	6.00	9.00

For the first six weeks of the introduction, there was an introductory offer, which meant that each time a retailer purchased a 200-tablet pack for ₦6.00 he received a 20-tablet pack free. If the retailer sold all 220 tablets at five kobo each, he would make a profit of ₦5.00. NHL expected that sometimes the salesmen would not pass on the 20-tablet package but instead sell the package and keep the profit. Management believed that the power of the Nigerian profit motive probably contributed significantly during the selling-in exercise.

A 2½ percent discount for cash payment was available to wholesalers who purchased a specified minimum volume of tablets and paid in cash. Most sales were on a cash, not credit, basis.

At the time of introduction, competitive prices were as follows:

Product	Pack size	Wholesale price/pack
Panadol	24 tablets	₦ 0.67
	96	2.67
Cafenol	50	0.59
Novalgin	10	0.82
(ethical)	20	1.43
	1,000	42.50
Phensic	50	0.53
	144	1.40
PR Tabs	10	0.21
	30	0.47
	50	0.75

Daga Results

NHL management initially hoped that 1981 Daga sales would equal the ₦665,000 promotional budget planned. However, sales developed much faster than anticipated, resulting in temporary stockouts of the small pack on two occasions. By year-end, Daga results were roughly three times better than projected, with about 66 million tablets sold. In its first year, Daga accounted for 13 percent of total Hoechst human ethical and OTC turnover, second only to Novalgin, which accounted for 40 percent of turnover with 72 million tablets sold. Table 5 shows quarterly and year-end results as well as projections for 1982.

NHL management predicted that Daga tablet sales would reach ₦5 million by the end of 1983 and ₦8 million by the end of 1986. Total Daga sales including the line extensions were expected to reach ₦15 million by the end of 1986.

Product H

In late 1981, Mr. Ford and Mr. Woerpel had discussed the desirability of a second NHL analgesic positioned in the OTC market to capture additional market share. Mr. Revier thought of it this way:

> The Daga success was wonderful, and Jeff Ford did a fantastic job. Now that I'm here, I have an even more interesting and complicated marketing job. We've got another analgesic of almost equal composition and cost that we hope to market in such a way as to be seen as quite different from Daga. We want as high a share of the analgesic market as we can get because the competition has come alive after Daga's introduction and they're beginning to fight back with advertising and promotion, too. The television stations have more than doubled their rates because of the demand for commercial time.
>
> The introduction of Product H will have to be carefully done because of the possibility of cannibalism with Daga. I think some form of marketing research is essential even though it's tough to do in this country.

Product H already existed. Its composition was aspirin, 200 mg; paracetamol, 200 mg; and caffeine, 50 mg. This meant that Product H delivered pain and fever relief roughly to the same extent as Daga. The caffeine gave the user a lift. "There's not that much difference," remarked Mr. Ford. "It's much

TABLE 5 Daga sales results and projections

Quarter	20s volume (000)	₦ (000)	200s volume (000)	₦ (000)	Total ₦ (000)
1	206	₦117	34	₦176	₦ 293
2	334	193	41	213	406
3	264	153	53	274	427
4	688	400	43	222	622
Total	1,492	₦863	171	₦885	₦1,748

	1981	1982 (estimated)
Gross sales	₦1,748,000	₦3,000,000
Gross margin	874,000	1,485,000
Direct costs	40,000	60,000
Interest costs	50,000	75,000
Promotion	665,000	620,000
Contribution to indirect costs and profit	119,000	760,000

like the distinction between one and two cups of coffee. But it will be noticeable.'' NHL management were intrigued by the product in part because there were no other analgesics of comparable composition and in part because they perceived that ''fast-acting'' would be a claim of interest to Nigerians.

Product H would be produced at the NHL factory, and early indications were that its cost would be less than Daga because the change in formulation favoured the less expensive ingredients. Mr. Revier was working at this point in time with an estimate of 10 percent less for cost of goods sold compared to Daga at its time of introduction.

There were still many questions to answer and decisions to make. For example, Product H could be made in an oblong tablet form and coated with a film to enable easier swallowing. Product H could be packaged in blister packs of clear plastic instead of the aluminum foil packages used when Daga was introduced. Mr. Revier learned that these changes would not change Product H costs in any significant way. Mr. Revier wondered how many tablets should be in a package, how many different package sizes, what name to give the product, and what theme to use to promote it:

> My objective is to gain a sales level of ₦1 million for Product H in its first year after introduction. I estimate the OTC analgesic market will be about ₦49 million in 1983 because of import difficulties expected. I'm not sure how to estimate cannibalism. I do want to increase sales of both Daga and Product H; doing anything else will not be accepted by my superiors.

Mr. Revier was particularly concerned about pricing. Daga had been increased in price to 6.5 kobo per tablet in early 1982 without any apparent problem from customers. This meant that as of early 1982, the following retail prices generally prevailed (note: two tablets was the common dosage for all of the brands):

Novalgin	17.0 kobo per tablet
Daga	6.5
Panadol	5.0
PR Tabs	5.0
Phensic	2.3
Cafenol	1.8
Top Tabs	1.0
Pengo	1.0

Mr. Revier felt he should price Product H in relation to Daga, but he had not decided whether to be above, the same, or below Daga:

> I've got to put together a complete marketing plan for Product H because it will be reviewed here by my superiors and back in Frankfurt by Mr. Helms and others. I know of a major Nigerian marketing institute that maybe could do some research for us in six months if I decide what I want, but I can't wait too long before submitting my plan. Even if I order research, I'll have to start now to prepare my first draft of a plan. And, I have to keep working on Daga, too.

Part 5

Distribution Decisions

Marketers must make decisions on how to present the products they produce to their ultimate purchasers. Most producers do not present their products to end consumers themselves. They tend to make use of wholesalers and retailers.

The marketing decision maker has a number of decisions to make with respect to the distribution of a product. These include:

1. The types of wholesale and retail intermediaries to use.
2. The number of wholesale and retail intermediaries to use of each type.
3. The number of levels in the channel (degree of directness).
4. The ways to motivate existing channel members to perform effectively.

The first cases in this section deal with these issues. Beyond these decisions are a series of decisions concerning the physical distribution of the product. These include: customer service level, inventory size, order quantities, reorder points, warehouse locations, and transportation.

The next section of this note is a short reminder of some of the concepts related to each of these decision points.

Types of Intermediaries

There are many different types of wholesale and retail intermediaries. They vary on the types of products they carry and the services that they are able to perform. The decision on which types of intermediaries to utilize is related to the services that a firm desires to have performed. This is in turn related to the resources and skills of the firm and the needs and behavior of the ultimate consumer.

The Number of Intermediaries

The firm must decide whether to have intensive, selective, or exclusive distribution at the wholesale and retail levels. This decision is related to the quality of support these intermediaries will give in each situation, the ability of the firm to service the intermediaries, and the behavior of the ultimate consumer. For example, a wholesaler whom you want may only be willing to carry your products on an exclusive basis, or you may not be able to afford to contact all the retailers of a particular type. Alternatively, consumers may demand that your product be available at all outlets. This may force you into an intensive distribution situation.

Number of Channel Levels

The decision on how direct a channel from producer to ultimate consumer should be related to the cost of alternative channels, the service and control provided, the characteristics of the end consumer in terms of their numbers and geographic location, the perishability and bulkiness of the product, plus the characteristics of the firm, and competitive activity.

Motivation

Once a channel is selected, motivating its members to perform effectively is an important activity. Motivating vehicles include monetary things such as margins, allowances, and cooperative programs; service activities such as training and technical advice, inventory taking, and display management; and provision of physical items such as racks. Also important here are the interpersonal relationships among the people in the intermediaries and in your firm.

Physical Distribution Management

Physical distribution management is a complex area where management science techniques have become important. In simple terms, the decision maker sets a customer service level (for example, deliver 95 percent of all orders within seven days) and then makes inventory, warehousing, and transportation decisions to reach this service level at minimum cost. The customer service level is set by considering costs, consumer behavior, and competitive activity.

Case 16 _____

Chaebol Electronics Company, U.S.*

In mid-1984, Mr. Park Sung-Il, grandson of the founder of Chaebol Industries, Inc., and president of Chaebol Electronics Company, U.S., was deciding how his company should enter the U.S. videocassette recorder (VCR) market. As of March 1985, the agreement signed by his company—which gave it access to the proprietary technology of the Japanese company Japan Victor Corporation (JVC) for the manufacture of VCRs but limited sales to only the domestic Korean market—would expire. After that date, Chaebol was free to market VCRs worldwide. The decision had already been made to begin selling Chaebol VCRs in the United States as soon as possible. The decision Mr. Park faced was that of marketing his company's VCRs as it was already selling its televisions or positioning this new product line differently, selling it through different channels of distribution.

History of Chaebol Industries, Inc.

Chaebol Industries, Inc., had its beginnings with a small construction firm started by Mr. Park Kyung-Yung in 1945. After gaining several large port construction projects following the Korean War, Mr. Park expanded the firm into shipbuilding and through this into the exporting business. While Chaebol was growing in these areas, other large Korean conglomerates, such as Lucky-Goldstar, Samsung, and Hyundai, diversified their corporations into such fields as chemicals, oil refining, textiles, appliance manufacture, and electronics manufacturing. Each of these firms developed its own foreign distribution capabilities and became very successful in worldwide markets. As a result, these other Korean firms began to become strong competitors for Chaebol's exporting business.

In 1965, Mr. Park Kyung-Yung retired and his son, Mr. Park Taik-Cha, became president of Chaebol. Looking at the successes of his competitors and their impact on Chaebol's business, Mr. Park decided in 1966 that the time had

---

* This case was prepared by Constance M. Kinnear, Research Associate, with the assistance of Thomas C. Kinnear, Professor of Marketing, both at the Graduate School of Business Administration, The University of Michigan. Copyright © 1986 by the authors.

come for Chaebol to expand its areas of operation into the electronics field. In 1967, Chaebol Electronics Company was established, and began producing black-and-white televisions. Room air conditioners, washing machines, refrigerators, and electric typewriters were added to Chaebol's list of products by 1970. As each new product was added to the Chaebol line, it was marketed only in Korea. However, the Korean market consisted of only 41 million people, with a per capita income of just under $2,000 per year. Faced with intense competition from the other large Korean conglomerates for its domestic market, Mr. Park soon became aware that his company would have to begin exporting its products to gain economies of scale in their manufacture.

Mr. Park hoped that Chaebol's long experience in exporting would give it a competitive advantage in foreign markets. To build on this experience, Chaebol first marketed its black-and-white TVs in the United States in 1975 through Johnson Importers of Atlanta, Georgia, the importer that had handled the export goods the company had transported for years. Since this importer was used to handling only low-cost items carried mainly by discounters, Chaebol offered only its lower-cost, lower-priced 12-inch and 19-inch black-and-white models for export. Johnson Importers found a market for 25,000 Chaebol sets in 1975, sold under the PKY brand name, in discount stores in Georgia, Alabama, and Florida. These stores on average priced the 12-inch sets at $105 and the 19-inch sets at $120 each. These stores included a 20 percent margin in these prices. Johnson Importers made a 15 percent margin on its sales of TVs to these outlets. Chaebol priced its 12-inch sets at $71.50 and its 19-inch sets at $81.50 each. Encouraged by this acceptance, Chaebol increased its production capacity in late 1975 from 300,000 to 400,000 sets per year.

In 1976, Johnson Importers was able to increase the sale of PKY sets to a total of 60,000 sets throughout the South. Mr. Park believed that similar success in the sale of Chaebol's TVs could be found in discount chains in other parts of the country. To achieve this, Mr. Park sent two Chaebol sales representatives to establish a sales office and arrange for warehousing facilities in Atlanta. These sales representatives received $25,000 in salary each, and it was budgeted that their sales expenses would come to another $15,000 each per year. These direct Chaebol employees contacted several large discount chains in the Northeast and Midwest. In 1977, sales to these chains, all employing private labels, were 50,000 units, increasing total company sales that year to 115,000 units. In 1978, Chaebol's salespeople were able to land the sale of 100,000 sets to K mart Corporation under K mart's KC brand name. As part of the arrangement for these sales, Chaebol agreed to open a service center to which sets could be sent by the retailer for repair. This center was located in Atlanta. As a result, total sales in 1978 jumped to 240,000 sets. Korean production capacity was increased to 600,000 units per year to handle these sales. In 1979, sales reached 275,000 units. In 1980, with additional private label sales to discounters in the West and constantly increasing sales to previous customers, Chaebol sold 375,000 units.

In 1981, Chaebol increased its number of U.S. sales representatives to five and opened a second sales office, warehouse facility, and service center in

5 × 37,000

Chicago. These sales representatives were now being paid a salary of $37,000 per year and had $20,000 a year in expenses each. Chaebol's salespeople began approaching large department store chains, such as Sears and Montgomery Wards, to increase sales. Again, the TVs sold to these accounts carried the retailers' own labels. 1981 total sales were 450,000 units. Of this total, only 100,000 sets carried the PKY brand name, and these were sold primarily to independent discounters who operated only a few stores each in regional areas.

In 1979, Mr. Park had directed Chaebol to begin manufacturing color TVs. As with Chaebol's previous products, these were first marketed only in Korea. By 1981, Mr. Park was ready to bring three color models, 9-inch, 13-inch, and 19-inch sets, to the United States. The decision to introduce color sets was brought on by a shift in sales patterns in the U.S. marketplace. By 1980, annual total sales of black-and-white TVs was dropping, by an average of 6 percent per year. Along with this drop in total sales, black-and-white set prices were dropping steadily, causing profit margins on the products to fall. Nineteen-inch black-and-white models were no longer desired in the market; buyers preferred to spend their money on a smaller color set than on a large black-and-white set. Furthermore, the color TV market was growing steadily, with growth rates of nearly 15 percent per year. Half of Chaebol's capacity was shifted to color TV production, and within black-and-white sets, 19-inch sets were dropped while small, portable 9-inch sets were added to the line. Cost information on Chaebol's export TV product line in 1981 is shown in Exhibit 1.

Chaebol marketed its color TVs through the same discount channels it was using for its black-and-white models. However, with color, Chaebol's U.S. salespeople were able to have its sets sold using the PKY label at K mart and two other large discounters. Color TV sales began with 100,000 units in 1981 and grew to 300,000 units in 1982. Forty percent of these color sets carried the PKY label. (See Exhibits 2 and 3 for competitive market shares).

120,000 PKY

In late 1982, Chaebol drastically changed its approach to the U.S. TV market. Great pressure in the press was being brought upon Korean TV producers, with many accusations of TV dumping by these companies within

EXHIBIT 1 Cost information on 1981 export television sets

	Black-and-White		Color		
	9-inch	*12-inch*	*9-inch*	*13-inch*	*19-inch*
Direct material	$ 57.85	$32.70	$102.30	$121.35	$147.05
Labor	1.40	1.00	2.40	2.95	3.45
Overhead	2.50	1.40	4.00	5.00	5.80
Transportation	5.10	6.25	5.20	6.30	6.85
Duty	3.15	1.90	5.35	6.40	7.70
Total costs	$ 70.00	$43.25	$119.25	$142.00	$170.85
Chaebol's selling price to channel	$100.00	$60.00	$195.50	$232.00	$280.00
Average retail selling price of Chaebol sets	$125.00	$75.00	$230.00	$290.00	$350.00
Retail price of leading domestic brand	$156.00	$95.00	$271.50	$345.00	$415.00

EXHIBIT 2 Black-and-white TV market—retail brand shares and market size, 1981–1984

	1981	1982	1983	1984
Domestic manufacturers				
RCA	16.3	16.3	15.5	12.5
Zenith	15.5	15.4	13.6	10.2
General Electric	8.9	8.2	8.4	7.5
North American Phillips	5.8	6.9	8.2	10.3
Other domestic	2.6	2.0	2.7	2.7
Total domestic	49.1	48.8	48.4	43.2
Japanese				
Panasonic	6.0	5.9	7.0	8.1
Sony	4.4	3.9	3.5	5.3
Sanyo	3.6	3.2	3.3	3.2
Hitachi	1.3	0.9	0.7	0.5
Sharp	1.0	1.6	1.0	1.4
Toshiba	0.5	0.6	0.2	0.4
Other Japanese	1.0	1.4	0.8	0.4
Total Japanese	17.8	17.5	16.5	19.3
Far East				
Samsung (Korea)	2.1	2.4	2.9	3.5
Goldstar (Korea)	1.8	1.9	2.3	2.5
Chaebol (Korea)	1.7	1.9	2.5	3.3
Other Far East	0.5	0.6	0.9	1.2
Total Far East	6.1	6.8	8.6	10.5
Private label (Sears, J. C. Penney, Montgomery Ward, K mart, etc.)	20.2	20.0	18.5	17.5
All other	6.8	6.9	8.0	9.5
Market size in units (000)	5,806	5,597	5,488	4,717

the U.S. market. In accusing them of dumping, it was being alleged that Korean manufacturers were selling TVs in the United States for prices below those charged for the same product in the domestic market. Mr. Park decided not to wait for the decision from the U.S. International Trade Commission on the dumping charges. He began construction in November 1982 of TV assembly and production facilities in Marietta, Georgia. Initial capacity of 100,000 units per year came online in June 1983. An additional 200,000 units of capacity was scheduled for 1985. Cost figures for 1983 production of 13-inch color TV sets in the United States as compared to in Korea was as follows:

	Korean production	U.S. production
Direct material	$101.20	$113.40
Labor	2.40	5.25
Overhead	4.25	5.85
Transportation	5.85	
Duty	5.35	
Total cost	$119.05	$124.50

EXHIBIT 3 Color TV market—retail brand shares and market size, 1981–1984

	1981	1982	1983	1984
Domestic manufacturers				
RCA	20.0%	20.1%	18.9%	18.1%
Zenith	18.7	18.9	16.8	16.2
General Electric	8.0	7.8	7.6	6.4
North American Phillips	12.4	11.8	10.5	10.2
Other domestic	4.7	3.8	3.9	3.5
Total domestic	64.0	62.4	57.7	54.4
Japanese				
Sony	7.7	6.9	7.5	6.7
Panasonic	2.6	3.7	4.0	3.9
Sharp	1.4	2.0	2.4	3.1
Hitachi	2.5	2.8	2.8	3.0
Sanyo	1.2	1.2	1.7	1.5
Other Japanese	3.1	3.0	3.0	4.2
Total Japanese	18.5	19.6	21.4	22.4
Far East				
Samsung (Korea)	0.2	0.5	1.6	1.6
Gold Star (Korea)	0.5	0.7	0.8	0.9
Chaebol (Korea)	0.7	1.1	1.3	1.7
Other Far East	0.5	0.8	0.7	0.8
Total Far East	1.9	3.1	4.4	5.0
Private label (Sears, J. C. Penney, Montgomery Ward, K mart, etc.)	13.4	12.7	13.2	12.9
All other	2.2	2.2	3.3	5.3
Market size in units (000)	10,641	11,567	13,608	15,646

Even though Chaebol's costs were higher when TVs were produced in the United States, management believed these U.S. costs were approximately 10 percent below those of domestic TV producers.

In conjunction with the establishment of U.S. production facilities, Mr. Park established Chaebol Electronics Company, U.S., and sent his son, Mr. Park Sung-Il, to the United States to head the company. The younger Mr. Park hired six new American sales representatives to work in three new sales offices in Denver, Los Angeles, and New York. Warehouse facilities and service centers were also established in these cities. Chaebol's five warehouses cost an average of $250,000 per year each. Service costs were one-quarter percent of sales in 1984. Mr. Park's goal was to expand TV sales into new markets. In late 1983, Chaebol U.S. succeeded in gaining contracts to sell its TVs in 9-inch black-and-white and 13-inch color to two major catalog showroom companies. These sets were all to carry the PKY label.

Chaebol's sales revenue in 1981 from sales of black-and-white TVs was $36.2 million. In 1983, sales revenue from black-and-white sets was $39.2 million, while sales of color sets brought in $83.75 million. Profit on these 1983 sales was $4.91 million.

EXHIBIT 4 Types of electronics products sales outlets; Number and percent of electronics market sales by type

Type of outlet	1975		1984	
	No. of stores	Percent sales	No. of stores	Percent sales
Radio/TV/appliance	50,152	31.4%	30,004	54.1%
Discount chains	17,887	25.0	5,764	12.4
Department stores	11,240	19.7	4,217	9.3
Furniture stores	38,732	15.9	29,609	3.7
Catalog/mail order	7,671	4.8	16,347	11.8
Auto/home supply	—	—	40,729	3.6
Drug/variety	—	—	60,516	3.3
Home centers	—	—	24,837	1.2
Hardware stores	—	—	19,870	0.6
Other	9,874	3.2	—	—
Total	135,556	100%	231,893	100%

The Electronics Market in 1984

Exhibit 4 shows the types of retail stores that sold electronic products in 1975 and 1984. It also shows the number of each type of store and the percentage of total electronic products sold in the United States in that year by that type of store. As the exhibit shows, there has been a significant increase not only in the total number of outlets selling electronic products but also in the variety of store types that carry this kind of product.

Although Exhibit 4 shows that the total number of radio/TV/appliance stores has greatly decreased since 1975, the importance of this type of outlet within the electronics market grew to the point where radio/TV/appliance stores sold more of these products than all the other outlet types combined. The key characteristics of this type of store were wide selection, low price, and high volume. The major appliance stores stocked virtually every model of every major mass market line. It was common to find up to 150 different TV models and 100 VCRs. The stores advertised low prices and often guaranteed that they would meet any price offered by a competitor in their market area. The salespeople were usually quite knowledgeable and were paid on commission. Thus, they were aggressive in selling their higher-margin models. Price cutting was a necessity, and dealers often bought in large quantity lots, watching for deals, damaged-model sales, and other ways to cut costs. The average margin for this type of outlet was about 22 percent. These stores commonly had extensive service departments.

Discount chains, such as K mart stores, had been handling electronic products for 15 years. They bought in large quantity at lowest possible cost. The manufacturers were usually willing to cut prices in order to obtain large volume orders. Some of the larger chains also engaged in private branding, from which they were able to gain very favorable terms from manufacturers. For example, a U.S. manufacturer who engaged in private branding for one of the large chains obtained an average margin of 19 percent versus 34 percent for national brand sales. Chains usually required the customer to contact the company or independent service facility for warranty service. Some stores supported "service centers," which would simply accept the set and send it on to the manufacturer for repairs. With low overhead and low margins (18 percent), the salespeople were usually few in number and rarely informed about electronics or the differences in major lines. These stores also carried very small lines of a few manufacturers, concentrating for the most part on the low end of the model line.

Department stores carried a limited variety of brands and models of electronic products. They usually did not carry either the lowest- nor the highest-priced models, but concentrated on the largest sales models of well-known brand names. The salespeople were quite knowledgeable, and engaged in a fair amount of trying to get the customer to "trade up." Prices were sometimes discounted, particularly in larger chains. The department stores usually got about a 30 percent margin. In addition, they were eager to seek "deals" on quantity buys, closeouts, and so on. Only the national department store chains, such as Sears, J. C. Penney, and Montgomery Ward, had their own service facilities or carried their own private brands.

Furniture stores were only involved in the sales of console model TVs. Their salespeople were well informed about cabinetry and styling, but usually not too knowledgeable about electronics. These outlets usually sold at suggested retail price, and thus gained about a 37 percent margin on their sales. Furniture stores offered no in-store service facilities. With the introduction of the wide variety of electronic products since 1975, the importance of this type of outlet to the total sales of these products had decreased greatly.

Catalog/mail-order sales outlets usually sold a limited range of models from well-known brands. Unlike department stores, the range of models offered by catalog/mail-order stores went from the lower- to mid-priced models. It was also common for catalogs to offer lesser-known brands that could be priced at a significantly lower price than national brands as long as they offered high quality for that price. Catalog/mail-order outlets usually had a 15 percent margin on sales. Little selling at point of purchase was available. No repair services were offered. This type of sales outlet was of increasing importance for electronic product categories that had reached the point of mass acceptance in the marketplace.

Auto/home supply stores tended to carry only specialty products to fit the needs of small segments of the electronics market. Therefore, models and brands offered limited, and prices and margins were relatively high. Salespeople were very knowledgeable, and these stores often offered repair services.

Drug/variety, home centers, and hardware stores had many characteristics in common. They all carried lower-priced, basic models of electronic products that were commonly purchased only through "special deals" so that low prices were possible. The variety of products and models sold by any given outlet in this group varied greatly from time to time, but usually they carried only radios, small black-and-white TVs, and accessory items like stereo speakers. The

EXHIBIT 5   U.S. videocassette recorder market—retail brand shares, 1984

	1984 share
Domestic manufacturers	
RCA (VHS)	15.1%
General Electric (VHS)	6.2
Quasar (VHS)	5.1
Magnavox (VHS)	4.1
Zenith (VHS/Beta)	3.2
Sylvania (VHS)	1.4
Curtis-Mathes (VHS)	1.3
Total domestic	36.4%
Japanese	
Panasonic (VHS)	12.8
Sony (Beta)	6.8
Sanyo (Beta)	6.3
Sharp (VHS)	4.6
Hitachi (VHS)	3.7
MGA (VHS)	2.7
JVC (VHS)	4.1
Toshiba (Beta)	1.6
Total Japanese	42.6%
Private label	9.5%
Other	11.1%

VCR market—Number of brands and models and price ranges by type of outlet

Type of outlet	*No. of brands offered*	*No. of models offered*	*Price range*
Radio/TV/appliance	12	60	$259–$1,100
Discount chains	5	7	$257–$459
Department stores			
National chains	3	11	$269–$599
Regionals and independents	6	12	$399–$799
Catalog/Mail-order stores	6	9	$278–$650

salespeople at these outlets had little knowledge of electronics. Margins for this group averaged 25 percent. No service facilities were offered on these products.

The VCR Market in 1984

The VCR market in the United States had grown very quickly from the time of the product's introduction in 1979. In 1981, 1.7 million units were sold. This number grew to 2.0 million units in 1982, 3.75 million units in 1983, and nearly 7.5 million units in 1984. The market shares of the major firms selling VCRs in 1984 are shown in the first part of Exhibit 5. The second part of the exhibit shows the number of brands and models of VCRs sold at each type of electronics outlet and the range of prices charged at each kind of store in 1984. Of the units sold in 1984, 48 percent sold for under $500, 20 percent for between $501 and $600, 17 percent for between $601 and $800, 13 percent for between $801 and $1,000, and only 2 percent for more than $1,000. The average price of VCRs sold in the United States had dropped by over $550 since their introduction in 1979. Typical features offered on low-, medium-, and high-priced VCRs in 1984 are shown below:

Low-priced models (under $400)	Medium-priced models ($400–$750)	High-priced models (over $750)
2 video heads	2 video heads	4 video heads
1 audio head	1 audio head	2 audio heads—stereo, hi-fi
Varactor tuner (preset 12–14 channels)	Varactor tuner (preset 80–99 channels)	Direct access quartz tuner
1-event/7-day programmability	4-event/14-day programmability	8-event/1-year programmability
8-hour/3-speed recording	8-hour/3-speed recording	8-hour/3-speed recording
8-function remote (many wired)	10-function wireless remote	13–17 function wireless remote
Not cable ready	107-channel cable capability	133-channel cable capability

The total U.S. market for VCRs in 1985 was expected to be between 11 and 12 million units. With this level of sales, VCRs will have succeeded in penetrating 25 percent of the product's total market potential (households with televisions) by the end of 1985. Because of the quickness with which VCR sales reached this sales level, industry analysts did not foresee much future growth for the product line, although they did predict sales levels maintaining a 10 million to 11 million unit-per-year pace for the next five years.

The quick growth of VCR sales has had long-reaching effects on the development of the market for these products. After only five years on the market, the demographics of VCR buyers were already broadening. Originally, VCRs were most commonly purchased by upper-income (over $32,000), well-educated, married heads of household between the ages of 35 and 49. In 1984, 27 percent of VCR units were purchased by 18-to-24-year-old singles with average income between $27,000 and $32,000. The amazing sales growth of VCRs attracted many new entrants to the market each year, so that by 1984 there were over 70 VCR brands available. Many brands offered extensive VCR lines. For example, RCA, the market share leader, offered 25 VCR models ranging in suggested retail price from $330 to $1,300. The more entrants there were to the market, the stronger price competition became. This led to progressively lower and lower margins and profitability for both manufacturers and retailers. This margin loss was greatest on the lower-price-range products. To counteract this, many manufacturers were adding VCRs with greater features and capabilities to their lines—VCRs that were higher priced but also more profitable.

In late 1984, market analysts expressed the belief that Korean VCR manufacturers would enter the U.S. market using the same strategy that had gained them market share in TV sales: that of offering low-priced products that would allow them to take advantage of their lower labor costs. Thus, their expectations were that Korean VCRs would be priced $50 to $75 below the

1984 $400 mid-priced Japanese units with the same features. Furthermore, analysts believed that this kind of price differential would require retailers to pick up the Korean models. However, many analysts felt retailers would only carry these models as advertising draws and would often try to get customers to buy up from these low-priced VCRs to more profitable models.

Chaebol's Decision

Mr. Park Sung-Il had narrowed down Chaebol's VCR entry strategy to between one of two alternatives.

Strategy I

The first entry strategy alternative involved using distribution channels and retail outlets for VCRs similar to those Chaebol had employed for TV sales. For VCRs, Mr. Park wanted to limit distribution to only high-volume buyers. Thus, if this strategy was employed, Chaebol would only seek sales to large discount chains and catalog/mail-order retailers. Mr. Park planned to produce three models for these outlets. All would be two video head, one audio head models, with varactor tuning allowing 12 stations to be preset. The lowest-cost model, Model CHA, would also feature one-event/one-week programmability, wired remote, auto rewind, and would not be cable ready. Model CHA would cost Chaebol $143.50 to produce. The next step up in Chaebol's offerings would be Model CHB, which would have 1-event/14-day programmability, an eight-function wireless remote, auto rewind, and be cable ready. Model CHB would cost $201 to manufacture. Model CHC, the highest-priced model offered under this strategy, would feature 1-event/14-day programmability, 12-function remote control, auto rewind, frame advance, a sharpness control, and would be cable ready. Model CHC would cost Chaebol $247.90. Mr. Park believed Chaebol's costs on these products would allow its customers to price these models 15 percent below similar VCRs on the market.

Since Chaebol salespeople were already calling on these customers, Mr. Park believed this alternative would have few additional costs over Chaebol's present expenses. Additional warehouse space and service personnel would have to be acquired, but no new sales offices would be needed. Mr. Park believed that most of these sales would be low-priced, private brand VCRs, although he hoped that those customers who were purchasing PKY brand TVs would purchase PKY brand name VCRs. Mr. Park estimated he could sell 225,000 VCRs in 1985 with this strategy, 70,000 carrying the PKY name. He believed private label sales would carry a 27 percent gross margin for Chaebol, while the PKY brand sales would bring a 34 percent gross margin.

Strategy II

Mr. Park's alternative to the above strategy was to use Chaebol's cost advantage, arising from lower labor coats than either U.S. or Japanese competitors, to

association with PKY?

gain admission to the TV/radio/appliance outlets that had the largest share of VCR sales and sold only brand name products. Mr. Park believed Chaebol's cost advantage would allow it to produce VCRs that carried more features than competitors' products at each price point in the market. Selling VCRs in this channel would enable Chaebol's products to be distinguished from the 50 or more brands of low-cost, low-priced VCRs, and firmly establish the PKY brand name. In the future, he hoped to move Chaebol TVs into this channel where there were higher margins for producers and retailers. His dream was to have the PKY brand obtain the same quality reputation that Sony and Panasonic had achieved.

The models Chaebol would offer under this strategy were as follows:

Model	Chaebol cost	Features
CHC	$247.90	Two video heads, 1 audio head, 1-event/14-day programmability, varactor tuning for 12 preset stations, 12-function wireless remote, auto rewind, frame advance, sharpness control.
CH1A	$286.15	Two video heads, 2 audio heads, stereo, 5-event/14-day programmability, varactor tuning for 50 preset stations, 14-function wireless remote, auto rewind, tape memory, memory backup, time-remaining indicator, 107-channel cable ready.
CH1B	$367.90	Four video heads, 2 audio heads, stereo/hi-fi/Dolby, 8-event/1-year programmability, quartz tuning, 133-channel cable ready, 17-function wireless remote, auto rewind, tape memory, time-remaining indicator, one-touch recording, slow motion, frame advance, video dub, audio dub, sharpness control.
CH1P	$388.30	All of the features of the CH1B Model plus portable.

Mr. Park estimated that these models would sell at retail for considerably less than competitive products with similar features. On Model CH1B, he believed the retail price difference could be as much as $350. With this kind of differential, Mr. Park believed he would find many TV/radio/appliance store-owners eager to take on his products since they would allow the retailer to gain larger margins than other brands. Chaebol expected to make nearly a 44 percent gross margin on models sold to this type of outlet.

Mr. Park was considering two approaches to getting his company's VCRs in TV/radio/appliance outlets. The first was to sell directly to the owners of these stores. This approach would require a significant expansion of Chaebol's marketing organization. Since the number of TV/radio/appliance stores to be reached was large and geographically dispersed, new sales offices would have to be established in Boston, Indianapolis, Dallas, St. Louis, and Seattle. Each sales office would have three salespeople. In addition, three regional sales managers would have to be hired to help organize the now diverse and large sales function of the company. Furthermore, the establishment of a high recognition for Chaebol's PKY brand name would have to come from extensive advertising. Mr. Park estimated that the expenditure of $6 million on advertising in 1985 would be minimal to achieve the results he desired.

+5

As an alternative, Mr. Park knew this market could also be approached through the employment of distributors who were already selling the VCRs of other manufacturers to TV/radio/appliance stores. Under this plan, no new sales offices would need to be opened, but one new salesperson would be added to the staff of each existing office. These five salespeople would be charged with maintaining relationships with the 10 geographically dispersed consumer electronics distributors that Chaebol's head office would choose to carry its VCRs. These distributors would work first on getting PKY brand VCRs into the largest regional and national TV/radio/appliance chains. Chaebol's salespeople would also call on PKY retailers in their areas, working on incentive programs with outlet salespeople, solving any problems that might arise, and checking that the services expected from the distributors were being adequately performed. Using distributors would cost Chaebol 11 percent of its margin; that is, the distributors would get an 11 percent margin on sales while Chaebol's margin would drop to approximately 33 percent on these sales. Under this approach, no additional warehouses over those proposed under Strategy I would be required. However, since this approach required the establishment of the PKY brand name, the advertising cost of $6 million would still be necessary.

Mr. Park believed Chaebol could achieve sales of 120,000 VCRs in 1985 using the direct approach and 150,000 VCRs using distributors. Though these figures were lower than the initial sales that could be achieved under the first strategy, Mr. Park believed the long-term strength of the company was better served by the firm establishment of a brand name and a strong position in TV/radio/appliance outlets.

A comparison of the costs involved in the plans considered by Mr. Park is shown in the table below:

Expense area	Cost of each new unit	Strategy I	Strategy II	
			Direct	Distributors
Sales offices	$ 25,000/yr.	—	5	—
Salespeople	$ 42,000/yr. salary			
	$ 23,000/yr. expenses	—	18	5
Warehouses	$300,000/yr.	3	5	3
Service facilities		.25% sales	.33 sales	.33 sales
Average margins		27%, 34%	44%	33%
Advertising		$1.5 million	$6 million	$6 million

As Mr. Park worked on estimating the relative costs of these alternatives, he wondered if there was another approach to the market that might lead to success both now and in the future for Chaebol Electronics Company, U.S.

Thompson Respiration Products, Inc.*

Victor Higgins, executive vice president for Thompson Respiration Products, Inc. (TRP), sat thinking at his desk late one Friday in April 1986. "We're making progress," he said to himself. "Getting Metro to sign finally gets us into the Chicago Market . . . and with a good dealer at that." *Metro,* of course, was Metropolitan Medical Products, a large Chicago retailer of medical equipment and supplies for home use. "Now, if we could just do the same in Minneapolis and Atlanta," he continued.

However, getting at least one dealer in each of these cities to sign a TRP Dealer Agreement seemed remote right now. One reason was the sizeable groundwork required—Higgins simply lacked the time to review operations at the well over 100 dealers currently operating in the two cities. Another was TRP's lack of dealer-oriented sales information that went beyond the technical specification sheet for each product and the company's price list. Still another concerned two conditions in the Dealer Agreement itself—prospective dealers sometimes balked at agreeing to sell no products manufactured by TRP's competitors and differed with TRP in interpretations of the "best efforts" clause. (The clause required the dealer to maintain adequate inventories of TRP products, contact four prospective new customers or physicians or respiration therapists per month, respond promptly to sales inquiries, and represent TRP at appropriate conventions where it exhibited.)

"Still," Higgins concluded, "we signed Metro in spite of these reasons, and 21 others across the country. That's about all anyone could expect—after all, we've only been trying to develop a dealer network for a year or so."

The Portable Respirator Industry

The portable respirator industry began in the early 1950s when polio-stricken patients who lacked control of muscles necessary for breathing began to leave

* This case was written by Professor James E. Nelson and DBA Candidate William R. Woolridge, the University of Colorado. This case illustrates neither effective nor ineffective administrative decision making. Some data are disguised. © 1984 by the Business Research Division, College of Business and Administration and the Graduate School of Business Administration, University of Colorado.

treatment centers. They returned home with hospital-style iron lungs or fiberglass chest shells, both being large chambers that regularly introduced a vacuum about the patient's chest. The vacuum caused the chest to expand and, thus, the lungs to fill with air. However, both devices confined patients to a prone or semiprone position in a bed.

By the late 1950s, TRP had developed a portable turbine blower powered by an electric motor and battery. When connected to a mouthpiece via plastic tubing, the blower would inflate a patient's lungs on demand. Patients could now leave their beds for several hours at a time and realize limited mobility in a wheelchair. By the early 1970s, TRP had developed a line of more sophisticated turbine respirators in terms of monitoring and capability for adjustment to individual patient needs.

At about the same time, applications began to shift from polio patients to victims of other diseases or of spinal cord injuries, the latter group existing primarily as a result of automobile accidents. Better emergency medical service, quicker evacuation to spinal cord injury centers, and more proficient treatment meant that people who formerly would have died now lived and went on to lead meaningful lives. Because of patients' frequently younger ages, they strongly desired wheelchair mobility. Respiration therapists obliged by recommending a Thompson respirator for home use or, if unaware of Thompson, recommending a Puritan-Bennett or other machine.

Instead of a turbine, Puritan-Bennett machines used a bellows design to force air into the patient's lungs. The machines were widely used in hospitals but seemed poorly suited for home use. For one thing, Puritan-Bennett machines used a compressor pump or pressurized air to drive the bellows, much more cumbersome than Thompson's electric motor. Puritan-Bennett machines also cost approximately 50 percent more than a comparable Thompson unit and were relatively large and immobile. On the other hand, Puritan-Bennett machines were viewed by physicians and respiration therapists as industry standards.

By the late 1970s, TRP had developed a piston and cylinder design (similar in principle to the bellows) and placed it on the market. The product lacked the sophistication of the Puritan-Bennett machines but was reliable, portable, and much simpler to adjust and operate. It also maintained TRP's traditional cost advantage. Another firm, Life Products, began its operations in 1981 by producing a similar design. A third competitor, Lifecare Services, had begun operations somewhat earlier.

Puritan-Bennett

Puritan-Bennett was a large, growing, and financially sound manufacturer of respiration equipment for medical and aviation applications. Its headquarters were located in Kansas City, Missouri. However, the firm staffed over 40 sales, service, and warehouse operations in the United States, Canada, United Kingdom, and France. Sales for 1985 exceeded $100 million while employment was just over 2,000 people. Sales for its Medical Equipment Group (respirators, related equipment, and accessories, service, and parts) likely exceeded $40 million for 1985; however, Higgins could obtain data only for the period 1977–1980 (see Exhibit 1). Puritan-Bennett usually sold its respirators through a system of independent, durable medical equipment dealers. However, its sales offices did sell directly to identified "house accounts" and often competed with dealers by selling slower-moving products to all accounts. According to industry sources, Puritan-Bennett sales were slightly more than three fourths of all respirator sales to hospitals in 1985.

However, these same sources expected Puritan-Bennett's share to diminish during the late 1980s because of the aggressive marketing efforts of three other manufacturers of hospital-style respirators: Bear Medical Systems, Inc.; J. H. Emerson; and Siemens-Elema. The latter firm was expected to grow the most rapidly, despite its quite recent entry into the U.S. market (its headquarters were in Sweden) and a list price of over $16,000 for its basic model.

Life Products

Life Products directly competed with TRP for the portable respirator market. Life Products had begun operations in 1981 when David Smith, a TRP employee, left to start his own business. Smith had located his plant in Boulder, Colorado, less than a mile from TRP headquarters.

He began almost immediately to set up a dealer network and by early 1986 had secured over 40 independent dealers located in large metropolitan areas. Smith had made a strong effort to sign only large, well-managed durable medical equipment dealers. Dealer representatives were required to complete Life Product's service training school, held each month in Boulder. Life Products sold its products to dealers (in contrast to TRP, which both sold and rented

EXHIBIT 1 Puritan-Bennett Medical Equipment Group sales

	1981	1982	1983	1984
Domestic sales:				
Model MA-1:				
Units	1,460	875	600	500
Amount ($ millions)	8.5	4.9	3.5	3.1
Model MA-2:				
Units	—	935	900	1,100
Amount ($ millions)	—	6.0	6.1	7.8
Foreign sales:				
Units	250	300	500	565
Amount ($ millions)	1.5	1.8	3.1	3.6
IPPB equipment ($ millions)	6.0	6.5	6.7	7.0
Parts, service, accessories				
($ millions)	10.0	11.7	13.1	13.5
Overhaul ($ millions)	2.0	3.0	2.5	2.5
Total ($ millions)	28.0	34.0	35.0	37.5

Source: The Wall Street Transcript.

products to consumers and to dealers). Dealers received a 20 to 25 percent discount off suggested retail price on most products.

As of April 1986, Life Products offered two respirator models (the LP3 and LP4) and a limited number of accessories (such as mouthpieces and plastic tubing) to its dealers. Suggested retail prices for the two respirator models were approximately $3,900 and $4,800. Suggested rental rates were approximately $400 and $500 per month. Life Products also allowed Lifecare Services to manufacture a respirator similar to the LP3 under license.

At the end of 1985, Smith was quite pleased with his firm's performance. During Life Products' brief history, it had passed TRP in sales and now ceased to see the firm as a serious threat, at least according to one company executive:

> We really aren't in competition with Thompson. They're after the stagnant market and we're after a growing market. We see new applications and ultimately the hospital market as our niche. I doubt if Thompson will even be around in a few years. As for Lifecare, their prices are much lower than ours but you don't get the service. With them you get the basic product, but nothing else. With us, you get a complete medical care service. That's the big difference.

Lifecare Services, Inc.

In contrast to the preceding firms, Lifecare Services, Inc. earned much less of its revenues from medical equipment manufacturing and much more from medical equipment distributing. The firm primarily resold products purchased from other manufacturers, operating out of its headquarters in Boulder as well as from its 16 field offices (Exhibit 2). All offices were stocked with backup parts and an inventory of respirators. All were staffed with trained service technicians under Lifecare's employ.

Lifecare did manufacture a few accessories not readily available from other manufacturers. These items complemented the purchased products and, in the company's words, served to "give the customer a complete respiratory service." Under a licensing agreement between Lifecare and Life Products, the firm manufactured a respirator similar to the LP3 and marketed it under the Lifecare name. The unit rented for approximately $175 per month. While

EXHIBIT 2 Lifecare Services, Inc., field offices

Augusta, Ga.	Houston, Tex.
Baltimore, Md.	Los Angeles, Calif.
Boston, Mass.	New York, N.Y.
Chicago, Ill.	Oakland, Calif.
Cleveland, Ohio	Omaha, Nebr.
Denver, Colo.	Phoenix, Ariz.
Detroit, Mich.	Seattle, Wash.
Grand Rapids, Mich.*	St. Paul, Minn.

* Suboffice.
Source: Trade literature.

Lifecare continued to service the few remaining Thompson units it still had in the field, it no longer carried the Thompson line.

Lifecare rented rather than sold its equipment. The firm maintained that this gave patients more flexibility in the event of recovery or death and lowered patients' monthly costs.

Thompson Respiration Products, Inc.

TRP currently employed 13 people, 9 in production and 4 in management. It conducted operations in a modern, attractive building (leased) in an industrial park. The building contained about 6,000 square feet of space, split 75/25 for production/management purposes. Production operations were essentially job shop in nature: skilled technicians assembled each unit by hand on work benches, making frequent quality control tests and subsequent adjustments. Production lots usually ranged from 10 to 75 units per model and probably averaged around 40. Normal production capacity was about 600 units per year.

Product Line

TRP currently sold seven respirator models plus a large number of accessories. All respirator models were portable but differed considerably in terms of style, design, performance specifications, and attendant features (see Exhibit 3). Four models were styled as metal boxes with an impressive array of knobs, dials, indicator lights, and switches. Three were styled as less imposing, "overnighter" suitcases with less prominently displayed controls and indicators. (Exhibit 4 reproduces part of the specification sheet for the M3000, as illustrative of the metal box design.)

Four of the models were designed as *pressure machines,* using a turbine pump that provided a constant, usually positive, pressure. Patients were provided intermittent access to this pressure as breaths per minute. However, one model, the MV Multivent, could provide either a constant positive or a constant negative pressure (i.e., a vacuum, necessary to operate chest shells, iron lungs, and body wraps). No other portable respirator on the market could produce a negative pressure. Three of the models were designed as *volume machines,* using a piston pump that produced intermittent, constant volumes of pressurized air as breaths per minute. Actual volumes were prescribed by each patient's physician based on lung capacity. Pressures depended on the breathing method used (mouthpiece, trach, chest shell, and others) and on the patient's activity level. Breaths per minute also depended on the patient's activity level.

Models came with several features. The newest was an assist feature (currently available on the Minilung M25 but soon to be offered also on the M3000) that allowed the patient alone to "command" additional breaths without having someone change the dialed breath rate. The sigh feature gave patients a sigh, either automatically or on demand. Depending on the model, up to six alarms were available to indicate a patient's call, unacceptable low pressure, un-

EXHIBIT 3 TRP respirators

Model*	Style	Design	Volume (cc)	Pressure (cm. H_2O)
M3000	Metal box	Volume	300–3,000	+10 to +65
MV Multivent	Metal box	Pressure (positive or negative)	n.a.	−70 to +80
Minilung M15	Suitcase	Volume	200–1,500	+5 to +65
Minilung M25 Assist (also available without the assist feature)	Suitcase	Volume	600–2,500	+5 to +65
Bantam GS	Suitcase	Pressure (positive)	n.a.	+15 to +45
Compact CS	Metal box	Pressure (positive)	n.a.	+15 to +45
Compact C	Metal box	Pressure (positive)	n.a.	+15 to +45

Model	Breaths per minute	Weight (lbs.)	Size (ft.³)	Features
M3000	6 to 30	39	0.85	Sigh, four alarms, automatic switchover from AC to battery
MV Multivent	8 to 24	41	1.05	Positive or negative pressure, four alarms, AC only
Minilung M15	8 to 22	24	0.70	Three alarms, automatic switchover from AC to battery
Minilung M25 Assist (also available without the assist feature)	5 to 20	24	0.70	Assist, sigh, three alarms, automatic switchover from AC to battery
Bantam GS	6 to 24	19	0.75	Sigh, six alarms, automatic switchover from AC to battery
Compact CS	8 to 24	25	0.72	Sigh, six alarms, automatic switchover from AC to battery
Compact C	6 to 24	19	0.50	Sigh, four alarms, automatic switchover from AC to battery

Note: n.a. = not applicable.

* Five other models considered obsolete by TRP could be supplied if necessary.

Source: Company sales specification sheets.

acceptable high pressure, low battery voltage/power failure, failure to cycle, and the need to replace motor brushes. All models but the MV Multivent also offered automatic switchover from alternating current to either an internal or an external battery (or both) in the event of a power failure. Batteries provided for 18 to 40 hours of operation, depending on usage.

Higgins felt that TRP's respirators were superior to those of Life Products. Most TRP models allowed pressure monitoring in the airway itself rather than in the machine, providing more accurate measurement. TRP's suitcase-style models often were strongly preferred by patients, especially the polio patients who had known no others. TRP's volume models offered easier volume adjustments and all TRP models offered more alarms. On the other hand, he knew that TRP had recently experienced some product reliability problems of an irritating—not life threatening—nature. Further, he knew that Life Products had beaten TRP to the market with the assist feature (the idea for which had come from a Puritan-Bennett machine).

EXHIBIT 4 The M3000 Minilung

THOMPSON

M3000 MINILUNG

PORTABLE VOLUME VENTILATOR

What it can mean to the User...

• The M3000 is a planned performance product designed to meet breathing needs. It is a significant step in the ongoing effort of a company which pioneered the advancement of portable respiratory equipment.

• This portable volume ventilator sets high standards for flexibility of operation and versatility in use. The M3000 has gained its successful reputation as a result of satisfactory usage in hospitals, for transport, in rehabilitation efforts and in home care. This model grew out of expressed needs of users for characteristics which offer performance PLUS. It is engineered to enable the user to have something more than just mechanical breathing.

• Now breathing patterns can be comfortably varied with the use of a SIGH, which can be obtained either automatically or manually.

• Besides being sturdy and reliable, the M3000 can be adjusted readily.

• Remote pressure sensing in the proximal airway provides for more accurate set up of the ventilator pressure alarms.

• This model has the option of a patient-operated call switch.

• AC-DC operation of the M3000 is accomplished with ease because automatic switch-over is provided on AC power failure, first to external battery, then to internal battery.

THOMPSON takes pride in planning ahead.

See reverse for specifications.

Innovators in Respiratory Equipment for Over 25 Years
Thompson Respiration Products, Inc.   1680 Range Street   Boulder Colorado 80301   303/443-3350

M3000 MINILUNG
Portable Volume Ventilator

SPECIFICATIONS:

300 to 3000 ml adjustable volume

10 to 65 cm. water pressure

6 to 30 breaths per minute

Automatic or Manual Sigh

Alarms:
  Patient operated call alarm
  Low Pressure alarm and light
  High Pressure alarm and light
  Low Voltage light with delayed alarm
  Automatic switchover provided on AC power failure, first to external battery, then to internal battery
  Alarm delay switch

Pilot lamps color-coded and labeled

Remote pressure connector

Self-contained battery for 2 hour operation — recharges automatically

Power sources:
  120 volt, 60 hz; 12 volt external battery; and internal battery

Size: 12⅝ W x 11¼ D x 10¾ inches H

Weight: 39 pounds (Shipping weight: 48 pounds)

EXHIBIT 5 TRP dealer locations

Bakersfield, Calif.	Salt Lake City, Utah
Baltimore, Md.	San Diego, Calif.
Birmingham, Ala.	San Francisco, Calif.
Chicago, Ill.	Seattle, Wash.
Cleveland, Ohio	Springfield, Ohio
Fort Wayne, Ind.	Tampa, Fla.
Greenville, N.C.	Tucson, Ariz.
Indianapolis, Ind.	Washington, D.C.
Newark, N.J.	
Oklahoma City, Okla.	Montreal, Canada
Pittsburgh, Pa.	Toronto, Canada

Source: Company records.

TRP's line of accessories was more extensive than that of Life Products. TRP offered the following for separate sale: alarms, call switches, battery cables, chest shells, mouthpieces, plastic tubing, pneumobelts and bladders (equipment for still another breathing method that utilized intermittent pressure on a patient's diaphragm), and other items. Lifecare Services offered many similar items.

Distribution

Shortly after joining TRP, Higgins had decided to switch from selling and renting products directly to patients to selling and renting products to dealers. While it meant lower margins, less control, and more infrequent communication with patients, the change had several advantages. It allowed TRP to shift inventory from the factory to the dealer, generating cash more quickly. It provided for local representation in market areas, allowing patients greater feelings of security and TRP more aggressive sales efforts. It shifted burdensome paperwork (required by insurance companies and state and federal agencies to effect payment) from TRP to the dealer. It also reduced other TRP administrative activities in accounting, customer relations, and sales.

TRP derived about half of its 1985 revenue of $3 million directly from patients and about half from the dealer network. By April 1986, the firm had 22 dealers (see Exhibit 5) with 3 accounting for over 60 percent of TRP dealer revenues. Two of the three serviced TRP products as did two of the smaller dealers; the rest preferred to let the factory take care of repairs. TRP conducted occasional training sessions for dealer repair personnel but distances were great and turnover in the position high, making such sessions costly. Most dealers requested air shipment of respirators, in quantities of 1 or 2 units.

EXHIBIT 6 Current TRP respirator price list

| | Suggested retail | | Dealer Rent/month | Dealer price | |
Model	Rent/month	Price		1–2	3 or more
M3000	$380	$6,000	$290	$4,500	$4,185
MV Multivent	270	4,300	210	3,225	3,000
Minilung M15	250	3,950	190	2,960	2,750
Minilung M25	250	3,950	190	2,960	2,750
Bantam GS	230	3,600	175	2,700	2,510
Compact CS	230	3,600	175	2,700	2,510
Compact C	200	3,150	155	2,360	2,195

Source: Company sales specification sheets.

Price

TRP maintained a comprehensive price list for its entire product line. (Exhibit 6 reproduces part of the current list.) Each respirator model carried both a suggested retail selling price and a suggested retail rental rate. (TRP also applied these rates when it dealt directly with patients.) The list also presented two net purchase prices for each model along with an alternative rental rate that TRP charged to dealers. About 40 percent of the 300 respirator units TRP shipped to dealers in 1985 went out on a rental basis. The comparable figure for the 165 units sent directly to consumers was 90 percent. Net purchase prices allowed an approximate 7 percent discount for orders of three or more units of each model. Higgins had initiated this policy early last year with the aim of encouraging dealers to order in larger quantities. To date one dealer had taken advantage of this discount.

Current policy called for TRP to earn a gross margin of approximately 35 percent on the dealer price for 1–2 units. All prices included shipping charges by United Parcel Service (UPS); purchasers requesting more expensive transportation service paid the difference between actual costs incurred and the UPS charge. Terms were net 30 days with a 1.5 percent service charge added to past due accounts. Prices were last changed in late 1985.

Consumers

Two types of patients used respirators, depending on whether the need followed from disease or from injury. Diseases such as polio, sleep apnea, chronic obstructive pulmonary disease, and muscular dystrophy annually left about 1,900 victims unable to breathe without a respirator. Injury to the spinal cord above the fifth vertebra caused a similar result for about 300 people per year. Except for polio, incidences of the diseases and injury were growing at about 3 percent per year. Most patients kept one respirator at bedside and another mounted on a wheelchair. However, Higgins did know of one individual who kept eight

Bantam B models (provided by a local polio foundation, now defunct) in his closet. Except for polio patients, life expectancies were about five years. Higgins estimated the total number of patients using a home respirator in 1981 at

Polio	3,000
Other diseases	6,500
Spinal cord injury	1,000

Almost all patients were under a physician's care as well as that of a more immediate nurse or attendant (frequently a relative). About 95 percent paid for their equipment through insurance benefits or foundation monies. About 90 percent rented their equipment. Almost all patients and their nurses or attendants had received instruction in equipment operation from respiration therapists employed by medical centers or by dealers of durable medical equipment.

The majority of patients were poor. Virtually none were gainfully employed and all had seen their savings and other assets diminished to varying degrees by treatment costs. Some had experienced a divorce. Slightly more patients were male than female. About 75 percent lived in their homes with the rest split between hospitals, nursing homes, and other institutions.

Apart from patients, Higgins thought that hospitals might be considered a logical new market for TRP to enter. Many of the larger and some of the smaller general hospitals might be convinced to purchase one portable respirator (like the M3000) for emergency and other use with injury patients. Such a machine would be much cheaper to purchase than a large Puritan-Bennett and would allow easier patient trips to testing areas, X-ray, surgery, and the like. Even easier to convince should be the fourteen regional spinal cord injury centers located across the country (Exhibit 7). Other medical centers that specialized in treatment of pulmonary diseases should also be prime targets. Somewhat less promising but more numerous would be public and private schools that trained physicians and respiration therapists. Higgins estimated the numbers of these institutions at:

EXHIBIT 7 Regional spinal cord injury centers

Birmingham, Ala.	Houston, Tex.
Boston, Mass.	Miami, Fla.
Chicago, Ill.	New York, N.Y.
Columbia, Mo.	Philadelphia, Pa.
Downey, Calif.	Phoenix, Ariz.
Englewood, Colo.	San Jose, Calif.
Fishersville, Va.	Seattle, Wash.

General hospitals (100 beds or more)	3,800
General hospitals (fewer than 100 beds)	3,200
Spinal cord injury centers	14
Pulmonary disease treatment centers	100
Medical schools	180
Respiration therapy schools	250

Dealers

Dealers supplying homecare medical products (as distinct from dealers supplying hospitals and medical centers) showed a great deal of diversity. Some were little more than small areas in local drugstores that rented canes, walkers, and wheelchairs in addition to selling supplies like surgical stockings and colostomy bags. Others carried nearly everything needed for home nursing care—renting everything from canes to hospital beds and selling supplies from bed pads to bottled oxygen. Still others specialized in products and supplies for only certain types of patients.

In this latter category, Higgins had identified dealers of oxygen and oxygen-related equipment as the best fit among existing dealers. These dealers serviced victims of emphysema, bronchitis, asthma, and other respiratory ailments, a growing market that Higgins estimated was about 10 times greater than that for respirators. A typical dealer had begun perhaps 10 years ago selling bottled oxygen (obtained from a welding supply wholesaler) and renting rather crude metering equipment to patients at home under the care of a registered nurse. The same dealer today now rented and serviced oxygen concentrators (a recently developed device that extracts oxygen from the air), liquid oxygen equipment and liquid oxygen, and much more sophisticated oxygen equipment and oxygen to patients cared for by themselves or by relatives.

Most dealers maintained a fleet of radio-dispatched trucks to deliver products to their customers. Better dealers promised 24-hour service and kept delivery personnel and a respiration therapist on call 24 hours a day. Dealers usually employed several respiration therapists who would set up equipment, instruct patients and attendants on equipment operation, and provide routine and emergency service. Dealers often expected the therapists to function as a sales force. The therapists would call on physicians and other respiration therapists at hospitals and medical centers, on discharge planners at hospitals, and on organizations such as muscular dystrophy associations, spinal cord injury associations, and visiting nurse associations.

Dealers usually bought their inventories of durable equipment and supplies directly from manufacturers. They usually received a 20 to 25 percent discount off suggested list prices to consumers and hospitals. Only in rare instances might dealers instead lease equipment from a manufacturer. Dealers aimed for a payback of one year or less, meaning that most products began to contribute to profit and overhead after 12 months of rental. Most products lasted physically for upwards of 10 years but technologically for only 5 to 6: every dealer's warehouse contained idle but perfectly suitable equipment that had been superseded by models demanded by patients, their physicians, or their attendants.

Most dealers were independently owned and operated, with annual sales ranging between $5 million and $10 million. However, a number had recently been acquired by one of several parent organizations that were regional or national in scope. Such chains usually consisted of from 10 to 30 retail operations located in separated market areas. However, the largest, Abbey Medical, had begun operations in 1924 and now consisted of over 70 local dealers. Higgins estimated 1985 sales for the chain (which was itself acquired by American Hospital Supply Corporation in April 1981) at over $60 million. In general, chains maintained a low corporate visibility and provided their dealers with working capital, employee benefit programs, operating advice, and some centralized purchasing. Higgins thought that chain organizations might grow more rapidly over the next 10 years.

The Issues

Higgins looked at his watch. It was 5:30 and really time to leave. "Still," he thought, "I should jot down what I see to be the immediate issues before I go— that way I won't be tempted to think about them over the weekend." He took a pen and wrote the following:

1. Should TRP continue to rent respirators to dealers?
2. Should TRP protect each dealer's territory (and how big should a territory be)?
3. Should TRP require dealers to stock no competing equipment?
4. How many dealers should TRP eventually have? Where?
5. What sales information should be assembled in order to attract high-quality dealers?
6. What should be done about the "best efforts" clause?

As he reread the list, Higgins considered that there probably were still other short-term-oriented questions he might have missed. Monday would be soon enough to consider them all.

Until then, he was free to think about broader, more strategic issues. Some reflections on the nature of the target market, a statement of marketing objectives, and TRP's possible entry into the hospital market would occupy the weekend. Decisions on these topics would form a substantial part of TRP's strategic marketing plan, a document Higgins hoped to have for the beginning of the next fiscal year in July. "At least I can rule out one option," Higgins thought as he put on his coat. That was an idea to use independent sales representatives to sell TRP products on commission: a recently completed two-month search for such an organization had come up empty. "Like my stomach," he thought, as he went out the door.

Case 18

Laramie Oil Company: Retail Gasoline Division*

In April 1980 George Thomas, vice president in charge of domestic automotive gasoline distribution for the Laramie Oil Company, was considering what action he should take with regard to the company's 12,400 franchised and lessee-operated service stations. A number of developments that indicated discontent among franchisees and lessees had recently occurred. Although he was unsure as to what extent these developments indicated real widespread discontent, Mr. Thomas was wondering what might be causing it, and what action he should take at the present time, and in the long run.

Company Background

The Laramie Oil Company was a fully integrated petroleum company with operations in 21 countries. In 1979 domestic sales were $8.79 billion, and net income was $823.4 million. The Laramie product line included automotive gasoline, aviation fuels, distillates, lubricants, and assorted agricultural and industrial chemicals. Sales of automotive gasoline and related products accounted for 52 percent of revenues earned and 64 percent of net profit.

Both the international and domestic American Head Offices were situated in New York City. As distribution vice president, George Thomas had responsibility for the overall maintenance of a strong network of retail outlets. This responsibility involved the setting of policies concerning lease terms, the selection of dealers, the training of dealers, the motivation of dealers, the dismissal of dealers, and any other factors involving the maintenance of dealer morale and overall effectiveness. Mr. Thomas only had responsibility for the company's Laramie brand stations. Laramie Oil also operated about 50 discount outlets and expected to open more in the near future. These outlets operated under a different brand name.

George Thomas described his objective as distribution vice president as follows:

---

* This case was written by Thomas C. Kinnear and C. Merle Crawford, Professor of Marketing, University of Michigan. Copyright © 1985 by Thomas C. Kinnear.

We've done a great deal of research to determine why gasoline purchasers use one brand of gasoline or another. In almost every instance, the consumer's perception of the gasoline retail outlet was a very significant determinant in brand selection. It appears that we're halfway to first base if we can keep our outlets modern and clean, plus provide the service that the consumer desires. By service, I mean more than just good, fast, competent pump island work. Service includes having outlets open when consumers need them, and making sure that outlets handle our national promotions. There is nothing more irritating to a customer who expects to receive a glass or coupon than to find that the station that he happens to be in isn't participating in the national promotion. That is one of the best ways to lose customers for good.

Our whole retail distribution policy is directed toward providing a consistent type of physical outlet and service from one end of the country to the other. That's how gasoline is sold.

Implementation of Distribution Policies

George Thomas's control over the implementation of his department's policies was quite indirect. A general manager in each of five geographical divisions had responsibility for all marketing activities in his division, including retail distribution. Each division had a distribution manager whose responsibilities included the day-to-day implementation of corporate policies in regard to service station operations. The division distribution manager reported directly to the division general manager. The corporate and divisional distribution managers did, however, maintain informal contact with each other. Each divisional distribution manager had a number of district sales managers reporting directly to him. Direct contact with service station operators was maintained by company sales representatives, each of whom reported to a district sales manager. The sales representative was the final link in the chain of implementation between George Thomas's office and the service station operator. (See Exhibit 1 for a partial organization chart.)

Type of Service Stations

Laramie Oil Company distributed its automotive products through three types of service stations:

1. *Company operated.* These stations were owned or leased by Laramie Oil who hired the service station personnel to operate them on a straight salary basis. Laramie controlled the retail price and all other aspects of all products sold through these stations. About 100 of Laramie's 12,400 stations were operated in this manner.

2. *Franchised dealers.* The station site and all physical facilities of franchised dealer operations were owned by the dealers themselves. Laramie did, however, provide financing, so that an individual dealer could commence operation by putting up as little as $2,000. The company, or local financial institutions, held mortgages on the land and physical facilities. About 500 outlets were in this category.

EXHIBIT 1 Partial organization chart

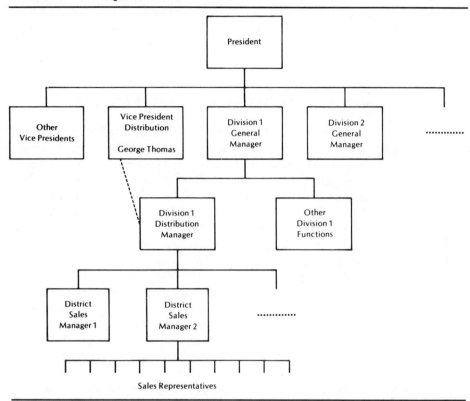

-----Indicates an informal communications link.

3. *Lessee operated.* Lessee operators were dealers who leased their service station from Laramie Oil. The stations, in these cases, continued to be owned by Laramie Oil. The lessee purchased petroleum products from Laramie but was free to set his own operating policies as related to such things as hours, prices, and brands of accessories carried. The lessee's cost price of gasoline was based on a "tank wagon price" which included all taxes and delivery charges to the lessee's station. Typical lessee operators were charged per gallon, as shown in the accompanying table.

Transport price (except tax)	$0.660
Plus: State and federal taxes	0.450
Transport price (including tax)	1.110
Plus: Jobber margin	0.085
Tank wagon price	1.195
Plus: Rent paid to Laramie	0.055
Lessee's margin	0.070
Retail price	$1.320

The cost price of gasoline to franchised dealers closely approximated the lessee cost arrangement, except that rent charges were not included. For most franchisees, interest charges on their mortgages tended to make up this cost difference.

A Closer Look at Two Laramie Lessee Dealers

1. Jerry Williamson's Laramie service station, Dearborn, Michigan. Jerry Williamson's service station was located at one of the main intersections in the Detroit suburb of Dearborn. His customers were drawn mainly from local residents and commuters who drove through Dearborn on their way to and from their work in Detroit. Williamson was a class A automobile mechanic who had worked for a Ford dealership for eight years before becoming a Laramie dealer in 1964. He had put up $9,500 of his own money to obtain the right to be the Laramie lessee for his Dearborn location. Most of the $9,500 had been used to finance product inventories and tools, while some had been used to physically upgrade the station.

Williamson did a large automobile repair business. Over the years he had built up an excellent reputation among the residents of Dearborn for providing competent and reliable repair service. As a result of this business and his good location for attracting gasoline customers, he did an annual sales volume of slightly over $494,000. His profit statement for 1979 is presented in Exhibit 2.

Williamson took great pride in the fact that he had been able to build a very successful business operation. He thought of himself as being a part of the community as he took part in community work through his memberships in the Lion's Club and the Chamber of Commerce. In the latter organization he had risen to the position of vice president, and was looking forward to being president at some time.

When he was asked if there were any negative aspects to being a Laramie dealer, Williamson replied as follows:

> Well . . . not really; it's tough to complain a lot when you're making $33,000 a year. The only thing I really have to complain about is that Laramie pressures me to buy most of my repair parts and accessories from their own supply company or from company-approved jobbers. I think I could get slightly better margins from other jobbers, as the company takes a percentage rake-off from the approved jobbers. However, it's really a small complaint when you consider all the pluses that Laramie gives. Overall, I'm extremely pleased.

2. Fred Shaw's Laramie service station, Detroit, Michigan. Fred Shaw's service station was located in an industrial section of Detroit, with most of his customers being people who worked in the plants in the surrounding area. Prior to becoming the lessee of his current station, Shaw had worked as an employee in a suburban Laramie station. He had always wanted to be in business for himself, and whenever he heard that a station was available, he

EXHIBIT 2 Percentage profit statements for Jerry Williamson's and Fred Shaw's service stations for 1979

	Jerry Williamson	Fred Shaw
Sales	100.00%	100.00%
Cost of goods sold	75.36	75.24
Gross profit	24.64	24.76
Expenses:		
Labor for outside work	0.46	0.29
Supplies	0.75	0.79
Wages (excluding owner)	8.38	8.69
Repairs and maintenance	0.34	0.24
Advertising	0.79	0.93
Delivery	0.41	0.42
Bad debts	0.02	0.02
Administrative	0.38	0.35
Miscellaneous	0.96	0.72
Rent	2.60	2.00
Insurance	0.47	0.46
Utilities	0.96	1.00
Taxes	0.74	0.66
Interest	0.10	0.11
Depreciation	0.60	0.65
Total expenses	17.96	17.33
Net profit	6.68%	7.43%
Inventory turnover × 1 year	17.26	12.88

would approach the sales representative involved to see if he could obtain the station. Most of the stations had required too much capital, but finally he was able to obtain his current station by putting up $8,500 for the required inventories.

Although managing his station required long hours for Shaw, he preferred it to a very great extent over working for another dealer. It was in a very real sense to him the fulfillment of his dream of being his own boss.

Due to the nature of the surrounding environment, Shaw's station was quiet most of the day except when the shifts changed and then it was extremely busy. This constant changing from feast to famine made proper staffing extremely difficult, and required long hours to cover all shift changes.

Shaw's station was not as productive in either gasoline sales or repair service as was Jerry Williamson's. As a result, his 1979 sales volume was just under $190,000. Exhibit 2 presents his 1979 profit statement.

Hank Homes was the Laramie sales representative in Shaw's district, and on one of his weekly visits recently he asked Fred to take part in a special Bicentennial china giveaway promotion. Part of the conversation between the two men went as follows:

Hank: This looks to me to be one of the best promotions the company has ever put together. They're going to put about $2.5 million in advertising behind it. You should draw a pile of customers.

Fred: Come on, Hank. The type of customer who buys from my outlet isn't interested in bone china. It may be fine for other outlets, but I don't want in on this one. Besides, since the gasoline shortage of '73 and '74, I can't believe anyone wants to start these rotten giveaways again.

Hank: I disagree, Fred. I'm sure you'd do well with it. Why don't you let me sign you up. I think you'd be pleased with the results. We pretested this in Denver and it went well. Think about it for a few minutes while we discuss a few other things. It looks to me as if your station could use a new coat of paint this spring. If we let it go any longer, it will chase customers away.

Fred: I don't think I can afford to put out for the paint right now, Hank. You know what a problem I'm having making ends meet here.

Hank: Well, maybe I can help you out on that score. If I work on them at the regional office, they might let me absorb part or even all of the expense for you. . . . Think about the china promotion, Fred, and I'll drop back tomorrow.

Franchisee and Lessee Discontent

The following dealer comments were taken from meetings of several Laramie retail dealer associations in various parts of the United States. Laramie retail dealer associations were groups of Laramie dealers who had gotten together on their own for such purposes as: the discussion of mutual problems, the collective purchasing of products from independent suppliers, and the undertaking of various social activities. Not all Laramie dealers belonged to associations and the strength and activity level of the associations varied greatly.

Lessee 1: The company claims that we can set our own prices, but that damn sales rep comes into my place and tells me I can't sell at more than a four-cent markup. I can hardly scrape from one week to the next at that rate. . . . I know for sure he'll drop my lease if I don't set these prices. Our dealer association has had economists do studies that showed that on the average it takes a gross profit margin of nine cents a gallon to operate profitably. Margins today run from about three cents to eight cents with the average at about five and a half cents. That's just not enough.

Lessee 2: What really bugs me is those stupid premium offers I have to put up with. They advertise them like mad on TV, so I have to carry them or the customers start screaming. . . . I don't get any more business with them—all my competitors are running some premium too—all they do is add to my costs. It's really frustrating. I thought the oil crisis had finished these things. I guess I was wrong.

Lessee 3: I couldn't be more satisfied. I make a really good living. If some of you guys stopped complaining and started working, you could do the same.

Lessee 4: You know I'd really like to close my place down at night . . . the only reason I'm open nights is 'cause the sales rep said he wouldn't renew my lease if I didn't keep his hours—imagine that, I've worked for Laramie for 15 years as a dealer and they'd drop me just like that. I can't afford to lose my station but I'm losing money by staying open.

Lessee 5: What's really got me worried is that they are going to turn my station into a company-owned and -operated outlet. Where would I be then?

Lessee 6: The company is more interested in their gallonage than our profits, and those one-sided leases let them dictate what we'll charge and what products we'll sell. They also use the lease to ride herd on our prices.

Lessee 7: I had hoped that the Supreme Court rulings prohibiting forcing their TBA (tires, batteries, and accessories) brands on us would have helped; however, all it's done is to make their methods more subtle.

Franchisee 1: I thought when I put up my bucks I was going to be in business for myself—fat chance—that sales rep is in my place all the time suggesting what hours to work, how to work, what price to set. . . . If I object, he starts talking about revoking my franchise. I know the Laramie name draws customers but some of his suggestions are unreasonable.

Franchisee 2: This business of them running their own discount stations in competition with me has really got me bugged, too.

Comments of Sales Representatives (SR)

The following comments were taken from individual interviews with selected sales representatives:

SR 1: Sure, I set hours and prices and procedures; if I didn't, some of those dolts would be out of business tomorrow.

SR 2: To get the volume out of my territory that the district manager demands, I have to pressure the dealers. Talking about the lease is always effective. However, I've never actually threatened any of my dealers with the loss of the lease.

SR 3: If you're honest and friendly with your dealers and show them what they will gain from following what you suggest, then you don't have to threaten them to get cooperation.

SR 4: You can bet your life I'm out pushing our TBA line to dealers. That right hasn't been taken away from us. However, that doesn't mean we're going to club them over the head if they don't.

Comments by George Thomas

(Made before a congressional committee.)

It isn't our policy to require dealers to maintain company-directed hours or prices. The whole idea is that the dealer has the right to establish his own hours and prices.

I'd fire any sales representative found pressuring dealers on matters like prices or hours or contests.

It seems to me that what we have here is a situation completely analogous to the normal arrangement between the landlord and tenant. We have up to $200,000 invested in large stations, and if the dealers are mismanaging them we have a right and a duty to protect our investment.

Developments in 1980

A number of developments that concerned George Thomas took place in 1980.

1. A group of dealers in Chicago filed a suit against Laramie, alleging that Laramie violated the Sherman Act by using short-term leases to intimidate

the dealers into following suggested retail prices. No decision had been handed down yet by the court.

2. A Laramie Marketing Research Staff report indicated that the turnover rate among Laramie dealers had increased significantly in the last few years. This problem of dealer turnover was common throughout the oil industry. Estimates indicated that approximately one third of all service stations in the United States change management every year. The Laramie turnover rate was below the national average, but was still very high. This high turnover was considered to be a very serious problem by George Thomas. Also disturbing was the fact that a significant number of long-service Laramie dealers had left to join cut-rate chains who guaranteed station managers at least $1,500 income per month.

3. The Automotive Retail Trade Association had requested the Federal Trade Commission (FTC) to charge the seven major oil companies (including Laramie) with misrepresentation, breach of contract, and promotion of price wars. The writ alleged misrepresentation of "exclusive" franchise agreements and breach of contract because the oil companies have opened "off-brand" stations near franchise service stations. The association charged that the off-brand stations sell at prices lower than the wholesale prices charged to the franchise dealers. The association wants an injunction to stop oil companies from creating subsidiary stations in direct competition with franchised dealers.

The writ also criticized the oil companies for nondisclosure of fees or profits received by oil companies from firms which supply automobile products to the service stations. The association wanted to know this information since service station lessees are requested to buy the accessories only from designated dealers.

Finally the writ criticized promotional gimmicks and giveaways as a financial burden to operators and alleged that oil companies "demanded" cooperation and participation under threat of nonrenewal of leases.

4. The Central States Automotive Retailers Association presented a brief to the governors of six states asking for legislation to prohibit gimmicks and giveaways connected with gasoline selling. The association alleged that an end to giveaways could reduce the selling price of gasoline by one or two cents a gallon. The brief also asked that oil companies be required to sell gasoline at one price to all customers. At present, wholesale price varies from customer to customer, with the highest charged to leased gas stations.

5. Laramie had recently closed many marginal stations as a result of gasoline shortages in 1979. A group of dealers dispossessed in this process had brought suit against Laramie charging violations of their franchise agreement and conspiracy to restrain trade.

Mr. Thomas reflected on these developments and wondered what alternative courses of action were available to him, and what action he should take both in the short run and in the long run. He also wondered what factors had caused the current problems.

Case 19

U.S. Pioneer Electronics Corporation*

In fall 1977 Bernie Mitchell, president of U.S. Pioneer Electronics, placed an ad featuring a portrait of William Shakespeare in several trade magazines. It was an open letter from Shakespeare and Mr. Mitchell to several "dissident" dealers franchised to sell Japanese-made Pioneer products in the United States.[1] The ad, shown in Exhibit 1, alleged that "a few dealers" had resorted to "disparagement of Pioneer products and 'bait and switch' advertising" and threatened dealer investigations to protect Pioneer's reputation.

Mr. Mitchell hoped these "unjustifiable practices" were the sporadic misconduct of only "an unwise few" and could be dealt with individually. But if they represented an overall erosion of dealer support for Pioneer products, he was determined (a) to take immediate steps to prevent further erosion and (b) to establish a new long-run distribution strategy to ensure U.S. Pioneer's continued leadership in the hi-fi industry.

Industry Background

The U.S. hi-fi industry was started in the 1960s by a few engineers who, according to industry legend, left their positions (mostly in the aerospace industry) to pursue their hobby of building amplifiers and speakers in their garages and basements. By the late 1960s, larger component manufacturers were beginning to broaden their product lines.[2] For instance, Scott, previously identified solely with electronics, was building its reputation in the speaker business. Sherwood, also an electronics manufacturer, introduced an automatic turntable in 1969.

---

* Copyright © 1978 by the President and Fellows of Harvard College.

This case was prepared by Hirotako Takeuchi as the basis for class discussion rather than to illustrate either effective or ineffective handling of an administrative situation. Reprinted by permission of the Harvard Business School.

[1] The words *retailers* and *dealers* are used interchangeably in this case.

[2] Components were combinations of different audio equipment, which reproduced sound highly faithful (i.e., high-fidelity or hi-fi sound) to the original record or tape. Consumers created component systems of their choice by combining (a) an inlet source, such as a turntable, tape deck, or FM tuner; (b) a control center, such as an amplifier or receiver, which was an amplifier and FM tuner combined into one unit; and (c) an outlet, such as speakers. In audio terminology, receivers and amplifiers were called "electronics."

EXHIBIT 1

AN IMPORTANT MESSAGE FROM WILLIAM SHAKESPEARE AND PIONEER.

"Who steals my purse steals trash . . .
But he that filches from me
my good name
Robs me of that which not
enriches him
And makes me poor indeed."

The Immortal Bard said it over three hundred years ago. It's still true today.

It has come to our attention at Pioneer that a few dealers of high fidelity products, acting in what they believe to be their best interest, have taken up the practice of disparagement of Pioneer products and "bait and switch" advertising, often using Pioneer's hard earned reputation in the industry as the "bait."

This tactic hurts Pioneer, hurts the consumer and ultimately hurts all dealers since it will damage the credibility of our high fidelity business in the eyes of consumers. To protect our legitimate dealers, Pioneer will conduct frequent investigations of this practice, and we will take appropriate steps to protect and defend our reputation on behalf of the great majority of our dealers against the unjustifiable practices of an unwise few.

Respectfully,

William Shakespeare, *Stratford upon Avon*
Bernie Mitchell, *U.S. Pioneer Electronics*

KLH, which had started out making speakers, turned to stereo compacts about the same time.[3]

Japanese hi-fi manufacturers such as Pioneer, Kenwood, Sansui, and Teac also entered the U.S. market in the late 1960s. At the same time most original founders of the hi-fi companies, who had operated in a "club-like" business atmosphere, were leaving the industry.

The 1970s saw a new attitude among hi-fi manufacturers. As Mr. Mitchell told one trade magazine reporter,

> Six years ago . . . we only wanted to sell our product to a certain select group of people who had to qualify somehow intellectually and technologically. We didn't want to sell . . . to kids or to ordinary people, only to superpeople. It was a real elitist attitude, and terribly dangerous. We've changed it from an elitist business that didn't really want to grow to an industry that has some pride in itself and its products and says, "These products are so good we won't be happy until we tell everybody." (*Crawdaddy*, July 1976.)

Company Background

Pioneer Electronics Corporation was founded in Tokyo in 1938. It started with capital of $235 and had expanded to $843 million in worldwide sales by 1977. Overseas sales surpassed domestic sales in 1974 and, in 1977, accounted for 65 percent of the total. Net income (pretax) in 1977 was nearly $61 million.

U.S. Pioneer was established in March 1966 under Ken Kai, vice president, then 26 years old. He had joined the parent company in Tokyo after graduating from college and was sent to New York a year later as Pioneer's U.S. liaison. In 1966, U.S. Pioneer had less than $200,000 in sales and fewer than 30 dealers.

Bernie Mitchell joined the company in 1970. He was an economist by training and a music buff, as well as a member of the boards of directors of the New Jersey Symphony and the Metropolitan Opera. He had worked previously with Westinghouse, Toshiba, and Concord Electronics.

To help U.S. Pioneer grow, Mr. Mitchell and Mr. Kai took on the task of developing the market—making more people aware of and knowledgeable about hi-fi products. U.S. Pioneer sponsored hi-fi shows on college campuses and became the first hi-fi company to advertise in such magazines as *Playboy, National Lampoon,* and *The New Yorker.* U.S. Pioneer ads featured music, sports, and other celebrities.

The company also strengthened its distribution network. U.S. Pioneer was supplied by its parent in Japan. Commission sales representatives sold to its retail dealers. In 1972, U.S. Pioneer had six independent sales representative

---

[3] Compacts were preassembled audio systems that usually consisted of two units—one containing a turntable, receiver, and/or tape player and the other a pair of speakers. A compact system usually cost less and was smaller than a component system. It reproduced stereo sound (i.e., sound reproduced through two separate channels) but not necessarily high-fidelity sound.

offices, which sold only Pioneer products (with the exception of accessories, complementary items, and very high-priced lines of electronics that did not directly compete with Pioneer). Each office had its own sales force and served a given region. Each had from four to seven salespeople paid an average annual salary of $20,000. They assisted retailers with merchandising and display, store operations, and sales training. By 1975, U.S. Pioneer had added 10 independent sales representative offices and 4 company-owned offices—in New York, Washington, D.C., Florida, and Missouri. These ''captive'' offices were paid the same commission as the independents—but were not allowed to carry product lines of direct or indirect competitors.[4]

By 1977, the number of retail outlets carrying Pioneer products had grown to almost 3,600 from approximately 500 in 1970. Retailers had to sign franchise agreements with U.S. Pioneer. Mr. Mitchell thought they did not hesitate to sign because the company's strong national and local cooperative advertising created considerable consumer pull. Five percent of U.S. Pioneer sales was allocated to local ads featuring its products. In addition, the firm offered dealers attractive gross margins and credit terms.

Fair Trade[5] versus Free Market

FTC Action

Just as market expansion and distribution building were starting to generate higher net sales ($80 million in 1974), the Federal Trade Commission (FTC) issued a complaint against U.S. Pioneer and three other competitors. It alleged that Sansui, Sherwood, Teac, and U.S. Pioneer granted dealerships to retailers only if they agreed to maintain suggested retail prices, directed their sales representatives to report on retailers who failed to maintain such prices, and delayed shipments to retailers who cut prices. These practices violated Section 5 of the Federal Trade Commission Act, which prohibited ''unfair methods of competition . . . and unfair or deceptive acts or practices in commerce.'' Their effect, the FTC charged, was to inflate consumer prices.

---

[4] Before 1974, U.S. Pioneer sales representative offices received a 10 percent commission. That year the rate was reduced to 5 percent, comparable with that of other manufacturers.

[5] Fair-trade (or resale price maintenance) laws permitted a manufacturer or distributor of trademarked products to determine their resale price. Although on the surface such laws seemed to support a manufacturer's desire to influence retail prices, they had initially been advocated by small, independent retailers seeking protection from direct price competition by large chains. The first such state law was passed in 1931, and by 1941 all but three states had such laws. In 13 states a ''nonsigner clause'' bound all retailers selling a fair-traded product to the contract if one retailer in the state signed an agreement. The Miller-Tydings Act, passed in 1937, applied resale price maintenance to interstate commerce.

Fair-trade practice and enforcement began to decline steadily in the early 1950s. By 1975 fair trade was being used only for certain brands of hi-fi equipment, television sets, jewelry, bicycles, clothing, cosmetics, and kitchenware. Major efforts to repeal state laws started in 1974. In December 1975, the Consumer Goods Pricing Act terminated interstate fair-trade regulations.

Consent Decree

In August 1975, the four companies signed consent decrees with the FTC. They did not admit guilt, but did promise not to engage in the alleged practices. Specifically, they were prohibited from fair trading their products for five years in the 21 states where the practice was still permitted and from using suggested list prices for two years in any part of the country. They also could not ask consumers the price of purchased products on warranty registration forms. Finally, the companies were required to distribute copies of the consent order to all their dealers and to give any dealer whose franchise had been terminated an opportunity to regain it.

U.S. Pioneer's Response

Asked why U.S. Pioneer decided not to contest the FTC decree, Mitchell replied:

> I don't mind being a crusader. In fact, I kind of enjoy it. But I like to crusade for something that makes some long-term sense.
>
> The FTC is asking us not to violate the law. It has never been our intention to violate the law. They are asking that we no longer fair trade our products. We had already unilaterally made the decision that fair trade wasn't viable anymore anyhow. . . . The third thing they are asking us is that we not conspire to fix prices, either among dealers or among ourselves, and we had no intention of doing that.
>
> We did try to fix retail prices at the dealer level as long as fair trade lasted; that was the purpose of fair trade statutes. When we fair traded, we did it pretty darn well. But when we decided to go off fair trade, we decided we were going to be the best there was at free market practices. (*Electronics Retailing,* October 1975.)

To implement this new goal, Pioneer replaced the price sheet in effect during fair trade (see Exhibit 2) with a list that replaced the words "fair trade resale price" with "approximate nationally advertised value" and added optional retail prices under gross margins of 15 percent, 20 percent, 25 percent, 30 percent, 35 percent, 40 percent, and 45 percent (see Exhibit 3).

According to *Home Furnishings Daily* (August 27, 1975), "Most of the dealers and manufacturers contacted scorned [Pioneer's] list because they felt it was, in the words of one manufacturer, 'an open invitation to cut the hell out of prices.'" Mr. Mitchell said in the same article that the initial response was fear and that dealers did not understand the significance of the change from fair-trade to free-market prices.

> Too often, under the fair-trade environment, dealers felt, "If we have a very fine mix of products, and people come in and we tell them wonderful stories about each of those products, they will tell us which products they want. They'll sort of self-sell in an enlightened environment."
>
> I don't really think that's a very good way to run a business. Dealers have to identify what needs the consumer has, acquaint him very quickly with options,

EXHIBIT 2 Price list of selected products, April 22, 1975

Stereo Receivers	Description	Fair Trade Resale	1-3 pcs.	4-more	Case	Shipping Weight
SX-1010	AM/FM Stereo Receiver	$699.95	$466.60	$420.00	1	60 lbs.
SX-939	AM/FM Stereo Receiver	599.95	400.00	372.00	1	51 lbs.
SX-838	AM/FM Stereo Receiver	499.95	333.40	310.00	1	44 lbs.
SX-737	AM/FM Stereo Receiver	399.95	266.60	248.00	1	35 lbs.
SX-636	AM/FM Stereo Receiver	349.95	233.30	217.00	1	29 lbs.
SX-535	AM/FM Stereo Receiver	299.95	200.00	186.00	1	27 lbs.
SX-434	AM/FM Stereo Receiver	239.95	160.00	148.80	1	22 lbs.

U.A. Series	Description	Fair Trade Resale	1-3 pcs.	4-more	Case	Shipping Weight
Spec 1	Stereo Pre-Amplifier........	$499.95	$333.40	$300.00	1	30 lbs.
Spec 2	Stereo Power Amplifier......	899.95	600.00	540.00	1	60 lbs.
SA-9900	Integrated Stereo Amp.	749.85	500.00	450.00	1	50 lbs.
SA-9500	Integrated Stereo Amp.	499.95	333.40	300.00	1	44 lbs.
SA-8500	Integrated Stereo Amp.	399.95	266.60	240.00	1	32 lbs.
SA-7500	Integrated Stereo Amp.	299.95	200.00	180.00	1	30 lbs.
SA-5200	Integrated Stereo Amp.	138.95	93.30	84.00	1	23 lbs.
TX-9500	AM/FM Stereo Tuner	399.95	266.60	240.00	1	24 lbs.
TX-7500	AM/FM Stereo Tuner	249.95	166.70	150.00	1	21 lbs.
TX-6200	AM/FM Stereo Tuner	139.95	93.30	84.00	1	18 lbs.
RG-1	RG Dynamic Expander	179.95	120.00	108.00	1	15 lbs.
SR-202W	Stereo Reverb. Amp.	139.95	93.30	84.00	1	12 lbs.
SF-850	Electronic Crossover	199.95	133.30	120.00	1	16 lbs.
SD-1100	Quad/Stereo Display	599.95	400.00	360.00	1	34 lbs.
WC-UA1	Walnut Cabinet*	34.95**	23.30	21.00	1	11¼ lbs.

* Walnut Cabinet for SA-8500, SA-7500, TX-9500, TX-7500 only.   ** Suggested Resale

Turntables	Description	Fair Trade Resale	1-3 pcs.	4-more	Case	Shipping Weight
PL-71	2-Speed, DC Brushless Servo Motor, Anti-skating Direct-Drive	$299.95	$200.00	$180.00	1	33 lbs.
PL-55X	2-Speed, DC Brushless Servo Motor, Anti-skating, Direct-drive Automatic Turntable	249.95	166.60	150.00	1	31 lbs.
PL-A45D	2-Speed, Automatic Turntable 2-motor, Belt-drive, Anti-skating	169.95	113.30	105.40	1	26 lbs.
PL-15D/II	2-Speed, Automatic Turntable with Hysteresis Synchronous Motor, Belt-drive, Anti-skating	129.95	87.10	83.20	1	20 lbs.
PL-12D & PL-12D/II	2-Speed, Hysteresis Synchronous Motor, Belt-drive, Anti-skating	99.95	70.00	66.00	1	19 lbs.

EXHIBIT 3 Price list of selected products, July 1, 1975

STEREO RECEIVERS	Description	DEALER COST 1-3 pcs.	4- more	Case	Shp. Wt.	15% Margin	20% Margin	25% Margin	30% Margin	35% Margin	40% Margin	45% Margin	Approx. Nationally Adv. Value	Your Price	Model Number
SX-1010	AM/FM Stereo Rec.	$466.60	$420.00	1	60 lbs.	$494.00	$525.00	$560.00	$600.00	$646.00	$700.00	$764.00	$700.00	_____	SX-1010
SX-939	AM/FM Stereo Rec.	400.00	372.00	1	51 lbs.	438.00	465.00	496.00	531.00	572.00	620.00	676.00	600.00	_____	SX-939
SX-838	AM/FM Stereo Rec.	333.40	310.00	1	44 lbs.	365.00	388.00	413.00	443.00	477.00	517.00	564.00	500.00	_____	SX-838
SX-737	AM/FM Stereo Rec.	266.60	248.00	1	35 lbs.	292.00	310.00	331.00	354.00	382.00	413.00	451.00	400.00	_____	SX-737
SX-636	AM/FM Stereo Rec.	233.30	217.00	1	29 lbs.	255.00	271.00	289.00	310.00	334.00	362.00	395.00	350.00	_____	SX-636
SX-535	AM/FM Stereo Rec.	200.00	186.00	1	27 lbs.	219.00	233.00	248.00	266.00	286.00	310.00	338.00	300.00	_____	SX-535
SX-434	AM/FM Stereo Rec.	160.00	148.80	1	22 lbs.	175.00	185.00	198.00	213.00	229.00	248.00	271.00	250.00	_____	SX-434

U.A. SERIES	Description	1-3 pcs.	4- more	Case	Shp. Wt.	15% Margin	20% Margin	25% Margin	30% Margin	35% Margin	40% Margin	45% Margin	Approx. Nationally Adv. Value	Your Price	Model Number
Spec 1	Stereo Pre-Amplifier	$333.40	$300.00	1	30 lbs.	$353.00	$375.00	$400.00	$429.00	$462.00	$500.00	$545.00	$500.00	_____	Spec 1
Spec 2	Stereo Power Amp.	600.00	540.00	1	60 lbs.	635.00	675.00	720.00	771.00	831.00	900.00	982.00	900.00	_____	Spec 2
SA-9900	Integ. Stereo Amp.	500.00	450.00	1	50 lbs.	529.00	563.00	600.00	643.00	692.00	750.00	818.00	750.00	_____	SA-9900
SA-9500	Integ. Stereo Amp.	333.40	300.00	1	44 lbs.	353.00	375.00	400.00	429.00	462.00	500.00	545.00	500.00	_____	SA-9500
SA-8500	Integ. Stereo Amp.	266.60	240.00	1	32 lbs.	282.00	300.00	320.00	343.00	369.00	400.00	436.00	400.00	_____	SA-8500
SA-7500	Integ. Stereo Amp.	200.00	180.00	1	30 lbs.	212.00	225.00	240.00	257.00	277.00	300.00	327.00	300.00	_____	SA-7500
SA-5200	Integ. Stereo Amp.	93.30	84.00	1	23 lbs.	99.00	105.00	112.00	120.00	129.00	140.00	153.00	140.00	_____	SA-5200
TX-9500	AM/FM Stereo Tuner	266.60	240.00	1	24 lbs.	282.00	300.00	320.00	343.00	369.00	400.00	436.00	400.00	_____	TX-9500
TX-7500	AM/FM Stereo Tuner	166.70	150.00	1	21 lbs.	176.00	189.00	200.00	214.00	231.00	250.00	273.00	250.00	_____	TX-7500
TX-6200	AM/FM Stereo Tuner	93.30	84.00	1	18 lbs.	99.00	105.00	112.00	120.00	129.00	140.00	153.00	140.00	_____	TX-6200
RG-1	RG Dyn. Expander	120.00	108.00	1	15 lbs.	127.00	135.00	144.00	154.00	166.00	180.00	196.00	175.00	_____	RG-1
SR-202W	Stereo Reverb. Amp.	93.30	84.00	1	12 lbs.	99.00	105.00	112.00	120.00	129.00	140.00	153.00	150.00	_____	SR-202W
SF-850	Electronic Crossover	133.30	120.00	1	16 lbs.	141.00	150.00	160.00	171.00	185.00	200.00	218.00	200.00	_____	SF-850
SD-1100	Quad/Stereo Display	400.00	360.00	1	31 lbs.	424.00	450.00	480.00	514.00	554.00	600.00	655.00	600.00	_____	SD-1100
WC-UA1	Walnut Cabinet†	23.30	21.00	1	11 lbs.	25.00	26.00	28.00	30.00	32.00	35.00	38.00	35.00	_____	WC-UA1
													†Walnut cabinet for SA 8500, SA 7500, TX 9500 & TX 7500 only		
WC-UA2	Walnut Cabinet‡	26.70	24.00	1	11 lbs.	28.00	30.00	32.00	34.00	37.00	40.00	44.00	40.00	_____	WC-UA2
													‡Walnut cabinet for SA 9900 & SA 9500 only		

TURN-TABLES	Description	1-3 pcs.	4- more	Case	Shp. Wt.	15% Margin	20% Margin	25% Margin	30% Margin	35% Margin	40% Margin	45% Margin	Approx. Nationally Adv. Value	Your Price	Model Number
PL-71	2-Sp., DC Brushless Servo Motor, Anti-skating, Direct drive	$200.00	$180.00	1	33 lbs.	$212.00	$225.00	$240.00	$257.00	$277.00	$300.00	$327.00	$300.00	_____	PL-71
PL-55X	2-Sp., DC Brushless Servo Motor, Anti-skating, Direct drive, Auto. Turntable	166.60	150.00	1	31 lbs.	176.00	188.00	200.00	214.00	231.00	250.00	273.00	250.00	_____	PL-55X
PL-A45D	2-Sp., Auto. Turntable 2 motor, Belt drive, Anti-skating	113.30	105.40	1	26 lbs.	124.00	132.00	141.00	151.00	162.00	176.00	192.00	175.00	_____	PL-A45D
PL-15D/₁₁	2-Sp., Auto. Turntable w/Hysteresis Synch Motor, Belt drive, Anti-skating	87.10	83.20	1	20 lbs.	98.00	104.00	111.00	119.00	128.00	139.00	151.00	125.00	_____	PL-15D/₁₁
PL-12D & PL-12D/₁₁	2-Sp., Hysteresis Synch. Motor, Belt drive, Anti-skating	70.00	66.00	1	19 lbs.	78.00	83.00	88.00	94.00	102.00	110.00	120.00	100.00	_____	PL-12D PL-12D/₁₁

suggest an option they think he ought to take, and bear down very hard to lead him to take that option. That's called selling.

Effects on Sales and Prices

The immediate impact of the consent decree, according to *Home Furnishings Daily,* was a "price war which lowered dealer profit margins to 5 or 6 percent in many parts of the country." The newspaper also said that "many retailers began to criticize manufacturers for 'abandoning' them and called for them to control the fluctuating markets." Some softening of the market, according to an FTC spokesperson, was expected as a "backlash." But "prices won't stay as low as they are now and higher margins will eventually return. [In the meantime] I expect to see greater sales at discount prices and the good dealers will survive."

In 1976 retail dollar sales jumped 12.6 percent and unit sales increased 9.4 percent over the previous year (see Exhibit 4). In 1975, on the other hand, the increases had been 1.6 percent and 2.2 percent, respectively. According to Mr. Kai, the much smaller percentage increase between 1974 and 1975 probably resulted from the recession and consumer decisions to delay purchases until fair-trade laws were repealed. In New York and New Jersey repeal had been rumored as early as August 1975.

In the meantime, U.S. Pioneer net sales increased from $80 million in 1974 to $87 million in 1975. In addition, its market share increased between 1974 and 1975 in all hi-fi product categories except turntables and speakers (see

EXHIBIT 4 Unit and dollar sales of hi-fi components, 1974–1977

	1974	1975	1976	1977
Unit sales (000s)				
Total components	7,799	7,971	8,719	9,539
Receivers	960	970	1,050	1,185
Amps, pre-amps, tuners	231	263	275	320
Turntables (except OEM)	1,767	1,709	1,866	2,015
Speakers	2,500	2,550	2,800	3,125
Tape decks (cassette and open reel)	341	399	428	494
Headphones	2,000	2,080	2,300	2,400
Dollar sales ($ millions)				
Total components	$1,056	$1,073	$1,208	$1,390
Receivers	336	306	341	392
Amps, pre-amps, tuners	69	76	81	97
Turntables (except OEM)	168	179	222	252
Speakers	300	319	350	416
Tape-decks (cassette and open reel)	113	120	133	147
Headphones	70	73	81	86

Source: *Merchandising,* March 1978, p. 51.

EXHIBIT 5 U.S. Pioneer market share data*

Product category	1971	1972	1973	1974	1975	1976
Receivers	7%	15%	23%	22%	25%	25%
Tuners	3	5	25	18	23	18
Amplifiers	3	5	8	9	12	10
Turntables	3	3	3	11	10	11
Speakers	2	1	4	5	3	7
Headphones	10	5	4	7	9	9
Cassette decks	—	—	4	11	26	20
Open reel tape decks	—	—	—	5	9	9

* Pioneer's overall market share in the hi-fi component market was 18 percent to 20 percent in 1977.
Source: Company data.

Exhibit 5). All Pioneer's market share percentages in 1976 were equal to or higher than those of 1974.

Market Growth and Changes

The hi-fi market was growing, and there was evidence that buyer profiles for component parts were changing. As shown in Exhibit 6, there were fewer women, more young adults (ages 18 to 24), more Pacific area residents, more college graduates, and more households with incomes of $25,000 and over purchasing stereo component parts in 1975 than in the previous year.

Realizing a shift in buyer demographics, U.S. Pioneer undertook extensive research to determine (a) the market potential of hi-fi products compared with low-fi products, such as compacts or consoles[6] and (b) the purchasing behavior of hi-fi component buyers.

An independent research firm found that sales of components were growing faster than sales of compacts and consoles. But in sheer volume, compacts outsold components and consoles by a wide margin. In 1975, 3.5 million units of compacts were sold in the United States, compared with 1.5 million component systems and 400,000 consoles. To Mr. Mitchell, this meant that 3.9 million U.S. buyers were taken off the hi-fi market. Once they had purchased compacts and consoles, these customers were not expected to consider replacing them with hi-fi components for several years.

"Also, every time a compact or console is sold, you lose the potential of an additional speaker, add-on tape deck, upgraded receiver, tuner, turntable, and more," said Mr. Mitchell. The research revealed that this add-on market was larger than expected. In 1975, add-on sales accounted for 55 percent of

---

[6] Consoles were preassembled, all-in-one audio systems that were larger and cost more than most component systems. Their sound reproduction was generally considered poorer than that of components.

EXHIBIT 6 Demographic profile of buyers of stereo component parts*

	1974		1975	
	United States (139,778,000)	Stereo components buyers (3,400,000)	United States (141,622,000)	Stereo components buyers (2,788,000)
Sex				
Men	47.3%	73.4%	49.6%	76.4%
Women	52.7	26.6	50.4	23.6
Age				
18–24	18.1%	42.5%	18.5%	47.6%
25–34	20.6	31.8	21.2	26.9
35–49	24.6	18.0	24.2	15.0
50–64	22.4	6.8	21.7	9.9
65 or over	14.2	1.0	14.4	0.5
Residence				
New England	3.9%	4.4%	5.9%	6.6%
Mid-Atlantic	22.2	18.6	20.6	18.8
East Central	13.1	16.9	14.2	15.1
West Central	16.5	19.8	15.2	16.6
Southeast	18.0	14.0	19.1	14.9
Southwest	10.6	10.4	10.1	7.1
Pacific	15.6	15.9	14.8	20.8
Education				
Graduated college	11.9%	16.3%	12.5%	25.6%
Attended college	14.0	30.8	14.7	27.5
Graduated high school	37.7	39.5	38.0	36.2
Did not graduate high school	36.4	13.4	34.8	10.7
Household income				
$25,000 or more	8.8%	11.5%	11.3%	20.9%
$20,000–$24,999	7.5	9.3	8.4	9.1
$15,000–$19,999	17.1	21.4	18.6	22.7
$10,000–$14,999	24.1	21.5	23.2	21.1
$ 8,000–$ 9,999	9.2	9.8	8.7	8.5
$ 5,000–$ 7,999	14.4	10.8	13.3	11.3
Less than $5,000	18.8	15.7	16.5	6.4
Family life cycle				
Single	16.2%	38.8%	17.3%	41.9%
Married	69.5	50.4	67.9	52.2
Widowed/divorced/separated	14.3	10.8	14.9	6.0
(Parents)	(43.7)	(36.0)	(42.4)	(37.6)

* Buyers of stereo component parts within the past year.

Source: 1975 and 1976 issues of *Target Group Index*, published by Axiom Market Research Bureau, Inc. Sample sizes were approximately 25,000 for 1974 and 30,000 for 1975.

total dollars spent on hi-fi components. New system sales made up the remaining 45 percent.

Buying Influences

Consumer research showed that buyers of different audio systems were influenced by different factors, in order of importance:

Component buyers	Console buyers	Compact buyers
1. Lifelike sound reproduction.	1. Esthetics.	1. Lower price.
2. Superior electronics.	2. Adequate electronics.	2. Small size.
3. Add-on capability.	3. No involved hookup.	3. No involved hookup.
4. Status symbol.	4. A lot for the money.	4. Ease of operation.

The research also found that component buyers:

> Depended heavily on advice of family and friends.
>
> Thought they knew just enough about hi-fi components to get by (only 8 percent thought they knew "a lot").
>
> Shopped around, especially for the initial purchase.
>
> Paid either $350–$400 or $650–$750 for initial purchase of system.
>
> Replaced or upgraded components approximately one to two years after their initial purchase.

New Marketing Strategy

On the basis of this research, Mr. Mitchell established the goal of "doubling the number of people owning and buying any brand of hi-fi components next year." He said,

> We'd rather see a consumer buy a Marantz, Sansui . . . yes, and even a Technics than a fancy fruitwood console, or plastic compact, both of which deliver less than true high fidelity.

To implement this goal, he asked dealers to persuade prospective compact or console buyers to consider lower priced hi-fi components. He argued that this could be best accomplished by prominently displaying low-end components and explaining their advantages over compacts and consoles. To support this dealer effort, Pioneer introduced lower priced components. It also allocated $6 million for national advertising for 1976. Of this, $2 million was earmarked for persuading consumers that only hi-fi components produced true high-fidelity sound. Head copy for one of the ads read, "BAD SOUND IS AN UNNECESSARY EVIL." The ad referred by name to some of Pioneer's competitors—Marantz, Kenwood, and Sansui—as dedicated companies trying to reproduce high-quality sound.

Mr. Mitchell also asked dealers to use direct mail to tap the replacement and add-on markets. Ads were mailed to customers who had purchased audio systems one and two years before.

Results

Mr. Mitchell and Mr. Kai were very satisfied with their new strategy as Pioneer's sales increased from $87 million in 1975 to $135 million in 1976. Although their goal of doubling the number of hi-fi owners and buyers was not

EXHIBIT 7 Unit sales of compacts and components, 1974–1977 (000s)

Compact systems	1973	1974	1975	1976
Cassette tape recorder bimode	32	36	38	44
Cassette tape recorder trimode	103	190	197	233
8-track tape player bimode	652	528	525	527
8-track tape player trimode	1,234	798	843	910
8-track tape recorder bimode	549	590	555	569
8-track tape recorder trimode	480	1,024	1,100	1,183
Changer bimode	377	325	324	337
Total	3,427	3,491	3,582	3,803
Components parts (total)	7,799	7,971	8,719	9,539

Source: *Merchandising,* March 1978, p. 51.

achieved, they felt that more people were buying components than compacts and consoles. The number of compact systems sold in the United States increased from 3.4 million in 1975 to 3.6 million in 1976, whereas component *unit* (not system) sales increased from 8.7 million in 1975 to 9.5 million in 1976 (see Exhibit 7).

They were also impressed by the findings of a Gallup Organization consumer survey for U.S. Pioneer.[7] The survey, conducted in the first half of 1977, measured consumer brand preference for different hi-fi component categories (receiver, FM tuner, amplifier, turntable, speaker, and tape deck). As shown in Exhibit 8, prospective component purchasers preferred Pioneer over all other brands in every category except tape decks.

Retailer Dissidence

Just as Pioneer's "franchise" with consumers was strengthening, Mr. Mitchell came across a number of reports suggesting that relationships with its franchised dealers were starting to deteriorate. In particular, he was concerned about sales representatives' reports about (*a*) disparaging Pioneer products by misrepresenting product specification sheets or manipulating sound demonstrations, and (*b*) using an illegal and unethical tactic known as "bait and switch."[8]

Pioneer Field Investigation

Disparagement of Pioneer products was spotted in continuous field work by employees (mostly part time) who visited Pioneer's franchised stores posing as

---

[7] Gallup Organization was an independent research firm that specialized in survey research and had gained its reputation through political polls.

[8] "Bait and switch" refers to advertising a product at bargain price to draw customers into the store and sell them something similar to, but more expensive than, the advertised item. Pioneer products were good *bait* because of their strong consumer pull—created through national advertising and favorable word-of-mouth communication. In one Pioneer survey, 98 percent of Pioneer component owners interviewed said they were satisfied and would buy the brand again.

EXHIBIT 8 Brand preference data for hi-fi components

Brand of receiver	All prospective purchasers (percent)	Brand of FM tuner	All prospective purchasers (percent)
Pioneer	26	Pioneer	28
Marantz	15	Marantz	18
Sony	13	Sansui	14
Sansui	12	Fisher	6
Kenwood	7	Kenwood	6
Fisher	2	Dynaco	3
Harman-Kardon	2	Technics	1
Technics	1	Sherwin	0
Sherwood	1	Rotel	0
Other	2	Other	1
Don't plan to buy	5	Don't plan to buy	5
Don't know	14	Don't know	18
Total	100	Total	100
Brand of amplifier		Brand of turntable	
Pioneer	29	Pioneer	24
Marantz	17	Garrard	19
Sansui	9	Dual	12
Kenwood	8	BSR	8
Harman-Kardon	5	Technics	6
Superscope	3	Sansui	5
Crown	1	Bang & Olufsen	2
Dynaco	1	B.I.C.	1
Technics	1	JVC	1
Other	2	Other	3
Don't plan to buy	6	Don't plan to buy	4
Don't know	18	Don't know	15
Total	100	Total	100
Brand of speaker*		Brand of tape deck	
Pioneer	32	Teac	21
Jensen	11	Pioneer	17
JBL	11	Sony/Superscope	15
AR	5	Sansui	9
Infinity	5	Fisher	6
KLH	4	Akai	5
B.I.C.—Venturi	3	Bekorder	1
Technics	3	Harman-Kardon	1
Dynaco	1	Technics	0
Other	3	Other	2
Don't plan to buy	4	Don't plan to buy	9
Don't know	18	Don't know	14
Total	100	Total	100

Note: National probability sample of 196.

* Among the different component parts, speakers usually offered the highest gross margin to dealers. One industry source estimated the margin spread between speakers and other components (branded products) to be 10 percent to 20 percent. This spread differed by brand and by type of retail outlets.

Source: Gallup Organization, July 12, 1977.

interested shoppers for Pioneer products, interacted with store personnel, and prepared "shopping reports" for the company. (See Exhibit 9.)

In one report, a U.S. Pioneer employee visited a midwestern hi-fi specialty store and asked for a Pioneer tape deck, but was persuaded by the salesperson to buy a competing brand (see Exhibit 9). The report noted that (*a*) the store salesperson made a comment on how "he could produce copies of letters that dealers had written to Pioneer complaining about service"; (*b*) Pioneer's tape deck (CT-F7272) was missing from its display area; (*c*) the store salesperson, when asked for a CT-F7272 specification sheet, handed him that of a competing brand but did not have one for Pioneer; and (*d*) the store salesperson set the playback sound control at maximum volume for the competing brand but at less than maximum for Pioneer.

To counter these objectionable practices, Pioneer placed the Shakespeare ad (Exhibit 1) in major trade publications to appeal to dealers. The company also asked the presidents of all its sales representative offices to identify the "most blatant, most persistent" disparagement and bait-and-switch offenders in their territories.

Audio Warehouse Suit

U.S. Pioneer filed a suit against Audio Warehouse, a five-store chain with 1977 sales of $10 million, and its advertising agency, both of Akron, Ohio in July 1977. It charged them with using bait-and-switch tactics, advertising without sufficient inventory, and disparaging Pioneer products to customers. A temporary restraining order barred Audio Warehouse from engaging in these practices.

Ed Radford, the 34-year-old president of Audio Warehouse, told *Retail Home Furnishings* (September 26, 1977),

> Yeah, we're being sued (by U.S. Pioneer), but we're not taking this lying down— we're going to fight it. Pioneer surprised me because they got a temporary restraining order, and within one day, they had it in every newspaper in my state. As far as I'm concerned, Pioneer's trying to make me look bad. The public doesn't understand that a temporary restraining order doesn't mean anything. Anybody who puts up a bond can get one.

To prove his point, Mr. Radford (who was called "Fast Eddie" because of his hurried speech and quick rise to fortune) placed a full-page advertisement in two Ohio newspapers (see Exhibit 10).[9] The ad contained Audio Warehouse's version of the suit filed by U.S. Pioneer and offered sharply reduced prices on a number of Pioneer products.

Mr. Radford contended that "many dealers around the country were

---

[9] According to the *Sunday Tribune* (February 12, 1978), Ed Radford, who was orphaned at age five, was planning a "fast" retirement at age 49. He had started his business in 1973 with his life savings of $10,000. In 1978 "Fast Eddie" was a millionaire who still came to work in jeans and an "exploding blond Afro."

EXHIBIT 9 Shopping report

1. *Shopper's name:* John Smith
2. *Store visited:* ABC Sounds
3. *Salesperson and/or store attitude toward Pioneer:* Store's attitude generally negative. Salesperson was not really negative but went along with negative comment by another salesperson.
4. *Products they tried to get you to buy and discouraged:* Pushed Sankyo STD-1900 (a tape deck on sale for $218) and discouraged Pioneer CT-F7272 (a tape deck on sale for $208).
5. *Unfavorable statements toward Pioneer:* The salesperson made no derogatory remarks about Pioneer to me but became involved in a conversation with another store salesperson and prospective customer in which the other salesperson stated that he could produce copies of letters dealers had written to Pioneer complaining about service.
6. *Favorable statements toward competition:* Sankyo unit had much better frequency response and much cleaner sound. Sankyo was the second largest manufacturer of tape decks and manufactured components for Teac.
7. *How were Pioneer products displayed in comparison to competition?* I did not see any of the Pioneer equipment advertised in the paper displayed in the normal manner. Specifically, CT-F7272 was missing from where all other Pioneer decks were displayed. It was in another room with a Sankyo unit sitting on top of it.
8. *Other comments:* When the salesperson set up to play the tapes back I noted that the Sankyo playback control was set at maximum volume and that he adjusted the Pioneer control to about 6. He began playing the tapes back, switching from one deck to the other and commented on the very audible difference of sound created by the higher frequency response of the Sankyo deck. I made no comment but asked to see the spec sheets on the two units. He came back with the spec sheet on the Sankyo but not the Pioneer.

    During the time I spent in the store I overheard no less than six customers ask specifically for one of the Pioneer products advertised in the paper. In each case the customer was told that the particular item had been sold out but that they had lesser or better products in the Pioneer line or comparable products in other lines. I also heard another customer ask if ABC Sounds could order Pioneer's HMP-100s. The salesperson replied, "No, we can't." The customer dropped the idea at that point.

Source: Company data.

EXHIBIT 10 Audio Warehouse advertisement

EXHIBIT 10 Audio Warehouse advertisement

having difficulty maintaining margins on Pioneer equipment'' and charged that Pioneer didn't "seem to care whether we make a profit or not'' *(Retail Home Furnishings).*

Although Mr. Mitchell was confident that the suit would be settled in Pioneer's favor (especially because the attorney general of Ohio became a coplaintiff), he was concerned about the impact of Audio Warehouse's publicity on Pioneer's dealer outlets. At the same time he wondered whether to initiate legal action against other offenders and/or terminate their franchises.[10] (See Exhibit 11 for sample agreement.)

EXHIBIT 11

Dealer Franchise Agreement

AGREEMENT made   this   day of   19 , by and between U. S. PIONEER ELECTRONICS CORP. a Delaware Corporation, having its principal place of business in Moonachie, New Jersey (hereinafter called "PIONEER"), and

hereinafter called "Dealer"

Signer's name _____

Corporate name _____

dba _____

Address _____

City_____ State _____ Zip _____

Telephone No. (_____) _____

WITNESSETH:

WHEREAS Pioneer is the Distributor of certain quality products which are sold under the Pioneer brand name and trade marks (hereinafter referred to as "Products"); and

WHEREAS, Dealer desires to engage in the sale of Products at retail.

NOW, THEREFORE, Pioneer and Dealer mutually agree as follows:

1. Pioneer hereby appoints Dealer one of its Franchised Dealers in the continental limits of the United States only, and Dealer hereby accepts such appointment and agrees conscientiously and diligently to promote the sales of the above mentioned products.

2. Dealer shall purchase from Pioneer such Products for resale but all sales or agreements by Dealer for the resale of Pioneer Products shall be made by Dealer as principal and not as agent of Pioneer.

3. Prices to Dealer for such Products shall be set forth in the Pioneer Dealer Cost Schedules issued from time to time by Pioneer. Pioneer shall have the right to reduce or increase prices to Dealer at any time without accountability to Dealer in connection with Dealer's stock of unsold products on hand at the time of such change. When a new price schedule is issued by Pioneer it shall automatically supersede all such schedules on and after its effective date.

4. Dealer has represented to Pioneer, as an inducement to Pioneer for entering this agreement, that Dealer is at the time of entering into this agreement solvent and in a good and substantial financial position. Dealer shall from time to time when requested by Pioneer furnish such financial reports and other financial data as may be necessary to enable Pioneer to determine Dealer's financial condition.

5. Pioneer shall have the right to cancel any orders placed by Dealer or to refuse or to delay the shipment thereof if Dealer shall fail to meet payment schedules or other credit or financial requirements established by Pioneer and the cancellation of such orders or the withholding of shipments by Pioneer shall not be construed as a termination or breach of this agreement by Pioneer.

6. Pioneer will use its best efforts to make deliveries with reasonable promptness in accordance with orders accepted from Dealer, but it shall not be liable for any damages, consequential or otherwise, for its failure to fill orders or for delays in delivery or for any error in the filling of orders.

7. No territory is assigned exclusively to Dealer by Pioneer. Pioneer reserves the absolute right, for any reason whatever, to increase or decrease the number of Franchised Dealers in Dealer's locality or elsewhere, at any time without notice to Dealer.

8. Pioneer shall have the right at any time to discontinue the manufacture or sale of any or all of its Products and parts without incurring any liability to Dealer.

9. Pioneer is at liberty to change its service policies, its financial requirements and the design of its Products and parts thereof at any time without notice, and the Dealer shall have no claim on Pioneer for damage by reason of such change or changes.

10. Dealer agrees to forward promptly to Pioneer information concerning all charges, complaints or claims involving Products, by customers or accounts, that may come to its attention.

11. Dealer shall at no time engage in any unfair trade practices and shall make no false or misleading representations with regard to Pioneer or its Products. Dealer shall make no warranties or representations to customers or to the trade with respect to Products except such as may be approved in writing by Pioneer. Dealer shall hold Pioneer harmless from all damages caused by Dealer's violation of this paragraph. Any written representations respecting Pioneer products must first be submitted to Pioneer for its written approval.

12. Dealer will use its best efforts to resell Products purchased from Pioneer.

---

[10] Most of these dealer franchise agreements had been signed during the "fair-trade" days and did not fully reflect the changes resulting from the FTC consent order.

EXHIBIT 11 *(concluded)*

13. Dealer shall have no rights in the names or marks owned, used, promoted by Pioneer or in the names or marks of Products, except to make reference thereto in selling, advertising and promoting the sale of Products, which right shall be completely terminated upon the termination of this agreement.

14. Nothing herein contained shall be deemed to establish a relationship of principal and agent between Pioneer and Dealer, Dealer being an independent contractor, and neither Dealer nor any of its agents or employees shall be deemed to be an agent of Pioneer for any purpose, whatsoever and shall have no right or authority to assume or create any obligation of any kind, express or implied, on behalf of Pioneer except as specifically provided herein, nor any right or authority to accept service of legal process of any kind on behalf of Pioneer nor authority to bind Pioneer in any respect whatsoever.

15. All negotiations, correspondence and memoranda which have passed between Pioneer and Dealer in relation to this agreement are merged herein and this agreement constitutes the entire agreement between Pioneer and Dealer. No representations not contained herein are authorized by Pioneer and this agreement may not be altered, modified, amended, changed, rescinded or discharged, in whole or in part, except by a written memorandum executed by Pioneer and Dealer in the same manner as is provided for the execution of this agreement, except that the agreement may be terminated by either party as herein provided.

16. This agreement shall become effective only upon its execution by Pioneer in its executive offices at Moonachie, New Jersey, and no changes, additions or erasure of any printed portion of this agreement shall be valid and binding unless such change, addition or erasure is initialled by both Pioneer and Dealer.

17. This agreement supersedes and terminates any and all prior agreements or contracts, written or oral, if any, entered into between Pioneer and Dealer as of the effective date of this agreement with reference to all matters covered by this agreement.

18. Dealer is appointed a Franchised Pioneer Dealer by reason of Pioneer's confidence in Dealer, which appointment is personal in nature, and consequently this agreement shall not be assignable by Dealer, nor shall any of the rights granted hereunder be assignable or transferable in any manner whatsoever without the consent in writing of Pioneer.

19. This agreement shall be governed and construed in accordance with the laws of the State of Delaware. In the event of the provisions of this agreement, or the application of any such provisions to either Pioneer or Dealer with respect to its obligations hereunder, shall be held by a court of competent jurisdiction to be contrary to any State or Federal Law, the remaining portions of this agreement shall remain in full force and effect.

20. Either Dealer or Pioneer may terminate this agreement at any time by giving five days' written notice to the other and such termination may be made either with or without cause. Neither Dealer nor Pioneer shall be liable to the other for any damages of any kind or character whatsoever on account of such termination. Pioneer, at its option, shall have the right to repurchase from Dealer any or all Products in Dealer's inventory within a reasonable period from said notice of termination, at the net prices at which such Products were originally invoiced to Dealer less any allowances which Pioneer may have given Dealer on account of such Products. If such option to repurchase is exercised by Pioneer, Dealer agrees to deliver the inventory of Products so purchased to Pioneer, Moonachie, New Jersey, immediately after receipt of the exercise of such option.

21. Any notice which is required to be given hereunder shall be given in writing and shall either be delivered in person or sent by registered letter via United States mail to the respective addresses of the parties appearing above. If mailed, the date of the mailing shall be deemed to be the date such notice has been given.

22. Dealer shall not return merchandise without Pioneer's prior written authorization; and Pioneer shall assume no responsibility for returns made without prior written authorization.

IN WITNESS WHEREOF, the parties hereto have caused these presents to be executed the day and year first above written.

DEALER:

BY _____ U. S. PIONEER ELECTRONICS CORP.

Title: _____ BY: _____

Dealer Communication Program

Sales representatives suggested that U.S. Pioneer organize an extensive communication program to convince dealers that the company was concerned about their well-being and to demonstrate how effective selling of Pioneer products could improve their profits. The sales reps were increasingly confronted with complaints from dealers such as

Most of my customers ask for Pioneer. But I can't make money with Pioneer.

How can we compete with discounters or mail-order guys who are selling Pioneer for as low as 10 percent above cost?

We'd be better off selling products of smaller manufacturers like Advent and Bose, which still sell at list prices.

I'm making 50 percent to 60 percent margin on house brands; why should I push Pioneer?

Such comments concerned Mr. Mitchell, because he thought dealer support was crucial. When a recent consumer survey asked, "What factors had the greatest influence in your most recent purchase of hi-fi products?" respondents replied,

	Percent of respondents*
Recommendations of friends	29%
Dealers/salespeople	27
Advertising by manufacturers	15
Recommendations of family members	12
Advertising by dealers	8
Store display	7
All others	14
No answer	(n = 1,290)

* Percentages total over 100 because of multiple answers.

In a sales representatives' meeting, Bob Gundick, president of the company sales office in Florida, displayed a presentation package he had used successfully. A set of flip charts was shown to dealers during regular visits and handouts (similar in content) were left after the presentations. As shown in Exhibit 12, the package suggested ways the dealers could (*a*) cope with their competitors, (*b*) determine their product mixes, (*c*) creatively sell Pioneer products in combination with other brands, and (*d*) improve their businesses in general. Mr. Gundick offered his package for nationwide use.

Other suggestions during the meeting included

1. Direct mail brochures to all dealers.
2. More salespeople to increase the frequency of dealer visits.
3. Cash rebates or other incentive programs (such as a contest for dealers).
4. Organizing a "national dealers conference" at a resort.

Although the format of the sales communication program was yet to be determined, Mr. Mitchell felt it justified a budget of $3 million. He was uncertain, however, whether the budget should be incremental or whether some funds should be transferred from consumer advertising.

EXHIBIT 12 Sunshine Audio sales presentation program

MOST OF MY CUSTOMERS ASK FOR PIONEER!!!

I CAN'T MAKE MONEY WITH PIONEER!!!

HOW OFTEN HAVE WE HEARD, OR HAVE YOU MADE, THESE VERY STATEMENTS. IF YOU ARE INTERESTED IN INCREASING YOUR OVERALL BUSINESS AND YOU WANT TO INCREASE YOUR OVERALL PROFIT DOLLARS—READ ON.

You and your competitor

Your business is really not that different from that of the store down the street. You both sell hi-fi, you both are after the same consumer, you both have to make a profit, you both want your business to grow, and you both are competing against each other. Why?

View your competitor as an ally and see what happens to your perspective of the business. You are both fighting to get consumers' disposable income dollars from the TV dealer, the motorcycle dealer, the travel agent, the car dealer, and any number of places they can spend that extra $300–$700. You and other hi-fi retailers should run ads to make the hi-fi market in your town grow—not to "get the other guy" with a low-ball price. Think about it—how many people in your market know that a RZ105 receiver at $136 is a good buy (cost in fact)? Much less, how many know what a receiver is?

You and your sales

Think about this for a minute. Most of your business should be in systems—about 70 percent. Single-piece sales account for the 30 percent balance. Fifteen percent are high margin pieces or accessory sales, and 15 percent are low margin promotional pieces. Now, think about that margin. If you only sell 40 percent margin products and you are not a "discount" house, how come your balance sheet only shows your gross margin between 28 percent and 32 percent? Interesting.

You and Pioneer

Now for the sales pitch. When you put a Pioneer piece in a system you will sell more systems (better brand name recognition) at your usual system margin. Pioneer has plenty of products that sell at full margin all the time—SG-9500, RG-1, turntables with cartridges, component ensembles, RT-2022, and so on. Of course, we have promotional pieces too, CTF 2121, Project 60, 100a, and others. But how low a margin is a CTF 2121 at a cost of $124—with an advertised price of $139—when you sell the deck and its case for $179. This makes the margin 26 percent; sell tape and your margin is higher. I can't make money on Pioneer. Don't believe it! How about the SX1250 at $595—only a $50 profit. With the $50 rebate recently offered your real profit is $100. Sell an extra three SX1250s each week and we add over 15,000 profit dollars to your bottom line in a year. Even without the $50 rebate, the contribution to profit is $7,500 in one year.

EXHIBIT 12 *(concluded)*

Instead of using your energy not to sell, to down sell, or to sell off Pioneer, what would happen if you put that effort into creatively selling it?

You and your business

Some suggestions:

Put together systems with brand name products that can't be duplicated by any dealer in your market.

Sell the accessories with the promotional pieces or make them part of a system to increase profitability.

Sell brand name goods that customers want.

Think in terms of profit dollars, not always gross profit margin.

You and the industry

Pioneer will spend close to $7 million in advertising. Take advantage of this tremendous support. Without advertising and without brand names your business would dry up. Most hi-fi dealers have some exclusive lines. But limited distribution can mean limited market and limited growth. Pioneer in a system will help sell more JVC receivers; Bose, JBL, or Advent speakers; Technics turntables; or whatever your exclusive is, and your business will grow. Pioneer has a product and a model that will fit almost any system you can design. The quality has never been questioned. Sandy Ruby from Tech HiFi in a recent *Home Furnishings Daily* was quoted as saying, "We're actually not doing as much business in limited distribution lines as we were a few years ago. We've tried to look more toward what the market wants. We see surveys of what people are buying or what they say they plan to buy around the coun- try . . . and then we get that equipment. You can't just look at your sales figures. Sure, you may be selling a lot of private brand equipment, but what about the people who didn't buy from you?" What brand do they want? You've got to have a handle on the customers who walked. Pretty interesting stuff. How many of your customers walked? How many did your salespeople's paranoia scare away?

We can help.

Long-Run Strategy Options

Citing the broad changes occurring in the industry, several sales reps argued that the existing situation provided a timely opportunity to reconsider U.S. Pioneers' long-run distribution strategy.

Distribution Shift

One possibility was to shift retail distribution away from specialty stores to department stores and catalog showrooms. In 1977, 75 percent of U.S. Pi- oneer's dollar sales were accounted for by hi-fi specialty stores, 5 percent by department stores, 7 percent by catalog showrooms, and 13 percent by appliance/TV/hardware/furniture stores.[11] Department stores and catalog showrooms did not generally offer the extensive customer services provided by specialty stores, including professional sales assistance, demonstration, extended store warranty,[12] on-the-premises repair, home delivery and installation, and loaner component programs. They usually had, however, extensive credit facilities, strong consumer "pull" advertising, and lower prices. Industry sources predicted a substantial increase in the market shares of department stores and catalog showrooms.

Multiple Branding

Some sales reps suggested that one way to take advantage of the trend toward more mass-oriented retail outlets and, at the same time, "keep specialty stores reasonably happy" would be multiple branding. U.S. Pioneer would offer several product lines of varying quality and price points under separate brand names. Different product lines would be carried by different types of retail outlets. The "department store" line would presumably be of lower quality and price than a "regular" line. Supporters pointed out that multiple branding had been used in other industries[13] and that it would enable U.S. Pioneer to adapt most effectively to future changes in retail distribution.[14] Others were more concerned that such a strategy would tarnish Pioneer's reputation for selling only top-of-the-line products.

Company-Owned Stores

Another strategic option was to move toward operating its own retail stores. Some retailers in the low-fi market (such as Radio Shack and Sears) had been selling their own house brands for some time. More recently, house brands were starting to make inroads in the hi-fi market. For example, house brand sales by Pacific Stereo (a chain of 80 West Coast stores) were estimated to be 25 percent (unit basis). In other hi-fi specialty stores, house brands were believed to account for 5 percent to 10 percent of unit sales.

---

[11] In terms of the number of existing U.S. Pioneer retail outlets, 69 percent were hi-fi specialty stores, 2 percent department stores, 3 percent catalog showrooms, and 26 percent other stores.

[12] Many specialty stores extended the two-year Pioneer guarantee on parts and labor on its electronics to three years.

[13] For example, it was used in the watch industry. The Bulova Watch Company had three brand names—Bulova, Accutron, and Caravelle. The Bulova line was intended for jewelry and department stores, Accutron for the best stores carrying the Bulova line, and Caravelle predominantly for quality drugstores and specialty gift shops. In fact, Bulova had experienced considerable difficulty maintaining discrete channels for these lines.

[14] Should discount stores become a major force in hi-fi components sales, a new line with a new brand name could be added. Pioneer Electronics of America, a separate, wholly owned subsidiary of Pioneer Electronics Corporation of Japan, currently sold compacts and car stereos to discount stores under the "Centrex" brand name.

Some sales reps felt that house brands would seriously threaten U.S. Pioneer. Because the primary promoters of house brands were large specialty store chains, Pioneer risked being "squeezed out" of them. One way to counter this prospective threat would be to start Pioneer retail stores by acquiring existing one- or two-unit family-owned stores or converting nonaudio stores into "Pioneer shops."

The estimated U.S. Pioneer initial fixed investment for starting up, say, a 5,000-square-foot hi-fi store was to be about $50,000. Given the operating data for a comparable existing specialty store, shown in Exhibit 13, the initial invest-

EXHIBIT 13
HI-FI SPECIALTY STORE*
Income Statement

	1976
Income	$680,069
Cost of sales	509,182
Expenses:	
Advertising	34,803
Sales commissions (4 salespeople)	36,048
Payroll home office (administration)	12,875
Payroll home office (clerical)	767
Payroll taxes	1,770
Rent	18,780
Depreciation	1,831
Insurance	2,937
Taxes—other	237
Freight out	2,017
Store security	1,168
Outside labor	3,374
Travel and entertainment	1,336
Bad debts	3,313
Repairs and maintenance	579
Repairs to merchandise	57
Credit plan service charges	872
Telephone	5,318
Heat, light, and power	1,242
Bad checks	4,108
Recruiting expenses	889
Store supplies and expenses	3,055
Selling and promotion	115
Cleaning and rubbish removal	45
Cash over and short	442
Office supplies and expenses	1,058
Group insurance	257
Interest expense	857
Legal and accounting	3,648
Auto and truck expense	2,070
Rental commissions	130
Computer service expenses	44
Bank service charges	147
Officers' life insurance	193
Miscellaneous	916
Total expenses	146,120
Operating income before federal taxes	$ 24,767

* One of a four-unit chain on the East Coast.

EXHIBIT 14

U.S. PIONEER ELECTRONICS CORPORATION

(A wholly owned subsidiary of Pioneer Electronics Corporation)

Statement of Income and Retained Earnings

($000)

	1976*		1975*	
Net sales	$134,836		$87,105	
Other operating revenue	258		235	
Total revenue		135,094		87,340
Cost of goods sold (CGS) (primarily purchases from the parent company)	91,707		60,470	
Selling, general and administrative expenses (SG&A)	30,608		23,409	
Total CGS and SG&A		122,315		83,879
Income before income taxes		12,779		3,461
Provision for income taxes		6,530		1,716
Net income		6,249		1,745
Retained earnings at beginning of year		4,985		3,240
Retained earnings at end of year		11,234		$ 4,985

* Fiscal year ended September 30.

Source: Company data.

ment appeared to be recoverable in a short time. (U.S. Pioneer's income statement is provided in Exhibit 14.)

Conclusion

A few months after the sales rep meeting, Mr. Mitchell met with Mr. Kai to decide what action, if any, to take in the short run and the long run to ensure U.S. Pioneer's growth and profitability.

Part 6

Promotion Decisions

A. Advertising Decisions

Advertising is the most visible and controversial activity carried on in marketing. The first seven cases in this section focus their attention on this function.

Advertising is defined as all paid, nonpersonal forms of communication that are identified with a specific sponsor. It, therefore, includes expenditures on radio, television, newspaper, magazines, and outdoor billboards, plus the Yellow Pages. The largest absolute dollar spenders on advertising tend to be big consumer products companies, like Procter & Gamble, General Foods, and General Motors. The industries that spend the highest percentage of their sales on advertising are the drug and cosmetic companies, followed closely by packaged food products and soaps.

The marketing decision maker has a number of decisions to make with respect to advertising for a product. These include:

1. Setting advertising objectives.
2. Determining the advertising budget.
3. Deciding on what creative presentation should be used.
4. Selecting what media vehicles to use.
5. Selecting what scheduling pattern should be used.
6. Deciding how the advertising should be evaluated.

In the cases that follow in this section, the reader will work to make decisions in most of these areas. The next section of this note is a short reminder of some of the concepts related to each of these decision points.

Advertising Objectives

Advertising objectives should be stated in qualified terms with a specific time period designed for a specific market target. The objective may be in terms of profits, sales, or communications measures such as awareness, interest, and preference. The objective: ''increase brand awareness'' is obviously not as good a statement as ''increase brand awareness to 85 percent of all women 18–40, in the next six months.''

Advertising Budgets

Advertising budgets are difficult to set. That is why companies have fallen into using rule of thumb methods such as (1) the ''all we can afford'' method; (2) the percentage of sales method; and (3) the matching competitors method. We would prefer decision makers to proceed by defining the task they hope to accomplish and then have them calculate the cost of doing this. This is called the task approach. To do this method the advertiser must understand the functional relationship between his or her task and advertising expenditures.

Creative Development

Creative activity is usually done by an advertising agency. The final product is usually the result of much copy testing on dimensions such as attention getting and persuasiveness.

Media Decision

Media decisions are of two types. The first is the selection of broad classes of media to be considered for future analysis. This is done by matching the media characteristics with the needs of the advertiser. For example, television allows for good visual demonstration. This may be a desired characteristic for the campaign at hand.

The second stage involves the selection of specific media vehicles, for example, the NFL football game versus ''All in the Family'' versus a page in *Fortune*. The procedures for doing this are complex. Simply stated, vehicles are compared on the basis of their cost per thousand (CPM) target audience persons reached. The vehicle with the lowest CPM is selected. Audience sizes are then adjusted to allow for duplication between vehicles and new CPMs are calculated. Then the lowest CPM vehicle at that point is selected. This process continues until the budget is used up. A number of computer algorithms have been developed to handle the many calculations made in this process.

Scheduling Patterns

The advertisers must decide whether to (1) spend their budget continuously throughout the period; (2) concentrate it at a short interval; or (3) spend it intermittently throughout the period. There are no good rules of thumb to answer this question. The advertisers must experiment to find out which pattern makes the most sense for their products.

Evaluating Advertising

If the advertiser has specified quantitative objectives, one is then in a position to measure to see if the objectives were met. The procedure used should be specifically designed to fit the type of objective stated.

B. Sales Management Decisions

The last three cases in this section of the book deal with the management of the personal selling function. Personal selling is defined as all paid, personal forms of communication that are identified with a specific organization.

Organizations in the United States spend over one and one half times as much money on personal selling as they do on advertising. Effective management of personal selling activity is thus very important.

The marketing decision maker has a number of decisions to make with respect to personal selling for a product. These include:

1. Defining the selling job to be performed.
2. Establishing the desired characteristics of the salespersons who will do this job.
3. Determining the size of the sales force.
4. Recruiting and selecting salespersons.
5. Training salespersons.
6. Organizing the sales force.
7. Designing sales territories.
8. Assigning salespersons to territories.
9. Motivating salespersons.
10. Compensating salespersons.
11. Evaluating salespersons.

In the three sales management cases that are in this section, the reader will work to make decisions in most of these areas. Again, the next section of this note is a short reminder of some of the concepts related to each of these decisions.

Definition of the Selling Job

The beginning point of all sales management decisions is the definition of the selling job to be performed. For example, is the job basically just order taking or are there complex engineering presentations involved? In defining a particular selling job, one must keep in mind the role of personal selling in the overall marketing strategy and understand well the needs of the buyer or buyers involved. The competitive and physical environments of the job are also important considerations.

Desired Characteristics for Salespersons

Out of the definition of the selling job, the manager is able to establish a set of criteria for determining the type of person who should perform the selling job. One should list the personal background and individual skills and qualifications that are necessary to effectively perform the defined job. For example, in selling complex electrical equipment, the criteria might include the holding of a degree in electrical engineering, with strong oral communications skills to make presentations to customers.

Sales Force Size

Determining the necessary size of a sales force involves determining the effort level capabilities of an average salesperson and dividing that into a measure of the total selling job to be done. In doing so, judgments must be made on how many total accounts to serve, how often to call on them, and how many accounts an average salesperson can effectively handle.

Recruiting and Selecting Salespersons

The selection of the right salespersons basically involves generating a pool of prospects and evaluating those prospects using the criteria established for the selling job. Information is collected on prospects using application forms, personal interviews, and psychological tests.

Training

The basic objective of training is to bring a salesperson up to the required level of competence in those areas of the defined selling job that were deficient upon hiring. These might include product knowledge, oral presentation skills, field procedures, and so on. Decisions must be made as to who should do the training and where it should be done. Do we let current salespersons do the training in the field or have special people to do it at the office, or some combination?

Organizing the Sales Force

The sales force may be organized on a geographical, product, market, or some combination of these factors basis. If a salesperson can effectively handle all the company's products in a given geographic area then the geographical structure probably makes the most sense. Otherwise, the product or market basis seem appropriate. The selection between these two approaches depends on whether product or market knowledge is the most important.

Designing Sales Territories

No matter how a sales force is organized, each salesperson is assigned a product or market or geographic territory. The determination of the size of a territory involves the trade-off between equalizing the sales potential in each territory and equalizing the required salesperson effort in each territory. It is usually impossible to have all one's territories with equal potential and equal effort. Both potential and required effort change with time, requiring territories to be changed. The reaction of current salespersons must be considered in doing this.

Assigning Salespersons to Territories

Just who is assigned to a particular territory is a tough issue. The criteria necessary for success may vary by territory for a given company. Chicago is different from Provo, Utah. Individuals may be selected for a particular territory, requiring that the selection criteria reflect these differences.

Motivating Salespersons

Many techniques are used to motivate salespersons. These include sales meetings, nonfinancial incentives, special recognition, and just the interpersonal style of the sales manager. However, these activities are not likely to be effective unless the selection, training, organization, territory designing, and assignment procedures are effective.

Compensation

Compensation is a key motivator that deserves special attention. The compensation plan (salary and/or commission, and/or bonuses for sales over quota) must fit the defined selling task, and the behavior one is trying to stimulate. For example, it would seem to make little sense to pay one's salespersons all on commission if the selling requires a great deal of new customer work with long purchase decision lead times.

Evaluating Salespersons

Evaluation provides important feedback to the salespersons as to how they are performing against the standards that management holds to be important. These standards may include sales levels, sales versus quota, call frequencies, new accounts opened, work habits, and so on. Some subjective judgments are a necessity for some of these standards. The proper handling of this type of feedback is a strong motivator.

Case 20

South-West Pharmaceutical Company*

In August, Frank Van Huesen, vice president of the New Orleans-based advertising agency, Advertising Associates, was sitting in his skyscraper office contemplating a meeting scheduled for the next week. At that time, he was to meet with Mr. Lewis Spring, president of South-West Pharmaceutical Company (S.W.P. Company), to discuss agency recommendations for Gentle Care advertising for the next year. Although advertising expenditures for Gentle Care, a skin conditioner for pregnant women, were relatively small, the client was an important account for Advertising Associates, with about $700,000 in billings. Even though the number of pregnant women had been declining, Gentle Care had been experiencing a sudden, unexpected surge in sales. Therefore, planning its future strategy posed a definite challenge to Van Huesen's marketing and advertising expertise. Before the meeting, he had to come up with sound answers to such questions as: "How much to spend for advertising?"; "What media mix to employ?"; and "What to say in messages for Gentle Care?"

Company Background

The S.W.P. Company of New Orleans, Louisiana, is the oldest manufacturer of proprietary medicine products in the United States. It all began in Iberville, Louisiana, in 1826 when Captain N. L. Denard obtained the "formula" for a tonic from the Choctaw Indians. Formulation took place on south Louisiana plantations for many years until 1860 when Charles Thomas Spring, a pharmacist, bought the formula for $25 and started making and selling bottles of the tonic for $5. The company was moved to New Orleans in 1874 because of the city's better transportation facilities, and growth continued in a sporadic way. In 1955, the Stanfield Company was absorbed and with it another unique product, Gentle Care, joined the S.W.P. product line.

---

* This case was prepared by Kenneth L. Bernhardt and John S. Wright, Professor of Marketing, Georgia State University. Copyright © 1987 by Kenneth L. Bernhardt.

The company now manufactures and sells three principal products: Spring's Tonic, Ease Eye Drops, and Gentle Care. Exhibit 1 shows a partial product list, which includes package sizes, prices charged to retailers per dozen items, suggested "list" prices to be charged customers by retailers, as well as case sizes and weights. Wholesalers selling the products receive an 18 percent discount for performing their functions. Sales volume for the company was at an annual rate of less than $5 million, and had been growing about 10 percent per year.

The firm's products have traditionally been sold in retail drugstores, which received the merchandise through drug and specialty wholesalers. The company employs one salesman who calls upon present and prospective customers, primarily in the Southwest. Mr. Spring is active in several trade associations and spends much time traveling to cement trade relations. Management is keenly aware that customer buying patterns are changing and, therefore, efforts are being made to have company products stocked in discount stores, supermarkets, and chain drugstores. Consequently, many "direct" sales are made to large retailers and to rack jobbers. Of its 3,000 active accounts, 500 are large retail chains, and the remaining 2,500 are to a variety of middlemen including wholesale grocers, rack jobbers, and specialty jobbers.

The Product and Its Market

Gentle Care is also very old as products go, having been first sold in 1869. The product, which is a skin conditioner especially formulated for use during pregnancy to relieve tight, dry skin, was originally provided in liquid form. When massaged on the skin, it has a very soothing and relaxing effect on the muscles. Gentle Care's basic ingredients include winter-pressed cottonseed oil, soft-liquid soap, camphor, and menthol.

EXHIBIT 1 Product and price list for S.W.P. Company

Wholesale discounts: 18 percent on net billing	Quantity: 150-pound minimum prepaid shipment. Any assortment of S.W.P. Company products in original case lots can be combined to meet these shipping requirements.			Resale to retailers. At list less applicable wholesaler's cash discount when earned. Terms: 2 percent if paid within 30 days from date of invoice. Net and due after discount period.	
Product	Unit size	List dozen	List	Packed case	Case weight
Gentle Care liquid	3 oz.	$29.60	$3.70	3 doz.	9½ lbs.
Gentle Care cream	2 oz.	29.60	3.70	1 doz.	3 lbs.

In 1967, a line extension of the product was devised in the form of Gentle Care cream, whose ingredients include cottonseed oil, laury, myrestyl, cetyl, stearyl in absorption base, glycerin, sorbitol, perfume, and color. Currently the cream form comprises a small but growing percentage of Gentle Care sales.

Mr. Van Huesen describes the industry as ''body lotions and creams for use during pregnancy.'' Exhibit 2 shows the few other companies in the industry, along with the pricing they employ. It should be noted that the other brands are very small in comparison to Gentle Care, are sold primarily through maternity shops, and have only regional or local distribution. None advertises, nor do the brands pose a competitive threat to Gentle Care, which is believed to have better distribution for its sales volume than any other drug product in the United States. By its very nature, the product is a ''slow-mover'' at the store level, and smaller outlets order the product in half-dozen lots. No deals have been made available to the middlemen in the past; however, an experiment was planned for the fall when retailers would be offered a ''one free in five'' package deal.

Isolating the target market for Gentle Care may appear to be an obvious exercise—it consists of all pregnant women. Within that category of womankind, however, Mr. Van Huesen thought the prime target for such lotions and creams should be the first-time mother-to-be. If she decides to use such a product at that time, it is quite likely she will again use it during succeeding pregnancies. What role is played by ''influencers'' (the expectant mother's mother, older mothers in the neighborhood, aunts, nurses, maternity shop personnel, and so forth) in the purchase and use decision is not known.

Birthrates in the United States have been declining precipitously, and the United States is approaching a state of zero population growth, a point where deaths and births are in balance. Reference to Exhibit 3 shows, nevertheless,

EXHIBIT 2 Industry and pricing structure—body lotions and creams for use during pregnancy

Company	Product	Size	Retail price	Wholesale price per dozen
S.W.P. Company, New Orleans, La.	Gentle Care (liquid)	3 oz.	$3.70	$25.60
	Gentle Care (cream)	2 oz.	3.70	25.60
Leading Lady Foundations, Inc., Cleveland, Ohio	Anne Alt Body Lotion	8 oz.	3.00	n.a.
Mothers Beautiful, Miami Beach, Fla.	Mothers Beautiful Body Lotion	8 oz.	2.50	n.a.
Shannon Manufacturing Co., North Hollywood, Calif.	Mary Jane Maternity Lotion	8 oz.	3.00	n.a.
Maternity Modes, Niles, Ill.	Maternity Modes Protein Body Creme	4 oz.	3.00	n.a.

n.a. = not available.

EXHIBIT 3 Birthrate by age of mother and color, United States, 1961–1971

Ago (years)	Nonwhite			White		
	Ten years age	Now	Percent change	Ten years ago	Now	Percent change
15–19	15.3%*	12.9%	−16%	7.9%	5.4%	−32%
20–24	29.3	18.5	−37	24.8	14.5	−42
25–29	22.2	13.6	−39	19.4	13.5	−30
30–34	13.6	8.0	−41	11.0	6.6	−45
35–39	7.5	4.0	−47	5.3	2.7	−49
40–44	2.2	1.2	−45	1.5	0.6	−60

* Table is read as follows: Ten years ago, of all nonwhite women between 15 and 19 years of age, 15.3 percent gave birth.

that one woman in seven in the 20–24 age range does have a baby in a given year.

Little is known about the consumer decision to use these lotions and creams during pregnancy. How do women learn about such products? Are influencers important to the decision, or does advertising inform the expectant mother of the product's availability? In the absence of specific research into this area of consumer behavior, it was assumed by both Mr. Spring and Mr. Van Huesen that advertising plays a significant, if not *the* critical, role. The product recently had been experiencing large increases in sales, with this year's sales expected to be about 50 percent greater than the level of two years earlier, in spite of a decline in the market potential for the product category. Exhibit 4 gives the sales of Gentle Care for the previous seven years, as well as the advertising-to-sales ratio for that period. The large sales increases were being achieved by both the liquid and cream forms of Gentle Care.

Marketing Strategy

The marketing strategies employed by S.W.P. Company are reflections of the marketing philosophy of its president, Lewis Spring. Before joining the firm in

EXHIBIT 4 Gentle Care—advertising-to-sales ratios

	Sales	Advertising	A/S ratio
Seven years ago	$189,578	$140,512	0.74
Six years ago	195,664	82,092	0.42
Five years ago	205,102	69,390	0.34
Four years ago	250,314	69,050	0.28
Three years ago	253,818	40,902	0.16
Two years ago	264,286	68,176	0.26
Last year	315,918	65,706	0.21
Current year	400,000 (projected)	75,000	0.19

1969, Spring worked in promotional jobs in the petroleum and entertainment industries and he views promotion as an important part of his job. Technical people are hired to handle the manufacturing and physical distribution sides of the business, while Spring concentrates on the marketing-sales-advertising operations.

This circumstance simplifies Van Huesen's job. There are no layers of bureaucratic approval of S.W.P. Company. Once Van Huesen and Spring agreed on a strategy to be followed, it was implemented. The process involved a combination of Spring's ideas on how proprietary drugs should be promoted and Van Huesen's understanding of how advertising can be used to achieve the company's goals.

For a long time, Spring has maintained great faith in the importance of package design to the sales success of the kind of products manufactured by his company. The company once changed advertising agencies over this issue; Spring thought the Gentle Care package needed changing, while agency personnel felt that such a change would destroy the product's "image with the consumer."

Another of Spring's marketing guidelines is that the smaller company "must find the one single most important use for the product" and build the promotional program around that point. Closely related is another philosophical belief, namely that the firm "should do what the competition is not doing," whether it is in the area of media selection, creative strategy, or other promotional concerns.

The Advertising Budget

The company management does not have any "cut-and-dried" formula for arriving at the advertising budget. Advertising's importance to the sales of company products is recognized by Lewis Spring; nevertheless, as Exhibit 4 reveals, the advertising-to-sales ratio has been declining over the past decade without a consequent decline in sales. The relatively large budget seven years ago was due to the simultaneous introduction of the cream and a change in package design, which was accompanied by an increased budget to help secure greater distribution. The drastic cutback in advertising expenditures three years ago was due to an unsuccessful diversification into the cosmetic business that necessitated a recoupment of financial resources. The relative cutbacks this year and last year were in response to tight money conditions at the time and to a management decision to "make this year a year of profit." Spring believes, however, that such cutbacks can be only a temporary phenomenon; in respect to advertising he holds that "you must be everlastingly at it."

Media Strategy

As has been characteristic of the proprietary drug industry for generations, Gentle Care was traditionally advertised by means of small space ads placed in newspapers. Twenty years ago it was realized that for a product whose market is as highly segmented as that for Gentle Care, this media strategy resulted in a great deal of "wasted circulation" of the advertising message; thereafter, advertising for the product was concentrated solely in magazines.

As shown in Exhibit 5, there exists an appreciable number of magazines which can be characterized as "baby oriented." Of course, within the category, those read during the prenatal stage are desired by the producers of pregnancy body skin conditioners. Once the child is born, the product is no longer needed, although it is possible that the woman will continue to use the product for other skin care purposes.

For many years, Gentle Care was featured in smaller-sized ads (one-sixth page to one-half page) in 8 or 10 magazines, one or two insertions per year. In other words, the emphasis was placed on the *reach* strategy—trying to get the message before as many different prospects as possible for a given expenditure of advertising dollars. This strategy was replaced with one aiming at greater *frequency;* fewer publications were used with more insertions in each magazine over the year. The rationale behind this change was based on the fact that there is no seasonality in the product's use; women become pregnant throughout the 12 months.

The current advertising schedule for Gentle Care is shown in Exhibit 6. One key change made last year was switching out of *Redbook,* where the product had been advertised every other month adjacent to the magazine's "expectant mother's" column. To ensure that position, larger space had to be purchased, so for the same amount of money, the entire McFadden Group of eight magazines was available, although for small-sized ads. The agency's media department felt that the McFadden Group would be a better match with the target market for Gentle Care than would *Redbook. Parents' Magazine* was

EXHIBIT 5 Baby-oriented magazines

Magazine	Frequency of publication	Circulation	CPM (B/W)	Page rate (B/W) one insertion
American Baby	Monthly	1,108,700	8.92	$ 9,890
Baby Care	Quarterly	575,785	7.49	4,310
Baby Talk	Monthly	1,021,693	8.28	8,460
Congratulations	Annually	2,624,120*	n.a.†	20,670
Expecting	Quarterly	855,013	9.11	7,790
Good Housekeeping	Monthly	5,703,732	3.94	22,765
Modern Romances	Monthly	752,339	3.48	2,645
Mothers' Manual	Bimonthly	913,085	8.77	8,010
Parents' Magazine and Better Family Living	Monthly	2,017,029	6.52	13,565
Redbook's Young Mother	Annually	1,519,888	4.77	19,345

* Distributed to specific places; CPM not determinable.

† n.a. = not available.

Source: SRDS *Consumer Magazines and Farm Publications.*

EXHIBIT 6 Gentle Care—current advertising plan

Magazine	Size ad	Cost per ad	Number ads	Total cost
Expecting	½ page (2¼ × 6¹⁵⁄₁₆ inches)	$6,620	2	$13,240
American Baby	1 col. (2⅜ × 5 inches)	3,640	3	10,920
Mothers' Manual	⅓ page (4⁹⁄₁₆ × 5 inches)	3,600	2	7,200
Parents' Magazine	1 col. (2¼ × 5 inches)	5,330	2	10,660
McFadden's Group	⅓ page (2¼ × 5¹⁄₁₆ inches)	6,082	4	24,328
True Story				
Photoplay				
TV-Radio Mirror				
True Confessions				
Motion Picture				
True Romance				
True Experience				
True Love				
Redbook				
Reserve for special regional availabilities				4,000
				$70,348
Estimated production				4,652
				$75,000

included in the media schedule primarily to allow the company to use the seal of approval in Gentle Care advertising, even though its impact on sales was undetermined.

Creative Strategy

Before Advertising Associates took over the account five years earlier, Gentle Care was advertised through ads which featured the product jar. A typical ad, as created by the former agency, is shown in Exhibit 7. This ad shows an attractive woman's head with her hand apparently rubbing her shoulder. The headline is very general in content; it is not until the reader sees the subheading does she learn that Gentle Care is for use during pregnancy. Seals of approval from two well-known certification agencies were also featured, which meant that advertisements had to be placed in *Good Housekeeping* and *Parents' Magazine*. Exhibit 8 shows the first advertisement in company history which prominently displays that the product is for use during pregnancy.

The new campaign inaugurated by Advertising Associates, an example of which is shown in Exhibit 9, was more direct; the reader could readily determine who used the product and for what purpose. One seal of approval, that of *Good Housekeeping* magazine, was dropped in the belief that the magazine's

EXHIBIT 7 Pre-Advertising Associates
ad for Gentle Care

EXHIBIT 8 First Gentle Care ad prominently featuring use during pregnancy

PREGNANT?
MAKE YOURSELF COMFORTABLE.

Treat your skin to a soothing beauty massage with Gentle Care. The rich lubricating liquid helps tight, dry skin stay soft and supple. It brings you ease and comfort while you wait. Look for Gentle Care at your Drug Counter. It's the Body Skin Conditioner that's especially recommended during pregnancy.

Gentle Care

EXHIBIT 9 First ad in the Advertising
Associates campaign

Make Yourself Comfortable.

Treat your skin to a soothing beauty
massage with GENTLE CARE. It's the
body skin conditioner that's especially
recommended during pregnancy. The rich,
lubricating liquid helps tight, dry
skin stay soft and supple. It
brings you ease and comfort
while you wait. Look for
GENTLE CARE
at your drug
counter.

Gentle
Care

EXHIBIT 10 Example of current advertising for Gentle Care

Don't let your tummy get out of shape while you're pregnant.

Give your tight, dry skin a soothing massage with Gentle Care. Its special formula will help relieve the taut feeling and minimize itching. And it will help your skin stay soft and supple. So make yourself comfortable. Look for Gentle Care in cream or liquid form at your drug counter.

audience was much older than the target market for Gentle Care. The decision was discussed at length because the role of older women in the purchase and use of the product was not known.

Changing standards and values in our society are reflected in the current campaign as shown in Exhibit 10. Here a nude model is seen actually applying the product as it would be done by the purchaser. Furthermore, the headline is direct and to the point. The *Parents' Magazine* seal is again featured, and the product package is illustrated in a subordinate position.

The New Advertising Plan

In mulling over the advertising history of his client, Van Huesen jotted down several questions which he felt needed answering before he could design the new advertising plan for Gentle Care:

1. What level of advertising should be recommended for next year?
2. What changes, if any, should be made in media strategy? Are specialized magazines the best media choice for Gentle Care? If so, are "baby-oriented" publications the best choice?
3. Is the frequency rather than the reach strategy to be continued for Gentle Care advertising next year?
4. Should the *Parents' Magazine* seal be retained?
5. What changes, if any, should Mr. Van Huesen recommend in the creative strategy for the product?

Once these questions were answered, Mr. Van Huesen felt he was ready to meet with Mr. Spring to present his recommendations for the Gentle Care advertising. Van Huesen knew from past experience that he could anticipate some probing questions from Mr. Spring concerning how the effectiveness of the advertising for Gentle Care could be measured.

Case 21

The Phoenix Suns (B)*

As opening day of the 1981–82 National Basketball Association season approached, Phoenix Suns' General Manager Jerry Colangelo found himself in an enviable, but frustrating, position. Colangelo was at the helm of one of the most successful and progressive franchises in the entire NBA. The Phoenix Suns had just completed their most successful campaign ever in terms of club wins (57 wins, .695 percent) fan attendance (92.9 percent of arena capacity), and the final standings (Pacific Division Champions).

The team was exceeded only by the World Champion Boston Celtics (62 wins, .756 percent), the Philadelphia 76'ers (62 wins, .756 percent), and the Milwaukee Bucks (60 wins, .732 percent) in total number of wins and won-lost percentage. In overall percent of arena capacity filled, the Portland Trail Blazers (100 percent), Milwaukee Bucks (98.9 percent), and Boston Celtics (94.8 percent) were the only NBA clubs to attain higher marks (see Table 1). In addition to these successes, Colangelo himself had been named NBA Executive of the Year by *The Sporting News*—the second time that he had been the recipient of this honor.

Yet, with all of this good fortune, Colangelo remained somewhat dissatisfied. The primary source of this dissatisfaction was the fact that his team had once again been disappointed in the NBA playoffs. A gritty Kansas City Kings club had defeated his Suns, four games to three, in the 1980–81 Western Conference semifinals. For Colangelo and the Suns the defeat represented the fifth time in the last six years that the Suns had made the playoffs but had failed to bring home the championship.

The upcoming season also posed a number of difficult off-the-court decisions that Colangelo did not look forward to making. The team's advertising agency had recently presented their recommendations for the 1981–82 Suns' advertising/promotional campaign and Colangelo found himself in disagreement with many of the agency's proposals. The agency had called for a substantial increase in the Suns' media budget and for a much expanded promotional effort. In view of the Suns' many accomplishments the previous year, Colangelo had serious doubts concerning the need for such an extensive program.

---

* This case was prepared by Professor Vincent J. Blasko, Arizona State University. The original version of the Phoenix Suns case was written by Charles H. Patti and appeared in *Advertising Management: Cases and Concepts,* by Charles H. Patti and John H. Murphy (Columbus, Ohio: Grid, 1978).

TABLE 1 1980–1981 NBA attendance figures and percent of arena capacity filled

		Total attendance	Average attendance	Arena capacity	Percent capacity
1.	Portland Trail Blazers	519,306	12,666	12,666	100.0
2.	Milwaukee Bucks	448,366	10,936	11,052	98.9
3.	Boston Celtics	595,454	14,523	15,320	94.8
4.	Phoenix Suns	482,693	11,773	12,660	92.9
5.	Golden State Warriors	413,480	10,084	13,239	76.2
6.	Los Angeles Lakers	537,865	13,119	17,505	74.9
7.	San Antonio Spurs	440,553	10,745	15,964	68.4
8.	New York Knicks	544,641	13,284	19,591	67.8
9.	Philadelphia 76'ers	469,355	11,448	18,276	62.6
10.	Utah Jazz	307,825	7,508	12,143	61.8
11.	Houston Rockets	385,354	9,399	15,676	59.9
12.	Denver Nuggets	423,307	10,325	17,271	59.8
13.	Seattle Supersonics	675,097	16,466	27,894	59.0
14.	Indiana Pacers	408,839	9,996	16,924	59.0
15.	Atlanta Hawks	595,454	8,846	15,700	56.3
16.	Chicago Bulls	389,718	9,505	17,374	54.7
17.	Kansas City Kings	336,585	8,209	16,638	49.3
18.	Washington Bullets	375,360	9,155	19,035	48.1
19.	Dallas Mavericks	319,347	7,789	17,134	45.4
20.	San Diego Clippers	257,597	6,283	13,841	45.4
21.	New Jersey Nets	302,059	7,367	21,100	34.9
22.	Cleveland Cavaliers	224,489	5,475	19,548	28.0
23.	Detroit Pistons	228,348	5,569	22,366	23.9

In evaluating the agency's performance over the last few seasons, Colangelo had also decided that the team's advertising had lacked a basic continuity and focus. This represented an additional area of concern for the Suns' management since the agency recommended the same overall strategies for the upcoming campaign.

Marketing Considerations

The Product

Jerry Colangelo and the Suns' top management have always strived to improve their product offering from year to year. Since the beginning of the franchise's history in 1968 (when the team struggled through their worst season ever—16 wins), Colangelo has worked tirelessly to improve all areas of the business. Fortunately, he has seen those efforts pay major dividends. That first season, a grand total of 753 season tickets were sold and attendance ran at a rather embarrassing 4,340 fans per home game. The team's second year saw season ticket sales jump to 1,752 and average home game attendance nearly doubled (7,617). From that point to the present, with the exception of the 1974–75 season, the Suns have steadily increased both their individual game ticket sales and their season ticket figures (see Table 2).

TABLE 2 Phoenix Suns' home attendance: 1968–1969 through 1980–1981

Year	Season ticket sales	Dates	Attendance	Average
1968–1969	735	37	160,565	4,340
1969–1970	1,752	37	280,868	7,617
1970–1971	3,204	41	332,945	8,120
1971–1972	3,510	41	342,922	8,364
1972–1973	4,396	41	342,117	8,444
1973–1974	4,503	41	284,424	6,934
1974–1975	2,900	41	253,103	6,173
1975–1976	3,500	41	295,293	7,202
1976–1977	5,030	41	411,294	10,032
1977–1978	5,500	41	470,009	11,463
1978–1979	6,800	41	465,010	11,342
1979–1980	8,010	41	480,659	11,723
1980–1981	8,026	41	482,693	11,773

The chief reason for the team's success at the gate is, of course, the overall success that the Suns have realized on the court over the past 13 seasons. Like most teams, the Suns have experienced their highs and lows—with most of the lows occurring between the dismal first year and the 1974–75 season. In that period, the Suns' record (including playoff contests) was 255 wins and 326 losses (.434 percent). The Suns had five coaches in those seven years and managed to make it to the playoffs one time—in the 1969–70 season.

The next six seasons (1975–76 through 1980–81) however, provided a totally different scenario. In that period, under Coach John MacLeod, the team notched an outstanding record. The Suns gained a playoff berth five times in those six years and earned a trip to the NBA World Championship Series in the 1975–76 season. In addition, the Suns' won–lost percentage, including playoff competition, rose to .575—a record exceeded by only Philadelphia, Los Angeles, and Boston for that same time period.

What is perhaps most impressive is the fact that this record was achieved without the presence of a true superstar on the team. While the Suns have had some very solid players, they have never built their attack around a specific individual. As a result, the Suns have gained the reputation for exciting team, rather than individual, performance.

In preparing for the coming 1981–82 season, the Suns' management made a number of transactions that they believe will add even more strength to the team's already impressive roster. Larry Nance and Craig Dykema, the Suns' number one and three draft picks in the 1981 college draft, were signed and second-year guard Dudley Bradley was acquired in a deal with the Indiana Pacers. Returning to the Suns are a number of standout performers including All-NBA defensive performer Dennis Johnson, all-star forward Walter Davis, and last year's impressive rookie, Kyle Macy. The Suns' aggressive, breakaway style and well-balanced attack, combined with these individual player personalities, make the Suns a very marketable product.

The Market

Fan Loyalty

In the formative years of the team's existence, General Manager Colangelo felt that the Phoenix market contained a number of negative characteristics with regard to the establishment of a successful NBA franchise. The most disturbing of these was the fact that the Phoenix area has been growing so rapidly that it was difficult to build true fan allegiance to the Suns. Many of the new Phoenix area residents (from the East and Midwest) still felt a strong loyalty to teams such as the Milwaukee Bucks, New York Knickerbockers, or Boston Celtics. In fact, a study conducted for the Suns in 1975 supported Colangelo's beliefs. Over one third of the study's respondents selected a team other than the Suns as their favorite NBA club.[1]

The problem of building a loyal following, however, seems to have been rectified as witnessed by the recent success of the team, near capacity attendance figures, and a later study which reported only 9 percent of the respondents selecting a team other than the Suns as "their favorite."[2] The study sampled 525 attendees at the first three home games of the 1978–79 season and was conducted by marketing research students at Arizona State University. The study was designed to answer the following two questions:

1. What demographic characteristics do the Phoenix Suns' fans possess?
2. What effect do various promotional activities have upon the fans' decision to attend the games?

See Tables 3 through 7 for the results of the study.

TABLE 3 Occupation characteristics of population attending Suns' first three home games in 1978

Occupation	Total number of responses	Percent of total
Laborer	28	5.3
Clerical	31	6.0
Professional	168	32.0
Technical	34	6.4
Service worker	26	5.0
Farm worker	4	.8
Sales	64	12.2
Student	54	10.3
Self-employed	48	9.1
Unemployed	21	4.0
Retired	19	3.6
Other	28	5.3
Totals	525	100.0

---

[1] McGuire Research Co., Dallas, Texas, December 1975.
[2] *Phoenix Suns Marketing Research Study,* College of Business Administration, Department of Marketing, Arizona State University, Tempe, Arizona, October 1978.

TABLE 4 Education characteristics of population attending Suns' first three home games in 1978

Education	Total number of responses	Percent of total
Finished grade school	16	3.0
1–3 years high school	37	7.0
Graduated high school	105	20.0
1–3 years college	189	36.0
Graduated college	178	34.0
Totals	525	100.0

TABLE 5 Income characteristics of population attending Suns' first three home games in 1978

Income	Total number of responses	Percent of total
No response	26	5.0
Under $8,000	52	10.0
$8,000–$14,999	100	19.0
$15,000–$24,999	137	26.0
$25,000–$39,999	121	23.0
$40,000 and more	89	17.0
Totals	525	100.0

TABLE 6 Age distribution of population attending Suns' first three home games in 1978

Age	Total number of responses	Percent of all sampled		
		Males	Females	Total
Under 18	39	4.8	2.6	7.4
18–24	78	9.8	5.2	15.0
25–35	141	17.5	9.3	26.8
35–49	179	22.0	12.0	34.0
50–64	64	8.1	4.1	12.2
65 and over	24	3.1	1.5	4.6
Total	525	65.3	34.7	100.0

TABLE 7 Effectiveness of promotions on fans' decision to attend Suns' games (data collected at Suns' first three home games in 1978)

	Reduced price tickets (percent)	Giveaways, T-shirts, etc. (percent)	Opposing team (percent)
Always influenced	36.0	16.0	53.0
Occasionally influenced	9.0	12.0	4.0
Never influenced	55.0	72.0	43.0
Total	100.0	100.0	100.0

Lack of Blue-Collar Market

Another major hurdle that the Suns have managed to negotiate successfully is the fact that a large portion of the Suns' spectators are employed in a professional capacity. This means the makeup of the Suns' target audience is quite a bit different from most NBA franchises. Typically, the blue-collar worker represents the largest portion of the professional sports team market; however, 32 percent of the Suns' audience are employed in a professional category. In addition, 70 percent of the Suns' home game attendees have attended college for one to three years or are college graduates.

Colangelo has been successful in turning this "disadvantage" into a marketing opportunity by employing an approach emphasizing season ticket institutional buys. Under this program, a large company purchases a block of season tickets and then uses the seats for various marketing and promotional activities (public and customer relations, employee incentives, customer contests, etc.). The Suns were the first NBA club to adopt this strategy—an approach now considered standard in the marketing of professional sports teams.

Stadium Expansion

Suns' management expects both season and individual ticket sales to be boosted even further with the expansion of the Phoenix Coliseum that was completed at the start of the 1981–1982 NBA season. A $1.2 million loan, approved by the Arizona State Legislature, allowed for the addition of 2,100 seats to the existing arena. The new capacity brings the total seating to approximately 15,000, a figure that closely parallels that of other NBA arenas.

Colangelo believes that the addition will increase season ticket sales by 1,000 and that overall attendance will be increased by 2,000 per game. It is estimated that an increase of 2,000 fans per game will mean over a half million dollars to the Suns in gate receipts.

Effects of a Championship

Colangelo feels that the best way for the Suns to increase attendance revenues would be to win the NBA World Championship. The experience of the Portland Trail Blazers, NBA Champions of 1977, would seem to confirm Colangelo's beliefs. The Portland club has consistently sold out their home dates since winning the championship and shows no signs of any attendance loss four years later (see Table 1). Colangelo also cites the 1976–77 season (the year following the Suns' defeat by Boston in the championship series) as proof of what that title could mean. Average attendance per game during the 1976–77 season jumped 39 percent (from 7,202 in 1975–76 to 10,032) and season ticket sales increased 25 percent (from 3,500 in 1975–76 to 5,030).

In addition to improving performance at the gate, Colangelo feels the championship would increase the profitability of the team's television market also. The Suns sell television rights to KPNX, a Phoenix TV station, and have also entered into a contract with the American Cable Company. American Cable will televise a total of 37 Suns' games (20 home, 17 away) beginning with the 1981–82 season. The NBA championship would undoubtedly increase the price of these rights substantially. The Suns' radio market is controlled by the team, who purchase the air time from KTAR, a Phoenix radio station. The Suns then sell the advertising time to produce profit from the broadcast. An NBA championship title would, of course, raise the price of that advertising time.

The Competition

The Suns find themselves in an excellent marketing position because there is only one other major league team in the Phoenix metropolitan area. The other professional sports franchise competing with the Suns is the Phoenix Inferno, a member of the Major Indoor Soccer League. The Inferno, who also play in the Phoenix Coliseum, began their second full season in 1981 and compete in 22 contests at home. Two other professional sports franchises, the Phoenix Racquets (World Team Tennis) and the Phoenix Roadrunners (World Hockey League), had been located in the market but both teams experienced only limited success, for various reasons, and were forced to discontinue play.

The Suns must also compete with a major collegiate sports power, Arizona State University, an institution located in nearby Tempe and well known for its top-flight baseball, football, and basketball teams. ASU is a member of the competitive PAC-10 Conference. In addition, ASU's stadium is the home of the Fiesta Bowl football game, which takes place every December.

In the spring four major league baseball teams (Oakland A's, Milwaukee Brewers, San Francisco Giants, and Chicago Cubs) make the Phoenix area their annual training ground. Also, the Phoenix Giants (the AAA minor league baseball team of the San Francisco Giants) play a 70-game home schedule that extends from April through August. See Exhibit 1 for a summary of team sports located in the Phoenix metropolitan area.

In addition to the organized team sports in the Phoenix area, Suns management realizes that the many outdoor recreational activities that the

EXHIBIT 1 Team sports in Phoenix

Team	Season	Home games	Average attendance	Ticket price*
Phoenix Suns	October–April	41	11,723	$4.50
Phoenix Giants	April–August	70	5,255	2.50
Phoenix Inferno	November–April	22	7,191	4.00
ASU football	September–December	6	63,683	7.25
ASU baseball	January–May	35	2,160	2.50
ASU basketball	November–March	14	8,703	5.00
Major league baseball (spring training)	February–April	40	2,500	3.00

* Denotes general admission ticket price.

Phoenix area is well known for must also be considered direct competition for the sports enthusiast's dollar. Because the weather in the area is comfortable throughout most of the year, the many activities (golf, hiking, boating, tennis, etc.) available to Phoenix residents comprise a negative factor with regard to professional sports attendance.

Past Marketing Efforts

Promotional Strategy

Basically, the Suns' management conducts two promotional campaigns. The first is geared toward the building of season ticket sales and the second attempts to increase individual game ticket purchases. Season ticket sales are promoted primarily through personal sales calls made by a Suns' representative on large Phoenix area businesses. The primary purpose of these visits is to discuss with company executives the advantages connected with the purchase of a large block of Suns' season tickets. The Suns' representative outlines a variety of promotional ideas and programs that these organizations can implement through the use of season tickets. Many large Phoenix firms (such as Armour Dial, Carnation, and First National Bank) take advantage of this program and have used the season seats to accomplish a variety of their own marketing and promotional objectives (increased traffic, better customer relations, and others). The Suns have also used newspapers and direct mail in the promotion of season tickets. These media, however, play a much less important role in the marketing of these seats since the majority (78 percent) of season purchases are made by area businesses.

Although the 1978 survey profiles the Suns' primary target audience quite well, Suns management believes that the market for individual home games is, in actuality, much broader than this. The Suns feel that any sports enthusiast who lives in the area and has the means available ($4.50) for a general admission ticket is an excellent prospect for a single game ticket sale. The Suns have used a number of promotions to help encourage attendance at individual games, including giveaway nights (team posters, T-shirts) and numerous discount ticket nights in cooperation with local businesses (Basha's Night, Circle K Night, and the like).

Other secondary markets that the Suns management feels are important in individual game sales are out-of-town businesses that will be holding conventions in the Phoenix area and the many area clubs and organizations that might be interested in a Suns outing. These prospects (convention directors and club officers) receive a mailer that offers selected home games at specific group rates. Since the target market for individual game tickets is a good deal broader than that for season tickets, the Suns rely more heavily on a wider range of media (television, newspaper, radio, and outdoor) to deliver their advertising message.

Creative Strategy and Execution

In attempting to increase attendance, for both season ticket sales and individual game ticket sales, the Suns have adopted a number of creative concepts which have served as a basis for their advertising executions. These concepts and executions have been built around a number of consumer sales points and consumer benefits. The majority of the Suns' advertising messages are delivered through radio and newspaper, with television, magazine, and outdoor also used but to a much lesser degree (see Table 8). A description of the creative themes and executions are outlined below.

1. Stars on other teams. Frequently, Suns' ads have featured prominent players on other teams, such as Julius "Dr. J" Erving of the Philadelphia 76'ers (see Exhibit 2) and Ervin "Magic" Johnson of the Los Angeles Lakers (see Exhibit 3). Used to promote individual games, this theme has highlighted the playing ability of NBA superstars as well as the personality of their respective teams.

2. Suns player/company discount promotions. The Suns have also used ads featuring their own team members (such as Walter Davis and Alvin Scott) in conjunction with company promotional nights to boost individual game attendance (see Exhibits 4 and 5). The strategy behind these ads is to capitalize on the performance/personality of the Suns players and to promote the company ticket discount. In addition, the Suns have promoted company discount nights quite frequently on radio.

3. Season ticket promotions. Ads intended to increase season ticket sales have generally centered around a specific Suns player (see Exhibit 6) or on the Suns' team personality (see Exhibit 7). Because the majority of season ticket sales are made to businesses (through personal sales and direct mail), these themes have been used rather infrequently in Suns advertising.

TABLE 8 Phoenix Suns' media expenditures: 1977–1981

Medium	1977–78*	1978–79†	1979–80‡	1980–81§
Newspaper	$52,100	$49,614	$40,984	$44,382
Radio	21,523	19,786	21,260	20,380
Magazine	855	988	71	185
Television	750	2,380	1,970	2,560
Outdoor	1,756	—	1,037	1,065
Totals	$76,984	$72,768	$65,322	$68,572

* Does not include $42,625 of media purchased by trading tickets for space and/or time.

† Does not include $40,757 of media purchased by trading tickets for space and/or time.

‡ Does not include $41,145 of media purchased by trading tickets for space and/or time.

§ Does not include $44,320 of media purchased by trading tickets for space and/or time.

EXHIBIT 2

THE DOCTOR MAKES A HOUSECALL!

Julius Erving

SUNS VS. 76ERS
Monday, Oct. 19 / 7:35

See Dr. J, Darryl Dawkins and the rest of the Sixers in one of only two Coliseum appearances this season. Get tickets early for best seat selection.

PHOENIX SUNS

TICKETS:
Suns office—2303 N. Central
Coliseum Box Office
Diamonds Box Office*

50¢ service charge per ticket at Diamonds

EXHIBIT 3

SUNS VS. LAKERS
SATURDAY / 7:35

Magic Johnson

PHOENIX SUNS

TICKETS:
Suns Office—2910 N. Central
Coliseum Box Office
Diamonds Box Office*

50¢ service charge per ticket at Diamonds

EXHIBIT 4

SUNDAY /7:05

SUNS
VS. WARRIORS

Walter Davis

ARMOUR DIAL NIGHT

Bring a wrapper from Dial soap to the Suns
office and get a $3 discount on $8 tickets, a
$2 discount on $6 or $7 tickets. Offer good
only at the Suns ticket office and is subject
to ticket availability.

**PHOENIX
SUNS**   2303 N. Central

EXHIBIT 5

THURSDAY/7:35
SUNS
VS. HAWKS

Only Coliseum appearance by Atlanta this season

Alvin Scott

BASKIN·ROBBINS
31 FLAVORS NIGHT
Ticket discount coupons available at
Baskin-Robbins 31 Flavors Ice Cream stores

$8 tickets — $3 discount per ticket with coupon
$6 & $7 tickets — $2 discount per ticket with coupon

Redeem coupons at any Suns ticket outlet,* including the
Coliseum right up till gametime. Subject to ticket availability. Children 12 years & under get $8, $7, or $6 adult
tickets FOR HALF PRICE.

PHOENIX SUNS

TICKETS:
Suns office – 2303 N Central
Coliseum
Diamonds Box Office*

*35¢ service charge per ticket at Diamonds

EXHIBIT 6

MACY!

In Indiana, his high school talents earned Kyle Macy the title of "Mr. Basketball." At the University of Kentucky, he was a three-time All American. As a pro with the Suns…the beat goes on.

And the best way to see it, is with your own season tickets. For your family. For your business.

Tomorrow, call or visit the Suns office to get complete information on the many season ticket packages available. It's the best entertainment around.

PHOENIX
SUNS

2303 N. Central
258-7111

EXHIBIT 7

Intensity!

You see it in every Phoenix Suns fast break, in every steal, in every John MacLeod time-out. And it's contagious!

Catch it yourself, 41 nights a year, with season tickets. There isn't a better entertainment act in town.

PHOENIX

2303 N. Central   **258-7111**

SUNS

4. Giveaway promotions. The Suns agency has also included the team's many giveaway nights in advertising designed to build single game attendance. These ads have featured such promotions as Team Poster Night (see Exhibit 8) and Suns T-Shirt Night (see Exhibit 9). These giveaways are usually advertised as part of an overall promotion being sponsored by a local company (other giveaway promotions include Coors Cup Night and Pepsi-Cola Tote Bag Night).

5. Family-oriented promotions. Top management has always felt it important to reinforce the belief that Phoenix Suns basketball is family entertainment, packaged in a highly appealing team, and augmented by numerous family-oriented promotion nights. This theme has been advertised through a variety of executions and in a variety of media (see Exhibit 10).

EXHIBIT 8

HOME OPENER!
PHOENIX   SAN ANTONIO
SUNS VS. SPURS
TUESDAY, NOV. 3 / 7:35 p.m.

CIRCLE K NIGHT
Save on tickets to the Suns' home opener with special discount coupons available at Circle K stores throughout the Valley. Or use the coupon below.

FREE SUNS CALENDAR POSTERS
to everyone attending the game, compliments of Circle K!

TICKETS:
Coliseum Box Office, Diamonds Box Office*
Suns Ticket Office—2303 N. Central
    (2910 N. Central effective Nov. 2)

SUNS TICKET DISCOUNT COUPON

SUNS VS. SPURS / Nov. 3

PHOENIX SUNS

This coupon good for a $2.00 discount on $7.00 adult tickets or a $2.50 discount on $9.50 adult tickets purchased for the above game. Discount ticket prices for children 12 years & under are one half the regular adult ticket price. To receive discount, coupon must be redeemed at the time of ticket purchase. Redeem the coupon at the Suns office, Diamonds Box Office* or at the Coliseum Box Office right up until game time. Offer is subject to ticket availability.

*50¢ service charge per ticket at Diamonds   Code B 1

EXHIBIT 9

Mike Bratz

CIRCLE K NIGHT
Ticket discount coupons available at all Valley Circle K locations

$8 tickets — $3 discount per ticket with coupon
$6 & $7 tickets — $2 discount per ticket with coupon

Redeem coupons at any Suns ticket outlet,* including the Coliseum right up till gametime. Subject to ticket availability. Children 12 years & under get $8, $7, or $6 adult tickets FOR HALF PRICE.

FREE SUNS T-SHIRTS

to the first 3,000 16 years & under at the game, compliments of Circle K.

TICKETS:
Suns office — 2303 N. Central
Coliseum
Diamonds Box Office*

*35¢ service charge per ticket at Diamonds

EXHIBIT 10

SUNDAY/1:45 p.m.

SUNS

New Jersey

VS. NETS

Alvan Adams

SMITTY'S FAMILY PLAN

Pick up Family Plan ticket discount coupons at any Valley Smitty's location. Redeem at a Suns ticket outlet and save $3 on $8 tickets; $2 on $6 & $7 tickets. Subject to ticket availability.

PHOENIX SUNS

TICKETS:
Suns office — 2303 N. Central
Coliseum
Diamonds Box Office*

*35¢ service charge
per ticket at Diamonds

Current Situation

As the Suns face the 1981–82 season, very few obstacles would seem to stand in the way of successful ticket sales and further improvement in attendance figures. However, there are two negative factors that must be considered when one begins to construct an objective-oriented advertising plan. These problem areas, as outlined by the Suns' advertising agency, are as follows:

1. *Lack of "choice" season tickets.* Because of excellent team performance in the past few seasons and a low season ticket attrition rate, many of the best season seats are no longer available for purchase.
2. *Economic factors.* Double-digit inflation, possible fuel shortages, and other demands on personal income are likely to cut into discretionary funds and impact leisure-time activities.

The Suns' agency has also pointed out that the team has a number of items in its favor. These are:

1. *Increase in attendance.* The previous year saw the team enjoy their best season in terms of overall attendance and season ticket sales.
2. *Team performance.* The Suns are also coming off their best year in terms of on-court performance, with the team recording a mark of 57 wins against only 25 defeats.
3. *Team charisma.* The Suns are a team characterized by youth, personality, and a breakaway style of play. These attributes combine to make the team a very marketable product.
4. *Realignment of NBA schedules.* The weighting of schedules toward more frequent play within conferences and divisions will serve to create two areas of opportunity:
    a. The more frequent exposure to teams within the division will heighten rivalries and place more significance on intradivision contests.
    b. One-time visits by top teams outside the conference (Boston, Milwaukee, Washington, and Chicago) will give tickets to these games a premium status.
5. *Promotional nights.* The various premium and discount offers conducted with local businesses provide an incentive for the occasional ticket buyer to become exposed to Suns basketball more frequently. This may heighten a fan's interest in the Suns and may also make the individual a prospect for future season tickets. (See Exhibit 11 for the agency's proposed promotion game schedule.)
6. *Healthier local economic outlook.* Despite the many negative influences nationwide, the Phoenix economy is likely to suffer less than other parts of the country. Local economic indications are quite strong, with personal income and employment figures at all-time highs.
7. *Additional 2,000 Coliseum seats.* The expansion of the Veteran's Memorial Coliseum provides an excellent market opportunity for the Suns in both season and individual game ticket sales.

EXHIBIT 11 Suns' promotion games: 1981–1982 Phoenix Suns

Date		Opposing team	Promotion
November	3	San Antonio	Circle K Night
			Poster Calendar Night
November	5	Dallas	Armour Dial Night
November	25	Houston	Bashas' Night
November	27	Chicago	Pepsi-Cola Night
December	1	San Diego	Armour Food Night
December	5	Utah	Phoenix Gazette Night
December	10	Portland	Sun Giant Night
			Coors Cup Night
December	12	Washington	Circle K Night
			Carnation YMCA Night
December	19	Kansas City	Pepsi-Cola Team Poster Night
December	23	Golden State	J. C. Penney Poster Night
December	30	Portland	Rossie Ford Night
January	2	Seattle	Greyhound Night
			Gorilla T-Shirt Night
January	14	New York	Carnation Night
January	16	San Diego	Circle K T-Shirt Night
January	19	San Antonio	Bashas' Night
January	22	New Jersey	Pepsi-Cola Tote Bag Night
January	23	Detroit	Carnation Girl Scout Night
February	3	Golden State	Checker Auto Night
February	10	Boston	Coors Cup Night
February	12	Atlanta	Earl's Sporting Goods Night
			Wristband Night
			Carnation Boy Scout Night
February	26	Denver	Circle K T-Shirt Night
March	3	Utah	Armour Food Night
March	5	Kansas City	Pepsi-Cola Night
March	7	Houston	Armour Dial Night
March	21	Seattle	Pioneer Take-Out Night
March	24	Dallas	Circle K Night
March	26	Milwaukee	Nike Poster Night
April	4	Kansas City	Bashas' Night
April	8	Portland	Circle K Night

8. *Influx of new residents*. As the Phoenix metropolitan area continues to grow, new markets for both season tickets and individual game ticket sales will be further expanded.

After evaluating the advertising and promotion plans prepared by the Suns' advertising agency for the 1981–82 season, General Manager Jerry Colangelo finds himself hesitant in approving the agency's recommendations. For the past three years the Suns have been spending between $65,000 and $73,000 for advertising media (see Table 8). The cost of giveaways, salaries, production, and media time and space purchased in exchange for tickets is not included in these figures. To further increase both season ticket sales and individual game ticket sales, the Suns' advertising agency is recommending (based on the aforementioned positive factors) a substantial increase both in the media budget (see Table 9) and in individual game promotions. (See Exhibit 11.)

TABLE 9 Proposed Phoenix Suns' media budget: 1981–1982

Medium	Proposed budget*
Newspaper	$55,000
Radio	31,000
Magazine	6,000
Television	6,000
Outdoor	2,000
Total	$100,000

* Does not include approximately $45,000 of media space and/or time that will be purchased by trading tickets.

The agency is recommending a $100,000 media budget and is also requesting an expanded promotional effort consisting of 29 promotion games. (This is an increase of 38 percent over the previous year, in which 21 promotion nights were held.) The agency feels that the Suns are a very salable commodity and that the current situation warrants increased expenditures to take full advantage of an excellent market opportunity. Mr. Colangelo, on the other hand, is not convinced that the agency's media and promotion recommendations are particularly sound. It is his feeling that the team is now in a position to rely more on its excellent record and proven personnel to increase attendance.

Mr. Colangelo has always believed that a team's success at the gate is directly related to its performance on the court. He backs up this contention by citing the 1970–71 and 1971–72 seasons, when team attendance was growing rapidly without large advertising expenditures (about $30,000) and with about half the number of promotions that are currently being recommended. During these two seasons the team had excellent records and therefore generated expanded interest and support. He also brings out the fact that after the Suns' exciting 1975–76 season, ticket sales soared and the team was spending only $50,000 on advertising media. It is Mr. Colangelo's contention that, after the Suns' best season ever, the fans will not have to be coaxed into coming to see the team play.

In addition, Mr. Colangelo has his doubts concerning the viability of the giveaway and discount ticket promotions. His feeling is that teams with excellent records should not have to rely so heavily on giveaways and discounts to attract fans. A successful team, in Colangelo's opinion, is the best promotion that management can possibly have. For these reasons, and the fact that the Suns are currently the only proven major league sports franchise in the area, Mr. Colangelo would like to see the media budget set at $50,000 and the number of promotions reduced by half of what the agency suggests.

Finally, the Suns' management feels that a clear statement of advertising objectives is needed to provide the team's overall communications effort with a basic focus and direction. Without these goals, Colangelo feels that a unified program is impossible.

Case 22

Law Offices of Gary Greenwald*

Gary Greenwald leaned back in his chair, daydreaming about what it was going to be like to become a daddy. His law practice had been growing since he started it nearly two years ago, and he was pleased that this year's gross income looked like it would be about 50 percent higher than he earned during his first year. He recognized, however, that he would have to convert some of his excess capacity to increased business if he was to be able to buy a house and adequately support his family. He decided to review the actions he had taken to increase the business over the past 18 months and do some thinking about marketing activities for the next year. He also thought he should review the Bar Association Canon of Ethics regarding marketing practices.

Background

From 1908 until 1977, the legal profession in the United States operated under a canon of ethics that formally banned any method of advertising or client solicitation. The ban, enforced by the American Bar Association (ABA), had historic precedent. Since the days of ancient Greece and Rome, solicitation by attorneys and judges had been both a written and unwritten taboo.

The prohibition of legal service advertising was initiated in the United States in 1908 for several reasons. First, it was felt that the advertising of certain legal services would cause an increase in the events that prompted the need for such service. For example, members of the legal profession thought that advertising of legal services for divorce proceedings would cause an increase in the number of divorces. Second, the American Bar Association felt that the demographic profile of the United States (at that time primarily a rural population) did not have a legitimate need for advertising. Most lawyers were general practitioners in small communities, and legal services were rendered with a one-to-one relationship between people who were known to each other and the community.

By the mid-1970s, the demographics of the country had changed dramatically from what they were in 1908. An equally important change had occurred

* This case was written by Kenneth L. Bernhardt and Bruce Bassett, Graduate Research Assistant, Georgia State University. Copyright © 1984 by Kenneth L. Bernhardt.

in the legal process of society and in the legal needs of the population. Gone were the days of general practitioners and one-to-one relationships between lawyers and clients/friends. Instead, there was a complex society in which legal regulations were rampant and legal specialization was a necessity. One thing that had not changed, however, was the advertising/solicitation prohibition in the ABA Canon of Ethics.

Changes in the Legal Environment

In 1973 and 1974, the ABA conducted a survey to analyze the public's level of knowledge about lawyers, the law, and the legal process. The survey showed that the public had difficulty recognizing when they needed legal services, finding a lawyer to provide such services, and determining what a lawyer would cost. This survey led the ABA to reexamine its restrictions against advertising.

In December 1975, the ABA Committee on Ethics and Professional Responsibility proposed a change in the Canon of Ethics which would allow advertising not containing a false, fraudulent, misleading, deceptive, or unfair statement or claim. However, at the 1976 midyear meeting of the ABA House of Delegates, the advertising proposal was rejected in favor of a limited code amendment. Under the revised amendment, lawyers were allowed to communicate certain information about themselves and their practice (such as name, address, nature of practice, and consultation fees) in legal directories, bar association directories, and the Yellow Pages of telephone books. Concerned that the ABA had not gone far enough, in June 1976, the U.S. Department of Justice initiated an antitrust suit against the ABA, alleging a conspiracy to prohibit advertising.

Responding to changes in the environment, there emerged in the late 1960s and early 1970s clinics of various sorts to meet the needs of society. These clinics ranged from psychological counseling centers to abortion clinics to health services clinics to legal clinics. Each type of clinic had as its avowed purpose the rendering of specific high-quality services to a large number of people at a low cost to the individual. The clinic concept had initially been part of the social and human rights movements and had been financed in large part with government funds. It slowly evolved from a publicly funded orientation into a private enterprise orientation—this was especially true for legal clinics. Private legal clinics sprang up to handle such routine matters as uncontested divorces, adoptions, simple personal bankruptcies, simple wills, and name changes.

The Bates Case

From 1974 through 1976, John Bates and Van O'Steen ran a legal clinic in Phoenix, Arizona. Their clinic handled routine legal matters and was able to keep costs low by utilizing standardized office procedures and forms. They also used automated typing equipment and relied heavily on paralegals.[1] Their idea was to charge low prices for their legal services but to make money by doing a high volume of work.

The issue of advertising was a hot topic in most local ABA circles, and Bates and O'Steen decided to use advertising to secure a steady flow of new business, which they felt was critical to the success of their clinic. They placed an ad in the February 26, 1976, *Arizona Republic Newspaper,* offering "legal services at very reasonable fees." The ad listed their fees for the various legal services they provided (see Exhibit 1). The ad violated the Arizona Bar Association Disciplinary Rule 2-101(B), which prohibited lawyers from publicizing themselves through print, radio, and television advertisements or any other means of commercial publicity.

Bates and O'Steen were summoned before the local ABA disciplinary committee which recommended that they be suspended for six months. The Board of Governors of the Arizona Bar Association, upon reviewing the proceedings, recommended a one-week suspension. The two lawyers took the case to the Arizona Supreme Court which held that the state board had acted within its rights. Bates and O'Steen then sought review of the decision by the U.S. Supreme Court.

In 1977, the U.S. Supreme Court agreed to review the case. In the opinion of the Court, there were several issues that dealt with the U.S. Justice Department's antitrust suit against the ABA and several issues that concerned advertising. It was the opinion of the Court that the public's need for information about availability and costs of legal services outweighed the concerns expressed by the Arizona bar that advertising would have a negative impact on professionalism, on the quality of service provided, and on the administration of justice.

Although allowing lawyers to advertise, there were certain restrictions on legal services advertising that the Court did not strike. The Court allowed continued restrictions on ads that were false, deceptive, or misleading and ruled that the time, place, and manner of lawyer advertising could be subjected to reasonable restrictions. In addition, the Court felt that in order to assume that a consumer would not be misled a disclaimer might be needed. In concluding, the Court avoided a stand on radio and television advertising, stating that "the special problems of advertising in the electronic broadcast media would warrant special consideration." In-person solicitation was not an issue in the Bates case and was reserved for future consideration by the Supreme Court.

Changes after Bates

In August 1977, the ABA responded to the Bates decision by creating the ABA Commission on Advertising. The commission developed two alternative pro-

---

[1] Paralegals are individuals who have had some specialized legal training but have not graduated from law school and are not certified by the ABA to practice law. They typically are paid much less than a new attorney just out of law school.

EXHIBIT 1
Ad at issue in *Bates* v. *State Bar of Arizona*

━━━ADVERTISEMENT━━━

DO YOU NEED A LAWYER?

LEGAL SERVICES
AT VERY REASONABLE FEES

* Divorce or legal separation--uncontested
  (both spouses sign papers)

  $175.00 plus $20.00 court filing fee

* Preparation of all court papers and instructions on how to do your own simple
  uncontested divorce

  $100.00

* Adoption--uncontested severance proceeding

  $225.00 plus approximately $10.00 publication cost

* Bankruptcy--non-business, no contested proceedings

  Individual
  $250.00 plus $55.00 court filing fee

  Wife and Husband
  $300.00 plus $110.00 court filing fee

* Change of Name

  $95.00 plus $20.00 court filing fee

Information regarding other types of cases
furnished on request

Legal Clinic of Bates & O'Steen
617 North 3rd Street
Phoenix, Arizona 85004
Telephone (602) 252-8888

posals for the regulation of legal advertising, allowing each state bar the option of adopting or not adopting each proposal. The states also had some latitude in changing the recommended codes to reflect their own perceived needs.

Proposal A was described as regulatory. It specifically authorized certain prescribed forms of lawyer advertising, listing the type of information that could be provided in attorney ads. The proposal permitted advertising in print, on radio, and (following a 1978 amendment) on television.

A less restrictive proposal, Proposal B, was also developed. Proposal B, which could be termed "directive," allowed publication of all information not "false, fraudulent, misleading, or deceptive." It provided guidelines for the determination of improper advertisements, which were subject to "after-the-fact" discipline by state authorities. Neither proposal allowed one-to-one solicitation.

A majority of states, including Georgia, adopted Proposal A, and developed "laundry lists" specifying the terms that could be used in ads. Some state codes included long lists of information about what was permissible within lawyer advertising; others created equally long lists of prohibited information. An attorney from Alabama ran into trouble with his state's regulations, for example, because he included the words *free parking* in his advertising, a term not on the state's list of approved terms.

But in a 1982 case, In re RMJ, the Supreme Court loosened restrictions by state bar associations on legal advertising, stating that they could be no broader than reasonably necessary to prevent deception. The case involved a young attorney who had opened for business in St. Louis, Missouri, in 1978, using advertising containing terms such as *personal injury* instead of the required *tort law*, and *real estate* instead of *property law*.

The attorney also used a mailing that went to potential new customers, not just friends and relatives as required by the Missouri law. After being reprimanded by the Missouri Supreme Court, the attorney appealed to the U.S. Supreme Court, which threw out Missouri's rule limiting lawyer mailings to "lawyers, clients, former clients, personal friends, and relatives." The Supreme Court indicated the state had not justified its interferences with truthful commercial speech and also rejected Missouri's insistence that lawyers limit ad claims to specific state-approved phrases.

In February 1983, the ABA House of Delegates approved a proposal to allow "written communication not involving personal contact" but also adopted a proposal that forbids a lawyer to "solicit professional employment from a prospective client by mail, in person, or otherwise, when a significant motive for the lawyer's doing so is the lawyer's pecuniary gain." Direct mail advertising thus would be permitted when distributed to "persons not known to need legal services, but who are so situated that they might in general find such services useful." This was interpreted by legal advertising scholars to indicate that a lawyer could not send direct mail pieces to 50 known survivors in an airplane crash, but he or she could send the mailing to heavy users of airline travel. By mid-1983, direct mail advertising was specifically allowed in only 11 states, with Georgia being one of the ones that had not changed its regulations in response to the Supreme Court decision and subsequent ABA code revision. Greenwald felt sure that the Georgia restrictions against direct mail would be loosened soon. In any case, he believed the restrictions would not hold up if challenged in the courts.

There were substantial variances in legal advertising regulations from state to state. The ABA had no authority to establish advertising policies at the state level, even though they had considerable influence on the state bar association's decisions regarding advertising policies. The state of Georgia followed the ABA Proposal A closely, requiring that the ads be dignified and allowing the listing of routine services offered. In-person solicitation, direct mail, billboards, handbills, and advertising of contingency fees were all prohibited. TV, radio, Yellow Pages, and newspapers were all specifically permitted.

Most attorneys were still opposed to advertising by lawyers. A recent survey of ABA members funded by the *American Bar Association Journal* revealed that only 3 percent of lawyers had advertised in 1978, only 7 percent had in 1979, and in 1981 only 10 percent had. The percentage had not grown much by the mid-1980s. The bulk of the advertising that had been done had been in the Yellow Pages or in newspapers. Many lawyers, especially established ones, felt that advertising lowers the professionalism of lawyers. The likelihood of advertising decreased as an attorney's income increased, with lawyers earning less than $25,000 five times as likely to advertise as those making over $50,000.

Background on Gary Greenwald

Gary Greenwald moved to Atlanta three years earlier after graduating from Potomac School of Law in Washington, D.C. During his first year in Atlanta, he served as a public defender practicing in the State Court of Fulton County, Georgia. During the first year as a public defender, he handled more than 200 court-appointed cases, with about 80 percent being criminal cases. After two years in business for himself, his practice had changed considerably. He had attained the state bar designation for practice in tax law, had several small-business clients, and had only about 20 percent of his business in criminal cases. His storefront office was on Peachtree Road, the main route from downtown to the affluent residential area called Buckhead.

Within a mile of his office on one side of Peachtree Road were several affluent residential areas made up of single-family homes worth well in excess of $100,000. On the other side of Peachtree Street were many apartments and condominiums housing young urban professionals. All along Peachtree Road were many retailers and office buildings containing small businesses of all types. Although his office was very visible from the street, with "Law Offices of Gary Greenwald" and his telephone number painted in large letters on the window, virtually no clients had come to him as a result of that visibility. Most of the cases that he did have, typically 15–20 at any one time, were referred to him by other attorneys. They sent him certain cases that were types their firms didn't handle such as criminal and personal injury cases.

In addition to the good location, another advantage of his offices was the low overhead. The rent was $290 per month. Telephone expenses were $200 per month. He spent $200 per month on law books and updates and had spent $5,000 initially for the books in his law library. Other expenses, including a part-time secretary, amounted to about $5,000 per year. The office was not plush, but it was functional. Greenwald believed that it was important for an attorney to meet the expectations people had of a successful lawyer, and therefore he did not see his long-term future in this office. Until he built up the practice, however, the large amount of space and very low rent were extremely attractive.

Greenwald enjoyed the flexibility and freedom associated with running his own law office. Currently, however, his case load was only taking about 25 percent of his time. Greenwald was anxious to increase the business and reduce his idle time and had tried many different things to accomplish this goal.

Recent Marketing Activities

About nine months earlier, Greenwald had put up a poster advertising his services on bulletin boards in about 60–70 locations in the area including supermarkets and apartment building laundryrooms. Each of the posters contained a number of his business cards which could be taken for later reference (see Exhibit 2). Greenwald had paid $100 for 400 of these posters. The effort generated six clients and about $2,000 in legal fees.

Several months earlier Greenwald had distributed 10,000 copies of the $8\frac{1}{2}'' \times 3\frac{1}{2}''$ advertisement shown in Exhibit 3, using a "Dow Pack" mailing for the distribution. The Dow Pack contained 10 other advertisements and cost him $400. Four people had come in for a free initial consultation, but as yet no new clients had been developed from the mailing.

Greenwald had also undertaken some advertising in the Georgia Tech and Georgia State University student newspapers and in *Creative Loafing*, a weekly tabloid newspaper containing entertainment listings which was distributed for free. The ads had not been successful in generating new business. For example, 8–10 weeks of classified advertising in *Creative Loafing*, which cost $100, had only generated one new client—a $650 divorce case.

He had also used a two-line classified ad for 10 weeks at a cost of $75 in a neighborhood weekly newspaper. The ad offered to write one letter on his stationery for a client for $12.50. The series of ads generated demand for five letters and four new clients.

Current Marketing Considerations

In thinking about his marketing plan for the next year, a lot of things were going through Greenwald's mind. He wondered what rates he should charge, if and

EXHIBIT 2 Poster advertisement

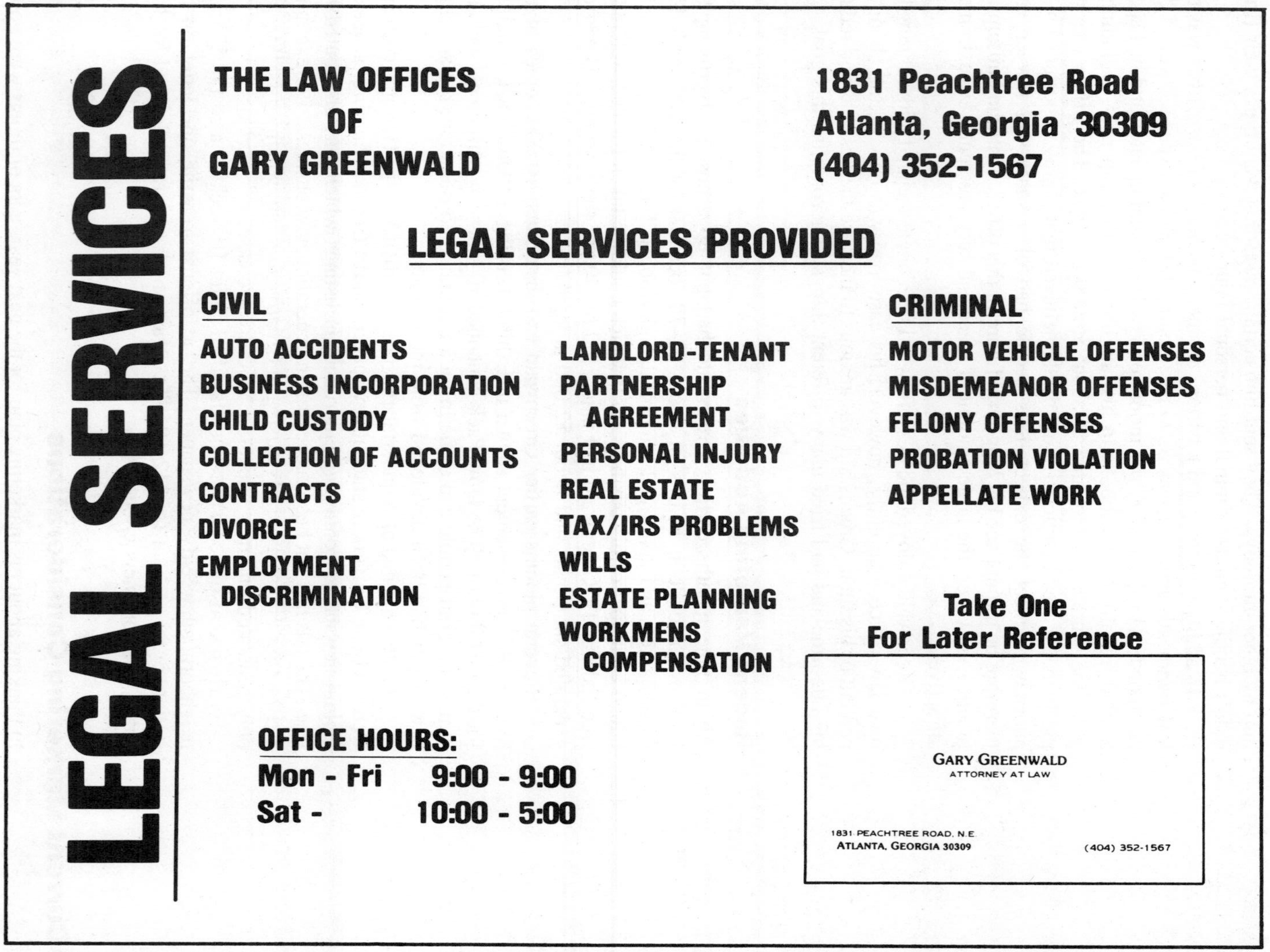

EXHIBIT 3 Direct mail ad

LEGAL SERVICES

THE LAW OFFICES OF GARY GREENWALD

A COMPREHENSIVE COORDINATED LEGAL PRACTICE FOR FAMILIES & BUSINESSES

TRIAL PRACTICE IN STATE & FEDERAL COURTS

LEGAL SERVICES PROVIDED

Personal

- Auto Accidents
- Family Law
- Personal Injury
- Estate Planning / Wills
- Taxation / IRS Problems
- Workmen's Compensation

Business

- Contracts
- Collection of Accounts
- Partnership Agreements
- Incorporations
- Taxation / IRS Problems

Criminal

- Traffic Offenses
- Misdemeanor Offenses
- Felony Offenses
- Probation Violations
- Appeals

Present This Ad For Your FREE Initial Consultation

1831 Peachtree Rd. • Atlanta • Mon. - Fri. 9 - 9, Sat. 10 - 5 • By Appointment Only • 352-1567

how to target his market, and what promotion strategy he should use to communicate to his potential market.

Originally he had offered new clients an initial consultation for free. Recently he had been charging $15 for an initial consultation for individuals and $25 for businesses. His hourly rate varied considerably, depending upon the client and the task. For example, for tax work he charged some clients $40 per hour. He charged others $75 per hour and billed two clients at $120. He was on the list of attorneys taking cases from the juvenile court, and he received only $25 per hour for this work. Greenwald did take a few cases for a fixed fee, typically $500–$600. He only did this when he could accurately forecast the amount of time it would take for the case. Also, he did a number of cases for free when a client could not afford his services, telling the client to pay him when he or she could scrape up the money.

The biggest fee he ever received was $32,000 for a criminal case which lasted 14 months. His next biggest fee was $6,000. He had 10 personal injury cases pending, including a rape, a broken tooth incident, and several car accidents. He anticipated eventually receiving about $20,000 in total from these cases which were all being handled on a contingency basis.[2]

Greenwald had grossed $40,000 his first full year and expected in the second year to gross $60,000. He knew there was considerable room for growth here, particularly if the number of clients could be increased. That led him to thinking about the types of legal services he liked to perform. He had no interest in handling real estate or bankruptcy cases. He felt that the biggest money was to be made in personal injury cases. He liked doing tax work. Greenwald commented that criminal work was fantastic because the work was easy, most

---

[2] With a typical contingency case, an attorney received no fees if the client lost the case, but received one third of the damages awarded if the client won the case.

cases were plea bargained, and clients always paid in cash. Overall, Greenwald most liked the diversity of work that was possible in his profession.

Advertising

Greenwald reviewed the information he had gathered on various advertising alternatives. He had gathered information on direct mail, newspapers, business publications, radio, television, and the Yellow Pages. Some of this information is presented in Exhibit 4.

There were approximately 10,000 households within a couple of miles of his office. Greenwald could send out a postcard format advertisement, using third-class mail, to 5,000 households for $610, including the cost of the mailing list. He could send out a mailing to 10,000 households for $1,150. It was also possible to include a postcard advertisement in a Valpack. This was a mailing containing the ads from a number of different advertisers who shared the cost of the mailing, resulting in a cost less than half of a solo mailing. Valpack mailings were sent quarterly.

An ad in the Yellow Pages would cost about $4,000 for a small (2″ × 2″) ad. A large ad would cost approximately $10,000 per year. About 40–50 of the 9,000 lawyers in Atlanta had large ads in the Yellow Pages.

It would cost Greenwald about $1,500 to have a television ad produced before he even ran the ad one time. Ads on the major networks would cost thousands of dollars for each spot, although he could buy time on low-rated stations after midnight for about $50 per spot. Radio advertising was cheaper. He felt that he would have to run an ad at least twice per day, five days per week, for a month to have any impact. This would cost about $3,000, the minimum he felt was appropriate for a fair test. Greenwald knew that Hyatt Legal Services had been very successful with television advertising in Atlanta. Although the six offices in Atlanta had only been open for nine months, he had heard that each office was bringing in about 200 new clients per month as a result of the ads. Hyatt was spending about $8,000 per month on television. In addition, they had a very large ad in the Yellow Pages. Hyatt did not handle personal injury and certain other kinds of cases. They tended to concentrate on simple legal matters like wills, name changes, and uncontested divorces, and Greenwald felt that the average legal fee per client was under $200.

Consumer Analysis

Greenwald had seen the results of several studies that had been conducted to determine the consumer perspective on legal advertising. The studies typically showed that most users of legal services selected their attorney using recommendations by friends or personal acquaintance. Consumers also used the lawyer's area of specialization, integrity, quality of service, past experience, and reputation as selection criteria. Recommendations by other lawyers, promptness of service, and location of office were other selection criteria used.

EXHIBIT 4 Media costs per advertisement

1. *Atlanta Journal* and *Constitution* (major daily newspapers)

	Sunday	Morning and evening combination
Ad 4¼″ × 3⁷⁄₁₆″	$734.00	$660.96
Ad 2¹⁄₁₆″ × 2″	142.80	128.52
Services classified ad	5.55/line	4.52/line

TV Week supplement:	1 time	2 times	6 times
⅕ page	$735.00	$684.00	$625.00
¹⁄₂₀ page	212.00	197.00	180.00

2. *Atlanta Business Chronicle* (weekly tabloid business newspaper)

	1 time	4 times	13 times
1 inch	$ 49.00	$ 47.00	$ 44.00
⅛ page	290.00	275.00	260.00
Classified 1 inch	24.00	21.00	18.00

3. *Business Atlanta* (monthly business magazine)

	1 time	3 times	12 times
¹⁄₁₆ page	$275.00	$260.00	$225.00

4. Radio

	Morning drive time	Evening drive time
WGST (all news station):		
30 seconds	$ 96.00/spot	$ 68.00/spot
60 seconds	120.00	85.00
WPCH (easy listening):		
30 seconds	88.00	92.00
60 seconds	110.00	115.00
WSB–FM (middle of the road):		
30 seconds	323.00	191.00
60 seconds	380.00	225.00

5. TV (exclusive of production costs)

	Prime time	Late news
WAGA (CBS station):		
30 seconds	$2,200–$7,000/spot	$1,100/spot
WTBS (Channel 17 superstation):		
30 seconds	650–850/spot	450/spot
WANX (Channel 46 independent station):		
30 seconds	150–550/spot	n.a.

n.a. = not available.

Listings in the Yellow Pages, name of law school attended, years in practice, convenience of office hours, and cost of legal services were not among the top 10 selection criteria used by consumers. Overall, personal acquaintance and recommendation by a friend were overwhelmingly the most frequently used means of selecting an attorney.

It is not clear from the studies exactly why other criteria such as cost or advertising are not used more frequently. Unavailability of these sources of information in the past is one possible explanation. It is interesting to note, for example, that cost of legal services is mentioned as being very important to consumers, yet very few consumers use this as a factor in selecting their attorney.

Conclusion

Greenwald wondered whether he should invest some of the money that he had saved up for the down payment on a house in an advertising campaign to increase his business. With the baby coming, he and his wife really wanted to buy a house, so he didn't want to blow it all on advertising that might not work. He wondered how much he should spend and whether the advertising he had been using could be used or whether he should develop new copy. He wondered what media would be most appropriate and what services would be best to promote. He was also concerned about how big his ads should be and how frequently they should run. He also wondered how he could benefit more from the excellent storefront location he had and how he could generate more referrals.

After thinking about the effort that would be required to generate an effective marketing program, Greenwald wondered whether he should pack it in and go to work for a big law firm instead. He decided that he better not postpone thinking about these issues any longer and reached for the phone to call his wife to tell her that he would be late for dinner.

Case 23

Suburban CableVision*

Kim Harrison had joined Communications Industries, Inc., six months ago, following her graduation from a well-known midwestern business school. Now, in late 1986, she had been promoted to marketing manager for Suburban CableVision, a New England subsidiary of Communications Industries (CI), with the responsibility for marketing cable services in four suburban communities. Suburban CableVision had just been acquired, and a new management team had been put in place.

Ms. Harrison had been assigned the task of developing a marketing plan for 1987. Given that the new year was only a few weeks away, she realized that she did not have much time. The problem was complicated by the regulatory changes that were due to take place on January 1. The new regulations allowed considerably greater flexibility in packaging and pricing cable TV services. As she began to review the marketing files left by her predecessor, she realized that this holiday season was going to be very busy for her and very different than the previous few years when she was on Christmas break from her university studies.

Background on the Cable TV Industry

The cable television industry was born in 1948. At that time, Ed Parsons of Astoria, Oregon, lived at the foot of a mountain. The mountain was between his home, which contained a TV set with nothing but snow on the screen, and the transmitters for the television stations he wanted to watch. Parsons climbed the mountain with antenna in hand, secured it at the top, and strung a wire all the way back down to his TV set. As the only person in town with good picture quality, he soon had friends and neighbors at his house all of the time. When neighbors asked him if he would hook up their sets to his wire, he quickly agreed, allowing him and his wife to have time alone together for the first time since he had climbed the mountain.

After this birth of cable television, the industry grew very slowly. In areas where TV reception was poor, people put up towers and ran cable to those households willing to pay for better reception. By 1975, only about 10 percent

* This case was prepared by Kenneth L. Bernhardt and James Novo. Copyright © 1987 by Kenneth L. Bernhardt.

of U.S. television households were cable subscribers. RCA launched the first communications satellite, SATCOM I, in 1975. Programs from the East Coast could now be received by the West Coast instantaneously. Home Box Office became the first company to provide programming specifically aimed at cable subscribers. Others followed, and today there are over 150 programming sources. The rapid increase in programming led to a rapid growth in the number of cable subscribers.

Consumers were expected to spend more that $10 billion on cable television in 1986, more than they spend on going to the movies or renting home video programs. More than 77,000 people were employed by cable systems. The number of subscribers had doubled during the previous five years, and now totaled 42 million. More than three fourths of all TV households now had cable available to them, but only about 60 percent of those households able to receive cable actually chose to buy it.

The number of subscribers had grown at a compound annual growth rate of 14.2 percent between 1980 and 1985. This rate was expected to slow to under 5 percent between 1986 and 1990. An Arthur D. Little study indicated that spending on new cable systems would decline from a peak of $1.4 billion in 1982 to $160 million by 1990. Ms. Harrison recognized that the future of the industry lay in increasing the number of subscribers and revenue from existing systems rather than from laying new cable in areas that previously did not have cable TV available.

Planning for 1987 was complicated by the Cable Communications Policy Act of 1984 (CCPA). The act took away the power of state and local authorities to regulate the rates that cable companies charge subscribers for basic cable service. At the same time, the Federal Communications Commission was phasing out such regulations as the requirement that local cable systems carry all available local channels. Thus, starting January 1, 1987, local systems were free to raise rates and to put whatever programming they wanted on the channels.

The amount of money the average U.S. subscriber paid for cable TV services nearly doubled between 1980 and 1986, to $21 per month. One leading cable TV analyst recently estimated that the average monthly fee would grow to $28 in 1990 and $39 by 1995. Others in the industry were afraid that higher prices could drive away potential new subscribers and cause some existing subscribers to drop cable. A number of premium channels—such as Home Box Office (HBO), Showtime, and The Movie Channel—were already experiencing a slowing in their growth patterns as consumers appeared to be rejecting expensive cable bills that included multiple premium services.

Background on Communications Industries and Suburban CableVision

Communications Industries (CI) owned and operated four cable television systems servicing 43 cities in the states of Delaware, Connecticut, Rhode Island, and Massachusetts. The four systems had cable passing 315,000 homes,

EXHIBIT 1   1985 Statistics on Communications Industries, Suburban CableVision, and 10 largest cable companies

Rank	Company	Basic subscriptions (million)	Pay units (million)	Homes passed (million)	Percent basic /Homes passed*	Percent premium† /Basic
1	Tel-Communications	3.7	2.7	6.4	57	73
2	ATC (Time Inc.)	2.6	2.3	4.6	56	91
3	Group W	2.0	1.6	3.9	53	76
4	Cox Communications	1.5	1.5	2.7	57	97
5	Storer	1.5	1.5	2.7	56	95
6	Warner-Amex	1.2	.9	2.7	45	75
7	Times-Mirror	1.0	.8	2.0	49	87
8	Continental	1.0	1.1	1.8	54	114
9	Newhouse	.9	1.0	1.5	62	107
10	Viacom	.8	.6	1.5	54	78
35	Communications Industries	.2	.2	.3	62	83
NA	Suburban CableVision	.01	.02	.02	64	119

* Basic penetration = $\dfrac{\text{Basic subscribers}}{\text{Homes passed (those with access to cable)}}$

† Premium-to-basic ratio = $\dfrac{\text{Premium services subscribed to}}{\text{Basic subscribers}}$

196,000 of which subscribed to basic cable programming services. More than 113,000 (62 percent) also subscribed to premium programming services, such as movie channels or pay sports channels. CI was the 35th largest cable company but was very small compared to the larger firms in the industry (see Exhibit 1). Total revenues for CI were in excess of $100 million from four television stations, six radio stations, and outdoor advertising services in addition to the cable TV revenues.

Suburban CableVision marketed cable services in four communities. As

EXHIBIT 2   Profile of four towns

	Downing	Anderson	North Lexington–Middletown	
Basic penetration*	75%	58%	61%	
Premium-to-basic ratio†	1.00	1.26	1.26	
Proportion of total households	one third	one third	one third	
Demographics	Blue-collar, industrial	Very white-collar, managerial, elderly	Rural, farm areas rapidly being developed into far-out suburban subdivisions; young families; mixed demographics.	
Number of years system in operation	5	4	3	2

* Basic penetration = $\dfrac{\text{Basic subscribers}}{\text{Homes passed (those with access to cable)}}$

† Premium-to-basic ratio = $\dfrac{\text{Premium services subscribed to}}{\text{Basic subscribers}}$

EXHIBIT 3 Guide to the satellite and premium channels

Channel	Title	Description
2	Local origination	Programming produced locally for all subscribers.
3	Eternal Word	"Inspirational programming"; Catholic Cable Network.
4	Lifetime	Women-oriented programming; many subscriber call-in shows; exercise, lifestyles, star interviews.
5 and 6 (seen on 55 and 56)	Reuters News & Sports	(5 and 6 are a "channel lock," which keeps other channels in tune.) News and financial reports.
7	The Weather Channel	Local and world weather reports.
8	CNN (Cable News Network)	Live coverage of national and world news.
9	CNN Headline	"Around the world in 30 minutes"; for the busy news viewer.
10	C-SPAN (Cable Satellite Public Affairs Network)	Senate and House committee meetings from start to finish; viewer call-in programs.
11	Public access	"Your community channel"; Suburban CableVision supplies the equipment and training free of charge to anyone in the community who wishes to produce and cablecast a television show or event for the community.
12	Educational access	Channel reserved for use by the school system of the community.
13	Middletown College	Channel reserved for use by local college.
14–29		These channels are the network and independent broadcast stations in the area.
30	WOR 9, New York	Movie classics and television programming from the late 60s and 70s; New York news and sports with Nicks, Rangers, Islanders, Devils, Jets, and Mets.
31	CKSH 9, Canada	Canadian television station; broadcasting in French; programming similar to U.S. network stations.

described in Exhibit 2, the communities had very different profiles. Downing was a blue-collar, industrial town. Suburban had penetrated 75 percent of the homes in Downing with access to cable, which was the highest penetration of any of the cities in the area. However, the number of premium service subscriptions was lower than in the other areas. Some of the Suburban managers attributed this to the lower incomes of Downing's households—many could not afford basic plus several pay channels. They felt that the basic penetration was high because TV was a major form of entertainment for these people, and they were willing to pay for basic cable service.

The town of Anderson had a high percentage of the population employed in white-collar and managerial jobs. There was also a large elderly population. Suburban managers felt that these people would drive some distance to attend plays and the opera, so TV was less important to them. Those who did subscribe to basic cable, however, were likely to buy more pay services because of their relatively high incomes.

The towns of North Lexington and Middletown were rural, farm areas just beginning to be developed. Although these suburbs were relatively far from the

EXHIBIT 3 *(concluded)*

Channel	Title	Description
32	WTBS (Turner Broadcast System)	Movie classics and TV programming from the late 60s and 70s.
34	CBN (Cable Broadcast Network)	Family programming; specializes in movies and early television shows from the 50s and 60s.
35	Nickelodeon	Cable channel for kids of all ages; quality non-violent entertainment.
37	SPN	From movies to music to international entertainment.
38	Nashville Network	Sports, comedy, dance, and news about country-western favorites.
39	MTV–Music Television	Video music, music news, interviews with the stars.
40	Arts & Entertainment	Cultural programming.
41	USA Network	TV series from the 70s no longer seen on broadcast television.
42	ESPN	The total sports network.
44	Sports Channel	The best of Eastern sports; all home Celtics games live.
45	Bravo	International award-winning films; exciting theater productions featuring the world's best performers; opera, symphony, and ballet.
46	Showtime	Latest box office hits.
47	HBO	Hollywood blockbusters; original HBO premier films.
48	Cinemax	More movies than HBO and Showtime; late-night, adult-only films.
49	TMC (The Movie Channel)	More movies than HBO and Showtime.
50	HTN (Home Theatre Network	Family programming; the movie channel that doesn't have sex and violence.
51	Disney	Disney movies and classic cartoons.
52	NESN	New England's Sports Network; exclusive live coverage of Bruins and Red Sox.

downtown metropolitan area, a number of subdivisions were being created and many young families were moving into the area. The basic penetration and purchase of premium services were similar to the rates experienced in Anderson.

Although the population in Suburban's market area was growing relatively slowly, the company had experienced rapid growth. During 1985–86 the number of households with access to cable increased by only 1.4 percent. The system as a whole comprised 22,675 households, and 14,600 (64 percent) of these were basic cable subscribers. Although the number of basic subscribers had grown by 7.8 percent in the previous year, the number of pay channel subscriptions, 17,200, was up only 2 percent over the previous year.

Channels 2 through 42 contained a wide variety of basic cable programming. Included were several news channels, network and independent broadcast stations, and specialized channels devoted to local programming, movies, children's programs, and music and culture (see Exhibit 3). On channels 44 through 52, a number of premium channels were available for an extra charge above the basic cable service.

EXHIBIT 4 Pricing structure

Basic tiers/premium channels	Channels	Service	Cost/month
Tiers 1 and 2	2–29	Basic service	$ 7.25
Tier 3	30–32	Super stations	2.05
Tier 4	34–40	Family stations	3.10
Tier 5	41, 42	Sports stations	2.35
Sports Channel	44	Celtics and eastern sports	6.95
Bravo/HBO/Showtime/ Movie Channel/Cinemax	45–49	Movie channels	11.00 each
HTN	50	Family movies	7.95
Disney	51	Disney movies and cartoons	11.00
NESN	52	Bruins and Red Sox	7.95

Note: If subscribers order basic tiers 1–4, they get a $1 discount off of all $11 services (movie channels plus Disney) and HTN. If subscribers order any three premium channels, they get Bravo free.

Pricing

Suburban's pricing structure was very complex (see Exhibit 4). Basic service was broken down into five tiers. The lowest level of service generally available, basic service, consisted of tiers 1 and 2 (channels 2 through 29). Subscribers signing up for this basic service were charged $7.25 per month. The three other tiers available had options to add super stations (tier 3, $2.05 per month), family stations (tier 4, $3.10), and sports stations (tier 5, $2.35). In addition, eight premium channels were available at prices ranging from $7.95 per month to $11 per month.

Exhibit 5 shows a breakdown by level of service. Only 1,000 subscribers, 6.9 percent, subscribed to tiers 1 and 2 only. Ms. Harrison believed that the current system was much too complicated and caused problems in the development of advertising copy. In addition, it was difficult for Suburban's telephone sales representatives to explain the system to potential new subscribers. Thus, she felt that it was important to create a new system now that the company had the ability to change rates without having to get approval from each city council. She wondered whether she should include tier 3 as part of a basic subscriber package and felt that there was a marketing opportunity to simplify

EXHIBIT 5 Breakdown by level of basic service

	Number of subscribers	Percent of subscribers
Tiers 1 and 2 only	1,000	6.9%
Tiers 1, 2, and 3 only	4,550	31.1
Tiers 1, 2, and 4 only	100	.7
Tiers 1, 2, 3, and 4 only	2,950	20.2
Tiers 1, 2, 4, and 5 only	300	2.1
Tiers 1, 2, 3, and 5 only	150	1.0
Tiers 1, 2, 3, 4, 5	5,550	38.0
	14,600	100.0%

the system into basic and super basic (consisting of all five tiers). Other systems typically charged between $5 and $15 for basic service and anywhere from $7 to $12 for premium channels.

Ms. Harrison believed that Suburban made more money on basic service than on premium channels. The cost to Suburban for most of the premium movie channels was about $4 per subscriber per month, some being slightly more and some slightly less. The premium sports channels cost about $3. Many of the basic channels did not cost Suburban anything, and most of the others only cost about 25 cents per subscriber per month. Counting all costs for billing, maintaining subscriber records, and programming costs, the average variable cost per month for basic subscribers (tiers 1 through 5) was about $5.

Some cable executives believed that "basic subscriptions pay for the fixed costs of the system, and you make your profit from premium channel sales." Others felt that subscribers perceived more value in the basic channels and that premium channels were already priced about as high as they could be. In fact, many felt that if basic channel rates were raised, then premium channel rates should be decreased to prevent pricing people out of the cable market. These managers believed that instead of downgrading their service (for example, having one of the premium channels disconnected), many people would simply have the total cable service disconnected. Ms. Harrison had heard that some systems had substantially increased sales of the Disney channel by lowering the price to $7.95. Ms. Harrison knew that she would have to give considerable thought to the issue of how she packaged the channels together and how she priced them.

Advertising

Exhibit 6 contains a copy of the newspaper advertising that Suburban had been running. The campaign had only been moderately successful, and Ms. Harrison wondered whether newspaper advertising was just not effective or whether it was the copy itself that caused the poor results.

Suburban had been experimenting recently with the use of direct mail in cooperation with premium channel programming suppliers. For example, it had recently completed a test of a promotion with the Disney channel. The promotion, run in September, was centered around a free preview weekend. Direct mail and print ads informed consumers that they could preview the Disney channel for free, and if they decided to sign up, a 50 percent discount ($5) was given toward the $10 installation charge. While she had not had time to fully evaluate the promotion, she felt that it had been a success. The advertising and mailing costs had been $2,160, but the Disney co-op rebate had covered $783 of this. The Suburban customer service representatives were given 50 cents per new Disney subscriber as their commission. The gross margin (revenue less cost of programming) was $6 per subscriber per month. In addition, Suburban received the $5 installation fee per new subscriber to the Disney channel and incurred only about 25 cents in actual costs for the installation. Over the course

EXHIBIT 6 Sample newspaper ad

What's the difference between these two pictures?

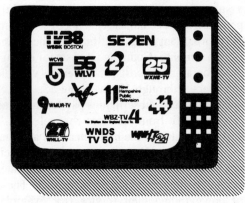 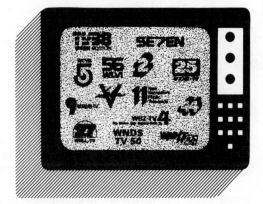

Cable Channels 2 - 29

SUBURBAN CABLEVISION

All area stations, *and MORE*

Less than 24¢ per day.

Including wireless remote control and monthly cable guide.

---

of the promotion, 188 subscribers took advantage of the offer and added the Disney channel to their service. This represented a 14 percent increase in the number of people subscribing to the Disney channel.

A similar offer from HBO and Cinemax was far less successful. This promotion was communicated to subscribers via print advertising only. Only 12 subscribers added HBO as a result of the offer, and nobody added Cinemax.

During the fall, Suburban also tested a heavy newspaper advertising campaign for adding The Movie Channel. New subscribers were given an AM/FM radio premium. Only 18 sales were attributable to the campaign, and Ms. Harrison thus had questions about the effectiveness of newspaper advertising and premiums.

A second direct mail campaign was tested, promoting the Sports Channel and the New England Sports Network. Sales of these two premium channels increased 25 percent and 17 percent, respectively, at a cost per new subscriber of $2.58. No discounts or premiums were used.

As a result of the successes with the premium channel direct mail promotions, Ms. Harrison decided to test targeted direct mail for basic subscriber acquisition. Eleven hundred mailers were sent to apartment addresses that had never had cable service. The mailers cost 25 cents each, and 3 percent of those receiving them signed up. In addition, the mailer was sent to 321 homes where cable had been disconnected because the residents were moving. These homes represented 30 percent of the moves; the other 70 percent had been reconnected when the new residents moved in. One sixth of those receiving the mailing signed up for cable. Ms. Harrison thought that there might be potential with direct mail targeted to subsegments of the nonsubscriber base, including the elderly, educators, managers, and those who disliked network TV.

In the early days of cable, there were a number of "truck chasers"—consumers who would actually chase after the cable television truck when it was in their neighborhood laying cable. They would beg to get hooked up immediately, and direct salespeople were used extensively to make door-to-door sales calls in neighborhoods where cable was being laid. With changing demographics, two-income families, and increased customer sophistication, Ms. Harrison doubted whether door-to-door salespeople would be effective today, but she wondered whether it would be worth testing. A good salesperson would probably cost $25,000, including benefits.

She also wondered whether it might make sense to use public relations to help sell cable subscriptions. She was aware of Toys For Tots campaigns in various cities. In return for bringing in a toy for an orphan, the installation fee for new subscribers would be waived.

Ms. Harrison's predecessor had recommended a public relations program shortly before he left, but a decision had not been made on the program. He had recommended that Suburban sponsor a telethon in North Lexington in support of raising money for the renovation of the local library. There were 1,200 households in North Lexington that had never subscribed to cable, and anyone from these households who donated $25 or more to the telethon would be given free cable installation. Ms. Harrison made a note to review this plan to see whether by changing or keeping its present form it would be a good promotional vehicle for the coming year.

Other Potential Segments

Ms. Harrison was unsure about exactly which segments should be targeted. Much emphasis in the industry had been devoted to increasing the amount of revenue per cable household. Adopting this as a goal would mean that efforts should be directed at increasing the number of services to each current subscriber household, thus increasing the total revenue.

One industry leader believed instead that it's easier to acquire a nonsubscriber than to get someone who is already paying $20 a month to pay $30.

This person recommended that cable systems target the "Young and Busies," conveying the message that cable provides a sense of control over one's viewing habits. He also recommended going after TV lovers already predisposed to the product category and promoting cable's variety and choices.

Still another target market recommended by others in the industry was videocassette recorder (VCR) owners. A recent study had shown a relationship between VCR ownership and cable subscriptions. Only 18.5 percent of non-subscribers owned a VCR versus 27 percent for basic-only subscribers. The percent owning a VCR increased to 33 percent for those who subscribed to one premium service, and to 34 percent for those who subscribed to two services.

Another recent study indicated that VCR ownership was related to cable subscriber behavior, depending on the degree to which the VCR owner rented tapes. As shown in Exhibit 7, light renters of VCR tapes were more likely than average to upgrade (add premium services), and much less likely than average to downgrade (cancel premium channels) or disconnect the cable service. Ms. Harrison had read in a trade journal about one leading cable company that had been testing a strategy of positioning itself as an expert consultant on video electronics. This cable company promoted a $15 VCR hook up kit, and even offered to come out and hook up a subscriber's VCR for a fee. The company offered technical assistance over the telephone to its subscribers, and had begun selling GE VCRs in several markets. The trade journal article reported that the company had sold 389 VCRs in one and one half months in a four-market test. Special discounts were offered, tied to a pay channel upgrade campaign. Given that industry projections indicated that 50 percent of the population would soon have VCRs, she wondered whether Suburban should target VCR owners in its advertising and promotional efforts.

Another potential market that she thought should be given some consideration was former subscribers. She thought a direct mail campaign targeted toward these households might have a high payoff. Many in the industry were concerned about "churn." Churn was a result of households downgrading their service or having it totally disconnected, and was computed by dividing the number downgrading or disconnecting each month by the total number of subscribers at the beginning of the month. Depending on the season (it was higher in the summer and lower in the winter), the churn percentage for Suburban had been running between 2 and 3 percent for basic service, and between 4 and 6 percent for premium channels. If she chose to concentrate on

EXHIBIT 7   Impact of VCR ownership on subscriber behavior (indexed against all cable subscribers)

	All cable subscribers	Non-VCR owners	VCR owners	Heavy renters	Light renters
Downgrade rate	100	100	100	115	50
Disconnect rate	100	105	89	114	55
Upgrade rate	100	112	88	54	132

Source: Cable Television Administrative and Marketing Society Newsletter 1, no. 3 (1985).

increasing retention of subscribers (thus reducing churn), there were a number of promotional techniques that could be used. Some cable systems had experienced success in mailing letters to new subscribers that explained all aspects of cable. Thus these better educated people were able to get more out of their subscriptions. She felt that it would be important to beef up customer service, since some people disconnected in frustration after having trouble getting billing and reception problems taken care of promptly and competently. Finally, she had heard that some cable systems had had some success in reducing churn by using advertising to inform people about programs on cable channels. Apparently, bringing these programs to the attention of subscribers through advertising made them appreciate the service more, and thus they were less likely to downgrade or disconnect. Suburban's churn rate was about average for the industry, and she wondered whether it made any sense to use her promotional budget to reduce churn.

Other Considerations

Suburban's system used the latest technology and was an ''addressable'' system. This meant that the subscriber's service could be changed by merely pushing a button at the central office. It also allowed the use of pay-per-view (PPV) television. Basically, PPV is just what the name implies—cable TV customers call their cable company and order a particular movie (or other program, such as a sports event) at one of the times it is offered. The cable company transmits the movie and bills the customer accordingly. This means that cable companies can offer subscribers the ability to watch a movie at home without having to pay a full month's price for such services as Home Box Office or Showtime. It is also more convenient than renting a videotape: you don't have to have a VCR, and you don't have to leave your house.

One leading industry consultant estimated that by the end of 1986, 2.6 million households will have PPV available, and industry revenues are projected to reach $70 million. The same consultant predicts that by the end of the decade, PPV will reach nearly 10 million cable subscribers and generate revenues of more that $350 million. The typical price of a PPV movie is $4.50 (ranging from $3.95 to $4.95, depending on the particular movie).

Currently, movies are shown first in the movie theaters and then are released on videotape to the tape rental stores. Finally, they become available on premium movie channels, such as HBO. With PPV it is sometimes shown on cable TV before it is released on videotape for rental. Suburban's technology would allow the introduction of PPV movies, and Ms. Harrison wondered whether that was the direction in which to go.

Thinking about all of the available alternatives, Ms. Harrison recognized the challenging opportunity in front of her. She realized that putting together the marketing plan for the new management team would be quite a job, and thought that she had better get started.

Rich's Department Store*

The Executive Committee meeting had been a lengthy session, lasting through most of the morning, but Mr. Dick Mills, vice president and sales promotion director of Rich's Department Store, had returned to his office knowing that a major advertising decision was still not ready to be made. And Mr. Mills realized that it would be his responsibility to submit a final recommendation on media strategy at the next meeting.

Mr. Mills stared at the two neatly bound research reports that he had placed side by side on his desk. The pair of documents represented summaries of the two presentations that had been made to the Rich's Executive Committee that morning. These studies had been based on exactly the same data, drawn from the same in-store survey of Rich's customers. Each report had been prepared by an experienced and professional marketing researcher. Mr. Mills had expected the strong self-interests of the researchers to be reflected in their presentations and interpretations of the survey results, but he was confident that neither man would misrepresent the actual facts.

Mr. Mills had to admit to himself that he had been very surprised at the apparent major contradictions between the two presentations that he had heard earlier that morning. Mr. Mills and the research director of Rich's, who had also attended the morning presentations by the two outside researchers, had discussed the situation briefly after the meeting. The two men had decided to separately review the written reports and, then, to meet later in the afternoon to decide what additional steps to take.

Before rereading the reports, Mr. Mills thought back over the events of the past three months that had eventually led to this situation.

Rich's Department Store was both the largest merchant and the largest single advertiser in Atlanta, Georgia. The store had been founded in 1867 and had grown to an annual sales volume of approximately $200 million through its downtown store and six branch stores located in major suburban shopping centers. The Rich's market share was 40 percent of department store sales in Atlanta and 25 percent of all general merchandise sales.

---

* This case was prepared by Kenneth L. Bernhardt. Copyright © 1987 Kenneth L. Bernhardt.

The Rich's advertising strategy in the past had been to emphasize newspaper advertising for specific sales items and to utilize broadcast media primarily for image purposes. Newspaper was also used for some image-oriented advertising, with occasional direct mailings used to promote specific sales items of merchandise. Rich's is the largest local advertiser in both print and broadcast media.

The two principal daily newspapers in Atlanta are *The Atlanta Journal* (evenings) and the *Atlanta Constitution* (mornings). These are two of the largest circulation newspapers in the South, and both have distinguished journalism traditions, including Pulitzer Prizes. Although both newspapers are owned by the same company, Atlanta Newspapers, Inc., there is little overlap of readership except for the combined Sunday morning edition.

There are 6 TV stations and 40 radio stations in the Atlanta market. However, broadcast media are dominated by WSB-TV and WSB Radio, both of which are owned by Cox Broadcasting Corporation.

Mr. Mills recalled that several months earlier, executives of Cox Broadcasting and of their two local stations had met with key executives of Rich's. One topic discussed at that meeting had been possible use of broadcast media to promote individual sales items. WSB had offered to participate with Rich's in a market test to determine the abilities of different media to sell specific items of merchandise.

As a result of these discussions, Mr. Mills had held a series of meetings with Mr. Jim Landon, research director of WSB-TV and Radio, and Mr. Ferguson Rood, research director of the Atlanta Newspapers, Inc., to design the market test. It was eventually decided to conduct the test during Rich's annual Harvest Sale, which has been the merchandising highlight of the year since 1925. This sale runs for two weeks each fall. The test was to center on 10 specific items of merchandise which would be advertised in both print and broadcast media during the first three days of the sale. During this same period, in-store interviews would be conducted by professional interviewers, with all purchasers of these 10 items in three representative stores (see appendixes for detailed survey design, sample questionnaire, and media plan).

At the conclusion of the survey period, the Research Departments of both Atlanta Newspapers, Inc., and WSB were furnished duplicate computer card decks by Rich's containing survey data. It was this data that served as the basis for the presentations that Jim Landon and Ferguson Rood had made to the Rich's Executive Committee. Excerpts from *The Atlanta Journal* and *Constitution* report are in Appendix A, and excerpts from the WSB report are presented in Appendix B.

These were the two presentations that Mr. Mills would have to reconcile to arrive at a decision about future media strategy for Rich's. Mr. Mills knew that a decision would have to be made quickly, in view of TV production lead times, if any change in media mix were to be considered for the upcoming Christmas sales season.

Appendix A   An Analysis of a Rich's In-Store Study of Advertising Effectiveness on Specific Purchase Decisions*

Foreword

This report is the result of an innovative research study conducted by Rich's Department Store in partnership with Atlanta Newspapers, Inc. and Cox Broadcasting Corporation.

The study was designed to measure:

1. The relative performance of newspapers, television, and radio as a source of influence on shoppers' decisions to purchase specific items.
2. Shoppers' exposure to specific item advertising messages.

The advertising period covered in this study consisted of three days (beginning Sunday, September 20) prior to Rich's annual Harvest Sale.

A total of 2,176 interviews were made on Monday and Tuesday, September 21 and 22. The interviews were made in three of Rich's seven stores—Downtown, Lenox Square, and Greenbriar, and focused on the 10 departments in each store where the advertised items were sold.

An Atlanta interviewing firm was employed by Rich's to interview shoppers in each department immediately after they made their purchase. To qualify for the survey, shoppers had to purchase the specific advertised item or a directly related item.

Summary and Interpretation

More than 9 out of 10 shoppers covered in this survey had the specific purchase in mind before going to Rich's, or knew it was *on special*.

Three fourths of all shoppers recalled being recently exposed to advertising messages for specific items.

More than half of all shoppers' decisions to purchase specific items were attributed to advertising.

Attributions to newspapers were more than twice those of television and radio combined in influencing specific item purchase decisions (71 percent versus 33 percent).

Dollar for dollar . . . newspapers delivered more than three times the influence on specific item purchase decisions than television and radio combined.

The advertising schedule placed in newspapers . . . was conspicuously more effective and more efficient . . . in influencing specific purchase decisions . . . than the saturation schedule placed on television and radio.

---

* Presented by *The Atlanta Journal* and *Constitution* Research & Marketing Department.

See Exhibits A–1 through A–16.

EXHIBIT A-1 Newspaper advertising schedule*

	Sunday Journal and Constitution (inches)	A.M. Constitution (inches)	P.M. Journal (inches)
Sunday	1,064		
Monday		172	247
Tuesday		0	505
Total	1,064	172	752

* 1,989 column inches, the equivalent of 11.6 pages, made up the newspaper schedule covered in this survey.

EXHIBIT A-2 Broadcast schedule*

	Television			Radio		
	Sunday	Monday	Tuesday	Sunday	Monday	Tuesday
6 A.M.		X			X	X
7		X			X	X
8		X	X		X	X
9		X	X	X	X	X
10		X		X	X	X
11		X			X	X
12		X	X	X	X	X
1 P.M.	X	X	X	X	X	X
2	X	X	X	X	X	X
3	X	X	X	X	X	X
4	X	X	X	X	X	X
5	X	X	X	X	X	X
6	X	X		X	X	
7	X	X		X	X	
8	X	X				
9	X	X				
10	X	X				
11	X	X				
Total spots	42	86	49	53	121	87
Average number per schedule hour	3.8	4.8	6.1	5.3	8.6	7.2

* 438 30-second spots were scheduled to run on five television and five radio stations, for an average of 8 spots per hour, between 6 A.M. and 11 P.M., over the three-day period.

EXHIBIT A-3 Comparison of advertising schedule and budget

	Broadcast spots			Newspaper space (inches)
	TV	Radio	Total	
Hard goods:				
Mattress	12	19	31	35
Carpeting	12	23	35	150
Draperies	16	26	42	407
Vacuum sweeper	15	22	37	172
Color television*	0	0	0	150
Soft goods:				
Handbags	15	27	42	189
Girdles†	15	27	42	0
Shoes	15	27	42	398
Shirts*	56	64	120	86
Pant suits	21	26	47	400
Total 10 departments:				
Sunday	42	53	95	1,064
Monday	86	121	207	420
Tuesday	49	87	136	505
Total	177	261	438	1,989
Budget			$27,158	$16,910

* The original broadcast schedule included 20 TV and 24 radio spots for the color television sets to run Tuesday. Since all the sets were sold on Monday, this commercial time was switched to shirts.

† While no Playtex girdle ads were scheduled to run in newspapers, other foundation advertising during the test period supported the influence.

EXHIBIT A-4 Interviews

	Number	Percent
Total	2,175	100%
Women	1,764	81
Men	380	18
Couples	31	1
Under 35	963	44
35–49	817	38
50 and older	394	18
White	1,966	90
Nonwhite	209	10
Hard goods	527	24
Mattress	71	3
Carpeting	45	2
Draperies	123	6
Vacuum sweeper	134	6
Color television	154	7
Soft goods	1,649	75
Handbags	284	13
Girdles	249	11
Shoes	393	18
Shirts	483	22
Pant suits	240	11
Distribution of interviews by store		
Downtown	683	31
Lenox Square	848	39
Greenbriar	645	30

EXHIBIT A-5

"Before coming to Rich's today, did you have in mind buying this specific brand/item, or did you decide after you came into the store?"

63 percent of all shoppers had the specific purchase in mind before going to Rich's.

These shoppers described the following as sources of influence on their buying decision when asked: "What was it that gave you the idea to buy this brand/item?"

Advertising	52%
Needed or wanted it	23
Past experience with it	16
Outside source suggestion	6
Other	7

EXHIBIT A-6

"Was the store having a special on this specific brand/item today, or were they selling at the regular price?"

84 percent of all shoppers said the brand/item was on special.

These shoppers gave the following sources when asked: "Where did you learn about that?"

Advertising	63%
Store display/crowds	27
Outside source	6
Other	4

EXHIBIT A-7 Advertising influence

55 percent of all shoppers attributed their specific purchase decision to advertising. Of these, 71 percent attributed their purchase to newspapers, 33 percent to broadcasts (28 percent to television and 9 percent to radio), and 9 percent to mail circulars.

Newspapers and broadcast accounted for 94 percent of all advertising influence. 61 percent of these influences were attributed to newspapers exclusive of broadcast. 23 percent were attributed to broadcast exclusive of newspapers, and 10 percent were attributed to both.

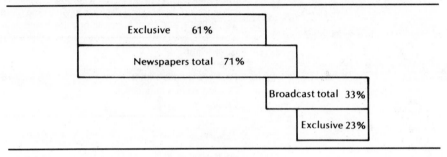

EXHIBIT A-8 Advertising influence

Newspapers and television accounted for 90 percent of all advertising influence. 62 percent of these influences were attributed to newspapers exclusive of television. 19 percent were attributed to television exclusive of newspapers, and 9 percent were attributed to both.

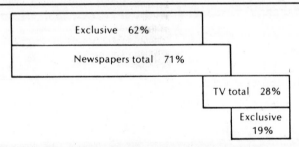

Newspapers and radio accounted for 77 percent of all advertising influence. 68 percent of these influences were attributed to newspapers exclusive of radio. 6 percent were attributed to radio exclusive of newspapers, and 3 percent were attributed to both.

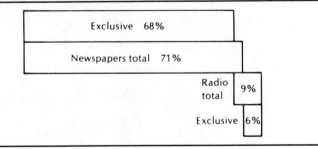

EXHIBIT A-9 Advertising influence—by shopper demographics (among the 55 percent of all shoppers who were influenced by advertising)

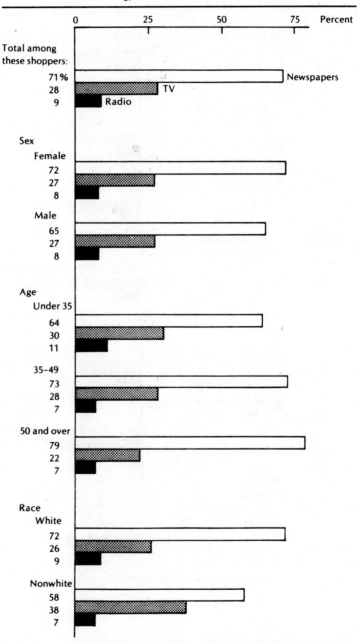

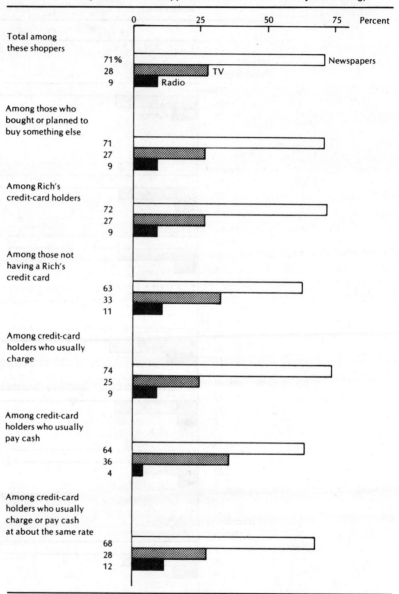

EXHIBIT A-10 Advertising influence—by shopping patterns (among the 55 percent of all shoppers who were influenced by advertising)

EXHIBIT A-11 Share of budget versus share of influence

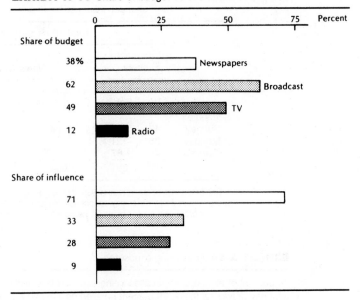

EXHIBIT A-12 Newspapers/broadcast—share of influence versus share of budget by departments

	Newspapers		Broadcast	
	Share of influence	Share of budget	Share of influence	Share of budget
Total	71%	38%	33%	62%
Hard goods	77	45	30	55
Mattress	43	11	69	89
Carpeting	83	39	23	61
Draperies	83	56	22	44
Vacuum sweeper	70	25	45	75
Color TV	99	100	1	—
Soft goods	68	34	34	66
Handbags	68	41	27	59
Girdles	28	—	74	100
Shoes	87	54	25	46
Shirts	63	12	36	88
Pant suits	82	53	16	47

EXHIBIT A-13 Comparison of advertising schedule/budget/ shopper influence*

	Total 10 departments				
	Broadcast spots		Newspaper space		
	TV	Radio	Journal—Constitution	Constitution	Journal
Schedule					
Sunday	42	53	1,064		
Monday	86	121		172	248
Tuesday	49	87		0	505
	177	261	1,064	172	753

* 438 broadcast spots versus 1,989 inches; budget—$27,158 for broadcast spots versus $16,910 for newspaper space; and shopper influence—33 percent for broadcast spots versus 71 percent for newspaper space.

EXHIBIT A-14 Advertising exposure

74 percent of all shoppers recalled being exposed to specific advertising messages within the past day or two. Of these, 79 percent recalled newspapers, 53 percent recalled broadcasts (46 percent television, 18 percent radio), and 24 percent recalled mail circulars.

Newspapers and broadcast accounted for 96 percent of all advertising messages. 43 percent recalled newspapers exclusive of broadcast. 17 percent recalled broadcast exclusive of newspapers, and 36 percent recalled both.

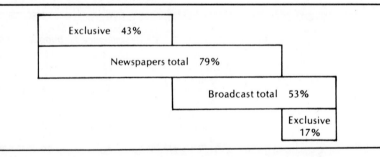

EXHIBIT A-15 Advertising exposure

Newspapers and television accounted for 93 percent of all advertising messages. 47 percent recalled newspapers exclusive of television. 14 percent recalled television exclusive of newspapers, and 32 percent recalled both.

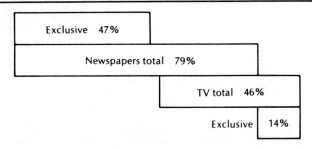

Newspapers and radio accounted for 85 percent of all advertising messages. 67 percent recalled newspapers exclusive of radio. 6 percent recalled radio exclusive of newspapers, and 12 percent recalled both.

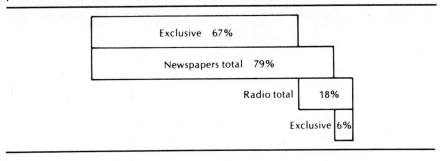

Questionnaire   HARVEST SALE IN-STORE CUSTOMER SURVEY

Interviewer Name: _____ (1-2) STORE: . . . . . . .Downtown . . . . . Lenox . . . . . Greenbriar   (3)
                                                              1   2   3

DATE: M   T   W   TIME OF INTERVIEW:_____ DEPARTMENT: _____   (6)
       1   2   3 (4)   (5)

Hello. We're conducting a short survey among RICH'S customers:

1.   What did you happen to buy in this department today?_____
                                                    (PROBE, BRAND, STYLE)
                                                                                                    (7-8)

2.   Before coming to RICH'S today, did you have in mind buying this specific brand/item, or did you decide after you came into the store?

         HAD IN MIND. . . .(☐)1   DECIDED IN STORE. . . . .(☐)2   SKIP TO Q. #3   (9)

         What was it that gave you the
         idea to buy this brand/item? _____

         (IF APPROPRIATE, ASK: Where did you learn about that?)_____

                                                                                                    (10-11)

3.   Was the store having a special on this specific brand/item today, or were they selling at the regular price?

         SPECIAL. . . . . . (☐)1   REGULAR PRICE. . . . . . .(☐)2   SKIP TO Q. #4   (12)

         Where did you learn about that?_____

                                                                                                    (13-14)

4.   Do you recall seeing or hearing any advertising within the past day or two on radio or television or in the newspapers or in a
     mail circular that may have reminded you or helped you decide to buy this _____today?

         YES. . . . .(☐)1   NO. . . . .(☐)2   SKIP TO Q. #5   (15)

         a. Where did you see or hear it? _____   (16)

	4a. UNAIDED RECALL	5. AIDED RECALL		
		YES	NO, DK	
RADIO.	1	1	2	(17)
NEWSPAPERS	2	1	2	(18)
TELEVISION.	3	1	2	(19)
MAIL CIRCULAR	4	1	2	(20)
OTHER, DON'T KNOW	5			

ASK FOR EACH MEDIUM NOT CHECKED IN Q. #4a.

5.   Did you happen to see or hear any of the following within the past day or two:
     A radio commercial for this specific _____? A newspaper ad for this
     specific_____? A television commercial for this specific _____?
     A mail circular for this specific _____?_____

6.   Have you bought anything else at RICH'S today, or do you plan to buy anything else at RICH'S today?

         YES. . . . .(☐)1   NO. . . . .(☐)2

7.   Do you (or your wife/husband) have a RICH'S credit card?   (21)

         YES. . . . .(☐)1   NO. . . . .,.(☐)2   (22)

         a. Do you usually charge or pay cash for most of your purchases at RICH'S?

         CHARGE . . . .(☐)1   CASH. . . . .(☐)2   SAME. . . . .(☐)3   (23)

8.   What is the name of the county where you live? _____ OUT-OF-STATE . . (☐) (24-25-26)

     ESTIMATE AGE: UNDER 35 YEARS. .(☐)1   SEX: FEMALE . . .(☐)1   RACE: WHITE . . . . .(☐)1   (27)
                    35 - 49 . . . .(☐)2   MALE. . . . .(☐)2   NON WHITE.(☐)2 (28)
                    50+ . . . .(☐)3   (29)

Appendix B Analysis of Rich's In-Store Survey*

Introduction

First, we would like to state that WSB television and radio were pleased to have the opportunity to participate in this research effort with Rich's. We have one basic characteristic in common with Rich's—both WSB-TV and WSB Radio, like Rich's, are dominant in the Atlanta market. Like Rich's, we are an Atlanta institution and have enjoyed dominance since our origination.

In this presentation, we will not attempt to interpret the results of your research from a marketing standpoint. You have your own market research department, and we are sure that they have done a capable job of analyzing and interpreting the results of the study from that aspect. Instead, we will concentrate on interpreting the results from a media standpoint, which is our particular area of experience.

The following pages contain our detailed analysis of this research for Rich's management.

Pre-Harvest Sale Advertising Weight

Rich's Pre-Harvest Sale was heavily promoted with a "mix" of three media: radio, TV, and newspaper.

On the broadcast side, Rich's ran 261 radio spots on five stations and 177 TV spots on five stations promoting 10 different items during a three-day period. It can be estimated that the total radio campaign reached about 90 percent of the Atlanta adult metro population, with the average listener exposed to seven commercial announcements (all products combined). The total television campaign also reached an estimated 90 percent of the Atlanta adult population, with the average viewer exposed to 10 commercial announcements.

The newspaper campaign consisted of 13 ads for the specific items and 11 ads for related[1] items, or a total of 24 ads representing 1,987 inches of space in the *Journal* and *Constitution*. Rich's also ran 6,140 inches of other newspaper advertising during the three-day period. We have no way of estimating the reach and frequency of the newspaper ads.

Pre-Harvest Sale a Success

Rich's total advertising effort helped make the store's pre-Harvest Sale a tremendous success.

Monday, September 21, and Tuesday, September 22, were two of Rich's biggest days of the year according to traffic and sales volume. As far as we

---

* Presented by WSB-TV, WSB Radio, and Cox Broadcasting Research.

[1] Same item but different price than in the radio and TV commercial.

know, the departments participating in the test were all up considerably in sales volume compared to a year ago.

Unfortunately, sales results for the *specific items* tested were not available. However, it is our understanding that the departmentwide sales results reflected the success of the individual items in those departments that were tested.

The advertising effort for the pre-Harvest Sale represented one of the few times that Rich's has used a media-mix for *item selling*. Radio and TV have been used extensively by Rich's for institutional advertising and to announce sale events, but item selling has been limited in the past primarily to newspaper and direct mail. *The media-mix for item selling worked from a sales results standpoint.*

Summary of Media Recall Findings

After analyzing the results of the survey, we found the following to be the most significant findings:

1. Because of the confusion and particularly the conditioning factor regarding newspaper, the three media cannot be completely compared in recall.
2. Recall for both radio and TV was significantly higher on Tuesday versus Monday, indicating that the broadcast media were building in impact on customers. Sales results were also generally better on Tuesday versus Monday.
3. Both radio and TV did *best* in recall (compared to newspaper) for items having the *least* amount of newspaper advertising. Radio and TV did *poorest* for items having the *greatest* amount of newspaper advertising.
4. In general, items where radio and TV did *best* in recall (compared to newspaper) had better sales results than items where radio and TV did poorest.
5. All three media performed better among high-priced items and for items where customers decided to buy before coming into the store.
6. Radio and TV balanced newspaper quite well by reaching younger adults than the print medium.

See Exhibits B–1 through B–3.

EXHIBIT B-1 Summary of newspaper recall

Item	Budget	Day/ads	Got idea	Learned of special	Direct recall
Draperies	$4,412	Sun.–2, Tues.–2	48%	68%	81%
Pant suits	3,359	Sun.–2, Mon.–1, Tues.–3	50	56	63
Shoes	2,834	Sun.–1, Mon.–2, Tues.–1	48	55	72
Handbags	1,670	Sun.–1, Tues.–1	30	30	60
Carpeting	1,503	Sun.–1	61	63	80
Color TV	1,503	Sun.–1	62	68	66

EXHIBIT B-1 (concluded)

Item	Budget	Day/ads	Got idea	Learned of special	Direct recall
Dress shirts	859	Sun.-1	40%	40%	54%
Vacuum cleaner	780	Mon.-4	36	62	64
Mattresses	260	Tues.-1	30	37	54
Career shirts	—	—	19	27	45
Girdles	—	—	12	15	16
Averages, all items*			42	51	64

* Excludes girdles (no ads), but includes career shirts because of ads for dress shirts, a related item.

EXHIBIT B-2 Summary of television recall

Item	Budget	Adult audience (000)	Got idea	Learned of special	Direct recall
Career shirts	$2,998	1,373.4	15%	16%	27%
Draperies	2,714	776.5	11	15	37
Pant suits	2,494	885.4	8	9	39
Playtex girdles	2,364	752.1	25	34	32
Dress shirts	2,028	824.8	16	16	29
Handbags	1,922	649.2	10	10	34
Shoes	1,909	724.7	11	14	41
Vacuum cleaner	1,867	627.4	19	36	42
Carpeting	1,790	624.5	8	12	29
Mattresses	1,627	691.9	40	48	49
Color TV	—	—	0	0	5
Averages, all items*			16	21	36

* Excludes color TV (no commercials).

EXHIBIT B-3 Summary of radio recall

Item	Budget	Adult audience (000)	Got idea	Learned of special	Direct recall
Career shirts	$903	489.1	2%	6%	17%
Draperies	560	654.3	1	2	8
Shoes	544	566.8	5	6	14
Pant suits	539	633.9	1	2	12
Carpeting	513	590.9	8	7	24
Dress shirts	498	496.4	4	5	12
Girdles	482	553.0	6	9	11
Mattresses	477	527.6	11	23	29
Handbags	476	475.1	2	3	20
Vacuum cleaner	453	482.1	7	8	10
Color TV	—	374.2	—	1	2
Averages, all items*			5	7	16

* Excludes color TV (no commercials).

Three Types of Media Recall in the Study

The questionnaire used in Rich's in-store survey obtained information about customers' recall of advertising media in three areas:

1. Idea to Buy

For customers purchasing the item being tested, those that indicated having in mind buying that specific merchandise before coming to the store were asked *what gave them the idea to buy the item*. In this question, answers involving media came from top-of-mind recall (not aided). Nonmedia answers to this question, such as "needed" item, "wanted" item or "had past experience" with item were accepted.

2. Learned of Special

Those customers who were aware of the store having a special on the specific item purchased were asked *where they learned about it*. In this question, answers involving media also came from top-of-mind recall and nonmedia responses such as "saw on display" or "friend told me" were accepted.

3. Direct Recall

Customers were also asked if they recalled seeing or hearing any advertising that may have reminded them or helped them decide to buy the specific item. If they answered in the affirmative, they were then asked *where they saw or heard it*. If radio, newspaper, TV, or mail circular were not mentioned by the respondent, they were also asked if they happened to hear a radio commercial, see a newspaper ad, and so on (aided recall). For purposes of analyzing the results, the unaided and aided answers to direct recall have been combined in this question.

Effect of Confusion and "Conditioning"

First, we would like to emphasize three points that should be taken into consideration when evaluating each advertising medium's performance based on the recall results of the study:

1. Because of the heavy amount of Rich's advertising activity in all media during the three-day period of interviewing, there was a certain amount of confusion that occurred among the customer-respondents regarding where they saw or heard advertising. This fact will be documented in the pages to follow.

2. Because Rich's traditionally has done the vast majority of its *item* advertising in newspaper, customers are "conditioned" to this particular medium; i.e., more inclined to think of Rich's merchandise being advertised in a newspaper.

3. During the three-day period of the study, *other department stores* were also running *newspaper* ads for items similar to Rich's items being tested. Some newspaper ad recall in this study could have been due to confusion with other stores' ads.

These points can all be substantiated by the following results.

Only Slight Confusion for Radio Commercials

There were *no* radio commercials for color TV sets, since the spots were canceled before they were scheduled to run on Tuesday afternoon.

0%	Claimed they got the idea to buy a color TV set from radio commercials.
1%	Thought they learned of color TV sets being on sale from radio commercials.
2%	Said they recalled hearing radio commercials for color TV sets.

Only Slight Confusion for TV Commercials

There were *no* TV commercials for color TV sets, since the spots were canceled before they were scheduled to run on Tuesday afternoon.

0%	Claimed that they got the idea to buy a color TV set from TV commercials.
0%	Thought they learned of color TV sets on sale from TV commercials.
5%	Said they recalled seeing TV commercials for color TV sets.

Some Confusion and "Conditioning" for Mail Circular

In the mail circular that Rich's distributed to its customers the week prior to the survey, there were *no* ads for any specific items, yet among the total sample of customer-respondents purchasing any of the 11 items tested:

3%	Claimed they got the idea to buy the specific item from a mail circular.
5%	Thought they learned of the specific item being on sale from a mail circular.
18%	Said they recalled seeing a mail circular for the specific item.

Greater Confusion and "Conditioning" for Newspaper Ads

There were *no* Rich's newspaper ads for Playtex girdles, yet:

12%	Claimed they got the idea to buy girdles from newspaper ads.
15%	Thought they learned of girdles being on sale from newspaper ads.
16%	Said they recalled seeing newspaper ads for girdles.

There were *no* Rich's newspaper ads for mattresses on either Sunday or Monday of the survey, yet among customers interviewed on Monday:

<u>27%</u>	Claimed they got the idea to buy a mattress from newspaper ads.
<u>30%</u>	Thought they learned of the mattress being on sale from newspaper ads.
<u>49%</u>	Said they recalled seeing newspaper ads for mattresses.

Caution in Comparing Media by Recall!

As you can see, the extent of erroneous recall of newspaper advertising ranged from a low of 12 percent to a high of 49 percent. For this important reason, it is impossible to derive any accurate yardstick for measuring the separate value of each medium, dollar for dollar. In addition, these results cannot be converted to any type of advertising-to-sales ratio.

Radio May Have Been Higher with More WSB Spots

Due to the problem created by trying to find enough availabilities on WSB only in morning and evening drive time (because of the agency's buying criteria) to handle commercials for 11 different items in three days, Atlanta's dominant radio station was not able to contribute as much weight as it should have to most of the media schedules. As a result, a higher proportion of spots ran on WQXI (primarily teens), WAOK (primarily ethnic) and WRNG (primarily 50+ listeners), and WPLO (lower socioeconomic level). A brief analysis of the number of radio commercials that ran for each item, showing the light proportion of WSB spots, is shown in the accompanying table.

	Total spots	WSB spots	WSB morning drive spots*
Career shirts	48	10	0
Carpeting	23	6	3
Color TV	—	—	—
Draperies	26	7	2
Dress shirts	15	6	2
Girdles	27	5	1
Handbags	27	5	1
Mattresses	19	6	2
Pant suits	26	8	2
Shoes	27	6	2
Vacuum cleaner	22	5	2
Total	260	64	17

* Monday or Tuesday.

Television versus Newspaper

While TV budgets were fairly even, newspaper budgets ranged from $260 for mattresses up to $4,412 for draperies. TV versus newspaper performance in all types of recall showed a good relationship to the amount of money spent in newspaper. The smaller the newspaper budget versus TV, the better TV performed versus newspaper in recall, and vice versa:

1. TV did *best* in all types of recall *compared to newspaper* for mattresses, career shirts, and vacuum cleaners. These items had the *smallest amount* of advertising space in the newspaper compared to the others.
2. TV did *poorest* in all types of recall *compared to newspaper* for draperies, pant suits, shoes, and carpeting. These items had the *greater amount* of advertising space in the newspaper.

Radio versus Newspaper

Again, radio budgets were fairly even compared to the wide range in newspaper budgets. Radio versus newspaper performance in all types of recall also showed a fairly strong relationship to the amount of money spent in newspaper. The smaller the newspaper budget versus radio, the better radio performed versus newspaper in recall, and vice versa:

1. Radio did *best* in all types of recall *compared to newspaper* for mattresses, vacuum cleaners, and career shirts. These items generally had the least newspaper space.
2. Radio did *poorest* in all types of recall *compared to newspaper* for draperies, pant suits, and handbags. These items generally had the greatest newspaper space.

Less Newspaper Space—No Harm to Sales Volume

We have just indicated that, as newspaper space was reduced, both radio and TV did better in recall.

How about Rich's Sales Volume?

There appeared to be little, if any, correlation between the amount of newspaper space and sales volume as measured by department sales increases. If anything, the reverse occurred:

	Monday	Tuesday
TV and radio did best (least newspaper space):		
Girdles	+7%	+92%
Career shirts	+151	+349
Mattresses	+43	+76
Vacuum cleaners	+98	+222
TV and radio did poorest (most newspaper space):		
Draperies	−0	+9
Pant suits	+17	+46
Shoes	−19	+14
Carpeting	−9	+526

Idea to Buy versus Direct Recall

One probable indication of the "conditioning" of Rich's customers to newspaper advertising comes from comparing initial "idea to buy" recall, where media responses came purely from top of mind, to the direct recall that came later in the interview, concentrating on each medium. All three media gained in regard to the proportion of customers recalling (from idea to buy to direct recall), but newspaper, having been recalled more from top of mind, gained the least, while TV and especially radio, in the background during top of mind "idea to buy," came to the surface more in the direct recall.

	Average recall, all items*		
	Idea to buy	Direct recall	Percent increase
Newspaper	42%	64%	+52%
TV	16	36	+125
Radio	5	16	+220

* Girdles were eliminated for newspaper and color TV sets were eliminated for radio and TV because of no advertising.

First Day versus Second Day Recall

Analysis of the direct recall results by day of interview produced an interesting fact. The impact of newspaper was initial, while both radio and TV performed significantly better on the second day. This is probably due to the nature of the broadcast media, which gain impact and effectiveness with *increased frequency* (as listeners and viewers are exposed to more commercials). In addition, sales results for all items were generally better on Tuesday than on Monday, compared to a year ago. This also indicates that, if spots had been spread more evenly over Sunday, Monday, and Tuesday (rather than concentrated on Sunday and Monday in most cases), and if interviewing had been extended through Wednesday, both radio and TV would have performed better in recall, at no increase in budget for either medium.

	Average recall, all items*		
	Monday	Tuesday	Tuesday percent difference
Newspaper	66%	62%	−6%
TV	33	38	+15
Radio	13	18	+38

* Mattresses were eliminated for newspaper as an invalid comparison, since there were no ads on Sunday or Monday. However, even though there were no radio or TV commercials for career shirts on Sunday or Monday, and no newspaper ads at all, this item was included in this comparison because there was advertising for dress shirts, a related item. Also girdles were eliminated for newspaper and color TV for radio and TV because of no advertising.

High-Priced versus Low-Priced Items

In order to analyze media performance by item *price range,* the items were divided into either a high-price (carpeting, color TV, draperies, mattresses, and vacuum cleaners) or a low-price (career shirts, dress shirts, girdles, handbags, pant suits, and shoes) group. All three media performed better among high-priced items compared to low-priced merchandise, especially radio and TV. However, the differences were greater regarding ''idea to buy'' recall and ''learned of special'' recall than with the direct recall. Customers who had made up their minds to buy a large ticket item were apparently more persuaded by advertising than those coming to Rich's for lower priced merchandise. However, whether in the market for high- or low-priced items, both type customers were exposed to advertising, as indicated in the direct recall.

	High-priced items	Low-priced items	High-priced percent difference
Idea to buy:			
Newspaper	47%	37%	+27%
TV	20	14	+43
Radio	7	3	+133
Learned of special:			
Newspaper	60	42	+43
TV	28	16	+75
Radio	10	5	+100
Direct recall:			
Newspaper	69	59	+17
TV	39	34	+15
Radio	18	14	+29

"Had in Mind" versus "Decided in Store"

In order to analyze media performance by the extent to which customers had in mind to buy the item before coming to the store, the items were divided into two groups: ''had in mind'' and ''decided in store,'' based on results to the question covering this aspect of purchasing. The four items where roughly half of the customers indicated deciding in the store (pant suits, dress shirts, career shirts, and handbags) were placed in the ''decided in store'' group. The other seven items, where significantly less customers indicated deciding in store, were placed in the ''had in mind'' group. All three media performed significantly better among items in the ''had in mind'' group, that is, for items where a greater proportion of customers made their decision in advance. The differences were greater regarding ''idea to buy'' and ''learned of special'' recall than with the direct recall.

	"Had in mind" items	"Decided in store" items	"Had in mind" percent difference
Idea to buy:			
Newspaper	48%	35%	+37%
TV	19	12	+58
Radio	6	2	+200
Learned of special:			
Newspaper	59	38	+55
TV	26	13	+100
Radio	9	4	+125
Direct recall:			
Newspaper	70	56	+25
TV	38	32	+19
Radio	16	15	+7

Broadcast Media Recall Reflected Younger Adults

By analyzing media recall by age of customer, it was determined that radio and TV balanced newspaper quite well by reaching younger adults. In all three types of recall, the under-35 age group was proportionately higher for broadcast, especially radio, than for newspaper. These figures are based on all items combined.

Age	Radio	TV	Newspaper
Got idea:			
Under 35	56%	44%	36%
35–49	31	38	44
50 and over	13	18	20
Learned of special:			
Under 35	50	43	36
35–49	34	41	41
50 and over	16	16	23
Direct recall:			
Under 35	49	44	41
35–49	33	38	41
50 and over	18	18	18

Note: Read table. Of those customers indicating that they "got the idea" to buy an item from radio commercials, 56 percent were in the under 35 age group.

Rich's Dominant Position in Atlanta

In concluding this presentation, we would like to announce the results of separate research that we have just completed that indicates the extent to which

Rich's dominates the department store market in Atlanta, a domination that we feel is due to:

Outstanding management.

Quality of merchandise.

Attention to customer service and satisfaction.

Efficient use of advertising and promotion, *especially the use of a media-mix.*

Presentation Summary

1. With use of media-mix for item selling, the pre-Harvest Sale was a success. All departments participating in the test were up in sales volume.
2. Because of confusion and conditioning factors, recall results are not completely comparable between media.
3. In general, as the amount of newspaper space was reduced, the proportion of recall for both TV and radio was increased, and sales results were generally more favorable.
4. Sales volume was up significantly on Tuesday versus Monday in all departments, indicating a relationship with broadcast media recall, also up significantly on Tuesday as frequency increased.
5. All media had higher recall for higher priced items and items where customer generally decided in advance.
6. Separate research confirms Rich's dominance of the Atlanta market, especially versus Davison's. Rich's uses radio and TV effectively, Davison's uses very little broadcast media.

Case 25

Exercise in Print Advertising Assessment*

One of the most important and most difficult marketing decisions is the choice of creative executions in advertising. The purpose of this exercise is to help you develop skills in determining what is a good and a bad creative execution.

In preparation for your class session using this exercise, we would like you to spend time looking at *print* advertising (newspaper and magazine advertising). We would like you to select what you think is the "best ad" you have seen and the "worst ad" you have seen. To aid you in this task you might ask yourself the following questions:

1. What is the sponsor's apparent target segment(s)?
2. What are the objectives of the ad?
3. Is the basic appeal, theme, and copy approach appropriate for these purposes?

To the bottom of each ad you selected attach a small piece of paper containing the following information:

1. Sponsor of the ad.
2. Publication in which the ad appeared.
3. Publication date.
4. Your reason(s) for selecting that ad as the best or worst.
5. Your name.

Staple or tape this information to the bottom of the ad but don't obscure any of the ad. Turn in your ads to your professor as required. In the class session you will get a chance to compare your choice of ads with those of your classmates.

---

* Copyright © 1987 Thomas C. Kinnear.

Case 26

Allied Food Distributors*

In April 1987, Ms. Elizabeth Ramsey, the district sales manager for the upper Midwest district of Allied Food Distributors, was preparing to hire a new salesperson for the southwest Indiana sales territory. The current salesperson in this territory was leaving the company at the end of June. Ms. Ramsey had narrowed the list of potential candidates to three. She wondered which of these applicants she should select.

Company Background

Allied Food Distributors was one of the largest food wholesalers in the United States. The company carried hundreds of different packaged food items (fruits, vegetables, cake mixes, cookies, powdered soft drinks, and so on) for sales to supermarkets and grocery stores. Allied carried items in two different circumstances. First, some small food companies had Allied carry their entire line in all areas of the United States. Allied was in essence their sales force. Second, some large food companies had Allied carry their lines in less populated parts of the country. These areas were not large enough to sustain a salesperson for each food company.

Allied operated in all 50 states. The country was divided into 20 sales districts. Ms. Ramsey's sales district included Michigan, Indiana, and Illinois. Each district was divided into a number of sales territories. A salesperson was assigned to each territory.

The Southwest Indiana Territory

The sales territory for which Ms. Ramsey was seeking a salesperson was located in the southwest corner of Indiana. Exhibit 1 presents a map of the territory. It was bordered on the south by the Ohio River and the state of Kentucky, on the west by the Wabash River and the state of Illinois, and on the

---

* This case was written by Thomas C. Kinnear. Copyright © 1987 Thomas C. Kinnear.

EXHIBIT 1 A map of the southwest Indiana territory

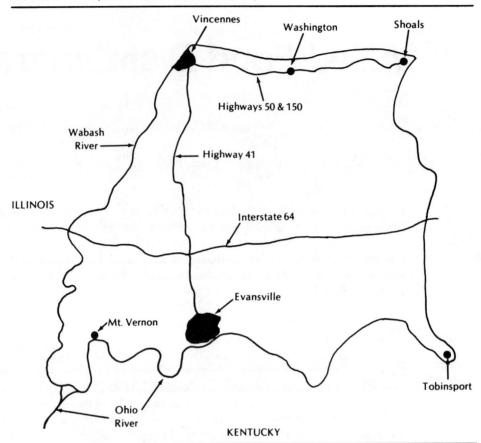

east by the Hoosier National Forest. The northern boundary ran a few miles north of Highways 50 and 150 that ran from Vincennes in the west through Washington to Shoals in the east. Evansville was the largest city in the area with a population of about 140,000. The salesperson for the territory was expected to live in Evansville, but would spend about three nights a week on the road. The only other reasonably large population concentration was in Vincennes with a population of about 20,000. Vincennes was located about 55 miles straight north of Evansville on Highway 41. Interstate Highway 64 ran the 80 miles east-west through the territory about 15 miles north of Evansville. Evansville was 165 miles southwest of Indianapolis, 170 miles east of St. Louis, Missouri, and 115 miles southwest of Louisville, Kentucky. The territory was very rural in character with agriculture being the dominant industry. The terrain was quite hilly, with poor soil. As a result, the farms in the area tended to be economically weak. There were many small towns and villages located throughout this basically rural environment.

The Selling Task

Allied maintained 75 active retail accounts in the southwest Indiana territory. About 10 of these accounts were medium- to large-sized independent supermarkets located in Evansville and Vincennes. The rest of the accounts were small, independent general food stores located throughout the territory.

The salesperson was expected to call on these accounts about every three weeks. The salesperson's duties included: checking displays and inventory levels for items already carried, obtaining orders on these items, informing retailers about new items, attempting to gain sales orders on these items, setting up special displays, and generally servicing the retailers' needs. Often, the salesperson would check the level of inventory on an item, make out an order, and present it to the retailer to be signed. The salesperson generally knew the store owner on a first name basis. The ordered goods were sent directly to the retailer from a warehouse located in Indianapolis.

The Selection Process

The responsibility for recruiting salespersons for the territories within a district was given to the district sales manager. The process consisted of the following steps:

1. An advertisement for the job was placed in newspapers in the state in question.
2. Those responding to the ad were sent job application forms.
3. The returned application forms were examined and certain applicants were asked to come to the district sales office for a full day of interviews.
4. The selection was then made by the district sales manager, or all applicants were rejected and the process started again.

Training

Allied did all its salesperson training on the job. The salesperson on the territory to which a new person would be assigned was given the task of training. Basically, this involved having the new person travel the territory to meet the retailers and to be shown how to obtain and send in orders. The district sales manager usually assisted in this process by traveling with the new salesperson for a few days.

Compensation

The current salesperson on the southwest Indiana sales territory was earning a straight salary of about $37,000 per year plus fringe benefits. Ms. Ramsey indicated that she was willing to pay between $19,000 and $40,000 for a new person depending on the qualifications presented.

The Choices

On the basis of application forms and personal interviews, Ms. Ramsey had narrowed the field of applicants down to three. A summary of the information on their application forms along with the comments she had written to herself are contained in Exhibits 2, 3, and 4. She wondered which person she should select for the position.

EXHIBIT 2 Information on Mr. Michael Gehringer

Personal information

Born July 15, 1945; married; three children ages 14, 16, and 19; height 5 feet, 10 inches; weight 205; excellent health; born and raised in Indianapolis.

Education

High school graduate; played football; no extracurricular activities of note.

Employment record

1. Currently employed by Allied Food Distributors in the warehouse in Indianapolis; two years with Allied; job responsibilities include processing orders from the field and expediting rush orders; current salary $2,200 per month.

2. In 1984–85 employed by Hoosier Van Lines in Indianapolis as a sales agent; terminating salary was $550 per month; left due to limits placed on salary and lack of challenge in the job.

3. In 1982–84 employed by Main Street Clothiers of Indianapolis as a retail salesperson in the men's department; terminating salary $1,500 per month; left due to boring nature of this type of selling.

4. Between 1965 and 1982 held six other clerical and sales type jobs, all in Indianapolis.

Applicant's statement

I feel that my true employment interest lies in selling in a situation where I can be my own boss. This job seems just right.

Ms. Ramsey's comments

Seems very interested in job as a career.

Well recommended by his current boss.

Reasonably intelligent.

Good appearance.

Moderately aggressive.

EXHIBIT 3 Information on Mr. Carley Tobias

Personal information

Born February 12, 1957; married; two children ages 1 and 4; height 6 feet, 2 inches; weight 170; excellent health; born in San Francisco; raised in Cleveland, Ohio.

Education

High school and Community College graduate in business administration; student council president at Community College; plus belonged to a number of other clubs.

Employment record

1. Currently employed by The Drug Trading Company in Cincinnati as a salesperson; job responsibility involves selling to retail drugstores; seven years with Drug Trading; current salary $3,300 per month.
2. In 1979–81 U.S. Army private; did one tour of duty in Germany.

Applicant's statement

I am seeking a new position because of the limited earning potential at Drug Trading, plus my family's desire to live in a less populated city.

Other information

He is very active in civic and church organizations in Cincinnati; he is currently president of the Sales and Marketing Executives of Cincinnati.

Ms. Ramsey's comments

Very personable.
Reasonably intelligent.
Good appearance.
He seems to like Cincinnati a lot.
Good experience.

EXHIBIT 4 Information on Mr. Arthur Woodhead

Personal information

Born May 26, 1965; single; height 6 feet; weight 180; excellent health; born and raised in Chicago.

Education

Will graduate in May 1987 from the University of Illinois, Chicago, with a B.B.A. Active in intramural athletics and student government.

Employment record

Summer jobs only; did house painting and gardening work for his own company. Earned $1,400 per month in summer of 1986.

Applicant's statement

I really like to run my own affairs, and selling seems like a good position to reach this objective.

Ms. Ramsey's comments

Well dressed and groomed.

Very intelligent.

Management potential, not career salesperson.

Not very aggressive.

Case 27

Outdoor Sporting Products, Inc.*

The annual sales volume of Outdoor Sporting Products, Inc., for the past six years had ranged between $6.2 million and $6.8 million. Although profits continued to be satisfactory, Mr. Hudson McDonald, president and chief operating officer, was concerned because sales had not increased appreciably from year to year. Consequently, he asked a consultant in New York City and the officers of the company to submit proposals for improving the salesmen's compensation plan, which he believed was the basic weakness in the firm's marketing operations.

Outdoor's factory and warehouse were located in Albany, New York, where the company manufactured and distributed sporting equipment, clothing, and accessories. Mr. Hudson McDonald, who managed the company, organized it in 1956 when he envisioned a growing market for sporting goods resulting from the predicted increase in leisure time and the rising levels of income in the United States.

Products of the company, numbering approximately 700 items, were grouped into three lines: (1) fishing supplies, (2) hunting supplies, and (3) accessories. The fishing supplies line, which accounted for approximately 40 percent of the company's annual sales, included nearly every item a fisherman would need such as fishing jackets, vests, caps, rods and reels of all types, lines, flies, lures, landing nets, and creels. Thirty percent of annual sales were in the hunting supplies line, which consisted of hunting clothing of all types including insulated and thermal underwear, safety garments, shell holders, whistles, calls, and gun cases. The accessories line, which made up the balance of the company's annual sales volume, included items such as compasses, cooking kits, lanterns, hunting and fishing knives, hand warmers, and novelty gifts.

While the sales of the hunting and fishing lines were very seasonal, they tended to complement one another. The January–April period accounted for the bulk of the company's annual volume in fishing items, and most sales of hunting supplies were made during the months of May through August. Typically,

---

* Adapted from a case written by Zarrel V. Lambert, Auburn University, and Fred W. Kniffin, University of Connecticut, Stamford. Used with permission.

the company's sales of all products reached their lows for the year during the month of December.

Outdoor's sales volume was $6.57 million in the current year with self-manufactured products accounting for 35 percent of this total. Fifty percent of the company's volume consisted of imported products, which came principally from Japan. Items manufactured by other domestic producers and distributed by Outdoor accounted for the remaining 15 percent of total sales.

Mr. McDonald reported that wholesale prices to retailers were established by adding a markup of 50 to 100 percent to Outdoor's cost for the item. This rule was followed on self-manufactured products as well as for items purchased from other manufacturers. The resulting average markup across all products was 70 percent on cost.

Outdoor's market area consisted of the New England states, New York, Pennsylvania, Ohio, Michigan, Wisconsin, Indiana, Illinois, Kentucky, Tennessee, West Virginia, Virginia, Maryland, Delaware, and New Jersey. The area over which Outdoor could effectively compete was limited to some extent by shipping costs, since all orders were shipped from the factory and warehouse in Albany.

Outdoor's salesmen sold to approximately 6,000 retail stores in small- and medium-sized cities in its market area. Analysis of sales records showed that the firm's customer coverage was very poor in the large metropolitan areas. Typically, each account was a one- or two-store operation. Mr. McDonald stated that he knew for a fact that Outdoor's share of the market was very low, perhaps 2 to 3 percent; and for all practical purposes, he felt the company's sales potential was unlimited.

Mr. McDonald believed that with few exceptions, Outdoor's customers had little or no brand preference and in the vast majority of cases they bought hunting and fishing supplies from several suppliers.

It was McDonald's opinion that the pattern of retail distribution for hunting and fishing products had been changing during the past 10 years as a result of the growth of discount stores. He thought that the proportion of retail sales for hunting and fishing supplies made by small- and medium-sized sporting goods outlets had been declining compared to the percent sold by discounters and chain stores. An analysis of company records revealed Outdoor had not developed business among the discounters with the exception of a few small discount stores. Some of Outdoor's executives felt that the lack of business with discounters might have been due in part to the company's pricing policy and in part to the pressures which current customers had exerted on company salesmen to keep them from calling on the discounters.

Outdoor's Sales Force

The company's sales force played the major role in its marketing efforts since Outdoor did not use magazine, newspaper, or radio advertising to reach either the retail trade or consumers. One advertising piece that supplemented the work of the salesmen was Outdoor's merchandise catalog. It contained a complete listing of all the company's products and was mailed to all retailers who were either current accounts or prospective accounts. Typically, store buyers used the catalog for purposes of reordering.

Most accounts were contacted by a salesman two or three times a year. The salesmen planned their activities so that each store would be called upon at the beginning of the fishing season and again prior to the hunting season. Certain key accounts of some salesmen were contacted more often than two or three times a year.

Management believed that product knowledge was the major ingredient of a successful sales call. Consequently, Mr. McDonald had developed a "selling formula," which each salesman was required to learn before he took over a territory. The "formula" contained five parts: (1) the name and catalog number of each item sold by the company; (2) the sizes and colors in which each item was available; (3) the wholesale price of each item; (4) the suggested retail price of each item; and (5) the primary selling features of each item. After a new salesman had mastered the product knowledge specified by this "formula" he began working in his assigned territory and was usually accompanied by Mr. McDonald for several weeks.

Managing the sales force consumed approximately one third of Mr. McDonald's efforts. The remaining two thirds of his time was spent purchasing products for resale and in general administrative duties as the company's chief operating officer.

Mr. McDonald held semiannual sales meetings, had weekly telephone conversations with each salesman, and had mimeographed bulletins containing information on products, prices, and special promotional deals mailed to all salesmen each week. Daily call reports and attendance at the semiannual sales meetings were required of all salesmen. One meeting was held the first week in January to introduce the spring line of fishing supplies. The hunting line was presented at the second meeting, which was scheduled in May. Each of these sales meetings spanned four to five days so the salesmen were able to study the new products being introduced and any changes in sales and company policies. The production manager and comptroller attended these sales meetings to answer questions and to discuss problems which the salesmen might have concerning deliveries and credit.

On a predetermined schedule each salesman telephoned Mr. McDonald every Monday morning to learn of changes in prices, special promotional offers, and delivery schedules of unshipped orders. At this time the salesman's activities for the week were discussed, and sometimes the salesman was asked by Mr. McDonald to collect past due accounts in his territory. In addition, the salesmen submitted daily call reports, which listed the name of each account contacted and the results of the call. Generally, the salesmen planned their own itineraries in terms of the accounts and prospects that were to be contacted and the amount of time to be spent on each call.

Outdoor's sales force during the current year totaled 11 full-time employ-

EXHIBIT 1 Salesmen: Age, years of service, territory, and sales

				Sales	
				Previous	Current
Salesmen	Age	Years of service	Territory	year	year
Allen	45	2	Illinois and Indiana	$ 330,264	$ 329,216
Campbell	62	10	Pennsylvania	1,192,192	1,380,240
Duvall	23	1	New England	—	414,656
Edwards	39	1	Michigan	—	419,416
Gatewood	63	5	West Virginia	358,528	358,552
Hammond	54	2	Virginia	414,936	414,728
Logan	37	1	Kentucky and Tennessee	—	447,720
Mason	57	2	Delaware and Maryland	645,032	825,088
O'Bryan	59	4	Ohio	343,928	372,392
Samuels	42	3	New York and New Jersey	737,024	824,472
Wates	67	5	Wisconsin	370,712	342,200
Salesmen terminated in previous year				1,828,816	—
House account				257,384	244,480
Total				$6,478,816	$6,374,816

ees. Their ages ranged from 23 to 67 years, and their tenure with the company ranged from 1 to 10 years. Salesmen, territories, and sales volumes for the previous year and the current year are shown in Exhibit 1.

Compensation of Salesmen

The salesmen were paid straight commissions on their dollar sales volume for the calendar year. The commission rate was 5 percent on the first $300,000, 6 percent on the next $200,000 in volume, and 7 percent on all sales over $500,000 for the year. Each week a salesman could draw all or a portion of his accumulated commissions. McDonald encouraged the salesmen to draw commissions as they accumulated since he felt the men were motivated to work harder when they had a very small or zero balance in their commission accounts. These accounts were closed at the end of the year so each salesman began the new year with nothing in his account.

The salesmen provided their own automobiles and paid their traveling expenses, of which all or a portion were reimbursed by per diem. Under the per diem plan, each salesman received $70 per day for Monday through Thursday and $42 for Friday, or a total of $322 for the normal workweek. No per diem was paid for Saturday, but a salesman received an additional $70 if he spent Saturday and Sunday nights in the territory.

In addition to the commission and per diem, a salesman could earn cash awards under two sales incentive plans that were installed two years ago. Under the Annual Sales Increase Awards Plan, a total of $10,400 was paid to the five salesmen having the largest percentage increase in dollar sales volume over the previous year. To be eligible for these awards, a salesman had to show a sales

EXHIBIT 2 Salesmen's earnings and incentive awards in the current year

	Sales		Annual sales increase awards		Weekly sales increase awards (total accrued)	Earnings*
Salesmen	Previous year	Current year	Increase in sales (percent)	Award		
Allen	$ 330,264	$ 329,216	(0.3%)	—	$1,012	$30,000†
Campbell	1,192,192	1,380,240	15.8	$3,000 (2d)	2,244	88,617
Duvall	—	414,656	—	—	—	30,000†
Edwards	—	419,416	—	—	—	30,000†
Gatewood	358,528	358,552	(0.1)	400 (5th)	1,104	18,513
Hammond	414,936	414,728	—	—	420	30,000†
Logan	—	447,720	—	—	—	30,000†
Mason	645,032	825,088	27.9	4,000 (1st)	3,444	49,756
O'Bryan	343,928	372,392	8.3	1,000 (4th)	1,512	19,344
Samuels	737,024	824,472	11.9	2,000 (3d)	1,300	49,713
Wates	370,712	342,200	(7.7)	—	612	17,532

* Exclusive of incentive awards and per diem.
† Guarantee of $600 per week or $30,000 per year.

increase over the previous year. These awards were made at the January sales meeting, and the winners were determined by dividing the dollar amount of each salesman's increase by his volume for the previous year with the percentage increases ranked in descending order. The salesmen's earnings under this plan for the current year are shown in Exhibit 2.

Under the second incentive plan, each salesman could win a Weekly Sales Increase Award for each week in which his dollar volume in the current year exceeded his sales for the corresponding week in the previous year. Beginning with an award of $4 for the first week, the amount of the award increased by $4 for each week in which the salesman surpassed his sales for the comparable week in the previous year. If a salesman produced higher sales during each of the 50 weeks in the current year, he received $4 for the 1st week, $8 for the 2d week, and $200 for the 50th week, or a total of $4,100 for the year. The salesman had to be employed by the company during the previous year to be eligible for these awards. A check for the total amount of the awards accrued during the year was presented to the salesmen at the sales meeting held in January. Earnings of the salesmen under this plan for the current year are shown in Exhibit 2.

The company frequently used "spiffs" to promote the sales of special items. The salesman was paid a spiff, which usually was $4, for each order he obtained for the designated items in the promotion.

For the past three years in recruiting salesmen, Mr. McDonald had guaranteed the more qualified applicants a weekly income while they learned the business and developed their respective territories. During the current year five salesmen, Allen, Duvall, Edwards, Hammond, and Logan, had a guarantee of $600 a week, which they drew against their commissions. If the year's cumulative commissions for any of these salesmen were less than their cumulative weekly drawing accounts, they received no commissions. The commission and drawing accounts were closed on December 31 so each salesman began the new year with a zero balance in each account.

The company did not have a stated or written policy specifying the maximum length of time a salesman could receive a guarantee if his commissions continued to be less than his draw. Mr. McDonald held the opinion that the five salesmen who currently had guarantees would quit if these guarantees were withdrawn before their commissions reached $30,000 per year.

Mr. McDonald stated that he was convinced the annual earnings of Outdoor's salesmen had fallen behind earnings for comparable selling positions, particularly in the past six years. As a result, he felt that the company's ability to attract and hold high-caliber professional salesmen was being adversely affected. He strongly expressed the opinion that each salesman should be earning $50,000 annually.

Compensation Plan Proposals

In December of the current year, Mr. McDonald met with his comptroller and production manager, who were the only other executives of the company, and solicited their ideas concerning changes in the company's compensation plan for salesmen.

The comptroller pointed out that the salesmen having guarantees were not producing the sales that had been expected from their territories. He was concerned that the annual commissions earned by four of the five salesmen on guarantees were approximately half or less than their drawing accounts.

Furthermore, according to the comptroller, several of the salesmen who did not have guarantees were producing a relatively low volume of sales year after year. For example, annual sales remained at relatively low levels for Gatewood, O'Bryan, and Wates, who had been working four to five years in their respective territories.

The comptroller proposed that guarantees be reduced to $250 per week plus commissions at the regular rate on all sales. The $250 would not be drawn against commissions as was the case under the existing plan but would be in addition to any commissions earned. In the comptroller's opinion, this plan would motivate the salesmen to increase sales rapidly since their incomes would rise directly with their sales. The comptroller presented Exhibit 3, which showed the incomes of the five salesmen having guarantees in the current year as compared with the incomes they would have received under his plan.

From a sample check of recent shipments, the production manager had concluded that the salesmen tended to overwork accounts located within a 50-mile radius of their homes. Sales coverage was extremely light in a 60- to 100-mile radius of the salesmen's homes with somewhat better coverage beyond 100 miles. He argued that this pattern of sales coverage seemed to result from a

EXHIBIT 3 Comparison of earnings in current year under existing guarantee plan with earnings under the comptroller's plan*

		Existing plan			Comptroller's plan		
Salesmen	Sales	Com-missions	Guar-antee	Earnings	Com-missions	Guar-antee	Earnings
Allen	$329,216	$16,753	$30,000	$30,000	$16,753	$12,500	$29,253
Duvall	414,656	21,879	30,000	30,000	21,879	12,500	34,379
Edwards	419,416	22,165	30,000	30,000	22,165	12,500	34,665
Hammond	358,552	18,513	30,000	30,000	18,513	12,500	31,013
Logan	447,720	23,863	30,000	30,000	23,863	12,500	36,363

* Exclusive of incentive awards and per diem.

desire by the salesmen to spend most evenings during the week at home with their families.

He proposed that the per diem be increased from $70 to $90 per day for Monday through Thursday, $42 for Friday, and $90 for Sunday if the salesman spent Sunday evening away from his home. He reasoned that the per diem of $90 for Sunday would act as a strong incentive for the salesmen to drive to the perimeters of their territories on Sunday evenings rather than use Monday morning for traveling. Further, he believed that the increase in per diem would encourage the salesmen to spend more evenings away from their homes, which would result in a more uniform coverage of the sales territories and an overall increase in sales volume.

The consultant from New York City recommended that the guarantees and per diem be retained on the present basis and proposed that Outdoor adopt what he called a ''Ten Percent Self-Improvement Plan.'' Under the consultant's plan each salesman would be paid, in addition to the regular commission, a monthly bonus commission of 10 percent on all dollar volume over his sales in the comparable month of the previous year. For example, if a salesman sold $40,000 worth of merchandise in January of the current year and $36,000 in January of the previous year, he would receive a $400 bonus check in February. For salesmen on guarantees, bonuses would be in addition to earnings. The consultant reasoned that the bonus commission would motivate the salesmen, both those with and without guarantees, to increase their sales.

He further recommended the discontinuation of the two sales incentive plans currently in effect. He felt the savings from these plans would nearly cover the costs of his proposal.

Following a discussion of these proposals with the management group, Mr. McDonald was undecided on which proposal to adopt, if any. Further, he wondered if any change in the compensation of salesmen would alleviate all of the present problems.

Case 28

Puritan Drug Company*

On May 1, 1984, David Thomas transferred to the Syracuse Division of the Puritan Drug Company as divisional sales manager. Prior to his transfer, Thomas served as assistant to the vice president of sales in the company's New York headquarters location.

At the conclusion of Thomas' first month-end sales meeting held on June 6, 1984, Harvey Brooks, a salesman in one of the division's rural territories, informed Thomas of his wish to retire, effective the following month. Thomas was surprised by Brooks' announcement because Robert Jackson, the division manager, informed him that Brooks had recently requested and received a deferment of his retirement until he reached his 66th birthday in July 1985. Brooks' sole explanation was that he had "changed his mind."

Brooks' retirement posed a significant territorial reassignment problem for Thomas.

Background of the Syracuse Division

David Thomas became the divisional sales manager at the age of 29. He had joined Puritan Drug as a sales trainee after his graduation from Stanford University in 1978. From 1978 to 1980 he worked as a salesman. In the fall of 1980, the sales manager of the company made Thomas one of his assistants. Thomas assisted the sales manager in arranging special sales promotions of the lines of different manufacturers.

Thomas' predecessor in Syracuse, Harry L. Schultz, had served as divisional sales manager for 15 years before his death in April 1984. "H. L.," as Schultz was called, had also worked as a salesman for the drug wholesale house that merged with Puritan Drug in 1964 and became its Syracuse Division. Although Thomas had made Schultz's acquaintance in the course of business, he did not know Schultz well. Over the past month many members of the divisional sales force often expressed their admiration and affection for Schultz. Several sales reps made a point of telling Thomas that "Old H. L." knew every druggist in 12 counties by their first name. Schultz, in fact, had died of a heart

* Copyright © 1985 by the President and Fellows of Harvard College

This case was prepared by Rowland T. Moriarty, Jr., as the basis for class discussion rather than to illustrate either effective or ineffective handling of an administrative situation. Reprinted by permission of the Harvard Business School.

attack while trout fishing with the president of the Syracuse Pharmacists' Association. Robert Jackson remarked that most of the druggists in town attended Schultz's funeral.

The Syracuse Division of Puritan Drug was one of 74 wholesale drug divisions in the United States owned by the firm. Each division acted as a functionally autonomous unit maintaining its own warehouse, sales, buying, and accounting departments. While the divisional manager was responsible for the performance of the division, there were a number of line functions performed by the regional and national offices of Puritan Drug. As divisional sales manager, for example, David Thomas maintained a relationship with the regional office in Albany, which was responsible for assisting him in implementing marketing policies established by the central office in New York.

As a wholesaler, the Syracuse Division sold to retail druggists a broad product line of approximately 18,000 items. The product line consisted of just about anything and everything sold through drugstores except fresh food, tobacco products, newspapers, and magazines. In the Syracuse trading area, Puritan Drug competed with two other wholesalers; one carried substantially the same line of products as Puritan Drug, and the other carried a more limited line of drug products.

The Syracuse Division operated as a profitable family-owned wholesale drug house before its merger with Puritan Drug in 1964. While the division operated profitably since 1964, it had not shown a profit on sales equal to the average for the other wholesale drug divisions of Puritan Drug. From 1973 to 1984 the net sales of the division rose each year. However, because competitors did not make available their sales figures, it was impossible to ascertain whether this increase in sales represented a change in the competitive situation or merely a general trend of increasing business volume in the Syracuse trading area. While Schultz was of the opinion that the increase had been at the expense of competitors, the Albany office maintained that since the trend of increase was less than that of other divisions in the northern New York region, the Syracuse Division may have actually lost ground competitively. A new technique for calculating the potential wholesale purchasing power of retail drugstores, adopted shortly before Thomas' transfer, indicated that the share of the wholesale drug market controlled by the Syracuse Division was below both the median and the mean for other Puritan Drug divisions.

Only a handful of the division's current work force was employed by the family-owned firm prior to its merger with Puritan Drug in 1964. H. L. Schultz was the one remaining executive whose employment in the Syracuse Division antedated the merger; only two sales reps, Harvey Brooks and Clifford Nelson, had sold for the predecessor company.

Many of the company executives and sales reps, although not employed by the predecessor company, nevertheless had employment histories with Puritan Drug going back to the 1960s and 1970s. Of those employees hired prior to 1974, only Robert Jackson, the division manager, had an undergraduate degree, earned at a local YMCA evening college. The more recently hired employees were, without exception, university or pharmacy college graduates. None of the younger employees were promoted when recent vacancies occurred for the jobs of divisional warehouse operations manager and divisional merchandise manager in Syracuse. Two of the younger employees, however, had recently been transferred to similar positions in other divisions.

The Syracuse Division Sales Force

From the time Thomas assumed Schultz's duties in early May, he had devoted four days a week to the task of traveling through each sales territory with the sales rep who covered it. He had made no changes in the practices or procedures of the sales force. Brooks' retirement request provided the first occasion where Thomas could make a nonroutine decision.

When Thomas took charge of the Syracuse Division sales force, it consisted of nine sales reps and four trainees. Four of the sales reps (Frederick Taylor, Edward Harrington, Grace Howard, and Linda Donnelly) had joined the company under the sales training program for college graduates initiated early in the 1970s. The other five sales reps had been with the company many years. Harvey Brooks and Clifford Nelson were the most senior in service. William Murray joined the company as a warehouse employee in 1960 at the age of 19. He became a sales rep in 1965. Walter Miller joined Puritan Drug as a sales rep in 1965 when the wholesale drug firm that he had previously worked for went out of business. Miller, who was 48 years old, had been a wholesale drug sales rep since the age of 20. Albert Simpson came to Puritan Drug after working as a missionary salesman for a manufacturer. Simpson, who joined the company in 1968 at age 26, had earlier served as an officer in the Army Medical Corps.

The four sales trainees graduated from college in June 1983. When Thomas arrived in Syracuse, they were in the last phase of their 12-month training program and were spending much of their time traveling with the experienced sales reps. Thomas believed that Schultz hired the trainees to cover anticipated turnover of sales reps and trainees and to implement the New York office's policy of getting more intensive coverage of each market area. The trainees expected to receive territory assignments, either in the Syracuse Division or elsewhere, on the completion of their training period at the end of June 1984.

Thomas had not seen very much of the sales reps as a group. His acquaintance with them had been formed by the one month-end sales meeting he attended and through his travels with them through their territories.

Walter Miller. Thomas was of the opinion that Walter Miller was a very easy-going, even-tempered person. He seemed to be very popular with the other sales reps and with his customers. Thomas thought that Miller liked him because he had commented to Thomas several times that his suggestions had been very helpful.

Harvey Brooks. Harvey Brooks had not been particularly friendly. Thomas observed that Brooks was well liked because of his good humor and friendly manner with everyone. Thomas did notice, however, that Brooks intimated that the sales manager should defer to Brooks' age, experience, and judgment. Brooks and his wife lived in the town of Oswego.

On June 4, 1984, Thomas traveled with Brooks, and they visited five of Brooks' accounts. Thomas filed a routine report with the Albany office on the sales rep's field work:

Points requiring attention: Not using merchandising equipment; not following weekly sales plan. Pharmaceutical business going to competitors because of lack of interest. Too much time spent on idle chatter. Only shows druggists what "he thinks they will buy." Tends to sell easy items instead of profitable ones.

Steps taken for correction: Explained shortcomings and demonstrated how larger, more profitable orders could be obtained by following sales plan—did just that by getting the biggest order ever written for Carthage account.

Remarks: Old-time "personality." Should do terrific volume if trained on new merchandising techniques.

On a similar form completed by H. L. Schultz on the basis of his travels with Brooks on March 3, 1984, the following comments were made:

Points requiring attention: Not getting pharmaceutical business. Not following promotion plans.

Steps taken for correction: Told him about these things.

Remarks: Brooks made this territory—can sell anything he sets his mind to—a real drummer—very popular with his customers.

Grace Howard. Grace Howard (age 29) was the oldest of the sales reps who had passed through the formal sales training program. Thomas considered her earnest and conscientious. Howard had increased her sales each year. Although Thomas did not consider Howard to be the "sales rep type," he noted that Howard was quite successful in using the merchandising techniques that Thomas wanted to implement.

William Murray. William Murray handled many of the big accounts in downtown Syracuse. Thomas believed that Murray was an excellent sales rep who considered himself "very smooth." Thomas had been surprised at the affront Murray had taken when he had offered a few suggestions to improve Murray's selling technique. William Murray and his wife were good friends of the Jacksons, as well as the merchandise and operations managers and their wives. Thomas suspected that Murray had expected to be Schultz's successor.

Clifford Nelson. Clifford Nelson appeared to Thomas to be an earnest and conscientious sales rep. He had been amiable, but not cordial to Thomas. Thomas' report on Nelson's calls on 10 accounts on June 5, 1984, contained the following statements:

Points requiring attention: Rushing calls. Gets want book and tries to sell case lots on wanted items. Carries all merchandising equipment, but doesn't use it.

Steps taken for correction: Suggested change in routing; longer, better-planned calls; conducted presentation demonstration.

Remarks: Hard-working, conscientious, good salesman, but needs to be brought up-to-date on merchandising methods.

Schultz's comments on his observations of Nelson on March 4, 1984, were:

Points requiring attention: Uses the want book on the basis of most sales. Not pushing promotions.

Steps taken for correction: Discussed shortcomings.

Remarks: Nelson really knows how to sell—visits every customer each week. Hard worker—very loyal—even pushes goods with very low commission.

On the day Thomas traveled with Nelson, the sales rep suggested that Thomas have dinner at the Nelsons' home. Thomas accepted the invitation, but at the end of the day Nelson took him to a restaurant in Watertown instead, explaining that he did not want to inconvenience his wife because his two daughters were home from college on vacation.

Albert Simpson. Albert Simpson caused Thomas considerable concern. Simpson continually complained about sales management procedures, commission rates, the "lousy service of the warehouse people," and similar matters at the sales meeting. Thomas believed that while most of his complaints were valid, the matters were usually trivial, and that the other sales reps did not complain about any of these matters. Thomas mentioned his difficulties with Simpson to Robert Jackson, the district manager. Jackson replied that Simpson had been very friendly with Schultz. Simpson seemed quite popular with his customers.

Frederick Taylor. Frederick Taylor was, in Thomas' opinion, the most ambitious, aggressive and argumentative sales rep in the division. He had been employed by the company since his graduation from the University of Rochester in 1980, first as a trainee, and then as a sales rep. Taylor had substantially increased the sales volume of his territory. He persuaded Schultz to assign him six inactive hospital accounts in July 1982. Within six months, he was able to generate sales to these accounts in excess of $50,000. While the other sales reps considered Taylor "cocky" and a "big spender," Thomas regarded Taylor's attitude as one of independence. If Taylor agreed with a sales plan, he worked hard to achieve its objectives; if he did not agree, he would not cooperate. Thomas thought that he had been successful in working with Taylor.

Linda Donnelly. Linda Donnelly impressed Thomas as being unsure of herself, confused, and overworked. Thomas attributed these difficulties to Donnelly's attempts to serve too many accounts in too large a territory. Donnelly was very receptive to Thomas' suggestions on how to improve her work. Thomas believed that, at age 24, Donnelly would improve with proper guidance. Donnelly had raised her sales to a point enabling her to move from salary to commissions in March 1984.

Edward Harrington. Edward Harrington (age 25) was the only sales rep who continued to work on a salary basis. His sales volume was insufficient to sustain the income of $1,500 a month, the company minimum for sales reps with more than one year's experience. Harrington was very apologetic about being on a salary. Thomas believed that Harrington's determination to "make good" would be realized through his conscientiousness. When he was assigned the territory in 1982, it consisted largely of uncontacted accounts. The volume of sales in the territory tripled over the past two years. Thomas felt that Harrington appreciated all the help given and that, in time, Harrington would be an excellent salesman.

Commission and Turnover Rates at Puritan Drug

Sales commission rates were paid to the sales force as follows:

Brooks and Nelson	2.375%
Miller and Donnelly	2.25
Murray and Simpson	2.125
Howard and Taylor	2

Expense accounts amounted to about .75 percent of sales. Thomas explained the differences in commission rates in terms of the differential product commissions set by the company. Higher commission rates were given on items the company wished to "push," such as pharmaceuticals and calendar promotion items.

While all four trainees seemed to be good prospects, they were somewhat of an unknown quantity to Thomas. He had held training conferences with them, and thought they performed rather poorly. He was concerned that Schultz had neglected their training, yet the reps were eager for assigned territories. They indicated this desire to Thomas at every possible opportunity.

The turnover of the Syracuse Division sales force had been quite low among the senior sales reps. Only six of the graduates of the sales training program had left the division since 1979. Two were promoted to department heads in other Puritan Drug divisions. The remaining four left to work for drug manufacturers. Drug manufacturers valued sales reps with wholesaling experience, and wholesalers who competed with Puritan Drug did not offer any training programs. Consequently, there were many opportunities for a sales rep who left Puritan Drug.

Sales Management at Puritan Drug

Throughout the month of May, Thomas devoted considerable thought to improving the sales performance of the Syracuse Division. He had accepted the transfer to this job at the urging of Richard Topping, vice president in charge of sales and his prior boss. Thomas was one of a dozen young employees whom Topping had brought into the New York office as assistants to the top sales executives. None of these young assistants remained in the New York office for more than three years. Topping had made a policy of offering them field assignments so that they could "show their stuff."

Thomas had observed the performance records of other divisional sales managers while he worked in New York. He knew that some sales managers had achieved substantial improvements on the past performances of their divisions. Thomas believed that the sales performance of his own division could be enhanced by improving the sales management plan. He also knew that the share of the Syracuse market for wholesale purchases of retail drugstores[1] held by Puritan Drug was 20.05 percent, compared to a 48 percent share for some of the other divisions.

Thomas remembered that Topping had regularly focused his staff's attention on the qualitative aspects of sales policy. Thomas had assisted Topping in implementing merchandising plans to utilize the sales reps' efforts to minimize the handling cost of their sales, and to maximize the gross margin.

The company promoted a three-step sales plan for increased profitability:

1. Sales of larger average value per line of the order were encouraged because the cost of processing and filling each line of an order was practically constant.
2. Sales of larger total value were encouraged because the delivery cost for orders having a total weight between 20 and 100 pounds was practically constant.
3. Because some manufacturers offered margins considerably larger than others, sales of higher margin items were encouraged. Sales commissions

---

[1] The New York market analysis section calculated the potential wholesale sales for retail drugstores. This market estimate, called the PWPP (potential wholesale purchasing power), was calculated for each county by adjusting retail drugstore sales to an estimate of the purchases of goods from wholesalers.

varied with the margins available to Puritan Drug on the products the sales reps sold.

The headquarters office also sought to increase the effectiveness of Puritan Drug promotions by setting up a sales calendar. The sales calendar coordinated the activities of all Puritan Drug divisions so that during a given calendar period, every company account could be solicited for those specific items which yielded attractive margins. The sales calendar required that the sales reps in each division follow a fairly prescribed pattern in selling to each individual account. The divisional sales managers were responsible for the coordination of the activities of their sales reps. Thomas believed that his predecessor had never really accepted the sales patterns prescribed by the New York office.

The national office also required each division to keep uniform sales and market analysis records. In the New York office, Thomas had developed a familiarity with the uses of these records. He inherited from Schultz a carefully maintained system of sales department records.

The division trading area formed the basis of the sales and market analysis record system. The economics of selling costs, transportation costs of delivery, and sales reps' traveling expenses determined the limits of the trading area. Thomas knew from his own experience, however, that delineation of trading areas was heavily influenced by tradition, geography, number of sales reps, number of possible sales contacts, estimated market potential, competition, and agreements with adjacent Puritan Drug divisions. The Rochester and Albany trading areas bordered the Syracuse Division on the east, south, and west; Canada bordered the division in the north. (A map of this division is included as Exhibit 1.)

Since his arrival, Thomas had formed the opinion that the present territories had been established without careful regard for the number of stores in the area, the sales potential, or the travel involved. Although he had not yet studied any one territory carefully, Thomas suspected that all his sales reps skimmed the cream from many of their accounts. He believed that they simply did not have adequate time to do a thorough selling job in each store. Exhibit 2 provides information on sales and sales potential by county. Exhibits 3 and 4 provide selected data on individual territory assignments and performance.

Sales Territories of Harvey Brooks and Clifford Nelson

Harvey Brooks' sales territory included accounts scattered through small towns in four rural counties northeast of Syracuse (see Exhibit 5). Brooks originally developed the accounts for the predecessor company. At the time he undertook this task in 1954, a competing service wholesaler had established a mail-order business with the area's rural druggists. Brooks "took to the road" to build sales with personal service. He had been hired specifically for this job because he was a native of the area and an experienced "drummer."

EXHIBIT 1 Syracuse Division trading area in upstate New York. Salesmen's assignments

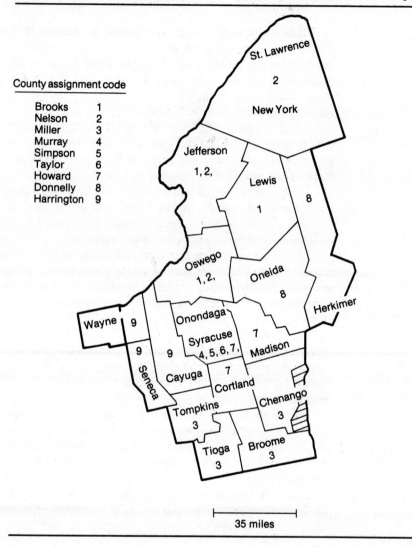

County assignment code

Brooks	1
Nelson	2
Miller	3
Murray	4
Simpson	5
Taylor	6
Howard	7
Donnelly	8
Harrington	9

35 miles

EXHIBIT 2   Selected data on sales and sales potentials, by counties

County	Salesman code[a]	Population (000s)	Percent of division	Retailers Sold	Retailers Inactive accounts	Retailers Accounts not sold	Retailers Total	Potential wholesale purchasing power (000s)	Percent of division PWPP	Sales (000s)[b]	Sales percent of PWPP	Hospitals Sold	Hospitals Not sold	Hospitals Sales (000s)	Miscellaneous sales (000s)
St. Lawrence	2	117.2	6.3%	23	1	2	26	$ 2,725	4.4%	$ 1,020	26.9%	2	4	$ 20	$ 15
Jefferson	1,2	90.2	4.9	34	—	—	34	3,265	5.3	918	28.2	2	2	10	—
Lewis	1	24.8	1.3	8	—	—	8	653	1.0	215	32.2	—	1	—	8
Herkimer	8	69.3	3.7	10	6	1	17	1,560	2.5	245	15.7	1	2	—	—
Oswego	1,2	97.8	5.3	25	1	—	26	3,350	5.5	933	27.1	—	2	—	25
Oneida	8	285.4	15.5	46	14	12	72	8,700	14.2	838	10.5	—	13	—	18
Wayne	9	76.6	4.1	4	—	1	5	618	1.0	138	22.3	—	—	—	68
Cayuga	9	75.6	4.1	12	4	—	16	1,403	2.3	253	18.0	2	—	10	—
Onondaga	4,5,6,7	474.8	25.8	98	9	13	120	19,118	31.2	5,415	28.7	6	9	270	480
Madison	7	59.7	3.2	12	2	3	17	3,125	5.1	653	20.9	2	1	15	—
Seneca	9	34.4	1.9	6	1	3	10	1,395	2.3	210	15.0	—	2	—	60
Cortland	7	45.4	2.5	6	2	1	9	1,275	2.1	403	31.5	—	2	—	—
Chenango	3	48.2	2.6	4	2	6	12	1,420	2.3	158	11.1	—	3	—	—
Tompkins	3	75.7	4.1	9	1	4	14	2,038	3.3	330	16.2	—	5	—	—
Tioga	3	46.2	2.5	4	—	7	11	805	1.3	200	24.8	—	—	—	—
Broome	3	225.3	12.2	22	2	13	37	9,925	16.2	633	6.4	—	8	—	45
Totals		1,846.6	100.0%	323	45	66	434	$61,375	100.0%	$12,562	20.5%	15	54	$325	$719

a County assignment code:

Brooks	– 1	Murray	– 4
Nelson	– 2	Simpson	– 5
Miller	– 3	Taylor	– 6

Howard	– 7
Donnelly	– 8
Harrington	– 9

b Excludes miscellaneous sales, sales to hospitals, and house sales.

EXHIBIT 3 Selected data on sales reps' territory assignments by county

Sales rep	County	Sales 1984[a]	Active[b] accounts	PWPP[c]	Assigned[b] accounts
Miller	Chenango	$ 154,755	4	$ 1,417	15
	Tompkins	332,250	9	2,038	19
	Tioga	199,195	4	805	11
	Broome	675,750	22	9,928	45
Total		1,361,950	39	14,188	90
Brooks	Jefferson	365,085	16	2,265	18
	Lewis	215,985	8	653	9
	Oswego	924,650	25	2,675	28
Total		1,150,720	49	5,593	55
Howard	Onondaga	572,543	14	2,275	14
	Madison	652,125	12	3,125	19
	Cortland	402,500	6	1,275	11
Total		1,627,168	32	6,675	44
Murray	Onondaga	1,890,383	33	5,563	44
Total		1,890,383	33	5,563	44
Nelson	St. Lawrence	1,020,440	25	2,725	32
	Jefferson	556,298	20	1,000	20
	Oswego	6,950	1	675	1
Total		1,583,688	46	4,400	53
Simpson	Onondaga	1,834,815	29	7,520	48
Total		1,834,815	29	7,520	48
Taylor	Onondaga	1,595,183	29	3,760	29
Total		1,595,183	29	3,760	29
Donnelly	Herkimer	242,650	10	1,560	19
	Oneida	937,500	46	8,700	85
Total		1,180,150	56	10,260	104
Harrington	Wayne	136,000	4	618	5
	Cayuga	317,500	14	1,403	18
	Seneca	271,950	8	1,395	13
Total		725,450	26	3,416	36
Hospitals	Taylor (Syracuse)	270,000			
	Nelson/ Harrington	55,000			
House accounts		$ 1,322,530			
Total division sales		$14,951,910			

[a] The figure by sales rep includes sales to chain and independent drugstores and to miscellaneous accounts, but do not include sales to hospitals or house accounts indicated at the foot of the table.

[b] Includes hospitals and other recognized drug outlets in the territory.

[c] No potential is calculated for hospitals or miscellaneous sales. However, where a county is divided among several sales reps, the potential sales figure for each rep is obtained by allocating the county potential in proportion to the total *number* of potential drugstore and miscellaneous accounts in that county assigned to that rep.

EXHIBIT 4 Summary data on sales reps' performance

	1984 sales (000s)	Percent of total sales	1984 PWPP[a] (000s)	Percent of total PWPP	Sales percent of PWPP	1984 active accounts[b]		1984 assigned accounts[b]		Active accounts percent of assigned	1984 sales per active account	PWPP per assigned account[c]	1984 commissions
						No.	Percent	No.	Percent				
I													
Miller	$ 1,363	10.2%	$14,188	23.2%	9.6%	39	11.5%	90	17.9%	43.4%	$35,000	$157,750	$30,675
Brooks	1,505	11.3	5,593	9.1	27.0	49	14.5	55	10.9	89.0	30,750	101,500	35,725
Murray	1,890	14.2	5,563	9.1	34.0	33	9.8	44	8.8	75.0	57,250	126,250	40,200
Nelson	1,585d	11.9	4,400	7.2	36.0	46	13.6	53	10.5	85.0	34,500	83,000	38,500
Simpson	1,835	13.8	7,520	12.2	24.5	29	8.6	48	9.5	60.5	63,375	156,750	39,000
Subtotal	$ 8,178	61.4%	$37,264	60.8%	22.0%	196	58.0%	290	57.6%	67.2%	$58,450	$128,500	
II													
Howard	$ 1,628	12.2%	$ 6,675	10.9%	24.4%	32	9.5%	44	8.7%	72.7%	$50,900	$151,500	$ 3,300
Taylor	1,595d	12.0	3,760	6.1	42.4	28	8.3	29	5.8	96.5	66,750	129,500	31,900
Donnelly	1,180	8.9	10,260	16.7	11.5	56	16.5	104	20.7	53.8	21,050	98,750	26,550
Harrington	725d	5.5	3,415	5.5	21.3	26	7.7	36	7.2	72.3	27,875	95,000	18,000
Subtotal	$ 5,128	38.6%	$24,110	39.2%	21.3%	142	42.0%	213	42.4%	66.7%	$36,188	$113,250	
Total	$13,306d	100.0%	$61,374	100.0%	21.7	338	100.0%	503	100.0%	67.0%	$39,325	$122,000	

Hospital sales by:
Taylor	$ 270
Nelson	30
Harrington	25
House sales:	1,322
Grand total	$14,953

a No potential is calculated for hospital or miscellaneous sales. However, where a county is divided among several sales reps the potential sales figure for each rep is obtained by allocating the county potential in proportion to the total *number* of potential drugstore and miscellaneous accounts in that county assigned to that rep.

b Includes hospitals and other recognized drug outlets in the territory.

c Understated since hospitals and miscellaneous accounts are included in the assigned accounts listed but not in the potential.

d Excluding hospital sales.

EXHIBIT 5 Counties sold by Brooks and Nelson

In 1959, Clifford Nelson, a friend of Brooks, became a division sales rep. At the suggestion of Brooks, he covered other accounts in the same four-county area. Nelson previously had been a sales rep for a proprietary medicine firm. He was seven years younger than Brooks. Since 1955, Brooks and Nelson each had had a number of accounts in the four-county area. (The list of their accounts appears as Exhibits 6 and 7.) Thomas noticed that the commission incomes Brooks and Nelson received had been stable over the years.

EXHIBIT 6   Accounts sold by Harvey Brooks, by counties, with 1984 purchases

Jefferson County			Oswego County			Lewis County		
Adams Center	D	$ 8,925	Calosse	D	$ 4,273	Beaver Falls	D	$ 9,525
(Alexandria Bay)	D	45,750	Central Square	D	4,643	Croghan	D	61,493
(Alexandria Bay)	D	39,475	Constantia	M	180	Harrisville	D	46,290
Bellville	D	5,250	Cleveland	M	975	Lowville	D	59,220
(Carthage)	D	152,500	(Fulton)	D	37,800	Lowville	D	10,785
Chaumont	D	1,510	(Fulton)	D	61,275	Lyons Falls	D	15,060
(Clayton)	D	26,575	(Fulton)	D	69,500	Port Leydon	D	5,813
(Clayton)	D	41,000	(Fulton)	D	96,000	Turin	M	7,800
Deferiet	D	923	Hannibal	D	9,725	County total:		$215,986
Dexter	D	29,175	Hastings	M	9,600	Territory total: $1,505,724		
Ellisburg	D	590	Lacona	M	1,155			
LaFargeville	D	1,305	Mexico	D	39,750			
Plessis	D	2,200	Oswego	D	30,188			
Redwood	M	270	(Oswego)	D	51,900			
Rodman	D	8,025	(Oswego)	D	60,250			
Sackets Harbor	D	1,613	(Oswego)	D	102,500			
County total:		$365,086	(Oswego)	D	109,750			
			(Oswego)	D	56,075			
			Oswego	H	38			
			Parish	M	12,900			
			Phoenix	D	24,325			
			(Pulaski)	D	21,875			
			(Pulaski)	D	72,700			
			Sandy Creek	D	35,325			
			West Monroe	D	11,950			
			County total:		$924,652			

Code: D = Independent drugstore; M = miscellaneous account; H = Hospital.

Note: Accounts in parentheses are those indicated by Nelson as the ones he wanted from Brooks. These accounts total $1,044,963 (87.7 percent of Brooks' sales in Jefferson County, 80 percent in Oswego County, or 69.4 percent of the territory total). Added to Nelson's 1983 sales, this would increase his volume 65 percent to $2,658,018. Brooks' old territory would be left with $460,758 in sales.

A Visit from Clifford Nelson

On the morning of June 9, three days after the June sales meeting, Thomas saw Clifford Nelson come in the front door of the Syracuse Division offices. Although Nelson passed within 30 feet of Thomas' desk, he did not appear to notice Thomas. Nelson walked through the office area directly to the partitioned space where Robert Jackson's private office was located. Twenty minutes later, Nelson emerged from the division manager's office and made his way to Thomas' desk.

"Hi there, young fellah!" he shouted as he approached.

"Howdy, Cliff. Sit down and chat awhile," Thomas replied. "What got you out of bed so early?" he asked, knowing that Nelson must have risen at 6 o'clock to make the drive to Syracuse from his home in Watertown.

Nelson squeezed his bulky frame into the armchair next to the desk. "It's a shame Harvey is retiring," he said. "I never thought he could stand to give it

EXHIBIT 7 Accounts sold by Clifford Nelson, by counties, with 1984 purchases

St. Lawrence County			Jefferson County			Oswego County		
Canton	D	$ 98,100	Adams	C	$ 4,713	Pulaski	C	$6,825
Edwards	D	5,040	Carthage	C	5,325			
Edwards	M	14,138	Evans Mills	D	5,525			
Gouverneur	D	1,695	Philadelphia	D	9,450			
Gouverneur	D	70,373	Watertown	D	75,500			
Gouverneur	D	123,898	Watertown	D	11,850			
Heuvelton	D	810	Watertown	D	22,000			
Massena	D	84,443	Watertown	D	76,700			
Massena	D	25,478	Watertown	D	46,100			
Massena	C	18,360	Watertown	D	65,750			
Massena	C	16,688	Watertown	D	95,500			
Massena	H	285	Watertown	D	57,500			
Madrid	D	10,740	Watertown	D	24,250			
Morristown	D	20,483	Watertown	D	2,135			
Norfolk	D	22,463	Watertown	D	28,300			
Norwood	D	23,543	Watertown	C	9,075			
Ogdensburg	D	60,675	Watertown	C	14,925			
Ogdensburg	D	169,163	Watertown	M	1,700			
Ogdensburg	D	54,023	Watertown	H	315			
Ogdensburg	D	25,350	Watertown	H	9,000			
Ogdensburg	M	1,118	County total:		$565,613			
Ogdensburg	H	19,898						
Potsdam	D	115,830						
Potsdam	C	55,283						
Potsdam Falls	D	2,753						
County total:		$1,040,630						

Territorial total: $1,613,068

Code: D = Independent drugstore; C = Chain drugstores; M = Miscellaneous account; H = Hospital.

up. I never knew anyone who enjoyed selling as much as Harvey—except maybe me.'' Nelson continued praising Brooks and telling anecdotes which illustrated his point until Thomas began to wonder whether Nelson thought that he was biased in some way against the retiring sales rep. Thomas recalled that he had made some critical remarks about Brooks to Jackson, but he could not recall any discussion of Brooks' shortcomings with the man himself, or any of the other sales reps. Nelson ended his remarks by saying, ''Old H. L. always said that Harvey was the best damn wholesale drug salesman he'd ever known.''

There was a brief silence, as Thomas did not realize that Nelson was finished. Finally Thomas said, ''You know, Cliff, I think we ought to have a testimonial dinner for Harvey at the July sales meeting.''

Nelson made no comment on Thomas' suggestion; instead, he went on to say, ''None of these green trainees will ever be able to take Harvey's place. Those druggists up there are old-timers. They would resent being high pressured by some kid blown up to twice his size with college degrees. No sir! You've got to sell 'em right in those country stores.''

Thomas questioned whether Nelson's opinion of the adaptability of the younger, college-educated sales reps was justified by the available evidence. He recalled that several of them with rural territories performed better against their May sales quotas than either Brooks or Nelson. Thomas was proud of his self-restraint when he commented, "Selling in a rural territory is certainly different."

"That's right, Dave. I wanted to make sure you understood these things before I told you." Nelson was nervously massaging his double chin between his thumb and forefinger.

Thomas looked at him with a quizzical expression. "Told me what?"

"I have just been talking to Robert Jackson. Well, I was talking to him about an understanding between Harvey and me. We always agreed that if anything should happen to the other, or he should retire, or something—well, we agreed that the one who remained should get to take over his choice of the other's accounts. We told H. L. about this and he said, 'Boys, what's OK by you is OK by me. You two developed that territory and you deserve to be rewarded for it.' Well, yes sir, that's the way it was."

Without pausing, Nelson went on, "I just told Jackson about it. He said that he remembered talking about the whole thing with H. L. 'Yes,' he said, 'Tell Thomas about it,' he said, 'Tell Thomas about it.' Harvey and I went over his accounts on Sunday. I went over his list of accounts with him and checked the ones that I want. Here is the list with the accounts all checked off.[2] I already know nearly all the proprietors. You'll see that—"

"Wait a minute, Cliff! Wait a minute!" Thomas interrupted. "You've lost me completely. In the first place, if there is any assignment of accounts to be made I'll do it. It will be done on a basis that is fair to the sales reps concerned, and profitable to the company. You know that."

"Dave, I'm only asking for what is fair." Nelson's face was flushed. Thomas noticed that the man he had always believed to be deliberately confident and self-possessed was now so agitated that it was difficult for him to speak. "I don't want my territory chopped up and handed to some green kid!"

Thomas noticed that everybody in the office was now watching Nelson. "Calm down, Cliff," he whispered to the sales rep, indicating with a nod of his head that others were watching.

"Don't talk to me that way!" replied Nelson. "I don't care. A man with 25 years' service deserves some consideration!"

"You're absolutely right, Cliff. You're absolutely right." As Thomas repeated his words, Nelson settled back in his chair. The typewriters started clattering again.

"Now, first of all, Cliff," as Thomas tried to return the conversation to a friendly basis. "Where did you get the idea that your territory was going to be 'chopped up'?"

---

[2] Nelson's selected accounts are the accounts in parentheses in Exhibit 6.

"You said so yourself. You said it at the sales meeting the other day when you made that speech about how you were going to boost sales in Syracuse." Nelson emphasized his words by pounding the side of the desk with his masonic ring.

Thomas reflected for a moment. He recalled his speech at the sales meeting called, "How We Can Do a Better Job for Puritan Drug." The speech was a restatement of the merchandising policy of the New York office. He had mentioned that getting more profitable business would require that a larger percentage of the purchases of each account would have to come to Puritan Drug; that receiving a larger share of the business from each store would require more selling time in each store; and that greater concentration on each account would require reorganization of the sales territories. He realized that his future plans entailed reorganization of the territories. He had not anticipated, however, Nelson's reaction.

Finally, Thomas said, "I do plan to make some territorial changes—not right away—at least not until I have looked things over pretty darn carefully. Of course, you understand that our first duty is to make greater profits for the company. Some of our territories would be a great deal more profitable if they were organized and handled in a different manner."

"What are you going to do about Harvey's territory?" asked Nelson.

Since Thomas had not yet looked over the information about the territory, he was anxious not to commit himself to any course of action relating to it. "Well, I just haven't had a chance to study the situation yet," he replied. "If I could make the territory more profitable by reorganizing it, I guess that is what they would expect me to do."

"What about the promises the company made to me about letting me choose the accounts I want?" Nelson asked.

"You don't mean the company's promise; you mean Schultz's promise," Thomas corrected him.

"Well, if Schultz wasn't 'the company,' I don't see how you figure that you are!" Nelson's face resumed its flush.

"OK, Cliff. How about giving me a chance to look over the situation. You know that I want to do the right thing. Let me go over the list of the accounts you want. In a few days I can talk intelligently about the matter." Thomas felt that there was no point in carrying the discussion further.

"All right, Dave," said Nelson, rising. The two men walked toward the front entrance of the office. As they reached the top of the steps leading to the front door, Nelson turned to Thomas and offered his hand. "Look, Dave, I'm sorry I got so mad. You just can't imagine what this means to me. I know you'll see it my way when you know the whole story." Nelson's voice sounded strained.

Thomas watched the older man leave. He felt embarrassed, realizing that Nelson's parting words had been overheard by several manufacturers' representatives standing nearby.

A Conversation with the Division Manager

Thomas decided he would immediately discuss his conversation with Nelson with Jackson. He walked over to Jackson's office, and hesitated upon reaching the doorway. Jackson looked up, and indicated with a gesture that Thomas should take a seat.

Thomas sat down and waited for Jackson to speak. Jackson was occupied for the moment unwrapping a cigar. After a few moments of silence, Thomas opened the conversation. "Clifford Nelson just stopped by to speak to me."

"Yeah?" said Jackson, removing bitten flakes of tobacco from the end of his tongue.

"He said something about getting some of Harvey Brooks' accounts when Harvey retired," Thomas said in a deliberately questioning manner.

"Yeah."

Thomas continued, "Well, this idea of his was based on a promise that he said H. L. had made."

"Yeah. He told me that, too."

"Did Schultz make such a promise?" Thomas inquired.

"Hell, I don't know. It sounds like him." Jackson tilted back in his swivel chair.

"What shall I do about it?"

"Don't ask me; you're the sales manager." Jackson paused, holding his cigar away from his lips as if he were about to speak. Just as Thomas was about to say something, Jackson lurched forward to flick the ashes from his cigar into his ash tray. "Look here, Dave. I don't want any morale problems around here. You're the first of the 'wonder boys' to be put in charge of a department in this division. I don't want you to do anything to mess up the morale. We never had any morale problems when Schultz was around. We don't want anything like that in this division."

Thomas was momentarily bewildered. He knew from the way that Jackson used the phrase "wonder boys" that he was referring to the managers brought into the organization by Richard Topping.

Jackson went on, "Why the devil did you tell the reps that you were going to reassign the sales territories without even telling me?"

"But you were there when I said it."

"Said what?"

"Well, at the sales meeting, that one of the ways we were going to get more business was to reorganize the sales territory," Thomas replied.

"I certainly don't remember anything like that. Dave, you gave a good inspirational talk, but I sure can't remember anything about reassigning territories."

"Actually, I just mentioned the reorganization of territories in passing," Thomas smiled.

"I'll be damned. That sort of thing is always happening. Here everybody is frothing at the mouth about something that they think we are going to do and we haven't the slightest idea why they think we're going to do it. You know, probably the real reason Harvey Brooks is retiring, instead of staying on as he planned, was this fear of sales territory reorganization. Both he and Nelson know that their retirement pension is based on earnings from their last five years of active employment. Now that I think of it, three or four of the other sales reps have stopped during the last couple of days to tell me what a fine job they were doing. They probably had this territory reassignment stuff on their minds, too.''

Jackson's cigar was no longer burning. He began groping under the papers on his desk for a match. Thomas took advantage of this pause in the conversation. ''Mr. Jackson, I think there are some real advantages to be won by adjusting the sales territories. I think—''

''You still think that after today?'' the division manager asked in a sarcastic tone.

''Why, yes! The profit made on sales to an individual account is related closely to delivery expense. The larger the total proportion of the account's business we get, the more profit we make because the delivery expense remains more or less constant.''

''Look, Dave, you college computer types always have everything figured out, but sometimes that doesn't count. Morale is the important thing. The sales reps won't tolerate having their territories changed. I know that you have four trainees that you'd like to put out on territories. If you put them out on parts of the territories belonging to some of the more experienced reps—bam! God knows how many of our good sales reps would be left. I've never had any trouble with sales force morale since I've been manager of this division. Old Schultz, bless his soul, never let me down. He wasn't any damn Ph.D., but he could handle sales reps. Don't get off on the wrong foot with them, Dave. With the labor situation in the warehouse being what it is, I've just got too much on my mind. I don't want you creating more problems than I can handle. How 'bout it, boy!''

Jackson ground out his half-smoked cigar, looking steadily at Thomas.

Thomas was extremely upset with the division manager's implication that he lacked concern for sales rep morale. He had always thought of himself as very considerate. He realized that at the moment his foremost desire was to get away from Jackson.

Thomas rose from his chair, saying, ''Mr. Jackson, you can count on me. I know you are right about this morale business.''

''Atta boy,'' said the division manager. ''It does us a lot of good to talk like this once in a while. Now, see if you can make peace with the sales reps. I want you to handle everything yourself.''

''Well, thanks a lot,'' said Thomas, as he backed out of the office door.

As he walked through the office, he saw two manufacturers' representatives with whom he had appointments. His schedule of appointments that day prohibited him from doing more than gathering the material pertaining to the Nelson and Brooks territories.

Thomas Goes Home

Thomas left the office shortly after 5 o'clock to drive to a suburb of Syracuse. It was a particularly hot and humid day. Pre-Fourth of July traffic lengthened the drive home by nearly 20 minutes. When he finally turned into his own driveway, he felt as though his skin were caked with grime and perspiration. He got out of the car and walked around to the terrace at the rear of the house. Beth, his wife, was sitting in a deck chair, working on some papers.

"Hello, Dave. You're late," she said, looking up with a smile.

"I know it. Even the traffic was bad today." He dropped his suit coat on a glass-topped table and sprawled out full length on a chaise lounge. "I'm exhausted. And, boy, I am disgusted with myself."

"Bad day?"

"Awful. You just can't imagine how discouraging it is trying to get this job organized. You would think it would be obvious to everyone that what ails the Syracuse Division is the organization of the sales force," said Thomas, arranging a pillow under his head.

"I didn't realize that you thought anything was wrong with the Syracuse Division."

"Well, what I mean is that we now get only 20 percent of the potential wholesale business. If I could organize the sales force my way—well, God knows, maybe we could get 40 percent of the business. That is what the New York office watches for. The sales manager who increases his division's share of the market gets the promotions when they come along. I know Topping transferred me to this division because he knew these possibilities existed."

"I don't understand. Is Mr. Topping still your boss, or is Mr. Jackson?"

"Beth, it's terribly discouraging. While Jackson is my boss, I'll never get anywhere in Puritan Drug unless Topping and the other people in New York promote me."

"Don't you like Mr. Jackson?"

"I had a run-in with him today."

"You didn't!" she said as she laid her papers aside.

Thomas didn't anticipate his wife's reaction. He gazed up at the awning as if he did not notice her intent expression. "We didn't argue particularly. He just—well, he doesn't know too much about sales management. He put his foot down on my plans to reorganize the territories."

"I can't understand why you would go and get yourself into a fight with your boss when you haven't even been here two months."

"Honest, Beth, I didn't have any fight. Everything is OK. He just—well, do you want me to be a divisional sales manager all my life?"

"You're tired," she said sympathetically. "Why don't you go up and shower."

"That sounds wonderful," he said, raising himself from the chaise lounge.

An Unexpected Caller

Thomas had just stepped out of the shower when he heard his wife calling to him. "Dave, Fred Taylor is here to see you."

"Tell him I'll be down in just a minute. Offer him a drink, Beth."

As he dressed, Thomas wondered why Fred Taylor had chosen the dinner hour to call. During the month since he had moved into his new home, no other sales rep had ever dropped by uninvited.

When Thomas came downstairs, he found Taylor sitting on the living room couch, a gin and tonic in his hand.

"Hello, Fred," said Thomas, crossing the room with his right hand extended. "You look as if you had a hot day. Why don't you take off your coat? If we go out to the terrace, you may get a chance to cool off."

"Thanks, Dave," the visitor said as they moved out to the terrace. "I'm sorry to barge in this way, but I thought it was important."

"Well, what's on your mind?" asked Thomas as they sat down.

"I heard about what happened at the office today. I thought I'd come over and tell you that we stand behind you 100 percent."

Thomas was perplexed by Taylor's words. He realized that Taylor probably was referring to his meeting with Nelson. Thomas said, "I'm not sure what you mean, Fred."

"I heard that you and Nelson had it out this morning about changing the sales territories," Taylor replied.

Thomas smiled. Two thoughts entered his mind. He was amused at the proportions that the brief morning conversation had assumed. At the same time, he was curious to know how Taylor, who had presumably been in the field selling, had heard about the incident so quickly. Without hesitation he asked, "Where did you hear about this, Fred?"

"Bill Murray told me! He was down at the warehouse with Walter Miller when I stopped off to pick up a special narcotics order for a customer. They are all excited about this territory business. Murray said Nelson came out to his house at lunch time and told him about it. Everybody figured that you were going to change the territories when you started traveling around with each of the reps, especially after what you said at the sales meeting."

"Well, the reason I went on the road with each of the reps, Fred," said Thomas, "was so that I could learn more about their selling problems while, at the same time, meet the customers."

Taylor smiled, "Sure, but when you started filling out a rating sheet on each account, I couldn't help thinking you had some reason for it."

Thomas realized that Taylor had spoken with irony in his voice, but he thought it was better to let the matter pass. Since he was planning to use the information he had gathered for the reorganization of the sales territories, he decided that he would be frank with Taylor. To find out what the young sales rep's reaction might be to territorial changes, he said, "Fred, I've thought a lot about making some changes in the territories—"

Taylor interrupted him. "That's terrific. I'm sure glad to hear that. I don't like to speak ill of the dead, but old Schultz really gave the trainees the short end of the stick when he put us on territories. He either gave us a territory of uncontacted accounts where it was like beating our heads against a stone wall. Some of us actually quit, like the two guys who trained with me. Or, Schultz gave us replacement territories where some of the best accounts had been handed over to the older reps. Well, I know for a fact that when I took over my territory from Mike Green, Bill Murray and Albert Simpson got 12 of Green's best accounts. And, damn it, I got more sales out of what was left than Green ever did; Murray and Simpson's total sales didn't go up. It took me a while, but I had the laugh at every sales meeting when our monthly sales figures were announced.''

"Is that right?'' said Thomas.

"Damn right! And I wasn't the only one. That's why those old duffers are so down on the four of us that have come with the division since the mid-1970s. We've beaten them at their own game.''

"Do you think that Harrington and Howard and Donnelly feel the same way?'' asked Thomas.

"Think, hell! I know it! That's all we ever talk about. If you reorganize those territories and give us back the accounts that Schultz took away, you'll see some real sales records. Take, for example, the Medical Arts Pharmacy out by Mercy Hospital. Bill Murray got that one away from my territory and he calls there only once a week. If I could get that one back, I'd get in there three times a week, and get five times as much business.''

Thomas had to raise his hands in a gesture of protest. "Don't you have enough accounts already, Fred, to keep you busy?''

"Dave, I spend 50 hours a week on the road and I love it; but I know damn well that if I put some of the time I spend in the 'two-by-four' stores into some of those big juicy accounts like Medical Arts Pharmacy, I'd do even more business.''

Thomas commented, "I'm not particularly anxious to argue now, but if you start putting time into Medical Arts Pharmacy, what's going to happen to your sales to the two-by-four stores?''

Taylor quickly replied, "Those druggists all know me. They'd go right on buying.''

Thomas did not agree with Taylor. He thought that Taylor realized this.

After a moment of silence, Taylor rose from his chair, saying, "I'd better scoot home. My family will be furious with me for being late when we have plans for the weekend.''

The two men walked to Taylor's car. As Taylor climbed into his car, he said, "Dave, don't forget what I said. Harrington, Howard, Donnelly, and I stand behind you 100 percent. You won't ever hear us talk about going over to a competitor!''

"Who's talking about that?'' asked Thomas.

"Well,'' said Taylor as he started the motor and shifted into gear, "I don't want to tell tales out of school.''

"Sure,'' Thomas said quickly. "I'm sorry I asked. So long, Fred. I'll see you soon.''

Part 7

Pricing Decisions

The cases in the pricing section of this book involve several different kinds of decisions. A firm's pricing strategy is extremely important because of the quickness with which a change can be implemented, because of the importance of price to consumers in their purchase decisions, and because of the direct impact of prices on profits.

The first important consideration in establishing a price for a product is the firm's pricing objectives. A firm striving for growth may utilize a totally different strategy from one who is seeking to discourage others from cutting prices or to desensitize consumers to price. Firms with objectives oriented around maximizing long-run profits may utilize different strategies than firms who are seeking to maximize short-run profits. Thus, the first step in establishing a price should be to clearly identify what the objectives are.

Two alternative strategies often utilized are skimming and penetration. A skimming strategy is one in which a high initial price is set, and the product is sold to all those consumers willing to pay this price. The price is then lowered somewhat, and the product is sold to those consumers willing to pay that price. This process continues for some time, ''skimming the cream'' off the top of the market with each price change. For example, when electronic calculators were first introduced, they were priced at more than $300. A number of scientific and engineering related organizations were willing to purchase the product at this price. The price was then lowered to the neighborhood of $150 to $200, and a number of other organizations were willing to purchase the product. Later, the price was reduced to the $50 to $100 range, and very many more buyers entered the market. Eventually, the price was lowered still further, and many more consumers entered the market.

A skimming strategy is appropriate when there are no close substitutes for the product and the demand is inelastic with respect to price. It is a very conservative policy allowing the marketer to recover as much of the costs as possible quickly in the event that demand is not that great. It also allows the marketer to accumulate money for aggressive penetration later when competition enters the market. A skimming strategy is an effective way to segment the market, as in the calculator example and in the case of the book market where a skimming strategy is used for hardcover books, and the paperback edition is later introduced using a penetration strategy.

A penetration strategy utilizes a low initial price in the hopes of penetrating a large proportion of the market in a short period of time. This strategy would be used when one or more of the following conditions existed:

a. High short-run price elasticity [for example, the low price of the Model-T Ford allowed many people to purchase a car for the first time].
b. Large economies of scale in production.
c. The probability of quick public acceptance.
d. The probability of quick competitive imitation.

The specific pricing decisions that have to be made include the price level to set, price variation including discount structure and geographic price differences, margins to be given to various intermediaries in the channels of distribution, and the determination of when to change the price structure.

A number of different pricing methods are utilized by organizations. Some use the cost-plus method, whereby a certain percentage is added to the firm's costs to establish their pricing. This method is often used by industrial marketers and by wholesalers and retailers. Other organizations use break-even analysis, marginal cost analysis, and/or marginal revenue analysis to determine their pricing structure. Still other organizations are price followers and use a strategy of meeting the prices of competitors.

The ideal way to determine the price that should be charged involves analyzing a number of variables before actually setting the price. Included would be:

1. *Consumer buying patterns.* What price would consumers expect to pay for this type of product? What are the important price points or price lines that different segments of the market desire?
2. *Product differentiation.* In what ways is the company's product different from the others on the market? What advantages does the product offer the consumer?
3. *What is the competitive structure* of the industry, and what stage of the product life cycle is the product in?
4. *How price sensitive* is total industry demand, and how price sensitive is demand for the individual firm's product? What is the size of the total market and what is the likelihood of economies of scale?
5. *What is the economic climate forecast,* and how sensitive is the demand of the product to changes in the economic climate?
6. *Legal and social considerations.* New interpretations of the Robinson-Patman Act (prohibiting price discrimination) and various state laws governing pricing must be taken into consideration.

7. *Cost structure of the firm.* The relationship between fixed costs and variable costs is extremely important in pricing decisions, as is the cost structure of the firm compared to competitors' pricing structure. Pricing strategy for a hotel, with a very low variable cost ratio, will of necessity be quite different than pricing strategy for a clothing manufacturer, which has a very high variable cost ratio.

8. *The overall marketing strategy for the product.* It is important to recognize that the pricing strategy must be consistent with all the other elements of the firm's marketing strategy.

Case 29

S.C. Johnson and Son, Limited (R)*

Four months ago, in November, George Styan had been appointed division manager of Innochem, at S.C. Johnson and Son, Limited[1] (SCJ), a Canadian subsidiary of S.C. Johnson & Son, Inc. Innochem's sole product line consisted of industrial cleaning chemicals for use by business, institutions, and government. George was concerned by the division's poor market share, particularly in Montreal and Toronto. Together, these two cities represented approximately 35 percent of Canadian demand for industrial cleaning chemicals, but less than 10 percent of Innochem sales. It appeared that SCJ distributors could not match the aggressive discounting practiced by direct-selling manufacturers in metropolitan markets.

Recently, George had received a rebate proposal from his staff designed to increase the distributor's ability to cut end user prices by "sharing" part of the total margin with SCJ when competitive conditions demanded discounts of 30 percent or more off the list price to end users. George had to decide if the rebate plan was the best way to penetrate price-sensitive markets. Moreover, he wondered about the plan's ultimate impact on divisional profit performance. George either had to develop an implementation plan for the rebate plan or draft an alternative proposal to unveil at the Distributors' Annual Spring Convention, three weeks away.

The Canadian Market for Industrial Cleaning Chemicals

Last year, the Canadian market for industrial cleaning chemicals was approximately $100 million at end user prices. Growth was stable at an overall rate of approximately 3 percent per year.

"Industrial cleaning chemicals" included all chemical products designed to clean, disinfect, sanitize, or protect industrial, commercial, and institutional

---

* Copyright © 1987, The University of Western Ontario. This case was written by Carolyn Vose under the supervision of Associate Professor Roger More for the sole purpose of providing material for class discussion at the School of Business Administration. Any use or duplication of the material in this case is prohibited except with the written consent of the School. Used with permission.

[1] Popularly known as Canadian Johnson Wax.

buildings and equipment. The label was broadly applied to general purpose cleaners, floor maintenance products (strippers, sealers, finishes, and detergents), carpet cleaners and deodorizers, disinfectants, air fresheners, and a host of specialty chemicals such as insecticides, pesticides, drain cleaners, oven cleansers, and sweeping compounds.

Industrial cleaning chemicals were distinct from equivalent consumer products typically sold through grocery stores. Heavy-duty industrial products were packaged in larger containers and bulk and marketed directly by the cleaning chemical manufacturers or sold through distributors to a variety of end users. Exhibit 1 includes market segmentation by primary end user categories, including janitorial service contractors and the in-house maintenance departments of government, institutions, and companies.

Building Maintenance Contractors

In Canada, maintenance contractors purchased 17 percent of the industrial cleaning chemicals sold during 1980 (end user price). The segment was growing at approximately 10–15 percent a year, chiefly at the expense of other end user categories. *Canadian Business* reported, "Contract cleaners have made sweeping inroads into the traditional preserve of in-house janitorial staffs,

EXHIBIT 1 Segmentation of the Canadian market for industrial cleaning chemicals

By end user category	
End user category	*Percent total Canadian market for industrial cleaning chemicals (end user value)*
Retail outlets	25%
Contractors	17
Hospitals	15
Industrial and office	13
Schools, colleges	8
Hotels, motels	6
Nursing homes	5
Recreation	3
Government	3
Fast food	2
Full-service restaurants	2
All others	1
Total	100% = $95 million

By product category	
Product category	*Percent total Canadian market for industrial cleaning chemicals*
Floor care products	40%
General purpose cleaners	16
Disinfectants	12
Carpet care products	8
Odor control products	5
Glass cleaners	4
All others	15
Total	100% = $95 million

selling themselves on the strength of cost efficiency."[2] Maintenance contract billings reached an estimated $1 billion last year.

Frequently, demand for building maintenance services was highly price sensitive, and since barriers to entry were low (small capitalization, simple technology), competition squeezed contractor gross margins below 6 percent (before tax). Variable cost control was a matter of survival, and only products bringing compensatory labour savings could command a premium price in this segment of the cleaning chemical market.

A handful of contract cleaners did specialize in higher margin services to prestige office complexes, luxury apartments, art museums, and other "quality-conscious" customers. However, even contractors serving this select clientele did not necessarily buy premium cleaning supplies.

In-House Maintenance Departments

Government

Last year, cleaning chemical sales to various government offices (federal, provincial, and local) approached $2 million. Typically, a government body solicited bids from appropriate sources by formally advertising for quotations for given quantities of particular cleaning chemicals. Although bid requests often named specific brands, suppliers were permitted to offer "equivalent substitutes." Separate competitions were held for each item and normally covered 12 months' supply with provision for delivery "as required." Contracts were frequently awarded solely on the basis of price.

Institutions

Like government bodies, most institutions were price sensitive owing to re-strictive budgets and limited ability to "pass on" expenses to users. Educational institutions and hospitals were the largest consumers of cleaning chemicals in this segment. School boards used an open-bid system patterned on the govern-ment model. Heavy sales time requirements and demands for frequent delivery of small shipments to as many as 100 locations were characteristic.

Colleges and universities tended to be operated somewhat differently. Dan Stalport, one of the purchasing agents responsible for maintenance supplies at The University of Western Ontario, offered the following comments:

> Sales reps come to UWO year 'round. If one of us (in the buying group) talks to a salesman who seems to have something—say, a labour-saving feature—we get a sample and test it. Testing can take up to a year. Floor covering, for example, has to be exposed to seasonal changes in weather and traffic.

---

[2] "Contract Cleaners Want to Whisk Away Ring-Around-the-Office," *Canadian Business*, 1981, p. 22.

> If we're having problems with a particular item, we'll compare the perform-ance and price of three or four competitors. There are usually plenty of products that do the job. Basically, we want value—acceptable performance at the lowest available price.

Hospitals accounted for 15 percent of cleaning chemical sales. Procure-ment policies at University Hospital (UH), a medium-sized (450-bed) facility in London, Ontario, were typical. UH distinguished between "critical" and "non-critical" products. Critical cleaning chemicals (i.e., those significantly affect-ing patient health, such as phenolic germicide) could be bought only on approval of the staff microbiologist, who tested the "kill factor." This measure of effectiveness was regularly retested, and any downgrading of product per-formance could void a supplier's contract. In contrast, noncritical supplies, such as general purpose cleaners, floor finishes, and the like, were the exclusive province of Bob Chandler, purchasing agent attached to the Housekeeping Department. Bob explained that performance of noncritical cleaning chemicals was informally judged and monitored by the housekeeping staff:

> Just last year, for example, the cleaners found the floor polish was streaking badly. We (the Housekeeping Department) tested and compared five or six brands—all in the ballpark price-wise—and chose the best.

Business

The corporate segment was highly diverse, embracing both service and man-ufacturing industries. Large volume users tended to be price sensitive—particularly when profits were low. Often, however, cleaning products repre-sented such a small percentage of the total operating budget that the cost of searching for the lowest cost supplier would be expected to exceed any realiza-ble saving. Under such conditions, the typical industrial customer sought efficiencies in the purchasing process itself, for example, by dealing with the supplier offering the broadest mix of janitorial products (chemicals, paper supplies, equipment, etc.). Guy Breton, purchasing agent for Securitech, a Montreal-based security systems manufacturer, commented on the time econo-mies of "one-stop shopping":

> With cleaning chemicals, it simply isn't worth the trouble to shop around and stage elaborate product performance tests. I buy all our chemicals, brushes, dusters, toweling—the works—from one or two suppliers . . . buying reputable brands from familiar suppliers saves hassles—back orders are rare, and Mainte-nance seldom complains.

Distribution Channels for Industrial Cleaning Chemicals

The Canadian market for industrial cleaning chemicals was supplied through three main channels, each characterized by a distinctive set of strengths and weaknesses:

EXHIBIT 2 Effect of geography on market share of different distribution channels

Supplier type	Share nationwide	Share in Montreal and Toronto
Direct marketers	61%*	70%
Private label distributors	14	18
National brands distributors	25†	12

* Dustbane	17%
G.H. Wood	13
All others	13
Total	61%
† SCJ	8%
N/L	4
Airkem	3
All others	10
Total	25%

a. Distributor sales of national brands.

b. Distributor sales of private label products.

c. Direct sale by manufacturers.

Direct sellers held a 61 percent share of the Canadian market for industrial cleaning chemicals, while the distributors of national brands and private label products held shares of 25 percent and 14 percent, respectively. Relative market shares varied geographically, however. In Montreal and Toronto, for example, the direct marketers' share rose to 70 percent and private labellers' to 18 percent, reducing the national brand share to 12 percent. The pattern, shown in Exhibit 2, reflected an interplay of two areas of channel differentiation, namely, discount capability at the end user level and the cost of serving distant, geographically dispersed customers.

Distributor Sales of National Brand Cleaning Chemicals

National brand manufacturers, such as S.C. Johnson and Son, Airkem, and National Labs, produced a relatively limited range of "high-quality" janitorial products, including many special purpose formulations of narrow market interest. Incomplete product range, combined with shortage of manpower and limited warehousing, made direct distribution unfeasible in most cases. Normally, a national brand company would negotiate with middlemen who handled a broad array of complementary products (equipment, tools, and supplies) by different manufacturers. "Bundling" of goods brought the distributors cost efficiencies in selling, warehousing, and delivery by spreading fixed costs over a large sales volume. Distributors were, therefore, better able to absorb the costs of after-hour emergency service, frequent routine sales and service calls to many potential buyers, and shipments of small quantities of cleaning chemicals to multiple destinations. As a rule, the greater the geographic dispersion of customers, and the smaller the average order, the greater the relative economies of distributor marketing.

Comparatively high gross margins (approximately 50 percent of whole-sale price) enabled national brand manufacturers to offer distributors strong marketing support and sales training along with liberal terms of payment and freight plus low minimum order requirements. Distributors readily agreed to handle national brand chemicals, and in metropolitan markets, each brand was sold through several distributors. By the same token, most distributors carried several directly competitive product lines. George suspected that some distributor salesmen only used national brands to ''lead'' with and tended to offer private label whenever a customer proved price sensitive, or a competitor handled the same national brand(s). Using an industry rule of thumb, George estimated that most distributors needed at least 20 percent gross margin on retail sales to cover sales commission of 10 percent, plus delivery and inventory expenses.

Distributor Sales of Private Label Cleaning Chemicals

Direct-selling manufacturers were dominating urban markets by aggressively discounting end user prices—sometimes below the wholesale price national brand manufacturers charged their distributors. To compete against the direct seller, increasing numbers of distributors were adding low-cost private label cleaning chemicals to their product lines. Private labelling also helped differentiate a particular distributor from others carrying the same national brand(s).

Sizable minimum order requirements restricted the private label strategy to only the largest distributors. Private label manufacturers produced to order, formulating to meet low prices specified by distributors. The relatively narrow margins (30–35 percent wholesale price) associated with private label manufacture precluded the extensive marketing and sales support national brand manufacturers characteristically provided to distributors. Private label producers pared their expenses further still by requiring distributors to bear the cost of inventory and accept rigid terms of payment as well as delivery (net 30 days, FOB plant).

In addition to absorbing these selling expenses normally assumed by the manufacturer, distributors paid salesmen higher commission on private label sales (15 percent of resale) than on national brands (10 percent of resale). However, the incremental administration and selling expenses associated with private label business were more than offset by the differential savings on private label wholesale goods. By pricing private label chemicals at competitive parity with national brands, the distributor could enjoy approximately a 50 percent gross margin at resale list, while preserving considerable resale discount capability.

Private label products were seldom sold outside the metropolitan areas where most were manufactured. First, the high costs of moving bulky, low-value freight diminished the relative cost advantage of private label chemicals. Second, generally speaking, it was only in metro areas where distributors dealt in volumes great enough to satisfy the private labeller's minimum order requirement. Finally, outside the city, distributors were less likely to be in direct local competition with others handling the same national brand, reducing value of the private label as a source of supplier differentiation.

For some very large distributors, backward integration into chemical production was a logical extension of the private labelling strategy. Recently, several distributors had become direct marketers through acquisition of captive manufacturers.

Direct Sale by Manufacturers of Industrial Cleaning Chemicals

Manufacturers dealing directly with the end user increased their gross margins to 60–70 percent of retail list price. Greater margins increased their ability to discount end user price—a distinct advantage in the price competitive urban marketplace. Overall, direct marketers averaged a gross margin of 50 percent.

Many manufacturers of industrial cleaning chemicals attempted some direct selling, but relatively few relied on this channel exclusively. Satisfactory adoption of a full-time direct-selling strategy required the manufacturer to match distributor's sales and delivery capabilities without sacrificing overall profitability. These conflicting demands had been resolved successfully by two types of company: large-scale powder chemical manufacturers and full-line janitorial products manufacturers.

Large-scale powder chemical manufacturers. Economies of large-scale production plus experience in the capital-intensive manufacture of powder chemicals enabled a few established firms, such as Diversey-Wyandotte, to dominate the market for powder warewash and vehicle cleansers. Selling through distributors offered these producers few advantages. Direct-selling expense was almost entirely commission (i.e., variable). Moreover, powder concentrates were characterized by comparatively high value-to-bulk ratios, and so could absorb delivery costs even where demand was geographically dispersed. Thus, any marginal benefits from using middlemen were more than offset by the higher margins (and associated discount capability) possible through direct distribution. Among these chemical firms, competition was not limited to price. The provision of dispensing and metering equipment was important, as was 24-hour servicing.

Full-line janitorial products manufacturers. These manufacturers offered a complete range of maintenance products, including paper supplies, janitorial chemicals, tools, and mechanical equipment. Although high margins greatly enhanced retail price flexibility, overall profitability depended on securing a balance of high- and low-margin business, as well as controlling selling and distribution expenses. This was accomplished in several ways, including:

Centering on market areas of concentrated demand to minimize costs of warehousing, sales travel, and the like.

Increasing average order size, either by adding product lines which could be sold to existing customers, or by seeking new large-volume customers.

Tying sales commission to profitability to motivate sales personnel to sell volume, without unnecessary discounting of end user price.

Direct marketers of maintenance products varied in scale from established nationwide companies to hundreds of regional operators. The two largest direct marketers, G.H. Wood and Dustbane, together supplied almost a third of Canadian demand for industrial cleaning chemicals.

S.C. Johnson and Son, Limited

S.C. Johnson and Son, Limited (SCJ), was one of 42 foreign subsidiaries owned by the U.S.-based multinational, S.C. Johnson & Son, Inc. It was ranked globally as one of the largest privately held companies. SCJ contributed substantially to worldwide sales and profits and was based in Brantford, Ontario, close to the Canadian urban markets of Hamilton, Kitchener, Toronto, London, and Niagara Falls. About 300 people worked at the head office and plant, while another 100 were employed in field sales.

Innochem Division

Innochem (Innovative Chemicals for Professional Use) was a special division established to serve corporate, institutional, and government customers of SCJ. The division manufactured an extensive line of industrial cleaning chemicals, including general purpose cleansers, waxes, polishes, and disinfectants, plus a number of specialty products of limited application, as shown in Exhibit 3. Last year, Innochem sold $4.5 million of industrial cleaning chemicals through distributors and $0.2 million direct to end users. Financial statements for Innochem are shown in Exhibit 4.

Innochem Marketing Strategy

Divisional strategy hinged on reliable product performance, product innovation, active promotion, and mixed channel distribution. Steve Remen, market development manager, maintained that "Customers know our products are of excellent quality. They know that the products will always perform as expected."

At SCJ, performance requirements were detailed and tolerances precisely defined. The Department of Quality Control routinely inspected and tested raw materials, work in process, packaging, and finished goods. At any phase during the manufacturing cycle, Quality Control was empowered to halt the process and quarantine suspect product or materials. SCJ maintained that nothing left the plant "without approval from Quality Control."

"Keeping the new product shelf well stocked" was central to divisional strategy, as the name Innochem implies. Products launched over the past three

EXHIBIT 3 Innochem product line

Johnson Wax is a systems innovator. Frequently, a new product leads to a whole new system of doing things—a Johnson system of "matched" products formulated to work together. This makes the most of your time, your effort, and your expense. Call today and see how these Johnson systems can give you maximum results at a minimum cost.

For all floors except unsealed wood and unsealed cork

Stripper:	**Step-Off**—powerful, fast action
Finish:	**Pronto**—fast-drying, good gloss, minimum maintenance
Spray-buff solution:	**The Shiner Liquid Spray Cleaner or The Shiner Aerosol Spray Finish**
Maintainer:	**Forward**—cleans, disinfects, deodorizes, sanitizes

For all floors except unsealed wood and unsealed cork

Stripper:	**Step-Off**—powerful, fast stripper
Finish:	**Carefree**—tough, beauty, durable, minimum maintenance
Maintainer:	**Forward**—cleans, disinfects, deodorizes, sanitizes

For all floors except unsealed wood and unsealed cork

Stripper:	**Step-Off**—for selective stripping
Sealer:	**Over & Under-Plus**—undercoater-sealer
Finish:	**Scrubbable Step-Ahead**—brilliant, scrubbable
Maintainer:	**Forward**—cleans, disinfects, sanitizes, deodorizes

For all floors except unsealed wood and cork

Stripper:	**Step-Off**—powerful, fast stripper
Finish:	**Easy Street**—high solids, high gloss, spray buffs to a "wet look" appearance
Maintainer:	**Forward**—cleans, disinfects, deodorizes
	Expose—phenolic cleaner disinfectant

For all floors except unsealed wood and unsealed cork

Stripper:	**Step-Off**—for selective stripping
Sealer:	**Over & Under-Plus**—undercoater-sealer
Finishes:	**Traffic Grade**—heavy-duty floor wax
	Waxtral—extra tough, high solids
Maintainer:	**Forward**—cleans, disinfects, sanitizes, deodorizes

General cleaning:
Break-Up—cleans soap and body scum fast
Forward—cleans, disinfects, sanitizes, deodorizes
Bon Ami—instant cleaner, pressurized or pump, disinfects
Toilet-urinals:
Go-Getter—"Working Foam" cleaner
Glass:
Bon Ami—spray-on foam or liquid cleaner
Disinfectant spray:
End-Bac II—controls bacteria, odors
Air freshener:
Glade—dewy-fresh fragrances
Spot cleaning:
Johnson's Pledge—cleans, waxes, polishes
Johnson's Lemon Pledge—refreshing scent
Bon Ami Stainless Steel Cleaner—cleans, polishes, protects
All-purpose cleaners:
Forward—cleans, disinfects, sanitizes, deodorizes
Break-Up—degreaser for animal and vegetable fats
Big Bare—heavy-duty industrial cleaner
Carpets:
Rugbee Powder & Liquid Extraction Cleaner
Rugbee Soil Release Concentrate—for pre-spraying and bonnet buffing
Rugbee Shampoo—for power shampoo machines
Rugbee Spotter—spot remover
Furniture:
Johnson's Pledge—cleans, waxes, polishes
Johnson's Lemon Pledge—refreshing scent
Shine-Up Liquid—general purpose cleaning
Disinfectant spray air freshener:
End-Bac II—controls bacteria, odors
Glade—dewy-fresh fragrances
Glass:
Bon Ami—spray-on foam or liquid cleaner
Cleaning:
Break-Up—special degreaser designed to remove animal and vegetable fats
Equipment:
Break-Up Foamer—special generator designed to dispense Break-Up cleaner
General cleaning:
Forward—fast-working germicidal cleaner for floors, walls, all washable surfaces
Expose—phenolic disinfectant cleaner
Sanitizing:
J80 Sanitizer—liquid for total environmental control of bacteria; no rinse necessary if used as directed

EXHIBIT 3 *(concluded)*

For all floors except asphalt, mastic and rubber tile.
Use sealer and wax finishes on wood, cork, and cured
concrete; sealer-finish on terrazzo, marble, clay, and
ceramic tile; wax finish only on vinyl, linoleum, and
magnesite.

Sealer:	**Johnson Gym Finish**—sealer and top-coater, cleans as it waxes.
Wax finishes:	**Traffic Wax Paste**—heavy-duty buffing wax
	Beautiflor Traffic Wax—liquid buffing wax
Maintainers:	**Forward**—cleans, disinfects, sanitizes, deodorizes
	Conq-r Dust—mop treatment
Stripper:	**Step-Off**—stripper for sealer and finish
Sealer:	**Secure**—fast-bonding, smooth, long-lasting
Finish:	**Traffic Grade**—heavy-duty floor wax
Maintainer:	**Forward or Big Bare**
Sealer-finish:	**Johnson Gym Finish**—seal and top-coater
Maintainer:	**Conq-r-Dust**—mop treatment

Disinfectant spray:
  End-Bac II Spray—controls bacteria, odors
Flying insects:
  Bolt Liquid Airborne or **Pressurized Airborne,**
    P3610 through E10 dispenser
Crawling insects:
  Bolt Liquid Residual or **Pressurized Residual,**
    P3610 through E10 dispenser
  Bolt Roach Bait
Rodents:
  Bolt Rodenticide—for effective control of rats
    and mice, use with Bolt Bait Box

EXHIBIT 4
S.C. JOHNSON AND SON, LIMITED
Profit Statement of the Division
(in thousands)

Gross sales:	$4,682
Returns	46
Allowances	1
Cash discounts	18
Net sales	4,617
Cost of sales	2,314
Gross profit:	2,303
Advertising	75
Promotions	144
Deals	—
External marketing services	2
Sales freight	292
Other distribution expenses	176
Service fees	184
Total direct expenses	873
Sales force	592
Marketing administration	147
Provision for bad debts	—
Research and development	30
Financial	68
Information resource management	47
Administration management	56
Total functional expenses	940
Total operating expenses	1,813
Operating profit	490

years represented 33 percent of divisional gross sales, 40 percent of gross profits, and 100 percent of growth.

Mixed Distribution Strategy

Innochem used a mixed distribution system in an attempt to broaden market coverage. Eighty-seven percent of divisional sales were handled by a force of 200 distributor salesmen and were serviced from 50 distributor warehouses representing 35 distributors. The indirect channel was particularly effective outside Ontario and Quebec. In part, the tendency for SCJ market penetration to increase with distances from Montreal and Toronto reflected Canadian demographics and the general economics of distribution. Outside the two production centres, demand was dispersed and delivery distances long.

Distributor salesmen were virtually all paid a straight commission on sales, and were responsible for selling a wide variety of products in addition to S.C. Johnson's. Several of the distributors had sales levels much higher than Innochem.

For Innochem, the impact of geography was compounded by a significant freight cost advantage: piggybacking industrial cleaning chemicals with SCJ consumer goods. In Ontario, for example, the cost of SCJ to a distributor was 30 percent above private label, while the differential in British Columbia was only 8 percent. On lower value products, the "freight effect" was even more pronounced.

SCJ had neither the salesmen nor the delivery capabilities to reach large-volume end users who demanded heavy selling effort or frequent shipments of small quantities. Furthermore, it was unlikely that SCJ could develop the necessary selling and distribution strength economically, given the narrowness of the division's range of janitorial products (i.e., industrial cleaning chemicals only).

The Rebate Plan

The key strategic problem facing Innochem was how best to challenge the direct marketer (and private label distributor) for large-volume, price-sensitive customers with heavy service requirements, particularly in markets where SCJ had no freight advantage. In this connection George had observed:

> Our gravest weakness is our inability to manage the total margin between the manufactured cost and consumer price in a way that is equitable and sufficiently profitable to support the investment and expenses of both the distributors and ourselves.
>
> Our prime competition across Canada is from direct-selling national and regional manufacturers. These companies control both the manufacturing and distribution gross margins. Under our pricing system, the distributor's margin at end user list on sales is 43 percent. Our margin (the manufacturing margin) is 50 percent on sales. When these margins are combined, as in the case of direct-

selling manufacturers, the margin becomes 70 percent at list. This long margin provides significant price flexibility in a price-competitive marketplace. We must find a way to profitably attack the direct marketer's 61 percent market share.

The rebate plan George was now evaluating had been devised to meet the competition head-on. "Profitable partnership" between Innochem and the distributors was the underlying philosophy of the plan. Rebates offered a means to "share fairly the margins available between factory cost and consumer price." Whenever competitive conditions required a distributor to discount the resale list price by 30 percent or more, SCJ would give a certain percentage of the wholesale price back to the distributor. In other words, SCJ would sacrifice part of its margin to help offset a heavy end user discount. Rebate percentages would vary with the rate of discount, following a set schedule. Different schedules were to be established for each product type and size. Exhibits 5, 6, and 7 outline the effect of rebates on both the unit gross margins of SCJ and individual distributors for a specific product example.

The rebate plan was designed to be applicable to new, "incremental" business only, not to existing accounts of the distributor. Distributors would be required to seek SCJ approval for end user discounts of over 30 percent or more of resale list. The maximum allowable end user discount would rarely exceed 50 percent. To request rebate payments, distributors would send SCJ a copy of the resale invoice along with a written claim. The rebate would then be paid within 60 days. Currently, Innochem sales were sold by distributors at an average discount of 10 percent off list.

Proponents of the plan maintained that the resulting resale price flexibility would not only enhance Innochem competitiveness among end users but would also diminish distributor attraction to private label.

As he studied the plan, George questioned whether all the implications were fully understood and wondered what other strategies, if any, might increase urban market penetration. Any plan he devised would have to be sold to distributors as well as to corporate management. George had only three weeks to develop an appropriate action plan.

EXHIBIT 5 Distributors' rebate pricing schedule: An example using Pronto floor wax

Code: 04055
Product description: Pronto Fast-Dry Finish
Size: 209-Litre
Pack: 1

EFF. DATE: 03-31-81
Resale price list 71 613.750
Distributor price list 74 349.837
Percent markup on cost with carload and rebate

Discount percent[1]	Quote (Federal sales tax included)[2]	Rebate Percent[3]	Rebate Dealers[4]	2% Net[5]	2% Markup percent[6]	3% Net	3% Markup percent	4% Net	4% Markup percent	5% Net	5% Markup percent
30.0	429.63	8.0	27.99	314.85	36	311.35	38	307.86	40	304.36	41
35.0	398.94	12.0	41.98	300.86	33	297.36	34	293.86	36	290.36	27
40.0	368.25	17.0	59.47	283.37	30	279.87	32	276.37	33	272.87	35
41.0	362.11	17.5	61.22	281.62	29	278.12	30	274.62	32	271.12	34
42.0	355.98	18.0	62.97	279.87	27	276.37	29	272.87	30	269.37	32
43.0	349.84	18.5	64.72	278.12	26	274.62	27	271.12	29	267.63	31
44.0	343.70	19.0	66.47	276.37	24	272.87	26	269.37	28	265.88	29
45.0	337.56	20.0	69.97	272.87	24	269.37	25	265.88	27	262.38	29
46.0	331.43	20.5	71.72	271.12	22	267.63	24	264.13	25	260.63	27
47.0	325.29	21.0	73.47	269.37	21	265.88	22	262.38	24	258.88	26
48.0	319.15	21.5	75.21	267.63	19	264.13	21	260.63	22	257.13	24
49.0	313.01	22.0	76.96	265.88	18	262.38	19	258.88	21	255.38	23
50.0	306.88	23.0	80.46	262.38	17	258.88	19	255.38	20	251.88	22
51.0	300.74	24.0	83.96	258.88	16	255.38	18	251.88	19	248.38	21
52.0	294.60	25.0	87.46	255.38	15	251.88	17	248.38	19	244.89	20
53.0	288.46	26.0	90.96	251.88	15	248.38	16	244.89	18	241.39	19
54.0	282.33	28.0	97.95	244.89	15	241.39	17	237.89	19	234.39	20
55.0	276.19	30.0	104.95	237.89	16	234.39	18	230.89	20	227.39	21

[1] Discount extended to end user on resale list price.
[2] Resale price at given discount level (includes federal sales tax).
[3] Percentage of distributor's price ($613.75) rebated by SCJ.
[4] Actual dollar amount of rebate by SCJ.
[5] Actual net cost to distributor after deduction of rebate and "carload" (quantity) discount.
[6] Effective rate of distributor markup.

EXHIBIT 6 Effect of rebate plan on manufacturer and distributor margins: The example of one 209-litre pack of Pronto floor finish retailed at 40 percent below resale list price

I. Under present arrangements

Base price to distributor	$349.84
Price to distributor, assuming 2 percent carload discount*	342.84
SCJ cost	174.92
∴ SCJ margin	$167.92
Resale list price	613.75
Resale list price minus 40 percent discount	368.25
Distributor price, assuming 2 percent carload discount	342.84
∴ Distributor's margin	$ 25.41

II. Under rebate plan

Rebate to distributor giving 40 percent discount off resale price amounted to 17 percent distributor's base price	$ 59.47
SCJ margin (minus rebate)	108.45
Distributor margin (plus rebate)	84.88

III. Competitive prices

For this example, George estimated that a distributor could buy a private brand "comparable" product for approximately $244.

* A form of quantity discount, which, in this case, drops the price the distributor pays to SCJ from $349.84 to $342.84.

EXHIBIT 7 Effect of end user discount level on manufacturer and distributor margins under proposed rebate plan: The example of 1 209-litre pack of Pronto Fast-Dry Finish*

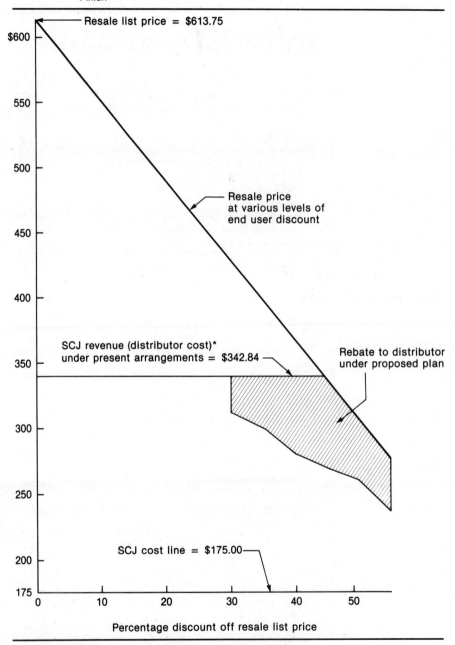

* Assuming 2 percent quantity ("carload") discount off price to distributor.

Case 30

United Techtronics*

In June 1977, United Techtronics faced a major pricing decision with respect to its new video screen television system. "We're really excited here at United Techtronics," exclaimed Mr. Roy Cowing, the founder and president of United Techtronics. "We've made a most significant technological breakthrough in large-screen, video television systems." He went on to explain that the marketing plan for 1978 for this product was now his major area of concern, and that what price to charge was the marketing question that was giving him the most difficulty.

Company History

United Techtronics (UT) was founded in Boston in 1959 by Mr. Cowing. Prior to that time Mr. Cowing had been an associate professor of electrical engineering at M.I.T. Mr. Cowing founded UT to manufacture and market products making use of some of the electronic inventions he had developed while at M.I.T. Sales were made mostly to the space program and the military. Sales grew from $100,000 in 1960 to $27 million in 1976. Profits in 1976 were $3.2 million.

The Video Screen Project

For a number of years beginning in the late 1960s, Mr. Cowing had been trying to reduce the company's dependency on government sales. One of the diversification projects that he had committed research and development monies to was the so-called video screen project. The objective of this project was to develop a system whereby a television picture could be displayed on a screen as big as 8 to 10 feet diagonally. In late 1976, one of UT's engineers made the necessary breakthrough. The rest of 1976 and the first few months of 1977 were spent producing working prototypes. Up until June 1977, UT had invested $600,000 in the project.

* This case was written by Thomas C. Kinnear. Copyright © 1980, Thomas C. Kinnear.

Video Screen Television

Extra-large screen television systems were not new. There were a number of companies who sold such systems both to the consumer and commercial (taverns, restaurants, and so on) markets. Most current systems made use of a special magnifying lens that projected a regular small television picture onto a special screen. The result of this process is that the final picture lacked much of the brightness of the original small screen. As a result, the picture had to be viewed in a darkened room. There were some other video systems that did not use the magnifying process. These systems used special tubes, but also suffered from a lack of brightness.

UT had developed a system that was bright enough to be viewed in regular daylight on a screen up to 10 feet diagonal. Mr. Cowing was unwilling to discuss how this was accomplished. He would only say that the process was protected by patent, and that he thought it would take at least two to three years for any competitor to duplicate the results of the system.

A number of large and small companies were active in this area. Admiral, General Electric, RCA, Zenith, and Sony were all thought to be working on developing large-screen systems directed at the consumer market. Sony was rumored to be ready to introduce a 60-inch diagonal screen system that would retail for about $2,500. A number of small companies were already producing systems. Advent Corporation, a small New England company, claimed to have sold 4,000, 84-inch diagonal units in two years at a $4,000 price. Muntz Manufacturing claimed one-year sales of 5,000, 50-inch diagonal units at prices from $1,500 to $2,500. Mr. Cowing was adamant that none of these systems gave as bright a picture as UT's. He estimated that about 10,000 large-screen systems were sold in 1976.

Cost Structure

Mr. Cowing expected about 50 percent of the suggested retail selling price to go for wholesaler and retailer margins. He expected that UT's direct manufacturing costs would vary depending on the volume produced. Exhibit 1 presents these estimates. He expected direct labor costs to fall at higher production volumes due to the increased automation of the process and improved worker skills.

EXHIBIT 1 Estimated production costs of UT's video screen system

	Volume		
	0–5,000	5,000–10,000	10,001–20,000
Raw materials	$ 480	$460	$410
Direct labor	540	320	115
Total direct costs	$1,020	$780	$525

Material costs were expected to fall due to less waste due to automation. The equipment costs necessary to automate the product process were $70,000 to produce in the 0–5,000-unit range, an additional $50,000 to produce in the 5,001–10,000-unit range, and an additional $40,000 to produce in the 10,001–20,000-unit range. The useful life of this equipment was put at five years. Mr. Cowing was sure that production costs were substantially below those of current competitors including Sony. Such was the magnitude of UT's technological breakthrough. Mr. Cowing was unwilling to produce over 20,000 units a year in the first few years due to the limited cash resources of the company to support inventories, and so on.

Market Studies

Mr. Cowing wanted to establish a position in the consumer market for his product. He felt that the long-run potential was greater there than in the commercial market. With this end in mind he hired a small economic research consulting firm to undertake a consumer study to determine the likely reaction to alternative retail prices for the system. These consultants undertook extensive interviews with potential television purchasers, and examined the sales and pricing histories of competitive products. They concluded that: "UT's video screen system would be highly price elastic across a range of prices from $500 to $5,000, both in a primary and secondary demand sense." They went on to estimate the price elasticity of demand in this range to be between 4.0 and 6.5.

The Pricing Decision

Mr. Cowing was considering a number of alternative suggested retail prices. "I can see arguments for pricing anywhere from above Advent's to substantially below Muntz's lowest price," he said.

Case 31

Consolidated-Bathurst Pulp and Paper Limited*

On the morning of September 28, 1973, Mr. John Andrew, president of Consolidated-Bathurst Pulp and Paper Limited, was evaluating the current price charged for newsprint to U.S. customers. A number of recent developments in the newsprint market had provoked this evaluation. Newsprint was in much shorter supply than in previous years due to a large increase in demand in the last two years. This increase had not been matched by increased industry capacity to produce. Also, a number of competitor's newsprint mills were shut down by strikes. Mr. Andrew was considering a change from Consolidated-Bathurst's current price of U.S. $175 per ton. He was aware that he would have to carefully consider both the customers' reactions and the competition's reactions to any changes that he might make.

Company Background

Consolidated-Bathurst Pulp and Paper Limited was a wholly owned subsidiary of Consolidated-Bathurst Limited, a fully integrated, multiproduct paper company. Mr. Andrew was a senior vice president of the parent company, besides holding the operating responsibility for the newsprint division.

In 1972, Consolidated-Bathurst Limited had sales of $348 million and had assets of $430 million. The company's sales and earnings performance record for the period 1966–72 is shown in Exhibit 1. In 1970 and 1971, the company operated at a loss. Throughout this period the newsprint operation, the firm's major product line, had remained profitable, but with insufficient return on investment to warrant the investment of additional capital to purchase a new newsprint machine. These machines cost about $120,000 per daily ton, if built at an existing mill site with wood handling facilities available. At a new site, the costs of developing this wood handling capacity would raise the cost to about $150,000 per daily ton. Thus, a machine that could produce 500 tons per day would cost about $75 million. Consolidated-Bathurst had made some capital investments in the last few years and as a result anticipated that their capacity

---

* This case was written by Thomas C. Kinnear and Stephen Becker. Copyright © 1974, the University of Western Ontario. Reproduced with permission.

EXHIBIT 1 Sales and earnings results ($000)

	1972	1971	1970	1969	1968	1967	1966
Net sales	$348,055	$343,362	$353,944	$348,087	$295,472	$242,198	$234,485
Earnings (before extraordinary items)	6,496	442	589	10,554	13,126	17,788	21,108
Per common share*	0.55	(0.45)	(0.42)	1.23	1.69	2.48	3.05
Net earnings (loss) per share after extraordinary items*	0.56	(8.70)	(2.30)	1.40	1.36	2.40	3.00

* Per common share earnings are stated after deducting application of preferred dividend requirements.

would increase by 70,000 tons per year at the end of 1973. This increase in capacity would come from an extension of their Belgo Division Mill in Shawinigan, Quebec. An old newsprint machine had been purchased and modified at a cost of $11 million to give this increase in capacity.

Governments, particularly provincial, had frequently distorted the industry's normal growth pattern. By means of grants and tax incentives, they had promoted expansion when it was not needed, sometimes in a locale which was not and never could be economic. Many of these ventures had proven to be disastrous. (Developments in Newfoundland and Manitoba were outstanding examples of this.)

Mr. Andrew was concerned that increased prices would be an incentive for competitors to develop new mills. The risks were that expansion by competitors would decrease Consolidated-Bathurst's share of the market and also that rapid expansion by many companies could result in significant overcapacity such as had existed some few years before.

In 1972, Consolidated-Bathurst recorded a newsprint sales volume of 912,000 tons, of which about two thirds was sold in U.S. markets. About 10 percent was sold overseas and the rest in Canada. Other Consolidated-Bathurst products included pulp, container board, kraft paper, boxboard, lumber, and packaging products. Overall, the company's total business was 56 percent basic mill products, 41 percent packaging, and 3 percent lumber.

The Newsprint Industry

Consolidated-Bathurst ranked fifth in newsprint capacity in Canada with 9.2 percent of the total capacity. Exhibit 2 shows the capacity and shares of the other Canada-based competitors in the industry. Operating capacity rates for the past nine years, as shown in Exhibit 3, were a major element in pricing decisions by members of the industry. There were also a number of significant U.S. producers of newsprint. Exhibit 4 shows their estimated capacities. The U.S. companies were very important in the pricing process for newsprint. Consolidated-Bathurst sales personnel felt that American publishers attached a higher degree of legitimacy to price increases originating with U.S.-based producers. At the present time, only Great Northern, Crown Zellerbach, and

EXHIBIT 2 Canadian newsprint producers (>200,000 tons) in order of size, by capacity and residual total (<200,000 tons) lumped

	Producer	Capacity (tons)	Share of industry (percent)
1.	MacMillan-Bloedel Ltd.	1,364,100	13.4%
2.	Canadian International Paper	1,154,100	11.3
3.	The Price Company Ltd.	1,058,400	10.4
4.	Abitibi Paper Co. Ltd.	1,044,200	10.2
5.	Consolidated-Bathurst Ltd.	936,600	9.2
6.	Ontario Paper Co. Ltd.	765,000	7.5
7.	Bowaters Canadian Corp. Ltd.	546,200	5.4
8.	Domtar Newsprint Ltd.	540,300	5.3
9.	Great Lakes Paper Co. Ltd.	432,200	4.2
10.	Anglo-Canadian Pulp & Paper	336,800	3.3
11.	Spruce Falls Power & Paper Co.	332,100	3.3
12.	Ontario-Minnesota Pulp & Paper Co.	322,200	3.2
13.	Donohue Co. Ltd.	257,000	2.5
14.	Crown Zellerbach Can. Ltd.	254,100	2.5
15.	B. C. Forest Products Ltd.	242,700	2.4
	Balance of producers (<200,000 ton producers)	607,600	5.9
		10,193,600	100.0

EXHIBIT 3 Canadian newsprint industry: Capacity, operating ratio, production, reserve capacity (1965 through 8 months 1973)

Year	Official capacity*	Indicated operating ratio	Production	Indicated reserve capacity
1965	8,420,800	91.7	7,719,700	701,100
1966	8,878,100	94.8	8,418,800	459,300
1967	9,293,900	86.6	8,051,500	1,242,400
1968	9,655,400	83.2	8,031,300	1,624,100
1969	9,611,500	91.1	8,758,400	853,100
1970	9,718,900	88.6	8,607,500	1,111,400
1971	10,050,400	82.6	8,297,000	1,753,400
1972	10,117,900	85.6	8,660,800	1,457,100
8 months—1973	6,795,100	90.5	6,130,100	665,000
12 months—1973	10,193,600†			

* Capacity figures shown are official, theoretically possible amounts. An approximate 95 percent is considered practically possible. Note also that these figures represent nondutiable (U.S. tariff) grades only and do not incorporate Groundwood Printing and Specialty Grades (dutiable) of which some 500,000 tons per annum are produced. Detailed capacities of the latter are not published and, indeed, some part of the above capacities can be shifted to produce dutiable grades as demand dictates and profit incentives exist.

† Estimated.

EXHIBIT 4 Major U.S.
newsprint
producers

Producer	Capacity (tons)
Southland Paper	470,000
Kimberly-Clark	420,000
Publishers Paper	360,000
Great Northern	360,000
Boise Cascade	135,000
Boise Price	150,000
Others	<100,000

Publishers Paper of the U.S. producers were placing their major sales emphasis in the prime market areas of the Canadian producers.

Most pulp and paper companies were experiencing increasing production costs. As shown in Exhibit 5, manufacturing costs as a percentage of sales were higher in 1972 than most of the previous seven years. Consolidated-Bathurst's manufacturing costs as a percentage of sales had risen sharply in the previous three years and in 1973 were above the industry average. An increase in the cost of labour in 1974 was expected to increase production costs even more. Although Consolidated-Bathurst did not have any workers on strike, the demands of wage parity with other firms that were on strike would certainly be a major factor in future negotiating sessions. The current industry labour position is shown in Exhibit 6. The seriousness of the situation was reported in the *Globe and Mail* on Friday, September 28, 1973:

> Despite recent settlements in Ontario, strikes in the Quebec pulp and paper industry continue to present a bleak contrast to an otherwise rosy prospect for that key Quebec industry.
>
> No end is in sight to strikes involving about 5,000 workers that began several weeks ago at five mills, three of them in Quebec, owned by Canadian Interna-

EXHIBIT 5 Ratio of
manufacturing
costs to gross
sales: Index
1965 = 100

Year	Industry
1972	108
1971	107
1970	103
1969	106
1968	108
1967	106
1966	102
1965	100

EXHIBIT 6 Eastern Canadian newsprint mills—strikes situation as of September 28, 1973

Company	Date strike began	Status
MacMillan Rothesay Ltd. (MacMillan-Bloedel Mill at Rothesay, Quebec)	September 9	Still out
E. B. Eddy	August 29	Ratified Sept. 14
Canadian Cellulose	August 1	Settled Aug. 5
C.I.P.—Gatineau, LaTuque, Trois Rivieres	July 27	Still out
C.I.P.—Hawkesbury	August 3	Still out
New Brunswick International Paper	August 8	Still out
Ontario and Minnesota Pulp and Paper—Fort Frances	July 3	Still out
—Kenora	July 9	Still out
Price Company—Alma and Kenogami	August 10	Still out

tional Paper Co. of Montreal, nor to strikes by about 1,800 employees that began in August at two Quebec mills of Price Co. Limited of Quebec City.

Meanwhile, the UPIU (United Paperworkers International Union) has resumed contract negotiations with the Eastern Canada Newsprint Group, which is bargaining on behalf of five mills owned by four Quebec companies and one in Nova Scotia. Negotiations involving several other Quebec mills remain in abeyance in their preliminary stages.

These strikes come at a time when sales have generally been ''Terrific'' for pulp and paper producers, says Paul E. Lachance, President of the Council of Pulp and Paper Producers of Quebec.

He considers the strikes particularly unfortunate because the industry could have been selling so much. He estimates that between CIP and Price, about $1 million a day of sales are being lost.

Dr. Lachance expects strong markets to continue in 1974.

The Market for Newsprint

About 50 percent of newsprint in the United States was consumed by major metropolitan papers and the rest by much smaller dailies and weeklies. Papers like the *New York Times* and the *Detroit News,* for example, would consume about 400,000 tons and 100,000 tons of newsprint every year, respectively. Consolidated-Bathurst sold mostly to larger papers or groups of papers. Their yearly contracts with the larger papers or groups of papers ranged from 20,000 tons to over 100,000 tons with an average of about 50,000 tons. Consolidated-Bathurst had a total of about 170 accounts with 10 percent of these accounting for almost 70 percent of sales and 25 percent accounting for over 90 percent of sales. In the United States some of the larger contracts were held with the *Baltimore Sun,* The Newhouse Group (including *Long Island Daily* and *Cleveland Plain Dealer*), the Knight Newspapers (including *Miami Herald, Beacon Journal,* Akron, Ohio, *Detroit Free Press*), the *Detroit News, Philadelphia Bulletin, Boston Globe, The Wall Street Journal,* and the *New York*

Daily News. Major Canadian customers included *La Presse Trans-Canada Newspapers,* the *Montreal Star,* and the *Toronto Star.* For large accounts, newsprint contracts were negotiated by Mr. Andrew and his immediate subordinates. The publisher and financial vice president usually represented the newspaper in these negotiations. Most other newsprint producers had about the same amount of account concentration as Consolidated-Bathurst.

In determining which newsprint producer received a particular volume of newsprint contract, publishers considered the printability and runability (amount of breakage in the press), delivery time, sales terms, and customer technical service to correct any problems. Personal relationship among negotiators was also considered to be very important. Almost all publishers had two or three sources of supply. Also, they quite often purchased some cut-price newsprint from smaller suppliers in Scandinavia or the United States.

About 85 percent of Canadian newsprint was produced in eastern Canada with the remaining 15 percent being produced in British Columbia. The major western producers were MacMillan-Bloedel Limited, Crown Zellerbach, and B. C. Forest Products. These producers sold mainly in the western United States and the Orient. MacMillan-Bloedel also had about 25 percent of its total capacity at Rothesay in eastern Canada and so competed directly with the eastern producers. The eastern producers sold mainly in the Northeast and Midwest United States, the United Kingdom, South America, and Canada.

Personnel at Consolidated-Bathurst estimated that in 1974, U.S. production would be 3.4 million tons out of a capacity of 3.6 million tons, and that Canadian production would be 9. 8 million tons out of a capacity of 10.6 million tons. U.S. exports were expected to be about 100,000 tons while Canadian overseas exports were expected to be about 1.7 million tons. Scandinavian imports into the United States were expected to be about 300,000 tons. Total U.S. demand for 1974 was estimated at 10.5 million tons, while Canadian demand was expected to be 900,000 tons. Another 200,000 tons were expected to be sold for inventory.

Mr. Andrew knew that a few competitors had started marketing a 30-pound grade of newsprint. An important factor was that the thinner sheet produced a 6 percent saving in wood consumption. This saving was important as the pulp and paper industry was quickly approaching the limit of low-cost, accessible wood resources. The impact of this thinner paper on publishers was not yet known.

Consolidated-Bathurst also made higher-quality newsprint grades, which sold at a 3 percent to 10 percent premium over the standard price.

History of Price Changes

Because of the competitiveness in the newsprint market, any price changes were made after much deliberation and with full anticipation of possible competitive moves. An outline of pricing activity in the U.S. newsprint market in recent years is shown in Exhibit 7. This exhibit only lists those firms that were in the

EXHIBIT 7 Outline of U.S. newsprint price changes (1965–1973) in U.S. dollars per ton

Date	Company (in order of announcement)	Announced increase or decrease	Effective price	Effective date	
March 1, 1966 (est.)	Domtar	$10	$145	April 1, 1966	
	Bowater Sales Corp.	10	145	April 1, 1966	
	Consolidated Paper (Consolidated-Bathurst's 1966 name)	10	145	April 1, 1966	
March 23, 1966	Domtar announces rollback	(5)	140	May 16, 1966	
	Bowater Sales Corp.	(5)	140	May 16, 1966	
	Great Lakes Paper	(5)	140	May 16, 1966	
April 20, 1966	All firms change effective date	(5)	140	June 1, 1966	
September 26, 1966	Crown Zellerbach Corp.	4	138	June 1, 1967	West Coast
October 25, 1966	MacMillan Bloedel	(3)	137	June 1, 1967	United States only
November 1, 1966	Crown Zellerbach	3	140	June 1, 1967	
March 15, 1967	Consolidated Paper	3	143	July 1, 1967	
March 17, 1967	International Paper Sales Co.	3	143	July 1, 1967	
September 27, 1968	International Paper Sales Co.	5	148	January 1, 1969	North
	International Paper Sales Co.	4	147	January 1, 1969	South*
	All others follow immediately after				
September 24, 1969	Bowater Sales Co.	4–5	152	January 1, 1970	Wipes out all price differential— universal price
November 20, 1969	(Consolidated-Bathurst is 4th company to announce price increase) $1 price differential to South reinstated	(1)	152	January 1, 1970	North
			151	January 1, 1970	South

Announcement Date	Company	Increase	Price	Effective Date	Market*
September 8, 1970	Anglo-Canadian	10	162	January 1, 1971	
	Consolidated-Bathurst	10	162	January 1, 1971	
	International Paper	10	162	January 1, 1971	
September 22, 1970	Boise-Cascade	10	162	January 1, 1971	South only
	Boise-Cascade	8	160	January 1, 1971	All markets
November 3, 1970	Abitibi	8	160	January 1, 1971	South
November 4, 1970	Southland Paper	7	159	January 1, 1971	
November 15, 1970	All majors	8	160	November 15, 1970	
December 6, 1970	All majors	8	160	April 1, 1971	Canada only
August 12, 1971	MacMillan-Bloedel	8	168	November 1, 1971	
	Price Company	8	168	November 1, 1971	
	(Consolidated-Bathurst is 5th company to announce price increase)				
August 15, 1971	Nixon imposes wage-price freeze. Price increase dropped.				
December 10, 1971 (Est.)	International Paper Sales Co.	8	168	December 1971	North
	(3.4%, or $5.25 price increase approved by U.S. Price Commission)	5.25	164.25	December 1971	South
	Consolidated-Bathurst	8	168	December 1971	North
December 1, 1972	Great Northern Paper Co.	5	170	February 1, 1973	
	Southland Paper Co.	5	170	February 1, 1973	
	(Consolidated-Bathurst is 4th company to announce price increase (December 19)).				
April 12, 1973	Bowater Sales Co.	5	175	July 1, 1973	
	Kruger Pulp and Paper	5	175	July 1, 1973	
	Consolidated-Bathurst	5	175	July 1, 1973	

* South includes Texas, Oklahoma, Louisiana, Arkansas, Missouri, and Kansas.

first group of firms to act on any price change. After a sorting-out period following a price change, most firms sold at the established market price within a particular geographic market. Usually a change was made effective from a future date which allowed both competitors and purchasers time to analyze and react to the change. The North-South distinction in the exhibit refers to the fact that major publishers in the southeastern states had bargained one firm against another to get a lower market price than existed in the northeastern states. This difference existed despite the increased distance and transportation costs.

Most sales contracts were for 5 to 10 years but provisions for price increases were outlined in clauses tying them to ''general although not necessarily universal'' industry prices. In relation to these contracts, members of the sales staff generally felt that the customer was not bound if the conditions under which the contract was signed should change.

Newsprint represented about 30 percent of the total costs to newspaper publishers, and consequently, newsprint price increases had to be passed on by the publisher, usually to advertisers, if he was to maintain his profitability. Timing of a price increase therefore was critical—if it came just after the publisher had revised his advertising rates (which were usually fixed for a certain period) then he would have no means of recouping the extra cost. Rate cards for major publishers were set at many different times throughout the year.

Newspaper publishers had in the past reacted in several ways to the announcement of a price increase for newsprint. The first reaction was sometimes emotional. Heated telephone calls, letters pleading for reconsideration, or speeches castigating the Canadian newsprint ''cartel'' were not uncommon.

Publishers could also take direct action by threatening to cancel their contracts. Some contracts actually had been cancelled using the price increase as an excuse, but the real reason might have been something else. More often, customers used the threat of cancellation to extract discounts from suppliers. This pressure was particularly effective when either of the following conditions existed:

a. The market was soft; that is, the industry was in a general state of oversupply. In this case, the customer would likely be able to find supply elsewhere, often at a reduced price.
b. The customer had more than one supplier. If one supplier was willing to grant a discount, the customer could use this as leverage to obtain concessions from the others. A prime example of this type of situation existed in the southern United States where a publisher-controlled newsprint company had influenced the establishment of a market price $2 less than the rest of the eastern United States. Because of this, Canadian mills charged a lower price to southern customers than to those in the North.

In August 1971, President Nixon imposed universal wage and price controls in the United States for 90 days. As of September 1973, the newsprint industry was operating under voluntary restraint on prices. Price increases were allowed, but were subject to review by the Cost-of-Living Council. If this council considered a price increase to be unreasonable, it could order the price rolled back.

The Future

Mr. Andrew was anxious to avoid any losses in the future especially in view of Consolidated-Bathurst's performance in previous years. In evaluating all the factors, Mr. Andrew knew that he would have to decide what the new price should be and when the change was to be made if he decided to make any price change at all. He also wondered if now was the time to make the investment in a new newsprint machine, and if so, what size of machine. He expected that production costs for newsprint on a new machine would be about 10 percent less than the current average total cost. Mr. Andrew knew that he was operating in a basically conservative commodity business. He was anxious to make good decisions both for his company and for his industry.

Big Sky of Montana, Inc.*

Introduction

Karen Tracy could feel the pressure on her as she sat at her desk late that April afternoon. Two weeks from today she would be called on to present her recommendations concerning next year's winter season pricing policies for the Big Sky of Montana, Inc.—room rates for the resort's accommodation facilities as well as decisions in the skiing and food service areas. The presentation would be made to a top management team from the parent company, Boyne U.S.A., which operated out of Michigan.

"As sales and public relations manager, Karen, your accuracy in decision making is extremely important," her boss had said in his usual tone. "Because we spend most of our time in Michigan, we'll need a well-based and involved opinion."

It'll be the shortest two weeks of my life, she thought.

Background: Big Sky and Boyne U.S.A.

Big Sky of Montana, Inc., was a medium-sized destination resort[1] located in southwestern Montana, 45 miles south of Bozeman, and 43 miles north of the west entrance to Yellowstone National Park. Big Sky was conceived in the early 1970s and had begun operation in November 1974.

The 11,000-acre, 2,000-bed resort was separated into 2 main areas: Meadow and Mountain Villages. The Meadow Village (elevation 6,300 feet) was located 2 miles east of the resort's main entrance on U.S. 191 and 7 miles from the ski area. The Meadow Village had an 800-bed capacity in the form of 4

---

* This case was prepared by Anne Senausky and Professor James E. Nelson for educational purposes only. It is designed for classroom purposes and not for purposes of research nor to illustrate either effective or ineffective handling of administrative problems. Some data are disguised. Copyright © 1978 by the Endowment and Research Foundation at Montana State University. Used with permission.

[1] Destination resorts were characterized by on-the-hill lodging and eating facilities, a national market, and national advertising.

condominium complexes (ranging from studios to 3-bedroom units) and a 40-room hostel for economy lodging. Additional facilities included an 18-hole golf course, 6 tennis courts, a restaurant, post office, a convention center with meeting space for up to 200 people, and a small lodge serving as a pro shop for the golf course in the summer and cross-country skiing in the winter.

The Mountain Village (elevation 7,500 feet) was the center of winter activity, located at the base of the ski area. In this complex was the 204-room Huntley Lodge offering hotel accommodations, 3 condominium complexes (unit size ranged from studio to 3-bedroom), and an 88-room hostel for a total of 1,200 beds. The Mountain Mall was also located here, next to the Huntley Lodge and within a five-minute walk of 2 of the 3 condominium complexes in the Mountain Village. It housed ticket sales, an equipment rental shop, a skier's cafeteria, two large meeting rooms for a maximum of 700 persons (regularly used as sack lunch areas for skiers), two offices, a ski school desk, and ski patrol room, all of which were operated by Boyne. Also in this building were a delicatessen, drug store/gift shop, sporting goods store/rental shop, restaurant, outdoor clothing store, jewelry shop, a T-shirt shop, two bars, and a child day-care center. Each of these independent operations held leases, due to expire in two to three years.

The closest airport to Big Sky was located just outside Bozeman. It was served by Northwest Orient and Frontier Airlines with connections to other major airlines out of Denver and Salt Lake City. Greyhound and Amtrak also operated bus and train service into Bozeman. Yellowstone Park Lines provided Big Sky with three buses daily to and from the airport and Bozeman bus station (cost was $4.40 one way, $8.40 round trip), as well as an hourly shuttle around the two Big Sky villages. Avis, Hertz, National, and Budget offered rent-a-car service in Bozeman with a drop-off service available at Big Sky.

In July 1976 Boyne U.S.A., a privately owned, Michigan-based operation, purchased the Huntley Lodge, Mountain Mall, ski lifts and terrain, golf course, and tennis courts for approximately $8 million. The company subsequently invested an additional $3 million into Big Sky. Boyne also owned and operated four Michigan resort ski areas.

Big Sky's top management consisted of a lodge manager (in charge of operations within the Huntley Lodge), a sales and public relations manager (Karen), a food and beverage manager, and an area manager (overseeing operations external to the lodge, including the mall and all recreational facilities). These four positions were occupied by persons trained with the parent company; a fifth manager, the comptroller, had worked for pre-Boyne ownership.

Business figures were reported to the company's home office on a daily basis and major decisions concerning Big Sky operations were discussed and approved by "Michigan." Boyne's top management visited Big Sky an average of five times annually, and all major decisions such as pricing and advertising were approved by the parent for all operations.

The Skiing

Big Sky's winter season usually began in late November and continued until the middle of April, with a yearly snowfall of approximately 450 inches. The area had 18 slopes between elevations of 7,500 and 9,900 feet. Terrain breakdown was as follows: 25 percent novice, 55 percent intermediate, and 20 percent advanced. (Although opinions varied, industry guidelines recommended a terrain breakdown of 20 percent, 60 percent, and 20 percent for novice, intermediate, and advanced skiers, respectively.) The longest run was approximately three miles in length; temperatures (highs) ranged from 15 to 30 degrees Farenheit throughout the season.

Lift facilities at Big Sky included two double chairlifts, a triple chair, and a four-passenger gondola. Lift capacity was estimated at 4,000 skiers per day. This figure was considered adequate by the area manager, at least until the 1980–81 season.

Karen felt that the facilities, snow conditions, and grooming compared favorably with that of other destination resorts of the Rockies. "In fact, our only real drawback right now," she thought, "is our position in the national market. We need more skiers who are sold on Big Sky. And that is in the making."

The Consumers

Karen knew from previous dealings that Big Sky, like most destination areas, attracted three distinct skier segments: local day skiers (living within driving distance and not utilizing lodging in the area); individual destination skiers (living out of state and using accommodations in the Big Sky area); and groups of destination skiers (clubs, professional organizations, and the like).

The first category was comprised typically of Montana residents, with a relatively small number from Wyoming and Idaho. (Distances from selected population centers to Big Sky are presented in Exhibit 1.) A 1973 study of four Montana ski areas performed by the advertising unit of the Montana department of highways characterized Montana skiers as:

1. In their early 20s and males (60 percent).
2. Living within 75 miles of a ski area.
3. From a household with two skiers in it.
4. Averaging $13,000 in household income.
5. An intermediate to advanced ability skier.
6. Skiing five hours per ski day, 20 days per season locally.
7. Skiing four days away from local areas.
8. Taking no lessons in the past five years.

Karen was also aware that a significant number of day skiers, particularly on the weekends, were college students.

EXHIBIT 1

A. Population centers in proximity to Big Sky (distance and population)

City	Distance from Big Sky (miles)	Population (U.S. 1970 Census)
Bozeman, Montana	45	18,670
Butte, Montana	126	23,368
Helena, Montana	144	22,730
Billings, Montana	174	61,581
Great Falls, Montana	225	60,091
Missoula, Montana	243	29,497
Pocatello, Idaho	186	40,036
Idaho Falls, Idaho	148	35,776

B. Approximate distance of selected major U.S. population centers to Big Sky (in air miles)

City	Distance to Big Sky*
Chicago	1,275
Minneapolis	975
Fargo	750
Salt Lake City	375
Dallas	1,500
Houston	1,725
Los Angeles	975
San Francisco	925
New York	2,025
Atlanta	1,950
New Orleans	1,750
Denver	750

* Per passenger air fare could be approximated at 20 cents per mile (round trip, coach rates).

Destination, or nonresident skiers, were labeled in the same study as typically:

1. At least in their mid-20s and males (55 percent).
2. Living in a household of three or more skiers.
3. Averaging near $19,000 in household income.
4. More an intermediate skier.
5. Spending about six hours per day skiing.
6. Skiing 11–14 days per season with 3–8 days away from home.
7. Taking ski school lessons.

Through data taken from reservation records, Karen learned that individual destination skiers accounted for half of last year's usage based on skier days.[2] Geographic segments were approximately as follows:

---

[2] A skier day is defined as one skier using the facility for one day of operation.

Upper Midwest (Minnesota, Michigan, North Dakota)	30 percent
Florida	20 percent
California	17 percent
Washington, Oregon, Montana	15 percent
Texas, Oklahoma	8 percent
Other	10 percent

Reservation records indicated that the average length of stay for individual destination skiers was about six or seven days.

It was the individual destination skier who was most likely to buy a lodging/lift package; 30 percent made commitments for these advertised packages when making reservations for 1977–78. Even though there was no discount involved in this manner of buying lift tickets, Karen knew that they were fairly popular because it saved the purchaser a trip to the ticket window every morning. Approximately half of the individual business came through travel agents, who received a 10 percent commission.

The third skier segment, the destination group, accounted for a substantial 20 percent of Big Sky's skier day usage. The larger portion of the group business came through medical and other professional organizations holding meetings at the resort, as this was a way to "combine business with pleasure." These groups were typically comprised of couples and individuals between the ages of 30 and 50. Ski clubs made up the remainder with a number coming from the southern states of Florida, Texas, and Georgia. During the 1977–78 season, Big Sky drew 30 ski clubs with membership averaging 55 skiers. The average length of stay for all group destination skiers was about four or five days.

A portion of these group bookings were made through travel agents, but the majority dealt directly with Karen. The coordinator of the professional meetings or the president of the ski club typically contacted the Big Sky sales office to make initial reservation dates, negotiate prices, and work out the details of their stay.

The Competition

In Karen's mind Big Sky faced two types of competition, that for local day skiers and that for out-of-state (i.e., destination) skiers.

Bridger Bowl was virtually the only area competing for local day skiers. Bridger was a "nonfrills," nonprofit, and smaller ski area located some 16 miles northeast of Bozeman. It received the majority of local skiers including students at Montana State University, which was located in Bozeman. The area was labeled as having terrain more difficult than that of Big Sky and was thus more appealing to the local expert skiers. However, it also had much longer lift lines than Big Sky and had recently lost some of its weekend business to them.

Karen had found through experience that most Bridger skiers usually "tried" Big Sky once or twice a season. Season passes for the two areas were

EXHIBIT 2 Competitors' 1977–1978 package plan rates,* number of lifts, and lift rates

	Lodge double (2)†	Two-bedroom condo (4)	Three-bedroom condo (6)	Number of lifts	Daily lift rates
Aspen, Colo.	$242	$242	$220	19	$13
Steamboat, Colo.	230	230	198	15	12
Jackson, Wyo.	230	242	210	5	14
Vail, Colo.	230	242	220	15	14
Snowbird, Utah	208	none	none	6	11
Bridger Bowl, Mont.	(no lodging available at Bridger Bowl)			3	8

* Package plan rates are per person and include seven nights lodging, six lift tickets (high season rates).

† Number in parentheses denotes occupancy of unit on which price is based.

mutually honored at the half-day rate for an all-day ticket, and Big Sky occasionally ran newspaper ads offering discounts on lifts to obtain more Bozeman business.

For out-of-state skiers, Big Sky considered its competition to be mainly the destination resorts of Colorado, Utah, and Wyoming. (Selected data on competing resorts is presented in Exhibit 2.) Because Big Sky was smaller and newer than the majority of these areas, Karen reasoned, it was necessary to follow an aggressive strategy aimed at increasing its national market share.

Present Policies

Lift Rates

It was common knowledge that there existed some local resentment concerning Big Sky's lift rate policy. Although comparable to rates at Vail or Aspen, an all-day lift ticket was $4 higher than the ticket offered at nearby Bridger Bowl. In an attempt to alleviate this situation, management at Big Sky instituted a $9 "chair pass" for the 1977–78 season, entitling the holder to unlimited use of the three chairs, plus two rides per day on the gondola, to be taken between specified time periods. Because the gondola served primarily intermediate terrain, it was reasoned that the chair pass would appeal to the local, more expert skier. A triple chair serving the bowl area was located at the top of the gondola, and two rides on the gondola would allow those skiers to take ample advantage of the advanced terrain up there. Otherwise, all advanced terrain was served by another chair.

However, if Big Sky was to establish itself as a successful, nationally prominent destination area, Karen felt the attitudes and opinions of all skiers must be carefully weighed. Throughout the season she had made a special effort to grasp the general feeling toward rates. A $12 ticket, she discovered, was thought to be very reasonable by destination skiers, primarily because Big Sky was predominantly an intermediate area and the average destination skier was of intermediate ability; also because Big Sky was noted for its relative lack of lift lines, giving the skier more actual skiing time for the money. ''Perhaps we should keep the price the same,'' she thought, ''we do need more business. Other destination areas are likely to raise their prices and we should look good in comparison.''

Also discussed was the possible abolition of the $9 chair pass. The question in Karen's mind was if its elimination would severely hurt local business or would it sell an all-lift $12 ticket to the skier who had previously bought only a chair pass. The issue was compounded by an unknown number of destination skiers who opted for the cheaper chair pass too.

Season-pass pricing was also an issue. Prices for the 1977–78 all-lift season pass had remained the same as last year, but a season chair pass had been introduced which was the counterpart of the daily chair lift pass. Karen did not like the number of season chair passes purchased in relation to the number of all-lift passes and considered recommending its abolition as well as an increase in the price of the all-lift pass. ''I'm going to have to think this one out carefully,'' she thought, ''because skiing accounted for about 40 percent of our total revenue this past season. I'll have to be able to justify my decision not only to Michigan but also to the Forest Service.''

Price changes were not solely at the discretion of Big Sky management. As is the case with most larger western ski areas, the U.S. government owned part of the land on which Big Sky operated. Control of this land was the responsibility of the U.S. Forest Service, which annually approved all lift pricing policies. For the 1976–77 ski season, Forest Service action kept most lift rate increases to the national inflation rate. For the 1977–78 season, larger price increases were allowed for ski areas which had competing areas near by; Big Sky was considered to be such an area. No one knew what the Forest Service position would be for the upcoming 1978–79 season.

To help her in her decision, an assistant had prepared a summary of lift rates and usage for the past two seasons (Exhibit 3).

Room Rates

This area of pricing was particularly important because lodging accounted for about one third of the past season's total revenue. It was also difficult because of the variety of accommodations (Exhibit 4) and the difficulty in accurately forecasting next season's demand. For example, the season of 1976–77 had been unique in that a good portion of the Rockies was without snow for the initial months of the winter including Christmas. Big Sky was fortunate in receiving as much snow as it had, and consequently many groups and individuals who were originally headed for Vail or Aspen booked in with Big Sky.

Pricing for the 1977–78 season had been made on the premise that there would be a good amount of repeat business. This came true in part but not as

EXHIBIT 3

A. 1977–78 lift rates and usage summary (136 days operation)

Ticket	Consumer cost	Skier days*	Number season passes sold
Adult all-day all-lift	$ 12	53,400	
Adult all-day chair	9	20,200	
Adult half day	8	9,400	
Child all-day all-lift	8	8,500	
Child all-day chair	5	3,700	
Child half day	6	1,200	
Hotel passes†	12/day	23,400	
Complimentary	0	1,100	
Adult all-lift season pass	220	4,300	140
Adult chair season pass	135	4,200	165
Child all-lift season pass	130	590	30
Child chair season pass	75	340	15
Employee all-lift season pass	100	3,000	91
Employee chair season pass	35	1,100	37

B. 1976–77 lift rates and usage summary (122 days operation)

Ticket	Consumer cost	Skier days	Number season passes sold
Adult all-day	$ 10	52,500	
Adult half day	6.50	9,000	
Child all-day	6	10,400	
Child half day	4	1,400	
Hotel passes†	10/day	30,500	
Complimentary	0	480	
Adult season pass	220	4,200	84
Child season pass	130	300	15
Employee season pass	100	2,300	70

* A skier day is defined as one skier using the facility for one day of operation.
† Hotel passes refers to those included in the lodging/lift packages.

EXHIBIT 4

A. Nightly room rates,* 1977–1978

	Low season range	High season range	Maximum occupancy
Huntley Lodge			
Standard	$ 42–62	$ 50–70	4
Loft	52–92	60–100	6
Stillwater Condo			
Studio	40–60	45–65	4
One-bedroom	55–75	60–80	4
Bedroom w/loft	80–100	90–100	6
Deer Lodge Condo			
One-bedroom	74–84	80–90	4
Two-bedroom	93–103	100–110	6
Three-bedroom	112–122	120–130	8
Hill Condo			
Studio	30–40	35–45	4
Studio w/loft	50–70	55–75	6

EXHIBIT 4 (concluded)

B. Nightly room rates, 1976–1977

	Low season range	High season range	Maximum occupancy
Huntley Lodge			
Standard	$ 32–47	$ 35–50	4
Loft	47–67	50–70	6
Stillwater Condo			
Studio	39–54	37–52	4
One-bedroom	52–62	50–60	4
Bedroom w/loft	60–80	65–85	6
Deer Lodge Condo			
One-bedroom	51–66	55–70	4
Two-bedroom	74–94	80–100	6
Three-bedroom	93–123	100–130	8
Hill Condo			
Studio	28–43	30–45	4
Studio w/loft	42–62	45–65	6

* Rates determined by number of persons in room or condominium unit and do not include lift tickets. Maximums for each rate range apply at maximum occupancy.

much as had been hoped. Occupancy experience had also been summarized for the past two seasons to help Karen make her final decision (Exhibit 5).

As was customary in the hospitality industry, January was a slow period and it was necessary to price accordingly. Low season pricing was extremely important because many groups took advantage of these rates. On top of that, groups were often offered discounts in the neighborhood of 10 percent. Considering this, Karen could not price too high, with the risk of losing individual destination skiers, nor too low, such that an unacceptable profit would be made from group business in this period.

Food Service

Under some discussion was the feasibility of converting all destination skiers to the American Plan, under which policy each guest in the Huntley Lodge would be placed on a package to include three meals daily in a Big Sky-controlled facility. There was a feeling both for and against this idea. The parent company had been successfully utilizing this plan for years at its destination areas in northern Michigan. Extending the policy to Big Sky should find similar success.

Karen was not so sure. For one thing, the Michigan resorts were primarily self-contained and alternative eateries were few. For another, the whole idea of extending standardized policies from Michigan to Montana was suspect. As an example, Karen painfully recalled a day in January when Big Sky "tried on" another successful Michigan policy of accepting only cash or check payments

EXHIBIT 5

A.   1977–1978 Lodge-condominium occupancy (in room-nights*)

	December (26 days operation)	January	February	March	April (8 days operation)
Huntley Lodge	1,830	2,250	3,650	4,650	438
Condominiums†	775	930	1,350	100	90

B.   1976–1977 Lodge-condominium occupancy (in room-nights)

	December (16 days operation)	January	February	March	April (16 days operation)
Huntley Lodge	1,700	3,080	4,525	4,300	1,525
Condominiums‡	600	1,000	1,600	1,650	480

C.   Lodge-condominium occupancy (in person-nights§)

December 1977 (1976)	January 1978 (1977)	February 1978 (1977)	March 1978 (1977)	April 1978 (1977)
7,850 (6,775)	9,200 (13,000)	13,150 (17,225)	17,900 (17,500)	1,450 (4,725)

* A room-night is defined as one room (or condominium) rented for one night. Lodging experience is based on 124 days of operation for 1977–78 while Exhibit Three shows the skiing facilities operating 136 days. Both numbers are correct.

† Big Sky had 92 condominiums available during the 1977–78 season.

‡ Big Sky had 85 condominiums available during the 1976–77 season.

§ A person-night refers to one person using the facility for one night.

for lift tickets. Reactions of credit card carrying skiers could be described as ranging from annoyed to irate.

If an American Plan were proposed for next year, it would likely include both the Huntley Lodge Dining Room and Lookout Cafeteria. Less clear, however, were prices to be charged. There certainly would have to be consideration for both adults and children and for the two independently operated eating places in the Mountain Mall (see Exhibit 6 for an identification of eating places in the Big Sky area). Beyond these considerations, there was little else other than an expectation of a profit to guide Karen in her analysis.

The Telephone Call

"Profits in the food area might be hard to come by," Karen thought. "Last year it appears we lost money on everything we sold." (See Exhibit 7.) Just then the telephone rang. It was Rick Thompson, her counterpart at Boyne Mountain Lodge in Michigan. "How are your pricing recommendations coming?" he asked. "I'm about done with mine and thought we should compare notes."

"Good idea, Rick—only I'm just getting started out here. Do you have any hot ideas?"

"Only one," he responded. "I just got off the phone with a guy in Denver. He told me all of the major Colorado areas are upping their lift prices one or two dollars next year."

"Is that right, Rick? Are you sure?"

EXHIBIT 6 Eating places in the Big Sky area

Establishment	Type of service	Meals served	Current prices	Seating	Location
Lodge Dining Room*	A la carte	Breakfast	$2–5	250	Huntley Lodge
		Lunch	2–5		
		Dinner	7–15		
Steak House*	Steak/lobster	Dinner only	6–12	150	Huntley Lodge
Fondue Stube*	Fondue	Dinner only	6–10	25	Huntley Lodge
Ore House†	A la carte	Lunch	.80–4.00	150	Mountain Mall
		Dinner	5–12		
Ernie's Deli†	Deli/restaurant	Breakfast	1–3	25	Mountain Mall
		Lunch	2–5		
Lookout Cafeteria*	Cafeteria	Breakfast	1.50–3.00	175	Mountain Mall
		Lunch	2–4		
		Dinner	3–6		
Yellow Mule†	A la carte	Breakfast	2–4	75	Meadow Village
		Lunch	2–5		
		Dinner	4–8		
Buck's T–4†	Road house restaurant/bar	Dinner only	2–9	60	Gallatin Canyon (2 miles south of Big Sky entrance)
Karst Ranch†	Road house restaurant/bar	Breakfast	2–4	50	Gallatin Canyon (7 miles north of Big Sky entrance)
		Lunch	2–5		
		Dinner	3–8		
Corral†	Road house restaurant/bar	Breakfast	2–4	30	Gallatin Canyon (5 miles south of Big Sky entrance)
		Lunch	2–4		
		Dinner	3–5		

* Owned and operated by Big Sky of Montana, Inc.

† Independently operated.

EXHIBIT 7 Ski season income data (percent)

	Skiing	Lodging	Food and beverage
Revenue	100.0	100.0	100.0
Cost of sales:			
Merchandise	0.0	0.0	30.0
Labor	15.0	15.9	19.7
Maintenance	3.1	5.2	2.4
Supplies	1.5	4.8	5.9
Miscellaneous	2.3	0.6	0.6
Operating expenses	66.2	66.4	66.7
Net profit (loss) before taxes	11.9	7.0	(25.2)

''Well, you know nobody knows for sure what's going to happen but I think it's pretty good information. He heard it from his sister-in-law who works in Vail. I think he said she read it in the local paper or something.''

''That doesn't seem like very solid information,'' said Karen. ''Let me know if you hear anything more, will you?''

''Certainly. You know, we really should compare our recommendations before we stick our necks out too far on this pricing thing. Can you call me later in the week?'' he asked.

''Sure, I'll talk to you the day after tomorrow; I should be about done by then. Anything else?''

''Nope—gotta run. Talk to you then. Bye,'' and he was gone.

''At least I've got some information,'' Karen thought, ''and a new deadline!''

Case 33

Midland Industries (A)*

In late 1986, the overall plastics molding industry was operating at less than two-thirds capacity[1] as shown in Exhibit 1. Lin Love, general manager of Midland Industries of Watertown, New York, was evaluating a potential opportunity to use some of his idle molding capacity by supplying plastic flower pots to customers of a large firm, Harris[2] Products of Toledo, Ohio. Harris had invited Midland and other molders to quote on an initial order of injection-molded flower pots, with the understanding that substantially larger orders could follow a successful bid.

Lin believed that the market for plastic flower pots was highly price sensitive at the wholesale level and was convinced that any bid which exceeded Harris' estimated cost of manufacture would likely be rejected. During the next few days, he had to decide whether Midland should bid on the Harris contract and, if so, under what terms. Midland was currently operating at 45 percent of capacity.

Midland Industries

In 1949, the Betty Lou Shoe Company integrated backward into the molding of plastic shoe parts. Nine years later, the captive molding operation of this company was acquired by Shoe Corporation of America, forming a new division, Midland Plastics. While continuing as a captive supplier, Midland began to use its idle machine capacity to solicit contract business outside the firm. Following acquisition by Pacific Petroleum in 1964, Midland's shift from captive to custom molding was complete.

---

[1] Molders minimized high set-up and purge costs by attempting round-the-clock operation. By industry convention, theoretical capacity was calculated for a work week of five 24-hour days (i.e., 120 hours per week).

[2] Disguised name.

EXHIBIT 1 Rate of capacity utilization in the plastics and rubber products industry

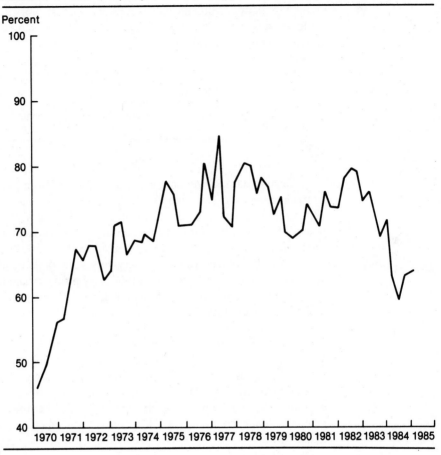

Midland Industries in 1986

Midland was recognized in the plastics molding industry as a leader. According to the trade journal *Plastics:*

> Willingness to experiment—to be first to try something and in the process establish a competitive edge—is the leadership trait that has marked Lin E. Love and the company he heads, Midland Industries, as an innovator in the plastics fields.
>
> For years, he and his company have been in the vanguard of advances in plastics processing—with learned lessons willingly shared among other molders.[3]

Midland had sales of $3.4 million in 1986, and employed 120 full-time

---

[3] Lyn Hamilton, "Taking Yet Another Step in Automatic Molding," *Plastics,* October, 1975, p. 22.

hourly plant workers (approximately 40 per shift) plus 31 salaried workers. As Exhibit 2 shows, Midland had one of the largest work forces in the plastics molding business. The 90,000-square-foot plant shown in Exhibit 3 was roughly allocated as follows:

Production	64,000 square feet
Raw material storage	15,000 square feet
Finished goods storage	5,000 square feet
Office	6,000 square feet

Despite its size, Midland was essentially a custom job shop, molding parts from clock faces to TV cabinets, electric fan blades, and designer tea kettles for 50 or more companies. The median annual business per client was approximately $60,000; however, the largest account approached $750,000 per year. Individual orders ranged in value from $2,000 to $50,000.

Custom molders were frequently very vulnerable to economic downturns, and so many had tried to develop proprietary products and components to boost capacity utilization. Midland, however, had remained strictly a custom contract molder, even through the early 80s recession.

It was no idle boast when Midland claimed to "custom mold plastics of every type into every variety of shape, size, and form utilizing every modern (plastics) manufacturing process." Exhibit 4 lists the varied equipment available for compression, injection, and transfer molding and numerous secondary operations including spray painting, silk screening, hot stamping, heat sealing, welding, and punching. Advanced quality control facilities enabled Midland to guarantee that each product would "consistently meet exact customer specifications." Midland was capable of producing within tolerances of ± .002 inch on many parts it molded.

Specialty molding contracts tended to be low volume. On average, individual runs lasted only two to three days (i.e., 48–72 machine-hours) and were therefore associated with high per unit manufacturing costs, high turnaround

EXHIBIT 2   Plastics fabricating operations: Distribution by size of work force

Number of employees	Percent operations within each category
1–9	30.3%
10–49	45.8
50–99	13.6
100–499	10.1
Over 500	.2
	100.0%

EXHIBIT 3   Floor plan of plant showing storage space available for lease to Midland

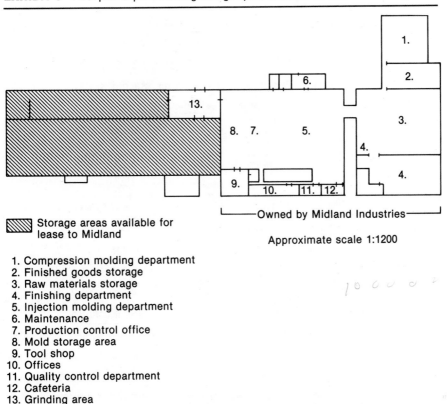

Owned by Midland Industries

Approximate scale 1:1200

Storage areas available for lease to Midland

1. Compression molding department
2. Finished goods storage
3. Raw materials storage
4. Finishing department
5. Injection molding department
6. Maintenance
7. Production control office
8. Mold storage area
9. Tool shop
10. Offices
11. Quality control department
12. Cafeteria
13. Grinding area

costs, substantial investment in raw materials inventory (different types, grades, and colors of resin), complicated production scheduling, and frequent work-in-process delays. Competition in the specialty segment was not entirely price based, and gross margins to the molder normally ranged between 15 and 20 percent. Lin identified the nine injection molders listed in Exhibit 5 as the major direct competitors for specialty contracts in New York.

In contrast, competitors were much more numerous in the molded plastic commodities market segment (drinking cups, combs, buttons, caps, closures, and other relatively low-cost standard design items). Almost 150 molders vied for commodity contracts. Relatively low barriers to entry (an active market in secondhand machinery, relatively simple technology, standard product design) favoured "basement" shops, which followed a low-capitalization, high-capacity utilization strategy. Conversely, firms such as Midland, with greater investment intensity and higher fixed costs, were seriously handicapped in this price-sensitive, high-volume segment.

EXHIBIT 4

General Description of Plant and Equipment

Plant Size — 90,000 square feet
Number of Employees — 150 approximately
Manufacturing Processes — Injection, Compression, Transfer, SMC, Decorating and Finishing

Injection Equipment – 19 Molding Machines

Quantity	Clamp	Shot Size	Type of Feed	Manufacturer
1	100 ton	3½ oz.	Screw	Trubor
1	175 ton	4 oz.	Screw	Reed-Prentice
1	175 ton	4 oz.	Plunger	Reed-Prentice
2	200 ton	8 oz.	Screw	Reed-Prentice
1	200 ton	14 oz.	Screw	Beloit
1	220 ton	14 oz.	Screw	H.P.M.
1	275 ton	8 oz.	Screw	Reed-Prentice
2	300 ton	20 oz.	Screw	Impco
1	300 ton	20 oz.	Screw	Watson-Stillman
1	325 ton	25 oz.	Screw	Beloit
1	375 ton	24 oz.	Screw	Reed-Prentice
1	375 ton	25 oz.	Screw	Beloit
1	400 ton	48 oz.	Screw	H.P.M.
1	450 ton	50 oz.	Screw	Fellows
1	500 ton	48 oz.	Screw	H.P.M.
1	650 ton	75 oz.	Screw	Fellows
1	750 ton	100 oz.	Screw	Beloit

Compression & Transfer Equipment–8 Molding Machines

1	150 ton	Bradley & Turton
1	250 ton	Biraghi
2	250 ton	Bradley & Turton
3	220 ton	Rodgers
1	350 ton	Viceroy

DECORATING & FINISHING EQUIPMENT

12 Spray Painting Booths
12 Hot Stamping Machines (up to 20 ton)
 3 Ultra-Sonic Welding Machines
 1 Heat Sealing Machine
 1 Shrink Tunnel
 1 Wheelabrator Deflasher
 1 Guyson Deflasher
   Drilling Equipment, Silk Screening
   Punching & Auxiliary Equipment

QUALITY CONTROL LABORATORY EQUIPMENT

1 Profile Projector Comparator	— Nikon
1 Daylight Comparator	— Macbeth
1 Flammability Testing Cabinet	— G.M.
1 Impact Testing Machine	— Tinius Olsen
1 Melt Indexer	— Slocomb
1 Moisture Balance	— Ohaus
1 Notching Machine	— Testing Mach.
1 Heat Testing Oven	— Blue M
1 Cold Testing Freezer	— So Low
Miscellaneous Auxiliary Equipment	

COMPUTER MONITORING AND PROCESS CONTROL EQUIPMENT

 Midland Industries

Pricing Policy at Midland Industries

A request for a bid quotation usually represented the starting point of buyer-seller negotiation. Midland submitted bid quotations to prospective buyers on the standard form reproduced in Exhibit 6. A molder's ratio of contracts to bids reflected selectivity in bidding as well as the level of competition from captive

EXHIBIT 5 Main competitors for
specialty molding business
in New York

Allied Plastics
General Electric
Somerville Plastics
Progressive Plastics
Plastomer
Custom Plastics
F and H Plastics
Mitchell Plastics
Plastmade

and custom molders, both domestic and foreign, and capacity utilization. Six
percent of Midland's quotations led to contracts, which was close to the industry
average.

At Midland, a quotation normally covered administrative overhead, selling expense, financial expense, and net profit of 20 percent plus "standard
factory cost." Standard factory cost computations were made as follows:

1. The physical volume of one piece, computed from blueprint dimensions,
    was multiplied by the known density of the molding compound to deter-
    mine weight per thousand and associated resin costs. A scrap allowance
    was then added to the material cost. In the case of the recyclable ther-
    moplastic resins used in injection molding, the material scrap allowance
    represented the expected cost of regrinding.
2. In general, the annual budgeted plant overhead (e.g., indirect labour,
    depreciation, plant salaries, taxes, utilities, repairs) was divided by the
    anticipated number of hours of machine operation during the year. Adjust-
    ments were made in the overhead rates of individual machines to reflect
    different machine sizes and capabilities. The hourly wages of direct labour
    were added to this hourly overhead rate, yielding the "machine-hour
    rate." The expected run length (Cycle times × Number of pieces required
    × Number of mold cavities) was added to allow for time lost while setting
    up the mold, starting up the run, molding imperfect parts, and purging the
    equipment. The total time was multiplied by the machine-hour rate and
    added to the total resin cost, yielding the standard cost estimate.

Lin outlined the Midland approach to bid pricing in a *Plastics* article
reproduced, in part, as Exhibit 7. Implementation of this "realistic full costing"
philosophy encountered practical difficulties such as imperfect cost information
and competition from molders with lower actual or apparent costs, or molders
who were milling, for a particular contract, to bid below their full costs or even
their variable costs in order to "win."

EXHIBIT 6

 Midland Industries   **QUOTATION**

TO   Date

Your Enquiry

Attention

MIL Part No.	ITEM:	Description/Blueprint No.	Production Run Quantity	Shipment(s) Release Period	Price/M

In accordance with Para. 1(a) (reverse side), for every $.01 per Kilogram change in resin cost, the above price(s) will change by $ _____ per M parts. Prices are based on resins costs as of

MOLD SPECIFICATIONS

Injection ☐   Transfer ☐

Compression ☐

Number of Cavities   _____

Complete Mold   _____

Cavities and Cores Only   _____

Approximate Tool Delivery	Tool Price
Estimated Delivery of Samples For Approval	

DESCRIPTION OF SPECIAL FIXTURES

MATERIAL SPECIFICATIONS

PACKAGING SPECIFICATIONS

QUALITY SPECIFICATIONS

Unless otherwise specified below, this quotation is based on 2.5 A.Q.L. to C.G.S.B. Standard 105 G.P.I. and 105 G.P. 2 Dated July 19, 1965 (U.S.A. MIL-Std. - 105D Dated April 29, 1963.)

TERMS:

1. F.O.B.—Our Plant Midland
2. All taxes extra
3. Merchandise—Net 30 days
4. Tooling—Subject to vendor terms
5. 2% per month charged on Overdue Accounts

EXHIBIT 7   Lin Love's views on costing: Excerpts from article published July 1984

Costing or Guessing

Most molders use a machine-hour rate, which includes all plant costs. We can call this "plant overhead," and it would include:

Indirect labor.

Depreciation.

Plant salaries.

Taxes.

Utilities.

Repairs.

It is impossible to go into the details of arriving at machine-hour rates, but generally the total plant overhead is spread over the anticipated hours you expect the plant to operate in a year. Add the direct labor and you have a rate. It sounds simple, but in reality it becomes a real problem because of different machine sizes and capabilities. However, regardless of how you do it, you must recover the total of your fixed and variable costs. All too often molders set their machine-hour rates by the going rate in the marketplace and with no regard for their own costs. What I would like to do is highlight a few areas that are sometimes overlooked and which, if not given serious consideration, may undermine your expected gross profit.

The obvious mechanics of estimating are relatively easy, taking into consideration material cost and packaging supplies. More difficult is estimating the cycle. You will either make money or lose money, depending on how realistic you are at this stage. Of the many variables involved in estimating, all of the major ones involve cycle. These are interrelated, and you must take them all into consideration. To do this, you must know the customer's requirements and quality standards. Otherwise you will find that you cannot perform to standard within the cycle used in your estimate.

Once you have determined the possible cycle, then check for what will be the "average" cycle. These are two entirely different figures and it is the latter one, "the average," that should go into your estimate.

And what about the nasty word *scrap*. Too many molders still think of scrap as a piece of material that can be reclaimed. Stop fooling yourselves about getting all that resin back and especially don't forget you lost machine time and thus lowered your average cycle.

Quantity	1,000	
Scrap	13%	1,130
Cavities		1
Cycle		36
Mlc. size		16 oz.

This first area of scrap allowance is vital if you are going to meet standard costs. Remember, each time you mold a piece of scrap, you must consider the lost machine time as well as lost material. Therefore, if we have a 13 percent scrap factor, we must allow enough machine time to mold 1,130 parts in order to end up with 1,000 good parts. This 13 percent factor is carried through the estimate sheet for material and molding time. How do we get that percentage?

EXHIBIT 7 *(continued)*

Scrap allowance formula

		Class 1 material	Class 2 material
		5%	10%
		Nylon	Acetate
		Polystyrene colors	Polycarbonate
		A.B.S.	Crystal or
		Polyethylene	white materials
High quality	5%	10%	15%
Medium quality	3	8	13
Standard quality	0	5	10

We rate materials and quality requirement of the article. You may not agree with our grouping of materials or scrap allowance. Naturally, if you are fortunate enough to be in production on a single material or exceedingly long runs, this can be modified. But for a custom shop with short runs using many materials, don't sell yourself short. You will need these allowances!

As outlined in the illustration above, if we cross reference a medium quality job with a 3 percent factor and a class 2 material with a 10 percent factor we end up with the 13 percent scrap allowance.

Original preparation costs must be absorbed into the job, regardless of length of run. These preparation costs must include mold set-up time, purging time, and purging material. For each a formula can be developed.

Mold set-up formula

Machine size	Hourly rate	Class 1 (average)	Class 2 (difficult)
4 oz.	$10	1.5 hrs. $15	3.0 hrs. $30
16 oz.	$14	2.5 hrs. $21	5.0 hrs. $70
50 oz.	20	4.0 hrs. 80	8.0 hrs. 160

Note: Rates shown are for example purposes only.

In the illustration above, mold set-ups are divided into two categories, average and difficult. Machine time for mold set-up is lost to you and must be charged to the job. Use your standard machine-hour rate for the size of machine required and multiply it by the number of hours. Thus on the right-hand side, a difficult mold that takes five hours to set up on a 16-oz. machine costs $70, and this becomes one part of your preparatory cost.

Purging formula

Machine size	Hourly rate	Class 1			Class 2		
		Hours	$	Pounds	Hours	$	Pounds
4 oz.	$10	2	20	25	4	40	65
16 oz.	$14	3	$42	50	6	$ 84	80
50 oz.	20	4	80	75	8	160	100

Note: Rates shown are for example purposes only.

In purging we refer back to the class of material previously used, multiply it by the standard machine-hour rate, and obtain the lost machine time during purging. Thus on the right-hand side again, a class 2 material costs $84 of machine time to purge plus 80 pounds of material. This cost must be spread over the total number of parts molded.

EXHIBIT 7 *(continued)*

Short-run penalty 1

Quantity ordered	1M
Hours allowed	15
Total cost	210.00

You never heard of a short-run penalty? Well, you should have! The estimator correctly figured the mold capable of running at a specific cycle. But how do you get the mold settled down to this cycle if the run will last for only three or four shifts? Here is what you can do.

Short-run penalty

Run hours	Penalty hours	4 oz. $10 hr.	16 oz. $14 hr.	50 oz. $20 hr.
30	5	$ 50	$ 70	$100
26	7	70	98	140
22	9	90	126	180
18	11	110	154	220
14	13	130	182	260
10	15	$150	$210	$300
8	16	160	224	320
6	17	170	238	340
4	18	180	252	360

Note: Rates shown are for example purposes only.

Starting at 30 hours use a reversal procedure. The shorter the run, the more hours you charge. By the time you get down to a 10-hour run you charge 15 hours penalty. If you think this is ridiculous, just put a true job costing on some of those short runs and remember it used just as many technicians and engineers to get it started, as a longer run.

	Pounds per 1,000			
Material 3	Net	Gross	Price per pound	
G.P. Styrene	480.7	543.2	.15	81.48
Red No. 2454				
Blue No. 1323				
Less reclaim		62.5	.075	4.69
Total				76.79

The only point in showing the illustration above is to emphasize the original scrap allowance. We previously said because of a 13 percent scrap allowance we would need to mold 1,130 pieces to get 1,000 good ones. Allow for this material and if you so wish you can credit this area for reclaimed scrap.

	Molding Hours per 1,000			
Cycle seconds	Total	Good	$ Rate	Std. cost
36	10.0	11.3	14.00	158.20

On molding extend the actual cycle by the time to mold those 130 extra pieces to arrive at the standard cycle for the job.

EXHIBIT 7 *(concluded)*

Quantity		1 000	4 000	10 000
Short-run penalty	1	210 00		
Preparation cost	2	102 75	25 69	10 28
Material	3	76 79	76 79	76 79
Molding	4	158 20	158 20	158 20
Die repair 5% of 158.20		7 91	7 91	7 91
Supplies	5			
Standard cost (000)	6	555 65	268 59	253 18

The recap, above, shows how the short-run penalty in the first column disappears after the quantity goes up in other columns. It also shows how the preparation costs, mold set-up, and purging are reduced as the quantity goes up. It puts the high cost of "getting going" on the short runs where it belongs. All other costs of material and molding remain constant.

Note that an allowance for the mold repair is based on a percentage of the hours the mold is running. This item eats into your gross profit if it is not specifically tied into the job.

Quantity		1 000	4 000	10 000
Preparation cost				
Molding cost	6	555 65	268 59	253 18
Assembly scrap	% of 6	16 67	8 06	7 60
Secondary operations	8	30 30	30 30	30 30
Supplies	9			
Standard cost		602 62	306 95	291 08

Beyond the molding level there may be secondary operations such as hot stamping, spray painting, or assembly. Many molders, starting into these operations in a small way, figure on absorbing their overhead on molding machine-hour rates. Thus they estimate direct labor only for these secondary operations. However, they do have overhead for these operations, such as supervision, floor space, and equipment costs, and it should be assessed to this operation properly.

Be sure to allow for scrap in this area based on the complete molded cost plus any extended labor or materials that have preceded.

Standard cost

Indirect labour
Plant salaries
Fringe benefits
Repairs
Plant supplies } Plant   Direct labour
Utilities   overhead + material   = Standard
Taxes   cost
Depreciation
Insurance

Finally, we have a standard cost estimate above. This represents, in our system, the manufacturing cost including all of plant expenses mentioned previously.

To arrive at the selling price we must add the following to the cost estimate:

Selling price = Standard cost + Administrative O/H, selling expense, financial expense, profit

These items are handled usually on a percentage basis, relative to your total sales budget forecast. Each firm must make its own decision, to achieve the desired return on investment.

To some extent, the terms of their standard molding contract protected Midland from cost overruns. The most important contract provisions dealt with price, quantity and material:

Price

a.   We reserve the right to increase our prices at any time if such increase(s) become necessary due to higher labour or material costs, or for other reasons beyond our control. However, unfilled orders or unfilled portions thereof which have been entered by us will be filled at the prices originally agreed upon, provided we are able to make shipment within the calendar quarter of order entry. All or part of an accepted order not shipped within the original calendar quarter will be invoiced at prices in effect during calendar quarter(s) in which shipments are made.

[For every $0.01 per kilogram change in resin cost, the quoted price(s) will change by $_____ per thousand parts. Prices are based on resin costs as of _____.]

b.   We also reserve the right to increase the price on any undelivered portion of any order by the amount seller's costs are affected by changes in federal or provincial sales taxes, duties, or rates or exchange.

c.   The prices quoted herein apply only to uninterrupted runs in the quantities specified and are subject to the seller's acceptance when the order is received.

d.   This quotation is subject to revision if not accepted within thirty (30) days from the date hereof.

Quantity

Delivery of 5 percent more or less than the quantity ordered shall constitute fulfillment of the order and any excess within this limit shall be accepted and paid for by the purchaser. If no underrun is specified, the overrun allowance will be increased to 10 percent. If no overrun is specified, the underrun allowance will be increased to 10 percent.

Materials

The purchaser is responsible for disclosing at the outset all pertinent engineering and design requirements and restrictions of the part. Any expense incurred by the seller due to failure of the purchaser to comply with the above will be the responsibility of the purchaser. The seller agrees to supply his professional engineering knowledge to advise the purchaser in every way possible and also draw on the specialized facilities of tool makers, designers, and material suppliers, but the final choice of the most suitable plastic material must ultimately be the responsibility of the purchaser.

Contracts were usually negotiated for large quantities to be delivered in several shipments (i.e., individual "orders") over the course of a year. Normally, each order was produced as a separate run. Orders were shipped as completed and clients billed net 30 days from date of shipment. In practice, Midland adopted a flexible policy with respect to total contract quantity.

Lin noted an industrywide tendency to underestimate or ignore costs in pricing decisions, a trend that was particularly prevalent in times of surplus capacity. Claiming that "competition-based pricing" was "spoiling the market," Lin became chief spokesman for "realistic full-costing plus reasonable return" in an address before the Society of Plastic Industries:

> One of the worst fallacies of the plastic processing industry is trying to plug up machine utilization with incremental costing. Naturally, a case can be made for incremental costing to help pick up the high fixed costs of our type of operation. However, the marketplace becomes flooded with the opportunity to buy at incremental prices. At this stage it becomes incremental no more—it becomes suicidal!
>
> Surely making a profit is the only way to stay in business. Surely it is the only way the customer will have a reliable source of supply. If the industry does not earn reasonable returns on investment, it will not continue to attract capital. If any industry needs capital, it is surely ours. Machinery, modernized and automated, adequate building space, research and control methods all take vast amounts of capital. This money can only come from the financial community, and it won't come from there unless we can prove that the return is forthcoming. Keep this in mind when pricing and don't be misled.

Harris Products

Harris Products marketed a line of flower pots to department stores, discount merchandisers, hardware chains, and nurseries across the United States and Canada. The pots were currently molded for Harris by an Ohio-based custom molding company. The current chain of distribution for the flower pots was as follows:

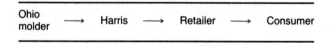

Ohio molder $\longrightarrow$ Harris $\longrightarrow$ Retailer $\longrightarrow$ Consumer

The U.S. market for flower pots and other garden accessories had seen explosive growth. According to *Merchandising Week:*

> It's no secret. Creeping charlies, boston ferns, diffenbachias are big business and the "greening" of housewares is accelerating at a phenomenal rate.
>
> Spurred by intense consumer interest in home horticulture plus the lure of fast turns and a high profit structure, housewares buyers are finding sales of pots, plants, and plant-related accessories sprouting all over the country.

Department stores and mass merchandisers have added or expanded these sections. . . . In fact, the category is growing at such a pace that it merits its own buyer in some stores.

Retail margins can run as high as 70 percent on plants (sometimes higher). . . . Planters can realize margins from 30 percent to 60 percent in assortments including plastic, ceramic, clay, wicker, basket, wood, and glass. Plastic and ceramic are said to be the number one and two most popular sellers. The key to . . . planters seems to be wide assortment with colorful designs balanced by those in natural tones.

A popular retail price point for plastic pots is about $1.50, while it's around $2.50 for ceramic. Baskets are popular near the $2 mark, while clay is good at $1 and under.[4]

The year 1986 had seen "continued strong growth" in U.S. demand and the emergence of a similar pattern in Canada. Harris had found a sales agent to promote and sell in New York State, where sales were weak. The agent predicted that Harris' sales would exceed 1 million flower pots in 1987 in New York, as shown in Exhibit 8. Their sales in 1986 had been 118,000 pots.

Equipped with 19 injection molding machines and a full-time work force

EXHIBIT 8   Harris forecast of their New York sales, 1987

Model		Forecast sales (000 units)
BP-11		30
BP-13		25
BP-15		22
LP-3		30
LP-4		55
LP-5		70
LP-6		80
LP-7	(item 1)	45
LP-11	(item 2)	45
#400		25
#430		25
#440		45
#450		40
#470	(item 3)	45
CS-4		65
CS-5		75
CS-6		80
CS-7		80
CS-8		70
CS-11		40
CS-13		30
CS-15		25
CS-17		25
Total		1,072

_____

[4] "Pots and Plants Bloom amid the Pots and Pans," *Merchandising Week*, October 6, 1985, p. 1.

of 140 employees, Harris' current Ohio molder could continue to handle the extra pot production caused by this sales growth, at least in the short term.

However, several factors weighed against this approach. Major Harris retail customers were highly price sensitive and demanded fast, direct delivery to minimize their inventory costs. Plastic finished goods from out of state were subject to a New York excise tax of 15 percent, which had to be paid by the retailer. Moreover, Harris was concerned that New York excise tax disagreements would cause competitively disadvantageous delays and expense. Operating a warehouse to service New York customers would add fixed costs in the order of $15,000 per year.

These problems had prompted Harris to consider New York pot manufacture for the New York market. They had sought a long-term relationship with a suitable custom injection molder willing to make, package, store, invoice, and ship flower pots to their retail customers, at an all-inclusive unit price comparable to their laid-in cost from Ohio.

Harris' basic requirements somewhat limited the number of New York molders eligible for bid consideration. Their prerequisites included:

1. A wide range of molding equipment—to accommodate all 23 sizes/styles in the Harris flower pot line.
2. Scheduling flexibility—to "work around" the production timetable of their molder. Harris owned only one set of flower pot molds. These were held in the custody of their molder. Since duplicate molds would cost an additional $15,000 each, Phillips intended to shuttle the molds back and forth across the state line, at an estimated cost of $50 per mold (round trip).
3. Storage space—to house raw materials (i.e., four colours of polypropylene resin and 20 different sizes of paper cartons) plus finished inventory.

In December 1986 Harris asked Midland to submit a quotation on an initial order for three flower pot models for 5,000 units of each. Harris would not guarantee purchase volume beyond this initial order. Lin also knew that Harris wanted a minimum margin themselves of about 20 percent in marketing the flower pots.

The Bid Pricing Decision

Lin Love believed Midland had the range of molding equipment and scheduling flexibility necessary to accommodate Harris. He was also confident that any additional area required to store resins, packaging materials, and finished goods could be leased on neighbouring property. Lin was less sure of Midland's ability to sell at a price agreeable to Harris and still make an acceptable return. As he reviewed the opportunity, he became more aware of the uncertainties in available cost/market information and wondered about the level of risk in the situation. On the other hand, Lin knew that any bid which grossly exceeded the laid-in cost of Ohio-produced pots would be rejected. He had made estimates of the Ohio molder's cost, but did not know its exact selling price to Harris. Harris would not reveal this information to him.

Harris flower pots were molded using a polypropylene resin, which was currently selling at 32.3 cents in New York compared to 26.5 cents per pound in Ohio. Prices of the various resins were volatile, reflecting a complex interplay of factors, including the capacity of resin producers, the demand for different resins, and the prices of petroleum feedstocks, among others.

Harris provided molding cycle times for each flower pot mold based on information from their supplier. Item 1 was molded in a double-cavity die, producing two pots every 46 seconds, while items 2 and 3 were molded singly every 40.6 seconds and 46.4 seconds, respectively. Although Midland had no previous experience molding flower pots, Lin was confident that it would be no more difficult than many other items they were molding.

The three flower pot models would be molded on separate machines, each assigned a different machine-hour rate:

	Variable	Fixed	Machine-hour rate
Item 1	$10.15	$18.95	$29.10
Item 2	7.40	7.80	15.20
Item 3	8.25	10.95	19.20

Lin believed Harris' current supplier's variable processing costs (mostly direct labor) more comparable to those at Midland. He was also fairly certain that, proportionately, annual fixed overhead was similar for both firms, although higher annual volume would lower the Ohio supplier's fixed costs on a per unit basis. Lin estimated machine-hour rates at the Ohio supplier as below:

	Variable	Fixed	Estimated machine-hour rate
Item 1	$10	$10	$20
Item 2	7	3	10
Item 3	8	4	12

Lin also expected Midland to match the Ohio supplier's "preparation" times (i.e., set-up and purge) but felt that shorter run lengths at Midland would raise per unit costs. The average run at Midland would be 5,000 flower pots, only one third the average run at the Ohio supplier.

Almost entirely variable, Midland's packaging expenses per thousand units were estimated as follows:

Item 1	$37.40
Item 2	40.60
Item 3	47.43

Lin knew packaging was less expensive in Ohio, since a recent study conducted by SPI had shown that New York molders spent approximately 25–30 percent more than their Ohio counterparts for equivalent packaging.

EXHIBIT 9 Estimated cost of producing initial order for Midland (cost per 1,000 units expressed in $)

	Item 1	Item 2	Item 3
Resin cost per pound	$ .323	$ .323	$ .323
Pounds of resin required/1,000 units*	580	604	620
Total resin cost/1,000 units	$187.34	$194.90	$200.26
Number of pots/cycle	2	1	1
Standard average cycle time	46 sec.	40.6 sec.	46.4 sec.
Gross molding hours/1,000 units*	6.4 hrs.	11.13 hrs.	12.9 hrs.
Machine-hour rate†	$ 29.10	$ 15.20	$ 19.20
Total machine cost/1,000 units	$186.25	$168.95	$247.70
Preparation time per run‡	1 hr.	1 hr.	1 hr.
Preparation time cost/1,000 units	$ 5.80	$ 3.05	$ 3.85
Packaging cost/1,000 units	$ 37.40	$ 40.60	$ 47.43
Total estimated factory cost	$416.79	$407.50	$499.24

* Includes 5 percent scrap allowance.

†

	Item 1	Item 2	Item 3
Variable	$ 10.15	$ 7.40	$ 8.25
Fixed	18.95	7.80	10.95
Total machine-hour rate	$ 29.10	$ 15.20	$ 19.20

‡ Assumes run of 5,000 units.

Midland had adequate storage space to accommodate the initial order. If, however, sales projections proved accurate, Midland would need approximately 1,000 square feet of additional space to accommodate subsequent orders. Room was available in an adjacent building for $4/square foot on a yearly basis. Storage costs would have to be fully absorbed into the unit price, as Harris refused to pay warehousing charges directly. Exhibit 9 summarizes the factory

EXHIBIT 10 Estimated molder cost of producing initial order at the current Ohio molder's plant (cost per 1,000 units expressed in $)

	Item 1	Item 2	Item 3
Resin cost per pound	$ .265	$ .265	$ .265
Pounds of resin required/1,000 units*	580	604	620
Total resin cost/1,000 units	$153.70	$160.05	$164.30
Number of cavities (i.e., pots/cycle)	2	1	1
Gross molding hours/1,000 units*	6.4	11.13	12.9
Machine-hour rate*	$ 26.00	$ 13.50	$ 16.50
Total machine cost	$166.40	$150.25	$212.85
Preparation time per run (hrs.)†	1	1	1
Preparation time cost/1,000 units	$ 1.70	$ .90	$ 1.10
Packaging/1,000 units	$ 29.20	$ 34.45	$ 40.20
Total estimated factory cost	$351.00	$345.65	$418.45

* Includes 5 percent scrap allowance.
† Assumes run of 15,000 units.

cost projections for Midland Industries. Similar estimates for Harris' current molder appear in Exhibit 10.

There would likely be no significant differences in selling and administration costs whether the pots were produced in New York or Ohio. Furthermore, the shipping charges on the finished flower pots (borne by Harris customers) were roughly the same FOB the Ohio supplier's plant as FOB Watertown, New York.

Lin questioned whether the differences between Harris' laid-in cost from Ohio and Midland's costs would ensure Midland "reasonable" profit, which he considered should be 20 percent. He reviewed the terms on the quotation sheet and wondered how much Midland could rely on the estimates. Lin had only three days to decide whether Midland should bid for the Harris business, and if so, on what terms. He knew that, given the excess capacity in the industry, competition for the business would be fierce.

Part 8

Marketing and Public Policy*

The current environment of the marketing manager is one undergoing rapid change and transition. Probably the most noteworthy of these developments, whether for better or for worse, is the increasing pervasiveness of "public" influences on marketing institutions and decision making. In this context, public influences are generally defined to include different levels of government (acting through legislation, regulation, or moral suasion), organized public groups (the consumerism movement, for example), individual advocates of change, and the force of changing public attitudes and opinion.

The cases in this section seek to develop an improved understanding of some of these trends and developments, and to provide practice for students in rendering decisions in the contemporary environment. The specific objectives of the cases are as follows:

1. To improve capacity for marketing decision making in situations where public influences are involved.
2. To explore the nature and extent of public influences on marketing institutions and decision making.
3. To develop conceptual foundations leading to an improved understanding of contemporary developments in marketing.

Approaches to decision making in the area of marketing and public policy are not well established. One possible approach makes three assumptions. They are as follows:

---

* This note draws heavily on the work of Professor Michael Pearce of the University of Western Ontario.

1. Marketing and public policy decisions are made in a bargaining arena containing many interest groups.
2. Either explicit or implicit bargaining takes place among the interest groups in this arena whenever a marketing decision involves public influences.
3. Better decisions will be made if the objectives, motivations, and behaviors of each interest group are understood.

With the assumptions in mind, we now shall present an approach to decision making in this area:

1. List and/or diagram the interest groups involved in a particular decision context. Note the interrelationships among them.
2. Identify the behavior of each group.
3. Attempt to explain this behavior by examining the objectives, motivations, and values of the people comprising the groups.
4. Identify what each group stands to lose or gain in the bargaining.
5. Identify what each group might be most willing to give up. What would they most want in return?
6. Based upon this analysis, predict the likely strategies of each group.
7. Make a decision based upon the anticipated reaction of each group to the alternatives you are considering. Be sure to have a contingency in case their reactions are not as you anticipated.

Case 34

F&F Sales Company*

Tom Frolik leaned back in his chair and reflected upon the events that had taken place earlier that day. His first day back to work after a long weekend over New Year's had really been hectic. Apparently while he had been on his skiing vacation, an article had appeared in the morning newspaper indicating that the Georgia State Troopers were upset about the effectiveness of radar detectors such as the Fuzzbusters that he marketed, and had encouraged several legislators to introduce a bill for the upcoming General Assembly outlawing these devices in Georgia. The phone had been ringing all day with many people calling to order a Fuzzbuster before their sale became illegal. Recognizing the potential consequences of this act for his company, he decided to develop a complete plan of action in the next few days.

Background on Radar Detector

The first radar detectors were marketed in the early 1960s. Typically, the units were not very high quality and sold for a price between $19.95 and $29.95. These units clipped onto the visor and would emit a beep when police radar was detected, allowing the driver to slow down before being caught in a radar trap. Although these units were relatively unsophisticated, several companies were somewhat successful in marketing them through mail-order advertising. With speed limits of 70 or 75 mph on most highways, however, most people did not have a need for these units.

Things changed dramatically beginning in 1973 with the fuel crisis and oil embargo. Speed limits were reduced nationally to 55 mph and were often enforced. The first response to this development was a dramatic increase in the sale of Citizens Band (CB) radios, which had been in existence for a number of years, but had experienced a very low level of sales. Many truckers purchased these units, and soon thereafter salesmen and other individuals who had to drive a great deal began purchasing CB units. By 1975, the general public started buying CB radios in great numbers.

There were several problems with the CB radios as a means of avoiding speeding tickets. First, as more and more amateurs started using their radios, the channels became very cluttered. Often it was hard to hear what people were

* Written by Kenneth L. Bernhardt. Copyright © 1980 by Kenneth L. Bernhardt.

saying, as many people tried to use the same channel. Second, the CB radio became less and less reliable as the police (Smokey the Bear) put CB radios in their cars also. Thus, they could receive the same messages that truckers and other drivers were sending to each other. Third, the CB radio became much less reliable at night with the users' inability to see the police speed trap in the dark.

In addition to the problems with the effectiveness of CB radios, the state of the art on radar increased substantially about this time. With the old police radar units, about all they could do was set up a radar trap. New mobile radar units were developed that allowed the policemen to get a radar reading on a speeding car while the police car was moving. Another dramatic development was the ability of police radar to determine the speed of a car even though the police car was going in the opposite direction. Thus, a police officer could detect a speeding car going in the other direction, make a U-turn and arrest the speeder, something that was unheard of previously.

It was in this environment of reduced speed limits, increased enforcement, reduced effectiveness of CB radios, and increased effectiveness of police radar that the Fuzzbuster was introduced by the Electrolert Company in 1975. The Fuzzbuster, a military-type, parametric radar receiver, is sensitive to one/one hundredth of one-millionth of one watt, approximately the strength of radar at three miles if not blocked or otherwise attenuated. The Fuzzbuster receives in the 10.5 GHz Amateur (ham microwave) Band.

Drawing less than one quarter of a watt power, the Fuzzbuster can be left on indefinitely. It is installed on the dash of the car and has a self-contained antenna. The unit plugs into the cigarette lighter. When radar is picked up by the receiver, a warning light goes on and at the same time, a high-pitched tone is generated. The tone cuts off after two to three seconds, but the lamp remains bright until the radar signal ceases. The Fuzzbuster provides this identification of radar up to three miles distant. A pamphlet describing the Fuzzbuster is reproduced in Exhibit 1.

Background on Tom Frolik and F&F Sales Company

Tom Frolik first became aware of Fuzzbusters in January 1976, when he was working as a consultant to a large truck stop on Interstate 75 in Georgia. At that time Fuzzbusters had a suggested retail price of $99.95 and were sold to the retailer for $75. The truck stop ordered one dozen and sold them. They then ordered another dozen, and these also sold quite rapidly. Mr. Frolik then contacted the Electrolert Company and worked out an arrangement to become a distributor. The truck stop had a warehouse distribution subsidiary which bought replacement parts for trucks, and this subsidiary became an Electrolert distributor. About this time some product improvements were made, the most important being the introduction of a flashing light in addition to the beep when radar was detected, and the retail price was increased to $109.95. The wholesale price was $79.

The price to the distributor was $59 per unit, but they had to order in gross

EXHIBIT 1

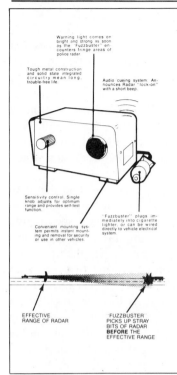

Warning light comes on bright and strong as soon as the "Fuzzbuster" encounters fringe areas of police radar.

Tough metal construction and solid state integrated circuitry mean long, trouble-free life.

Audio cueing system. Announces Radar "lock-on" with a short beep.

Sensitivity control. Single knob adjusts for optimum range and provides self-test function.

"Fuzzbuster" plugs immediately into cigarette lighter, or can be wired directly to vehicle electrical system.

Convenient mounting system permits instant mounting and removal for security or use in other vehicles.

EFFECTIVE RANGE OF RADAR

"FUZZBUSTER" PICKS UP STRAY BITS OF RADAR **BEFORE** THE EFFECTIVE RANGE

Complete protection for

$109.95

FUZZBUSTER

IS MADE EXCLUSIVELY BY

ELECTROLERT, inc.

Troy, Ohio 45373

DISTRIBUTED BY

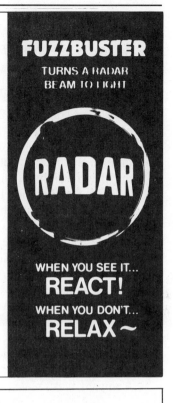

FUZZBUSTER

TURNS A RADAR BEAM TO LIGHT

RADAR

WHEN YOU SEE IT...
REACT!

WHEN YOU DON'T...
RELAX ~

FUZZBUSTER

Parametric Radar Receiver

Put a **Fuzzbuster** on your Dash and you can drive relaxed again. No watching for Radar lurking in the bushes, or trying to make sense out of the C.B. Radio chatter. And you don't have to put up with squeals or growls that warn you too late, or when there isn't any Radar around. Now you can enjoy the drive, anytime, anyplace . . . tension free.

The **Fuzzbuster** has been proven by tens of thousands of truckers over billions of miles, nationwide . . . so effective it has become a highway legend!

The **Fuzzbuster** was designed by a Speed Radar Manufacturer, and is a thoroughly engineered military type parametric radar receiver. Its performance is absolutely unparalleled. All solid-state integrated circuit construction insures extreme sensitivity and reliability.

The **Fuzzbuster** is equipped with a revolutionary audio cueing system which alerts you with a short beep each time the receiver locks on to a Radar signal. At the same time: the **Fuzzbuster** gives you positive visual indication of stationary or moving Radar ("New Vascar") two to ten times farther than the range of the Radar. You'll have ample time to slow down. With a little practice, the visual indicator can even tell you where and what kind of speed trap you are encountering.

The **Fuzzbuster** mounts quickly on the Dashboard and plugs directly into your cigar lighter, or you can wire it directly. It automatically adapts to positive or negative ground systems. The black matte finish prevents glare, and blends with any interior.

It works!

- **Sensitive** to 1/100th of a millionth of **one watt** microwave energy.
- **Many times** more **sensitive** and **selective** than nearest pretender.
- **Works two to ten times** farther than Radar **without** the frequent **false alarms** of other detectors.
- **Draws** less than ¼ **watt . . . indefinite life.**
- **12 volt positive** or **negative** ground.
- **No antenna — no involved installation.**
- **Receives** all **X-Band** Radars **in all states.**
- Especially **effective** on new **Moving Radar,** used by 40 states.
- **Works day** or **night . . . city** or **highway.**
- **Half the cost** of a good **C.B. Radio.**

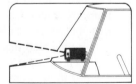

Give the **Fuzzbuster** a good view of the road ahead, and it will spot those electronic ambushes long before the Radar can spot you!

(a gross is 144 units). The manufacturer provided sample advertising mats and allowed $3 per unit for co-op advertising allowances. In March 1976, the truck stop ordered its first gross and at the same time, reduced the retail price to $84.95. Mr. Frolik recalled that they sold like hotcakes at this price, but because of complaints from those who had paid $109.95, and a feeling that a higher price would not hurt sales, they decided to raise the price to $89.95.

The truck stop distributor subsidiary made no attempt to sell Fuzzbusters through any other outlets, but did sell them through a second truck stop which they had recently purchased.

By October they had sold five gross (720 units) and were told that they had a big backup on the co-op advertising allowance. At the same time, the owner of the truck stop began to have some guilt feelings about marketing the product and decided he did not want to advertise it using his company name.

In late October, Tom Frolik announced that he was leaving the truck stop company to move to Atlanta to establish his own consulting firm and start several entrepreneurial enterprises. The owner of the truck stop suggested that Frolik market in the Atlanta area some of the products that the truck stop's distributor subsidiary handled. Frolik suggested that he be given the use of the advertising allowance credit for the Fuzzbuster, that he put in the time on the project, and that the truck stop owner and he split the profits on an equal basis. His proposal was accepted by the truck stop owner, and thus F&F Sales Company was created.

In November when Frolik came to Atlanta, the advertising allowance was up to $2,200. The Electrolert Company would pay 50 percent of all advertising expenditures for the Fuzzbuster up to this amount, but they would pay 100 percent of the expenses for newspaper advertising. Because of this provision, Frolik decided to take out some ads in *The Atlanta Journal* and *Constitution*. Exhibit 2 contains the ad that was approved by Electrolert. Mr. Frolik decided to run the ad four times—Sunday, December 12, the evening of December 16, the morning of December 17, and Sunday, December 19. These four ads, at an average of approximately $550 each, would utilize the full co-op advertising allowance available.

After the December 12 ad ran, with minimal response, Mr. Frolik changed the ad by inserting the telephone number of his office where people could call for further information or to place an order which would be charged to a bank credit card (using the truck stop's bank credit card mechanism). The four ads resulted in the immediate sale of 60 Fuzzbusters, with approximately half the people calling in for information before sending in their order. Mr. Frolik indicated that most of these buyers were salesmen, rather than truckers.

Three other outlets in Atlanta were advertising Fuzzbusters at this time. Two of these were retailers which took out small ads at a price of $99.95 and $109.95, with both stores requiring the consumer to come to the retail outlet to purchase the Fuzzbuster. The third source was a firm in Alabama that offered a toll-free number together with a coupon in the ad for ordering. This firm, which

EXHIBIT 2

accepted credit cards, charged $89.95 plus tax and handling ($3.50 for the tax and handling, the same as F&F Sales charged).

Although there were several other companies which marketed similar kinds of products, Mr. Frolik felt that the Fuzzbuster was the best radar detector available on the market. In the Atlanta area, these competitors had virtually no distribution.

Current Situation

As a result of the four ads in the middle of December, Mr. Frolik had been quite optimistic about sales of the Fuzzbuster. He had a number of ideas which he was planning to implement to increase sales, including taking out some classified advertising in the CB radio section of the classified ads. He also knew that Radio Shack stores did not stock Fuzzbusters or competitors, so he planned to write to the 43 Radio Shack store managers in his area and ask them to send any customers who requested this product to him.

Thus, all was very rosy for F&F Sales Company and Mr. Frolik when he left on Friday, December 24 for a 10-day skiing vacation. By the time he returned to the office on January 3, things were quite different. Exhibit 3 contains the article which ran in the morning *Atlanta Constitution* on Friday, December 31 describing the plan by the Georgia State Troopers to outlaw Fuzzbusters. Exhibit 4 contains the proposed legislation that would be introduced in the Georgia legislature. Mr. Frolik had read that the Virginia legislature had banned the devices several years earlier, but that the public outcry against such action had been so strong that legislation lifting the ban on radar detectors was under consideration in that state, and had a high likelihood of passing.

Mr. Frolik realized that his vacation was over and that he would have to develop a plan of action for the next few weeks. His first thought was that none of the cases he had studied during his M.B.A. program at a well-known eastern business school had dealt with this type of problem.

EXHIBIT 3 Fuzzbuster newspaper article

Fuzz Busters Really Work— Troopers Want Radar Detectors Outlawed

By Keeler McCartney

Georgia state troopers are up in arms over the latest gadgets some motorists are using to detect highway radar speed timers, and they want the upcoming General Assembly to do something about it.

Bill Wilson, information officer of the state Department of Public Safety, said the gadgets in question detect the presence of radar machines and warn drivers before the troopers have a chance to detect speeders.

"It just isn't fair," Wilson said.

He said the warning devices, usually mounted on the dashboards of autos and trucks, can be purchased for $99.95 under the suggestive trade names of "Fuzz Busters," "Bear Finders" and "Trooper Snoopers."

As they approach radar stations, drivers equipped with the devices are alerted by a variety of noises ranging from the wail of an upended talking doll to the buzz of an angry bee and the beep of a telephone answering service.

The safety department has prepared a bill to submit to the next General Assembly which would make it a misdemeanor to possess, manufacture, or sell the devices in Georgia.

Troopers have checked the devices and found that they do, indeed, give the driver ample warning to slow down to the legal 55-mile limit before he enters a radar field, Wilson declared.

State Patrol Capt. R. C. Womack, who conducted a series of the tests in the Thomson and Savannah areas, concluded his findings this way:

"These devices are very demoralizing to the trooper who works the road day after day attempting to enforce the national speed limit. It is also a pathetic situation when a $100 device can counteract a $2,000 piece of equipment being used by law enforcement officers."

The troopers may be down because of the radar warning detectors, but they definitely are not out. They've worked up a trick or two of their own to beat the gadgets.

One of their favorites is to keep the radar speed timer turned off until the driver is well within range and then flick it on.

"The warning device will sound, all right," Wilson grinned. "But it's too late. The driver has already been caught."

And troopers have figured out the Citizens' Band (CB) lingo that goes with the use of radar detectors.

A favorite among truck drivers is, "My bird dogs are barking."

While awaiting legislative action, the troopers are collecting advertisements of the warning gadgets.

"Put a——on your dash and you can drive relaxed again," one ad suggests.

"No watching for radar lurking in the bushes or trying to make sense out of the CB radio chatter," says another. "And you don't have to put up with squeaky bleeps that warn you too late. Now you can enjoy the drive."

Wilson said legislation which the safety department is seeking is similar to laws already passed in the states of Virginia and Connecticut and the cities of Denver, Colo., and Washington, D.C.

Reprinted with permission from *The Atlanta Constitution,* December 31, 1976, p. 1.

EXHIBIT 4 Proposed legislation

H.B. No. 545
By: Representatives Milford of the 13th, Coleman of the 118th, Smith of the 42nd, McDonald of the 12th and Childs of the 51st

A BILL TO BE ENTITLED

AN ACT

To prohibit the use of devices on motor vehicles used to detect the presence of radar upon highways; to prohibit the operation of motor vehicles so equipped; to prohibit the sale of such devices; to provide for penalties; to provide an effective date; to repeal conflicting laws; and for other purposes.

BE IT ENACTED BY THE GENERAL ASSEMBLY OF GEORGIA:

Section 1. Prohibiting use of devices on motor vehicles to detect presence of radar upon highways or operation of motor vehicles so equipped or sale of such devices. It shall be unlawful for any person to operate a motor vehicle upon the highways of this State when such vehicle is equipped with any device or mechanism to detect the emission of radio microwaves in the electromagnetic spectrum, which microwaves are employed by police to measure the speed of motor vehicles upon the highways of this State for law enforcement purposes; it shall be unlawful to use any such device or mechanism upon any such motor vehicle upon the highways; it shall be unlawful to sell any such device or mechanism in this State. Provided, however, that the provisions of this section shall not apply to any receiver of radio waves of any frequency lawfully licensed by any State or federal agency.

Section 2. Any person, firm, or corporation violating the provision of this Act shall be guilty of a misdemeanor and, upon conviction thereof, shall be punished as for a misdemeanor, and any such prohibited device or mechanism shall be forfeited to the court trying the case.

Section 3. The presence of any such prohibited device or mechanism in or upon a motor vehicle upon the highways of this State shall constitute prima facie evidence of the violation of this section. The State need not prove that the device in question was in an operative condition or being operated.

Section 4. This section shall not apply to motor vehicles owned by the State or any political subdivision thereof and which are used by the police of any such government nor to law enforcement officers in their official duties, nor to the sale of any such device or mechanism to law enforcement agencies for use in their official duties.

Section 5. This Act shall become effective upon its approval by the Governor or upon its becoming a law without his approval.

Section 6. All laws and parts of laws in conflict with this Act are hereby repealed.

Case 35

AUTOCAP*

On November 7, William Carey, vice chairman of the Georgia Automotive Consumer Action Panel (AUTOCAP), was reviewing files on the five cases to be discussed at AUTOCAP's regular monthly meeting the following day. Carey was one of three consumer representatives on the panel; the other four members of the seven-person panel, including the chairman, were automobile dealers. Each member came to the meetings prepared to discuss each of the cases and to suggest resolutions to the disputes involved.

The five cases to be discussed represented consumer complaints that had not already been successfully resolved by the staff of AUTOCAP. Each month several times this number of cases were successfully resolved by the staff without review by the full panel. In fact, it had been found that about 80 percent of the consumer complaints received by AUTOCAP could be resolved simply by establishing direct communication between the customer and the dealership's owner or general manager (rather than the sales or service departments). More often than not, the dealer was simply unfamiliar with the problem, and customer dissatisfaction could be traced to improper handling by dealership personnel, poor customer-dealership communication, or manufacturer defects.

In addition to reviewing the case files, Carey was reflecting upon the role of AUTOCAP in general, its effectiveness since its inception six months earlier, and consumer awareness of AUTOCAP, issues which he planned to bring up for discussion at the meeting.

History of AUTOCAP

In the past few years there has been rapid expansion in the number of consumer complaints. A variety of alternative complaint resolution mechanisms have been established, including state and local government agencies, trade association organizations such as the Better Business Bureaus and consumer action panels, private, nonprofit consumer organizations, corporate complaint handling departments, and the President's Office of Consumer Affairs in Washington. At the same time, the number of consumer-oriented bills introduced in Congress and major pieces of consumer legislation enacted by Congress have skyrocketed.

---

* This case was prepared by Kenneth L. Bernhardt and Sherri McIntyre. Copyright © 1987 by Kenneth L. Bernhardt. Names of consumers and auto dealers in the case have been changed.

AUTOCAP is an example of the attempt made in several industries (including the automobile, major appliance, and furniture industries) to handle their own consumer complaints by establishing consumer action panels and to reduce thereby the need for government intervention in industry affairs. The first AUTOCAP was introduced as a pilot program developed by the National Automobile Dealers Association and the Automotive Trade Association of the Nation's Capital, with the endorsement of the White House Office of Consumer Affairs. The basic objectives of AUTOCAP are:

1. To establish channels at the state and local levels for automotive customers to voice their complaints and obtain action.
2. To take automotive complaints out of the offices of congressmen and federal and state consumer agencies.
3. To demonstrate to government and consumers that automobile dealers can and will resolve customer problems.
4. To promote an improved dealer image, more satisfied customers, and less government interference in the affairs of the retail automobile business.

AUTOCAP strives to make the automotive retailing industry more responsive to the needs and desires of the consuming public and to alleviate the breakdown in communication between business and the public largely responsible for the frustration consumers can experience in today's marketplace.

The Georgia AUTOCAP was one of 35 AUTOCAPs throughout the country (22 state organizations and 13 city organizations). Establishment of the Georgia AUTOCAP by the Georgia Automobile Dealers Association in cooperation with the governor's office was met with some opposition. The controversy involved whether an industry can handle its own complaints or if state, local, and federal agencies are better able to resolve these consumer complaints, an issue that has caused a great deal of disagreement.

The major opponent of the Georgia AUTOCAP was the administrator of the governor's Office of Consumer Affairs, who was quoted as claiming that: (1) the panel was an "industry ploy" to dilute the effectiveness of his own agency; (2) if the panel met only once a month and had only one full-time staff member, it could not be effective; (3) the panel would be weighted toward the industry since four of its seven members would come from the automobile dealership business; and (4) information from consumer affairs offices around the country indicated that AUTOCAP did not work. The major proponent of the panel, the governor's chief assistant, argued that business was capable of resolving its own problems and should be encouraged to do so.

Operating Procedures of Georgia AUTOCAP

The Georgia AUTOCAP was established as a free-of-charge community service of the Georgia Automobile Dealers Association for handling complaints concerning its members. An 800 WATS line number was established for calling AUTOCAP toll-free from anywhere in the state of Georgia. Consumers were made aware of AUTOCAP's services mainly by means of brochures available at the dealerships and periodic announcements pertaining to the program released to the public by the Georgia Automobile Dealers Association through news releases sent to the various media.

The AUTOCAP panel was appointed by the president of the Georgia Automobile Dealers Association with the advice and approval of the board of directors. The chairman of the panel was selected from the board of directors and was appointed by the board. The terms of the chairman and each consumer panelist expired on the 31st day of December each year. The dealer members' terms were not specified, but it was expected that their terms would be less than a year to enable more dealers to have experience as a panel member.

The by-laws of the Georgia AUTOCAP stipulate that each of the three consumer panelists "shall be directly affiliated with an organization actively involved in the field of consumerism and shall not be employed in the automobile industry." The vice chairman of the panel was always to be a consumer panelist. Dealer panelists are selected from the approximately 600 members of the Georgia Automobile Dealers Association (GADA).

The chairman of AUTOCAP was assisted in his duties by the executive vice president of GADA and the full-time AUTOCAP staff person, who was responsible for administration of the activities of AUTOCAP and the preparation and dissemination of all communications relating to those activities.

Upon receiving a telephone call from a consumer voicing a complaint, AUTOCAP sent a form to the consumer to register the complaint. When AUTOCAP received the written complaint, it was immediately acknowledged and forwarded to the dealer concerned for a response. Dealers were given a maximum of 15 days to respond to official notification of a complaint from AUTOCAP before the complaint was automatically forwarded to the panel for consideration at its regular monthly meeting.

The staff person officially closed all cases which appeared to be resolved to the satisfaction of both parties, as indicated on a return postcard sent in by the consumer. When the consumer and the dealer could not agree on a satisfactory solution, the problem was referred to the AUTOCAP panel for informal arbitration and mediation. The staff person prepared a complete file on each case for the panel to examine before their regular monthly meeting. Personal interviews and meetings with complainants were not usually conducted by the chairman or any panel member. However, in special cases the complaint was assigned to one member of the panel who investigated the circumstances by meeting with both parties together and reported the case back to the full panel.

At any meeting a total of four panelists constituted a quorum; of this number, two had to be consumer panelists and two had to be dealer panelists. The panel attempted to arrive at recommendations by consensus, which had been possible in virtually all of the cases handled by the full panel since its inception. In the event that a consensus could not be obtained, an "official" AUTOCAP recommendation was determined by a majority vote of those present.

AUTOCAP did not attempt to determine the legal rights of the parties to any dispute and could choose not to attempt to mediate any dispute which had been litigated, was currently in litigation, or in which litigation appeared inevitable. In all instances, AUTOCAP strove to be objective. Under no circumstances was the status or economic condition of any party to a dispute considered relevant in reaching a solution.

The essence of AUTOCAP was the resolution of disputes to the mutual satisfaction of the customer and the dealer. In achieving this goal, all panelists were expressly charged with protecting the confidentiality of all information originating from AUTOCAP. Any panelist could be dismissed at any time for whatever reason if regular panelists determined that such a member was a detriment to the viability of AUTOCAP.

During the first four months of operation, AUTOCAP had closed 91 cases. As shown in Exhibit 1, 58 of these resulted in customer satisfaction, as indicated on the return postcards sent in by the consumers. In only 4 cases did AUTOCAP rule that the complaint was not valid and the desired remedy should be denied. The number of requests for assistance forms had been increasing recently and was expected to continue to increase as "the word got around."

EXHIBIT 1 AUTOCAP status report, October 25

Customer request for assistance forms mailed on request		229
Customer request for assistance forms not returned		92
Cases closed to customer satisfaction:		
Manufacturer's warranty repairs	21	
Dealer repairs	23	
New car sales	9	
Used car sales	5	
Cases closed—customer satisfaction unknown:		
Vehicle stolen from service lot (insurance claim)	1	
Customer no longer owns vehicle	3	
Customer retained an attorney	4	
Unable to contact consumer	3	
Panel concluded that complaint was not valid	4	
Complaint for record only—no action requested	5	
Dealer not a member of AUTOCAP	2	
Referred complaint to other organizations	11	
	91	91
Pending cases		46
		229

Cases to Be Discussed at the November Meeting

The first case William Carey had to review in preparation for the next day's meeting involved the complaint of one Gene Mitchell concerning the gas mileage he was getting with his new Mercury Monarch. Mitchell's complaint form and the subsequent correspondence are reproduced in Exhibit 2. In essence, Mitchell claimed that his 6-cylinder Monarch only averaged 12 to 12.5 miles per gallon and that he could not afford a car that got such low gas mileage. In order to solve his problem, he suggested that the dealership replace his 6-cylinder engine with an 8-cylinder engine and stated that he would be willing to pay the difference in the cost of the two engines. A service engineer from the parts and service division of the Ford Motor Company examined and adjusted Mitchell's Monarch but was unable to decrease the gas consumption of the car. In reply to Mitchell's suggestion, John Harris, the dealer's service manager who had been handling the problem, stated that such an exchange of engines would not only be economically unfeasible but would possibly be illegal. Harris concluded and wrote AUTOCAP that there was nothing that could be done to increase the gas mileage of this particular automobile or any so equipped.

EXHIBIT 2

CUSTOMER REQUEST FOR ASSISTANCE

AUTOCAP File #00118

Dealership: Kimbro Lincoln-Mercury

Address: 70 Pine Boulevard, Atlanta, Georgia

Customer's name: Gene Mitchell

Address: 2019 Village Circle, #4, Atlanta, Georgia   Phone: 821-4167

Make and model car: Mercury Monarch

In warranty? Yes __X__   Factory _____   (check one)

No _____   Used _____

Bought from: Kimbro Lincoln-Mercury

With whom at the dealership have you discussed the problem:

Service manager John Harris and salesman Bob Wilson

Nature of problem: Averaging 12 mpg to 12.5 mpg. Have been informed by the above gentlemen that the 6-cylinder Mercury Monarchs are overloaded and nothing can be done. I also spoke to a Mr. Jack Kinard, owner of a Lincoln-Mercury dealership known as Kinard's Lincoln-Mercury in Birmingham, Alabama, and he informed me that he will not handle the 6-cylinder Mercury Monarch because of the low miles per gallon. He further stated that in one case he changed carburetors several times and the best mileage he was able to get was 15 mpg on a trip.

NOTE: ATTACH COPIES OF ANY DOCUMENTS YOU FEEL PERTINENT.

EXHIBIT 2 (*continued*)

KIMBRO LINCOLN-MERCURY INC.
70 Pine Boulevard   Phone 226-4000
ATLANTA, GEORGIA 30321

Mr. Herman Watkins
Executive Vice President
AUTOCAP
1380 West Paces Ferry Road, N.W.
Atlanta, Georgia 30327

Dear Mr. Watkins:

I am writing in reference to your letter dated the 29th day of August and AUTOCAP File #00118. I am quite familiar with Mr. Gene Mitchell's problem. Initially, let me say that Mr. Mitchell has been extremely patient and cooperative throughout this experience. I hope he feels that we have reciprocated that cooperation.

My experience with this particular model automobile, equipped with a 250 C.I.D. engine, consistently falls short of any mileage estimates. After several attempts on our part to decrease Mr. Mitchell's gas consumption problem, we contacted the representatives of Ford Motor Company's parts and service division. They, in turn, sent Mr. Jack Adams, a service engineer, to examine and adjust as necessary Mr. Mitchell's automobile. After Mr. Adams had worked on the car, there again was no change in the gas consumption.

I contend that there is nothing that can be done to increase the gas mileage of this particular vehicle, or any so equipped. However, I am always open to any suggestions you may be able to offer in this matter.

Sincerely,

John Harris
Service Manager

cc: Mr. Bruce Kimbro
     Mr. Gene Mitchell

EXHIBIT 2 *(continued)*

2019 Village Circle, #4
Atlanta, Georgia 30309

Ms. Jean Spears
AUTOCAP
1380 West Paces Ferry Road, N.W.
Atlanta, Georgia 30327

Dear Ms. Spears:

I received a letter from Kimbro Lincoln-Mercury addressed to your Mr. Herman Watkins which indicated that nothing could be done to improve the mileage on my Mercury Monarch automobile. As I have stated in previous correspondence to the Ford Motor Company, I am perfectly willing to pay the difference in cost between my 6-cylinder and an 8-cylinder model, since I cannot afford a car which gives only 12 miles per gallon.

My car was checked at the Kimbro Mercury dealership by a service engineer for the Lincoln-Mercury parts and service division in order that they might check on the problem of mileage. He also said that nothing could be done to better the gas mileage on this model car.

I would greatly appreciate any assistance you may be able to afford me in this matter.

Very truly yours,

Gene Mitchell

EXHIBIT 2 *(concluded)*

KIMBRO LINCOLN-MERCURY INC.
70 Pine Boulevard   Phone 226–4000
ATLANTA, GEORGIA 30321

Ms. Jean Spears
AUTOCAP
1380 West Paces Ferry Road, N.W.
Atlanta, Georgia 30327

Dear Ms. Spears:

I am writing in response to your letter of October 2. You had enclosed a copy of a letter you received from Mr. Gene Mitchell concerning his Mercury Monarch.

In the letter Mr. Mitchell mentioned that he would be agreeable to replace his 6-cylinder engine with an 8-cylinder engine and he would pay the difference. Initially, let me say that we are eager to resolve Mr. Mitchell's problems. However, the proposal that you have suggested is not only economically unfeasible but possibly illegal.

The changeover would cost as much as $900 for the new engine alone. Then, in order to meet EPA specifications, new catalytic converters, exhaust pipes, and possibly a new differential would need to be installed.

I hope that I have shed some light on this particular problem and hope that we can work together in order to resolve Mr. Mitchell's problem.

Sincerely,

John Harris
Service Manager

The second case to be discussed at the monthly meeting of AUTOCAP involved the complaint of Dr. Charles Marvin (see Exhibit 3). Marvin had purchased a used Chevrolet Camaro with 3,914 miles on it for the use of his sons in college. The car was not covered by a warranty. Less than a month after purchase, Marvin's sons were on a weekend trip in the car when they looked out the window and saw the left rear wheel wobbling. Upon inspection, it was discovered that the car had a bent axle, apparently the result of a serious accident. The necessary repairs cost Marvin approximately $350. Although Marvin realized he had purchased the car out of warranty, he felt that the dealership had an obligation to insure that this and other cars were at least safe, and he felt that the dealer should be willing to pay for one half of the damages out of good faith. The dealer replied that although he regretted Marvin's problems he felt no obligation to repair any vehicle sold without a warranty.

EXHIBIT 3

CUSTOMER REQUEST FOR ASSISTANCE

AUTOCAP File #00131

Dealership: Fussell Volkswagen
Address: 4980 King Drive, Atlanta, Georgia 30216
Customer's name: Dr. Charles Marvin
Address: 747 Shannon Circle, Decatur, Georgia   Phone: 471-9140
Make and model car: Chevrolet Camaro
In warranty? Yes_____   Factory_____
           No_____   Used ___X___   (check one)
Bought from: Ben Johnson, salesman at Fussell VW
With whom at the dealership have you discussed the problem:
Ben Johnson and the sales manager (Mike O'Henry)

Nature of problem: The car was bought for my sons to use while attending school at the University of Virginia, Charlottesville, Virginia. The car had very low mileage (3,914 miles) when I bought it. I stated that this was unusual and said, "It hasn't been in a wreck, has it?" Ben Johnson said, "Not that I know of." I drove the car and it performed very well. My sons came home from summer school on the 6th of August and then drove the car back to Charlottesville on the 8th of August. They called me that night to say that they had arrived safely, and they said the car had performed fine; they got 20.2 mpg, etc. They did mention that when they stopped for gas and checked the tires, the left rear wheel lug nuts were loose; they could turn them with their fingers. They tightened them and had no further problem. I just assumed they were not tight to start with. On the 19th of August, I received a call from my sons who were en route to Alexandria, Virginia, for the weekend. They said while driving along the highway, they heard a clicking noise and looked out the window of the car, and the left rear wheel was wobbling. They checked the wheel, and the nuts were so loose they were about to drop off. They again tightened the lug nuts and proceeded 25 miles more to Alexandria, where they took the car to a garage and it was determined that the car had a bent axle. The garage stated that the bent axle had been caused by the car being in a fairly serious accident and proceeded to show my sons the tell-tale signs of repaired body work, etc. In addition, he stated that it would have been evident to anyone who had looked or examined the underside of the car, i.e., bottom was all scraped, gas tank bent, etc. I called Fussell VW on August 19th and informed them of the above. While they were sympathetic, they stressed that they had sold the car to me with no warranty and there was nothing they could do about it. I called them again on August 29th and advised that I was submitting this complaint to the Georgia Automobile Dealers Association. I have presently told my sons to have the car fixed, and the bill is going to be about $350. I feel an automobile dealer has the obligation to insure that a car he sells is at least safe. As the mechanic stated, all they had to do is look under the car, and it would have been immediately apparent that the car had been in a wreck. I feel Fussell should be willing to pay at least half of the costs I have incurred out of good faith. Hope you can help me out.

EXHIBIT 3 *(concluded)*

FUSSELL VOLKSWAGEN, INC.
4980 King Drive   622-9000
ATLANTA, GEORGIA 30216

Mr. Herman Watkins
Executive Vice President
AUTOCAP
1380 West Paces Ferry Road, N.W.
Atlanta, Georgia 30327

Dear Mr. Watkins:

This letter is a reply to yours dated September 9, concerning AUTOCAP File #00131.

Fussell Volkswagen, Inc., sold the subject vehicle with no warranty, expressed or implied. Dr. Marvin had ample opportunity to check out and drive subject vehicle prior to purchase. We do not offer a warranty of any type on any vehicles except Volkswagens.

We sympathize with Dr. Marvin and regret he has experienced a problem but we do not feel that we have any obligation to repair a vehicle that was sold without a warranty.

Sincerely,
FUSSELL VOLKSWAGEN, Inc.

R. L. Fussell, President

The third case awaiting review by the panel also involved a warranty problem although in this case a limited warranty on the vehicle had been issued and had expired (see Exhibit 4). Jack Cole, president of Cole and Patterson Battery Company, had purchased a used Ford van with 30,073 miles on it for his company. The van was covered by a 30-day or 1,000-mile warranty. Ten days after the warranty expired, the van broke down and required a complete transmission overhaul. Cole contacted both the dealer and Ford Motor Company concerning possible compensation for the repairs. He contended that no Ford van should require a major transmission overhaul 957 miles after purchase. The dealer and the manufacturer were unwilling to pay for any of the repairs, stating that the full extent of their obligation was set forth in the Dealer Limited Warranty accepted by Cole at the time of purchase.

EXHIBIT 4

CUSTOMER REQUEST FOR ASSISTANCE

AUTOCAP File #00180

Dealership: Bow-Mar Ford, Inc.

Address: 4000 Buchanan Highway, Atlanta, Georgia

Customer's name: Cole and Patterson Battery Company (Jack Cole)

Address: 614 Woodside Way, N.E., Conyers, Georgia   Phone: 696-1840

Make and model car: Ford E-100 Van

In warranty?   Yes X   Factory _____
               No _____   Used   X   (check one)

Bought from: Bow-Mar Ford

With whom at the dealership have you discussed the problem:

Salesman Roger Searcy

Nature of problem: See my letter, attached.

NOTE: ATTACH COPIES OF ANY DOCUMENTS YOU FEEL PERTINENT.

EXHIBIT 4 *(continued)*

COLE AND PATTERSON BATTERY COMPANY
614 Woodside Way, N.E.   Conyers, Georgia 30610
Telephone 696-1840

AUTOCAP
1380 West Paces Ferry Road, N.W.
Atlanta, Georgia 30327

Dear Sirs:

On May 14, my firm purchased a used Ford E-100 van from Bow-Mar Ford in Atlanta. At the time of the purchase there were 30,073 miles on the vehicle. On June 27, the vehicle was operating in the south Atlanta area and had total transmission failure. I personally called Roger Searcy, our salesman at Bow-Mar, to ask what could or should be done with the van. He advised me, after conferring with others at Bow-Mar, that they could do nothing since the vehicle was legally out of warranty. We then had the vehicle towed to the nearest Ford dealership, Mid-South Ford Truck Sales, Inc., who told us the transmission needed overhauling. I again called Searcy at Bow-Mar to see if they would like to send someone to look at the transmission prior to repairs, and when they declined, repair work was commenced.

On July 5, I mailed copies of all pertinent documents to Ronald Pickens at Ford's parts and service division and talked with him on the phone concerning possible compensation for the repairs. He told me that the matter would be researched and we should hear something in two or three weeks. A month later Mr. Pickens was again contacted, and he stated that in error he had forwarded the matter to the wrong person or division. Around September 2, I again contacted Mr. Pickens and was informed that the matter was still in progress. On October 3, Mr. Pickens was contacted and said that Mr. Bob Bates was now handling the matter. On October 4, I called and talked with Mr. Bates, who flatly stated that there was no possibility of aid and there never had been. I was left with the feeling after our brief conversation that he had neither researched nor heard of our case. On this same date I called Mr. Pickens again to tell him what had occurred and to ask him what else could be done. He stated that nothing else could be done.

What we are seeking is at least partial compensation for the repairs to the van. I realize that legally the van was 10 days out of warranty, but morally I feel that any Ford van should not require a transmission overhaul 957 miles after it rolls off a Ford dealer's used lot. Thank you in advance for your help in this matter.

Sincerely,

Jack Cole, President

EXHIBIT 4 *(continued)*

BOW-MAR FORD, INC.
4000 Buchanan Highway
ATLANTA, GEORGIA 30609
(404) 942–1900

AUTOCAP
Georgia Automobile Dealers Association
1380 West Paces Ferry Road, N.W.
Atlanta, Georgia 30327

Gentlemen:

Enclosed is a copy of the "Dealer Limited Warranty" which Mr. Jack Cole of Cole and Patterson Battery Company signed and accepted at the time of purchase of his vehicle.

Since our position is fully stated on the enclosed document, it would seem that no further reply would be required.

Very truly yours,
BOW-MAR FORD, INC.

Enclosure   Robert H. Bower, President

EXHIBIT 4 *(continued)*

DEALER LIMITED WARRANTY

ODOMETER MILEAGE ON DATE OF VEHICLE SALE __30,073__ VEHICLE DEALER: (WARRANTOR) __Bow-Mar Ford, Inc.__
ADDRESS: __4000 Buchanan Highway, Atlanta__ PURCHASER: __Cole and Patterson Battery Company__ ADDRESS: 614 Woodside Way, N.E. Conyers
DEALER SELLS TO PURCHASER THE VEHICLE BELOW IDENTIFIED SUBJECT TO THE FOLLOWING TERMS AND CONDITIONS:
VEHICLE INFORMATION

  MAKE __Ford__ SERIAL NUMBER __F02AMD48011__
  MODEL __E-100 Van__

1. Persons Capable of Enforcing the Limited Warranty. Dealer extends this warranty to any person who may reasonably be expected to use, or be affected by the goods, and who is injured by breach of the warranty.
2. Parts Covered by the Limited Warranty. The following parts are covered by this warranty, but only if their defect or malfunction is caused by a mechanical breakdown or failure (defined as inability of any covered part to perform its designed function) and only to the extent provided for in section 3.

A. Engine, including:
Cylinder block
Head
Internal parts
Water pump
Intake manifold

B. Transmission, including:
Case
Internal parts
Torque converter

C. Rear axle, including:
Differential
Internal parts

D. Propeller shaft, including:
Universal joints

E. Other parts covered: __N.A.__

3. Percentage of Repair Costs Covered. This warranty covers __50%__ of the total costs (parts and labor) for repairs under sections 2A, 2B, 2C, and 2D; and covers __N.A.__ % of the total costs (parts and labor) for repairs under section 2E.
4. Exclusions from the Warranty. All parts and systems that are not included in section 2 above are excluded from coverage under this warranty. Any malfunction resulting from failure to perform periodic maintenance in accordance with manufacturer's recommendations is excluded from this warranty. Any damage resulting to the vehicle that is not caused from a defect or malfunction is also excluded from this warranty.
5. Dealer's Obligations. During the period of this limited warranty (see section 6 below), Dealer will repair the parts as provided in section 2 above, and the only cost to Purchaser for these repairs will be the balance of the percentage amounts stated in section 3 above of the total repair costs (parts and labor), plus applicable sales taxes.
6. Period of the Warranty.

    A. The warranty coverage commences on the delivery date of the vehicle and extends to __30__ days after the delivery date, or for __1,000__ miles beyond the odometer reading, whichever occurs sooner.
7. Obligations of the Purchaser.

    A. Purchaser shall give notice to Dealer of any breach of contract or breach of express or implied warranty applicable to the goods within __twenty__

EXHIBIT 4 *(concluded)*

(20)   days after the notice of breach to allow the seller the opportunity to cure the said breach or the Purchaser shall be barred from any remedy for the breach.

B.   Purchaser must authorize the Dealer to make the repairs, and Purchaser must, upon redelivery of the repaired vehicle to Purchaser, pay the balance of the percentage amounts stated in section 3 above of the total repair costs (parts and labor), plus applicable sales taxes.

C.   If Purchaser is dissatisfied because he feels that Dealer has failed to conform to this warranty, he should contact:

Philip Sanderson   Phone Number   404/942-1900

at Dealer's above address.

IMPORTANT

8.   *Limitations on Implied Warranties and Exclusions as to Consequential Damages and Incidental Damages.* ALL IMPLIED WARRANTIES, INCLUDING THE IMPLIED WARRANTIES OF MERCHANTABILITY AND FITNESS FOR A PARTICULAR PURPOSE, ARE HEREBY LIMITED TO THE SAME DURATION OF TIME AS THE EXPRESS WRITTEN WARRANTY ABOVE STATED. PURCHASER SHALL NOT BE ENTITLED TO RECOVER FROM THE SELLING DEALER ANY CONSEQUENTIAL DAMAGES, DAMAGES TO PROPERTY, DAMAGES FOR LOSS OF USE, LOSS OF TIME, LOSS OF PROFITS, OR INCOME, OR ANY OTHER INCIDENTAL DAMAGES, EXCEPT IN JURISDICTIONS WHERE THE PROVISIONS OF ANY LAW PROHIBIT OR MAKE UNCONSCIONABLE THESE LIMITATIONS, AND THEN THAT PORTION OF THESE LIMITATIONS WHICH IS PROHIBITED OR DECLARED TO BE UNCONSCIONABLE SHALL BE OF NO EFFECT. SOME STATES DO NOT ALLOW LIMITATIONS ON HOW LONG AN IMPLIED WARRANTY LASTS, SO THE ABOVE LIMITATION MAY NOT APPLY TO YOU. SOME STATES DO NOT ALLOW THE EXCLUSION OR LIMITATION OF INCIDENTAL OR CONSEQUENTIAL DAMAGES, SO THE ABOVE LIMITATION OR EXCLUSION MAY NOT APPLY TO YOU.

9.   Purchaser's Legal Rights. This warranty gives you specific legal rights, and you may also have other rights which vary from state to state.

10.   Limited Warranty. This is limited warranty. It is not a service contract.

There is no other express warranty on this vehicle, and there is no agreement between Purchaser and Dealer relating to repairs of the vehicle except as set forth in this warranty.

Purchaser acknowledges that he has read, understands and accepts all of the provisions of the warranty statement covering the used vehicle above identified.

/s/ Jack Cole

Purchaser's Signature

/s/ Roger Searcy   /s/ Robert H. Bower

Witness   Dealer's Signature
(not valid unless signed by Dealer or his
authorized representative)

EXHIBIT 5

CUSTOMER REQUEST FOR ASSISTANCE

AUTOCAP File #00072

Dealership: Haverty Lincoln-Mercury Sales Inc.

Address: 2450 Peachtree Road, N.E., Atlanta, Georgia 30302

Customer's name: Mrs. Lynn Luxemburger

Address: 443 Janice Drive, Stone Mountain, GA 30348   Phone: 996–0619

Make and model car: Lincoln Continental Towncar

In warranty: Yes_____   Factory_____

No ___X___   Used _____   (check one)

Bought from: Venture Lincoln-Mercury Co., Spartanburg, S.C.

With whom at the dealership have you discussed the problem: Neil Simpson, service advisor, and Mr. Green, sales manager, at Haverty Lincoln-Mercury

Nature of problem: I left my car at Haverty Lincoln-Mercury for service on May 30, along with a written list of things to be done, which I gave to the service advisor, Mr. Simpson. Although I had an appointment for the work to be done and was promised one-day service, I had to wait a week before my car was ready. My car broke down on my way home from the service department. Furthermore, I was charged for things that were not done and that I did not authorize instead of the work I requested. My car is in worse condition now than when I brought it in. I recommend that someone from AUTOCAP examine my car to demonstrate that my charges are true, that the entire service bill be canceled, and that Haverty Lincoln-Mercury pay me for the hardship and inconveniences caused me by their negligence and inferior workmanship. I do not intend to carry my car back to Haverty for anything.

NOTE: ATTACH COPIES OF ANY DOCUMENTS YOU FEEL PERTINENT.

The fourth case involved service performed on Mrs. Lynn Luxemburger's Lincoln-Continental. Pertinent correspondence is reproduced in Exhibit 5. Mrs. Luxemburger left her car for servicing at the dealership, along with a list of items needing repair, and asked that she be provided an estimate. After the car was checked, it was determined that repairs costing in the neighborhood of $1,000 were needed. The dealer claims that Mrs. Luxemburger authorized the service department to proceed with the most needed repairs, not to exceed $500–$520. Mrs. Luxemburger denies this, claiming that she never authorized the $500 and was expecting the repairs to be around $300–$350. Furthermore, she says that she only authorized the repairs on her list, plus one additional repair authorized over the phone, and not the "most needed repairs" at the discretion of the service department. She also claims that much of the work she was charged for was not done. Mrs. Luxemburger's car broke down before she got home the day she picked it up from the dealership. She contends this was

EXHIBIT 5 *(continued)*

HAVERTY LINCOLN-MERCURY SALES, INC.
Telephone 821-6111   2450 Peachtree Road, N.E.
Atlanta, Georgia 30302

Georgia Automobile Dealers Association
1380 West Paces Ferry Road, N.W.
Atlanta, Georgia 30327

Attention: AUTOCAP

Gentlemen:

We have received your letters dated July 8 and 22, regarding a consumer complaint filed by Mrs. Lynn Luxemburger (AUTOCAP File #00072). The delay in responding to your letters has been occasioned by the fact that we have not been able to get Mrs. Luxemburger to bring her car in or to let us have it towed in. We enclose a report filed by our service manager concerning our contacts with Mrs. Luxemburger.

We feel that we have acted diligently and in good faith in our efforts to resolve this complaint. We stand ready to answer any questions Mrs. Luxemburger may have at any time; our offer to have the car brought in to our dealership to be checked by the several consumer affairs representatives she has contacted, along with our mechanic, is still open.

If Mrs. Luxemburger is not willing to meet us halfway or even part way in the interest of resolving this problem, we are prepared to defend whatever legal action she may take.

Sincerely,

G. M. Marvin
Executive Vice President and
General Manager

cc: Office of Consumer Affairs
    (Attention: Mr. Sumner)

due to the negligence and inferior workmanship of the service department; the service department believes that the breakdown was probably caused by the need for further alternator repairs that could not be made under the $500 limitation. AUTOCAP's file included several letters containing accounts of a number of subsequent contacts between the dealership and Mrs. Luxemburger that had been unsuccessful in clearing up the differences of opinion and fact discrepancies reported above. In settlement of her claim, Mrs. Luxemburger felt that the dealership should cancel the service bill and also should pay her for the inconveniences and hardship it had caused her.

EXHIBIT 5 *(continued)*

Mr. Ralph Bumgarner
WXTM—Atlanta

TO WHOM IT MAY CONCERN:

On May 30, Mrs. Lynn Luxemburger brought her Lincoln to Haverty for service. When she brought the car in, Mrs. Luxemburger requested that we check the car over and provide her with an estimate. She provided a list of items she felt needed to be done, as listed below:

Rear end bumpy
Using lots of oil
Power steering does not seem to work
Repair right rear arm rest
Brakes squeak
Check exterior lights, both front and rear
Check windshield washer fluid
Check starter

After checking the car, it was discovered that the following items needed to be done:

Shock absorbers
Upper inner shaft bushings
Power steering pump and steering gear
Brake job
Alternator
Fuel pump
Hoses
Alignment

Mrs. Luxemburger was called and advised of these repair needs and that these repairs alone would involve a repair bill of approximately $991. She authorized us to proceed with the most needed repairs with the stipulation we not exceed $500–$520.

Accordingly, we proceeded and performed the following repairs:

Replaced upper inner shaft bushings
Adjusted steering gear preload
Completed brake job
Replaced bearing on alternator (*)
Replaced fuel pump
Replaced all hoses and flushed system
Aligned wheels

(*) A notation was made on the repair order by the mechanic that the alternator still needed a stator and rotor; however, this was not done due to limitations placed on the repair bill to be incurred.

EXHIBIT 5 *(continued)*

The total repair bill for the work performed was $527.57, which Mrs. Luxemburger paid when she picked up her car on July 5. On the same day she called and stated that her car had stopped running—which was probably the result of the faulty alternator, although we cannot be sure because Mrs. Luxemburger has not permitted us to bring the car back in to our shop. Mrs. Luxemburger was told to have the car towed back to Haverty, and that if we had done something wrong we would pay the towing bill and would make the repair at no charge, but that if the cause was due to the *additional* work needed to be done, she would be responsible for the repair charges. I then gave her the number of our towing service. Later in the day Mrs. Luxemburger called and said she had taken the car to a service station and that *none* of the things she had paid for had been done. I told her I would like to verify this for myself and again asked her to have the car towed to Haverty, reminding her that an additional $500 in repairs was still necessary to put the car in good condition. She had been forewarned by the service writer and the mechanic that she could possibly have problems. She said that she was going to contact some consumer groups and file a legal action and that she would never bring her car back to Haverty Lincoln-Mercury. I replied that we would be perfectly willing to have her car checked at our dealership with whatever consumer representatives she desired present. Since that time, we have tried unsuccessfully on numerous occasions to meet with Mrs. Luxemburger and to resolve this complaint.

Neil Simpson
Service Manager

EXHIBIT 5 *(concluded)*

443 Janice Drive
Stone Mountain, Georgia 30348

AUTOCAP
Georgia Automobile Dealers Association
1380 West Paces Ferry Road, N.W., Suite 230
Atlanta, Georgia 30327

RE: AUTOCAP File #00072

Gentlemen:

Thank you for your letter of August 4 and the information therein.

The accounts given by Mr. Simpson and Mr. Marvin are inadequate and filled with half-truths and nontruths. My complaint is a simple one. I feel that I have been charged for parts and services allegedly done on my car which I did not authorize. The work which I authorized was submitted to the service department by me in written form at the time I left my car for service, with the exception of the alternator, which I authorized by telephone. In addition, I have been charged for work which was not done. The starter is an example. I was specifically told that the starter had been repaired when I picked the car up. The car stalled on me before I could get home from Haverty Lincoln-Mercury on July 5 with the same starter problem.

When I left my car, I was told specifically that a rough estimate of the repairs on my list would be approximately $300–$350. A couple of days later I called and was told my car was not ready; even at that time I was not told that the car would be over $500. My first knowledge of this amount was when I went to pick the car up on Tuesday, July 5.

I do not see how my car could possibly have needed $1,000 of work since it is a one-owner car, and I have always had it serviced in accordance with the manual and by a Lincoln-Mercury dealership.

Mr. Marvin did invite me to his office to discuss the matter. As I told him then, transportation is a problem for me. I have been without the use of my car now for over a month.

I am willing to have the car inspected by any impartial inspector, but I will not take it back to Haverty Lincoln-Mercury. I do hope you will put my case on the agenda for your next meeting and appreciate the interest you have put forth in trying to work out a solution to this frustrating problem.

Respectfully,

Lynn Luxemburger (Mrs.)

The last case is somewhat different from the rest in that it involved a complaint alleging deceptive and misleading advertising (see Exhibit 6). Ben Harrell, the complainant, had seen a newspaper advertisement advertising an F-100 pickup truck for only $3,395. Harrell had been comparing prices on the F-100 pickup, and $3,395 was considerably lower than anything he had seen elsewhere. For this reason Harrell went to Stokes Ford the following day planning to purchase the truck. As he examined the sticker price on the truck at the dealership, Harrell noticed a list price of $3,895, rather than the $3,395 he had seen in the ad. When he asked a salesman about this, it was pointed out that the $3,395 did not include the $500 down payment and that the cash price listed

EXHIBIT 6

CUSTOMER REQUEST FOR ASSISTANCE

AUTOCAP File #00194

Dealership: Stokes Ford, Inc.

Address: 7280 Russell Road, Atlanta, Georgia

Customer's name: Ben F. Harrell

Address: 929 Rosedale Avenue, Atlanta Georgia 30308 Phone: 862-0126

Make and model car: Ford F–100 Pickup

Yes_____ Factory_____

In warranty? No _____ Used _____   (check one)

Bought from: Not Applicable

With whom at the dealership have you discussed the problem:
Charlie Stikeleather, salesman

Nature of problem: I went to Stokes Ford on Monday, October 9, planning to purchase an F-100 pickup I had seen advertised in the Sunday paper (10/8) for $3,395; a copy of the advertisement is attached. I had been shopping around, and this price was quite a bit lower than any I had seen. At the dealership I was examining the items included on the sticker on the truck when I noticed a list price of $3,895, rather than the $3,395 I had seen advertised. When I asked a salesman about this, I was informed that the $3,395 price did not include the $500 down payment and that I had misread the ad. It was pointed out to me by Mr. Stikeleather that the cash price of the truck included in the ad was $3,895. This price was included in the *fine print*. In my opinion, this ad clearly says, "You pay only $3,395." I do not as a habit read the fine print in advertisements, nor do I believe that this is where important facts should be revealed. I feel this type of advertising is misleading and ought to be stopped. I would not do business with a company that uses such deceptive practices. I believe AUTO-CAP's review of this matter is warranted.

NOTE: ATTACH COPIES OF ANY DOCUMENTS YOU FEEL PERTINENT.

EXHIBIT 6 *(continued)*

STOKES FORD, INC.
7280 Russell Road, Atlanta, Georgia 30601
404/759–9050

Mr. Herman Watkins
Executive Director
AUTOCAP
1380 West Paces Ferry Road, N.W.
Atlanta, Georgia 30327

Dear Mr. Watkins:

This is in response to your letter of October 19, concerning the complaint of Mr. Ben Harrell. Mr. Harrell questions our advertising practices, in particular the advertisement we included in the *Atlanta Journal* on Sunday, October 8, a copy of which is already in your file.

We disagree that this advertisement is in any way deceptive. The terms advertised of "$500 down" are in very large print at the top of the ad, and the cash price clearly reads $3,895. Mr. Harrell obviously misread the ad; we have had no other problems or misunderstandings concerning it.

Please don't hesitate to call me at 759-9050 if you have any further questions in this regard.

Sincerely,

Kenneth Stokes

in the ad was $3,895 rather than $3,395. Harrell did not purchase the truck. However, he filed a complaint with AUTOCAP claiming that such advertising was misleading and should not be permitted. Stokes Ford replied to AUTOCAP that its advertisement was not deceptive, that all of the information was included in the advertisement, and that Harrell had simply misinterpreted it.

EXHIBIT 6 *(concluded)*

Case 36

Nestlé and the Infant Food Controversy (A)*

In October 1978, Dr. Fürer, managing director of Nestlé S.A., headquartered in Vevey, Switzerland was pondering the continuing problems his company faced. Public interest groups, media, health organizations, and other groups had been pressuring Nestlé to change its marketing practices for infant formula products, particularly in developing countries. Those groups had used a variety of pressure tactics, including consumer boycott in the United States over the past eight years. Critics of Nestlé charged that the company's promotional practices not only were abusive but also harmful, resulting in malnutrition and death in some circumstances. They demanded Nestlé put a stop to all promotion of its infant formula products both to consumers and health personnel.

Nestlé management had always prided itself on its high quality standards, its efforts to serve the best interests of Nestlé customers, and its contribution to the health and prosperity of people in developing countries. Nestlé management was convinced their infant formula products were useful and wanted; they had not taken the first signs of adverse publicity in the early 1970s very seriously. By 1978, massive adverse publicity appeared to be endangering the reputation of the company, particularly in Europe and North America. Despite support from some health officials and organizations throughout the world, Nestlé management in Vevey and White Plains, New York (U.S.A. headquarters) were seriously concerned. Dr. Fürer had been consulting with Mr. Guerrant, President of Nestlé U.S.A. in an effort to formulate a strategy. Of immediate concern to Nestlé management was the scheduled meeting of the National Council of Churches (USA) in November 1978. On the agenda was a resolution to support the critics of Nestlé who were leading the consumer boycott against Nestlé products in the United States. The National Council of Churches was an

* This case was written by Aylin Kunt, research assistant under the supervision of Professors Christopher Gale and George Taucher in 1979. The earlier work of Professor James Kuhn of Columbia University is gratefully acknowledged. This version is a substantial revision of the earlier case and was prepared by Professor Michael R. Pearce. Copyright © 1981 by l'Institut pour l'Etude des Methodes de Direction de l'Enterprise (IMEDE), Lausanne, Switzerland and The School of Business Administration, University of Western Ontario, London, Ontario, Canada. It is intended for classroom discussion and is not intended as an illustration of good or bad management practices.

important, prestigious organization which caused Nestlé management to fear that NCC support of the boycott might further endanger Nestlé.

Also of concern was the meeting of the World Health Organization (WHO) scheduled in the fall of 1979 to bring together the infant food manufacturers, public interest groups, and the world health community in an attempt to formulate a code of marketing conduct for the industry. Nestlé management, instrumental in establishing this conference, hoped that a clear set of standards would emerge, thus moderating or eliminating the attacks of the public pressure groups.

Dr. Fürer was anxious to clear up what he thought were misunderstandings about the industry. As he reviewed the history of the formula problem, he wondered in general what a company could do when subjected to pressure tactics by activist groups, and in particular, what Nestlé management should do next.

Nestlé Alimentana S.A.

The Swiss-based Nestlé Alimentana S.A. was one of the largest food products companies in the world. Nestlé had 80,000 shareholders in Switzerland. Nestlé's importance to Switzerland was comparable to the combined importance of General Motors and Exxon to the United States. In 1977, Nestlé's worldwide sales approximated 20 billion Swiss francs. Of this total, 7.3 percent were infant and dietetic products; more specifically, 2.5 percent of sales were accounted for by infant formula sales in developing countries.

Traditionally a transnational seller of food products, Nestlé's basic goal had always been to be a fully integrated food processor in every country in which it operated. It aimed at maintaining an important market presence in almost every nation of the world. In each country, Nestlé typically established local plants, supported private farms and dairy herds and sold a wide range of products to cover all age groups. By the end of 1977, Nestlé had 87 factories in the developing countries and provided 35,610 direct jobs. Nestlé management was proud of this business approach and published a 228-page book in 1975 entitled *Nestlé in Developing Countries*. The cover of this book carried the following statement:

> While Nestlé is not a philanthropic society, facts and figures clearly prove that the nature of its activities in developing countries is self-evident as a factor that contributes to economic development. The company's constant need for local raw materials, processing, and staff, and the particular contribution it brings to local industry, support the fact that Nestlé's presence in the Third World is based on common interests in which the progress of one is always to the benefit of the other.

Although it neither produced nor marketed infant formula in the United States, the Nestlé Company, Inc. (White Plains) sold a variety of products such as Nescafé, Nestea, Crunch, Quik, Taster's Choice, and Libby and McNeil & Libby products throughout the United States.

With over 95 percent of Nestlé's sales outside of Switzerland, the company had developed an operating policy characterized by strong central financial control along with substantial freedom in marketing strategy by local managers. Each country manager was held responsible for profitability. Through periodic planning meetings, Nestlé management in Vevey ("the Centre") reviewed the broad strategy proposals of local companies. One area of responsibility clearly reserved by Vevey was the maintenance of the overall company image, although no formal public relations department existed. Marketing plans were reviewed in part by Vevey to see if they preserved the company's reputation for quality and service throughout the world.

Nestlé and the Infant Formula Industry

The international infant formula industry was composed of two types of firms, pharmaceutically oriented ones and food processing ones. The major companies competing in the developing countries were as follows:

Company	Brands
A. Pharmaceutical	
(U.S.) Wyeth Lab (American Home Products)	SMA, S26, Nursoy
(U.S.) Ross Lab (Abbott Laboratories)	Similac, Isomil
(U.S.) Mead Johnson (Bristol-Myers)	Enfamil, Olac, Prosobee
B. Food processing	
(U.S.) Borden	New Biolac
(Swit.) Nestlé	Nestogen, Eledon, Pelargon Nan, Lactogen
(U.K.) Unigate	

In addition to these six firms, there were about another dozen formula producers chartered in 1978 throughout the world.

The basic distinction between pharmaceutically oriented formula producers and food processing oriented producers lay in their entry point into the formula business. In the early 1900s, medical research laboratories of major pharmaceutical firms developed "humanized formulas," leading their parents into marketing such products. Essentially, a humanized formula was a modification of normal cow's milk to approximate more closely human milk. Generally speaking, the food processing companies had begun offering infant food as an extension of their full milk powdered products and canned milk.

As early as the 1800s, Nestlé had been engaged in research in the field of child nutrition. In 1867, Henri Nestlé, the founder of the company and the great-grandfather of infant formula, introduced the first specifically designed, commercially marketed infant weaning formula. An infant weaning formula is basically a cereal and milk mixture designed to introduce solids to a child of five–six months of age.

As of the 1860s, both Nestlé and Borden had been producing sweetened and evaporated milk. Nestlé very quickly recognized the need for better artificial infant food and steadily developed a full line of formula products in the early 1900s (for example, Lactogen in 1921, Eledon in 1927, Nestogen in 1930). Although it was a food processing company, Nestlé's product development and marketing were supervised by physicians.

In the United States in the early 1900s, the infant formula products developed by the medical laboratories were being used primarily in hospitals. Over time, the industry developed the distinction of formula products for "well babies" versus for "sick babies." In the latter category would be included special nutritional and dietary problems, such as allergies to milk requiring babies to have totally artificial formulas made from soybeans. Approximately 2 percent of industry volume was formula designed for "sick babies."

In the late 19th century and early years of the 20th century, Nestlé had developed a commanding position in the sweetened and evaporated milk market in the developing countries (also referred to as "the Third World"). Demand for these products was initially established among European colonials and gradually spread throughout the world and into the rising middle classes in many nations. Nestlé's early marketing efforts focused on switching infant feeding from the previously common use of sweetened and condensed milk to a more appropriate product, humanized infant formula.

By promoting a full product line through doctors (medical detailing), Nestlé achieved an overwhelmingly dominant market position in the European colonies, countries which later became independent "Third World" countries. Meanwhile, most of the competition developed quickly in the industrialized countries, so much so that Nestlé stayed out of the U.S. formula market entirely. Only late in the 1950s did significant intense competition, mainly from American multinationals, develop in Nestlé's markets in developing countries. These markets with their high birth rates and rising affluence became increasingly attractive to all formula producers. After the entry of American competitors, Nestlé's share of markets began to erode.

As of 1978, Nestlé accounted for about one third to one half of infant formula sales in the developing countries while American companies held about one fifth. The size of the total world market for infant formula was not exactly known because data on shipments of infant formula were not separated from other milk products, especially powders. Some sources guesstimated world sales to be close to $1.5 billion (U.S.), half of that to developing countries.

Traditional Methods of Promotion

Several methods had been used over the years to promote infant products in developing countries. Five major methods predominated:

1. Media advertising—all media types were employed including posters in clinics and hospitals, outdoor billboards, newspapers, magazines, radio, television, and loudspeakers on vans. Native languages and English were used.

2. Samples—free sample distribution either direct to new mothers or via doctors was relatively limited until competition increased in the 1960s. Mothers were given either formula or feeding bottles or both, often in a "new mother's kit." Doctors in clinics and hospitals received large packages of product for use while mother and baby were present. The formula producers believed this practice helped educate new mothers on the use of formula products, and hopefully, initiated brand preference. In some instances, doctors actually resold samples to provide an extra source of income for themselves or their institutions.

3. Booklets—most formula marketers provided new mothers with booklets on baby care which were given free to them when they left the hospitals and clinics with their newborn infants. These booklets, such as Nestlé's *A Life Begins,* offered a variety of advice and advertised the formula products and other infant foods, both Nestlé and home made.

4. Milk nurses—milk nurses (also known as mothercraft nurses) were formula producer employees who talked with new mothers in the hospitals and clinics or at home. Originally, they were all fully trained nurses, instructed in product knowledge, then sent out to educate new mothers on the correct use of the new formula products. This instruction included the importance of proper personal hygiene, boiling the water, and mixing formula and water in correct quantities. These became a major part of many firms' efforts; for example, at one time Nestlé had about 200 mothercraft employees worldwide. The majority of milk nurses were paid a straight salary plus a travel allowance, but over time, some were hired on a sales-related bonus basis. Some companies, other than Nestlé, began to relax standards in the 1960s and hired nonnursing personnel who dressed in nurses' uniforms and acted more in a selling capacity and less in an educational capacity.

5. Milk banks—milk bank was the term used to describe a special distribution outlet affiliated with and administered by those hospitals and clinics which served very low income people. Formula products were provided to low income families at much reduced prices for mothers who could not afford the commercial product. The producers sold products to those outlets at lower prices to enable this service to occur.

PAG 23

Nestlé management believed the controversy surrounding the sale of infant formula in developing countries began in the early 1970s. Many international organizations were concerned about the problem of malnourishment of infants in the developing countries of South Asia, Africa, and Latin America. In Bogota (1970) and Paris (1972), representatives of the Food and Agricultural

Organization (FAO), the World Health Organization (WHO), UNICEF, the International Pediatric Association, and the infant formula industry including Nestlé all met to discuss nutrition problems and guidelines. The result was a request that the United Nations Protein-Calorie Advisory Group (PAG), an organization formed in 1955, set guidelines for nutrition for infants. On July 18, 1972, the PAG issued Statement 23 on the "Promotion of special foods for vulnerable groups." This statement emphasized the importance of breast-feeding, the danger of over-promotion, the need to take local conditions into account, the problem of misuse of formula products, and the desirability of reducing promotion but increasing education.

Statement 23 included the following statements:

> Breast milk is an optimal food for infants and, if available in sufficient quantities, it is adequate as the sole source of food during the first four to six months of age.

> Poor health and adverse social circumstances may decrease the output of milk by the mother . . . in such circumstances supplementation of breast milk with nutritionally adequate foods must start earlier than four to six months if growth failure is to be avoided.

> It is clearly important to avoid any action which would accelerate the trend away from breast-feeding.

> It is essential to make available to the mother, the foods, formulas, and instructions which will meet the need for good nutrition of those infants who are breast-fed.

Nestlé management regarded PAG 23 as an "advisory statement," so management's stance was to see what happened. None of the developing countries took any action on the statement. Nestlé officials consulted with ministers of health in many developing countries to ask what role their governments wished Nestlé to play in bringing nutrition education to local mothers. No major changes were requested.

At the same time, Nestlé Vevey ordered an audit of marketing practices employed by its companies in the developing nations. Based on reports from the field, Nestlé management in Vevey concluded that only a few changes in marketing were required which they ordered be done. In Nigeria, the Nigerian Society of Health and Nutrition asked Nestlé to change its ads for formula to stress breast-feeding. Nestlé complied with this request, and its ads in all developing countries prominently carried the phrase "when breast milk fails, use . . ."

The British Contribution

In its August 1973 issue, the *New Internationalist,* an English journal devoted to problems in developing countries, published an article entitled "The Baby Food Tragedy." This was an interview with two doctors: Dr. R. G. Hendrikse, Director of the Tropical Child Health Course, Liverpool University, and medical researcher in Rhodesia, Nigeria, and South Africa and Dr. David Morley, Reader in Tropical Child Health, University of London. Both doctors expressed concern with the widespread use of formula among impoverished, less literate families. They claimed that in such cases, low family incomes prevented mothers from buying the necessary amount of formula for their children. Instead, they used smaller quantities of formula powder, diluting it with more water than recommended. Further, the water used was frequently contaminated. The infant thus received less than adequate nutrition, indeed often was exposed to contaminated formula. The malnourished child became increasingly susceptible to infections, leading to diarrheal diseases. Diarrhea meant the child could assimilate even less of the nutrients given to him because neither his stomach nor intestines were working properly. This vicious cycle could lead to death. The two doctors believed that local conditions made the use of commercial infant formula not only unnecessary, but likely difficult and dangerous. Breast-feeding was safer, healthier, and certainly less expensive.

The article, in the opinion of many, was relatively restrained and balanced. However, it was accompanied by dramatic photographs of malnourished black babies and of a baby's grave with a tin of milk powder placed on it. The article had a strong emotional impact on readers and reached many people who were not regular readers of the journal. It was widely reprinted and quoted by other groups. The journal sent copies of the article to more than 3,000 hospitals in the developing nations.

The two doctors interviewed for the article had mentioned Nestlé and its promotional practices. Accordingly, the editors of the *New Internationalist* contacted Nestlé S.A. for its position. The company response was published in the October issue of the *New Internationalist* along with an editorial entitled "Milk and Murder."

Nestlé S.A. responded in part as follows:

> We have carefully studied both the editorial and the interviews with Dr. Hendrickse and Dr. Morley published in the August edition of the *New Internationalist*. Although fleeting references are made to factors other than manufacturers' activities which are said to be responsible for the misuse of infant foods in developing countries, their readers would certainly not be in a position to judge from the report the immense socioeconomic complexities of the situation. . . .
>
> It would be impossible to demonstrate in the space of a letter the enormous efforts made by the Nestlé organization to ensure the correct usage of their infant food products, and the way in which the PAG guidelines have been applied by the Nestlé subsidiaries. However, if the editor of the *New Internationalist* (or the author of the article in question) wishes to establish the complete facts as far as we are concerned, then we should be happy to receive him in Vevey on a mutually agreeable date in the near future. We should certainly welcome the opportunity to reply to some of the sweeping allegations made against Nestlé either by implication or by specific references.

The editor of the *New Internationalist* refused the invitation to visit Nestlé's Vevey headquarters. Further they maintained that PAG 23 guidelines were not being observed and did not have any provisions for enforcement.

In March 1974, War on Want published a pamphlet entitled *The Baby Killer*. War on Want was a private British group established to give aid to Third World nations. In particular, they were devoted ''to make world poverty an urgent social and political issue.'' War on Want issued a set of recommendations to industry, governments, the medical profession, and others to deal with the baby formula problem as they saw it. See Exhibit 1.

EXHIBIT 1 War on Want's recommendations

Industry
1. The serious problems caused by early weaning onto breast milk substitutes demand a serious response. Companies should follow the Swedish example and refrain from all consumer promotion of breast milk substitutes in high risk communities.
2. The companies should cooperate constructively with the international organisations working on the problems of infant and child nutrition in the developing countries.
3. Companies should abandon promotions to the medical profession which may perform the miseducational function of suggesting that particular brands of milk can overcome the problems of misuse.

Governments of developing countries
1. Governments should take note of the recommendations of the Protein Advisory Group for national nutrition strategies.
2. Where social and economic conditions are such that proprietary infant foods can make little useful contribution, serious consideration should be given to the curtailment of their importation, distribution, and/or promotion.
3. Governments should ensure that supplies are made available first to those in need—babies whose mothers cannot breast feed, twins, orphans, etc.—rather than to an economic elite, a danger noted by the PAG.

British Government
1. The British Government should exercise a constructive influence in the current debate.
2. The Government should insist that British companies such as Unigate and Glaxo set a high standard of behaviour and it should be prepared to enforce a similar standard on multinationals like Wyeth who export to developing country markets from Britain.
3. The British representative on the Codex Alimentarius Commission should urge the commission to consider all aspects of the promotion of infant foods. If necessary, structural alterations should be proposed to set up a subcommittee to consider broader aspects of promotion to enable the commission to fulfill its stated aims of protecting the consumer interests.

Medical profession
There is a need in the medical profession for a greater awareness of the problems caused by artificial feeding of infants and of the role of the medical profession in encouraging the trend away from breast-feeding.

EXHIBIT 1 *(concluded)*

Other channels

Practicing health workers in the Third World have achieved startling, if limited, response by writing to local medical journals and the press about any promotional malpractices they see and sending copies of their complaints to the companies involved. This could be done by volunteers and others not in the medical profession but in contact with the problem in the field.

In Britain, student unions at a number of universities and polytechnics decided to ban the use of all Nestlés products where they had control of catering following the initial exposé by the *New Internationalist* magazine. Without any clear objective, or coordination, this kind of action is unlikely to have much effect.

However, if the companies involved continue to be intransigent in the face of the dangerous situation developing in the Third World, a more broadly based campaign involving many national organisations may be the result. At the very least, trade unions, women's organisations, consumer groups, and other interested parties need to be made aware of the present dangers.

There is also a clear need to examine on a community scale, how infant feeding practices are determined in Britain today. There is a long history of commercial persuasion, and artificial feeding is now well entrenched.

As has been shown, there are still risks inherent in bottle feeding even in Britain. The available evidence suggests that both mother and child may do better physically and emotionally by breast-feeding. An examination of our own irrational social practices can help the Third World to throw a light on theirs.

The Baby Killer was written by Mike Muller as an attempt to publicize the infant formula issue. Mr. Muller expanded on the *New Internationalist* articles, and in the view of many observers, gave reasonable treatment to the complexity of the circumstances surrounding the use of formula products in the developing countries. On the whole, it was an attack against bottle-feeding rather than an attack against any particular company.

Part of *The Baby Killer* was based on interviews the author had with three Nestlé employees: Dr. H. R. Müller, G. A. Fookes, and J. Momoud, all of Nestlé S.A. Infant and Dietetics Division. These Nestlé officials argued that Nestlé was acting as responsibly as it could. Further, they said, that abuses, if they existed, could not be controlled by single companies. Only a drastic change in the competitive system could check abuses effectively. Mr. Muller apparently was not impressed by this argument, nor did he mention Nestlé management's stated willingness to establish enforceable international guidelines for marketing conduct. In *The Baby Killer*, Mr. Muller revealed he was convinced that Nestlé was exploiting the high birth rates in developing countries by encouraging mothers to replace, not supplement, breast-feeding by formula products. Mr. Muller offered as support for his stance a quotation from Nestlé's 1973 Annual Report:

. . . the continual decline in birth rates, particularly in countries with a high standard of living, retarded growth of the market. . . . In the developing countries our own products continue to sell well thanks to the growth of population and improved living standards.

Dr. Fürer's reaction to *The Baby Killer* was that Mr. Muller had given too much weight to the negative aspects of the situation. Mr. Muller failed to mention, for example, that infant mortality rates had shown very dramatic declines in the developing countries. Some part of these declines were the result of improved nutrition, Dr. Fürer believed, and improved nutrition was partly the result of the use of formula products. Despite his strong belief that Nestlé's product was highly beneficial rather than harmful, Dr. Fürer ordered a second audit of Nestlé's advertising and promotional methods in developing countries. Again, changes were made. These changes included revision of advertising copy to emphasize further the superiority of breast-feeding, elimination of radio advertising in the developing world, and cessation of the use of white uniforms on the mothercraft nurses.

At the same time, on May 23, 1974, WHO adopted a resolution that misleading promotion had contributed to the decline in breast-feeding in the developing countries and urged individual countries to take legal action to curb such abuses.

The Third World Action Group

In June 1974, the infant formula issue moved into Switzerland. A small, poorly financed group called the Third World Action Group located in Bern, the capital of Switzerland, published in German a booklet entitled *Nestlé Kills Babies (Nestlé Totet Kinder)*. This was a partial translation of the War on Want publication *The Baby Killer*. Some of the qualifying facts found in Mr. Muller's booklet were omitted in *Nestlé Kills Babies,* while the focus was changed from a general attack on bottle-feeding to a direct attack on Nestlé and its promotional practices.

Nestlé top management was extremely upset by this publication. Dr. Fürer immediately ordered a follow-up audit of Nestlé's marketing practices to ensure stated corporate ethical standards were being observed. Nestlé management also believed that the infant formula issue was being used as a vehicle by leftist, Marxist groups intent on attacking the free-market system, multinational companies in general, and Nestlé in particular. Internal Nestlé memoranda of the time reveal the material available to management that supported their belief that the issue went beyond infant formula promotion. For example:

Having a closer look at the allies of the AG3W in their actions, we realize that they happen to have the same aim. There are common actions with the leninist progressive organizations (POCH), who are also considered to be pro-Soviet, with the Swiss communist party (PdA) and the communist youth organization (KJV), as well as with the revolutionary marxist alliance (RML). Since the

AG3W has tried to coordinate the support of (only pro-communist) liberation movements with representatives of the communist block, it is not surprising that they also participate at the youth festival in Eastern Berlin.[1]

Believing the issue to be clearly legal, Nestlé management brought suit in July 1974 against 13 members of the Third World Action Group and against two newspapers who carried articles about *Nestlé Kills Babies*. Nestlé charged criminal libel, claiming that the company had been defamed because "the whole report charges Nestlé S.A. with using incorrect sales promotion in the third world and with pulling mothers away from breast-feeding their babies and turning them to its products." More specifically, Nestlé management claimed the following were defamatory:

The title "Nestlé Kills Babies."

The charge that the practices of Nestlé and other companies are unethical and immoral (written in the introduction and in the report itself).

The accusation of being responsible for the death or the permanent physical and mental damage of babies by its sales promotion policy (in the introduction).

The accusation that in less developed countries, the sales representatives for baby foods are dressed like nurses to give the sales promotion a scientific appearance.

The trial in Bern provided the Third World Action Group with a great deal of publicity, giving them a forum to present their views. Swiss television in particular devoted much time to coverage of the trial and the issues involved. The trial ended in the fall, 1976. Nestlé management won a judgment on the first of the libel charges (because of lack of specific evidence for the Third World Action Group), and the activists were fined 300 Swiss Francs each. Nestlé management dropped the remaining charges. In his judgment, the presiding judge added an opinion that became well-publicized:

the need ensues for the Nestlé company to fundamentally rethink its advertising practices in developing countries as concerns bottle-feeding, for its advertising practice up to now can transform a life-saving product into one that is dangerous and life-destroying. If Nestlé S.A. in the future wants to be spared the accusations of immoral and unethical conduct, it will have to change its advertising practices.

The Controversy Spreads

While the trial was in process, various interest groups from all over the world became interested and involved in the infant formula controversy. In London, England Mr. Mike Muller founded the Baby Foods Action Group. Late in 1974, the World Food Conference adopted a resolution recommending that developing-nation governments actively support breast-feeding. The PAG had been

---

[1] Third World Action Group (AG3W) *Der Zürichbieter,* August 15, 1973.

organizing a number of international regional seminars to discuss all aspects of the controversy. For example, in November 1974, during the PAG regional seminar in Singapore, the PAG recommended that the infant formula industry increase its efforts to implement Statement 23 and cooperate to regulate their promotion and advertising practices through a code of ethics.

The world health organizations kept up the pressure. In March 1975, the PAG again met:

> to discuss together the problem of deteriorating infant feeding practices in developing countries and to make recommendations for remedying the situation. The early discontinuance of breast-feeding by mothers in low-income groups in urban areas, leading to malnutrition, illness, and death among infants has been a serious concern to all.

In May 1975, WHO at its 14th plenary meeting again called for a critical review of promotion of infant formula products.

In response, representatives of the major formula producers met in Zürich, Switzerland in May 1975 to discuss the possibility and desirability of establishing an international code of ethics for the industry. Nine of the manufacturers, with the notable exceptions of Borden, Bristol-Myers, and Abbott, created an organization called the International Council of Infant Food Industries (ICIFI) and a code of marketing conduct. This code went into effect November 1, 1975. Some firms also adopted individual codes, including Nestlé, with standards higher than the ICIFI code.

The ICIFI code required that ICIFI members assume responsibility to encourage breast-feeding, that milk nurses be paid on a strict salary basis and wear company uniforms, and that product labels indicate breast milk as the best infant food. At this time, Nestlé began to phase out use of mass media for infant formula in developing countries, but continued to distribute educational materials and product information in the hospitals and clinics. Nestlé management believed such advertising and promotion was of educational value: to ensure proper use of formula and to decrease usage of sweetened and condensed milk for infant feeding.

ICIFI submitted its code of ethics to the PAG who submitted it to a number of third parties. On the basis of their opinions, the PAG refused to endorse the code saying it did not go far enough, that substantial amendments were required. ICIFI rejected these suggestions because of difficult antitrust considerations, so the PAG withheld its approval of the code.

An important exception to ICIFI membership was Abbott Laboratories. While Abbott representatives had attended the meeting that led to the establishment of ICIFI, they decided not to join. Abbott, having recently had difficulties with the U.S. Food and Drug Administration regarding the marketing of cyclamates and artificial sweeteners, felt ICIFI was not an adequate response to the public pressure:

> the most important area is to reduce the impact of advertising on the low-income, poorly educated populations where the risk is the greatest. The ICIFI code does not address this very important issue.

> Our company decided not to join ICIFI because the organization is not
> prepared to go far enough in answering this legitimate criticism of our industry.
> We feel that for Abbott/Ross to identify with this organization and its code would
> limit our ability to speak on the important issues.

Abbott acted largely independently of the other producers. Later in 1977,
Abbott management announced its intention to commit about $100,000 to a
breast-feeding campaign in developing nations and about $175,000 to a task
force on breast-feeding, infant formula, and Third World countries.

Developments in the United States

Although Nestlé U.S. neither manufactured nor marketed formula, management
found itself increasingly embroiled in the controversy during the mid-1970s.
The first major group to bring this matter to the public was the Interfaith Center
on Corporate Responsibility (ICCR). The ICCR, a union of 14 Protestant
denominations and approximately 150 Catholic orders and dioceses, was a
group concerned about the social responsibility behaviour of corporations. The
ICCR advised its members on this topic to guide decisions for the members'
combined investment portfolio of several billion dollars. Formerly known as the
Center of Corporate Responsibility, the ICCR was established under the tax-
exempt umbrella of the American National Council of Churches when the U.S.
Internal Revenue Service revoked the CCR tax exemption.

The ICCR urged its members to investigate the marketing practices of the
leading American formula producers, American Home Products, Abbott Laboratories, and Bristol-Myers. Stockholder groups demanded from these companies, as they were entitled to do by American law, detailed information
regarding market shares, promotion and advertising practices, and general
company policies concerning the infant formula business.

Nestlé management believed that the ICCR was interested in ideology
more than in baby formula. As support, they pointed to a statement made in a
January edition of ICCR's *The Corporate Examiner:*

> the motivations, ethos, and operations of transnational corporations are inimical to
> the establishment of a new economic order. Both justice and stability are under-
> mined in the fulfillment of their global vision.

Perhaps the major vehicle used by ICCR to get attention was a half-hour
film entitled *Bottle Babies*. Well-known German filmmaker Peter Krieg began
this film shortly after the Bern trial began. Nestlé Vevey management believed
that the film was partially sponsored by the World Council of Churches to
provide a public defense for the Third World Action Group position. Most of
the filming was done in Kenya, Africa in 1975 in a "documentary" style,
although Nestlé management pointed out that the film was scripted and in their
opinion, highly emotional and misleading. A letter (Exhibit 2) that Nestlé
management later received written by Professor Bwibo of the University of
Nairobi supported management's views about the *Bottle Babies* film.

EXHIBIT 2

14th April, 1978

Miss June Noranka
644 Summit Avenue
St. Paul
Minnesota 55105

Dear Miss Noranka:

Following your visit to Kenya and my office I write to inform you, your group, your colleagues, and any other person interested that the film Peter Krieg filmed in this department and the associated teaching areas, did not represent the right aspects of what we participated in during the filming.

The film which was intended to be a scientific and educational film turned out to be an emotional, biased, and exaggerated film—and failed to be a teaching film. It arouses emotions in people who have little chance to check these facts. No wonder it has heated the emotions of the Activists groups in America and I understand now spreading to Europe. I wish I was in an opportunity to be with your groups and we view the film together and I comment.

As a pediatrician, I would like to put on record that I have not seen the Commercial baby food companies pressure anybody to use their brands of milk. As for Nestlé, we have discussed with their Managing Directors, starting much earlier than the time of the film in 1971, as to the best way of approaching baby feeding and discussed extensively advertisement especially the material to be included. The directors have followed our advice and we are happy with their working conditions.

We are interested in the well-being of our children and we are Medical Scientists. So anything of scientific value we will promote but we will avoid imagined exaggerated and distorted views.

I am taking the liberty to copy this letter to Mr. Jones, managing director of Food Specialty in Nairobi who produce and make Nestlé's products here, for his information.

Yours sincerely,

NIMROD O. BWIBO
Professor & Chairman

ICCR distributed copies of the *Bottle Babies* film to church groups throughout the United States. Typically, the film was shown to a gathering of church members followed by an impassioned plea to write letters of protest and a request for funds to further the campaign. Since the film singled out Nestlé for attack in its last 10 minutes, Nestlé became symbolic of all that was wrong in the infant formula controversy in the minds of these religious groups. Nestlé management, however, was seldom asked for, or given an opportunity to present, its position on the issues.

While Nestlé felt the growing pressure of *Bottle Babies,* the major American formula producers faced a variety of ICCR-shareholder initiatives. ICCR requested detailed information from American Home Products, Abbott Laboratories, and Bristol-Myers. Each company responded differently.

American Home Products.   After refusing to release all the information ICCR requested, AHP faced a resolution to be included in its proxy statement. ICCR dropped the resolution the day before printing, when AHP management agreed:

To provide the requested information.

To send a report to its shareholders saying that many authorities believe misuse of infant formula in developing countries could be dangerous, that the company promotes breast-feeding while making available formula for mothers who cannot or do not choose to breast-feed, that the company would promote to medical professionals only and that AHP was a member of ICIFI which was developing a voluntary code of promotional practices.

Abbott Laboratories.   After a year and a half of meetings with ICCR, Abbott released most of the information ICCR wanted. Still, to obtain the rest of the data, ICCR shareholders filed a shareholder resolution. This proposal received less than the three percent of the vote required by the Securities and Exchange Commission (SEC) in order to resubmit the proposal at a later time. Thus, it was not resubmitted.

Bristol-Myers.   Bristol-Myers would not cooperate with ICCR so one church shareholder with 500 shares, Sisters of the Precious Blood, filed a shareholder resolution in 1975 asking that the information be released. After receiving 5.4 percent of the vote and having aroused the concern of the Ford Foundation and the Rockefeller Foundation, it appeared the resolution would be launched again the next year. In August 1975, Bristol-Myers management published a report "The Infant Formula Marketing Practices of Bristol-Myers Co. in Countries outside the United States." The 1976 proxy included the Sisters' resolution and a statement entitled "Management's Position." The Sisters maintained the statement was false and misleading and filed suit against management; statements appearing in a proxy statement are required by law to be accurate.

In May 1977, a U.S. district court judge dismissed the case, saying the Sisters had failed to show irreparable harm to themselves as the law requires.

The judge would not comment on the accuracy of the company's proxy report. The nuns appealed with the support of the SEC. In early 1978, the management of Bristol-Myers agreed to send a report outlining the dispute to all shareholders and to restrictions on company marketing practices including a ban on all consumer-directed promotion in clinics, hospitals, and other public places and a stop to using milk nurses in Jamaica.

In 1977, Abbott management agreed to revise their code of marketing conduct and to eliminate the use of nurses' uniforms by company salespeople despite the fact some were registered nurses.

ICCR and its supporters also persuaded Representative Michael Harrington, Democrat–Massachusetts to cosponsor a federal resolution requiring an investigation of U.S. infant formula producers.

The campaign against the formula producers took on a new dimension in mid-1977. A group called the Third World Institute, led by Doug Johnson at the University of Minnesota, formed the Infant Formula Action Coalition "IN-FACT" in June 1977. INFACT members were encouraged by ICCR and the Sisters, but felt that significant progress would not be made until Nestlé was pressured to change. INFACT realized that legal and shareholder action against a foreign-based company would be futile, so on July 4, 1977 INFACT announced a consumer boycott against those infant formula companies whose marketing practices INFACT found abusive. Despite the boycott's original target of several companies, Nestlé was the main focal point especially after the other major companies made concessions to ICCR. INFACT began the boycott in front of Nestlé's Minneapolis offices with a demonstration of about 100 people. INFACT urged consumers to boycott over 40 Nestlé products.

Nestlé management in White Plains was not sure what response to take. Nestlé U.S. was not at all involved with infant formula, but was genuinely concerned about the publicity INFACT was getting. Nestlé S.A. management on the other hand originally did not think the boycott campaign would amount to anything, that it was a project of some college kids in the United States based on misinformation about events in other parts of the world.

In September and October 1977, Nestlé senior managers from Vevey and White Plains met with members of INFACT, ICCR, the Ford Foundation, and other interested groups. Nestlé management had hoped to resolve what they thought was a problem of poor communication by explaining the facts. Nestlé management argued the company could not meet competition if it stopped all promotion, which would mean less sales and less jobs in the developing nations. Further, management claimed: "We have an instructional and educational responsibility as marketers of these products and, if we failed in that responsibility, we could be justly criticized." INFACT members stated they found the talks useful in clarifying positions, but concluded Nestlé was unwilling to abandon all promotion of its formula products.

In November 1977, INFACT decided not only to continue the boycott, but also to increase it to a national scale. INFACT held a conference in Minneapolis on November 2–4, for more than 45 organizers from 24 cities. These organizers represented women's groups, college hunger-action coalitions, health professionals, church agencies, and social justice groups. A clearinghouse was established to coordinate boycott efforts and information collection. The group also agreed to assist ICCR in its shareholder pressure campaign and to press for congressional action. Later, INFACT petitioned all U.S. government officials, state and federal, for support of the boycott. On November 21, the Interfaiths Hunger Coalition, a group affiliated with INFACT, demonstrated in front of Nestlé's Los Angeles sales office with about 150 people chanting "Nestlé kills babies." This demonstration received prominent media coverage as did other boycott activities. The combination of INFACT's boycott, ICCR's shareholder efforts, the exhibition of *Bottle Babies,* and the strong support of other U.S. activists (including Ralph Nader, Cesar Chavez, Gloria Steinem, and Dr. Benjamin Spock), resulted in an increasingly high profile for the infant formula controversy, even though Nestlé management believed there had been as yet no adverse effect on sales.

In early 1978, an unofficial WHO working group published the following statement:

> The advertising of food for nursing infants or older babies and young children is of particular importance and should be prohibited on radio and television. Advertising for mother's milk substitutes should never be aimed directly at the public or families, and advertising for ready-made infant food preparations should show clearly that they are not meant for less than three-month-old infants. Publicity for public consumption, which should in any case never be distributed without previous recommendation by the competent medical authority, should indicate that breast milk should always constitute the sole or chief constituent of food for those under three months. Finally, the distribution of free samples and other sales promotion practices for baby foods should be generally prohibited.

Nestlé management met again with INFACT representatives in February 1978. No progress was made in reconciling the two sides. Nestlé management could not accept statements from INFACT such as:

> The corporations provide the product and motivate the people to buy it, and set into motion a process that may cause the death of the baby. The corporations are responsible for that death. When the outcome is death, the charge against the corporation is murder.

Nonetheless, management learned what INFACT wanted:

> Stop all direct consumer promotion and publicity for infant formula.
>
> Stop employing "milk nurses" as sales staff.
>
> Stop distributing free samples to clinics, hospitals, and maternity hospitals.
>
> Stop promoting infant formula among the medical profession and public health profession.

To further publicize their campaign, INFACT representatives and their allies persuaded Senator Edward Kennedy, Democrat–Massachusetts, to hold Senate hearings on the infant formula issue in May 1978. CBS decided to make a TV report of the entire affair. To prepare for the hearings, INFACT organized a number of demonstrations across the United States. At one meeting on April 15, 1978, Doug Johnson said:

> The goal of the Nestlé's Boycott Campaign and of the entire infant formula coalition is to get the multinationals to stop promotion of infant formula. We're not asking them to stop marketing; we're not asking them to pull out of—out of the countries; we're simply asking them to stop the promotion, and in that I think we're—we're in agreement with a number of prestigious organizations. The World Health Organization recently asked the corporations to stop consumer advertising and to stop the use of free samples, and the International Pediatric Association did that several years ago. So, I think we're asking a very reasonable thing: to stop promoting something which is inappropriate and dangerous.

CBS filmed these demonstrations, but did not air them until after the Kennedy hearings.

The Kennedy Hearings and CBS Report

Senator Kennedy was chairman of the Subcommittee on Health and Scientific Research on Infant Nutrition. Both critics and members of the infant formula industry appeared before the Kennedy Committee in May 1978. Nestlé S.A. management decided not to send headquarters management or management from Nestlé U.S. Instead, they asked R. Oswaldo Ballarin, president and chairman of Nestlé, Brazil to represent Nestlé at the hearings. Dr. Ballarin began with a statement prepared by Nestlé U.S., but Senator Kennedy soon interrupted him as the following excerpt from the testimony indicates:

Dr. Ballarin: United States Nestlé's Company has advised me that their research indicates this is actually an indirect attack on the free world's economic system: a worldwide church organization with its stated purpose of undermining the free enterprise system is at the forefront of this activity.

Senator Kennedy: Now you can't seriously expect . . . [Noise in background: gavel banging] We'll be in order . . . we'll be in order now please. We'll be in order. Uh, you don't seriously expect us to accept that on face value, after we've heard as . . . as you must've, Doctor . . . if I could just finish my question . . . the . . . the testimony of probably 9 different witnesses. It seemed to me that they were expressing a very deep compassion and concern about the well-being of infants, the most vulnerable in this . . . face of the world. Would you agree with me that your product should not be used where there is impure water? Yes or no?

Dr. Ballarin: Uh, we give all the instructions . . .

Senator Kennedy: Just . . . just answers. What would you . . . what is your position?

Dr. Ballarin: Of course not. But we cannot cope with that.

Senator Kennedy: Well, as I understand what you say, is where there's impure water, it should not be used.

Dr. Ballarin: Yes.

Senator Kennedy: Where the people are so poor that they're not gonna realistically be able to continue to purchase it, and which is gonna . . . that they're going to dilute it to a point, which is going to endanger the health, that it should not be used.

Dr. Ballarin: Yes, I believe . . .

Senator Kennedy: Alright, now . . . then my final question is . . . is what do you . . . or what do you feel is your corporate responsibility to find out the extent of the use of your product in those circumstances in the developing part of the world? Do you feel that you have any responsibility?

Dr. Ballarin: We can't have that responsibility, sir. May I make a reference to . . .

Senator Kennedy: You can't have that responsibility?

Dr. Ballarin: No.

Dr. Ballarin's testimony continued (for example of excerpts, see Exhibit 3), but Nestlé management believed little attention was paid to it. Mr. Guerrant,

---

EXHIBIT 3 Further excerpts from Dr. Ballarin's testimony

Nestlé recognized that even the best products will not give the desired results if used incorrectly. We, therefore, placed great weight on educational efforts aimed at explaining the correct use of our product. Our work in this field has received the public recognition and approval of the official Pediatric Associations in many countries. Such educational efforts never attempt to infer that our product is superior to breast milk. Indeed, we have devoted much attention to the promotion of breast-feeding, and educational material has always insisted that breast-feeding is best for the baby.

Nevertheless, many factors militate against exclusive breast-feeding in the rapidly growing cities of Brazil as well as other developing countries, and our products are seen today as filling a valid need, just as they did when they were first introduced over 50 years ago. In recognition of this, all such products are subject to strict price control, while in many countries which do not have a local dairy industry, they are classified as essential goods and imported free of duty. In many cases, official agencies establish what they consider to be a fair margin for the manufacturers.

It must be stressed that many problems remain to be solved. Our production is far from reaching the total needs of the population. Hence, many mothers in the poorer population groups continue to supplement breast-feeding with foods of doubtful quality. Owing to the lack of adequate medical services, especially in the rural areas, misuse of any supplement can occur and we are very conscious of the need to improve our efforts. These efforts depend on continued cooperation between the infant food industry and health professionals. We have to be more and more conscious of our responsibility to encourage breast-feeding while researching new foods and safer methods for feeding babies who cannot be exclusively breast-fed. The dilemma facing industry and the health service alike, is how to teach these methods without discouraging breast-feeding.

---

president of Nestlé U.S. was very angry and wrote a letter to Senator Kennedy on May 26, 1978 protesting against the way he had treated Dr. Ballarin (Exhibit 4).

CBS aired its program on July 5, 1978. Again, Nestlé management was upset. In their view CBS had selected portions of the testimonies to make Nestlé

EXHIBIT 4 Excerpts from Mr. Guerrant's letter to Senator Kennedy

---

I am angry but more important deeply concerned about the example of our governmental processes exhibited this week by the Human Resources Subcommittee on Health and Scientific Research.

It was the general consensus of several people in the audience that your position toward the manufacturers was "you are guilty until you prove your innocence." Objectivity would have been more becoming, Senator.

Secondly, it seemed equally probable that prior to the hearing the prepared statements were reviewed and you were quite prepared to rebuff Dr. Ballarin on his statement "undermining the free enterprise system." Unaccustomed to television and this type of inquisition, Dr. Ballarin, who appeared voluntarily, was flustered and embarrassed.

Probably, for this gathering, the statement was too strong (though nothing to compare with their theme "Nestlé kills babies") and should have been more subtle. But the point is well made, and your apparent denial of this possibility concerns me.

As you may know, this whole issue gained its greatest momentum a few years ago in Europe fostered by clearly identified radical leftist groups. Their stated purpose is opposition to capitalism and the free enterprise system. I submit that they are not really concerned with infants in the Third World but are intelligent enough to know that babies, especially sick and dying, create maximum emotional response. Further, they are clever enough to know that the people most easy to "use" for their campaign, to front for them, are in churches and universities. These are good people, ready to rise against oppression and wrong-doing without, regrettably, truthful facts for objective research. I know, as my father is a retired Presbyterian minister, and I have a very warm feeling toward members of the church, Protestant and Catholic.

People with far left philosophies are not confined to Europe and are certainly represented in many accepted organizations here and abroad. (Please take the time to read the enclosed report of the 1977 Geneva Consultation of the World Council of Churches.) Associated with the World Council is the National Council of Churches, and one of their units is the Interfaith Centre for Corporate Responsibility. One of their major spokespersons appears to be Leah Margulies, who was present in your hearing.

Now, just briefly to the very complex infant food issue. As the U.S. Nestlé Company does not manufacture or sell any infant food products, we are unhappy with the attempted boycott of our products—at least 95 percent of these manufactured in the United States. The jobs and security of about 12,000 good U.S. employees are being threatened.

From our associates in Switzerland, and Nestlé companies in the Third World, we

EXHIBIT 4 *(concluded)*

have gathered hundreds of factual documents. Neither Nestlé nor the U.S. companies in this business claim perfection. Companies are comprised of human beings. However, virtually every charge against Nestlé has proved to be erroneous. Distorted "facts" and just pure propaganda have been answered by people with undeniable integrity and technical credentials. Quite some time ago, because of the accusations, Nestlé world headquarters in Switzerland studied every facet of their total infant food business, made immediate changes where warranted and established new and very clear policies and procedures regarding the conduct of this business.

I might add that Nestlé infant foods have undoubtedly saved hundreds of thousands of lives. There is not even one instance where proof exists that Nestlé infant food was responsible for a single death. The products are as essential in the Third World as in the industrialized world. Though the accusers use some statements by apparently qualified people, there is an overwhelming amount of data and number of statements from qualified medical, technical, and government representatives in the Third World confirming Nestlé's position.

At your hearing this week were the same identical charges made against Nestlé and the others years ago. These people will not recognize the changes made in marketing practices nor the irrefutable facts of the real infant health problems in the Third World. They continue to push the U.S. Nestlé boycott and continue to distribute the fraudulent film "Bottle Babies." (Please read Dr. Bwibo's letter enclosed.) Sincere, well-meaning church people continue to be used, as they have not had all the real facts available for analysis.

The above situation made me believe that the organizers must have some motivation for this campaign other than what appears on the surface. If it could possibly be what I think, then our representatives in government should proceed with caution, thorough study, and great objectivity, as your ultimate position can be of critical consequence. I am not a crusader, but I do feel the free enterprise system is best.

---

management look inept and confused. Mr. Guerrant wrote a letter of protest to CBS president Richard Salant (Exhibit 5).

Following the Kennedy hearings, representatives of Nestlé S.A., Abbott, Bristol-Myers, and American Home Products met privately with Senator Kennedy to explore a suggestion for a further hearing. Meanwhile, the president of ICIFI wrote Kennedy, pointing out that this was an international and not a U.S. domestic issue—and should therefore be discussed at a forum sponsored by WHO. Kennedy accepted ICIFI's suggestion and requested the Director General of WHO to sponsor a conference at which the question of an international code could be discussed.

A consensus emerged that a uniform code for the industry was required and that Kennedy and ICIFI would suggest that WHO sponsor a conference with that aim in mind. The conference would be comprised of WHO officials, ICIFI members and other companies, health and government officials from the

EXHIBIT 5 Excerpts from Mr. Guerrant's letter to CBS President Salant

In the first minute of the program the infant formula industry has been tried and convicted of causing infant malnutrition. The remainder of the program is devoted to reinforcing Mr. Myer's conclusion. Tools of persuasion include the emotionality of a needle sticking in a child's head and the uneasy answers of cross-examined industry witnesses who are asked not for the facts but to admit and apologize for their "guilt."

But CBS Reports chose to concentrate on the "rhetoric of concern" and the claims which permeate the rhetoric. Industry's response to the rhetoric is not glamorous but hits into the root causes of infant malnutrition—the poverty, disease, and ignorance existing in the areas of developing and developed countries. Those conditions are not easy for anthropologists, economists, scientists, or medical people to trace or explain. And certainly the reasons for them are not as identifiable as a major corporation. But in 30 minutes Mr. Myers and Ms. Roche identified four companies as a major reason for infant malnutrition.

One way Nestlé has attempted to meet the responsibility is by making capital investments in and transferring technology to the developing countries. Nestlé began this effort in 1921 in Brazil and now has almost 40,000 local employees working in 81 manufacturing facilities in 25 developing countries. Not only does Nestlé have a beneficial impact on those directly employed, the company also encourages and assists the development of other local supporting industries, such as the dairy industry and packaging plants.

Another way Nestlé meets its responsibility is to work with local governments and health authorities in educating consumers. Clinics, pamphlets, posters, books, and product labels emphasize the superiority of breast-feeding, demonstrate proper sanitation and diet for breast-feeding, and show in words and pictures how to correctly use formula products.

Neither of these positive approaches was covered in CBS Reports nor was there mention of the fact that infant mortality has declined worldwide over the past 30 years, nor that lack of sufficient breast milk is a major cause of infant malnutrition, nor that tropical diseases cause millions of deaths per year in developing countries. Any one of these facts would have provided some balance to the Myers-Roche report.

developing countries, and all appropriate concerned public groups. WHO accepted the idea and announced the conference date in the fall of 1979. Shortly after Nestlé management met with Kennedy, the National Council of Churches, comprised of about 30 major religious groups in the United States, announced that the question of supporting INFACT and ICCR would be discussed and decided at the NCC national conference in November 1978.

The Situation in October 1978

Dr. Fürer knew all senior Nestlé management felt personally attacked by critics of the industry. Not only was this the first major public pressure campaign ever encountered by Nestlé, but also Nestlé management felt its critics were using unfair tactics. For example, again and again they saw in boycott letters and articles a grotesque picture of a wizened child with a formula bottle nearby. Eventually this picture was traced to Dr. Derrick Jeliffe, an outspoken critic of the industry. He admitted to *Newsweek* he had taken the picture in a Caribbean hospital in 1964. Even though it seemed the media and many respected companies were against Nestlé, Dr. Fürer stated publicly:

> No one has the right to accuse us of killing babies. No one has the right to assert that we are guilty of pursuing unethical or immoral sales practices.

Nonetheless, under U.S. law a company is regarded as a public person which meant that the First Amendment applied; that is, Nestlé could not get legal relief against charges made by the critics unless the company could prove those charges were both wrong and malicious.

Further, Dr. Fürer was struck by the fact that all the demands for change were coming from developed countries. In fact, Nestlé had received many letters of support from people in the developing countries (Exhibit 6). Mr. Ernest Saunders, Nestlé vice president for infant nutrition products summarized his view as follows:

> Government and medical personnel tell us that if we stopped selling infant foods we would be killing a lot of babies.

EXHIBIT 6 Examples of support for Nestlé

1. I have been associated with the medical representatives of Nestlé in Kenya for the last five years. We have discussed on various occasions the problems of artificial feeding, in particular the use of proprietary milk preparations. We have all been agreed that breast-feeding should always come first. As far as I am aware, your representatives have not used any unethical methods when promoting Nestlé products in this country.

   M. L. Oduori, Senior Consultant
   Pediatrician
   Ministry of Health
   Kenyatta National Hospital, Nairobi
   Kenya, Dec. 23, 1974

2. You are not "killing babies," on the contrary your efforts joined with ours contribute to the improvement of the Health Status of our infant population.

   We consider your marketing policies as ethical and as not being opposite to our recommendations. We note with pleasure that you employ a fully qualified nurse and that during discussions with mothers she always encourages breast-feeding, recommending your products when only natural feeding is insufficient or fails.

   Dr. Jerry Lukowski
   Chief Gynecologist, Menelik Hospital
   Ethiopia, Dec. 3, 1974

EXHIBIT 6 *(continued)*

3. Over several decades I have had direct and indirect dealings with your organisation in South Africa in relation to many aspects of nutrition among the nonwhite population who fall under our care, as well as the supply of nutriments to the hospital and peripheral clinics.

    I am fairly well aware of the extent of your Company's contributions to medical science and research and that this generosity goes hand in hand with the highest ethical standards of advertising, distribution of products, and the nutrition educational services which you provide.

    At no time in the past have my colleagues or I entertained any idea or suspicion that Nestlé have behaved in any way that could be regarded as unethical in their promotions, their products or their educational programmes. On all occasions when discussion of problems or amendments to arrangements have been asked for, full cooperation has been given to this department.

    Your field workers have given and are giving correct priorities in regard to breast feeding, and, where necessary, the bottle feeding of infants.

    The staff employed to do this work have shown a strong sense of responsibility and duty towards the public whom they serve, no doubt due to the educational instruction they have themselves received in order to fit them for their work.

    > S. Wayburne, Chief Pediatrician
    > Baragwanath Hospital
    > Associate Professor of Pediatrics,
    > Acting Head of Department of
    > Pediatrics, University of
    > Witwaterbrand/South Africa
    > Dec. 18, 1974

4. I have read about the accusation that "Nestlé Kills Babies" and I strongly refute it, I think it is quite unjustifiable.

    On my experience I have never seen any mother being advised to use artificial milk when it was not necessary. Every mother is advised to give breast foods to her baby. It is only when there is failure of this, then artificial foods are advised.

    I, being a working mother have brought up my five children on Nestlé Products and I do not see anything wrong with them. I knew I would have found it difficult to carry on with my profession if I had nothing to rely on like your products.

    Your marketing policies are quite in order as I knew them and they are quite ethical. As they stress on breast milk foods first and if this is unobtainable then one can use Nestlé's Products.

    > Mrs. M. Lema, Nursing Officer
    > Ocean Hospital
    > Dar-es-Salaam/TANZANIA
    > Dec. 16, 1974

EXHIBIT 6 *(concluded)*

5. On behalf of the Sisters of Nazareth Hospital, I thank you heartily for your generous contribution in giving us the Nestlé products in a way that we can assist and feed many undernourished children freely cured and treated in our hospital.

Trusting in your continuous assistance allow me to express again my sincerest thanks, and may God bless you.

Nazareth Hospital
Nairobi, Kenya
September 9, 1978

6. I am very grateful for this help for our babies in need in the maternity ward.

Another mission has asked me about this milk gift parcels, if there would be any chance for them. It is Butula Mission and they have a health centre with beds and maternity and maternal child health clinics. There is a lot of malnutrition also in that area, so that mothers often do not produce enough milk for their babies. It would be wonderful if you could help them also.

Nangina Hospital
Medical Mission Sisters
Funyula, Kenya
June 15, 1976

7. As a doctor who has practiced for 18 years in a developing country, I was angered by the collection of half-truths, judiciously mixed with falsehoods put out by the Infant Formula Action Coalition as reported in the *Newsweek* article on breast-feeding. Whether we like it or not, many mothers cannot or will not resort to breast-feeding. I do not believe that advertising has played any significant part in their decision. It is an inescapable necessity that specific, nutritionally balanced formulas are available. Otherwise, we would witness wholesale feeding with products that are unsuitable.

I carry no brief for companies like Nestlé, but have always found it to be a company with the highest regard to ethical standards. Infant formulas have saved many thousands of lives. What alternative are their critics proposing?

D. C. Williams, M.D.
Kuala Lumpur
Malaysia

8. Surely, Nestlé is not to blame. There have been similar problems here but through the efforts of the Save the Children Fund and government assistance, feeding bottles can only be purchased through chemists or hospitals by prescription. In this way, the decision of whether to breast-feed or not is decided by qualified personnel.

I would think that Americans would have better things to do than walk around disrupting commerce with placards.

Gail L. Hubbard
Goroka, Papua New Guinea

Dr. Fürer also believed that the scientific facts underlying the breast versus bottle controversy were not being given adequate attention (for example, see Exhibit 7) nor were the changes Nestlé and the other companies had made. Nestlé's policies regarding infant formula products were apparently not well known. Exhibit 8 includes excerpts from the latest edition, dated September 1, 1977.

EXHIBIT 7 Examples of supplementary information on breast-feeding versus bottle-feeding

1. Findings of the Human Lactation Center (HLC).

The HLC is a scientific research institute, a nonprofit organization dedicated to worldwide education and research on lactation. The HLC entered the breast/bottle controversy between the infant formula industry and the anti-multinational groups in an attempt to clarify certain issues. Eleven anthropologists, all women, studied infant feeding practices in 11 different cultures, ranging from a relatively urbanized Sardinian village to a very impoverished Egyptian agricultural village. Their findings:

> Poverty is correlated with infant morbidity (disease). Child health is associated with affluence.

> Infant mortality had decreased in the three decades prior to 1973 when food prices began to escalate.

> Breast milk is the best infant food but breast-feeding exclusively for most *undernourished* women in the less developed countries is inadequate beyond the baby's third month. Lack of sufficient food after this time is a major cause of morbidity and mortality whether or not the infant is breast-fed.

> Mixed feeding is an almost universal pattern in traditional cultures; that is, breast-feeding and supplementary feeding from early on and often into the second year.

> The preferred additional food for the very young child is milk. Most milk is fresh milk, unprocessed.

> *Most* women still breast-feed though many do not. The popular assumption that breast-feeding is being reduced has not been verified.

> Third World women with the least amount of resources, time or access to health care and weaning foods, have no choice but to breast-feed.

> More than half the infants they bear do not survive due to lack of food for themselves and their children.

> Women who are separated from close kin, especially the urban poor, lack mothering from a supportive figure. They find themselves unable to lactate adequately or lose their milk entirely. Without suitable substitutes, their infants die.

> Middle class women in the less-developed countries, market women, the elite and professional women are moving towards bottle feeding with infant formula in much the same way women turned from breast to bottle feeding in the western countries.

EXHIBIT 7 *(continued)*

The current literature on breast-feeding in the developing countries is meager. Information on mortality, the incidence of breast-feeding, the content of infant food, and the amount of breast milk, tend to be impressionistic reports by well-meaning western or western trained persons often unaware of the complexities of feeding practices and insensitive to the real-life situation of the mothers. Judgments for action based on these inconclusive data could be dangerous.

Mothers have a sensitive and remarkable grasp of how best to keep their infants alive. Neither literacy nor what has been called "ignorance" determine which infants live and which die except as they are related directly to social class.

In seeking solutions to the problems of infant well-being in the developing world, we must listen to the mothers and involve them in the decisions which will affect their lives.

2. *The Feeding of the Very Young: An Approach to Determination of Policies*, report of the International Advisory Group on Infant and Child Feeding to the Nutrition Foundation, October 1978:

"Two basic requirements of successful feeding are: (1) adequate milk during the first four to six months of life, and (2) adequate complementary foods during the transition to adult diets. It is imperative that all societies recognize these requirements as a major component of nutrition policy. The extent to which mothers are able to meet both of these requirements will vary under different cultural and sociological circumstances. In all societies there will be some proportion of mothers who will not be able to meet them without assistance, and policy must be developed to protect those children who are at risk of malnutrition resulting from inadequacy in either one or both of these basic requirements."

Source: Nestlé memoranda.

EXHIBIT 7 *(concluded)*

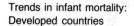

Trends in infant mortality:
Developed countries

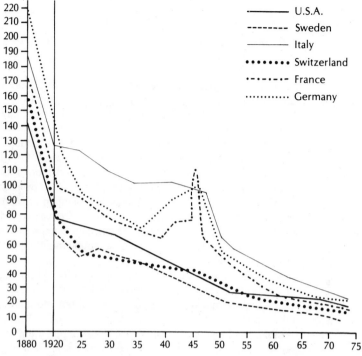

Trends in infant mortality:
Developing countries

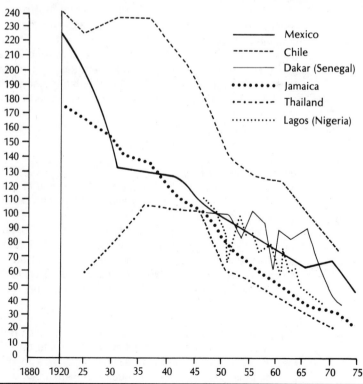

Source: Demographic Yearbook, United Nations.

EXHIBIT 8 Excerpts from Nestlé directives on infant and dietetic products policy

Infant milks

It is recognized that breast milk is the best food for a baby. Our baby milks are therefore not intended to compete with breast milk, but to supplement breast feeding when the mother's own milk can no longer cover the baby's needs or to replace it when mothers cannot, or elect not to breast feed.

Three to four months after birth, the quantities of breast milk produced by the average mother become insufficient to satisfy the growing needs of the baby. The baby needs a supplement of water and food. From this moment on, in the poor communities of developing countries this baby is in danger because water is sometimes polluted and local foods, like plantain or manioc, are nutritionally inadequate. They are starchy foods with little food value and a young baby cannot digest them. Thus the highest infant mortality occurs precisely in areas where babies receive only mother's milk plus a supplement of unboiled local water and/or starchy decoctions.

This is not a Nestlé theory. This is a fact known by every Third World doctor and recently scientifically demonstrated by British researchers working in Africa.

The alternative to traditional local supplement is a properly formulated breast milk substitute, preferably a humanized formula. It is true that there is a risk of misuse, but these risks exist with a local supplement too, although the baby has a better chance of survival when the starting point is of high quality.

It is precisely to reduce the risks of misuse and thereby increase the chances of survival that we had developed over the years a comprehensive programme of information and education: contact with doctors, educative advertising, booklets, nurses; all this had the purpose of making the alternative to local supplements known and ensuring a proper and safe use of our products when needed. Nestlé policies are designed to avoid the unnecessary replacement of breast milk.

The real issue is not breast milk versus formula, as so often pictured, but breast milk plus formula plus education versus traditional foods like manioc.

Products must be in line with internationally recognized nutritional criteria and offer definite consumer benefits.

Distribution policy

It is a rule that PID products are never sold to mothers directly by us; distribution aims at making products available to prescribers and users under optimum safety and price conditions.

Within the limits set by the law and by the distribution structure, we practice mixed distribution (pharmacies and general food stores) and use the normal market channels. On the other hand, dietetic specialties and products designed for delicate or sick babies, which are basically sold on medical prescription, are sold only through pharmacies, unless special local conditions warrant mixed distribution.

Communication policy—direct contact with mothers

Medical representatives must not enter into direct contact with mothers, unless they are authorized to do so in writing by a medical or health authority and provided that they are properly qualified. Films may be shown with the agreement of the medical or public health authorities concerned.

EXHIBIT 8 *(concluded)*

Visits to mothers in their homes are not allowed unless the responsible medical authority has made a written request for a visit to take place.

Personnel policy

The main task of the medical promotion personnel consists in contacting the medical and paramedical professions and hospitals. They are not concerned with direct sales to mothers and cannot sell dietetic products other than, exceptionally and exclusively, to the trade or institutions.

Specialized training must be given to such staff, to enable them to render a genuine service to the medical and paramedical professions and give them scientific and unbiased information on product characteristics and utilization.

No sales-related bonus will be paid to any staff engaged in medical promotion or having direct contact with mothers. If a bonus is to be paid, it must depend on elements other than sales, such as personal qualities and qualifications.

Many members of management believed the attack against Nestlé was ideologically based. They gathered information about and quotations from many of the activist groups to support their position (for example, see Exhibit 9). Whatever their foundation, the critics seemed to Dr. Fürer to be gaining publicity and momentum. INFACT claimed at least 500 separate action committees in the United States, support in about 75 communities in Canada, as well as support in about 10 other countries. "The movement is snowballing," reported Gwen Willens of INFACT. "We're getting over 300 letters of support every day."

As Dr. Fürer consulted with senior management in Nestlé, he wondered what further steps Nestlé might take to deal with the controversy surrounding the marketing of infant formula products in the developing countries.

EXHIBIT 9 Examples of comments concerning the ideology of the activist group

Sue Tafler and Betsy Walker, "Why Boycott Nestlé?" in *Science for the People*, January/February 1978.

> Unfortunately, the power in many developing countries is not held by the people themselves, and local ruling elites often want to encourage corporate investment. . . . What the boycott will not do is overthrow capitalism. . . . The boycott can unite well-meaning groups that see themselves as apolitical with more openly political groups. . . . We can have the effect of politicizing others working in the coalition. If Nestlé does make some concessions to the demands of the boycott, the sense of victory can give encouragement to the organizers of the boycott to continue on to larger struggles.

T. Balasusiya, Centre for Society and Religion, Colombo, Sri Lanka, participant at the World Council of Churches meeting, January 1977.

EXHIBIT 9 *(concluded)*

The capitalist system is the main cause of the increasing gap and within that system multinationals are a main form. Ideology of wealth is the practical religion of capitalist society. Churches are legitimizers of the system, so their first job is self-purification. There can be no neutrality between money and God.

Our function is not to judge persons, but we have to judge systems. . . . What alternative solutions do countries propose that have rejected the capitalist system, e.g., USSR, China, Cuba, Tanzania? Capitalism is inherently contradictory to the Gospel.

M. Ritchie, at a conference, "Clergy and Laity Concerned," August 1978.

It's not just on babies, it's not just multinational corporations, it's class conflict and class struggle. Broadening the constituency both of people interested in the infant formula issue . . . how the infant formula campaign and the people there link up completely in terms of support and action with other types of campaigns. . .

I think ultimately what we're trying to do is take an issue-specific focus campaign and move it in conjunction with other issue-specific campaigns into a larger very class-wide very class-conscious campaign and reasserting our power in this country, our power in this world.

Douglas Johnson of INFACT, at an address in Washington, September 1978.

Our hope is that we can use this [boycott] campaign as the forerunner of legislation for control of multinational corporations.

Source: Nestlé internal memoranda.

Case 37

Litton Industries, Inc.*

Introduction

Fridays were always the worst day of the week for Marc Stillwell. As an administrative law judge for the Federal Trade Commission, he frequently considered his workload burdensome, but Fridays always seemed the worst. While many civil servants spent the afternoon clearing off their desks preparing to start off fresh the following Monday, Stillwell was cramming his briefcase with case files and court briefs that would require his attention over the weekend. He felt he'd be lucky if he could spare the time to watch a little football on Sunday, judging by the bulge in his briefcase.

The Litton Industries case decision had to be made soon, and as the presiding administrative law judge, he would have to prepare a detailed decision including his reasoning for the conclusions reached. The FTC staff attorneys and the Litton attorneys had both filed their final statements containing their arguments and findings of fact, and he would have to sort out from these conflicting documents what was actually correct.

Although it was not surrounded by the heavy publicity that characterized some of the more dramatic cases he had worked on in the past, the Litton case was important because it contained some important issues concerning the use of surveys in advertising, and the increasing use of comparisons between competitors in advertising with actual names of competitors being used. He knew it was commission policy to encourage advertising that uses factual data such as that obtained from surveys and that the agency also wanted to encourage comparison advertising. At the same time he had to decide if in this case these goals conflicted with another FTC policy—that no advertising should be unfair or deceptive.

In addition to deciding if Litton had engaged in unfair or deceptive advertising and if they had adequate substantiation for the claims made, he also had to determine an appropriate remedy if the company was found guilty. A proposed order had been recommended by the FTC staff attorneys, and he would have to decide if it was reasonable or whether some other order would be better.

* This case was prepared by Kenneth L. Bernhardt and Larry M. Robinson, Assistant Professor of Marketing, Georgia State University. Copyright © 1984 by the authors.

The Company

Litton Industries, Inc., was founded in November 1953 as a small electronics firm in San Carlos, California. Revenues that year were less than $3 million. By the end of fiscal 1978, Litton was the 99th largest U.S. corporation with revenues exceeding $3.65 billion.[1] But Litton's management still held to a strategy laid out in the company's first annual report:

> The company's management [has] planned first to establish a base of profitable operations in advanced electronic development and manufacturing. Utilizing this base, the plan contemplates building a major electronics company by developing new and advanced products and programs and by acquiring others having potential in complementing fields. . . . This plan is designed to establish strong proprietary product values and a "broad base" on which to grow—a profitable balance between commercial and military customers and an integrated but diversified line of electronic products.[2]

By 1980, Litton had grown to become a widely diversified, international industrial conglomerate with 175 manufacturing and research facilities in the United States and around the world employing over 90,400 people. The corporation produced such products as business computer systems, business furniture, calculators, copiers, Royal typewriters, Sweda cash registers and POS/retail information systems, machine and hand tools, material-handling systems, specialty metal products, electronic components, biomedical equipment, paper and printed products, medical professional publications including the *Physicians Desk Reference,* textbook publications, airborne navigation systems, electronic signal surveillance equipment, and so on. Litton's Ingalls Shipbuilding subsidiary built U.S. Navy destroyers and nuclear submarines. Exhibit 1 contains Litton's sales by product line.

As can be seen, Litton Industries produced primarily commercial, industrial, and defense-related products. However, the company's electronic and electrical products division successfully produced and marketed at least one major consumer good—microwave ovens.

Microwave Ovens

Microwave cooking was first developed shortly after World War II as an offshoot of advancements in radar technology. Although microwave ovens were introduced as early as 1954 principally for institutional and commercial use, consumer models were not mass marketed until early 1970. Improvements in production technology corresponded in time with tremendous demand for convenience goods and fast-food services. In 1970 the industry sold about 40,000 microwave ovens. The Association of Home Appliance Manufacturers estimated that by the end of 1978 market penetration for microwave ovens in

---

[1] "The Forbes 500s," *Forbes,* May 14, 1979, p. 234.

[2] Litton Industries, Inc., *Annual Report, Fiscal 1978,* p. 4.

EXHIBIT 1 Litton's sales breakdown ($000)

Sales and service revenues by product line—continuing operations (unaudited)

	Year ended July 31,				
	1978	*1977*	*1976*	*1975*	*1974*
Business systems and equipment					
Business machines and retail information systems	$ 448,109	$ 373,489	$ 389,970	$ 431,941	$ 450,805
Typewriters and office copiers	321,970	302,078	284,903	284,385	302,344
Office products, furniture, and fixtures	177,510	157,899	147,408	143,396	151,638
Intrasegment eliminations	(855)	(1,134)	(1,394)	(9,821)	(2,881)
	946,734	832,332	820,887	849,901	901,906
Industrial systems and services					
Machine tools	282,475	252,238	223,678	242,909	219,453
Resource exploration	235,494	161,206	159,632	177,436	135,705
Material handling	95,559	79,705	81,513	91,423	96,677
	613,528	493,149	464,823	511,768	451,835
Electronic and electrical products					
Microwave cooking products	179,640	160,104	129,400	69,431	50,585
Medical and electronic products	160,964	187,762	220,776	217,163	192,527
Electronic and electrical components	398,241	336,742	305,389	313,395	306,880
Intrasegment eliminations	(6,759)	(8,492)	(7,527)	(4,800)	(3,346)
	732,086	676,116	648,038	595,189	546,646
Paper, printing, and publishing					
Specialty paper, printing, and forms	215,561	194,108	199,630	190,517	165,126
Educational and professional publishing	74,924	64,676	57,888	61,593	64,488
	290,485	258,784	257,518	252,110	229,614
Advanced electronic systems					
Navigation and control systems	315,045	276,719	286,278	248,034	212,935
Communications and electronic data systems	222,427	203,809	187,236	205,154	185,761
Intrasegment eliminations	(7,520)	(5,502)	(4,797)	(4,725)	(5,241)
	529,952	475,026	468,717	448,463	393,455
Marine engineering and production	616,069	792,213	794,142	906,851	642,618
	3,728,854	3,527,620	3,454,125	3,564,282	3,166,074
Intersegment eliminations	(89,935)	(96,852)	(120,429)	(153,433)	(164,191)
Miscellaneous	14,290	12,156	20,856	1,340	898
Sales and service revenues—continuing operations	$3,653,209	$3,442,924	$3,354,552	$3,412,189	$3,002,781

The above table sets forth the sales and service revenues of continuing operations by classes of similar products or services within the business segments.

Source: Litton Industries, Inc., 1978 Annual Report.

American households would reach 10 percent. Over 2.8 million ovens were sold in 1979, representing sales of over $1.25 billion.

The working principle of microwave cooking is actually quite simple. Microwaves are electromagnetic or radio waves in the gigahertz (in excess of one billion hertz or cycles per second) frequency range with wave lengths between one and one hundred centimeters. The Federal Communication Commission, which regulates all forms of electromagnetic transmissions, has set aside a frequency range equal to 2.45 gigahertz for the use of microwave ovens.

The device inside of these ovens that emits the microwave energy is known as a "magnetron microwave generator." Microwaves, if applied with sufficient energy, will cause the water molecules within food substances to become agitated and start to vibrate. This vibrating action generally begins, unlike conventional cooking, deep within the middle of whatever is being cooked. The vibrating molecules create friction which heats the food, generally in one fourth the time it would take conventionally.

All microwave ovens work on this simple principle, although most manufacturers have added features to facilitate the process further or that overcome some of the inherent problems in microwave cooking. Generally, foods cooked in a microwave oven are more nutritional and have a better, more natural flavor than conventionally prepared foods due to less water and natural vitamin content loss. Of course, the most desired feature remains the faster cooking speed.

Microwave cooking is not suitable for all types of food, a factor that ensures conventional ovens will not become obsolete in the near future. Meats and bread products are notable "problem" foods: Meat because it cooks from the inside out in a microwave oven and tends not to brown on the outside; and bread products because the water content quickly evaporates causing it to harden or not to rise properly. Manufacturers are trying to overcome these problems. Older model ovens generally were powered at a fixed energy level. Newer models, with a variable temperature feature, can emit microwaves intermittently or at different power settings up to the FCC maximum of 625 watts, which assists in more uniform cooking.

In the 1970s advancements in another type of technology took place that vastly affected the nature of microwave cooking. The development of silicon chips and microcircuitry was quickly adopted by the appliance industry to simplify and automate many procedures. Many of today's microwave ovens incorporate such "minicomputers" to facilitate cooking processes. For example, Litton's newest microwave oven, the model 560 Meal-In-One Oven, uses a microprocessor with four levels of memory. This oven "knows" how to cook, reheat, or defrost 47 types of frequently prepared foods with just a touch of a button on a keyboard-like control panel.

Litton's history in electronic technology allowed the company to be one of the first manufacturers of consumer microwave ovens. By 1979 the company was the largest manufacturer with a 25 percent market share. Amana, a division of the Raytheon Corporation and also an early pioneer in the microwave cooking field, was the second largest producer with 20 percent of the market, followed by Sharp, General Electric, and Tappan with 15, 10, and 10 percent shares respectively. Litton's microwave sales contributed almost $180 million in revenues to the company in 1978.

Primary Demand

Until 1978 microwave oven sales for the industry had been increasing at an annual rate exceeding 45 percent, and it has been estimated that by 1985 almost 50 percent of American households would be using the product. Microwave ovens were capable of handling over 80 percent of a household's normal cooking.

Demand for microwaves began to fall off sharply in mid-1978, surprising analysts who expected sales to begin to decline only after market penetration of America's 80 million households exceeded the 20 percent level. In the first six months of 1978, unit sales were only 14 percent ahead of the same period in the previous year. Comparatively, the growth rate for the first six months of 1977 was 43 percent. This represented a shakeout period in the industry with two manufacturers, Farberware and Admiral, dropping out of the American microwave market.

Industry experts generally concurred on several reasons for the unexpected slump. By 1978 there were 35 different manufacturers with microwave models on the U.S. market. The proliferation of brands, each with its own array of special features, was believed to have injected a great deal of confusion into consumer purchasing decisions. The complicated controls on many of the models also was believed to have scared off potential buyers.

Because it was a new and fairly expensive product, the proper marketing strategy called for knowledgeable salespeople to explain and demonstrate the microwave oven's many uses. Industry analysts pointed out that by 1978 most dealers were not putting enough effort into actual cooking demonstrations and other "push type" marketing strategies. This became especially true as mass merchandise retail chains began selling the product. Such stores had neither the time nor the trained salespeople to devote to the kind of personal selling required for such a product.

Another speculation as to the cause for the sudden slump in sales was related to market segmentation. As the manufacturers struggled to differentiate their products from those of their competitors, they began to upgrade their products by adding such items as probes that could automatically cook meat to the correct temperature, rotating carousels to ensure uniform cooking, browning units, defrosting cycles, variable temperature controls, memory storage, delayed timing controls, and so forth. Most manufacturers continued to market the basic, no frills oven models, but emphasis was placed on the deluxe-type models with all the added features. There was a good reason for this, since the fastest growing market segment, representing 32 percent of dollar volume sold, was for the expensive model ovens with retail prices of $450 and up. Litton's Model 560, for example, retailed for $629 and had been very popular.

To date, therefore, there had been very little incentive for manufacturers and retailers to lower prices to encourage demand. Members of the market segment for the more expensive models tended to have higher incomes and better educations, and were more likely to be familiar with the microwave principle, and to have seen it in actual use by friends or relatives. Such consumers were less likely to misunderstand the safety-related factors that had caused much apprehension in the early introductory stages.

Industry experts had begun to wonder whether sales to this particular market segment had reached the saturation level. Many felt that it was time that microwave manufacturers began to concentrate on selling to the larger, more price-conscious market segment which had remained mostly untapped. Research studies over a period of several years showed that there was a large segment of the market (86 percent) who consistently had stated that they had no plans to purchase a microwave oven. Trade analysts felt that many of these people could be encouraged to buy if prices were lower.

Although it remained slightly ahead of the industry with a 20 percent growth rate in 1978, Litton felt the effects of the general sales slump. The company reacted aggressively. The 1978 advertising budget already had been increased by 13.5 percent to over $21.5 million. To counter declining demand, the 1979 ad budget was increased to about $50 million. The company decided to stress product education as the key to market growth, and a large portion of the budget was earmarked for sales training, dealer promotions, and in-store demonstrations. Over 2,000 home economists were hired across the country to demonstrate the product in appliance and department stores, shopping malls, and grocery chains.

The Federal Trade Commission complaint

On January 31, 1979, the Federal Trade Commission formally issued a complaint against Litton stating that some of their earlier advertisements constituted "unfair and deceptive acts or practices in or affecting commerce and unfair methods of competition in or affecting commerce in violations of Section 5 of the Federal Trade Commission Act."[3] The complaint concerned a series of 1976 and 1977 ads in such publications as *Newsweek* and *The Wall Street Journal* that featured the results of an "independent" survey. The FTC charged the ads claimed that:

1. The majority of independent microwave oven service technicians would recommend Litton to their customers.
2. The majority of independent microwave oven service technicians are of the opinion that Litton microwave ovens are superior in quality to all other brands.
3. The majority of independent microwave oven service technicians are of the

---

[3] Federal Trade Commission Complaint, Docket No. 9123, January 31, 1979, p. 5.

opinion that Litton microwave ovens require the fewest repairs of all microwave brands.

4. The majority of independent microwave oven service technicians have Litton microwave ovens in their homes.[4]

The FTC stated that such claims were deceptive and unfair and that there was "no reasonable basis of support for the representations in those advertisements, at the time those representations were made."[5]

The FTC formally alleged that the survey in no way could be described as "independent." They claimed that Litton hired Custom Research, Inc., to conduct the survey but that Litton designed the survey instrument and analyzed the results themselves and that Custom Research had only engaged in telephoning the respondents who were selected from a list of names supplied by Litton.

The FTC also claimed that the list of respondents were drawn exclusively from a list of Litton-authorized microwave service agencies. The surveys also failed to show that the respondents knew enough about competing brands of microwave ovens to make a comparison to Litton's ovens. The commission also stated that the base number of respondents was too small to have any statistical significance.

In summary, "the sample surveyed was not representative of the population of independent microwave oven service technicians and the survey was biased."[6] (Refer to Exhibit 2 for a copy of the Federal Trade Commission complaint. Exhibit 3 shows a sample copy of the Litton advertisements in question.)

The filing of the FTC complaint was accompanied with the usual notice stating the time and place of an administrative hearing at which time Litton had to show cause why it should not be subject to a cease and desist order. Litton did not choose to enter into a consent agreement, whereby the company would not have admitted any of the charges and would have negotiated an order outlining an agreed upon remedy.

At the time the complaint was originally issued, a Litton spokesman made the following public response to the charges:

> We employed an independent research firm to survey our authorized independent microwave service agencies numbering over 500 throughout the U.S. Litton surveyed only those servicemen who repaired at least two brands of ovens and tabulated their response only as to the brands they serviced. Litton feels the claims made in the ads, that up to 80 percent of the servicemen would recommend purchase of Litton microwave ovens, were accurately represented, and that the FTC's concerns are unfounded.[7]

---

[4] Ibid., p. 2.

[5] Ibid., p. 4.

[6] Ibid.

[7] "Litton Industries, Inc.'s Microwave Oven Ads Deceptive, FTC Says," *The Wall Street Journal,* February 2, 1979, p. 4.

EXHIBIT 2 Litton complaint and proposed order

UNITED STATES OF AMERICA
BEFORE FEDERAL TRADE COMMISSION

In the Matter of
LITTON INDUSTRIES, INC.,
a corporation.

DOCKET NO. 9123

COMPLAINT

Pursuant to the provisions of the Federal Trade Commission Act, and by virtue of the authority vested in it by said Act, the Federal Trade Commission, having reason to believe that Litton Industries, Inc., a corporation (hereafter "Respondent" or "Litton"), has violated the provisions of said Act, and it appearing to the Commission that a proceeding by it in respect thereof would be in the public interest, hereby issues its complaint stating its charges in that respect as follows:

PARAGRAPH ONE: Litton Industries, Inc., is a corporation, organized, existing, and doing business under and by virtue of the laws of the State of Delaware, with its executive office and principal place of business located at 360 North Crescent Drive, Beverly Hills, California 90210. Litton's Microwave Cooking Products Division is located at 1405 Xenium Lane North, Minneapolis, Minnesota 55441.

PARAGRAPH TWO: Litton is now, and for some time in the past has been, engaged in the manufacture, distribution, advertising, and sale of various products including microwave ovens.

PARAGRAPH THREE: Respondent Litton causes the said products, when sold, to be transported from its place of business in various states of the United States to purchasers located in various other states of the United States and in the District of Columbia. Respondent Litton maintains, and at all times mentioned herein has maintained, a course of trade in said products in and affecting commerce. The volume of business in such commerce has been and is substantial.

PARAGRAPH FOUR: In the course and conduct of said business, Litton has disseminated and caused the dissemination of advertisements for microwave ovens manufactured by Litton, by various means in or affecting commerce, including magazines and newspapers distributed by the mail and across state lines, for the purpose of inducing and which were likely to induce, directly or indirectly, the purchase of said microwave ovens.

PARAGRAPH FIVE: Typical and illustrative of the advertisements so disseminated or caused to be disseminated by Litton are the advertisements attached as Exhibits A, B, C and D, designated as the "initial consumer microwave independent technician survey advertisement," the "revised consumer microwave independent technician survey advertisement," the "initial commercial microwave independent technician survey advertisement," and the "revised commercial microwave independent technician survey advertisement," respectively.

EXHIBIT 2 *(continued)*

PARAGRAPH SIX: In Exhibit A, the "initial consumer microwave independent technician survey advertisement," printed in *The Wall Street Journal,* October 25 and December 13, 1976, and elsewhere, and in Exhibit B,* the "revised consumer microwave independent technician survey advertisement," printed in *HFD Retailing Home Furnishings,* August 22, 1977, and in other advertisements substantially similar thereto, Litton has represented, directly or by implication, that:

1. The majority of independent microwave oven service technicians would recommend Litton to a friend.
2. The majority of independent microwave oven service technicians are of the opinion that Litton microwave ovens are the easiest to repair of all microwave oven brands.
3. The majority of independent microwave oven service technicians are of the opinion that Litton microwave ovens are superior in quality to all other microwave oven brands.
4. The majority of independent microwave oven service technicians are of the opinion that Litton microwave ovens require the fewest repairs of all microwave oven brands.
5. The majority of independent microwave oven service technicians have Litton microwave ovens in their homes.
6. Representations 1–5 were proved by a survey independently conducted by Custom Research, Inc., in June 1976.

PARAGRAPH SEVEN: In Exhibit C,* the "initial commercial microwave independent technician survey advertisement," printed in *Hospitality (Restaurant),* November 1976, and elsewhere, and in Exhibit D,* the "revised commercial microwave independent technician survey advertisement," printed in *Restaurant Business,* September 1977, and elsewhere, and in other advertisements substantially similar thereto, Litton has represented, directly or by implication, that:

1. The majority of independent microwave oven service technicians would recommend Litton to their customers.
2. The majority of independent microwave oven service technicians are of the opinion that Litton commercial microwave ovens are superior in quality to all other microwave oven brands.
3. The majority of independent microwave oven service technicians are of the opinion that Litton commercial microwave ovens are the easiest to repair on location of all microwave oven brands.
4. The majority of independent microwave oven service technicians are of the opinion that Litton commercial microwave ovens require the fewest repairs of all microwave oven brands.
5. The majority of independent microwave oven service technicians are of the opinion that Litton commercial microwave ovens are the least costly to maintain in operation over time of all microwave oven brands.

* Not included here.

EXHIBIT 2 *(continued)*

6. Representations 1–5 were proved by an April 1976 survey independently conducted by Custom Research, Inc.

In addition, in Exhibit C,* Litton has represented, directly or by implication, that Litton is the best commercial microwave oven to buy and that this representation was proved by the above referenced survey.

PARAGRAPH EIGHT: In Exhibits A and B,* and in other advertisements substantially similar thereto, Litton has represented, directly or by implication, that:

1. Litton microwave ovens are superior in quality to all other microwave oven brands.
2. Litton microwave ovens are the easiest to repair of all microwave oven brands.
3. Litton microwave ovens require the fewest repairs of all microwave oven brands.

PARAGRAPH NINE: In Exhibits C* and D,* and in other advertisements substantially similar thereto, Litton has represented, directly or by implication, that:

1. Litton commercial microwave ovens are superior in quality to all other microwave oven brands.
2. Litton commercial microwave ovens are the easiest to repair on location of all microwave oven brands.
3. Litton commercial microwave ovens require the fewest repairs of all microwave oven brands.
4. Litton commercial microwave ovens are the least costly to maintain in operation over time of all microwave oven brands.

PARAGRAPH TEN: In truth and in fact, the April and June 1976 technician surveys conducted for Litton by Custom Research, Inc., do not prove the representations listed in PARAGRAPHS SIX and SEVEN, for reasons including but not limited in the following:

a. The survey respondents were drawn exclusively from the list of Litton authorized microwave oven service agents. As such, the sample surveyed was not representative of the population of independent microwave oven service technicians and the surveys were biased.
b. The surveys failed to establish that the survey respondents possessed sufficient expertise with either (1) microwave ovens or (2) competitive brands of microwave ovens to qualify as respondents for a microwave oven comparative brand survey.
c. In some paired comparisons, the results lacked statistical significance because the base number was too small.

* Not included here.

EXHIBIT 2 *(continued)*

> d. The surveys conducted for Litton by Custom Research, Inc., were not in fact independent surveys. The surveys were designed and analyzed by Litton employees. The role of Custom Research was limited to placing the telephone calls, from a list of names supplied by Litton, and conducting the interviews, from a questionnaire supplied by Litton.

For the above reasons, representation 6 in PARAGRAPHS SIX and SEVEN is false. Therefore, representation 6, contained in Exhibits A, B,* C,* and D,* was, and is, deceptive and unfair.

PARAGRAPH ELEVEN: In Exhibits A, B,* C,* and D,* and other advertisements substantially similar thereto, Litton has represented, directly or by implication, that it had a reasonable basis of support for the representations contained in those advertisements at the time those representations were made. In truth and in fact, for the reasons enumerated in PARAGRAPH TEN, Litton had no reasonable basis of support for the representations listed in PARAGRAPHS SIX, SEVEN, EIGHT, and NINE at the time those representations were made. Therefore, the representations listed in PARAGRAPHS SIX, SEVEN, EIGHT, and NINE were, and are, deceptive and unfair.

PARAGRAPH TWELVE: In the course and conduct of the aforesaid business, and at all times mentioned herein, Litton has been and is now in substantial competition in commerce with corporations, firms, and individuals engaged in the sale and distribution of microwave ovens of the same general kind and nature as those sold by Litton.

PARAGRAPH THIRTEEN: The use by Litton of the aforesaid unfair and deceptive statements, representations and practices has had, and now has, the capacity and tendency to mislead members of the consuming public into the purchase of substantial quantities of microwave ovens manufactured by Litton.

PARAGRAPH FOURTEEN: The aforesaid acts and practices of Litton, as herein alleged, were, and are, all to the prejudice and inquiry of the public and of respondent's competitors and constituted, and now constitute, unfair and deceptive acts or practices in or affecting commerce and unfair methods of competition in or affecting commerce in violation of Section 5 of the Federal Trade Commission Act.

WHEREFORE, THE PREMISES CONSIDERED, the Federal Trade Commission on this 31st day of January 1979 issues its complaint against said respondent.

NOTICE

Notice is hereby given to the respondent hereinbefore named that the 19th day of March 1979 at 10:00 o'clock A.M. is hereby fixed as the time and Federal Trade Commission Offices, Gelman Building, 2120 "L" Street, Northwest, Washington, D.C. 20580, as the place when and where a hearing will be had before an administrative law judge of the Federal Trade Commission, on

* Not included here.

EXHIBIT 2 *(continued)*

the charges set forth in this complaint, at which time and place you will have the right under said Act to appear and show cause why an order should not be entered requiring you to cease and desist from the violations of law charged in this complaint.

You are notified that the opportunity is afforded you to file with the Commission an answer to this complaint on or before the thirtieth (30) day after service of it upon you. An answer in which the allegations of the complaint are contested shall contain a concise statement of the facts constituting each ground of defense, and specific admission, denial, or explanation of each fact alleged in the complaint or, if you are without knowledge thereof, a statement to that effect. Allegations of the complaint not thus answered shall be deemed to have been admitted.

If you elect not to contest the allegations of fact set forth in the complaint, the answer shall consist of a statement that you admit all of the material allegations to be true. Such an answer shall constitute a waiver of hearings as to the facts alleged in the complaint, and together with the complaint will provide a record basis on which the administrative law judge shall file an initial decision containing appropriate findings and conclusions and an appropriate order disposing of the proceeding. In such answer you may, however, reserve the right to submit proposed findings and conclusions and the right to appeal the initial decision to the Commission under Section 3.52 of the Commission's Rules of Practice for Adjudicative Proceedings.

Failure to answer within the time above provided shall be deemed to constitute a waiver of your right to appear and contest the allegations of the complaint and shall authorize the administrative law judge, without further notice to you, to find the facts to be as alleged in the complaint and to enter an initial decision containing such findings, appropriate conclusions and order.

The following is the form of order which the Commission has reason to believe should issue if the facts are found to be as alleged in the complaint. If, however, the Commission should conclude from the record facts developed in any adjudicative proceedings in this matter that the proposed order provisions as to Litton Industries, Inc., a corporation, might be inadequate to protect fully the consuming public, the Commission may order such other relief as it finds necessary or appropriate.

ORDER

IT IS ORDERED, that respondent Litton Industries, Inc., a corporation, (hereinafter "Litton") and its successors, assigns, officers, agents, representatives, and employees, directly or through any corporation, subsidiary, division or other device, in connection with the advertising, offering for sale, sale, or distribution of any commercial microwave oven, any consumer microwave oven, or any other consumer product, in or affecting commerce, as "commerce" is defined in the Federal Trade Commission Act, do cease and desist from:

1. Representing, directly or by implication, that any commercial microwave oven or consumer microwave oven or any other consumer product:
    a. Is able to perform in any respect, or has any characteristic, feature, attribute, or benefit; or

EXHIBIT 2 *(continued)*

    b. Is superior in any respect to any or all competing products; or

    c. Is recommended, used, chosen, or otherwise preferred in any respect more often than any or all competing products,

unless and only to the extent that respondent possesses and relies upon a reasonable basis for such representation at the time of its initial and each subsequent dissemination. Such reasonable basis shall consist of competent and reliable scientific surveys or tests, and/or other competent and reliable evidence.

2. Advertising the results of a survey unless the respondents in such survey are a representative sample of the population referred to in the advertisement, directly or by implication.

3. Representing, directly or by implication, by reference to a survey or test, that experts recommend, use, or otherwise prefer any commercial microwave oven, any consumer microwave oven, or any other consumer product unless:

    a. Such individuals or experts in fact possess the expertise to evaluate such product(s) with respect to such representation;

    b. Such experts actually exercised their expertise by comparatively evaluating or testing the product(s) and based their stated preferences, findings, or opinions on such exercise of their expertise;

    c. Such representation, to the extent it expresses or implies that such product(s) is superior to competing products, is supported by an actual comparison by such experts, and a conclusion therefrom that such product(s) is superior in fact to the competing products with respect to the feature(s) compared.

    For purposes of this order, an "expert" is an individual, group, or institution held out as possessing, as a result of experience, study or training, knowledge of a particular subject, which knowledge is superior to that generally acquired by ordinary individuals.

4. Making representations, directly or by implication, by reference to a survey and/or test, or to any portions or results thereof, concerning the performance or any characteristic, feature, attribute, benefit, recommendation, usage, choice of, or preference for any commercial microwave oven, any consumer microwave oven, or any other consumer product unless:

    a. Such survey and/or test is designed, executed, and analyzed in a competent and reliable manner so as to prove the claims represented;

    b. In regard to any claims of superiority based thereon, such survey and/or test establishes that such product is superior to each compared product in respect to which the specific representation is made to a degree that will be discernible to or of benefit to the persons to whom the representation is directed; and

    c. Such survey and/or test is represented as fully as necessary to assure that all results which are material to the consumer with respect to the specific representations made are disclosed.

    For purposes of this order, a survey or test conducted in a "competent and reliable manner" is one in which one or more persons, qualified by professional training and/or education and/or experience, formulate and conduct the survey or test and evaluate its results in an objective manner,

EXHIBIT 2 *(concluded)*

using procedures which are generally accepted in the profession, to attain valid and reliable results. The survey or test may be conducted or approved by *(i)* a reputable and reliable organization which conducts such surveys or tests as one of its principal functions, *(ii)* an agency or department of the government of the United States, or *(iii)* persons employed or retained by Litton Industries, Inc. Provided, however, such organization, agency, or persons must be qualified (as defined above in this paragraph) and conduct and evaluate the survey or test in an objective manner.

5. Misrepresenting in any manner, directly or by implication, the purpose, content, validity, reliability, results, or conclusions of any survey and/or test.

6. Failing to maintain accurate records, which may be inspected by Commission staff members upon reasonable notice,

   a. Which contain documentation in support or contradiction of any claim included in advertising or sales promotional material disseminated or caused to be disseminated by respondent insofar as the text is prepared, authorized, or approved by any person who is an officer or employee of respondent, or of any division, subdivision or subsidiary of respondent, or by any advertising agency engaged for such purpose by respondent, or by any of its divisions or subsidiaries;

   b. Which provided or contradicted the basis upon which respondent relied at the time of the initial and each subsequent dissemination of the claim; and

   c. Which shall be maintained by respondent for a period of three years from the date such advertising or sales promotional material was last disseminated by respondent or any division or subsidiary of respondent.

IT IS FURTHER ORDERED, that the respondent shall, within sixty (60) days after service upon it of this order, file with the Commission a report in writing, setting forth in detail the manner and form in which it has complied with this order.

IT IS FURTHER ORDERED, that the respondent shall forthwith distribute a copy of this order to each of its operating divisions.

IT IS FURTHER ORDERED, that respondent notify the Commission at least thirty (30) days prior to any proposed change in the corporate respondent such as dissolution, assignment or sale resulting in the emergence of a successor corporation, the creation or dissolution of subsidiaries, or any other change in the corporation which may affect compliance obligations arising out of this order.

By the Commission

SEAL

ISSUED: January 31, 1979

Carol Thomas
Secretary

EXHIBIT 3

The Federal Trade Commission

The Federal Trade Commission is an independent law enforcement agency charged by the Congress with protecting the public—consumers and businessmen alike—against anticompetitive behavior and unfair and deceptive business practices.

The commission has authority to stop business practices that restrict competition or that deceive or otherwise injure consumers, as long as these practices fall within the legal scope of the commission's statutes, affect interstate commerce, and involve a significant public interest. Such practices may be terminated by cease and desist orders issued after an administrative hearing or by injunctions issued by the federal courts upon application by the commission.

In addition, the FTC defines practices that violate the law so that businessmen may know their legal obligations and consumers may recognize those business practices against which legal recourse is available. The commission does this through Trade Regulation Rules and Industry Guides issued periodically as "do's and don'ts" to business and industry and through business advice—called Advisory Opinions—given to individuals and corporations requesting it.

When law violations are isolated rather than industrywide, the FTC exercises its corrective responsibility also by issuing complaints and entering orders to halt false advertising or fraudulent selling or to prevent a businessperson or corporation from using unfair tactics against competition. The commission itself has no authority to imprison or fine. However, if one of its final cease and desist orders or trade regulation rules is violated, it can seek civil penalties in federal court of up to $10,000 a day for each violation. It can also seek redress for those who have been harmed by unfair or deceptive acts or practices. Redress may include cancellation or reformation of contracts, refunds of money, return of property, and payment of damage.

The commission defines its role, in its literature, as:

> protecting the free enterprise system from being stifled or fetted by monopoly or anticompetitive practices and protecting consumers from unfair or deceptive practices.[8]

The remedies available to the FTC are described in Exhibit 4.

Deceptive Practices

Deceptive or fraudulent trade practices affecting consumers have centered around the misuse of advertising. The trend in the agency has been to identify and counter the more subtle forms of false advertising. Businesses, in arguing against the FTC's jurisdiction, have relied heavily on the First Amendment's

---

[8] This section is based on *Your FTC: What It Is and What It Does* (Washington, D.C.: The Federal Trade Commission).

EXHIBIT 4 FTC remedies

I. Assurance of voluntary compliance (nonadjudicative)

If the commission believes the public interest will be fully safeguarded, it may dispose of a matter under investigation by accepting a promise that the questioned practice will be discontinued. A number of factors are considered by the commission in the rare cases in which it accepts such a promise, including (1) the nature and gravity of the practice in question, and (2) the prior record and good faith of the party.

II. Consent order

Instead of litigating a complaint, a respondent may execute an appropriate agreement containing an order for consideration by the commission. If the agreement is accepted by the commission, the order is placed on the public record for sixty (60) days during which time comments or views concerning the order may be filed by any interested persons. Upon receipt of such comments or views, the commission may withdraw its acceptance and set the matter down for a formal proceeding, issue the complaint and order in accordance with the agreement, or take such action as it may consider appropriate. Respondents in consent orders do not admit violations of the law, but such orders have the same force and effect as adjudicative orders.

III. Adjudicative order

An adjudicative order is based on evidence of record obtaining during an adjudicative proceeding that starts when a complaint is issued. The proceeding is conducted before an administrative law judge who serves as the initial trier of facts. After the hearings the judge within 90 days issues his initial decision, which is subject to review by the commission on the motion of either party or on the commission's own motion. Appeals from a final commission decision and order may be made to any proper court of appeals and ultimately to the Supreme Court.

IV. Preliminary injunctions

The Federal Trade Commission has statutory authority to seek preliminary injunctive relief in federal district court against anyone who is violating or about to violate any provision of law enforced by the FTC.

Source: *Your FTC: What It Is and What It Does* (Washington, D.C.: Federal Trade Commission), p. 26.

protection, specifically freedom of speech. In 1976 the U.S. Supreme Court held in *Virginia State Board* v. *Virginia Citizens Consumer Council* that:

> Although an advertiser's interest is purely economic, that hardly disqualifies him from protection under the First Amendment. . . . It is a matter of public interest that [private economic] decisions, in the aggregate, be intelligent and well informed. To this end, the free flow of commercial information is indispensable.[9]

The Court was reaffirming the First Amendment rights of business enterprises through the right of the public to know facts relevant to decision making in the marketplace.

---

[9] William Sklar, "Ads Are Finally Getting Bleeped at the FTC," *Business and Society Review*, September 1978, p. 41.

The Supreme Court, however, held in *Bates* v. *State of Arizona* in 1977 that this First Amendment protection of advertising was entirely dependent upon its truthfulness. "The public and private benefits from commercial speech derive from confidence in its accuracy and reliability."[10] In other cases the courts have gone on to say that truthfulness in advertising includes completeness of information, as well as the absence of misleading or incorrect information.

The key legal requirement of advertising is that the advertiser have a "reasonable basis" to substantiate the claims made before an ad has been run. Not having a reasonable basis beforehand has been found by the courts to be a violation of Section 5 of the FTC Act as an unfair marketing practice, even if the ad is not deceptive.

It has long been argued that the FTC's simple enforcement power to issue cease and desist orders in regard to false advertising was largely ineffectual since it occurred after the fact and offered no remedial sanctions. Unscrupulous advertisers could get by with a simple admonition to "go and sin no more." Recently, however, the FTC has been increasing the use of such remedial actions as corrective advertising, the most severe of possible penalties facing legitimate marketers.

In 1975, for example, the FTC ordered the Warner-Lambert Company to include a corrective message in their $10 million of advertising. The message would have to say that Listerine was not effective against colds and sore throats, a statement which contradicted the company's earlier advertising. The commission argued that if, under Section 5(b) of the FTC Act, it had:

> the authority to impose the severe and drastic remedy of divestiture in antitrust cases in order to restore competition to a market, surely it had the authority to order corrective advertising to restore truth to the marketplace.[11]

On April 3, 1978, the Supreme Court upheld the FTC order by denying a request to review a lower court's decision.

The FTC, as a rule, has required corrective advertising only when it found that such ads are necessary to present to the public "the honest and complete information" about an advertised product to dispel "the lingering effects of years of false advertising."[12] Without such measures, advertisers would:

> remain free to misrepresent their products to the public, knowing full well that even if the FTC chooses to prosecute they will be required only to cease an advertising campaign which by that point will, in all likelihood, have served its purpose.[13]

---

[10] Ibid., p. 42.

[11] "Corrective Ad Order not Antifree Speech: FTC," *Advertising Age,* September 13, 1976, p. 2.

[12] Ibid.

[13] Ibid.

Summary of FTC's Arguments against Litton

In a national advertising campaign which stretched over a year and a half in at least 26 states, Litton Microwave Cooking Products promoted the results of a survey of microwave oven service technicians. (See the sample ad in Exhibit 3.) The advertisements represented the majority of service technicians as recommending Litton microwave ovens on the basis of quality, fewest repairs, and ease of repairs. These advertisements are held by the Federal Trade Commission to be unfair and deceptive in that the survey as conducted does not substantiate the advertisements' claims.

The survey is represented as an independent survey conducted by Custom Research, Inc. In fact, Litton designed the survey, developed the questionnaire, provided the sampling frame, and analyzed the results. Custom Research personnel made the actual phone interviews.

Errors exist in the survey design which biased the results of the study, thus precluding the results being projected to the population of service technicians as represented in the ads. Litton was aware of these biases prior to the implementation of the ad campaign but ran the advertisements anyway. A memorandum sent to executives by Litton's manager of marketing analysis noted that the surveys were likely to be biased and recommended that the source of the sample be kept confidential. The sample used for survey was limited to those service technicians on a list of 500 Litton authorized service agencies. No attempt was made to draw a sample from technicians authorized to service other brands of microwave ovens.

Only one technician from each agency and that technician selected by the person answering the phone was interviewed. Even with this limited, easily accessible sample, response rates were between 42 and 47 percent. Little was done to improve the response rate, and what was done is uncertain since no written interviewer instructions were provided.

With the majority of respondents authorized only by Litton, their familiarity with Litton products would tend to bias their responses. In addition, no screening was conducted to determine if the respondent had recently or ever serviced Litton or the brand compared, thereby failing to establish a level of expertise necessary for answering the questionnaire.

With the survey biased to the point that it cannot be held to substantiate the advertisements' claims, the FTC has proposed an order for Litton Industries, the parent corporation, and all divisions to cease and desist advertisements and representations based on faulty survey techniques or testing. This "strong order" which refers to all of Litton's consumer products and representations is necessary to "protect the public interest and to deter respondents from future unfair and deceptive acts."

Details of the specific FTC arguments are included in Exhibit 5.

EXHIBIT 5 FTC case against Litton

The findings as developed by the FTC are summarized by the following outline:

A. The FTC has *jurisdiction* over the alleged misleading advertisements since substantiation provided by Litton does not constitute a reasonable basis for the advertisement claims.
B. The advertisements are misleading in representing the results of the survey as *projectable to the total population.* Problems exist relative to:
   1. Survey design and statistical significance of the results.
   2. Deficiencies in sampling.
   3. Low response rate.
   4. Representing survey as "independent" survey.
   5. Respondents' possession of "necessary expertise."
   6. Respondents' familiarity with Litton as basis for answers.
   7. Definition of "independent technician."
C. The FTC has the right to issue a "strong order."

The national advertisement distributed by Litton has represented, directly or by implication, that the majority of independent microwave service technicians:

Would recommend Litton to a friend.
Are of the opinion that Litton microwaves are the easiest to repair.
Are of the opinion that Litton microwaves are superior in quality to other brands.
Are of the opinion that Litton microwave ovens require the fewest repairs.
Have Litton microwaves in their homes.

A. Jurisdiction

Litton is "engaged in the manufacture, distribution, advertising, and sale of various products including microwave ovens."

Litton causes their products "to be transported from their place of business . . . to purchasers located in various other states."

Litton has been and is now "in substantial competition in commerce with corporations, firms, and individuals engaged in the sale" of microwave ovens similar to those sold by Litton.

National advertisements based on the service technician surveys were disseminated in 4 magazines, 28 newspapers, and 6 trade publications.

One hundred fourteen ads ran during a year and a half period.

Litton Industries is a proper respondent to this proceeding since it owns and controls Litton Systems of which Litton Microwave Cooking Products is a division.

B. Survey results as advertised are misleading

The advertisements represent the results of the surveys as projectable to the entire population of independent microwave oven service technicians.

The disclaimer attempts (the use of "technicians surveyed" or "of those surveyed") in no way limit the representations of the ads as projectable to all technicians.

"The ad does not state that those service technicians actually interviewed . . . are in any way different from or might hold differing views than the general population of service technicians."

The many defects in the surveys preclude their results from being capable of supporting "*any* conclusions about the attitudes of . . . microwave oven service technicians."

EXHIBIT 5 *(continued)*

The surveys do not substantiate the advertised claims.

1.   Deficiencies in survey design limit the use of the survey.

There were no written interviewer instructions.

The screening questions on Litton's survey were ambiguous in whether the questions applied to "your company" or "you yourself."

Litton failed to test whether the survey results were statistically significant.

2.   Deficiencies in *sampling* procedure preclude projecting results to the population.

The surveys "do not provide accurate and reliable results because the surveys suffer from basic deficiencies in sample design."

All sampling was from lists of Litton approved service agencies. (Litton had in its possession but did not use lists of Magic Chef and Sharp technicians. Lists were also available for other technicians. Technicians not on Litton's authorized list had no chance of being interviewed.)

Litton asserted that samples obtained from their lists of authorized technicians were representative of all independent service technicians.

Litton vastly underestimated the universe of independent microwave oven service agencies. Litton's national field service manager estimated their list of 500 Litton authorized technicians represented 85–90 percent of all microwave service technicians and that there were not more than 100 independent agencies servicing microwave ovens that were not on the Litton list. But, in addition to the list of 500 used as a sampling frame, Litton had a list of 1,700 servicing dealers who repaired Litton microwave ovens under warranty. Other dealers' service networks included numerous additional service agencies: Sharp, 1,480; General Electric, 5,000; Amana, 2,500; Magic Chef, 1,323. These numbers do not include service networks for additional suppliers such as Tappan, Panasonic, Frymaster and Hobart.

From the results of a survey by an independent research company for the FTC, it is estimated that Litton excluded from its consumer survey between 414 and 715 (low and high projections) agencies which serviced Litton plus at least one other brand. At most, 421 service agencies were included in Litton's study. Therefore, Litton excluded at least as many service agencies which service Litton and another brand as it included.

Less than half the technicians surveyed were authorized to service the brand they compared to Litton. They were therefore comparing a brand for which they were authorized with one for which they were not authorized, a source of substantial bias.

Litton's survey methodology of interviewing only one technician per agency and that technician selected by the person answering the phone further limited the possibility of a technician in the population being interviewed and led to biases:

a.   Small firms may have been overrepresented.
b.   Technicians who work in the field would have been excluded (Litton's policy was to do warranty work in the home).

3.   The *response rates* in the Litton surveys were low (47 percent for the consumer survey, 42 percent for the commercial survey) leading to nonresponse biases.

4.   "The Litton consumer and commercial surveys were not independent sur-

EXHIBIT 5 *(concluded)*

veys," as the ads suggested. Custom Research merely placed telephone calls to agencies on a list provided by Litton and asked questions from a questionnaire designed by Litton.

    5. "Litton failed to establish that the respondents to the . . . surveys possessed the necessary expertise or relied upon that expertise to compare various brands of microwave ovens."

    6. The Litton survey respondents, as Litton-authorized technicians, were likely to have expressed preferences for Litton microwave ovens because they were most familiar with that brand.

    7. The term "independent microwave oven service technicians" in the ad headlines conveys the meaning of technicians working for independent agencies not owned by a manufacturer. The footnote stating only technicians who served Litton microwaves were interviewed does not qualify the representation of the headline. In fact, a Litton executive was unable to read the fine print of the footnote when asked to do so in court.

C. "The proposed order is required to protect the public from further deceptive and unfair practices." The respondents' conduct justifies a broad order to protect the public, since:

    1. Litton disseminated a large-scale deceptive advertising campaign.
    2. The survey claims are a prominent and material component of the advertisements.
    3. Litton knowingly disseminated results of a biased study.
    4. Litton is a leader in the advertising and marketing of microwave ovens.
    5. Litton sells a number of consumer products to the public.

Summary of Litton's Defense

The original complaint in this action challenged certain advertisements run by Litton Industries as being in violation of Section 5 of the Federal Trade Commission Act. The complaint was preceded by a two-year investigation of a limited number of magazine and newspaper ads run in October through December of 1976 and August and September of 1977.

Complaint counsel has not met the burden of proving that the advertisements were "deceptive" within the meaning of Section 5. Complaint counsel and their witnesses did nothing more than identify "potential" deviations from *ideal* survey procedures which "might" have influenced the survey results. The procedures used were perfectly reasonable, were in accord with generally accepted survey practice, and yielded reliable results.

Even if one were to assume that a technical violation of Section 5 has occurred, the unintentional, minor nature of any such violation, and the public policy implications of the proposed order dictate that no order should be issued. The proposed order covers all products of Litton Industries. As such, it is punitive in nature, sweeping far beyond the violations, if any.

In essence, the complaint charges that the ads contained three categories of representations: (1) alleged representations concerning the actual superiority of Litton microwave ovens over competitor brands, (2) alleged representations concerning the opinions of the "majority" of independent microwave oven service technicians relative to the superiority of Litton microwave ovens over competitive brands, and (3) alleged representations that the Litton surveys "proved" the first two representations. Only the third category is alleged to be false and misleading. Complaint counsel did not seek to prove that Litton was *not* superior to competitive brands on the attributes listed or even that independent service technicians were *not* of that opinion. The main issue was not the specific allegations in the ads but, rather, the sufficiency of the surveys upon which the ads were based.

The key issues, then, are (1) were the ads interpreted by the readers of those ads in the manner alleged in the complaint and (2) if so, did the survey provide a "reasonable basis" for any representations which were made. On both issues, complaint counsel bears the burden of proof. A careful examination of the record reveals that complaint counsel misconceived the nature of their burden of proof and fell far short of meeting it. What the record does reveal is that Litton Industries attempted in good faith to conduct reliable surveys aimed at guiding its future marketing and engineering decisions. The surveys were designed and conducted in a manner which would lead to results upon which a "reasonably prudent businessman" could rely.

The surveys were designed and conducted as part of the business planning function at Litton. Specifically, the surveys were in response to advertising and point-of-sale literature by Amana which directly and implicitly raised questions concerning the quality of Litton microwave ovens. These Amana ads emphasized the fact that Amana had received an exemption from a warning label requirement and caused certain Litton dealers to question the quality of Litton microwave ovens. As a result of the Amana ads, Litton dealers began encountering problems on the sales floors. Their concerns were communicated to Litton management.

The problems caused by Amana's attacks on the quality of Litton microwave ovens persisted. As a result, product quality became a frequent subject of discussion. The Litton marketing division president and Litton microwave consumer products president became very concerned that perhaps the quality of Litton microwave ovens was in fact deteriorating and that they were not being adequately informed. Thus, in the early spring of 1976, Litton decided to investigate the quality of Litton microwave ovens through market research studies.

It was only after Litton conducted its studies for internal management purposes and analyzed the results that the idea of incorporating the results into advertising germinated. That possibility was not even seriously considered until September 1976. In fact, the ads were not included in the advertising budget for 1976–77. As a result, special approval had to be obtained from the president of Litton microwave consumer products in order to prepare the ads.

The advertising copy which ultimately emerged from the surveys fairly presented the results, at a level of detail so complete that it threatened their effectiveness as an advertising tool. The decision to present the data fully was made so that the ads would withstand any subsequent scrutiny.

This case was chosen by Federal Trade Commission staff as a "test" case for establishing industrywide standards for the advertising of survey results and for the procedures which must be followed in such surveys. Indeed, the commission press release announcing the issuance of the complaint identified it as a test case which would set standards for advertising surveys and tests. Thus, the key issue is whether Litton had a "reasonable basis" upon which to make the claims included in the ads.

The arguments made by Litton as their defense are summarized in Exhibit 6.

EXHIBIT 6 Summary of Litton's defense

A. Litton acted in good faith in designing and conducting the surveys.

Litton confined the surveys to independent microwave oven service agencies servicing multiple brands, including Litton.

Litton followed the definition of independent microwave service agency commonly used in the industry: one which services but does not sell microwave ovens (this definition excluded over 1,700 Litton dealers who serviced Litton microwave ovens).

Independent service technicians eliminated a potential source of bias since they have no special tie to one manufacturer and are experienced in servicing many makes of microwave ovens.

Litton used a list of independent service agencies identified by a nationally known expert as the most reliable source. This list was nearly exhaustive and thus was representative of the universe of independent service agencies.

Interviewers were specifically instructed to ask for an experienced service technician. The respondent had to have worked for the agency for at least one year. The agency had to have serviced microwave ovens for at least one year. Only technicians who serviced at least two brands, including Litton, were interviewed.

To ensure unbiased representation of all brands serviced by the technicians surveyed, those comparisons were made between Litton and other brands only if the respondents serviced both brands.

A reputable outside organization, Custom Research, Inc., conducted the surveys.

Litton's identity as the research sponsor was never disclosed to the respondents. Also, the interviewers were not aware of the survey purpose.

In each ad, the headline prominently states that results pertain only to those "independent microwave service technicians surveyed."

The ads carefully delineate the groups surveyed and that the survey was conducted by Custom Research, Inc.

The ads were targeted to a special audience of businessmen and microwave oven purchasers who were characterized by complaint counsel witnesses as upscale, sophisticated, and knowledgeable.

EXHIBIT 6 *(continued)*

The total cost of all the survey ads was $215,384.29, only 2.1 percent of the Litton microwave advertising budget for the 1976–1977 year.

When the FTC challenged the initial ads, Litton modified the ads in response to the criticisms.

B. The specialized audience interpreted the representations in a distinctly limited manner.

Complaint counsel, under Section 5 of the FTC Act must prove that the ads were interpreted by the audience in a way which suggests "the capacity or tendency to mislead." Yet complaint counsel developed no empirical data nor called any expert to testify on the issue.

Expert testimony concluded that the small portion of the audience which attached any significance to the ads would merely perceive that a study had been done, that it involved people with major biasing ties to a manufacturer who were qualified to service microwave ovens, and that their opinions were obtained on various characteristics of microwave ovens.

The most which the ads could have possibly done was to convince a small number of readers who were otherwise uncertain that Litton was one of the brands worthy of further consideration.

The ads did not state, as alleged in the complaint, that a "majority" of *all* independent service technicians preferred Litton.

The combination of *low* public trust in surveys, the *lower* public trust in surveys conducted by private companies, the inherent cautiousness of readers of ads generally, and the even greater caution exercised by "upscale" readers lead to the conclusion the interpretations alleged in the complaint did not occur.

C. The surveys were conducted in accordance with generally accepted practices in the survey research community.

To prove that the Litton surveys did not provide a "reasonable basis" for representations made in the ads, complaint counsel had to establish that (1) generally accepted standards for survey and market research exist within the industry, (2) the procedures followed by Litton represent substantial, unreasonable deviations from those standards, and (3) such deviations resulted in demonstrable biases favoring Litton and thus in advertising which was "deceptive" within the reasoning of Section 5 of the FTC Act. Complaint counsel met *none* of the three requirements.

Expert witnesses were unable to define generally accepted survey research standards.

The Litton survey was, in the opinion of expert witnesses, "indicative of typical industry practice."

D. The surveys were conducted in an accurate and unbiased manner.

The universe was carefully defined to eliminate any significant risk or bias.

The Litton surveys were an attempted census of the ascertainable agencies in the universe.

EXHIBIT 6 *(concluded)*

The procedures to respond to the survey were reasonable and produced reliable results.

The use of Litton's authorized service agency lists was proper and introduced no bias into the survey results.

The questionnaires used adequately qualified respondents and produced accurate results.

Response rates were within normal and accepted ranges and did not create any biases.

Tests of statistical significance were neither necessary nor proper.

Litton's role in the surveys was consistent with normal survey procedures and with the advertised claims.

Interviewer instruction and supervision was entirely adequate.

Part 9

Marketing Programs and Strategy

This section contains seven cases which are comprehensive in nature, requiring the student to make a number of decisions in several different marketing decision areas. Thus, a great deal of integration is necessary. A decision in one of the marketing areas may have a significant impact on the other decisions which must be made to complete the marketing program.

In developing a complete marketing program for a product, one must start with the firm's overall goals and objectives. Then all the environmental factors such as demand, competition, marketing laws, distribution alternatives, and cost structure must be analyzed. At this point, a number of opportunities as well as potential problems will have been identified, and specific marketing objectives can be established.

The marketer must make a clear definition of the target market(s) to be served. This can be determined only after a thorough evaluation of all the alternative segments of the market, their needs, wants, attitudes and behavior, the strengths and weaknesses of the firm's products and those of competitors, and the potential profitability of various alternatives.

The next step in developing the marketing program is to search for the optimal marketing mix; that is, what is the best combination of product strategy, pricing strategy, promotion strategy, and distribution strategy? Typically, there will be a number of possible alternatives for each of these, so the marketer must determine the interrelationships among them and choose the optimal combination based upon a complete situation analysis.

The last step in the development of a marketing program is to create a plan for implementing the program. Without adequate implementation, even the best designed plans will fail.

Case 38

Greenwood Federal Savings and Loan*

In early October 1986, Ms. Jenny Harris was reviewing the results of the latest research that had been conducted by Greenwood Federal Savings and its advertising agency. Ms. Harris had been asked by the chairman of the board, Paul Robinson, to prepare a strategic marketing plan for Greenwood Federal. Annual marketing plans had been prepared in previous years, but these tended to be tactical in nature. Many changes had taken place in the previous year, necessitating a longer-term look at the organization's marketing planning. Ms. Harris grabbed several items off her bookshelf, including new research study results, last year's marketing plan, and the latest financial reports available documenting Greenwood's recent performance. She then reached for the phone to call her husband to tell him that she would be home very late that evening.

Background

Greenwood Federal Savings (GFS) is one of the nation's larger savings and loan associations. It was founded in 1927 in the largest milk-producing county south of Wisconsin. At the time, the county was beginning to emerge from an agricultural economy into a semi-urban economy oriented toward a major fast-growing city, Sunbelt City, located six miles to the west. The founder was an attorney, state legislator, and business and community leader who was president of the Chamber of Commerce and many civic and charitable groups. The board of directors consisted of a number of leading citizens in the community, and their goal was to make the city the finest residential city in the region. To ease unemployment and provide some new homes during the Depression, the Association pioneered in making construction loans. To ensure the quality of the homes built, the officers of Greenwood developed a code of minimum specifications and named an inspector to see that the homes complied with it.

From the beginning, those who directed the policies of Greenwood Federal were concerned with people and for the environment in which members

---

* This case was prepared by Kenneth L. Bernhardt for the purpose of class discussion. Names and selected data have been disguised. Copyright © 1986 by Kenneth L. Bernhardt.

of the Association lived. A commitment was made to serve all citizens without prejudice. The first loan to a black citizen was made in 1928. A close relationship with builders and developers was established and has been maintained throughout the years. In the early years, movies and slide presentations of land developments in other parts of the country kept the community's builders abreast of the latest developments. The first branch was established in 1952, when assets had grown to more than $25 million. During the 1960s the Association expanded its services, adding college education loans, home improvement loans, and FHA and VA loans. The officers were concerned that people in moderate and low-income categories should have adequate housing.

Greenwood was seeking to help the people of the community achieve "the good life," including the privilege of home ownership. Over the years, Greenwood was always on the forefront as an ethical, caring organization. For example, it was the last financial institution in the area to raise rates on loan assumptions. All employees were trained and continually reminded that their role was to satisfy customers. Greenwood had a strong corporate creed outlining its commitment to excellence. The officers and employees of Greenwood believed in the creed, which is reproduced in Exhibit 1.

Greenwood Federal Savings grew rapidly during the 1970s and 1980s, mirroring the growth of the city of Greenwood and the metropolis of Sunbelt City. In 1972 the first branch outside the city of Greenwood was opened, representing the Association's 10th office. During the mid- and late 1970s savings offices were opened in four regional malls, and by the end of the decade Greenwood had offices in five counties throughout the metropolitan area. In the early 1980s Greenwood moved statewide through a series of mergers. In 1984, faced with severe losses, the board of directors decided to concentrate on the Sunbelt City metropolitan area and the northern part of the state, and sold off some of the offices purchased earlier.

An organization chart is shown in Exhibit 2. Jenny Harris reported directly to the chairman of the board and CEO, and was responsible for all aspects of marketing, advertising, and product management. Since her arrival from a major packaged goods company several years earlier, Greenwood had introduced automated teller machines, discount brokerage services, homeowner's and personal lines of credit, automobile loans, credit cards, and checking accounts.

Competitive Environment

Many changes took place in the competitive environment for GFS in 1985. On June 10, 1985, the U.S. Supreme Court handed down a decision upholding regional banking. During the next several months, the major banks in Sunbelt City all merged with or acquired other large banks in surrounding states, resulting in the creation of "super banks." Other regulations resulted in a blurring of the distinction between banks and savings and loan institutions. In addition, large national organizations such as Sears, CitiCorp, Merrill Lynch,

EXHIBIT 1

GREENWOOD FEDERAL
SAVINGS & LOAN ASSOCIATION

Commitment to Excellence: A Corporate Creed

Greenwood Federal Is Committed:

To the pursuit of a leadership position in the delivery of financial services and to the belief that quality is more important than size.

To be innovative in all that we do, including products we design and support services we render.

To understanding the value of customer confidence and realizing that achieving this goal is only outweighed by the need to maintain it.

To the setting of sound financial policies that protect the future while enhancing the present.

To be human, open, friendly, and sincere and to recognize that results should never be achieved at the expense of human dignity.

To specialize in product areas where the future appears strongest and the Association is best able to excel.

To our employees by rewarding merit, by providing an environment for growth, by creating a team spirit by encouraging open, two-way communications, and by enabling them to feel pride in the products and services we provide.

To honest, fair, and enduring relationships with suppliers and associates.

To the concept of corporate social responsibility to our local communities through individual and company participation.

To all of these precepts because they are not only intrinsically right but also happen to be good business.

---

and several major insurance companies all expanded their financial service offerings and entered the Sunbelt City market in a big way.

Like most savings and loan associations, GFS concentrated on the "middle market," which comprised the bulk of its deposits and loans. GFS did not get much patronage from very high-income consumers or from low-income consumers. Competition for this retail middle market had become intense in recent years. There were 20 S&Ls in the Sunbelt City metropolitan area, and most of these, especially the major competitors, concentrated on the middle market. In addition, two of the three largest banks in town concentrated on this market, as did many of the national organizations that had recently entered the market. Jenny Harris recognized the problems created by the intense competition for this middle market, and knew that it would be important for GFS to segment the market even more finely than it had in the past. The key,

EXHIBIT 2   Greenwood's organization chart, 1986

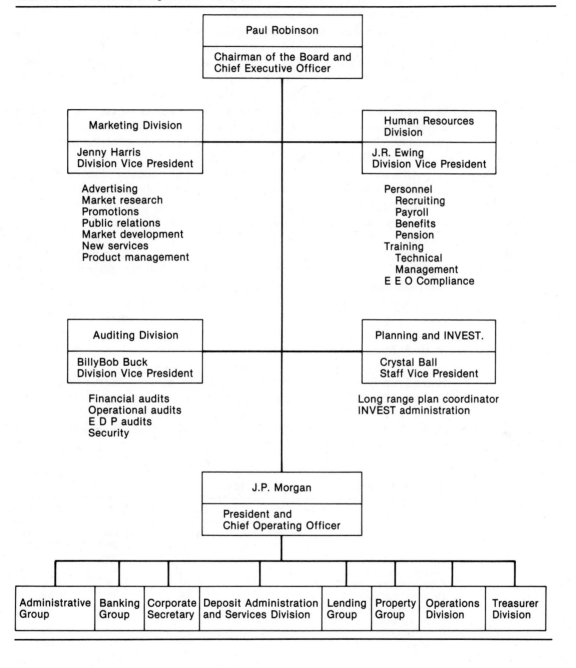

she thought, was to identify target markets where GFS could do a better job than competitors in meeting consumer needs.

Exhibit 3 shows GFS's market share and the shares for each of the major competitors. The data in Exhibit 3 comes from a study that GFS had conducted among residents living within three miles of each of its branches. The results show that about one quarter of the people living near its branches have one or more accounts with GFS. Only 9 percent of the residents, however, indicate the GFS is their primary financial institution. Information on each of the major competitors is presented in Exhibit 4. GFS's growth in assets, advertising expenditures, and number of branches are all below those of the major competitors, with the exception of Home Federal.

GFS was a major factor in construction lending due to its long-term strong relationship with builders and its excellent image in the construction community. GFS did not have the lowest interest rates, and over the years had been very conservative in its appraisals and the amount of its loans. It worked with the cream of the builders, catering to them and to the realtors in the community, who recognized that there would be fewer hassles in working with GFS. The organization was very "loan oriented," and almost all the senior management had come from the loan side of the Association.

In 1985 GFS became profitable again, following four straight years of losses. The reserve ratio (net worth/total assets) had deteriorated from 6.3 percent in 1980 to 2.7 percent in 1984. It had increased to 3 percent by the end of 1985. Most of GFS's savings and loan competitors had converted to stock organizations or were in the process of converting as a result of the 1985 Federal Home Loan Bank Board Regulations raising the required reserve ratio from 3 percent to 6 percent over the next five years. The easiest way to comply with this regulation would be to sell stock, thus raising a substantial amount of equity. GFS management believed that they could achieve the required ratio if they concentrated on increasing the profitability of the organization. Top man-

EXHIBIT 3 Market share analysis by competitor

	Percent who have relation- ship with institution	Percent indicating primary institution	"Primary" as a percent of "have relationship"
City National Bank	32%	19%	59%
First National Bank	28	10	36
Greenwood Federal	24	9	38
Heritage Trust	24	15	63
Sunbelt Federal	13	5	38
Home Federal	8	3	38
Credit Unions	24	7	29
All others	NA*	32	NA*
		100%	

Note: Table is interpreted as follows: 32 percent of the population living within three miles of Greenwood branches have a relationship with City National Bank; 59 percent of those with a relationship with City National (19 percent of the population) indicate City National is their primary financial institution.

*NA = not available.

EXHIBIT 4 Information on major competitors ($ in billions)

	Greenwood Federal Savings & Loan	Sunbelt Federal Savings & Loan	First National Bank	Heritage Trust Bank	City National Bank	Home Federal Savings & Loan
Total assets, 12/31/85	$1.3	$2.0	$12.7	$13.9	$ 9.8	$ 1.4
Percent growth in assets 1985 versus 1984	4.0%	20.6%	12.7%	22.9%	15.3%	5.4%
Total deposits, 12/31/85	$ 1.1	$ 1.5	$ 9.1	$10.6	$ 6.9	$ 1.3
Percent growth in deposits 1985 versus 1984	6.9%	4.0%	13.2%	15.1%	9.3%	4.6%
Net worth/assets, 12/31/85	3.0%	6.2%	5.8%	5.6%	5.9%	1.9%
Return on assets, 1985	.6%	1.0%	1.2%	1.0%	1.0%	(loss)
1985 Advertising expenditures ($ millions)	$ 0.7	$ 1.4	$ 1.5	$ 1.6	$ 1.4	*
Number of branches in Sunbelt City area	19	30	55	41	63	15

* Figure not available.

agement was concerned that if they converted to stock ownership it would not be clear how stockholders would fit in versus employees and customers. They feared they would lose flexibility in marketing and would need to direct a great deal of attention to investor relations and the stockbroker community.

Detailed financial information for Greenwood Federal, its number of accounts, and the structure for its savings and its loans are presented in Exhibit 5. Comments on the competitive situation for each of the major product categories follow.

Savings Certificates

The primary competitors for savings certificates are local banks, savings and loans, and credit unions. In the last year, First National Bank and several of the smaller banks and savings and loans have been particularly aggressive in their pricing. Banks especially are able to pay higher rates on certificates because of their greater ability to match assets and liabilities. Brokerage firms and insurance companies must also be considered competitors for these savings dollars. GFS has always been a leader in the savings certificate product area with high awareness levels. Recent strategy has been to replace 91-day and six-month certificates with long-term certificates in the portfolio.

Checking Accounts

Commercial banks, savings and loans, and credit unions are also direct competitors for both regular checking and NOW accounts. The source of business for checking accounts has been commercial banks, and Sunbelt Federal has been particularly aggressive in its marketing of checking accounts. The banks

EXHIBIT 5   GFS financial data and savings structure, July 31, 1986 (year to date)

Total assets .... $1.34 billion
Total savings deposits .... $1.18 billion
Number of savings accounts 140,144
Total loans... $1.14 billion
  Number of first mortgage loans 27,387
  First mortgage loans (average yield 10.0 percent) .... $1.07 billion
  Second mortgage loans, including home equity loans (home equity yield 10.5
    percent) .... $24.5 million
  Education loans (average yield 10.1 percent) .... $11.1 million
  Consumer loans (average yield 13.0 percent on unsecured and 11.6 percent
    on secured) .... $19.7 million
  Savings account loans .... $8.4 million
  Other loans .... $10.0 million
Operating income as percent of assets 11.75%
Average cost of all funds—July 8.2%
Average cost of new funds acquired—July 6.4%
Operating expenses 2.6%
Return on assets 6%

Savings structure	Dollars (millions)	Percent of total
Passbook savings	$ 61.2	5.2%
NOW accounts	37.9	3.3
Super NOW accounts	112.0	9.5
Money market accounts	202.7	17.0
Certificates:		
Jumbo	12.8	1.1
3-month	12.6	1.1
6-month	108.2	9.2
12– 24-month	145.9	12.5
25–36-month	170.0	14.4
Greater than 36-month	234.7	20.0
Retirement accounts	78.6	6.7
	$1,176.6	100.0%

have a definite convenience advantage, and they possess the majority of checking accounts. Many, however, are demarketing the smaller-deposit checking accounts through the use of high service fees. Ms. Harris felt there was opportunity to attract new checking accounts, with pricing as an important part of the strategy.

Money Market Accounts

Competitors for money market deposit accounts (MMDA) include commercial banks, savings and loans, money market funds, and bond and equity funds. For a large number of consumers the MMDA has actually replaced the passbook as the primary savings relationship. Ms. Harris thought that with its large base of savings customers, GFS had some competitive advantage here, but marketing of the MMDA had not been very aggressive since its introduction in late 1982. Competitors in the Sunbelt City market were not actively marketing these accounts.

Credit Lines

Commercial banks, savings and loans, mortgage bankers, and brokerage firms have all marketed home equity and personal credit lines aggressively during the past two years. GFS introduced its homeowners line of credit (HOLOC) in 1984, and a personal line of credit product was introduced in 1985. Jenny Harris felt that GFS had a tremendous marketing opportunity with the home equity product because of GFS's large pool of mortgage loan customers and because of changes in the federal tax laws expected to occur in 1987.

Residential Mortgage Loans

GFS is the leader among mortgage bankers, savings and loans, and commercial banks in the mortgage loan market. The market has changed dramatically in the past few years, with a large number of new competitors in the local market. Ms. Harris believed the tradition of good service and market leadership at GFS, together with its entrenched position with the real estate professional target market, provided excellent opportunities for continued success for GFS.

Consumer Loans

GFS has a weak competitive position in the consumer loan product area. Commercial banks have much greater experience with consumer loans and higher awareness. Finance companies, credit unions, and other savings and loans also compete for loan volume. GFS has tried in a modest way to build awareness of the availability of the consumer loan product. Ms. Harris thought there were opportunities to build this volume by differentiation based on product features rather than on the interest rate. None of the major competitors had developed an aggressive, innovative way to market consumer loans.

Brokerage Services

GFS was an equity partner in INVEST, a discount brokerage service. The service became profitable for GFS in 1985, with over 2,000 new accounts and $43 million in sales. INVEST was not an exclusive service, and several savings and loans in the area, including Sunbelt Federal, offered the service. The competition for this service included traditional brokerage firms, discount brokers, insurance companies, and depository institutions.

Strategies of Major Competitors

The major competitors employed different strategies and tactics, depending on the product involved. Ms. Harris's perceptions of some selected competitors are discussed below.

Sunbelt Federal Savings operated almost 60 offices in 20 communities, with 30 of the offices in the Sunbelt City metropolitan area. Most of its recent marketing effort focused on checking accounts and consumer loans. It has priced its checking account lower than most competitors and is actively seeking younger checking account customers. Focus groups conducted by GFS showed that consumers perceived Sunbelt Federal as dynamic, progressive, friendly, having low service charges, and a good place for savings.

Ms. Harris felt that First National Bank had earned the reputation as an innovative retail bank and had begun in earnest to cultivate a position as a rate leader. The bank has experienced dramatic growth in consumer deposits during the past year, at the expense of lower interest margins. A major strength is its extensive branching network, with over 75 offices (55 in the Sunbelt City metropolitan area). Its current advertising campaign, "If your bank isn't First, you should have second thoughts," is more aggressive than previous campaigns. In two television commercials First National Bank compares its performance on investment products with that of Heritage Trust and City National Bank. First National aggressively markets VISA cards throughout the South and is among the top 10 VISA banks in the country. Key image attributes for First National Bank mentioned by the participants in the focus groups include efficient, innovative, flashy, colorful, and convenient.

Heritage Trust had successfully positioned itself as the bank for upwardly mobile people, according to Ms. Harris. Its advertising had enjoyed high awareness levels and had served as an umbrella for product advertising, stressing how well the bank suits the needs of its customers. Heritage Trust had aggressively attracted newcomers to the market through strong corporate relationships. Its upscale banking program had been in operation for years, and was considered by Ms. Harris as one of the best in the region. Attributes for Heritage Trust identified by the focus group respondents included "pinstriped," educated, professional, confident, successful, convenient, and smart.

City National Bank is the largest commercial bank in the state and has a very strong retail presence through over 75 offices (63 in the Sunbelt City metropolitan area). City National had traditionally been a strong consumer lender and had recently been directing its advertising at the baby boom generation with its campaign, "Think of your future with City National." Product advertising had stressed simple interest loans, discount brokerage services, and Ready Equity (their equity-based credit line). City National's image as profiled by focus group respondents included convenience but also some negative attributes, such as "bully," impersonal, and greedy.

The image of GFS, as perceived by the attendees at the focus group sessions, is "established," conservative, friendly, and older. GFS had, in fact, attracted a market somewhat older than that of the banks.

Exhibit 6 presents data on the importance of various features to consumers, together with the ratings of GFS and four competitors on each of the features. The consumers in the study were asked to rate the importance of each of the features using a scale of 0–10. They were then asked to give a rating to each financial institution on each feature, again using a scale of 0–10 (with 0 being poor and 10 extremely good). Overall, the most important features for a financial institution include:

EXHIBIT 6 Importance of features and comparative ratings

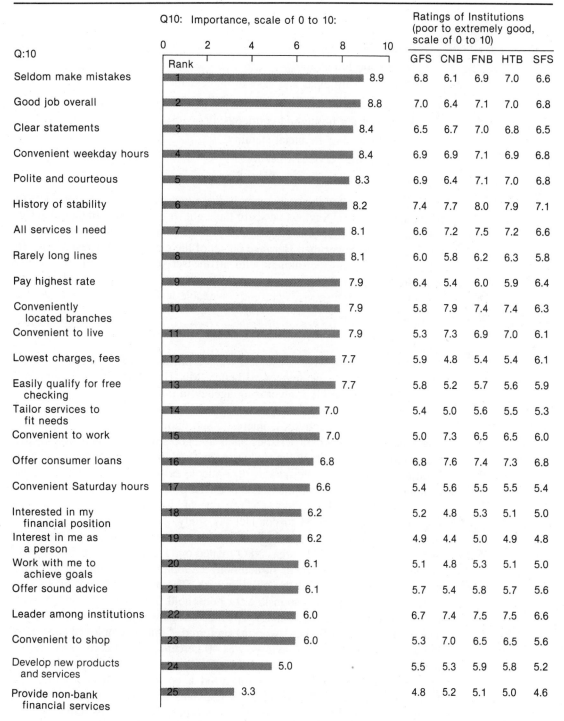

Q:10	Q10: Importance, scale of 0 to 10: Rank	Ratings of Institutions (poor to extremely good, scale of 0 to 10)				
		GFS	CNB	FNB	HTB	SFS
Seldom make mistakes	1 — 8.9	6.8	6.1	6.9	7.0	6.6
Good job overall	2 — 8.8	7.0	6.4	7.1	7.0	6.8
Clear statements	3 — 8.4	6.5	6.7	7.0	6.8	6.5
Convenient weekday hours	4 — 8.4	6.9	6.9	7.1	6.9	6.8
Polite and courteous	5 — 8.3	6.9	6.4	7.1	7.0	6.8
History of stability	6 — 8.2	7.4	7.7	8.0	7.9	7.1
All services I need	7 — 8.1	6.6	7.2	7.5	7.2	6.6
Rarely long lines	8 — 8.1	6.0	5.8	6.2	6.3	5.8
Pay highest rate	9 — 7.9	6.4	5.4	6.0	5.9	6.4
Conveniently located branches	10 — 7.9	5.8	7.9	7.4	7.4	6.3
Convenient to live	11 — 7.9	5.3	7.3	6.9	7.0	6.1
Lowest charges, fees	12 — 7.7	5.9	4.8	5.4	5.4	6.1
Easily qualify for free checking	13 — 7.7	5.8	5.2	5.7	5.6	5.9
Tailor services to fit needs	14 — 7.0	5.4	5.0	5.6	5.5	5.3
Convenient to work	15 — 7.0	5.0	7.3	6.5	6.5	6.0
Offer consumer loans	16 — 6.8	6.8	7.6	7.4	7.3	6.8
Convenient Saturday hours	17 — 6.6	5.4	5.6	5.5	5.5	5.4
Interested in my financial position	18 — 6.2	5.2	4.8	5.3	5.1	5.0
Interest in me as a person	19 — 6.2	4.9	4.4	5.0	4.9	4.8
Work with me to achieve goals	20 — 6.1	5.1	4.8	5.3	5.1	5.0
Offer sound advice	21 — 6.1	5.7	5.4	5.8	5.7	5.6
Leader among institutions	22 — 6.0	6.7	7.4	7.5	7.5	6.6
Convenient to shop	23 — 6.0	5.3	7.0	6.5	6.5	5.6
Develop new products and services	24 — 5.0	5.5	5.3	5.9	5.8	5.2
Provide non-bank financial services	25 — 3.3	4.8	5.2	5.1	5.0	4.6

Key: GFS = Greenwood Federal   CNB = City National Bank   FNB = First National Bank
     HTB = Heritage Trust Bank   SFS = Sunbelt Federal Savings

Seldom make mistakes.

Do a good job overall.

Statements are clear and easy to understand.

Open at convenient hours during the week.

Personnel are polite and courteous.

Long history of financial stability.

Offer all the services I need.

Sufficient tellers to avoid long lines.

GFS is not rated the best on any of these factors, although it is rated better than Sunbelt Federal Savings on six of the eight. It is also rated higher than City National Bank on four of the eight. GFS is rated lower than First National Bank on all eight and lower than Heritage on six of the eight. The biggest "gap" for GFS is in providing consumers with all the services they need. Ms. Harris wondered whether this perception could be changed by increasing the promotion of many of the services currently available at GFS.

To learn more about what consumers wanted in financial services and how the overall market could be segmented better, Ms. Harris had commissioned, in cooperation with the GFS advertising agency, a major consumer segmentation study. The research was designed to provide several clusters of consumers (segments) based on activities, interests, and opinions rather than on conventional demographic characteristics such as age, sex, or income. Ms. Harris wanted to use the results of the study to help develop a market niche for GFS, to identify appropriate target markets, to evaluate existing and new products, and to improve marketing communications for GFS.

National Family Opinion (NFO), one of the nation's largest marketing research firms, was used to conduct the study. NFO maintains a nationally representative consumer panel of 150,000 households, with over 3,000 in the Sunbelt City metropolitan area. NFO mailed out 1,250 questionnaires, and 57 percent, 712, were returned. In addition, a supplemental sample of 122 GFS customers also completed the questionnaire. The study included results only from persons primarily responsible for household financial decisions (approximately half male and half female). The median age was just under 45 years old. The proportion classified as "working preferred," that is, employed and reporting a minimum of $5,000 savings, was 40 percent, a level considered normal based on previous studies conducted by GFS.

Slightly over half, 57 percent, used a commercial bank as the main financial institution, 23 percent used a savings and loan, 12 percent used a credit union, and 18 percent listed all other types of institutions. GFS's market share for the main study was 15 percent (having any account, not "primary" institution).

The questionnaire presented 100 opportunities for each respondent to record his or her attitudes or opinions about financial matters and about his or her banking habits and preferences. Examples of questions include "I like to pay cash for almost everything I buy," "I'm always looking for a way to make more interest on my money," and "I need very little advice when making decisions about the types of financial services I should use." In addition, each person was presented with 25 questions concerning the importance to them of individual banking practices and services, together with questions concerning the rating of the individual financial institutions.

A large mainframe computer then was used to perform advanced statistical analysis of the questionnaire data. The objective was to cluster or group the 712 respondents into meaningful segments based on commonality of their attitudes rather than into groups based on age, income, or other demographic characteristics. The computer program identified five clusters or segments similar enough in their attitudes to be classified as distinct survey segments. These segments were then given names to help describe them. Most segmentation studies of this type attempt to group people according to lifestyles, thus ending up with such groupings as "yuppies," "young suburbia" or "gray power." Here the groupings were based on the way the respondents think and act about money, credit, banking, and financial services. Five clusters were identified and named:

> Secure Steve (self-confident and self-assured).
> Retiring Richard (72 percent employed, but the highest proportion of retirees).
> Fast Lane Phil (overspending, undersaving youth).
> Minimal Martha (highest proportion of females, but not necessarily female; users of a minimum of products and services).
> Single-Minded Sam (desire for one-stop banking at a full-service convenient institution).

Exhibits 7 through 10 present data from the two samples concerning the five segments, including size of the segments, demographics, amount of savings, and financial attitudes. Exhibits 11 through 13 present data from the study concerning each segment's rating of Greenwood Federal and usage of various products and services. The share of market for GFS and its major competitors by segment is included in Exhibit 14. Selected findings for each segment are discussed below.

Minimal Martha

This segment was the largest identified, with one third of all consumers and 30 percent of GFS customers included. Minimal Martha had the least usage of financial products and institutions among the five segments. This was the only segment where the financial decision maker was most often female and the

EXHIBIT 7 Descriptions and size of each segment

	GFS customers 100%	Total segmentation study 100%	% of segmentation that were W.P.** 40%
High assets, high checking Wants single account, single interest Wants security, personal attention Organized, disciplined Budgets, saves High TV and radio, high newspaper	Singleminded Sam 7%	Singleminded Sam 11%	32%
Oldest, most affluent High assets Well managed, highly organized Wants security, does not shop No ATM Uses many services Low checking, high savings High newspaper, high magazine	Retiring Richard 17%	Retiring Richard 13%	47%
Middle aged, well educated Good income Technical/Sales/Administrative Undisciplined, uninvolved, wife handles Has difficulty managing, overspends Low assets, low savings High TV, moderate other media	Fastlane Phil 15%	Fastlane Phil 19%	28%
Middle aged Married Likely male Educated Managerial/Professional High income, high savings High investments Self-confident Uses ATM Shops for rate Actively involved in managing finances Low checking balance Likely S & L Customer Age 25 - 49 Low TV and radio, high magazine	Secure Steve 30%	Secure Steve 22%	44%
Decision maker - female Pays cash, avoids credit Distrustful Low ATM usage Offices not convenient Lowest income (51% U 25K) Lowest savings Low education Blue collar Daytime TV, low radio, low news Age 25 - 55	Minimal Martha 30%	Minimal Martha 33%	28%
Base	106	712	*
% of total	15%	100%	*

*Each segment total

**Note: W.P. means working preferred, those employed with
at least $5000 in savings.

EXHIBIT 8 Demographics of the segmentation study

Sex of the Segments

Total survey		Martha	Steve	Phil	Rich	Sam
Women	46%	55	32	48	40	45
Men	54%	45	68	52	60	55
Base: 712		235	158	136	91	78
%: 100.0%		33.0%	22.2%	19.1%	12.8%	11.0%

Age of the Segments

Total survey		Martha	Steve	Phil	Rich	Sam
65 +	10%	8	8	1	22	21
55 - 64	20%	19	13	15		21
45 - 54	14%	16	14	15	39	12
35 - 44	26%	22	31	35		24
18 - 34	30%	35	35	33	12	23
					14	
					13	
Base: 712		235	158	136	91	78
%: 100.0%		33.0%	22.2%	19.1%	12.8%	11.0%

Household Income of the Segments

Total survey		Martha	Steve	Phil	Rich	Sam
$50 +	15%	7	25	12	17	18
$35 - 49.9	23%	22		23	31	18
$25 - 34.9	21%	20	22	23	21	12
$10 - 24.9	41%	51	26	42	31	53
			27			
Base: 712		235	158	136	91	78
%: 100.0%		33.0%	22.2%	19.1%	12.8%	11.0%

EXHIBIT 8 *(concluded)*

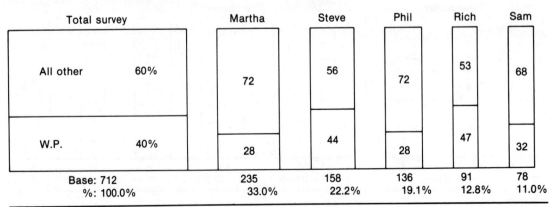

Occupation of the Segments

Total survey		Martha	Steve	Phil	Rich	Sam
Retired	11%	7	8	4		19
Other	11%	13	11	8	27	
			7	12		10
Blue collar	14%	23			11	13
					6	
White collar	64%	57	74	76	56	58
Base: 712		235	158	136	91	78
%: 100.0%		33.0%	22.2%	19.1%	12.8%	11.0%

Savings of the Segments

Total survey		Martha	Steve	Phil	Rich	Sam
$25,000 +	22%	13	24	8	53	31
				25		
$5,000 - 24,999	29%	30	33			25
				67	33	
Under $5,000	49%	57	43			44
					14	
Base: 712		235	158	136	91	78
%: 100.0%		33.0%	22.2%	19.1%	12.8%	11.0%

Working Preferred Status

Total survey		Martha	Steve	Phil	Rich	Sam
All other	60%	72	56	72	53	68
W.P.	40%	28	44	28	47	32
Base: 712		235	158	136	91	78
%: 100.0%		33.0%	22.2%	19.1%	12.8%	11.0%

EXHIBIT 9 Average amount of savings (by study segments)

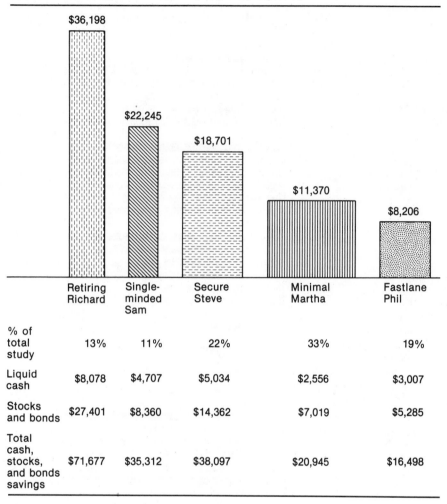

	Retiring Richard	Single-minded Sam	Secure Steve	Minimal Martha	Fastlane Phil
% of total study	13%	11%	22%	33%	19%
Liquid cash	$8,078	$4,707	$5,034	$2,556	$3,007
Stocks and bonds	$27,401	$8,360	$14,362	$7,019	$5,285
Total cash, stocks, and bonds savings	$71,677	$35,312	$38,097	$20,945	$16,498

banking chores were also handled most often by the female head of household. Minimal Martha generally manages her personal finances by paying cash, keeping funds in separate accounts, and avoiding credit. She is less comfortable and trusting of financial institutions. The convenience of a financial institution is probably the major determinant in its selection. Martha has a low income, less education, and is more likely to be married with a larger household and a blue-collar husband than other segments.

Secure Steve

The second largest segment is Secure Steve, who is upscale (managerial, professional, well educated, high income, high savings, high investment) and

EXHIBIT 10 Agreement with various attitudinal statements

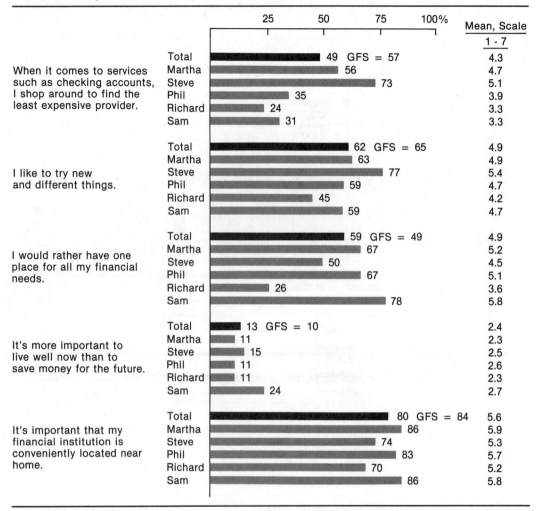

	25	50	75	100%	Mean, Scale 1 - 7

When it comes to services such as checking accounts, I shop around to find the least expensive provider.

		Mean
Total	49 GFS = 57	4.3
Martha	56	4.7
Steve	73	5.1
Phil	35	3.9
Richard	24	3.3
Sam	31	3.3

I like to try new and different things.

Total	62 GFS = 65	4.9
Martha	63	4.9
Steve	77	5.4
Phil	59	4.7
Richard	45	4.2
Sam	59	4.7

I would rather have one place for all my financial needs.

Total	59 GFS = 49	4.9
Martha	67	5.2
Steve	50	4.5
Phil	67	5.1
Richard	26	3.6
Sam	78	5.8

It's more important to live well now than to save money for the future.

Total	13 GFS = 10	2.4
Martha	11	2.3
Steve	15	2.5
Phil	11	2.6
Richard	11	2.3
Sam	24	2.7

It's important that my financial institution is conveniently located near home.

Total	80 GFS = 84	5.6
Martha	86	5.9
Steve	74	5.3
Phil	83	5.7
Richard	70	5.2
Sam	86	5.8

innovative. Secure Steve shops for low charges and high interest with self-confidence. He rejects frills and is unwilling to pay to get personal attention. Typically, Secure Steve is in the prime of his career, aged 25–49, married, with a confident, ambitious outlook. He maintains the minimum in checking, shops for the best terms, and is willing to try new products. He actively shops around for the ''best'' financial products and is more willing to change institutions to get the best deal. He represents 22 percent of the sample and 30 percent of GFS customers.

EXHIBIT 10 *(concluded)*

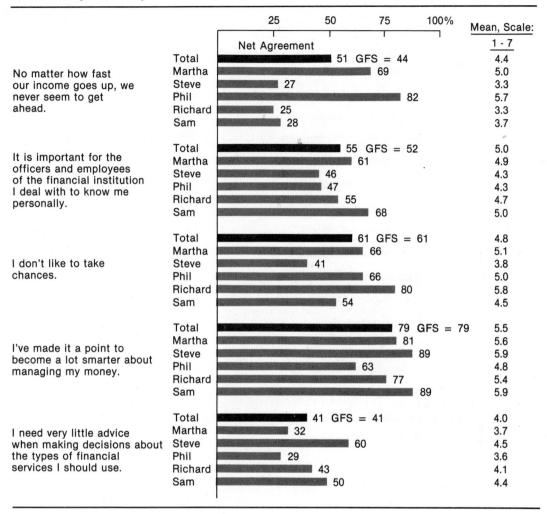

		Net Agreement	Mean, Scale: 1 - 7
No matter how fast our income goes up, we never seem to get ahead.	Total	51 GFS = 44	4.4
	Martha	69	5.0
	Steve	27	3.3
	Phil	82	5.7
	Richard	25	3.3
	Sam	28	3.7
It is important for the officers and employees of the financial institution I deal with to know me personally.	Total	55 GFS = 52	5.0
	Martha	61	4.9
	Steve	46	4.3
	Phil	47	4.3
	Richard	55	4.7
	Sam	68	5.0
I don't like to take chances.	Total	61 GFS = 61	4.8
	Martha	66	5.1
	Steve	41	3.8
	Phil	66	5.0
	Richard	80	5.8
	Sam	54	4.5
I've made it a point to become a lot smarter about managing my money.	Total	79 GFS = 79	5.5
	Martha	81	5.6
	Steve	89	5.9
	Phil	63	4.8
	Richard	77	5.4
	Sam	89	5.9
I need very little advice when making decisions about the types of financial services I should use.	Total	41 GFS = 41	4.0
	Martha	32	3.7
	Steve	60	4.5
	Phil	29	3.6
	Richard	43	4.1
	Sam	50	4.4

Fast Lane Phil

Phil likely can be found in the fast lane at Household Finance Corporation, but is not found among the jet set in the fast lane at the airport. The segment is undisciplined, and they are poor managers of financial affairs. Three out of four in this segment report less than $5,000 in savings. Phil frequently overspends with credit cards and often makes purchases with personal installment loans. He has the highest usage of checking accounts *without* interest and passbook accounts, but the lowest usage of other savings or investment products. This

EXHIBIT 11 Rating of Greenwood Federal Savings (poor to extremely good; scale of zero to ten)

	GFS Rating: Total Study	Minimal Martha	Secure Steve	Fastlane Phil	Retirng Richard	Single Sam
	Rank (importance)					
Seldom make mistakes	1 — 6.8	6.3	7.2	6.7	7.2	6.6
Good job overall	2 — 7.0	7.0	7.0	6.8	7.5	7.1
Clear statements	3 — 6.5	6.4	6.5	6.3	6.9	6.7
Convenient weekday hours	4 — 6.9	7.1	6.6	6.6	7.5	7.1
Polite and courteous	5 — 6.9	6.6	7.3	6.5	7.2	6.9
History of stability	6 — 7.4	7.5	7.2	6.9	8.3	7.8
All services I need	7 — 6.6	6.8	6.9	6.2	6.5	6.4
Rarely long lines	8 — 6.0	5.7	6.1	6.0	6.3	6.0
Pay highest rate	9 — 6.4	6.4	6.5	6.1	6.5	6.8
Conveniently located branches	10 — 5.8	5.7	5.8	5.5	6.5	5.8
Convenient to live	11 — 5.3	5.0	5.6	5.2	6.1	5.1
Lowest charges, fees	12 — 5.9	5.9	6.0	5.6	5.8	5.9
Easily qualify for free checking	13 — 5.8	5.4	6.3	5.3	6.3	6.2
Tailor services to fit needs	14 — 5.4	5.6	5.2	5.3	5.4	5.4
Convenient to work	15 — 5.0	5.1	4.8	4.7	5.8	4.6
Offer consumer loans	16 — 6.8	6.9	6.9	6.6	6.6	7.1
Convenient Saturday hours	17 — 5.4	5.3	5.8	4.9	5.3	5.8
Interested in my financial position	18 — 5.2	5.3	4.8	5.2	5.4	5.3
Interest in me as a person	19 — 4.9	4.9	4.5	4.9	5.1	5.5
Work with me to achieve goals	20 — 5.1	5.2	4.9	4.9	5.1	5.5
Offer sound advice	21 — 5.7	5.8	5.5	5.7	5.5	5.8
Leader among institutions	22 — 6.7	6.7	6.4	6.3	7.3	7.2
Convenient to shop	23 — 5.3	5.1	5.4	5.1	5.7	5.4
Develop new products and services	24 — 5.5	5.6	5.5	5.1	5.9	5.6
Provide non-bank financial services	25 — 4.8	4.9	4.9	4.3	5.0	5.2

EXHIBIT 12 Product Usage: Segmentation study: January 25—March 18, 1985

	Total study	GFS Customers	Martha	Steve	Phil	Richard	Sam
M/C Visa card	77	83	64	84	84	90	76
ATM	69	67	60	81	77	55	78
Passbook/statement	69	81	66	67	79	68	65
Home mtg. loan	61	75	58	70	60	62	53
Checking without	60	50	64	48	69	64	58
Checking with	54	69	46	73	41	58	49
Safe deposit	48	61	40	53	38	73	47
Auto loan	42	45	37	49	52	35	35
Stock	35	46	24	55	29	57	17
IRA	35	57	26	47	25	53	37
American Express	27	29	21	33	36	29	18
U.S. Bonds	26	25	24	31	29	25	18
CD More than year	24	46	25	20	13	44	23
Personal instl. loan	23	17	17	25	35	14	29
CD Year or less	23	40	23	22	12	45	22
MMDA BK/S&L	20	26	16	23	15	34	19
Other tax def.	15	22	10	25	13	22	13
MMF, Broker	14	19	9	20	8	29	9
Other mutual fund	13	19	6	17	13	23	12
Second mortgage	11	11	14	11	14	3	12
Corp/Gov. bonds	11	11	10	16	7	20	8
T-bills/Notes	4	3	3	4	2	4	3
Trust service	3	5	2	3	2	6	6

segment represents 19 percent of the total sample and 15 percent of GFS customers.

Retiring Richard

This segment has by far the highest savings. They prefer low risk to high interest and like personal attention. The Richard segment contains the highest proportion of retirees, 28 percent, more than double the average for the total

EXHIBIT 13 Service Usage

	Total study	GFS customers	Martha	Steve	Phil	Richard	Sam
Automatic deduction from checking	35	34	30	41	45	26	37
Direct deposit of payroll	29	23	7	51	40	31	33
Overdraft protection	29	32	23	35	34	23	39
Unsecured line of credit	19	15	11	27	21	21	25
Stock brokerage other than Bk/S&L	12	14	8	20	9	22	5
Automatic transfer saving to checking	11	6	8	13	12	7	20
Card that automatically deducts purchases	7	4	6	9	7	4	14
Secured line of credit	5	5	4	4	7	1	6
Telephone bill paying	5	2	4	4	4	4	5
Automobile leasing	3	4	3	3	5	2	4
Financial advice and counseling	3	4	2	6	1	3	3
Stockbrokerage at bank or S&L	1	3	1	1	2	2	1

Scale (Total study): 40% 30 20 10 / (GFS customers) 10 20 30 40%. Segments columns: Martha, Steve, Phil, Richard, Sam. Value "8" appears at bottom of Total study axis.

sample. His financial affairs are well established, and he is somewhat resistant to changing them. Retiring Richard has the highest usage of most financial products and is the oldest and most married of the five segments. The segment represents 13 percent of the total sample and 17 percent of GFS customers.

Single-Minded Sam

This segment, representing 11 percent of the sample and 7 percent of GFS customers, has the strongest preference for a single integrated account with one financial institution. This segment likes the security of a big institution, especially banks, and personal attention is very important. One-stop banking is more important than low fees or a high interest rate on savings. Sam is the second oldest and the most divorced, widowed, or separated of the segments.

EXHIBIT 14   Share of market (by study segments)

		25%	50%	Index
Total	GFS	15		100.0
	CNB	31		100.0
	FNB		38	100.0
	HTB	24		100.0
	SFS	21		100.0
Martha	GFS	14		91
	CNB	31		102
	FNB	31		82
	HTB	21		87
	SFS	18		89
Steve	GFS	20		136
	CNB	30		98
	FNB		42	112
	HTB	23		94
	SFS	28		136
Phil	GFS	12		79
	CNB	33		107
	FNB		40	105
	HTB	26		106
	SFS	18		90
Richard	GFS	20		133
	CNB		38	124
	FNB		37	99
	HTB	23		94
	SFS	24		118
Sam	GFS	9		60
	CNB	23		74
	FNB		47	125
	HTB	28		116
	SFS	12		56

Ms. Harris felt that the key to finding a niche for GFS and for differentiating it from the competition could be found in Exhibits 7 through 14. She planned to spend considerable time interpreting the meaning of this data.

Marketing Strategy Considerations

The senior management of Greenwood Federal had recently developed a mission statement. It read, ''The mission of Greenwood Federal is to discover and provide needed financial services to consumers in a manner consistent with their reasonable expectations and consistent with the achievement of reasonable earnings.'' Given the change in regulations that had taken place in the past year and the mission statement, Ms. Harris felt that she should develop a strategic marketing plan to provide ''controlled growth orchestrated to the beat of profitability, protecting assets and net worth while directing a positive course of profits.'' The Association had always used conservative policies, and loan delinquencies over the years had been consistently low because of the relatively strict loan underwriting standards. She felt it was important to maintain a conservative posture, but still felt there was considerable opportunity to increase consumer lending with new products, such as the homeowners line of credit, the personal credit line, and a new type of auto loan, the ''Payment Shrinker.'' Exhibit 15 contains copy the ad agency had developed for a brochure to explain how the Payment Shrinker auto loan works.

To help determine the relative importance of the various products offered by GFS, Ms. Harris had developed a product hierarchy ranking matrix. This is presented in Exhibit 16, together with the key used to give the ratings. According to her analysis, money market deposit accounts, certificates of deposit, IRAs, mortgage loans, and regular savings accounts were the products that should receive the highest priority. Ms. Harris was very uncomfortable with what she had done, and wondered whether the results were accurate. For example, she had weighted each of the factors equally and was now having some second thoughts about this decision. She vowed to take another look at the product hierarchy rankings as she started to develop the strategic marketing plan.

EXHIBIT 15

Payment Shrinker Auto Financing Cuts Monthly Payments up to 49 Percent

Now you can afford to drive the automobile you really want. GFS Federal makes it possible with Payment Shrinker, the auto loan that can reduce your monthly payments by 25 to 49 percent.

Here's How Payment Shrinker Reduces Monthly Payments

GFS Federal Payment Shrinker combines the lower monthly payment advantages of auto leasing with the ownership and tax benefits offered by conventional car loans.

Depending on your choice of terms, your monthly payments will extend over 24, 36, or 48 months. The final payment amount will be determined at the time you make the loan and will be based on the residual value of the car* at the end of the loan.

Interest is computed on the full amount of the loan, but your monthly payments are lower because the residual car value is subtracted from the purchase price. The monthly principal payments are based upon the difference.

* The residual value of the automobile is determined by *Automotive Lease Guide*, a published residual value book, in effect at the time the loan is originated. The residual value represents the estimated value of the vehicle after the 24- to 48-month loan is completed.

EXHIBIT 15 *(concluded)*

The interest that is charged on the full amount of the loan is tax deductible, as well as any sales tax you pay. This tax benefit is not available for personal automobile leases.

Four Options at End of Loan Term

At the end of the loan term, you'll have a choice of four options regarding your final payment: If you wish to keep your car, you may (1) pay off the residual car value amount figured in with the last monthly payment or (2) refinance the residual. If you would like another car, you may (3) sell or trade your car and keep the profit you make over and above the residual value or (4) return the car in good working condition (subject to condition and mileage requirements) to GFS Federal with no further obligation except to pay a nominal return fee.

Example of How Payment Shrinker Auto Loan Works

Purchase price of the car you want	$13,528
Less: Down payment (10%).	1,353
Amount to be financed over 36 months at	
13¾%† annual percentage rate	$12,175
Residual value of car at end of 36 month loan term.	$ 6,935

Monthly payments are composed of two parts:
1. Principal and interest payable on $5,240
   ($12,175 minus the $6,935 residual value) $178.44
2. Interest payments on the $6,935 residual car value . . . . $ 79.46

Total monthly payment	$257.90

Monthly payment with conventional auto loan at

12¼%† annual percentage rate	$405.86
Monthly payment with Payment Shrinker	$257.90
Amount saved per month	$147.96

† This is an example. Actual rate may vary.

Compare Monthly Payments—
Payment Shrinker versus Conventional Financing

Amount financed	Conventional auto loan (monthly)	Payment Shrinker auto loan (monthly)
$24,000		
24 months	$1,132.57	$712.24
36 months	$ 800.01	$573.31
48 months	$ 634.96	$501.72
$16,000	—	—
24 months	$ 755.05	$474.82
36 months	$ 533.34	$382.21
48 months	$ 423.31	$334.48
$8,000	—	—
24 months	$ 377.52	$237.41
36 months	$ 266.67	$191.11
48 months	$ 211.65	$167.24

Note: The monthly payment chart shown is based on the following assumptions: Payment Shrinker auto loan: **13.75% annual percentage rate;** Conventional auto loan: **12.25% annual percentage rate.** Assume residual value is 50% of sticker price for 24 months, 45% of sticker price for 36 months, 40% of sticker price for 48 months. Amount financed is 90% of purchase price.

EXHIBIT 16 Product hierarchy

	WP* usage	WP hot button	Comp. opp.†	GFS position	Profit	Commitment	Total
MMDA	3	3	3	2	3	2	16
CDs	3	3	2	2	3	3	16
IRA	3	3	1	2	2	3	14
Mortgage loans	3	2	1	3	2	3	14
Regular savings	3	1	3	2	3	2	14
Checking	3	2	2	1	1	3	13
HOLOC	1	3	1	3	3	1	12
INVEST	3	3	1	2	1	2	12
Consumer loans	2	3	2	1	1	3	12
Super NOW	1	2	3	2	2	1	11
Safe Deposit	3	2	3	1	2	1	11
Credit card	3	2	1	1	2	1	10
Travel company	1	1	3	1	1	2	9

Product Hierarchy Key

Working Preferred Usage:
  1 = Less than 30 percent use the product.
  2 = 30–50 percent use the product.
  3 = More than 50 percent use the product.

Working Preferred Hot Button:
  1 = Low priority—not likely to move or open account.
  2 = Medium priority—might move or open if offer is strong.
  3 = High priority—will move or open if offer is strong.

Competitive Opportunity:
  1 = Competitors are actively marketing the product.
  2 = Some competitive activity.
  3 = No competitive activity.

Greenwood Federal's Position:
  1 = Weak position.
  2 = Potential for unique position.
  3 = Strong position.

Profitability:
  1 = Significant losses on product.
  2 = Product is losing money but has potential.
  3 = Product is profitable.

Commitment:
  1 = Little or no resources have been committed in the past.
  2 = Some resources have been committed in the past.
  3 = Major resources have been committed in the past.

* WP = Working preferred (employed and savings of $5,000 and up).
† Comp. Opp. = Competitive opportunity.

The advertising agency had recommended several new campaigns for her consideration. The "25K Account" proposal is included in Exhibit 17. The goal of this ad is to attract larger accounts, and the campaign would use the tag line "your partner."

Exhibit 18 contains an ad the agency had developed to attract more consumer loans. This ad made use of the proposed alternative tag line "Experience the Partnership." Finally, Exhibit 19 contains the third proposal from the

EXHIBIT 17

Greenwood Federal Announces
A Golden Opportunity.

THE 25K ACCOUNT.

Take a moment to review your investments. If you aren't currently earning a preferred rate on any amount of $25,000 or more, you should consider investing in Greenwood Federal's 25K Account. With 25K you'll earn our highest money market account rate. A fiercely competitive figure you'll rarely find bested. One that changes with market conditions

to keep you head and shoulders above the crowd.

Your 25K Account is easily accessible every seven days. And federal insurance makes it as safe as, well, money in the bank.

your partner
GREENWOOD FEDERAL

The 25K Account. It's designed for those who are already experienced in recognizing golden opportunities. And for those interested in smaller investments, we offer competitive rates on a regular money market account with a minimum balance of $2,500. We invite you to come in to any Greenwood Federal office and seize the opportunity today.

Substantial Penalty for early withdrawal.

EXHIBIT 18

AFFORDABLE LOANS.
ACADILLACABLE LOANS.
APONTIACABLE LOANS.
APOOLABLE LOANS.
ANEWPORCHABLE LOANS.
AVACATIONABLE LOANS.
ACOLLEGEABLE LOANS.
ASPEEDBOATABLE LOANS.

Available loans. We've got plenty. Everything from auto loans, boat loans, home improvement loans, lines of credit, and of course, mortgage loans. In fact, we've always been a leader in mortgage lending. And that leadership carries over into all the other loans you need.

Agreeable loans. We're there to make it easier for you. With convenient terms, a variety of services, quick responses, simple interest, no prepayment penalties and service with a smile.

Affordable loans. Don't worry. We'll make sure your monthly payments are well within your reach.

A whatever-you-wantable loans. You'll find all you need at Greenwood Federal.

GREENWOOD FEDERAL

Experience The Partnership.

Member F.S.L.I.C.

EXHIBIT 19

Gifts for the Good Life.

Get a special bonus now with your new Greenwood Federal savings certificate ... you'll still get interest later.

RCA 20" ColorTrak TV w/Remote.

Sony 8mm Camera w/Recorder.

Pearl Grandfather Clock w/Chimes.

Apple Macintosh Personal Computer.

Litton Space Saving Microwave.

Cannon Typewriter.

Fisher Deluxe VCR.

Lawn-Boy Self-Propelled Mower.

CERTIFICATE TERMS AND DEPOSIT LEVELS

GIFT DESCRIPTION	7 : Years	5 : Years	3 : Years
Toshiba Gourmet Coffee Maker, OR Pulsar Quartz Watch—Men's/Ladies'	$2,500	$3,500	$5,000
Cannon Typewriter w/Adaptor, OR Litton Space-Saving Microwave	$4,000	$5,000	$8,000
GE 13" Portable Color TV	$5,000	$6,500	$10,000
Zenith 13" Color TV w/Remote, OR Magic Chef Deluxe Microwave w/Turntable	$7,000	$9,500	$15,000
RCA 20" ColorTrak TV w/Remote, OR GE VCR w/Wireless Remote	$9,500	$13,000	$20,000
Lawn-Boy Deluxe Self-Propelled Mower, OR Fisher Deluxe VCR w/MTS Stereo	$11,500	$16,000	$25,000
RCA 26" ColorTrak Console TV w/Remote	$14,500	$20,000	$30,000
Pearl Grandfather Clock w/Westminster Chimes	$19,000	$25,500	$40,000
Fisher Stereo Home Entertainment Center	$23,000	$32,500	$50,000
Sony 27" Console TV w/Stereo	$28,000	$38,000	$60,000
Sony 8mm Handycam Camera/Recorder	$32,500	$45,000	$70,000
Apple Macintosh Personal Computer	$35,000	$50,000	$80,000

Greenwood Federal announces a new, special kind of savings certificate. It pays you part of your interest income now, in the form of a luxury gift. You'll receive one or more of the gifts listed here, for yourself or to give as a gift. And your money will still earn interest compounded annually. For current rates, call 373-SAVE. So if you have money to invest, come to Greenwood Federal where your investment is rewarded handsomely ... and immediately.

Offer limited. Interest rates, qualifying deposit levels, and items of merchandise subject to change without notice. • Items of merchandise represent interest, therefore, the value of the merchandise will be reported as interest earned in the year received. • Allow minimum of 4 weeks for delivery. • This offer not applicable to IRA or KEOGH accounts. • A substantial penalty, which will include the value of merchandise received, may be imposed for early withdrawal of certificate funds.

GREENWOOD FEDERAL
FOR THE GOOD LIFE

"Why don't you get your grandson a TV set?"   *"I'm giving him the Apple computer."*

ad agency, "For the Good Life." This ad was designed to attract high dollar volumes for longer periods of time through the use of attractive premiums. These new certificates of deposit were to be priced 35 basis points below comparable three-, five-, and six-year certificates, with interest to be paid and compounded annually rather than quarterly. The agency proposed that advertising previously scheduled for high-interest checking be switched to this premium promotion and that newspaper ads and radio also be used.

As shown in Exhibit 20, the majority of GFS customers used only one type of product from among the offerings available, although a number of households had more than one account within the type (two or more savings accounts in the household, for example). Ms. Harris thought that there was great opportunity to "cross sell more services to more households." GFS had recently established a small telemarketing operation and she wondered if this might be used for this purpose. She wondered how to direct mail to customers or prospects and if advertising might work to increase cross-selling opportunities. To determine what had happened recently with some of the newer products she pulled out the report in Exhibit 21 which contained information on new loan production and consumer loans outstanding as of July 1986 (the latest report available).

Lots of things were popping into Ms. Harris's mind. She was concerned about how much attention she should pay to the short run versus the long run. For example, she knew that for GFS to devote strong emphasis to increase its penetration in the small business market would take a long time, given the lack

EXHIBIT 20 Types of accounts held by GFS customers

Account type	Percent of GFS households	Average number of GFS products per household
Savings only	28	
Mortgage only	18	
Checking only	7	
Consumer loan only	3	
Total one product type	56	1.4*
Checking and savings	16	
Mortgage and savings	5	
Consumer loan and savings	3	
Consumer loan and checking	2	
Consumer loan and mortgage	2	
Checking and mortgage	0	
Total two product types	28	3.1
Checking, savings, and mortgage	5	
Checking, savings, and consumer loan	3	
Savings, mortgage, and consumer loan	3	
Checking, mortgage, and consumer loan	1	
Total three product types	12	4.6
All four types	4	6.8
	100	2.5
Any savings	67	
Any checking	39	
Any mortgage	38	
Any consumer loan	21	
Any deposit	83	
Any loan	46	

* This number is greater than 1.0 because many households had more than one account (although all were the same type of account).

EXHIBIT 21 Banking group monthly report for July 1986

Consumer loans production:	Number		Total dollar amount
Real estate loans			
Second mortgages	19		$ 358,800.00
Equity line	39		1,145,100.00
Total	58		$ 1,503,900.00
Installment and single pay loans			
Payment Shrinker	10		118,763.86
Auto	184		1,239,500.10
Personal, secured and unsecured	291		2,145,839.73
Personal LOC	80		760,100.00
Total	565		4,264,203.69
Total production for July	623		$ 5,768,103.69

Consumer loans outstanding:	Total available credit	Number	Total dollar amount
Unsecured		1,234	$ 3,280,607.34
Secured other		704	3,718,010.66
Auto		3,106	15,147,248.45
Payment Shrinker		106	1,409,657.19
Subtotal		5,150	23,555,523.64
Equity line	12,493,481.68	1,086	17,383,580.59
Personal LOC	5,348,844.40	760	2,552,124.24
Total		6,996	43,491,228.47

	Number	Total	
2nd mortgages	795	9,219,720.55	
Less participated 2nds	419	−4,956,014.39	
Total 2nd mortgages	376	4,263,706.16	
Grand total	7,372		$47,754,934.63
Second mortgages maintained on mortgage loan system	726	$12,488,112.80	

Credit life insurance − Net income for July: $8,374.52.

Delinquencies:	Over 30 days	Over 60 days
Real Estate	11	4
Other	60	27
Total	71 .8%	31 .3%

Charge-offs in July—$11,382.62.   Recoveries—$198.00.

of history in marketing to this segment. Likewise, a strong commitment to home banking using personal computers would be a long-run effort. On the other hand, increasing the emphasis on the Payment Shrinker auto loan, the homeowners line of credit (HOLOC), personal line of credit, or consumer loans would be easy to accomplish in the short run, given that the products had already been developed.

She wondered how much emphasis to put on INVEST, the discount brokerage service. A recent study GFS had conducted showed that 77 percent of the money invested through INVEST came out of other sources and that 23 percent came from GFS accounts. Some of the management at GFS felt that the money pulled out of the accounts would have been invested in stock or bonds anyway, so that at least with INVEST some fees were generated. Also, heavy promotion of INVEST, which had just recently become profitable, could reduce the asset base for the Association while generating some fees, enabling a rise in the reserve ratio. Other GFS managers were more skeptical about this happening.

Ms. Harris had seen potential in the segmentation study for high-interest checking products with several of the segments. She also thought that the proposed tax law, which would remove deductions for consumer loans, could have a big impact on her strategic planning. Did it mean, for example, that emphasis should not be put on automobile loans (even the Payment Shrinker) and other consumer loans? Did it mean that homeowner equity loans were the wave of the future? She had seen Internal Revenue Service data indicating that only 38 percent of all taxpayers itemized deductions on their 1984 returns. Did this suggest that consumers simply will not care enough about tax savings to establish a home equity credit line when they are ready to buy a car? Home-owner equity lines typically cost $500–$700 in closing cost alone. She had heard rumors that several of the Sunbelt City banks were considering waiving the fees, and wondered how GFS should respond if this in fact happened in the near future. She also had heard rumors that one or more of the banks might lower the rates, currently two percentage points above prime, to prime or even below for several months to attract new accounts with home equity loans.

Finally, Ms. Harris thought about the advertising agency. It had been bugging her for some time to give it more direction. Did GFS intend to become a full-service financial institution in the mold of a traditional commercial bank, or did it plan to continue to specialize in the consumer savings and mortgage lending areas? Which niche would be appropriate for GFS to seek relative to other financial institutions? What competitive differences could be used to set GFS apart from the competition? She wondered whether it might just be simpler to become a stock company, which would be the quickest and easiest way to raise the net worth/total assets ratio to 6 percent.

Case 39

Dutch Food Industries Company (A)*

In early September, Jan de Vries, product manager for Dutch Food Industries' new salad dressing product, was wondering what strategy to follow with respect to this new product. His assistant had prepared information concerning alternative promotional methods to use to introduce the new product, and he was concerned with exactly which of these he should recommend for the product's introduction. He also wondered what price the new product should retail for and when the company should introduce the new product. Mr. de Vries had to decide these issues in the next couple of days, as his report containing his recommendations on the introduction of the new salad dressing was due on the desk of the director of marketing the following Monday.

Company Background

The Netherlands Oil Factory of Delft, The Netherlands, was founded in 1884. This firm, which supplied edible oils to the growing margarine industry, merged in 1900 with a French milling company. The new firm then operated under the name Dutch Food Industries Company (DFI).

From this origin, the brand name DFI became increasingly strong and was eventually given to all of the company's branded products. More recently, the name was registered for use internationally.

In the course of the 1920s, DFI became an important factor in the margarine market. The company was a troublesome competitor for the Margarine Union, the company formed by the merger in 1927 of the two margarine giants, Van den Bergh and Jurgens. In 1928, an agreement was reached by which DFI joined the Margarine Union.

In 1930, the interests of the Margarine Union were merged with those of International Industries Corporation—a large, diversified, and international organization. It was in this way that DFI became a part of the International Industries complex of companies.

---

* This case was written by Kenneth L. Bernhardt and James Scott assisted by Jos Viehoff, graduate student, Netherlands School of Economics. Copyright © 1987 by Kenneth L. Bernhardt.

International Industries Corporation (IIC) is a worldwide organization with major interests in the production of margarine, other edible fats and oils, soups, ice cream, frozen foods, meats, cheeses, soaps, and detergents.

The total sales of IIC were more than $1 billion.[1] Profits before taxes were $56 million.

Within IIC, DFI proceeded with its original activities after its margarine factory was closed, namely developing its exports of oils and fats, its trade in bakery products, as well as a number of branded food products. The following list indicates the range of consumer products which the company marketed: table oil, household fats, mayonnaise, salad dressing (several varieties), tomato ketchup, peanut butter, and peanuts.

DFI's total annual sales were between $14 million–$28 million. Profits before taxes were between $1.4 million–$2.8 million.

Background on the Dressing Market

A large and growing percentage of Holland's population eats lettuce, usually with salad dressing, with their meals. Estimates indicated that 82 percent of the people ate lettuce with salad dressing regularly. The salad dressing market has extreme seasonal demand as shown in Exhibit 1. This seasonal pattern coincides with the periods of greatest production of lettuce in Holland. Thus, 50 percent of the total year's volume for the salad dressing market occurs in the four months beginning in April. During this period, lettuce is plentiful and sells for approximately $0.46 per head.

The total salad dressing market was growing at approximately 7 percent per year. DFI's share of the market had declined from 20.7 percent to 16.6 percent over the last five years. The total market for salad dressings at manufacturer's level was currently estimated at between $7 million and $8.4 million. The company was looking for ways to halt the decline in market share and, in fact, increase DFI's share of the growing market.

Historically, the salad dressing market was composed of two segments. The first was a 25 percent oil-based salad dressing, which comprised 90 percent of the total market. The other 10 percent of the market consisted of 50 percent oil-based salad dressing, a slightly creamier product. Previously, DFI, in an effort to increase its market share, had introduced a new product which was 50 percent oil based. Up to that time, DFI sold only 25 percent oil-based salad dressing. The product, called Delfine, was not successful in obtaining the desired volume and profit. While DFI still marketed Delfine, almost all of DFI's volume came from its 25 percent oil-based product, Slasaus.

A research study was conducted to help the DFI marketing executives determine why Delfine was not successful. Several reasons emerged:

1. The potential of the 50 percent oil-based market was much smaller than

---

[1] All financial data in this case are presented in U.S. dollars.

EXHIBIT 1 Seasonal analysis of salad dressing market (percentage of annual total market sales—bimonthly periods)

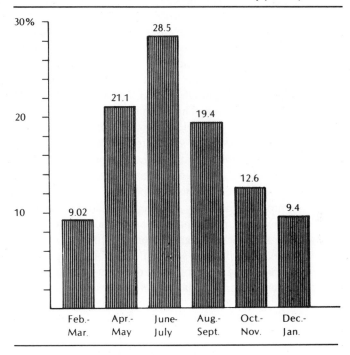

originally anticipated, and only a small percentage of the total population was even interested in this product.

2. The consumers could detect only a small difference between the 25 percent oil-based and the 50 percent oil-based varieties when blind-tested. The difference was not noticeable enough for the consumers to prefer the 50 percent oil-based product.

3. The 50 percent oil-based salad dressing was more expensive, and the consumer was not willing to pay the difference for an apparently almost imperceptible difference.

Because the Delfine sales were well below expectations, DFI removed the heavy promotion support which it had been giving the product. The executives decided to wait for a significant breakthrough of a product with unique advantages. The Delfine experience indicated to them that it would take a totally new type of product for DFI to increase its market share significantly.

Background and Development of Slamix

Every two years, the company conducted a housewives' habits study in which a panel of 700 consumers was asked about their household and their food preparation habits. In August two years before, the company received the most recent study, called PMC-11. The housewives were asked how they prepared their lettuce and what ingredients they used. The results showed that an extremely large percentage of the housewives added not only salad dressing to lettuce, but also added other ingredients such as salt, pepper, eggs, onion, gherkins, and so on. Thus DFI executives got the idea that putting some of these ingredients in the salad dressing would result in a real convenience for the housewife, and DFI would have the significant new product for which they had been searching. The laboratory, in August of the same year, began developing a "dressed" salad dressing which included some of the ingredients which many housewives were accustomed to adding.

Early in the next year, a committee called the Slamix Committee,[2] was formed to make sure that every part of the company was involved in the development of this new product. The committee, which was headed up by the product manager, had representatives from various parts of the company, including development, production, and marketing. The committee studied production problems, laboratory findings, and in general, was charged with the responsibility of seeing that the development progressed as scheduled. The committee did not have decision-making powers but either invited decision makers to important meetings or wrote reports to the people who were in a position to make the required decisions.

After several product tests concerned with taste and keeping properties were conducted at the factory, the company, one year after laboratory work began, undertook its first consumer test of the new "dressed" salad dressing. A panel of housewives was shown a bottle of the new product which was a salad dressing containing pieces of gherkins, onions, and paprika. Several conclusions emerged from this study:

1. The "dressed" salad dressing was seen by the housewives as more than a salad dressing with ingredients. It was seen as a completely new product.
2. There were two sides to this newness:
   a. By looking at the product, they thought that it had a new taste.
   b. The convenience aspect was strongly stressed by the housewives.
3. The housewives thought that the new product would be good for decorating the lettuce. With its new color (light red with colorful ingredients), they thought that they could decorate the lettuce much better than with present salad dressings which were creme-colored and very similar to mayonnaise.
4. When asked about the ingredients, one half of the housewives were favorable toward paprika, and half were against it. This apparently was a troublesome ingredient. However, because of the convenience aspect, gherkins and onions were favored by the housewives.

Later, a second consumer study was conducted by the Institute of House-

---

[2] Literally translated, Slasaus means "lettuce sauce," and Slamix is literally "lettuce mix."

hold Research in Rotterdam. A sample of 140 housewives who actually used salad dressing on lettuce was given a bottle of the new product to take home. Then, they were visited in their homes. Much useful information emerged from this study. After looking at the product, but before trying it, the housewives said that it looked like a fun product, it made them happy, and they thought that it would taste good. When asked what they thought the product contained, they said tomatoes, red paprika, celery, gherkins, and green paprika.

However, the company was disappointed with the housewives' overall evaluation of the product. Only 20 percent of the housewives said that they thought the product was very good, 11 percent did not like the product, and 69 percent of the housewives said that there were some favorable and some unfavorable aspects of the product. The main reason for the 80 percent unfavorable reaction was the consistency of the new salad dressing. It was too thin. The housewives could pour it too easily and it rapidly went to the bottom of the bowl. Because it fell to the bottom, the housewives said that it was much harder to decorate their salad. It was also uneconomical because they felt that they would put too much on if the product was that thin. There were also problems with taste. Many of the housewives thought it was too sour or too sharp. The paprika was the main reason for the dissatisfaction.

In spite of the above problems, there were several aspects of the study which encouraged the company to proceed with the development of this new product. When asked how they would change the ingredients in the "dressed" salad dressing, only 47 percent of the housewives suggested changes. Most recommended that more onions be added. The housewives were asked for their preference between DFI's Slasaus and the new "dressed" salad dressing. As shown in Exhibit 2, the housewives preferred the new product, except for its consistency. Sixty percent of the housewives said that they would buy the product if it were possible to buy it in the store. Since this was a very high positive response, the company was very encouraged.

The marketing, production, and development groups, coordinated by the Slamix Committee, began work on incorporating the required changes made evident by this consumer study. DFI's development group experimented with changes in the consistency, taste, and ingredients. The production group experimented with a new production process. DFI had intended to introduce the new "dressed" salad dressing in a few months. However, the top corporate executives decided that, before the new product could be introduced, an extensive test

EXHIBIT 2 Preference test: Slasaus versus "dressed" salad dressing

Prefer	Taste	Appear-ance	Decoration aspects	Con-sistency	Con-venience
"Dressed" salad dressing	59%	73%	46%	18%	50%
Slasaus	38	20	44	65	20
No preference/no difference	3	7	10	17	30
	100%	100%	100%	100%	100%

of its keeping properties (vulnerability to deterioration) would have to be conducted.

The keeping-properties test showed that after several months the light red-colored product changed to a pink color. The difference in color was only slight, but DFI executives thought that the consumer reaction to this change should be tested. They decided that at the same time they would conduct a consumer test to find a name for this new product. A sample of 180 housewives from the Institute of Household Research was used to get at these questions. Only 2 out of the 180 housewives saw that there was a difference in color between the two bottles of the new product. When they were told that there was a slight difference and were shown the two bottles together, most of the housewives could not see the color change, and those that could were not unhappy about it.

The housewives were then asked what the name for this product should be. The phrase "mixed salad dressing" kept coming up. The housewives were then asked what they thought of two names which the company had screened, "Slamix" (lettuce mix) and "Spikkeltjessaus" (sauce with little spots). Eighty-one percent thought that Slamix was a very good name. Only 26 percent thought that Spikkeltjessaus was a good name. The name Slamix was chosen for the new product. Interestingly, that was the name that the company had used internally for the new product when it was first being developed.

A short time later, DFI had solved the color-change problem. The company now thought that it had a product ready to be marketed, so a final consumer test was undertaken to test the effect of all of the changes that had been made during the previous year.

Two versions of Slamix, a white one and a pink one, were tested at the Institute for Household Research. One hundred eighty housewives were asked what they thought of the product and whether they would buy it or not. The negative reactions to the product were minimal. Almost no negative comments were voiced. The problems of consistency, color, taste, and ingredients had apparently been solved. When asked if they would buy the product, 76 percent of those shown the pink product, and 70 percent of those shown the white product responded in a positive manner. After tasting the two versions of Slamix, the housewives revealed a strong preference for the pink Slamix. The DCI executives felt that the product was now ready to be marketed.

DFI executives next reviewed the financial projections prepared by Mr. de Vries, the product manager. Almost no capital investment would be required as the Slamix would be produced by using present production facilities. Only a few machines, at a total cost of $11,000, would be required.

At an early stage in the development of the product, Slamix sales had been forecasted at 3.7 percent of the total market at the end of the first year. Encouraged by the results of the consumer tests, DFI executives revised their estimate of sales. The new forecast was for approximately 6.7 percent of the market. (See Exhibit 3.)

EXHIBIT 3 Forecast sales of Slamix

Year	Share of market (percent)
Original estimates	
Year 1	3.7%
Year 2	3.9
Year 3	4.4
Revised estimates	
Year 1	6.7
Year 2	11.7

The directors of the company thought that they finally had the product for which they had been waiting. The consumer tests were complete, and the product had found very high favor with the consumers. There was significant technological development involved in the product, and DFI executives thought that it would take considerable time for the competition to duplicate the product. The product manager's projected sales seemed reasonable. Mr. de Vries was asked to prepare a comprehensive report concerning the introductory marketing strategy to be used to introduce the new product.

Pricing Strategy

The first problem that the product manager had to resolve concerned the suggested retail price that the company should charge for Slamix. To help Mr. de Vries make his recommendation, the assistant product manager had made a list of the following considerations:

1. The company's total cost for a 0.30-liter-size bottle of Slamix was $0.20. This was 20 percent higher than DFI's regular salad dressing, Slasaus.
2. The gross margin for Slasaus was 22 percent. Because of the unique qualities of Slamix, large development costs, and possible substitution with Slasaus, a higher gross margin for Slamix might be considered.
3. DFI gave the wholesalers a 12.5 percent margin and retailers a 14.3 percent margin for Slasaus. Possibly these should be increased for Slamix to encourage greater acceptance and promotion by the trade channels of distribution.
4. The two leading salad dressings, Salata by Duyvis and Slasaus, both had a retail price of $0.28 for the 0.30-liter bottle. The retail price for the 0.60-liter bottle was $0.48. Private label salad dressings were $0.22 for a 0.30-liter bottle. The average price for all salad dressings was approximately $0.26.
5. DFI had conducted some research on the optimal price of Slamix. After using a sample of the product, 140 housewives were asked what price they would be willing to pay for Slamix. Their responses, by percent, were:

	Percent
$0.31 or less	45%
Between $0.31 and $0.40	41
$0.40 or more	14
Total	100%

The average price mentioned was $0.34.

The assistant product manager also prepared the table shown in Exhibit 4. The first column shows the retail price, and gives data that allows one to calculate trade margins and gross margin for Slasaus. The remaining six columns show alternative retail prices for Slamix, resulting from different trade margins and gross margins. Mr. de Vries wondered which of these prices he should recommend to the board of directors.

EXHIBIT 4 Alternative prices for Slamix*

	Slasaus	Slamix					
		1	2	3	4	5	6
Retail price	$0.28	$0.32	$0.34	$0.34	0.36	$0.37	$0.38
Price to retailer	0.24	0.28	0.28	0.29	0.295	0.31	0.316
Price to wholesaler	0.21	0.25	0.25	0.26	0.26	0.28	0.28
Cost	0.165	0.20	0.20	0.20	0.20	0.20	0.20

* Selected figures in this table have been disguised.

Promotion Alternatives

The board of directors told the product manager that he had $203,000 for his promotion budget. Of this, $7,000 was to be allocated as Slamix's share of the general corporate advertising which aided all DFI products. The $203,000 was determined by using a percentage of the "expected gross profit of the first year" for Slamix.[3] DFI's policy was to break even in the third year of the new product, attaining a total payback within five years. The company was generally willing to spend the gross profit for the first year as part of the total investment.

The company had already given considerable thought to the sales message and the brand image desired for Slamix. The information below was sent to the advertising agency to help in planning the promotional program of the company:

> *Sales message.* It is now possible, in a completely new way, to make delicious salad. Sla + Slamix = Sla Klaar. (Lettuce + Slamix = Lettuce Ready)

---

[3] It was possible that the percentage could be greater than 100 percent. This would mean that the company was willing to spend more than the first year's gross profit for initial promotion.

Supporting message. Slamix is a salad dressing with pieces of onion, gherkins, and paprika.

Desired brand image. With Slamix you can make, very easily and very quickly, a delicious salad that also looks nice. Slamix is a complete, good, handy product. DFI is a modern firm with up-to-date ideas.

Thus, the company wanted to get across three principal points. They are (1) that Slamix is a completely new product, (2) that it is convenient, and (3) that it is a salad dressing with ingredients making it a complete salad dressing.

The product manager was undecided as to how to divide the $196,000 among the following alternatives:

1. Television.
2. Radio.
3. Newspaper advertising.
4. Magazines.
5. Sampling.
6. Coupons.
7. Price-off promotion.
8. Key chain premiums.
9. Trade allowances.

Television

The product manager thought that television would be advantageous because of the ability to show the product in actual use—a housewife pouring Slamix onto the lettuce. The cost of using the television medium is shown in Exhibit 5. The company did not have a choice among the seven blocks of time, but had to take whatever was available. For planning, however, they figured an average cost of a 30-second ad would be $1,800. Mr. de Vries felt that at least 25 advertisements were necessary before the TV advertising would have maximum impact.

EXHIBIT 5 Data on Dutch television media

Station	Block number	Time	Cost of 30-second ad
Nederland 1	1	Before early news	$2,300
Nederland 1	2	After early news	2,300
Nederland 1	3	Before late news	2,950
Nederland 1	4	After late news	2,950
Nederland 2	5	After early news	500
Nederland 2	6	Before late news	840
Nederland 2	7	After late news	840
Average cost per 30-second TV ad			$1,800
Production cost for a TV ad			7,000

TV coverage per 1,000 households = 850 or 85 percent. Only about one half of the homes can receive Nederland 2.

Radio

The chief attraction of radio was its extremely low price. Each 30-second radio ad cost $126 on Radio Veronica, a popular station during the daytime. Production costs for a radio ad were approximately $840. Only 60 percent of the households could receive Radio Veronica, mainly in the western part of the country. Mr. de Vries felt that if radio were used, a minimum of 100 spots should be purchased.

Newspapers

Mr. de Vries thought the main advantages of newspapers would be the announcement effect and its influence with the local trade. Nationally, the cost of each half-page insertion would be $14,000.

Magazines

Magazines would be a desirable addition to the promotional program for several reasons. Due to the ability to use color, the company could show the product as it actually looked on the shelf. By using several women's magazines, the company could reach a select audience of people reading the magazine at its leisure. Data on selected Dutch magazines are shown in Exhibit 6. Mr. de Vries thought that if they were to use a magazine campaign, at least 10 insertions would be necessary before the advertising would be very effective. Of the

EXHIBIT 6 Data on selected Dutch magazines

				Price for full-page ad		
Magazines	*Type*	*Circulation*	*Frequency*	*Black and white*	*Color*	*Cost per 1,000 circulation**
Eva	Women's	375,000	Weekly	$ 770	$1,408	$3.75
Margriet	Women's	825,000	Weekly	2,100	3,440	4.15
Libelle	Women's	570,000	Weekly	1,416	2,340	4.10
Prinses	Women's	213,000	Weekly	660	1,175	5.55
Panorama	General	403,000	Weekly	1,300	2,150	5.40
Nieuwe Revu	General	261,000	Weekly	920	1,540	5.90
Spiegel	General	175,000	Weekly	710	1,325	7.55
Het Beste	Digest	325,000	Monthly	965	1,615	4.90
Studio	TV guide	575,000	Weekly	1,525	2,420	4.20
NCRV-gids	TV guide	482,000	Weekly	1,420	2,290	4.75
Vara-gids	TV guide	504,000	Weekly	1,500	2,370	4.70
AVRO-Televizier	TV guide	950,000	Weekly	2,600	3,870	4.05
Combination of *Eva*, *Margriet*, and *AVRO-Televizier*				4,900	7,785	3.65

* Cost of one-page color ad, divided by circulation in thousands. With *Eva* as an example, cost per 1,000 circulation = $1,408/375 = $3.75.

possibilities in Exhibit 6, the agency thought that the combination of *Eva, Margriet,* and *AVRO-Televizier* would be most effective for DFI, since the combination would reach a large number of people at a relatively low cost.

Sampling

Although he realized that it was very expensive, Mr. de Vries considered the use of direct-mail sampling. A small 12 cm. by 18 cm. (approximately 5 × 7 inches) folder could be mailed to Holland's 3.7 million households for $20,000. The cost, however, would increase substantially if a small bottle of the product were to be included in the direct mailing. This cost would be 20 cents for handling, plus 75 cents for the actual sample. Thus, it would cost $980,000 to sample the whole country.

Coupon

Mr. de Vries was considering whether or not to include a coupon good for $0.04 off the purchase of Slamix with one of the other DFI products—mayonnaise, for example. He estimated that 900,000 coupons would be distributed. At a redemption rate of 5 percent, the cost would, thus, be approximately $1,700.

Price-Off Promotion

DFI made use of a reduced retail price for most of its new product introductions. Thus, the product manager thought it quite normal to consider the use of reducing the retail price by U.S. $0.07 per bottle and identifying this price reduction on the label of the product. It was felt that this reduced price would encourage the housewives to try Slamix. It was also quite normal to follow up this sales promotion with a similar price reduction approximately five months after the product was introduced. This would encourage those who had still not tried the product to purchase a bottle and would encourage those who had already bought one bottle to continue purchasing the new product. The cost of this price-off promotion is shown in Exhibit 7.

EXHIBIT 7

Introduction:	
720,000 bottles at 25 cents (U.S. $0.07) off each	$50,400
Handling and display materials	2,800
Total	$53,200
Follow-up five months later:	
600,000 bottles at 25 cents (U.S. $0.07) off each	$42,000
Handling and display materials	2,800
Total	$44,800

Key Chain Premium

It was very unusual to use a free premium to introduce a new product, but Mr. de Vries was considering this alternative for several reasons. Many products in Holland at this time were using key chains as a premium. As shown in Exhibit 8, an extremely large percentage of the people in Holland were collecting key chains. The details of the research showed that mothers and daughters were more likely to collect key chains, especially if the children were between 8 and 11 years of age. Mr. de Vries felt that if he used key chains as premiums for the introduction of Slamix he could have a follow-up promotion five months later using either key chains or price-off deals. Selected cost information on the key chain promotion is shown in Exhibit 9.

Trade Allowances

The product manager also considered the use of trade allowances to encourage the retailers to accept and promote the new product. The company traditionally offered $0.28 per case of 12 bottles. Thus, if it was decided that trade allowances were desirable, the cost would be $16,800 for the initial introduction and an additional $14,000 used during the follow-up promotion five months later. Trade allowances could be used together with either the price-off promotion or the key chain promotion. The product manager felt that trade allowances would not be very effective without one of the two consumer sales promotions.

EXHIBIT 8 Percentage of households collecting key chains

	June	July	September
Households with children	45	n.a.	n.a.
Households without children	5	n.a.	n.a.
Total (weighted average)	34	37	41

n.a. = not available.

EXHIBIT 9

Introduction:	
720,000 bottles = about 220 metric tons	
750,000 key chains at $0.056	$42,000
Handling costs and display materials	16,800
Total	$58,800
Follow-up five months later:	
600,000 bottles = about 180 tons	
625,000 key chains at $0.056	$35,000
Handling costs and display materials	14,000
Total	$49,000

Distribution

Outside of the question of what trade margins to use and whether or not to use trade allowances during the consumer sales promotions discussed above, Mr. de Vries did not see any problems with distribution. DFI had a sales force of approximately 50 persons who regularly called on 10,000 outlets in Holland. It was felt that the sales force could handle the introduction of the new product with no problem.

The last problem the product manager faced concerned the timing of the introduction of Slamix. The product would be ready for introduction in October. Mr. de Vries wondered whether the seasonal nature of the demand for the product would make it more desirable to hold off the introduction until March of the next year.

Case 40

Prime Computer*

As he finished examining the financial forecasts for the fourth quarter, it was painfully obvious to CEO Joe Hanson that 1984 would be a difficult year for Prime Computer.

Looking out of his Natick, Massachusetts, office, Hanson thought back to the 27 years he spent at IBM learning this business. He was excited by the challenge of taking over Prime after its charismatic founder, Kenneth Fisher, suddenly departed in the summer of 1981 in a disagreement with his board of directors. The challenge, however, was growing each day.

Prime, in its 10-year history, had been one of the hottest success stories on Wall Street following its development in 1975 of a powerful 32-bit super-minicomputer. However, the industry that had fueled the explosive growth of Prime was in the midst of rapid change and shakeout. The strategic direction that Hanson and his competitors were to take over the next few months would direct the successes of these firms for years to come.

Supermini Computer Product

Over the past 30 years, the computer industry has evolved into a highly complex business offering a wide range of hardware, software, and technology-based services. The computer hardware product itself can be classified according to five measures of performance: *internal memory capacity, computer word length, speed of calculation, price,* and *application base.* The internal memory capacity of a machine indicates the amount of addressable memory that the computer can configure in main storage at one time. This directly determines the amount or complexity of work that is possible on a particular machine. Memory capacity is measured in terms of thousand-byte amounts (1K equals 1,024 byte units) and in terms of million-byte amounts (1M equals 1,024,000 byte units). A computer's word length denotes how much information a CPU can receive or send at one time. For example, the maximum number of storage locations that can be directly addressed by a 16-bit word is only 2 raised to the 16th power, or 65,536 storage locations. A 32-bit address, however, can specify up to 2 raised to the 32nd power, or 4.29 billion distinct storage

---

* This case was prepared from public sources by Chris S. Thomas and Kevin D. Tucker under the supervision of Thomas C. Kinnear. Copyright © 1987 by Thomas C. Kinnear.

locations within the computer's main memory. Therefore, the longer word length significantly expands a system's direct addressing capabilities and more effectively utilizes the computer's main memory. The speed of calculation is measured in *millions* of *instructions per second*, or MIPS. The application base refers to the primary need for the machine, such as scientific or commercial uses. The price of the computer generally follows the complexity of these other factors. For example, a Timex Sinclair computer may cost as little as $59, where a Cray supercomputer may exceed $25 million.

Given this basic classification format, a particular computer can be termed either a *microcomputer, minicomputer, superminicomputer,* or a *mainframe computer.* The following chart illustrates the basic differences:

	Micro	Mini	Supermini	Mainframe
MIPS	.01–.95	.40–2.20	.88–10.1	7.0–30
Memory	2K–512K	6K–512K	512K–16M	8M–64M
Word	8–16 bit	16 bit	32 bit	32–64 bit
Price	$50–$10K	$15K–$85K	$30K–$450K	$100K–$9M
Application	Home, small business	Office, distributed processing	Large office, scientific, distributed	Central corporate computer

The superminicomputer is best differentiated from the minicomputer in terms of word length. As previously discussed, this characteristic is significant in terms of the machine's processing capabilities. In relation to the larger mainframes, the supermini is more conducive to a multiuser, interactive processing environment due to its special internal architecture. In addition, they are easier to use, generally require less power, and do not need special environmental conditions.

Historical Development of the Supermini

The history of the supermini began long after such early "computer" pioneers as Xavier Thomas and Charles Babbage labored to develop sophisticated mechanical calculating machines in the early 1800s. It began as a natural progression from the large mainframe computers—such as Remington Rand's UNIVAC I, IBM's 701 and 360 series, and other associated computers—produced in the 1950s through the 1960s. The trend was the result of a growing market need for computers that would not cost millions of dollars, as did the mainframes, but would perform the wide variety of tasks needed by the scientific community.

Digital Equipment was the first to address this need with its PDP-8, the first mass-produced minicomputer. This product was introduced in 1966 at a price of under $20,000. The mini established a new way of looking at computerization. A computer could be applied to a single job no matter where that job existed. Computers became common in laboratories, in engineering design rooms, and on the factory floor. This development gave rise to the concept of distributed data processing: the idea that individual computers linked in a network could bear the brunt of a company's data processing without relying on one central computer facility.

The minicomputer was also the first computer to be sold outright rather than leased or rented. It then created the first major computer wholesale market, as thousands of small OEMs and systems houses began buying directly from the manufacturers and equipping them with extra hardware and software to make them appeal to different markets. Then, as minicomputers began to gain wide acceptance, small user applications started getting bigger, which meant users needed bigger and more versatile machines. In addition, memory prices began to fall rapidly. To increase overall system performance, most minicomputer producers stayed with the 16-bit word size but introduced complicated memory addressing techniques to allow more processing capacity.

In 1975 Perkin-Elmer introduced the first true 32-bit computer, the model 8/32, which was rated as fast as an IBM 370/158 mainframe in scientific applications but sold at much lower cost. At this point other mainframe computer manufacturers began efforts to enter this new market of enhanced minicomputers, and thus the era of the supermini arrived.

The Supermini Market

The computer industry's total revenues of $110 billion and 15 percent annual growth support predictions that it will soon pass the automobile industry as the second largest business behind the oil industry. Over the past three decades, the industry has become increasingly fragmented, driving off in dozens of different specialized market niches. Twenty years ago, the industry had but one product: the mainframe computer with a price of $2 million to $5 million. Today, there is a multitude of products designed for different market niches. Market growth in the computer industry depends on the particular segment since growth rates fluctuate radically. Some segments, such as artificial intelligence and voice response terminals, are just being introduced, while others, such as mainframes, are mature and intensely price/product competitive. Exhibit 1 shows estimated patterns of future growth for computer hardware.

The superminicomputer market segment accounted for almost $3 billion in sales during 1983, and is currently growing at a 30 percent annual rate. The market is dominated by nine manufacturers: Digital Equipment, Prime Computer, Perkin-Elmer, Wang Laboratories, Gould, Data General, Harris, Hewlett-Packard, and Apollo. Digital maintains a wide lead in the market, with a 30 percent overall share. Exhibit 2 illustrates the relative overall market shares of the segment. These figures could shift quite dramatically in the near future as larger players, such as IBM and AT&T, begin to attack the increasingly competitive supermini market segment. Historically, the mainframe makers have failed to threaten the mini market in an effort to avoid cannibalization of their profitable mainframe business. However, as consumers became more

EXHIBIT 1 1984 Computer growth rates

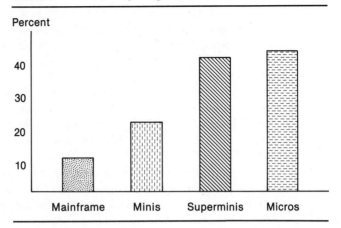

sophisticated and began to replace their smaller mainframes with superminis, this hands-off strategy began to change. IBM now markets several smaller mainframes that actually compete with these superminis in terms of price and performance. AT&T has also recently introduced products to enter this market. Neither is a major player—yet.

Market Segmentation

Superminis are being marketed for, and finding widespread user acceptance in, a broad spectrum of applications. The market for superminicomputers can be broken into three primary segments: *commercial, medium tech,* and *high tech.*

EXHIBIT 2 Supermini market share

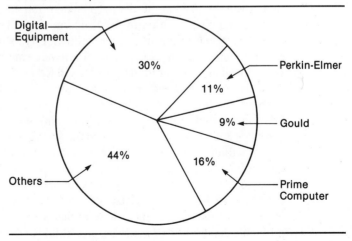

The high-tech segment, the original driver of traditional minicomputer demand, consists primarily of applications in scientific data acquisition, laboratory research, and the physical sciences. The medium-tech segment consists of computer-aided design (CAD) applications, graphics, and process control applications. This segment is gaining importance with the development of CAD software from a number of major vendors, including General Motors and Computervision. The third major segment, the commercial segment, is comprised primarily of distributed data processing and office technology applications. In terms of growth, the commercial segment is the leader, with a 40 percent annual increase in sales driven by the explosive demand for office automation.

During the last four years, the superminicomputer manufacturers have expanded their marketing horizons rather dramatically beyond scientific and technical uses into this growing commercial segment. Customers ranging from banks and service companies to all varieties of industrial firms have discovered that linking together several superminis is more economical than spending $3 million or more for a large centralized computer system. For example, Chase Manhattan recently purchased 10 superminis to track overtime and payroll costs, and Wells Fargo currently operates a series of superminis to manage investor portfolios. These activities would have been performed on mainframes five years ago.

Market Trends

The key to this supermini market in the future will be the increasing importance of software as well as the expected development of more efficient machines. Since the commercial segment is growing faster and offers greater growth potential than any other area of the 32-bit market, supermini vendors are striving aggressively to provide the appropriate software tools to turn their systems into efficient business data systems. In a survey released by Datamation, over 44 percent of the respondents rated software availability as the number one consideration in their supermini purchase decision.

The development of in-house software is extremely expensive and risky since the introduction of substandard software can damage the reputation of the firm as well as waste millions of dollars in R&D. The advantage will go to those firms that can afford such development or to those that are able to capitalize on cooperative arrangements with software producers on an OEM basis. The major orientation of this market will be to configure and market a "system" of hardware and software as opposed to marketing separate components. End users appear willing to pay a significant premium for a software/hardware package as opposed to developing the software themselves. As a result of this trend, almost every maker of superminis has reorganized its marketing and product development approaches to emphasize this software/hardware approach. An added incentive to the supermini makers is that such packages are inherently more profitable due to the extra charges of $50,000 or more for a packaged, complete system.

The expected introduction of 32-bit microprocessor chips will increase the pressures on supermini manufacturers to develop software links. With 32-bit microprocessors, the power of the present superminis will be pushed into smaller and smaller machines, leaving the machine as a commodity and the producers searching for other means to differentiate their products.

Environmental Analysis

The environment of the superminicomputer segment, like much of the computer industry, is undergoing tremendous change as technological, economic, and societal pressures come to bear on this growing business. Of the multitude of forces shaping the industry, four key trends that are driving this change can be isolated: *technology glut, turbulent growth patterns, economic sensitivity,* and the *development of a more sophisticated customer group.*

The tremendous infusion of technological research in the 1970s has provided the base for the onslaught of products in the 1980s. There are 14 different computer manufacturers producing products that match the description given for a supermini. These manufacturers range from IBM, with 1983 revenues of $46 billion, to three-year-old Apollo, with 1983 revenues of $80 million. The product life cycle of the superminis, which was recently 5 years, has been reduced to 2.5 years and continues to fall. Machines in some cases become outdated between announcement and delivery. Apollo recently began production on a system that is three times more powerful than its previous offering, at only 70 percent of the price. Such product improvements are becoming commonplace and placing tremendous pressure on firms to increase R&D expenditures. As previously mentioned, there is also considerable activity underway to develop a 32-bit microprocessor that will replace many of the proprietary supermini processors. If successful, this new chip would probably become an industry standard, much like the Intel 16-bit chip is to microcomputers. This would accelerate the supermini's direction as a commodity item and further pressure firms to offer other components, such as software, service, and marketing, to successfully differentiate their systems.

The rapid, spectacular growth of the superminicomputer market has produced a group of companies in fierce competition not only in the market but also with the analysts on Wall Street. Many of the supermini producers, such as DEC and, more recently, Prime, have attracted significant attention in the equity markets. This attention creates a short-term orientation toward profit and growth rate at the expense of the firm's market orientation. With the exception of Ken Olson at DEC, the founding pioneers of the supermini companies have relinquished command, leaving a less entrepreneurial management to compete in a very fast-paced, leading-edge marketplace. Both trends lead to slower market response on the part of the supermini manufacturers

The marketplace for superminis, although expanding nearly 40 percent annually, is experiencing a decline in the percentage of its sales growth. The supermini segment, as well as the entire industry, is becoming as sensitive to economic fluctuations as the users it serves. Soft demand in 1982 surprised

Digital and other supermini producers, causing a steep decline in profits. The superminis are particularly sensitive to economic fluctuations because over one third of their business is with original equipment manufacturers. These OEMs depend on a strong economy with low interest rates to attract sales of their general purpose systems.

Finally, the growing sophistication of consumers is impacting the trends in the superminicomputer segment. In 1983, over 7 million computer units were in use as compared with 24,000 in 1964. Computers are becoming more common, and consumers are expecting greater price/performance ratios each year. With more products to choose from and greater technological knowledge, consumers are pushing manufacturers to differentiate their products to an ever-increasing degree.

Distribution Channels

Superminis are marketed in two primary fashions: by original equipment manufacturers (OEMs) and directly to the consumer. The OEMs are typically small businesses that purchase superminis at a volume discount, augment the basic machine with extra hardware and software, and resell the final system to various end user markets. In recent years there has been an increased emphasis by the supermini producers to develop greater internal marketing to pursue the direct form of distribution, integrate their own software, and bypass the OEM market.

Market Barriers

There are significant barriers for new producers to overcome if they are to be successful in the superminicomputer market. A new firm must possess the marketing and distribution skills needed to enter and maintain a presence in the various segments of the market. It must also possess the technological complexity to develop the software needed to complete the supermini system. Most important, it must be able to configure and produce a 32-bit microprocessor that is of relatively high efficiency and low cost. Although development is under-way, the supermini marketplace does not have an industry-standard 32-bit microprocessor, which would eliminate this critical barrier. Finally, the capital required for a new firm to get established would be difficult to obtain as venture capitalists become more selective with their high-tech investments.

The primary barriers to exit are existing assets, various sunk research and development costs, and the various service agreements with customers. These agreements could be renegotiated with outside service firms at very little cost.

Vertical Integration

The vast majority of key components for the superminicomputer are purchased from supplier organizations rather than manufactured. The major exception is the memory chips, purchased primarily from Motorola, that are required to construct the 32-bit CPU configuration. Once commercial 32-bit micro-processors become standard, like Intel's 16-bit microprocessor in the micro-computer market, the sueprmini producers will become even less integrated. Digital Equipment is the only supermini manufacturer resisting the inevitable industry standard by developing its own 32-bit microprocessor for use with its VAX supermini line. Firms such as Motorola, Intel, National Semiconductor, and possibly AT&T will play major roles as primary 32-bit microprocessor suppliers.

The remaining components, such as hard disk drives, video display terminals, and other associated portions of the supermini system, are principally supplied by various component manufacturers in both America and Japan. Again, Digital produces the majority of its VAX system's peripheral devices but is the exception to the general market trend.

The key problem with becoming overly integrated in this market is related to the technological pace at which new products are introduced. It is less risky to purchase rather than manufacture those components that are subject to continual upgrades. By purchasing, the manufacturer ensures that the most modern components will be used in the system. This strategy also reduces fixed costs of the manufacturer and allows greater flexibility in cost cutting during economic downturns.

The strategic importance of a strong supermini product line makes the future of this key market segment of special interest to all computer manufactur-ers. The future may well depend on the actions of two firms that are not currently active participants in the supermini market but are nevertheless the most powerful players in the industry: IBM and AT&T. The supermini is important both in terms of its growth potential and the link it provides between smaller and larger computer systems.

Apollo

Apollo was started in 1980 by several former Prime employees. In a very short period of time, however, Apollo has established itself as the technology leader in superminis. 1980 sales were $80 million. Apollo has focused strictly on the computer market for modelers, scientists, designers, and programmers. Sys-tems for CAD comprise over 50 percent of total sales. In fact, three custom-ers—Auto-Trol, Calma (GE), and Mentor Graphics—account for 50 percent of sales.

The current Apollo products are called DOMAIN, which is the acronym for Distributed Operating Multi-Access Interactive Network. The units are equivalent in power to the DEC VAX series or the IBM 370/158 but sell at $13,000 for the desktop model and $80,000 for a larger model. The system is built on 32-bit VLSI architecture with low-cost RAM chips, high-resolution graphics, rigid disk drives, and the UNIX operating system. The Apollo units use high-level PASCAL language and can be linked together in networks.

For a company of its size, Apollo has built a fairly effective sales, maintenance, and service organization. A new supermini workstation introduced in 1983 offers a three-time improvement in the price-to-performance ratio compared to the previous product.

It is obviously too early to tell whether Apollo can survive the current upheaval in the supermini market. However, it is concentrating on a market niche where its considerable talents can be best exploited.

Data General

Data General is the third largest company concentrating on minicomputers. Like Digital, Data General has grown very rapidly. The company was founded in 1968 and had sales revenues of almost $830 million in 1983. Prior to 1980, Data General had experienced five consecutive years of 40 percent annual growth and 20 percent margins. All of DG's products were 8- and 16-bit minicomputers. The primary customers were OEMs. The company placed little emphasis on software, maintenance, or systems engineering.

To help alleviate some of its past problems, the company has hired several managers from IBM. DG has begun to concentrate on product development, technology, and building a sales force. A major marketing effort is still aimed at technical OEMs because of the superior price/performance ratio of the DG systems. This segment of the business, however, has dropped to one third of company sales from the previous high of almost 70 percent. Data General is now trying several different marketing approaches, distribution channels, and product configurations. The target markets include small businesses, factory automation, medical, scientific, and government. The new distribution channels being used include distributors for microprocessors and terminals, independent dealers for small business systems, and the DESKTOP Generation and system integrators.

There are currently six product lines being marketed at Data General. The NOVA family has five models based on 16-bit medium-, large-, and very-large-scale integration. The ECLIPSE Information Systems include three 16-bit models and five 32-bit supermini models, including the MV8000II, MN8000C, and MV10000 introduced in 1983. The Scientific ECLIPSE series has seven 16-bit models and five 32-bit models. There is also the MicroNOVA, which has four models.

The DESKTOP Generation includes a microECLIPSE-based CPU, main memory, keyboard, video display, floppy disk storage, and can be combined with up to four terminals. Commercial systems are developed with a CPU from the microNOVA, ECLIPSE, or NOVA series plus disk storage, a line printer, and video display terminal. These systems are primarily used for interactive data entry and inquiry.

DG also sells a variety of peripheral devices like printers that are manufactured in-house. Many other devices, including disk memories and line printers, are purchased from other suppliers. Data General also develops software and operating systems for its computers. An independent software vendor program was started in 1982 to encourage the development of application software by third parties. In addition, DG has developed the ADA compiler, which has been trademarked by the U.S. Department of Defense and is expected to become the designated computer language for all U.S. military branches, the European Economic Community, and NATO.

Finally, to improve its marketing and sales effectiveness, Data General is restructuring the entire organization. The Information Systems Division will be responsible for the sale of the ECLIPSE Information Systems and CS small business systems for office automation, distributed data processing, commercial OEMs, and small businesses. The Technical Products Division will sell the NOVA, Scientific ECLIPSE, and microNOVA products to technical OEMs and end users for the industrial, scientific, and technical markets. The DESKTOP Division will sell the DESKTOP Generation products to all customers. Finally, the Systems Division and Semiconductor Division will be responsible for developing systems, software, and semiconductors for all divisions.

Data General hopes that these significant changes along with the introduction of a new ECLIPSE series in early 1985 will solidify its position in the supermini market.

Perkin-Elmer

Perkin-Elmer was one of the pioneers of the superminicomputer, entering the market with the 1974 acquisition of Interdata Corporation. The total 1983 sales revenues for PE were $1.01 billion, with superminis contributing about $200 million.

Perkin-Elmer's business is broken into six operating divisions: Analytical Instruments, Electronic Data Systems, Semiconductor Production Equipment, Optical Group, Avionic Instrumentation, and Thermal Spray Equipment and Supplies. The company's strength in superminicomputers has always been in technical areas, but PE has recently announced new products, such as PENnet, aimed at the commercial markets. The recent emphasis has been to improve existing products. This includes the formation of a CAD/CAM operations unit to improve penetration in that market as well as the introduction of Edition VII of the UNIX operating system. The new 3200MPS is a top-of-the-line supermini that can be expanded by plugging in additional processors. The 3205 is the lowest priced supermini on the market and is aimed at broader business and technical markets. Finally, PE has entered the personal computer market with the 7500PC targeted at the scientific community.

Perkin-Elmer products are usually marketed through a direct sales force in the United States. However, foreign sales subsidiaries, representatives, or distributors are used for overseas marketing.

Hewlett-Packard

Hewlett-Packard is the world's third largest manufacturer of computers, with 1983 sales of $4.7 billion. The company is divided into four business segments: computer products, electronic test and measurement equipment, medical electronics equipment, and analytic instruments. Computer products were responsible for about 60 percent of the company's backlog in 1983. These products include business computers, engineering workstations, instrument controllers, data terminals, printers, disk memories, PCs, portable computers, and calculators. The HP9000 superminicomputer was introduced in 1982 as an engineering workstation targeted at the CAD market. This desktop unit was based on VLSI architecture, which allowed the use of 450,000 transistors per circuit-board compared to 130,000 per board for a 16-bit machine. The 9000 was originally priced at $28,250 and had the same power as the DEC VAX, which was priced at $84,000.

The HP9000 was introduced with an "end run strategy" to avoid direct confrontation with DEC. The product was marketed as a stand-alone workstation for scientists and engineers rather than for use in shared networks. Later, a local communications network helped the 9000 communicate directly with a VAX. Hewlett-Packard sells such products as calculators through dealers. Other products are sold through a direct sales force to users and OEMs. There are currently 220 sales and service locations in 75 cities in the United States and 30 foreign countries. Seventy-five distributors have also been established in 40 other foreign countries. The HP9000 engineering workstation has never been a serious contender in the CAD market. The product has received sporadic marketing support from HP and therefore has not challenged other competitors' products for significant market share.

Wang Laboratories

Wang, with 1983 sales of $1.54 billion, defines its business as products for the worldwide office automation market consisting of word processing, data processing, and advanced office automation. Wang is the world leader in distributed word processing, with a 1983 market share of approximately 49 percent.

Wang products for the word processing market are aimed at increasing the efficiency in text processing and repetitive typing. Products for this market include the Word Processing System, Office Information Systems, and Wang-writer. The small business and distributed data processing systems are intended to meet recordkeeping and financial data processing requirements for smaller businesses and government units and divisions of larger corporations. The Wang 2200 and VS series products are also used for distributed data processing in concert with telecommunications capability.

The advanced office automation products are aimed at increasing productivity for all levels of office workers. These products include the Wang PC, an integrated office system (Alliance 250), a broadband networking system (Wangnet), a remote office support for the VS series (VS Express), and an electronic mail system (Mailway). The company's line of superminicomputers contains the VS-90, VS-100, and VS-300. The VS-90 has 4 million bytes of main memory and 5.2 billion bytes of disk storage. This machine can be upgraded to the VS-100, which, on the other hand, has 8 million bytes of main memory storage and 10.2 billion bytes of disk storage. This system can accommodate up to 128 workstations and sells for up to $1 million. The VS-300 is a high-performance supermini, which rounds out Wang's product line.

Wang's sales organization consists of 4,500 sales, sales support, and administrative personnel in 195 cities in the United States. There are also 4,200 customer engineering personnel. In foreign markets, the company sells its products through wholly owned subsidiaries except in Italy and Mexico, which are partly owned. In 77 other foreign countries, distributors and trade organizations are used. Wang has recently begun using other distribution channels, including dealers and software vendors.

Wang usually assembles products from components and parts except for certain printers and mass storage devices, which are purchased pre-assembled. The tendency has been to broaden the in-house design and manufacturing capability of peripherals, including workstations and telecommunication devices. In an attempt to gain a technological and cost advantage, Wang tried to develop its own semiconductor manufacturing capability. This effort, however, was recently terminated. Instead of trying to develop this type of technology, Wang has recently purchased 15 percent of VLSI Technology for semiconductors and 20 percent of Intecom for PBXs.

Harris

Harris Corporation designs, produces, and markets advanced communication and information processing systems and equipment and components for the information technology market. Products are also produced for the voice and video communication markets. The sales revenue for Harris was $1.42 billion in 1983.

The company is currently divided into four business segments. Information Systems comprises approximately 22 percent of sales. Primary products include interactive terminals, superminicomputers, word processing systems, and digital and phone switches. Communications, responsible for 30 percent of sales, markets radio and television broadcasting equipment, two-way radios, and earth stations. The Semiconductor Segment, comprising 11 percent of sales, makes standard and custom printed circuitboards. Finally, Government Systems, which builds state-of-the-art prototypes, custom communication, and information processing systems, makes up 37 percent of Harris.

Harris markets a fully compatible line of superminicomputers for engineering, scientific, educational, and multipurpose applications. The prices for these products range from $70,000 to $500,000. Harris made a major attempt to become a force in the office automation market with its 1983 acquisition of Lanier Business Products. Lanier sells a line of dictating equipment, video display text-editing typewriters, and small business computers. In addition, Lanier distributes and services 3M copiers in most of the United States and 3M microfilm and visual products in the Southeast. The acquisition of Lanier will broaden the Harris product line and customer base as well as greatly improve its current distribution system.

Harris recently introduced word processing software called MUSE for use with its superminis. This is the first product introduction aimed specifically at the data processing user. Lanier uses a "building block" approach to the office automation market by concentrating on a limited number of products rather than complete systems.

Gould

Gould, with 1983 sales of $1.3 billion, is quickly changing from an electrical products manufacturer to an electronics company. The new business is based on three strategic technologies: computer science and software, signal processing and electronic devices, and materials. To accomplish this transformation Gould has recently divested the Electrical Products Group, the Battery Products Group, and the Power Conversion Division. Gould is currently involved in six different product areas: high-performance superminicomputers, computer-integrated factory automation systems, test and measurement instruments, medical instrumentation, defense systems, and components and materials for the electronic industry. Gould's overall strategy is to "interface the engineering automation environment with the computer-aided factory automation environment, where Gould products already have a leading market position. The company intends to provide single-vendor, integrated factory and engineering automation hardware and software systems."

Gould's focus in the supermini market has been with sophisticated users who need to process large volumes of data at high speeds. Gould entered this market with the 1980 acquisition of Systems Engineering Laboratories. Superminis contribute about 10 percent of Gould's annual sales.

Gould has continued to be one of the price/performance leaders in the industry. Seventy percent of all Gould superminis are used for simulation, laboratory computation, federal systems, or energy management. However, Gould plans to expand this focused, niche strategy with new products.

The Concept 32/67 series can perform up to three MIPs and sells for less than $200,000. This new series will use virtual memory and be based on the UNIX operating system. The PowerNode 6000 will also provide virtual memory for engineering and scientific applications. Finally, the new desktop microcomputer (Power Station 1000) can be used either as a stand-alone unit or in a network with other machines. Gould recently introduced the PN9000 supermini, which will use 32-bit virtual memory processors. This machine can process data 4 to 10 times faster than the VAX-11/780. The PN 9000 will use the Gould UTX/32 operating system. This computer can also be used with the Xerox Ethernet networking software. The system will sell for $245,000 to $385,000, and is targeted for the CAD/CAM, engineering administration, software database, and management support applications.

All of Gould's products continue to be sold through a direct sales force.

The U.S. government comprises almost 22 percent of the company's total revenue.

Digital Equipment Corporation

Digital Equipment Corporation is the second largest manufacturer of computers and associated peripheral equipment in the world behind IBM. DEC has been one of the major success stories in the computer industry, growing from sales of $25 million in 1966 to almost $4.3 billion in 1983. The superminicomputer has been a major factor in DEC's success, allowing the company to grow from sales of $1 billion in 1977 to its current size. The company has been driven by technology from the beginning and is, in fact, one of the few major computer firms still run by one of the original founders. Although DEC entered the supermini market after Perkin-Elmer and Prime, the emphasis on technology has allowed DEC to capture approximately 30 percent of the worldwide superminicomputer market.

The company's strategy has been to offer one of the broadest product lines in the computer industry. The current product line includes small microprocessors (such as the MICRO/T-11), a series of personal computers, and several minicomputers (such as the PDP-8, PDP-11, and VAX series, based on 12-bit, 16-bit, and 32-bit architecture, respectively). In addition, DEC markets two series of mainframes: the DECsystem-10 and the DECsystem-20. Other products currently marketed include magnetic tape transports, tape cassette and disk storage devices, cathode ray tubes, analog-to-digital converters, tape punchers and readers, and terminal and line printers. Several peripheral devices marketed are purchased from other suppliers.

Digital's products are intended for a wide variety of applications, including scientific research, computation, communications, education, data analysis, industrial control, word processing, office automation, health care, engineering, and simulation. Software includes operating systems, languages, data-handling services, and communications.

The VAX series is DEC's current superminicomputer offering. The product includes four models: the VAX-11/730, 750, 780, and 782. The prices for these products range from $20,000 for an entry-level version of the VAX-11/730 to $450,000 for a fully supported system using the VAX-11/782. A new series of VAX computers is scheduled to be introduced in 1985 to replace the current line. The new products will be completely compatible and range all the way from a microcomputer to mainframes, all based on the 32-bit architecture.

Digital has had mixed results in the past two years for several reasons. One of the major reasons has been a relatively weak sales organization. DEC products were in such great demand that they almost sold themselves. In addition, the sales force was paid strictly on salary while the rest of the industry continued to use quota systems. The Digital sales force was viewed as being not very aggressive and poorly organized. However, steps have been taken to correct these problems. The sales force is now organized according to customer (previously it had been by product line). New incentives are also being used to make the sales force more aggressive. Prices have also been reduced as new products have been introduced or existing products improved.

The current distribution system includes 200 sales offices located throughout the world using a direct sales force. Approximately 350 other locations are involved in the marketing, service, and distribution of DEC products. The company has established its own stores primarily to market its line of personal computers. Original equipment manufacturers continue to be an important outlet for products. As Digital continues to grow in size it will have to compete more directly with IBM. The major advantage that DEC has over some of the smaller companies in the computer industry will be its large and, for the most part, loyal customer base. However, to successfully compete DEC must improve the marketing effort and speed up the development of new products. In order to help speed up the development of new semiconductor technology, Digital recently purchased a 9 percent share in Trilogy Systems. Trilogy, founded by Gene Amdahl, is working on a breakthrough in wafer technology. Finally, Digital must penetrate the office automation market, where it has had very little presence up to this time. This last task will be extremely difficult against both IBM and Wang.

Prime

Prime was responsible for introducing the 32-bit superminicomputer in 1975. The initial product was basically a 32-bit minicomputer with a Honeywell mainframe operating system. Sales grew at approximately 78 percent per year, reaching $365 million in 1981 and $516 million in 1983. Prime offered a compatible line of small- and medium-sized general purpose interactive computer systems. Under the original CEO, Kenneth Fisher, Prime attempted to "attack all markets, to be all things to all people." This strategy resulted in Prime becoming spread too thin, with high initial development costs and declining customer relations. Fisher left Prime in 1981 in a dispute with the board of directors.

The new CEO, Joe Hanson from IBM, has directed Prime toward a "focused approach on CAD, using independent software developers to reduce fixed costs, and concentrating on networks." Prime has been working with Ford Motor Company and Compeda for computer-aided design products and with Convergent Technology for small computers.

The company's products are all based on the 50 series, which uses 32-bit architecture and the PRIMOS virtual memory operating system. There are seven current models, ranging from the 2250, a low-cost compact system designed for the office environment, to the 9950, which has technology usually found only in mainframes. Prime introduced two new intelligent workstations in 1983. The PW200 is a graphics workstation designed for remote CAD applications. The Prime Producer 100 is a microcomputer-based, desktop workstation designed for use with Prime's Office Automation System. Prime purchases most of the supporting peripheral devices from outside vendors. Prime continues to develop software internally but will place greater emphasis on cooperative development in the future. Important systems currently offered include DPTX, which allows Prime users to construct networks with IBM 3270 terminals and systems; PDGS, a product design graphics program; and PRIMENET, which enables Prime products to share resources.

Prime primarily markets its products through a direct sales force to end users. The entire organization includes almost 2,000 sales representatives, systems engineers, and other support personnel in 118 locations worldwide. Independent distributors are also used through the Authorized Distributor Program. Prices for Prime products range from $40,000 to approximately $500,000.

Strategic View of the Supermini

The strategic importance of a strong supermini product line makes the future of this key market segment of special interest to all computer manufacturers. The future may well depend on the actions of the two most powerful players in the industry: IBM and AT&T. The supermini is important both in terms of its growth potential and in the link it provides between smaller and larger computer systems.

The IBM Factor

International Business Machines Corporation is the absolute master of the computer industry. With 1983 revenues of $46 billion and profits of $6.5 billion, it is the most profitable Fortune 500 firm. It is also becoming one of the most aggressive. To put IBM in perspective, its profits were more in 1983 than its closest U.S. competitor's gross revenues. In fact, IBM's 1983 maintenance revenues alone will double the sales of Digital Equipment. No industrial company in history has approached the sheer dominance IBM has established over the markets in which it competes. The firm has set a corporate goal of becoming a $100 billion operation by 1990, which will require growth into those few markets it does not control.

One market that appears to be targeted is the supermini segment, where IBM has no current designated products even though its low-end mainframe 4300 series fits the profile of a supermini. The 4300 is well positioned to compete with the high-end DEC and Data General superminis. Further evidence that IBM is beginning to move in this market is the recent OEM pact with Computervision Corporation to provide hardware for Computervision-developed CAD/CAM software. To ensure integration within the commercial office systems market, IBM recently acquired 100 percent ownership in Rolm Corp., a leader in communication components that link computer systems. IBM is certain to continue its initial entry with a growing product line targeted especially toward the supermini market.

The impact of such a move from IBM could be critical to the producers of supermini products, who have significant market pressures just from the current players in the market. The seriousness of this projected move can best be illustrated by examining several IBM moves in the past three years:

After only two and one half years in the market, IBM sells 600,000 PCs a year.

IBM's plug compatible competitors have been severely crippled by a series of price cuts and product upgrades. Magnuson, Storage Technology, Memorex, and Amdahl have either been forced out of business or crippled.

Intel, a major producer of microprocessors for the industry, is partially owned by IBM, and appears destined to follow suit with Rolm as a takeover candidate.

Several Japanese competitors, such as Hitachi, Mitsubishi, and Fujitsu, Ltd., have become the victims of an organized legal attack from IBM over copyright infringements.

The Justice Department dropped its long-standing antitrust case against IBM.

IBM has announced wide-ranging price cutting on many products while introducing more advanced lines of computer hardware.

IBM has formulated a credit arm, IBM Credit Corp., to compete with third-party lessors for financing business. IBM will use its massive credit resources to attract low-cost funding to undercut the competition in the financing arena. It will market these financing arrangements through its sales force.

The concentration of this aggressive "New IBM" on the supermini market will cause considerable shifts in the marketing strategy of several supermini players. The pattern of future market evolution, if IBM brings its resources to bear, could best be predicted by examining the mainframe market segment, which IBM controls through strategic product introductions and associated price reductions on older models. The product life cycles for mainframes for the past decade have been five years, and the products have primarily been leased. These standards have come from IBM. During the past three years, however, IBM has converted to selling its products and has shortened the life cycles to an average of two years. As each new improved product is introduced, the old products are heavily discounted. The result of this action has been to eliminate time for competitor reaction, pressure the resources of competitors to "outresearch" IBM, reduce the importance of third-party lessors in the market, and force the competition into specialty niches. Given the relative number of competitors in the supermini market and the size of the segment, these actions from IBM would force the weaker firms from the market.

The AT&T Factor

The breakup of AT&T earlier in the year has allowed the communications giant to join the battle in the computer industry. This new AT&T is divided into two sectors: AT&T Communications and AT&T Technologies. The entire firm has assets of $34 billion and expects revenues from all operations to exceed $56 billion. It currently ranks number four on the Fortune 500.

In April 1984, AT&T brought out its first commercially available computers, including a family of 32-bit superminis called the 3B20 series. The machines are characterized by outstanding reliability (10 minutes downtime per year) and AT&T's unique UNIX operating system. This UNIX software is of key importance to AT&T's product line as it allows easier communication among computers and offers greater capability for computers to operate in parallel, key features in the future for office integration. UNIX could potentially become the industry standard for office products since DEC, Data General, Hewlett-Packard, NCR, and IBM have applied for UNIX licenses. AT&T's future patterns of concentration are as yet unclear, but the supermini office segment appears to be of prime importance if AT&T hopes to capitalize on its communications network strengths. Its marketing and support staffs are still in the process of development but, with some 40 products planned for introduction to the computer marketplace over the next three years, it is clear that they are serious competitors.

Key Industry Issues

In summary, the superminicomputer segment faces several critical issues:

Software is growing in importance in all phases of the computer industry. Integrated software/hardware systems are becoming a standard in the supermini business.

The introduction of a 32-bit microprocessor will transform the supermini hardware to commodity status.

Effective "systems marketing" directly to the end user is critical for success in this market.

A strong service organization is needed to build and maintain long-term customer relationships as well as initially market systems.

Entrepreneurial style management is needed to allow maximum flexibility in this rapidly changing marketplace.

Economic cycles are beginning to affect the computer industry.

Major competition with IBM and AT&T appears certain in the near future.

Prime's Marketing Strategy

Prime Computer has been a spectacularly successful entrant into the computer industry. Prime and Perkin-Elmer are generally credited with being the first firms to introduce the 32-bit superminicomputers. Prime, founded in 1972, held 16 percent of the $1.5 billion world supermini market in 1983. Total 1983 sales revenues were $516 million. Even in the poor economic conditions of 1981 and 1982, Prime continued to prosper. Kenneth Fisher, one of the original founders, left in 1981 in a dispute with the board of directors. Joe Hanson was brought in from IBM, but the shake-up didn't affect Prime's success. Sales and net income increased in every quarter of 1982, and orders were well ahead of 1981. Prime became one of the hottest stocks on Wall Street, increasing 46 percent in value in one year. In addition, Prime was preparing itself for the future with a 35 percent increase in investment in software development, acquisitions, new products, and R&D.

However, in 1983 the bubble burst. Prime's share of the supermini market, which was 33 percent in 1980, began to decline. First quarter earnings were lower than originally expected, and second quarter earnings dropped 41 percent as sales grew 16 percent. In July, six key marketing and sales executives left Prime to join Fisher in the startup of Encore Computer Corporation.

Prime's early success was based on selling very high-performance hardware to scientific and technical users. In fact, Prime's original products were so superior that very little selling effort was required. The market, however, was changing. Prime needed to switch from "selling hardware to selling major system solutions." Under Fisher, Prime had attempted to offer a wide variety of products to many different customer types. Hanson, however, has changed this strategy. Prime has started to focus attention on a smaller number of markets. These markets will include office automation, local area networks, and CAD/CAM. Prime has also made other revisions in its approach to the market. A greater emphasis will be put on attracting sales from larger customers by raising advertising budgets and increasing the sales and service organizations. In fact, Prime has increased its sales force 42 percent and its service staff 87 percent in the last two and one half years. Further, the advertising budget was increased to $4 million in 1983 from $800,000 in 1982. Prime hopes the increases to the sales and service organizations will allow the continuation of its premium pricing strategy.

Office Automation Marketplace

Wang is the current leader in the distributed word processing market, with a share of approximately 49 percent. IBM is the leader in stand-alone units. Prime, on the other hand, had less than 1 percent of the 1982 market of almost $307 million. This market is expected to grow to almost $2 billion in 1984.

Two basic strategies have emerged in the office automation market. Firms like Lanier (Harris) and Datapoint use a "building block" approach. This involves supplying one or two kinds of products rather than an entire system. NBI, for example, sees a need to integrate current technology with future customer needs. Its corporate communications manager says, "We hope to help customers solve office automation problems by providing the ability for users to migrate on a growth path from building block applications to well-integrated systems by supplying the simplest tools and interfaces for the users." The other strategy being used, "the top-down" approach, is typified by Wang and Prime. The intent with this strategy is to develop networks of different configurations to perform many different functions. Wang, for example, insists that an installation has top management support and a strategic plan. Wang intends to put information in the user's hands with easy-to-use tools by planning networks to handle all kinds of information on multiple levels. To further accomplish this goal, Wang is now attempting to make its products compatible with IBM products.

Prime actually ends up with a "sort of hybrid approach." The firm claims the approach is "relevant to a top-down approach but with strong emphasis on departmental needs and the individual user." Prime also attempts to provide user-friendly tools to accomplish a wide range of jobs by developing "processing subsets." The emphasis in the Prime software is to make sure the products appeal to non-DP experts and therefore English prompts are used. Unlike Wang, Prime continues to use a proprietary operating system.

In general, Prime remains weak in office automation. This position has been made worse because of a very late entry into the personal computer market as the PC is becoming a key component for success in the office automation market. Prime's insistence on using a proprietary operating system is also making further penetration difficult. Unless products can be effectively linked into networks with existing mainframes, particularly IBM, Prime's situation will remain difficult.

CAD/CAM Marketplace

This market segment represented about 16 percent or $65 million of Prime's sales in 1983. However, this is Prime's major target market, and it could account for 50 percent of the company's revenues in the next three to five years. Prime has taken a slightly unique approach to the CAD/CAM market. Major participants, such as Computervision and Calma (GE), buy computer hardware and peripherals from other companies, package the equipment with software, and sell the entire system. Prime, on the other hand, sells directly to the end user and encourages its customers to write their own software. Currently, Prime's incoming order rate is slower than that of other major competitors.

Prime believes that the CAD/CAM market is following the direction of office automation toward totally integrated systems. Prime sees customers opting for total solutions provided by systems suppliers when offered an opportunity to integrate CAD/CAM through application software, networks, and communications. Until recently, Prime has had a limited offering of CAD/CAM software. However, Compeda, Ltd., a British producer of software, was recently acquired in an effort to rectify this situation. Prime has also taken major steps toward success in the CAD/CAM market by filling out its line of computers with the new 9950 series and the purchase of Compeda for improved software. Prime also has agreements with Ford Motor Company to develop software and with Convergent Technologies for small computers.

A major stumbling block, however, may be Prime's reliance on a proprietary operating system (PRIMOS). The company believes the "exploitation of the CAD/CAM workstation technology will produce more sophisticated work-stations that will house more complex applications, leading to distributed CAD/CAM data systems." Prime indicates that its proprietary operating system, database management system, networking, and communications products will be an advantage in this integration process. Computervision, however, the current market leader, sees compatibility as one of the key elements to future success in CAD/CAM. Computervision recently announced a high-end system based on the IBM 4300 series computer. This system, unlike the Prime system, allows the CAD/CAM to access data on other IBM products throughout the organization.

Competitive Analysis

In evaluating the areas that denote success in the computer industry in general, key factors can be isolated. These factors are selling, service, software, being small and specialized, the style of management, stock financing, and systems compatibility.

Selling

Each of the first three success factors—selling, service, and software—will become even more critical as computer hardware becomes more of a commodity. The entire computer industry is experimenting with a large number of new distribution channels in order to prepare for the increased volume sales that must be attained for such a commodity market. The larger sales organizations will continue to be important in order to penetrate the specialized niche market areas. The direct sales force will continue to ensure that the features and benefits of the product, such as performance and reliability, are properly communicated to prospective customers.

The use of dealers and distributors could, however, harm the company's reputation and revenues results through dealers' and distributors' heavy discounting. The industry's recognition of the importance of the selling effort is evidenced by Prime's increasing its sales force by 42 percent in the last two and one-half years. In addition, both DEC and Data General have recently reorganized their marketing functions to better serve specific segments. Of the supermini manufacturers, Wang and Hewlett-Packard have the strongest sales organizations.

Software and Services

Software and services are the fastest-growing segment in the entire computer industry, with a growth rate of approximately 28 percent per year. As hardware prices continue to drop, it is apparent that the value added to products will be in the area of systems engineering, integration, software, and training. Each of these functions is expensive to develop effectively, easy to differentiate, and therefore highly profitable. This factor puts DEC and Hewlett-Packard, judged by the industry to have superior applications software, at an advantage. On the other hand, Perkin-Elmer is relatively weak in this area and therefore will be at a disadvantage.

Size and Specialization

As outlined previously, the supermini market is changing rapidly. New products with better performance and lower prices are constantly being introduced. These factors, along with IBM's dominant position in the market and the availability of semiconductors, dictate that firms will continue to pursue niches in the market. Further, firms must be able to react quickly to the changes taking place.

Smaller firms definitely have an advantage in this type of market since they are usually responsible for major innovations. These firms can introduce new products more rapidly without doing damage to an established product base.

Management Style

With the rapid changes of this industry, the management style of the organization also becomes critical to the success of the firm. It is extremely important that an entrepreneurial environment be encouraged and supported. This allows individuals to take the personal risks inherent in business, and both formal and informal communications can occur simultaneously to foster new product development and quick reaction to market developments.

There is also some indication that the leadership of the original founders is a crucial determinant of success. This leadership provides the organization with the direction and understanding of the specific firm's business that is often missing in "professionally managed" firms. Many of the supermini manufacturers have been able to foster the management style depicted here. Data General is known for its informal atmosphere, and HP for its emphasis on innovation. DEC and Wang are both run by the original founders, Ken Olson and An Wang, respectively. Prime, Gould, Harris, and Perkin-Elmer may be suspect when measured by this criteria. For example, Prime has recently installed a management team from IBM and has become highly structured. Perkin-Elmer and Gould both entered the supermini markets through acquisitions, and it may be difficult for the corporations to allow the divisions to continue to operate autonomously.

Finally, Harris is pinning its success in the office automation segment on the recent acquisition of Lanier Business Products. However, Lanier has specialized in narrow segments of the office market not necessarily synergistic with selling computer office automation.

EXHIBIT 3 1983 Financial results

	DEC	DG	PRIME	HP	GOULD	P-E	HARRIS	WANG	APOLLO
Sales	$4.3B	$830M	$516M	$4.7B	$1.3B	$1.0B	$1.4B	$1.5B	$80M
Profit/sales	6.6%	2.8%	6.3%	10.2%	4.8%	4.9%	3.9%	9.9%	16.3%
Cogs/sales	61%	57%	47%	47%	60%	58%	69%	—	40%
R&D/sales	11%	10%	10%	10%	12%	8%	6%	8%	13%
International sales	36%	34%	40%	41%	—	46%	24%	28%	—
ROE	8%	5%	12%	15%	7%	10%	9%	16%	17%
Debt ratio	.22	.44	.40	.31	.40	.42	.53	.44	.20
Debt to equity	3%	30%	6%	2%	26%	20%	—	39%	—
Current ratio	3.9	3.0	3.1	2.9	2.1	2.5	2.3	3.0	4.4
Quick ratio	2.2	2.0	2.2	2.0	1.4	—	1.7	2.0	3.2

Stock Financing

There is a distinct advantage to financing rapid growth through equity offerings or internally generated funds. By avoiding the fixed costs associated with debt financing, the firms allow the limited resources to be allocated to more important areas, such as R&D and marketing. The business risks in these markets are large enough without adding financial risk.

All of the companies in this market have very little debt, with the exception of Data General, Wang, and Harris, as shown in Exhibit 3.

Systems Compatibility

As the computer market continues to grow, there will be an increased emphasis on the ability to link products into networks. In addition, because of IBM's dominant position, it is becoming more important to be IBM compatible. Several of the companies in this market have developed their own networking systems, including WANGnet and DECnet. Others, such as Apollo, Prime, HP, and Data General, will develop products to use an existing system, such as Ethernet or UNIX.

Wang, in particular, has recently concentrated on making its products IBM compatible since the office automation systems will have to interface with IBM mainframes. Prime, on the other hand, will have to compete in the CAD/CAM market against Computervision, which has a marketing agreement with IBM for the 4300 series.

Summary

The marketplace for the superminicomputer is changing rapidly. The players in this arena have to make strategic market decisions without the flexibility for major error. Joe Hanson's Prime Computer has to make definitive moves to compete in this critical marketplace.

Case 41

The Stroh Brewery Company*

In April 1985, the headline in the *Detroit News* asked, "Why Can't Stroh Tap More of the Home Market?" The text went on to explain that while other leading brewers enjoy a generous share of the beer market on their home turf, the Stroh Brewery Company of Detroit, Michigan, had settled into a very distant third place in Detroit and Michigan, behind Budweiser and Miller. (See Exhibit 1 for state of Michigan beer sales.) "It's hard to describe why Stroh is not number one in Detroit," said Don Hill, president of City Marketing, Inc., a Detroit area beer distributor. "If you were to randomly call people and ask them which beer is number one here, they would say Stroh's," Hill said. "If you ask them what they drink, they'll name something else." During 1984, the Stroh brewery's total sales by volume declined 8.2 percent in the state of Michigan.

EXHIBIT 1 State of Michigan beer sales, top 13 brands *(barrels)*

	Brand	Percent total	1984 Sales	1984 Percent change	1983 Sales	1983 Percent change	1982 Sales
1.	Miller	15.9	1,074,375	−9.0	1,180,674	−9.5	1,304,621
2.	Budweiser	14.3	966,310	+12.4	859,993	+10.2	780,408
3.	Miller Lite	13.1	888,407	−1.7	903,405	+4.7	862,603
4.	**Stroh***	**11.5**	**779,712**	**−8.2**	**849,209**	**+3.9**	**817,373**
5.	Pabst	8.2	557,152	−23.0	723,874	−9.3	798,071
6.	**Schlitz†**	**4.5**	**305,520**	**−22.5**	**374,144**	**+13.7**	**328,967**
7.	Michelob	4.1	275,444	+12.8	244,082	−15.5	288,693
8.	Busch	3.2	215,828	+140.8	89,646	−11.2	100,908
9.	Michelob Light	3.2	213,581	−6.9	199,782	−11.3	255,227
10.	Budweiser Light	3.1	212,239	+31.4	162,011	+22.0	132,815
11.	Blatz	2.9	193,242	+24.7	203,727	+26.2	161,454
12.	Altes	1.8	121,488	−15.6	144,028	+22.5	177,566
13.	Colt 45	1.8	119,242	−12.7	136,560	+5.2	129,841

* Includes all Stroh brands.
† Includes all Schlitz brands.
Source: *The Michigan Brewery Record,* Investment Statistics Company, Detroit, 1985.

---

* This case was prepared from public sources by Susan A. Johnstal, under the supervision of Thomas C. Kinnear. Copyright © 1987 Thomas C. Kinnear.

Along the East and West Coasts, Stroh's beer, the flagship brand of the Stroh brewery, had a ritzy appeal similar to imported beers because of its unique fire-brewing process. It has been said that a case of Stroh's could be traded for any two cases of anything else in the East. In the Midwest, however, Stroh's was not a new name, and the hometown brew enjoyed no such mystique. In the Michigan home base, Stroh's was just another blue-collar thirst quencher. Bolstering the Midwest image of Stroh's and increasing share in its home market were priorities to Stroh management, as was the successful expansion of the flagship brand across the country.

However, the status of Stroh's national expansion was also a question. Stroh began to break out of its traditional Midwest distribution area by taking its flagship labels, Stroh's and Stroh Light, to a national level in 1984. Stroh advertised the two brands heavily with television commercials and outdoor billboards, further developed its wholesaler network, installed on-premise taps in bars and taverns, and sponsored local charity events. As a result, the Stroh geographic distribution area grew. By the end of 1984, Stroh officials were pleased with the preliminary results of the expansion effort. But Stroh's brand, as well as the entire list of Stroh brands, faced a faltering demand for beer in the United States (down .6 percent in 1984), and Stroh's nationwide 1984 beer sales by volume declined 1.6 percent. (See Exhibit 2 for Stroh production by brand.)

In addition to falling sales, management was concerned about several industry changes expected during the rest of the century. Consumer tastes were changing in the types of beer they preferred; imports and light beers were gaining sales volume at the expense of premium beers. Consumers' changing

EXHIBIT 2 Stroh production by brand (millions of barrels)

	1982	1983	1984
Old Milwaukee (popular priced)	6.0	7.6	7.1
Stroh (premium)	5.4	5.5	5.3
Schaefer (popular priced)	2.5	3.0	4.0
Schlitz Malt (malt liquor)	2.6	2.6	2.1
Schlitz (premium)	4.1	3.2	1.7
Old Milwaukee Light (popular light)	0.8	1.0	1.5
Stroh Light (premium light)	0.6	0.7	0.8
Goebel (popular priced)	0.3	0.3	0.6
Schlitz Light (premium light)	0.4	0.3	0.1
Erlanger (super premium)	0.1	—	—
Other	0.1	0.1	0.7
Schaefer L.A. (popular LA)			
Schaefer Light (popular light)			
Signature (super premium)			
Piels (premium)			
Piels Light (premium)			
Silver Thunder (malt liquor)			
Primo (premium)			
Total	22.9	24.3	23.9

Note: Capacity total = 29.5 million barrels.
Source: *Beverage Industry,* January 1985.

lifestyles included more often choosing wines and bottled water over beer. Demographic trends, including an aging society, threatened the popularity of beer as the number of people in the 18-to-35-year-old age bracket decreased. Increased consciousness of alcohol abuse brought about proposed legislation on banning beer advertising on television and radio. Within the beer industry, traditional beer wholesaler policies of exclusive territories were in question because of their anticompetitive nature. Finally, the efficiencies of national marketing and distribution were dictating that regional-only breweries could no longer compete as effectively against well-financed national brands, while consolidation of smaller brewers continued. These industry changes and Stroh's weakening position in its home market and lack of solid penetration in its new markets threatened to unseat Stroh from its 1985 number three spot on the list of largest national beer brewers.

History and Past Marketing Strategy

The Stroh family started brewing beer in the United States over 130 years ago. Bernhard Stroh, a German immigrant, opened his first successful brewery in 1865 in Detroit, Michigan. He brewed the beer in copper kettles over direct fire, a process that originated in Europe, while other brewers in America brewed over steam. The company grew in the Detroit area as a family business by delivering the brew to residents and local taverns. During Prohibition, the company survived by producing ice cream, malt extract, near beer, soft drinks, and ice. At the end of Prohibition, Stroh became a successful Midwestern beer brewer. Roger Fridholm, president of the Stroh brewery, attributes this success to quality, consumer service, packaging, and advertising. Also contributing to growing beer sales was the postwar baby boom, which produced 28 million additional Americans in beer brewers' prime age bracket, 18 to 35 years old. Stroh, as well as the entire beer-producing industry, could not help but grow as total beer consumption doubled in the next two decades.

In the 1960s, Stroh's was a popular-priced beer with a reputation for quality and taste generated by its fire brewing. Consumers were loyal to Stroh's because they believed, for the most part, that they were getting a premium beer at popular prices. Until 1979, Stroh had one brewery and essentially one brand: Stroh's (Bohemian style beer).

But during the 1970s, as the national brewers—Anheuser-Busch of St. Louis, Missouri, and the Miller Brewing Company of Milwaukee, Wisconsin— began to dominate the beer industry with tremendous advertising budgets, consolidation of smaller brewers sliced the number of beer producers in the country from approximately 171 to 45. In 1973, Stroh began raising the prices of Stroh's brand in hopes of repositioning it as a premium beer to compete directly with Budweiser and Miller. In the early 1980s, Anheuser-Busch (A-B) and Miller continued to grow without the aid of acquisition and forced many smaller brewers out of business. The Stroh brewery was forced to take on a defensive marketing strategy at that time. Stroh struggled to hold onto its existing Midwestern market and tried to offset the lack of sales growth by expanding into other beer segments and by producing new beer products. Stroh Light was introduced in 1979 as the first internally developed new product in the company's history, but serious production growth was severely hampered by the limits of Stroh's sole brewing plant.

"We woke up in the late 1970s to what was going on around us," says Chairman Peter Stroh, and that is when the brewery began its very aggressive expansion campaign. In 1979, Stroh acquired the F&M Schaefer Corporation, of Allentown, Pennsylvania, the eleventh largest brewer at the time. "We didn't buy a brand, we bought a brewery," explains Hunter Hastings, vice president of brand management. Although Stroh did not abandon the Schaefer brand, Stroh invested over $35 million to convert Schaefer's plant to fire brewing so that it could increase production of Stroh's brands. The Schaefer acquisition became Stroh's first move to dramatically expand the company.

In the summer of 1982, after a bitter battle, the Stroh Brewery Company, the seventh largest brewer in the nation, jumped to number three almost overnight when it acquired the Jos. Schlitz Brewing Company of Milwaukee, Wisconsin. Stroh borrowed $336 million to acquire the third largest brewer, thereby tripling its number of brewing plants to better compete at the national level. Stroh gained 1,250 wholesalers, 7,000 employees, and two very strong brand names: Old Milwaukee and Schlitz Malt Liquor.

Newspapers at the time quoted Peter Stroh's admiration for the Schlitz management. "I've been very impressed by their progress in overcoming the problems they inherited," exclaimed Peter. He was referring to the fact that during the five years before the merger, Schlitz's annual volume slid 35 percent, primarily because of quicker production techniques that noticeably cheapened the beer's quality. Peter Stroh believed his future as an independent brewer was in jeopardy, and the Schlitz failing position made it a prime candidate for takeover. With expansion for the Stroh brewery in mind, management concluded that acquisition was much cheaper than building new facilities. Building a brand new plant would have cost Stroh approximately $60 to $80 per barrel of plant capacity. Purchasing Schlitz cost only $25 per barrel. Schlitz's strategically located plants (see Exhibit 3 for a list of Stroh breweries) and its national, well-established distribution channels, including on-premise accounts in bars, off-premise network of retail stores, and wholesalers and distributors, were a few of the major reasons for Stroh's interest in Schlitz.

Stroh used the additional Schlitz plants nationwide to take advantage of economies of scale in production, distribution, and, probably most important, in advertising. Prior to 1982, as a regional brewer, Stroh had to pay a 50 percent premium on spot television to get the same results as A-B and Miller, who advertised nationally. "Every time we are forced to buy prime time regional spots, we take it on the chin," explained John Bissell, group vice president of marketing. To make up for this inefficiency prior to the Schlitz acquisition, Stroh and the Adolph Coors Company, a regional brewer out of Golden, Colorado, cleverly bought television air time together in the 1970s and split it

EXHIBIT 3 Stroh's breweries

Location	Capacity (million barrels)
Detroit, Michigan*	7.25
Allentown, Pennsylvania†	3.5
Longview, Texas‡	3.8
Van Nuys, California‡	2.95
Memphis, Tennessee‡	5.5
Winston-Salem, North Carolina‡	5.0
St. Paul, Minnesota§	1.5
Total	29.5

* Closed June 1985.
† Original Schaefer brewery.
‡ Original Schlitz brewery.
§ Exchanged with Pabst after Schlitz acquisition.

down the Mississippi River; Stroh commercials aired in the East, and Coors commercials aired in the West. After the Schlitz acquisition, as a national competitor Stroh could get even better representation on network television.

The Stroh brewery management proved its commitment to the growth of the company through its bold takeover of Schlitz. In reference to building the company as a national competitor, corporate Planning and Development Vice President Christopher W. Lole said, "You'd have to give credit to Peter. He's the visionary." But the fact remains that sales of Stroh products, both nationally and at home, have been falling, and Stroh management must further develop its marketing strategy to ensure the future of this independent family business.

Industry Environment

The Competition

The U.S. beer industry is highly competitive. In 1985, there were about 45 national, regional, and local brewers. Beer is an extremely mature product in the product life cycle, and as the industry shakeout continues, national brands are growing only at the expense of the smaller brewers.

Anheuser-Busch has traditionally dominated the beer industry through its sheer size and financial muscle. "The King of Beers" has been the largest brewer for over 25 years, and in 1984, A-B captured approximately 35.9 percent of the beer market, up from 33.6 percent the previous year. (See Exhibit 4 for brewers' estimated market shares.) A-B is the only domestic brewer to have meaningful growth in 1984: 6 percent growth in a total domestic market that declined 1.1 percent (or .6 percent, including imports). A-B's flagship brand, Budweiser, topped the most popular beer brands list in 1984 with 24.2 percent of the total beer sales, up from 22.8 percent in 1983. (See Exhibit 5 for the 1984 top 10 beer brands.) Also on the top 10 list was Michelob, the

EXHIBIT 4 Brewers' estimated market shares

	1979	1981	1983	1984E
Anheuser-Busch	26.8%	30.0%	33.6%	35.9%
Miller	20.8	22.2	20.8	21.3
Stroh*	**15.3**	**12.9**	**13.5**	**13.4**
Heileman	6.6	7.7	9.7	8.6
Coors	7.5	7.3	7.6	7.5
Pabst	12.3	10.5	7.1	6.6
Genesee	2.0	2.0	1.8	1.7
Schmidt	2.2	1.6	1.7	1.6
Pittsburgh	0.4	0.5	0.6	0.5
Others†	6.1	5.3	3.6	1.9
Total	100.0%	100.0%	100.0%	100.0%

* Includes Schlitz and Schaefer totals for all years.
† Includes imports and excludes tax-free sales.
Source: *Beverage Industry,* January 1985.

dominant super premium beer brand. New in 1984, Budweiser LA (without periods after the initials; LA is a logo protected by a trademark after Stroh unsuccessfully tried to use it for the Schaefer brand) is a low-alcohol brand with full-scale marketing support in the A-B lineup, with spending equivalent to all other A-B brands except Budweiser.

The Miller Brewing Company, a subsidiary of Philip Morris, was in a strong number two position. Miller's clever advertising and timely product development of Miller Lite, the first successful low-calorie beer, gave Miller almost 21.3 percent of the total beer market in 1984. The trend-setting Miller Lite brand beat its older brother, Miller High Life, for second position on the 1984 top 10 list of beer brands. Overall, Miller had a volume increase, up 1.3 percent in 1984, thanks to Miller Lite and Miller's new popular priced brands, Meisterbrau and Milwaukee's Best. Miller's flagship brand, Miller High Life, experienced declining sales, however, dropping from 17 million barrels in 1983 to 14.5 million in 1984. Problems with this brand have been widely speculated on. Some beer experts believe Miller used the ''It's Miller Time'' campaign

EXHIBIT 5 1984 Top 10 beer brands

Rank	Brand (brewer)	Market share	1984 Brand growth	Production (million barrels)
1	Budweiser (A-B)	24.2%	+3.7%	44.3
2	Miller Lite (Miller)	9.9	+.1	18.0
3	Miller High Life (Miller)	7.9	−14.7	14.5
4	Coors (Coors)	4.8	−10.0	8.7
5	**Old Milwaukee (Stroh)**	**3.9**	**−6.6**	**7.1**
6	Michelob (A-B)	3.7	−4.3	6.7
7	Pabst (Pabst)	3.6	−12.2	6.5
8	**Stroh (Stroh)**	**2.9**	**−3.6**	**5.3**
9	Old Style (Heileman)	2.8	−12.1	5.1
10	Coors Light (Coors)	2.5	+31.2	4.5

Source: *Beverage Industry,* January 1985.

long after its effectiveness had peaked, barely altering it for 10 years. Miller also raised the price of Miller High Life in 1980 in a slumping economy. Although Budweiser eventually followed, the higher price may have permanently driven countless High Life drinkers to Budweiser. In 1985, Miller reviewed several ad agencies in an attempt to pump life back into the brand's sagging sales. J. Walter Thompson USA won the six-month-long competition, and began promoting Miller with a ''Made the American Way'' campaign.

Although Miller had reported operating profits since being acquired by Philip Morris, according to *Fortune* (March 3, 1985) these profits have been so paltry that they have covered only the interest on the roughly $1 billion Philip Morris borrowed to build breweries and bottling plants in the 1970s. Miller had a $450 million brewery that it had never used as of 1985, and there was widespread speculation on Wall Street that Philip Morris would sell Miller. Yet, many brewing analysts believed The Miller Brewing Company was still the only serious competition A-B had in terms of market share and financial backing.

While A-B and Miller had faced little real competition in previous years, they had to contend in the 1980s with a trio of second-tier companies who were breaking out of their traditional regional boundaries in order to avoid losing market share. These brewers included Stroh, G. Heileman Brewing Company of La Crosse, Wisconsin, and the Adolph Coors Company. Like Stroh, Heileman and Coors were becoming more adept at competing with the leaders.

During the past decade, Heileman jumped from 15th place to 4th in the beer industry. The company has built its empire chiefly by acquiring and successfully revitalizing regional brands, including Old Style, its lead brand among the 24 brands it had. A strong brand identity was important for Old Style, which sought new markets as a means of improving brand share and becoming a national brand. Heileman had nine breweries and a mammoth wholesaler network. Overall, Heileman's marketing strategy, based on brand acquisitions and heightened price competition, added up to a rough year in 1984: Heileman sales declined over 11 percent.

Heileman also tried to merge with Schlitz in 1982, but the move was blocked by the Justice Department on antitrust grounds. In 1984 and 1985, Heileman attempted to acquire the ailing Pabst Brewing Company, the sixth largest brewer. This move was blocked by federal injunction after Stroh and the Christian Schmidt Brewing Company of Philadelphia, the number nine brewer, began a lawsuit alleging unfair competition.

Despite shrinkage of sales in its western base, Coors expanded outside of its traditional market into the Southeast in the 1980s. With a renewed financial position (Coors traditionally has no debt) after a disastrous labor strike in 1977, Coors established itself in a strong number five position among national beer brewers. Coors benefited from very strong brand identification for its premium Coors and Coors Light labels. These brews are unpasteurized and always shipped in refrigerated compartments, which contribute both to the brands' quality image and to customer confusion. Consumers were hesitant about buying Coors from unrefrigerated retail displays during large holiday promotions. As a result, in the summer of 1985, Coors advertised that while refrigeration certainly was desirable, it was not necessary to ensure the purity of Coors's taste.

1984 marked the first year that Coors had its two major brands in the list of top 10 most popular beer brands. Coors has not competed significantly in other beer segments. It seems the major limitation to Coors's expansion is that the company produces beer at a lone brewery in Golden, Colorado.

Beer Segmentation and the Consumer

For the first time in almost three decades, beer consumption in the United States declined in 1984. Consumption was 182.7 million barrels, down from 1983's 183.8 million barrels. Most industry researchers attribute this decline to changing lifestyles and social pressures. As brewing analysts predicted overall growth in domestic beer consumption to continue at 1 percent annually or less for the rest of the century, beer brewers sought to gain a larger portion of a steady-size pie through segment proliferation. Since many experts feel there really is no significant perceived difference among beer brands, especially after the first taste, brewers attempted to appeal to all different consumer backgrounds and introduced a brand image for almost every lifestyle, income, and taste.

1984 was a good year for light beer (for the more health-conscious consumer), popular priced beer (code term meaning inexpensive), and imported beers. Light beer sales increased its total industry share by 8 percent, moving up to 36.4 million barrels, or 19.9 percent of the total. Popular priced brands, the second most important segment, moved up to 42 million barrels, or 23 percent of the total. Imports accounted for 3.9 percent of total consumption, or 7.1 million barrels. (See Exhibit 6 for industry beer sales by market segment.)

However, the gains in these segments did not make up for the losses in the super premium segment (expensive beers of perceived higher quality), the premium segment (generally a brewer's flagship brand), and the malt liquor segment (beers with high alcohol content). Premium priced products, by far the largest beer segment, accounted for 82.3 million barrels sold, or 45 percent of

EXHIBIT 6 1984 Industry beer sales by market segment

	Barrels (millions)	Percent
Light beer	36.4	9.9%
Popular priced	42.0	23.0
Imports	7.1	3.9
Premium priced	82.3	45.0
Super premiums	9.1	5.0
Other (Malts, LA)	5.8	3.0
Total	182.7	100.0

Source: *Beverage Industry*, January 1985.

the total in 1984. Super premiums, generally priced higher on a par with imports, were down 1.3 million barrels, accounting for 9.1 million barrels in sales, or 5 percent of the total market. Stroh had representation in every beer segment and was committed to continuing this strategy.

The majority (83 percent) of the nation's beer drinkers are males. They are usually between the ages of 18 and 34, with per capita consumption declining rather steadily with age (see Exhibit 7). Demographic trends were less than favorable for beer producers in the 1980s as the postwar baby boom generation moved beyond the prime beer drinking age. The 18-to-34 age group was predicted to decline by 4 million people before 1990. Stroh reacted to this unfortunate trend by seeking national market penetration.

Changes in eating and drinking habits also impeded growth in beer sales. The most prevalent change centered around our society's health concerns. Light beers have been very successful in addressing consumer demands for low-calorie foods since Miller introduced Miller Lite in the mid-1970s. During the 10 years following Miller Lite's introduction, light beer sales grew to account for over 20 percent of total beer sales and two thirds of the total growth in beer consumption for the period. Stroh markets almost one third of its brands with light labels, including Stroh Light, Old Milwaukee Light, Schlitz Light, Schaefer Light, and Piels Light.

A large threat to increasing beer sales in this country in the 1980s was increased concern over alcohol abuse. Various community groups, especially Mothers Against Drunk Driving (MADD), opposed brewers for allegedly glamorizing drinking in their advertising. Peter Stroh said the drinking/driving problem was probably the single most important issue he faced in 1984. While many states raised the drinking age from 18 to 21, lawmakers also stiffened the

EXHIBIT 7 Consumer characteristics

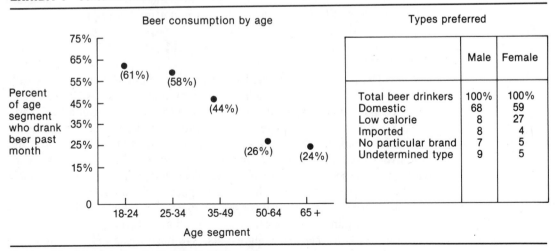

	Male	Female
Total beer drinkers	100%	100%
Domestic	68	59
Low calorie	8	27
Imported	8	4
No particular brand	7	5
Undetermined type	9	5

Source: *Advertising Age*, January 16, 1984, p. M-10.

penalty for driving while drunk. "This is an issue the beer industry cannot back away from. It is in the brewers' best interest to assist in educational efforts aimed against alcohol abuse," says Peter Stroh. Stroh has been very closely associated with efforts at Johns Hopkins and other leading universities to study health-related alcohol abuse effects.

On a related issue, consumer groups like SMART (Stop Marketing Alcohol on Radio and TV) were attempting to ban all alcoholic beverage advertising from TV and radio. Coalitions formed on both sides of the issue, and at Stroh, management felt brewers should work to shape any serious activity in this critical area rather than leaving the future of advertising laws only to the politicians. Stroh certainly did not want to see higher excise taxes to fund the fight against alcohol abuse, cigarette-type warning labels, or taglines on beer commercials warning consumers about the damage of abusing alcoholic beverages. Brewers traditionally imposed their own advertising standards, such as having actors in their ads who were over 25 years of age and never actually drank the beer on camera. Brewers claimed that there has been no credible scientific evidence to show that advertising encourages alcohol abuse and that the Supreme Court has previously ruled that truthful advertising has Constitutional protection. On the other hand, many legal scholars profess that a ban on advertising beer and wine on radio and television will withstand Constitutional law, and they point out the cigarette ruling as an example.

A-B addressed the alcohol-related issues by introducing a low-alcohol brand beer in 1984. Stroh quickly followed with Schaefer L. A. but was only distributing it on a limited basis until October 1985. In mid-1985, although A-B declined to give sales numbers for its low-alcohol beer, A-B called its LA "the bar call of the 80s" and did say that off-premise sales had been stronger than anticipated. Since exact sales figures on low-alcohol brands are not readily available, experts can only estimate that low-alcohol beers had only a negligible share of the beer market in their first year after introduction. Many analysts predict low-alcohol beers will not become a major market segment.

Advertising

"The Big Two," A-B and Miller, have capitalized on their high volumes with economies of scale in both production and distribution. This has allowed them to increase advertising expenditures well beyond what others can afford. (See Exhibit 8 for some national advertising expenditures by brand.) In an industry where savvy marketing is a key success factor, A-B and Miller secured the major live-action sports telecasts in the early 1980s with exclusive network advertising contracts that prohibited other beer competitors from airing their ads. The audience that watches live-action sports is the audience beer makers everywhere strive to attract: males aged 18 to 35. Stroh believed that network exclusive pacts hurt company business. "We have all the tools to compete, except for access to these sporting events. We have made offers to purchase time based on the terms and conditions customary to the television industry,"

EXHIBIT 8 Some national advertising expenditures by brand ($000s)

Brand	Medium	1982	1983	1984
Budweiser and Bud	Magazines	$ 2,560	$ 5,208	$ 2,907
Light (A-B)	Newspapers	1,929	2,242	2,246
	Network TV	50,479	68,165	93,421
	Spot TV	21,905	30,094	29,087
	Network radio	4,572	4,052	2,179
	Spot radio	20,261	19,804	17,660
	Outdoor	3,191	2,217	2,123
Total		$104,897	$131,782	$149,623
Miller High Life and	Magazines	$ 1,555	$ 1,352	$ 1,870
Miller Lite (Miller)	Newspapers	490	1,556	1,279
	Network TV	74,651	84,082	104,930
	Spot TV	19,868	22,374	18,514
	Network radio	—	—	—
	Spot radio	16,051	5,194	17,449
	Outdoor	661	470	657
Total		$113,276	$125,028	$144,699
Michelob and Michelob	Magazines	$ 13,993	$ 6,371	$ 2,040
Light (A-B)	Newspapers	11,657	980	812
	Network TV	22,355	19,760	49,566
	Spot TV	14,653	2,209	6,643
	Network radio	—	503	2,017
	Spot radio	1,867	7,746	3,445
	Outdoor	74	30	252
Total		$ 64,599	$ 37,602	$ 64,775
Coors and Coors Light	Magazines	$ 56	$ 29	$ 46
(Coors)	Newspapers	1,153	1,016	657
	Network TV	7,069	9,746	11,218
	Spot TV	11,367	18,658	24,398
	Network radio	—	—	—
	Spot radio	8,081	21,209	18,528
	Outdoor	451	547	517
Total		$ 28,179	$ 51,205	$ 55,364
Stroh's and Stroh	**Magazines**	**$ 260**	**$ 255**	**$ 1,988**
Light (Stroh)	**Newspapers**	**113**	**242**	**450**
	Network TV	**3,578**	**24,962**	**27,780**
	Spot TV	**7,649**	**7,014**	**5,936**
	Network radio	**—**	**—**	**—**
	Spot radio	**1,842**	**3,472**	**6,141**
	Outdoor	**610**	**951**	**2,642**
Total		**$14,052**	**$36,896**	**$44,937**
Heineken (Van	Magazines	n/a	$ 4,708	$ 5,006
Munching)	Newspapers		15	150
	Network TV		2,895	3,004
	Spot TV		5,532	7,143
	Network radio		1,645	548
	Spot radio		7,659	12,983
	Outdoor		—	—
Total			$ 22,454	$ 28,834

EXHIBIT 8 *(concluded)*

Brand	Medium	1982	1983	1984
LA (A-B)	Magazines			$ 742
	Newspapers			1,618
	Network TV			19,218
	Spot TV			783
	Network radio			2,036
	Spot radio			558
	Outdoor			872
Total				$ 25,827
Lowenbrau (Miller)	Magazines	$ 111	$ 130	$ 454
	Newspapers	131	81	18
	Network TV	16,096	15,918	12,387
	Spot TV	6,412	4,748	5,762
	Network radio	—	—	—
	Spot radio	1,359	4,020	3,045
	Outdoor	6	18	14
Total		$ 24,115	$ 24,915	$ 21,680
Meister Brau (Miller)	Magazines		—	—
	Newspapers		$ 1,028	$ 41
	Network TV		8,300	18,336
	Spot TV		2,887	2,906
	Network radio		—	—
	Spot radio		—	
	Outdoor		9	25
Total			$ 12,224	$ 21,308

Source: *Marketing and Media Decisions,* 14th Annual Report, "The Top 200 Brands."

explained Christopher Lole. The inability to reach a target audience through major network sports programs has critical trade implications also. Not having a presence on major sporting events makes it harder for local wholesalers to compete against those wholesalers whose product gets plenty of national exposure, and therefore it is more difficult to get ample shelf space from retailers.

After persistent efforts by Stroh management, including Peter Stroh himself, lengthy negotiations with the networks, and an investigation by the Department of Justice, the networks changed their policies on ad exclusivity in 1984. While no lawsuits were actually filed, Stroh made it clear that it would sue the networks on a restraint of trade basis if the two sides could not come to an agreement. Stroh was able to buy enough network time in 1984 to put off litigation over the matter. In fact, the networks actually offered Stroh more time than it could afford, according to Hunter Hastings, vice president of brand management. Stroh contracted to sponsor ABC's "Monday Night Baseball" on a nonexclusive basis for 1984. In addition, Stroh bought time on two NBC boxing matches and a CBS auto racing series.

In June 1985, the Stroh brewery introduced the "Stroh's Circle of Sports." For two hours every weekend for 13 weeks, Stroh's pursued a strategy of "going where the big guys ain't" on the USA cable network and a broadcast TV syndicate. The show featured interviews, analyses, opinions, historical flashbacks, and an "event of the week" shown from the perspective of a sports participant. The "Stroh's Circle of Sports" signaled that the brewer would look for advertising niches instead of always going head-on against A-B and Miller. This also represented the first example of Stroh's efforts to target audiences at a lower cost by creating its own programming. Stroh spent an estimated $200 million for advertising and sales promotions in 1985, but still could not match the spending of A-B and Miller.

Domestic beer brewers spent an estimated $575 million on advertising their products in 1984, which does not include the costs of promotion and distribution. Beer has gone from emphasizing traditional taste and quality claims to heavy consumer imagery. Certainly quality is an important factor in selling beer (as Schlitz found out only too late), but advertising, especially on TV, is the strategy of choice for the big beer makers.

Promotion

Brewers' promotional tactics came in many forms. Sporting events around the country throughout the year were usually the events of choice for national brewers—again, as a way of attracting young beer drinkers to their brands. Stroh sponsored the "Stroh Thunderfest," a hydroplane race in Detroit in which *Miss Budweiser* was often the boat favored to win. Other sponsorships by major brewers included bowling teams, auto races, rodeos, and track-and-field events. Budweiser was the official beer of the 1984 Olympics.

Many brewers sponsored special events such as rock concerts or symphonies to associate their beers with the lifestyles of those who participated in the events. Signature was the official beer of the 1982 World's Fair in Knoxville, Tennessee. Many brewers also sponsored charity events, including raising money for the renovation of the Statue of Liberty and making local donations to children's hospitals.

Brewers, in cooperation with local distributors, were very aggressive in providing quality point-of-purchase displays in retail outlets. Brewers attracted consumers in liquor and party stores with permanent and temporary illuminated prestige signs, nonilluminated plaques, and neon signs. Decorated mirrors with company logos were universally found in taverns and bars.

Stroh's very successful retail merchandising programs included the 10-year-old "Stroh a Party" campaign, which Stroh implemented to build sales of Stroh's and Stroh Light during the high-volume, peak summer selling season. The "Strohman"—a large plastic, stand-alone snowman—gave retailers a high-visibility display for Stroh's and Stroh Light during the winter holiday season. The "Strohman" program included not only the familiar snowman but also six-pack toppers, price cards, and cooler stickers for use in every display setting.

Super premium beers and malt liquors generally did not discount their prices to wholesalers in order to protect their upscale image. However, premium beers and popular priced brands often discounted their prices to wholesalers who in turn passed the savings on to retailers who, hopefully, sold the beers at sale prices during promotional campaigns. One of the wholesaler's jobs was to keep tabs on retail prices. Old Milwaukee offered periodic cents-off coupons, mail-in refund offers, and sweepstakes. These promotions were offered through newspapers, point of purchase, and direct mail.

Distribution and Pricing

Stroh brands, like all beers, were distributed through a three-tiered distribution system:

1. The brewery sold to wholesalers, who were independent, local businesspeople.
2. Wholesalers sold to retailers (bars and stores).
3. Retailers sold to consumers.

A brewery could not legally sell to retailers or to consumers.

Stroh officials, as described in a company document, believed the three-tiered system worked well because wholesalers agreed to provide service to all accounts, from mom-and-pop stores to high-volume chain stores. The wholesalers must maintain Stroh's strict standards of product quality by never selling beer over 90 days old and by keeping the product in temperature-controlled warehouses. In return, Stroh signed territorial agreements with wholesalers, giving them exclusive rights to sell Stroh products in their territories. From the brewery's point of view, this meant that the company did not have to pit wholesalers against one another. This industrywide practice was controversial because of its anticompetitive aspects.

Brewers set their prices of low-margin, popular priced beers to wholesalers based on a cost plus profit method. Brewers set prices of super premium beers, on the other hand, on a more consumer-oriented approach. Wholesalers and retailers were free to set their own prices based on their usual markups, but brewers hit certain price points by establishing a price to the wholesalers that, when marked up by the wholesalers and retailers, would match the desired retail price. (See Exhibit 9 for 1985 typical domestic retail beer brand prices.)

Laws governing promotional pricing varied widely from state to state. When a brand offered a lower promotional price, some states required it to stick with that price for as long as 120 days. For regular retail prices, most brands followed the segment leader's pricing strategy in any particular geographical market.

Current Marketing Strategy and Brand Management at Stroh

The Stroh Brewery Company's objective in 1985 was to keep a strong and growing number three position in the beer industry, with the ultimate goal of unseating the second largest industry leader, Miller. Industry experts predicted that consolidation of brewers in the next few decades would leave only four or

EXHIBIT 9 1985 Typical retail beer brand prices
(six-pack of 12-ounce bottles or cans)*

Brand	Brewer	Price
Popular priced		
Blatz	Heileman	$2.50
Busch	Anheuser-Busch	2.49
Carling Black Label	Heileman	2.50
Goebel	**Stroh**	**2.25**
Meisterbrau	Miller	2.49
Natural Light	Anheuser-Busch	2.49
Old Milwaukee	**Stroh**	**2.39**
Old Milwaukee Light	**Stroh**	**2.39**
Premium		
Budweiser	Anheuser-Busch	$2.98
Bud Light	Anheuser-Busch	2.98
Miller High Life	Miller	2.98
Miller Lite	Miller	2.98
Old Style	Heileman	2.98
Pabst	Pabst	2.98
Schlitz	**Stroh**	**2.98**
Schlitz Light	**Stroh**	**2.98**
Stroh	**Stroh**	**2.98**
Stroh Light	**Stroh**	**2.98**
Super premium		
Erlanger	**Stroh**	**$3.39**
Lowenbrau	Miller	3.49
Michelob	Anheuser-Busch	3.39
Signature	**Stroh**	**3.39**
Malt Liquor		
Colt 45	Heileman	$2.98
Schlitz Malt Liquor	**Stroh**	**2.98**

* Price does not include sales tax or bottle deposit.

five major beer producers. Although the company policy in 1985 did not include long-term planning of five years or more, Stroh was determined to be one of those few.

With the purchase of Schaefer, Stroh became a company in transition. Hunter Hastings said the company had to "make the switch from being a production company to a marketing company." In 1985, the entire marketing department was only six years old. The company recruited many young marketing MBAs, but most of the senior marketing executives came from other marketing-oriented firms. J. Wayne Jones, formerly with Coca-Cola, accepted the newly created position of executive vice president of sales and marketing in 1984, and John Bissell, group vice president of marketing, came from General Mills. Before the mid-1970s, Stroh did not bring outside talents into the company.

A-B and Miller relied on the "block buster brand" approach to the beer market for many years with their hugely successful Budweiser and Miller brands, respectively. Stroh, on the other hand, used the portfolio theory of brands after gaining so many different brands from acquisitions, and focused on the many segments in the beer market. Stroh had a brand of beer for all popular beer segments in the 1980s: popular priced, premium, malt liquor, etc. Stroh also concentrated on special niches, including demographics (Blacks and Hispanics) and geographics (targeting different states and cities with unique campaigns).

In 1984, Stroh concentrated its energy on taking its flagship brands—Stroh's and Stroh Light—nationwide. Stroh planned to market Schaefer nationwide in 1985 and have Signature not far behind. Other brands, such as Schlitz Malt Liquor and Old Milwaukee, already made Stroh a national firm through the Schiltz acquisition. But in 1984, Roger Fridholm hoped Stroh's brand penetration nationwide would broaden its 13.4 percent market share to 15 percent. Fridholm did not, however, pin down a time frame for this objective.

The Stroh marketing strategy contained six priorities for the company:

1. Maintain and grow Stroh's and Stroh Light as national competitors.
2. Maintain Old Milwaukee as the market leader in the popular priced segment.
3. Maintain and grow Schlitz Malt Liquor as the clear leader in the malt liquor segment.
4. Maintain leadership as the only beer company to specifically target the needs of Blacks and Hispanics.
5. Establish a super premium beer brand.
6. Continue the company's effort in new product development.

To support these six priorities, Stroh devoted almost 75 percent of its financial budget to 6 of its 15 brands: Stroh's, Stroh Light, Old Milwaukee, Old Milwaukee Light, Schlitz Malt Liquor, and Signature.

Stroh's and Stroh Light

For the best possible financial efficiencies, Stroh's and Stroh Light came under the same brand manager, had the same budgets, and were advertised in the same advertising campaigns (a strategy that had worked well with Old Milwaukee and Old Milwaukee Light). Stroh gave these flagship brands the same consumer positioning as the heavyweights in the premium beer category, Budweiser and Miller High Life. But Stroh wanted this image to carry a few discerning characteristics. Stroh's and Stroh Light were brewed with Stroh's unique fire-brewing process, which the company believed gave these beers the finest taste. In the 1980s, Stroh's and Stroh Light targeted what the company called the "type A" beer drinker. This was someone who drank at least a case of beer per week: the heavy user. Therefore, Stroh was careful to package the Stroh's brands in colorful, bright cartons and cans to attract this young, fun-loving consumer. Beginning in 1969, Stroh's used the advertising theme "From One Beer Lover to Another, Stroh's." In 1984, Stroh's was extremely successful with its clever "Alex the Dog" television advertising campaign (see Exhibit 10

EXHIBIT 10

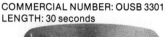

CLIENT: Stroh Brewery Co.
TITLE: Alex the dog

COMMERCIAL NUMBER: OUSB 3301
LENGTH: 30 seconds

POKER PLAYER: I'd sure like another Stroh's.
HOST: No, wait. Alex!

DOG: ARF

HOST: Two cold Stroh's.

DOG: ARF
HOST: Wait till you see this.

(SFX REFRIGERATOR DOOR OPENING)
He just opened the refrigerator.

(SFX BOTTLE OPENING)

He just opened one bottle.
(SFX BOTTLE OPENING)
He just opened the other.

(SFX STROH'S BEING POURED INTO GLASS)
Now he's pouring yours.

(SFX OTHER STROH'S BEING POURED)
Now he's pouring mine.
(SFX DOG DRINKING)

Alex, you better be drinking your water.

MUSIC

From one beer lover to another.

for a copy of Stroh's television photoboard). Stroh believed humor makes these brands more memorable. Budweiser and Miller High Life did not use humor to advertise in this premium segment. Budweiser long used its familiar tagline, ''For all you do, this Bud's for you!'' and Miller began using a new theme song for its television commercials in 1985; ''Miller's made the American Way, born and brewed in the USA, just as proud as the people who are drinking it today, Miller's made the American Way!''

In May 1984, Stroh's and Stroh Light became nationally distributed in Stroh's big push to become a national brewer. 1984 consumption of Stroh's and Stroh Light was 6.1 million barrels, which captured 7.4 percent of the national premium market. The two beers became available in all 50 states, but total sales for these two brands were down over 1 percent nationally in 1984, and sales in Michigan were off 8.2 percent for the same year.

Taking Stroh's and Stroh Light national had an advantage in that it allowed the company to address the key Hispanic populations in the West like no one else had before. Stroh appointed a new national manager of Hispanic market development in 1984 and spent over $4 million in the ethnic market with heavy advertising in radio, outdoor displays, and newspapers. Other brewers also attempted to capture the Hispanic market in the West and Southwest, but Stroh was emerging with the first major effort to court the Hispanic market. Stroh's success in this area is yet to be evaluated.

Old Milwaukee and Old Milwaukee Light

Old Milwaukee (OM) and Old Milwaukee Light (OM Light) was the best-selling duet of Stroh brands at 8.6 million barrels in 1984. The goal for these two original Schlitz brands was to continue to dominate the popular priced beer brands with a national image that says OM and OM Light have everything premium but the price. Stroh spent heavily to create this image and has attracted drinkers from other competitors. In a stagnant industry, OM's brands grew 16.9 percent in 1983. OM was the fifth most popular brand in 1984, climbing from number seven the previous year. OM and OM Light's large volumes were very important for assuring the utilization of full plant capacities, but at their popular prices, OM and OM Light did not provide very large profit margins.

Stroh emphasized image and taste rather than price when advertising OM on radio and television. Stroh believed Miller was making a mistake when it mentioned low prices in the advertising of its new popular priced Meisterbrau, OM's chief competition from Miller. Meisterbrau ended its television commercials in the early 1980s by claiming Meisterbrau ''Tastes as good as Budweiser, at a better price!'' Stroh believed advertising low prices did not reflect the proper image for quality.

OM and OM Light came in premium packages: tall bottles with colorful cartons and cases. (For pictures of OM and OM Light containers as well as of the rest of the Stroh line, see Exhibit 11.) They were carefully merchandised with premium point-of-purchase signs and premium print advertising. In televi-

EXHIBIT 11   Stroh bottles and cans

Source: Stroh media pamphlet.

sion ads, Stroh differentiated OM through a ''hard play/reward'' theme rather than the ''hard work/reward'' style of Meisterbrau. The characters in those OM television commercials were younger, vibrant types who enjoyed stone crab fishing in the Gulf of Mexico or bar-hopping in New Orleans, just the type of events that are capped off with Old Milwaukee. At the end of each commercial, the characters observed, ''It doesn't get any better than this!'' (See Exhibit 12.)

OM used many techniques to promote the beer. Charles Powell, brand manager for OM and OM Light, explained that ''While a lot of beer is consumed by men, it's actually bought [off premise] by women. So we try to provide incentives for women to buy our beer.'' OM capitalized on the gatekeeper effect by stressing refunds and product discounts. OM set trends with coupons on a more extensive basis than has been seen before. OM sponsored five in-store promotions each year, including sweepstakes and give-aways. OM ran ads on all three networks in prime time slots during big league

EXHIBIT 12

BBDO

Client: STROH BREWERY   Batten, Barton, Durstine & Osborn, Inc.   **Time:** 30 SECONDS

Product: OLD MILWAUKEE DUAL BRAND   **Title:** "SUMMER SKIING"   **Comml. No.:** SZDB 4053

VO: Mount Hood, Oregon and Old Milwaukee

both mean something great to these guys.

Mount Hood means the best summer skiing

in America.

And Old Milwaukee means a great beer.

Cold, crisp Old Milwaukee beer.

And smooth, golden

Old Milwaukee Light.

SONG: OLD MILWAUKEE

VO: And Old Milwaukee Light.

SONG: TASTE AS GREAT AS THEIR NAME.

GUY: Man, it doesn't get any better than this.

sporting events. OM also constantly tried to get retail trade attention through heavy advertising in trade publications.

Schlitz Malt Liquor

Schlitz Malt Liquor (SML) was clearly the brand leader in the malt liquor segment with a 40 percent market share in 1984 and 2.1 million barrels sold. Schlitz achieved this position with a superior product, and Stroh maintained it with ongoing taste tests to achieve the best flavor in this segment. Stroh stressed specific consumer targeting techniques for SML. Blacks consume almost 75 percent of this specialty product, so Stroh featured top Black pop groups like Kool and the Gang in television commercials. Malt liquors contain more alcohol and have a fuller, more robust flavor. For many years Schlitz used the strength of a bull crashing through a brick wall to create this imagery. All of SML's advertising copy showed celebration and times when people want more alcohol. (See Exhibit 13 for a sample Schlitz Malt Liquor television photoboard.) Because it produced the dominant product in malt liquors, Stroh used leadership pricing techniques and never resorted to discounts. However, SML sales were down .5 percent in 1984 as were sales of the entire malt liquor segment.

Signature

Signature was introduced in 1982 as the second new internally developed product in Stroh's history. Only in limited distribution in 1985, Stroh planned to expand this super premium product on a national level in the near future. The objective was to gain a significant share of the super premium segment. This segment, however, has traditionally been completely dominated by A-B's very popular Michelob brand, which sold almost 74 percent of the beer in this segment in 1984. Miller's Lowenbrau sold another 13 percent.

Signature, brewed from 100 percent European hops through the Stroh fire-brewing process, closely targeted the high-priced super premium segment with what the company believed was a fine-tasting product (200 recipes were rejected before Signature was personally chosen by Peter Stroh) that combined drinkability with a definite, distinctive flavor that was smoother and less bitter than other premiums. Signature tried to be distinctive not only in flavor but on other levels as well. Although Signature was on a parity pricing schedule with Michelob, Signature really focused on packaging, and Stroh proclaimed that Signature had a better shelf life than Michelob. Signature came in a uniquely shaped, old-fashioned-type bottle with gold foil around the top and elegant gold-trimmed labels. This package won Signature the coveted Clio award for packaging.

Signature bears the signature of former Chairman John W. Stroh, and the Stroh family history told through print ads (see Exhibit 14) conveyed to consumers why they should pay more for this product.

EXHIBIT 13

BENTON & BOWLES
909 THIRD AVENUE
NEW YORK, N.Y
(212) 758-6200

CLIENT: SCHLITZ
PRODUCT: MALT LIQUOR
TITLE: "BACHELOR PARTY/FP"
COMM'L NO.: SZML 0108
LENGTH: 30 SECONDS

(MUSIC UNDER)
FOUR TOPS SING: Tonight you're still a
bachelor, tomorrow's almost here.

So while you're still a free man, let's
bring on the beer . . .

KOOL AND THE GANG: Bull!

FOUR TOPS: Bull???

KOOL AND THE GANG SING: On this
night to remember, it's so clear.

You deserve to celebrate with more taste
than beer.

The bull's got a taste so big, so bold,
so smooth.

Let's all party with the Schlitz Malt
Liquor Bull.
ALL SING: Don't say beer, say Bull.

BACHELOR: Hey Gang how about
another Bull?

(SFX: CRASH)

(SFX: CRASH)

ALL SING: No one does it like the Bull!

EXHIBIT 14

Johann Stroh 1775-1810

Georg F. Stroh 1810-1850

Bernhard Stroh 1850-1882

Julius Stroh 1882-1939

Gari Stroh 1939-1950

John W. Stroh 1950-1982

Peter W. Stroh 1982

There's a lot of Stroh behind the great taste of Stroh Signature.

This exceptional premium beer is a product of over 200 years of Stroh family brewing experience.

Our family began brewing in Kirn, Germany in 1775. Three quarters of a century later, Bernhard Stroh introduced Stroh's Beer to America. Through the years, Stroh has come to represent the highest standards of the brewer's art.

We believe that Stroh Signature is as fine a beer as can be produced. It contains none but the choicest ingredients, including 100% imported European hops.

I personally hope you enjoy it.

John W. Stroh
Chairman

© 1985, Stroh Brewery, Detroit, Michigan

Michelob specifically targeted the yuppie crowd (young, urban professionals). This was quite evident in Michelob television advertising, which professed, "There's a style in your life, no one can ever deny. You're on your way to the top, and along the way you've always known just who you are. Where you're going, it's Michelob!"

Signature concentrated on the same young, financially stable age group in a somewhat different fashion with television commercials that featured independent, bearded role models who left corporate America to become entrepreneurs in such exciting fields as scuba diving and car racing. (See Exhibit 15 for a sample of Signature television advertising.) John Bissell, group vice president of Stroh marketing, described the target audience for Signature as "carefree, independent, self-confident, well-educated, and successful young men and women—the people who tend to dress differently than others, go into business for themselves, and, while viewed as responsible individuals, are definitely free-thinkers."

All the Rest

The Stroh Brewery Company had 11 other brands in 1985: Goebel, Schaefer, Schaefer Light, Schaefer L.A., Piels Beer, Piels Light, Schlitz, Schlitz Light, Erlanger, Silver Thunder, and Primo. These brands combined received only 25 percent of all the financial support of the company. Most of the brands competed on price, especially Goebel.

Stroh was repositioning its super premium beer, Erlanger (a label originated by Schlitz), for the 1980s as a specialty beer parity priced with imported beers. Erlanger management planned to make its brew available on a limited basis in upscale retail and on-premise accounts. Erlanger planned for three new labels on a rotating schedule and a new bottle in order to take advantage of high gross margins in this segment, although total industry sales in this segment declined in 1984.

Stroh took advantage of regional tastes, making Piels brands available in the East, Primo in Hawaii, and Goebel in the Midwest. As of the summer of 1985, Stroh intended to expand the popular priced Schaefer brands' distribution area, breaking them out of their original distribution area in 14 eastern states.

The Schlitz Problem

One of Stroh's biggest challenges after the Schlitz acquisition was to develop a new marketing program to breathe life into the ailing Schlitz brands, which sold only 1.8 million barrels in 1984. Stroh management monitored Schlitz sales, which slumped 26 percent in 1982, the first year under Stroh. Christopher Lole noted that "the first step to revitalizing the brand is to slow the erosion." Analysts say "The Beer That Made Milwaukee Famous" lost over one million faithful Schlitz drinkers after the company reformulated the Schlitz brewing process, which made the brew taste "funny." Schlitz again revised the brew's

EXHIBIT 15

STROH SIGNATURE

"CAR BUILDER"

MAN: (VO) I gave up a great job with an auto company

to do what I always wanted--design and build race cars.

(MUSIC)
SINGERS: WHEN A MAN HAS SOMETHING EXTRA DEEP INSIDE HIS SOUL. . .

IT SHINES LIKE A DIAMOND

AND IT'S WORTH MORE THAN GOLD.

MAN: (VO) This is the way to make a living.

SINGERS: SO HERE'S TO THE MAN

WHO LOOKS DEEP INSIDE.

AND HERE'S TO THE MAN

WHO FINDS SOMETHING EXTRA.

ANNCR: (VO) Stroh Signature is something extra.

You have our name on that.

MCA ADVERTISING, LTD.

formula and claimed that it was even better than the original Schlitz product. However, despite Schlitz's extensive advertising efforts, the old crop of regular Schlitz drinkers did not return.

Stroh began the new Schlitz campaign with a makeover of the Schlitz packaging. The new Schlitz brand marketing team replaced the ''government-issue'' yellow packing cartons with a more colorful design and also redesigned the Schlitz logo and bottle configuration. ''The major change was just brightening it up so it didn't look like it was only available for people over the age of 60,'' said Marketing Vice President John Bissell. ''I don't think we spent more than $25,000 on the research, because we needed to move fast.''

Apparently, Stroh did not pump big money into Schlitz until revitalization signs warranted more financial backing. Stroh did, however, continue to support promotional efforts in Schlitz's 28 strongest southern states, especially in Texas. Although many analysts thought Stroh was merely milking Schlitz, management insisted in 1984 that it would not drop the Schlitz name. ''Any brand that can generate some reasonable sales and profits determines its own viability,'' said Bissell.

Special Products Division

The Stroh Brewery Company instituted a new special products division at corporate headquarters in 1985. Although Stroh had continually marketed Stroh's ice cream since Prohibition, Stroh was definitely less diversified than the other major brewers, who owned everything from a major league baseball team (Anheuser-Busch owned the St. Louis Cardinals as well as many other nonbeer ventures) to cigarette companies (Miller, for example, was a subsidiary of Philip Morris, the tobacco company that also owned 7UP). Stroh was very busy developing a nonbeer beverage in early 1985: White Mountain Cooler. It is a flavored malt beverage similar to a wine cooler, targeted especially at women and nonbeer drinkers. Stroh was also investigating an all-natural flavored water beverage and the possibility of producing baked goods or snack foods since these products all require essentially the same ingredients Stroh already used in beer and could be distributed through some of the same retail beer channels.

Position in Home Market

The lag in home market sales was a puzzle for Stroh officials. In 1984, all Stroh brands captured approximately 16 percent of the Michigan market, down 10 percent from 1983. This compares unfavorably with a 28.91 percent Michigan market share for the Miller Brewing Company and 28.9 percent for Anheuser-Busch. Meanwhile, A-B commanded a 51 percent share of the market in its native Missouri in 1984. In Wisconsin, Miller beat another local brewer, G. Heileman Brewing Company, for the top slot, gaining 28.6 percent of the market to Heileman's 27.8 percent: a total of 56.4 percent for the home team.

Stroh closed its original brewery in Detroit in June 1985, which greatly disappointed many Stroh loyalists, although Stroh had long been a conscientious corporate citizen and involved in Michigan special events. Previous to the brewery's closing, Stroh had not been a firm that sought headlines. Detroit newspaper writers attributed this to the low profile Chairman Peter Stroh traditionally took because he didn't want to pat himself on the back. But during the summer the local brewery closed, Stroh published full-page ads in the Detroit area enumerating Stroh's community activities, apparently responding to Michigan consumers' anger. (See Exhibit 16 for a reprint of those advertisements.)

As the Stroh Brewery Company pondered the current state of the beer industry, both at home and nationally, management knew that it could institute long-range and risky plans without worrying about impressing any shareholders since the company was privately owned. The corporate management style was open and aggressive. But as the company grows, in Peter Stroh's words, ''The thing to keep our eyes on is not so much our size, but the size of the guys we're up against.''

EXHIBIT 16

We Are Still Here

Dear Michigan Consumers and Retailers,

The Stroh Brewery Company was founded in Detroit in 1950. Since then, the names "Stroh" and "Detroit" have become linked in the minds of people throughout the United States and, in fact, throughout the world.

Our difficult decision to close the least-efficient plant in our seven-brewery system was not a severance of that link. It was a decision made to ensure our future in a highly competitive industry. That future will show that the Stroh Brewery Company's commitments to Detroit and to Michigan remain as strong, if not stronger, than before.

Possibly the most visible sign of our sustaining commitment is our River Place corporate headquarters, a major development along the Detroit waterfront that will be a long-term asset to this city and its people. When the offices, shops, restaurants, and residences open at River Place, our 750 corporate employees will be joined by thousands of Detroiters sharing in the beauty and excitement River Place offers.

Other Stroh commitments are seen in our support of civic and cultural events. If you enjoy the Detroit-Montreux Jazz Festival or the Signature concerts at Meadowbrook; if you're in the stands for the hydroplane "Thunderfest" or the Detroit Formula One Grand Prix; if you watch "Late Night America" or "Michigan Outdoors;" if you attend the Detroit Symphony, or visit the Detroit Institute of Arts; then you are touched by the Stroh commitment to our home.

These are but a few of our commitments to Detroit and to Michigan. There is one more, which is perhaps the most important of all. That is our commitment to you that the brewing of fine beers will continue to be our top priority. Our Michigan distributors will continue to provide this state with the finest, and we intend to share it with the people of Michigan regardless of where you may live.

Sincerely,

Peter W. Stroh
Chairman
The Stroh Brewery Company

EXHIBIT 17
THE STROH BREWING COMPANY
Selected Financial Data*
Year Ended March 31
(amounts in $000s)

	1983	1982	1981
Barrels of beer sold	22,900	9,100	8,900
Brewery capacity	29,550	12,250	11,000
Sales	$1,535,126	$593,444	$561,578
Sales net of excise taxes	1,317,986	499,124	467,292
Earnings (loss) from operations	1,228	(6,172)	2,973
Discontinued operations	—	—	4,863
Change in accounting principles	—	11,774	—
Net earnings	1,228	5,602	7,836
Pro forma net earnings (loss)	1,288	(6,172)	10,716
Depreciation	39,868	19,724	15,918
Working capital	45,666	14,369	22,891
Year-end working capital	(46,502)	(19,370)	25,946
Property, plant, equipment	456,876	168,210	139,882
Total assets	721,142	263,433	231,588
Long-term debt†	321,328	72,996	69,648

* Includes operations for Schlitz from 1982 and Schaefer from 1980.
† Includes redeemable preferred shares of Schaefer.
Source: The Stroh Brewery Company 1983 Form 10-K.

It was against this background that the management at the Stroh Brewery Company developed its strategy to slow the erosion of sales in the home market. At the same time, meaningful penetration of the Stroh and Schaefer brands in the national market was certainly one of Stroh's top objectives, and further refinement of its implementation techniques was appropriate. Stroh's market planners knew where they wanted their expansion strategy to take them: closer to the top of the list of national competitors. However, while analyzing the effectiveness of the national expansion efforts thus far (see Exhibit 17), Stroh did not have the financial strength to take on all potential successful projects at once. Stroh had to establish which alternatives claimed the highest priorities, while balancing them against a declining beer market and powerful competition.

Case 42

Cool-Ray Sunglasses*

total strategy

Hugo Powell reached down and picked up the sunglasses from his desk and looked at them one more time, turning them over and over in his hands.

"These are absolutely excellent sunglasses," he said to himself, "yet people seem to be turning away from Cool-Ray and buying Foster Grant's or some other kind. We seem to have the competition beaten on all counts— product quality, distribution, sales force, advertising, and commanding higher prices—yet all the forecasts predict that we will lose market share. If we pick up this Cool-Ray line, we'd have to do something to protect our share of the market."

? high prices

Hugo Powell was to meet the following week with Steve Wilgar, president of Warner-Lambert Canada Limited. In that meeting on May 5, Hugo would present his recommendations on what should be done about the possible acquisition of the Cool-Ray line of sunglasses. As he looked out his window at the rush-hour traffic in the street, Hugo recalled the events that had led to this present assignment.

The previous year he and the marketing managers of the other divisions of Warner-Lambert had sat down with Mr. Wilgar in the boardroom to discuss the new corporate strategy. They had decided that they wanted to maintain earnings growth at 10 percent per year, and they had developed a three-part strategy to accomplish this. First, they concluded that they could develop their existing brand franchises. This might involve adding advertising support where it was needed, starting new consumer promotions, or improving products. Second, they could develop new brands that met new consumer needs. Third, they could plug gaps in existing product lines by manufacturing products under license (or by acquiring whole product lines or companies). Acquisitions were quite desirable because they represented a source of cash flow from which funds could be obtained for advertising expenditures on existing products or investment in new product research. Any firm that Warner-Lambert Canada Limited planned to acquire would have to allow the company to exploit two of what they considered to be their three main resources: selling, marketing, and manufacturing.

10% yr growth

2 of 3

---

* This case was written by Professor David D. Monieson of Queen's University and by Ronald Jamieson. Used by permission.

Wilgar had handed Hugo a file the company kept on prospective firms for acquisition and asked him to review those firms (and any others he might choose) and to present his recommendations within 12 months. After that meeting Hugo had called a young product manager from consumer products division, Bruce Pope, into his office and asked Bruce to assist him in his search for a firm to acquire.

About three weeks after they had started their search, Hugo had picked up the morning paper and read on the front page that a National Foreign Investment Review Agency (FIRA) was to be established in April of that year to oversee acquisitions and mergers involving Canadian companies and foreign-owned operations. The agency was to be empowered to examine any such situation involving a Canadian company with $250,000 in assets and $3 million or more in annual sales. The Foreign Investment Review Act's definition of a takeover was acquisition of 5 percent of the shares of a public company or 20 percent of a private company. Furthermore, FIRA was expected to extend its authority in the future and to start screening expansions into new lines of business by companies that were already foreign controlled. Acquisition of Canadian firms by foreign companies also had to be compatible with provincial development goals. Highest priority was given to the creation of jobs in underdeveloped areas and preservation of existing jobs.

Over the course of the next six weeks Hugo and Bruce had spent considerable time with corporate lawyers, assessing the political sensitivities of several potential acquisitions. After dropping several firms from the list because acquisition would have led almost certainly to a FIRA investigation, Hugo and Bruce had recommended that Warner-Lambert Canada Limited look further into acquiring the Cool-Ray line of sunglasses from American Optical Company. The risk of an investigation by FIRA was minimized because American Optical already was owned by Warner-Lambert's parent company in the United States; thus, it was expected that acquisition of Cool-Ray would be interpreted as the transfer of a business line from one subsidiary to another. Although it was possible that the decision for transfer of management of the Cool-Ray line from American Optical to Warner-Lambert would be done only in Canada, it would have to be cleared by the parent company, involving the presidents of the Pan American management centre and the international division, as well as the president of the Warner-Lambert Company.

The Canadian Market for Sunglasses

Two years ago Canadian sales of sunglasses amounted to 6.5 million units, or $26 million at retail, but dropped to 5.2 million units and $24 million in the current year. Unit sales were expected to grow at only 1.5 percent per year, while dollar sales were forecast to grow at 12 percent each year (see Exhibit 1).

Cool-Ray was the dominant figure in the market, holding 31 percent of the unit volume but 49 percent of the revenue. Although Foster Grant, Cool-Ray's

EXHIBIT 1 Canadian sunglass market comparison with the United States

	United States	Canada
Market development		
Reported/estimated sunglass units	87,300,000	6,523,000
Population	210,400,000	22,095,000
Market development (sunglasses/ thousand population)	414.9	295.2
Index: Canadian market development versus U.S. market development	100	71
Retail price		
Reported/estimated average retail	$8.50	$9.60
Index: Canadian versus U.S. average	100	113
Cool-Ray average retail price	$10.00*	$10.70
Index versus total market average	142	134
Index: Canadian versus U.S. average	100	107
Factory price		
Reported/estimated average factory cost	$2.80	$4.26
Index: Canadian versus U.S. average	100	152
Cool-Ray average factory price	N.A.	$4.62†
Index versus total market average	N.A.	135
Factory dollars		
Reported/estimated total factory value	$244,400,000	$30,008,000
Population	210,400,000	22,095,000
Market development (factory $/thousand population)	$1,163.8	$1,361.6
Index: Canadian market development versus U.S. market development	100	117

N.A. = Not applicable.
* Average unit price of polarized sunglasses.
† Before any discounts for early bookings.
Source: Company records.

[handwritten margin notes: "—why so high.", "Will Canada even be like sun glasses also?", "—Different mkt for Canada", "driving & skiing"]

principal competitor, held a 24 percent market share in the United States, in Canada it held only 4 percent of the market. The rest of the market in Canada was made up of a number of imported products, despite import duties of 12.5 percent plus another 12 percent. Some of the imports were European products, but the majority were manufactured in the Far East.

Sales of sunglasses were typically seasonal, peaking in the summer months. About 45 percent of the sales were made from May to August. However, people in the sunglass trade felt that the seasonality was becoming less pronounced and that sales would be more or less even through the year. "People don't see sunglasses as part of the summer anymore," they said. "Skiers buy them for the winter and automobile drivers buy them for year-round protection from the sun whenever they're driving."

Consumer Behaviour

Hugo had asked Bruce Pope to go out into the field during the summer to see what he could learn about consumers' buying habits through discussion with people in the sunglass trade.

"Well, between 60 and 70 percent of the population wear sunglasses," Bruce stated, "although only about 30 percent buy a new pair in any single year. I spoke with a buyer from one of the big department stores downtown, and he said most sunglass purchases were made by women. He mentioned that unisex and neutral styles were also big sellers in his stores. This buyer thought that the major influence on choice was appearance. Price, brand name, and lens quality he thought were of lesser importance. While I was out in the store with him, I noticed that people were trying on six or seven pairs before deciding on one they would buy. According to this chap, that is not unusual."

"Sounds like styling is pretty important."

"Yes. The buyer told me he thought that firms in the sunglass market need to be extremely close to the fashion industry and to be aware of changing fashion trends. Styles can be very faddish—in one year, out the next."

"Did customers just try on different styles of one brand name?"

"That would seem to be very unusual. I approached a few customers and asked them if they came into the store looking for any particular brand. For the most part they said that they were looking for something that appealed to them and bought the style they liked most regardless of brand. When I asked them what they liked about the last pair they owned, they usually talked about colour, style, or protection; while the things they liked least about their last pair usually were such things as quality of construction or materials."

An American study published a few years earlier revealed that purchasers had mentioned protection and styling with equal frequency as a reason for purchasing. However, now about 40 percent indicated styling was a major reason for purchasing and only 30 percent mentioned protection. Exhibits 2 and 3 show the data from the American study.

About 35 percent of sunglasses in Canada were sold in drugstores, 40 percent through department stores and mass merchandisers, 8 percent through department stores, and the remaining 17 percent through variety stores, tobacconists, and other small retailers. Over several years buyers in the sunglass trade had noted a decline in the importance of variety stores as outlets for sunglasses and had attributed this to a trend toward higher sunglass prices and the variety of styles available at other outlets.

Distribution and Sales

"When you spoke with people in the sunglass trade, did you find out anything about how the sales force is employed?" Hugo asked.

"Not all of the sunglass manufacturers use a sales force in Canada," said Bruce. "When I spoke with a representative of a larger association of independent wholesalers he said that there were three ways to obtain distribution: sell

EXHIBIT 2 The sunglass market consumer information*

	Past (percent)	Current (percent)
Incidence of sunglass wearing	62%	67%
Incidence of sunglass purchasing	39	41
Unaided brand awareness		
Cool-Ray	61	63
Foster Grant	21	26
Total brand awareness		
Cool-Ray	86	89
Foster Grant	50	57
When sunglasses brand decision made		
While in store	61	56
Before entering store	31	33
Not specified	8	11
Major reasons for purchasing		
Protection	38	30
Appearance	36	42
Forced choice: styling versus protection		
Styling	33	26
Protection	60	70
Average price paid per pair	$4.47	$5.34
Average number of pairs owned	1.6	1.6
Average number of pairs purchased at one time	1.4	1.4

(handwritten margin note: unaided vs total?)

* Based on U.S. data.

EXHIBIT 3 The sunglass market consumer perceptions of major
      brands*

	Cool-Ray (percent)	Foster Grant (percent)	Imports (percent)
Brand image			
Best brand overall	48%	12%	10%
Finest lens quality	54	19	18
Fashionable styles	42	31	32
Scratch-resistant lenses	28	10	9
Excellent frame fit	35	18	15
Excellent eye protection	55	17	14
Prestige brand	47	22	18
Expensive	27	12	22
Major reason(s) for purchasing last pair			
Like the style/shape	25	44	57
Eliminate glare/are polaroid; polarized	39	7	10
Fit well/are comfortable	29	7	24
Inexpensive	9	28	27
Lenses are nicely tinted	13	43	21
Why purchase decision made			
Wanted additional/different pair	24	11	28
Broken last pair	25	25	25
Lost or forgotten previous pair	16	17	23
First pair purchased	14	4	9

EXHIBIT 3 *(concluded)*

	Cool-Ray (percent)	Foster Grant (percent)	Imports (percent)
Major reason(s) for liking last pair purchased			
Fit well/are comfortable	43%	42%	37%
Eliminate glare/are polaroid; polarized	45	11	20
Cut down on glare	44	11	15
Provide protection from sunlight	16	11	20
Like the style/shape	5	20	23
Major reason(s) for disliking last pair purchased			
Are plastic/scratch easily	11	18	8
Not sturdy/fell apart	5	6	9
Consumer perceptions of brand differences			
Eliminate/cut down glare	44	8	2
Are a good (quality) product	11	7	9
Are clearer/offer more visibility	10	1	1
Are better/good for eyes	9	2	—
Provide protection from sun/protect eyes	8	2	1

* Based on U.S. data.

Source: Company records.

through a wholesaler and his sales force; employ a sales broker using a central warehouse; or sell direct to retailers with your own sales force. Because sunglasses are sold through so many different kinds of outlets, nearly all sunglass merchants use one or the other of the first two methods I described. This fellow said that Cool-Ray was the only sunglass manufacturer using its own sales force in Canada. Foster Grant and Riviera both used sales brokers. Other suppliers went to Europe to obtain exclusive distributionships in Canada for the high-style, high-price 'prestige' lines.

"The sunglass salesperson tries to call on a retail account twice a week during the summer peak period. In the off season, the salesperson's call pattern is more random, perhaps once every two months. Call frequency depends a lot on the size of the store. At the wholesale level the sunglass salesperson calls three or four times a year on the larger wholesalers and only once a year on the smaller wholesalers.

"The reason for such a low number of calls to wholesalers was that the salespeople, in addition to calling on wholesalers, spent a good portion of their time filling in retail accounts on the latest styles, prices, and so on. They would also drop ship[1] for the wholesaler in order to keep the store's racks full. While

---

[1] Drop shipment is one means of delivering merchandise to a retailer. Salespeople would typically have a supply of merchandise in their car that they could deliver to the retailer to replenish his/her stocks.

the salesperson actually made the delivery to the retailer, billing was done through the wholesaler by prior arrangements.''

Hugo said, ''It sounds like a sunglass salesperson's calls are more complicated than our salesperson's calls. At least we don't have to deal with the wholesaler because of our sell-direct policy. How exactly does a sunglass sales call go, Bruce?''

''One of the wholesalers arranged for me to meet some of the Cool-Ray salespeople, and I went with them on a few sales calls. When the salesperson entered the store, he/she went directly to the sunglass display. He'd/she'd count the sunglasses on hand and note down the styles and colours that were out of stock. The other sunglass manufacturers put their sunglasses on a Cool-Ray rack wherever they find the space, so the salesperson has to look the rack over very carefully to be sure only the Cool-Rays were counted.

''The salesperson then draws up an order based on what he/she thinks will move most quickly, and then talks with the store buyer. The buyer can either sign the order and wait for delivery from the warehouse or ask the salesperson to restock the racks from the stock in the trunk. The buyer tells the salesperson if any glasses have been lost or stolen while on the rack and returns any broken or faulty sunglasses. The sunglass salesperson can cover the retailer's losses on the spot and exchange good sunglasses for faulty ones. Often the salesperson makes up a credit voucher to compensate the retailer for lost and broken merchandise. If the retailer's requirements are too large for the salesperson to handle from trunk stock, he/she arranges to drop ship the merchandise on the next visit to the retailer.''

The salesperson was very important to the manufacturer because his/her expertise could influence the volume the manufacturer could move through certain outlets. It was usually the salesperson who determined the styles displayed on the racks. His/her knowledge of fashion trends was quite valuable because sunglass styles had a tendency to follow the latest fashions. The larger retail chains wanted to keep their merchandise turning over, and if the salesperson did not manage to keep the sunglasses moving, the supplier might be discontinued the following year. If one line of sunglasses was moving faster than another, the retailer might limit the volume the supplier of the slow-moving line could sell through the stores in the chain. The supplier of the fast-moving line might find that the retailer would allow him/her more space in the store and would allow him/her to sell a higher volume of sunglasses through the chain.

Display and Promotion

Sunglasses were displayed—usually prepriced by the manufacturer—on racks. While the retailer had the option of purchasing a standard display rack for his store(s), very often the retailer bought the rack already filled with sunglasses, and the cost of the rack was covered by the cost of the sunglasses. The retailer could also buy on consignment and return unsold sunglasses to the supplier at the end of the season. A counter rack by itself usually cost a manufacturer such as Cool-Ray about $70, while a floor rack cost $150. A floor rack held about 130 pairs of sunglasses.

Couponing, "cents off" deals, and other consumer promotions were not common practice in the sunglass trade. Occasionally promotions were directed at the wholesalers or retailers. A few of the large sunglass manufacturers relied on advertising to complement their coverage by the salesforce and would direct some of this advertising at consumers as well as at the trade.

One wholesale tobacconist said that the most important factors in selecting a supplier of sunglasses were the reputation of the supplier, their advertising policies, and their sales and exchange policy. Retailers wanted reliable suppliers whose merchandise was immediately and readily available so that the racks would be kept stocked. Advertising helped to maintain a high level of consumer brand awareness, which would result in a high level of consumer demand. Finally, the retailer wanted a guarantee that the glasses would sell and didn't want to be stuck with unsold or unpopular styles.

Warner-Lambert Company, Inc.

Warner-Lambert Company, Inc. (the U.S. parent company), was number 95 on *Fortune's* list of 500 industrials, with sales of $2.17 billion and net income of $165 million. Its earnings had grown at a rate of 10 percent per year for 10 years, assisted by several acquisitions during that period. Warner-Lambert was the product of a 1955 merger between the Lambert Company and Warner-Hudnut. The latter company was founded in 1856 as Warner-Chilcott, a manufacturer of prescription drugs, but later expanded to include DuBarry cosmetics and Richard Hudnut toiletries. The Lambert Company marketed toothpastes and toiletries, and it was probably best known for its Listerine mouthwash. The 1956 acquisition of the Emerson Drug Company added Bromo-Seltzer to Warner-Lambert's product line, and the 1962 acquisition of the American Chicle Company added confectionery products such as Chiclets, Dentyne, Rolaids, and Certs. Many other acquisitions were made by Warner-Lambert during this period, but these few illustrate the flavour of the company and outline its major divisions.

One of the largest acquisitions was American Optical Company, which marketed more than 2,000 products designed to extend and protect the physical senses of man. Some years prior to the merger, American Optical had sought to expand its lines of optical lenses and frames by diversifying into sunglasses. It had entered into an exclusive agreement with Polaroid Corporation for a process to coat lenses with a polarizing material. The result was the Cool-Ray line of sunglasses.

Warner-Lambert Canada Limited

Warner-Lambert Canada Limited had sales of $60 million. The company was organized into four divisions: Warner-Chilcott Pharmaceuticals, Adams Brands

EXHIBIT 4 Distribution channels in Canada

	Drug	Food	Discount	Department	Wholesalers	Others
Total number of accounts	5,000	31,700	1,000	300	450	
Consumer Products coverage	2,754	3,668	812	220	405	620
Adams Brands coverage	4,775	26,945	N.A.	240	432	
Cool-Ray coverage	3,693	360	624	179	50	260

Confectioneries, Consumer Products, and DuBarry. Manufacturing took place in three Toronto plants: the Adams plant, the main plant, and the Schick plant. Instead of reporting to Warner-Lambert Canada Limited, the Canadian management of American Optical reported to the head office of American Optical International in Massachusetts. In Canada, American Optical manufactured frames at the Nicolet, Quebec, plant and imported lenses from the United States for assembly at the Belleville plant. During the peak period the Nicolet plant employed about 140 people, of which 70 were part-time employees.

In considering which of the four divisions might adopt the sunglass line, Hugo decided that Cool-Ray would not be compatible with the distribution channels used by Warner-Chilcott Pharmaceuticals. Warner-Chilcott had fairly good penetration in the drug trade but was not really present to a significant extent in food stores or mass merchandisers. Moreover, Warner-Chilcott salespeople spent much of their time detailing physicians rather than selling to retail outlets. As it happened, Warner-Lambert had just divested the DuBarry division. Accordingly, Hugo was considering Adams Brands or Consumer Products as possible sources of management for the Cool-Ray line.

Because of the diversified nature of the Consumer Products and Adams Brands product lines, these divisions had achieved intensive distribution through food chains, department stores, drugstores, and intermediates such as wholesalers and jobbers (see Exhibit 4).

Warner-Lambert Canada employed 182 salespeople in the Adams and Consumer Products divisions. Exhibit 5 shows the number of salespeople in Consumer Products, Adams Brands, American Optical, and major Canadian

EXHIBIT 5 Comparison of sales forces

	Consumer Product	Adams Brands			American Optical Canada (Cool-Ray)	Foster Grant	Polaroid*	Riviera
		Gum	Candy	Both				
Salespeople	46	46	45	20	8	Use a broker	9	Use a broker
Sales managers	12		15		1		1	
Total	58		126		9		10	

* This represented the camera sales force; film was sold through a broker.

.13 x

.40 x

competitors. Adams Brands had 46 salespeople who sold gum exclusively (Dentyne, Chiclets, Trident, and the like) and 45 salespeople who sold confectioneries exclusively (such as Certs, Clorets, and Hall's Mentholyptus Cough Drops). Another 20 salespeople handled both gum and confectioneries. Consumer Products had a sales force of 46 people.

The Adams Brands line consisted of a number of confectionery items sold through food, drug, mass merchandisers, and variety stores. The most likely locations for an Adams display were the candy counter or a rack by the checkout counter to enhance last-minute purchases. The retailer usually received a discount of between 30 and 45 percent off the consumer list price as his margin for carrying this line. The risk of pilferage and spoilage contributed to the size of this markup.

The Consumer Products line was quite diverse, and thus this division's products were scattered throughout a store. While some products might be in with home remedies, others such as the Schick line might be among men's toiletries or displayed on a rack. This meant that a Consumer Products salesperson had to visit several areas of a store on one call, whereas a salesperson from Adams Brands visited only one or two areas. The discounts on Consumer Products were about the same as on Adams Brands.

Salespeople for Adams Brands made an average of 22 calls per day, whereas salespeople for Consumer Products made roughly 11 calls per day. The difference was attributed to the more complex Consumer Products sales presentation and the need for the Products salespeople to visit several sections of the customer's store. While the Adams salespeople could talk exclusively about gum or candy, the Products salespeople had to be able to talk about mouthwash, toothpaste, razor blades, stomach remedies, and so on. One study on Hugo's desk stated that the addition of sunglasses to the sales call was expected to reduce the call frequency to 16 per day from 22 for Adams salespeople and to 9 per day from 11 for Products salespeople.

Hugo recalled from his past experiences in accompanying salespeople on their sales calls that it seemed to take some special talent for a salesperson to service rack merchandise. The salesperson had to be able to look over the rack very quickly, identify items low in stock or out of stock, and then organize the rack so that products were in their proper locations and prepare an order for the items that were out of stock. Warner-Lambert was considered to have considerable expertise in rack servicing and rack design and thus made extensive use of this form of product display.

Sales of Adams and Products lines had a slight seasonality, with about one third of sales taking place between September and November. April to July was the "slow" period for their sales.

The Cool-Ray Operation

Cool-Ray was the originator of the polarized sunglass as it is known today. It manufactured the lenses using a process that was licensed from Polaroid

Corporation. Cool-Ray paid Polaroid a royalty of 4.3 percent of factory sales value and used the Polaroid name prominently in its advertising and on products and labels. The Cool-Ray line was one of many product lines of American Optical, and in Canada the line was sold by eight salespeople and a sales manager. According to people in the sunglass trade, Cool-Ray's major strength was its expertise in rack merchandising and pricing.

Cool-Ray had about 5,100 retail accounts and 130 headquarters accounts,[2] but 70 percent of Cool-Ray sales were to wholesalers. Of the seven or eight calls per day a Cool-Ray salesperson might make, two would be to retail outlets. Cool-Ray depended upon the wholesaler's sales force to supplement its coverage of retail accounts and had to accept the fact that the wholesalers sold more than just sunglasses on their sales calls to retailers. Two large wholesalers accounted for 38 percent of Cool-Ray's sales, and the larger of these two had just negotiated a sales agency agreement that was not cancellable for two years. To improve the coverage of retail accounts by its salespeople, Cool-Ray executives had drawn up a plan for a 35-person part-time sales force to service retail accounts.

Cool-Ray sunglasses were sold through 75 percent of all drugstores and 60 percent of the discount stores in Canada. Cool-Ray was typically strong in drugstores and weak in department stores, while variety stores and mass merchandising sales were close to average. Cool-Ray dealt with only about 10 percent of the food wholesalers and had extremely poor coverage of food stores. Exhibit 6 compares Cool-Ray distribution to the national averages in the United States and Canada.

Cool-Ray offered retailers a discount of 40 percent from the suggested list price; Foster Grant, Sahara, and other sunglass marketers offered the retailers a discount of 50 percent. Trade discount to wholesalers averaged between 10 and 15 percent of the prices paid by the retailers. Some marketers, such as Foster Grant, allowed wholesalers a further discount of 5 percent if they placed their orders early (usually before the spring). Cool-Ray offered wholesalers a 10 percent discount and would give a further 10 percent discount for orders booked three to six months early.

EXHIBIT 6 Comparison of U.S. versus Canadian sunglass sales distribution

	U.S Cool-Ray	U.S. market	Cool-Ray Canada	Canadian market
Drug stores	62%	24%	55%	35%
Department stores	1	20	5	8
Mass merchandisers	13	17	15	20
Food stores	2	8	5	20
Variety/other	22	31	20	17
Total	100%	100%	100%	100%

---

[2] Headquarters accounts were usually large national chains that had a center purchasing department and dealt with the Cool-Ray sales manager.

EXHIBIT 7 Cool-Ray analysis, sales seasonality comparison

	Dollar sales ($000)			Percentage sales		
	Consumer Products	Cool-Ray	Consumer Products plus Cool-Ray	Consumer Products	Cool-Ray	Consumer Products plus Cool-Ray
December–February	3,020.0	600	3,620.0	19.3%	11.2%	17.2%
March–May	3,708.5	860	4,568.5	23.7	16.1	21.8
June–August	2,560.7	468	4,028.7	22.7	8.8	19.2
September–November	5,367.2	3,420	8,787.2	34.3	63.9	41.8
Total	15,656.4	5,348	21,004.4	100.0%	100.0%	100.0%

Source: Company records.

Spiffs[3] could be paid to the retailer or to the wholesaler's sales force, depending on how distribution was organized. They were used to compensate the wholesaler or broker salespeople for keeping the racks stocked. Sahara paid a spiff of 3.3 percent of invoiced cost to the retailer or wholesaler; Foster Grant paid 1.75 percent; and Cool-Ray paid about 1.1 percent. Cool-Ray had a fairly generous policy of dating orders[4] anywhere from three to six months. Warner-Lambert did not know what sort of dating policy (if any) was used by other sunglass distributors.

While in theory, discounts of 40 and 10 percent meant that for every dollar of list sales price the retailer got 40 cents and the wholesaler 6 cents, in practice this was not necessarily the case. Chains typically received discounts of more than the usual retailer discount. If merchandise were sold direct to the chain's outlet, the retailer discount applied; if it were shipped to the chain's warehouse, the chain also received some or all of the usual wholesaler's trade discount.

Approximately 60 percent of Cool-Ray's shipments took place during October and November when retailers placed their orders for the following year. The peak period for in-store servicing was from May to August, and business was pretty even over the rest of the year. Exhibit 7 compares the seasonality of Cool-Ray and Warner-Lambert sales. About 85 percent of Cool-Ray's sales represented sales to stores of sunglasses on full racks, while the other 15 percent of sales came about as a result of rack replenishment during the May–August period.

To complement the efforts of its sales force, Cool-Ray spent approximately 11 percent of its sales revenue on advertising and promotion. Of the total sales and promotion budget, $250,000 was spent on media advertising, and

---

[3] Spiffs, or "push money," were payments made by a manufacturer to a retailer or a salesperson to provide an incentive to sell his/her products rather than a competitor's.

[4] Dating of orders was one means of extending credit to a customer. For example, if a customer receives goods in August and the order is dated November, he doesn't have to pay for the merchandise until November.

Cool-Ray was recognized by the sunglass trade as the only major national advertiser of sunglasses in Canada. The Cool-Ray copy platform had traditionally focussed on the glare-reduction (protection) feature of the lens (see Exhibit 8). Styling had been Foster Grant's copy platform for many years.

EXHIBIT 8 Advertisement for Cool-Ray sunglasses

ADVERTISEMENT FOR COOL-RAY SUNGLASSES

you won't believe your eyes.

You won't believe how great you'll look in Cool-Ray®Sunglasses. Over 125 eye-catching styles and colors! From our new polarized Gradient and Mirrored lenses to our Tortoise Stripe Frames, they're out of sight!

They're also specially designed to conform to your face, so they fit just as beautifully as they look. What's more, every pair of Cool-Ray Sunglasses is polarized to give you the glare-protection you simply can't get with ordinary sunglasses. Cool-Ray, with suggested retail prices from $2.50 to $12. They're America's No. 1 sunglasses. And it's easy to see why.

COOL-RAY sunglasses. You won't believe your eyes.

Cool-Ray typically sold its product at a premium price relative to its competitors. In contrast, the lowest priced sunglasses landed in Canada at as low a price as 50 cents per pair. For Cool-Ray the cost of goods at the factory represented about 50 percent of the factory selling price, while the factory cost of Foster Grant sunglasses was estimated to be 30 percent of the factory selling price. Cool-Ray's cost of goods was higher than Foster Grant's because Cool-Ray attempted to put more ophthalmic features such as top-quality lenses, frames, and materials into its products and manufactured to very close tolerances. For example, it was estimated that Cool-Ray's average factory price in Canada was $5.78, which was approximately 35 percent more than the Canadian average and double the U.S. average. It was generally acknowledged in the trade that Cool-Ray's biggest weakness was in its knowledge of styles and fashion. Its sunglasses were believed to be somewhat utilitarian and without great flair to them.

In the highly fragmented sunglass market Cool-Ray considered its main competition to come from Foster Grant. While Foster Grant had a 24 percent share of the U.S. market, it had only 4 percent of the Canadian market. The Foster Grant line was promoted on the basis of styling. For example, Foster Grant caught on to the popularity of aviator-style sunglasses and became the leader in this style, which accounted for 12 percent of Foster Grant's sales and was the most successful of its 60-odd styles. Foster Grant had developed a polarized lens of its own and had begun promoting its line of polarized sunglasses. It spent about 4 percent of its annual sales on advertising and kept market promotional cost at a low level by using a sales broker in Canada.

''The latest on Foster Grant is that they plan to establish a direct sales force here in Canada this year or next,'' Bruce Pope mentioned when Hugo asked him for an update. ''I expect that by putting in such effort they will be able to double their share of the market in the first year and add another 60 percent to that in the second year. However, I'm really worried about Polaroid. They're planning on introducing their own line of polarized sunglasses about the same time as Foster Grant puts on its big push. From what I've heard, they expect to grab 5 to 10 percent of the sunglass market in the first year and double that in the second year. Not only that, but they have manufacturing capacity available and a sales force already in Canada. The sales force handles cameras, and I don't know if they plan to add sunglass salespeople or have the nine salespeople at present handle sunglasses too.''

''Since American Optical plans to drop the Polaroid name from the Cool-Ray line about that time, I guess Polaroid is just trying to fill the vacuum by keeping their name present in the sunglass trade,'' said Hugo. ''The competition definitely appears to be more aggressive now. I had some of our salespeople look over the Cool-Ray racks in their territories during the summer. In their spot checks they reported that between 20 and 30 percent of the rack space was empty, and this was in the urban areas. The sales force said that other times they would go and look at a Cool-Ray rack to find that 25 to 90 percent of the space was filled with competitors' products.''

What's selling?

Cool-Ray executives had just completed a series of moves intended to strengthen the company's position. They had increased their allowance to the retail trade from 40 percent to 50 percent of retail price and had increased their early booking discount from 10 percent to 15 percent. They had instituted a policy of dating orders for five months after delivery and had added a 5 percent allowance to retailers for cooperative advertising. However, they had increased their wholesale prices by an average of 36 percent during a period in which some customer segments were switching to lower priced products. Finally, they had just decided to expand their product line from 130 to 180 items.

By May of the next year Cool-Ray executives found that returns, which were as low as 4 percent last year, shot up to 18 percent of sales. They were also accumulating an inventory worth almost $2 million at retail prices.

In talking with other managers in Warner-Lambert, Hugo learned about the problems in the acquisition of the DuBarry line. Some changes in DuBarry operations had been made so that they would conform to Warner-Lambert practices and standards. As a result of these changes in practices a number of costs were incurred by Warner-Lambert in the year that it acquired DuBarry. Hugo's assessment of the Cool-Ray acquisition was that immediate changes would have to be made in several areas of Cool-Ray's operations.

Based on Bruce Pope's survey of the sales force and his own judgment, Hugo estimated that 25 percent of Cool-Ray's inventory was unsalable because certain styles were out of fashion. He further estimated that 90 percent of the returned merchandise should be destroyed and not recycled (as had been the Cool-Ray practice) for the same reason. Although Cool-Ray held substantial inventory for delivery to customers the following year, it reported that sale of the merchandise had taken place in the present year. To offset what he thought was an excessive price increase, Hugo felt that prices might have to be decreased by 10 to 15 percent. Because most of next year's merchandise had already been delivered to the wholesalers and retailers, credit vouchers would have to be issued to them in order to realize such a price rebate.

Again drawing on the past experiences in Warner-Lambert, Hugo was apprehensive of the consequences of any move from a lengthy distribution channel (one with wholesalers or brokers between manufacturer and retailer) to a ''sell-direct'' policy. The wholesale trade would not be pleased by such a development.

Hugo was not certain if he had sufficient human resources in Warner-Lambert to accommodate Cool-Ray. There were promotional campaigns planned for next year to improve market share for several major brands such as Listerine. Considerable human resources and funds would be dedicated to these efforts. Furthermore, a staff group was studying the implications of the federal government's new Anti-Inflation Board (AIB), which was formed in October. The preliminary guidelines, as published in Canadian financial journals, called for firms to maintain their profit margins at no more than the percentage gross profit margin achieved during the last complete fiscal year.

Wage and price increases were limited to a maximum of 12 percent. Firms that achieved "unusual productivity gains" were expected to be allowed to keep the increased profit, although the interpretation of "unusual" was unknown. The AIB regulations did not seem to cover mergers or acquisitions.

If firms could allocate costs to individual products, price changes were expected to match cost changes. Firms that could not allocate costs to individual products were to price their products in such a way as to leave percentage pretax net profit margin no higher than 95 percent of their average percentage pretax net profit margin in the last five completed fiscal years.

Despite these obstacles, Hugo felt that Cool-Ray could benefit a great deal from Warner-Lambert control in Canada. By combining the Cool-Ray sales force with the sales force from either Consumer Products division or Adams Brands, Hugo felt that it would be possible to increase replacement sales by 50 percent and to expand distribution through new accounts and improve coverage of existing accounts. For example, he thought it possible to quadruple sales through food stores and to increase sales by 3 percent through other outlets. Such a combined sales force would eliminate the need for discounts to the wholesaler trade and virtually eliminate spiffs. To direct the entire Cool-Ray line, Hugo thought, a product manager would be required to assist the present sales manager. Exhibit 9 shows the structure of the Consumer Products and Adams Brands divisions.

Finally, Hugo turned to Bruce and said,

> We've really got to pull all this together—and fast! If I'm going to stand up in front of Steve (Mr. Wilgar, the president) and say that we should or should not acquire Cool-Ray, I'd better have some good reasons. Cool-Ray's profits are very large right now, and we could use that money to support our development of new brands. If I say that we should acquire Cool-Ray, Steve is going to want to know which division should handle it and where Cool-Ray is expected to go in the future. He's also going to want to know what we will be able to do to maintain Cool-Ray's profitability if we take it on.

EXHIBIT 9

A. Organization chart for the Consumer Products division

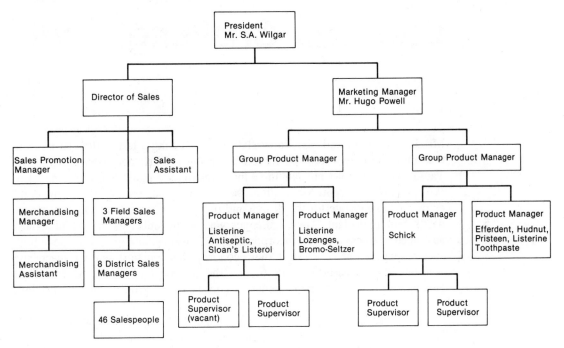

B. Organization chart for Adams Brands divisions

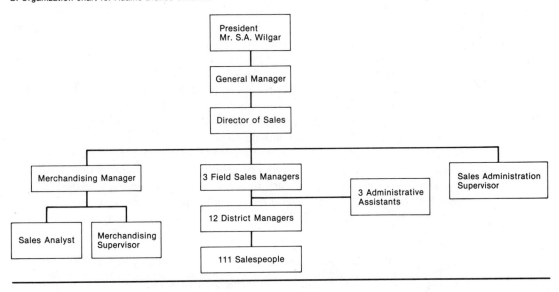

Case 43

Canadair Challenger Jet*

Mr. James Taylor and Mr. Harry Halton were taking a last-minute look at the marketing strategy developed for Canadair's new Challenger business jet. Mr. Taylor was head of Canadair Inc., the Challenger's marketing arm located in Westport, Connecticut. Mr. Halton, the executive vice president, was the chief engineer, responsible for the design and production of the Challenger at Canadair's Montreal plant. The Challenger was being touted as the world's most advanced business aircraft, incorporating the latest technologies to achieve high speed, longest range, greatest fuel economy, and greatest seating space and comfort. It was early July 1976, and the president of Canadair, Mr. Fred Kearns, wanted senior management's consensus on product design, pricing, advertising, and approach to selling.

The preliminary design of the Challenger was generally complete, but Mr. Halton continued to receive suggestions for additional features from Mr. Taylor and his marketing group, from prospective customers, and from project engineers. Rather than build prototype models by hand, Mr. Halton had decided to begin setting up a full-scale production line. Eventually, three preproduction models of the Challenger would be constructed for testing and demonstration.

Canadair management was considering a number of pricing options. Some executives advocated a very competitive initial price to hasten customer orders, with subsequent price increases. Another group of top executives believed that the Challenger should bear a premium price to reflect its superiority and to recover $140 million in development costs. The advertising agency's proposed copy for the Challenger's print advertisements was feared to be too controversial and the marketing group wondered whether some "softening" of the copy might be advisable. Selling direct to customers, selling direct to customers with a supplementary dealer network, or selling entirely through a dealer network were three possible approaches to sales. Finally, executives recognized that plans for service facilities required to maintain the Challenger "in the field," which could mean anywhere in the world, were very sketchy.

---

* This case was prepared by Mr. Larry Uniac, research assistant, under the direction of Professor Kenneth G. Hardy. Case material of the Western School of Business Administration is prepared as a basis for classroom discussion. Copyright © 1979, The University of Western Ontario.

Canadair executives wanted 50 orders by September 30, 1976, before committing fully to the Challenger program. However, the major marketing decisions had to be finalized before the sales blitz could begin. If sales by September 30 fell in the range of 30 to 40 units, management might grant an extension on the deadline. However, sales of fewer than 30 units probably would result in scrapping the Challenger program.

General Background

Canadair's objective was to sell 410 units, or 40 percent of the market for large business jets over the period from 1978 to 1988. Business jets were changing the way companies conducted business, as executives learned the competitive advantages that a corporate aircraft could provide. What critics had once scorned as a "toy of executive privilege" was increasingly seen as a desirable and advantageous management tool. "Probably more than ever, most businessmen agree with Arco's vice chairman Louis F. Davis, that 'there's nothing like face-to-face communications to keep a business running.' "[1] One observer commented:

> As big as corporate flying has become in recent years, there are strong signs that its role will continue to expand rapidly in years to come. Of the largest 1,000 U.S. companies, only 502 operate their own airplanes versus 416 five years ago. That leaves a sizable virgin market, which sales people from a dozen U.S. and foreign aircraft builders are tripping over each other to develop.[2]

Competitors were skeptical that the Challenger could meet its promised specifications. The unloaded Challenger would weigh only 15,085 pounds compared to 30,719 for the Grumman Gulfstream II (GII), a head-on competitor that was the biggest corporate jet flying, yet still provide a wider cabin. The Challenger would be propelled by less powerful engines than the GII, yet theoretically would fly faster and consume only 50 percent as much fuel. "The Canadians seem to know something the rest of the industry doesn't," commented Ivan E. Speer, group vice president of Aerospace at Garret Corp., the major builder of corporate jet engines.[3] The Challenger was to be powered by Avco-Lycoming engines, a competitor to the Garret Corp.

More simply, it was not known how well the Challenger would fly. Although Canadair had made jets for the military, the company had never built a business jet. Beyond these concerns, production problems could arise with a project of this nature and magnitude, but little could be done to anticipate how and when these problems would occur.

---

[1] "Corporate Flying: Changing the Way Companies Do Business," *Business Week*, February 6, 1978, p. 64.

[2] Ibid., p. 62.

[3] Ibid., p. 64.

Company Background

Originating as the aircraft division of Canadian Vickers Ltd. in the 1920s, Canadair assumed its own identity in 1944 following a reorganization brought about by the Canadian government. In 1947, Canadair was acquired by Electric Boat Company of Groton, Connecticut, forming the basis for an organization that became General Dynamics Corp. in 1952. Canadair reverted to Canadian government ownership in January 1976 under a government plan for restructuring the Canadian aerospace industry. In 1975, *Interavia* magazine described Canadair as follows: "Once a flourishing company, Canadair is the 'sick man' of the national aerospace industry; employment has steadily dropped since 1970, when 8,400 were on the books, and could fall below 1,000 sometime this year unless new work is found rapidly."[4]

However, uneven employment was characteristic of the entire aircraft industry. In terms of deliveries, quality, innovation, and steady profits, Canadair had an enviable record. Located at Cartierville Airport in St. Laurent, Quebec, approximately 10 miles from the center of Montreal, the plant was one of the largest and most versatile aerospace-manufacturing facilities in Canada. Canadair's activities included the design and development of new aircraft, and contracting for major modifications to existing types of aircraft. Subcontracts for the manufactured component parts and subassemblies for military and commercial aircraft in production such as the Boeing 747 accounted for a substantial volume of the company's business (Table 1). Exhibit 1 supplies data on earnings for Canadair from 1973 to 1976. Canadair's President reflected on the activities of the company:

> We at Canadair are not really known as a major influence in the international aerospace industry. For various reasons, we have been a major subcontractor or producer of other people's aircraft over a large span of our existence, and our native designs have not been more than a small portion of our overall effort. You may imagine that the elder statesmen of the aerospace industry smiled indulgently when they heard about this radical new aircraft that Canadair was developing.

TABLE 1 Canadair's estimated sales from 1973 through 1976 by class of business

	1976		1975		1974		1973	
	Dollars (000)	Per-cent	Dollars (000)	Per-cent	Dollars (000)	Per-cent	Dollars (000)	Per-cent
Aircraft	20,410	46	15,520	42	38,808	68	22,006	63
Component subcontracts	7,783	17	6,716	18	2,945	5	2,967	9
Surveillance systems	9,367	21	6,958	19	9,620	17	8,542	25
Other	7,034	16	7,938	21	5,744	10	1,113	3
Total	44,954	100%	37,132	100%	57,117	100%	34,628	100%

---

[4] *Interavia*, February 1975, p. 150.

EXHIBIT 1

CANADAIR LIMITED AND SUBSIDIARIES
Consolidated Statement of Income
($000)

	Year Ended December 31			
	1976*	1975	1974	1973
Sales	$44,594	$37,132	$57,117	$34,628
Cost of sales	41,325	42,421	53,264	31,702
Income (loss) from operations	3,269	(5,289)	3,853	2,926
Other income (expense):				
Interest income	240	260	248	356
Miscellaneous income	9	30	61	71
Interest expense	(2,056)	(3,203)	(1,755)	(1,001)
	(1,807)	(2,913)	(1,446)	(574)
Income (loss) from operations before provision for income taxes, loss on discontinued operations of a subsidiary, extraordinary items and share of earnings of Asbestos Corporation Limited	1,462	(8,202)	2,407	2,352
Provisions for federal and provincial income taxes	642	6	1,122	1,056
Income (loss) before loss on discontinued operations of a subsidiary, extraordinary items and share of earnings of Asbestos Corporation Limited	820	(8,208)	1,285	1,296
Loss on discontinued operations of a subsidiary	(385)	(165)	(260)	(280)
Income (loss) before extraordinary items and share of earnings of Asbestos Corporation Limited	435	(8,373)	1,025	1,016
Extraordinary items:				
Income tax reduction	638	—	1,100	1,041
Gain on exchange	—	1,957	—	—
Provision for disposal of a subsidiary company's assets	(988)	—	—	—
Total extraordinary items	(350)	1,957	1,100	1,041
Income (loss) before share of earnings of Asbestos Corporation Limited	85	(6,416)	2,125	2,057
Share of earnings of Asbestos Corporation Limited	—	7,368	6,063	520
Net income	$ 85	$ 952	$ 8,188	$ 2,577

Consolidated Statement of Earned Surplus (deficit—$000)

	Year Ended December 31			
	1976*	1975	1974	1973
Balance at beginning of year	$(14,059)	$ 49,683	$41,495	$38,918
Net income	85	952	8,188	2,577
	(13,974)	50,635	49,683	41,495
Dividend paid	—	25,000	—	—
Unrecovered portion of investment in Asbestos Corporation Limited, representing the excess of carrying value over the amount paid by General Dynamics Corporation	—	39,694	—	—
	—	64,694	—	—
Balance at end of year	$(13,974)	$(14,059)	$49,683	$41,495

* Estimated results for 1976.

The Canadian Aerospace Industry[5]

The Canadian aerospace-manufacturing industry had specialized capabilities for the design, research and development, production, marketing, and in-plant repair and overhaul of aircraft aero-engines, aircraft and engine subsystems and components, space-related equipment and air and ground-based avionic systems and components.

Approximately 100 companies were engaged in significant manufacturing work, but 40 companies accounted for 90 percent of the industry's sales in 1975. Three companies (including Canadair) were fully integrated, having the capability to design, develop, manufacture, and market complete aircraft or aero-engines. With aggregate sales of $785 million in 1976, the Canadian aerospace industry shared fifth place in western world sales with Japan, after the United States, France, the United Kingdom, and the Federal Republic of Germany.

It was economically impractical for Canadian industry to manufacture all the diverse aerospace products demanded on the Canadian market. Through selective specialization, the Canadian industry had developed product lines in areas related to Canadian capabilities and export-market penetration. In 1975, 80 percent of the industry's sales were in export markets, an achievement attained under strong competitive conditions.

The Canadian industry was fully exposed to the competitive forces of the international aerospace market. In some cases, its hourly labour rates were higher than those in the United States. The industry's export-market penetration was vulnerable to the economic forces associated with competitor's industrial-productivity improvements. The industry, like most world aerospace industries, was manufacturing high-cost and high-risk products. There were many hazards: a relatively long-term payback cycle, sporadic government purchasing decisions, tariff and nontariff barriers, monetary inflation, and rapid technological obsolescence.

Aerospace industries throughout the world generally received government support, particularly in the areas of research, development, and equipment modernization. For example, the U.S. aircraft industry benefitted from the annual $10 billion Department of Defense budget and the annual $6 billion NASA budget. By contrast, during the nine years ended March 31, 1976, the Government of Canada had provided $349 million to the Canadian aerospace industry through several programs. In short, the Canadian aircraft industry was not subsidized.

There were indications in 1976 that the Canadian aerospace industry was entering a growth cycle. The trend lines of Canadian sales and exports encouraged an optimistic outlook.

---

[5] Source: Chairman D. C. Lowe, *A Report by the Sector Task Force on the Canadian Aerospace Industry,* June 30, 1978.

The Business Jet Industry

Continued expansion of business-aircraft activities was expected to continue into the 1980s in what business aviation officials described as the "best growth climate in years."[6] Booming sales of business aircraft in Europe, the Middle East, and Africa were giving rise to a belief that the business aircraft was becoming a true business tool in these regions, much as it had in the United States about a decade earlier.

All forecasts pointed to an enormous upsurge in the sale of business jet aircraft. Exhibit 2 graphs the trends in the U.S. business jet industry from 1956 to an estimate of 1976 and beyond. Exhibit 3 illustrates the trends in world deliveries of all corporate aircraft from 1965 to 1975, with delivery estimates through 1981. Many factors were contributing to increase the desire for private business aircraft:

> Commercial airlines were reducing service drastically as they added the "jumbo" jets. In six years, the number of U.S. cities served by commercial airlines dropped from 525 to 395.

EXHIBIT 2 Growth trends in U.S. business flying (semilog paper)

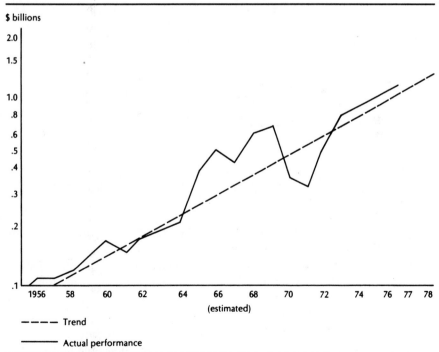

Source: *Aviation Week and Space Technology.*

---

[6] *Aviation Week and Space Technology,* September 11, 1978, pp. 46–56.

EXHIBIT 3 Unit worldwide corporate jet deliveries (all models)

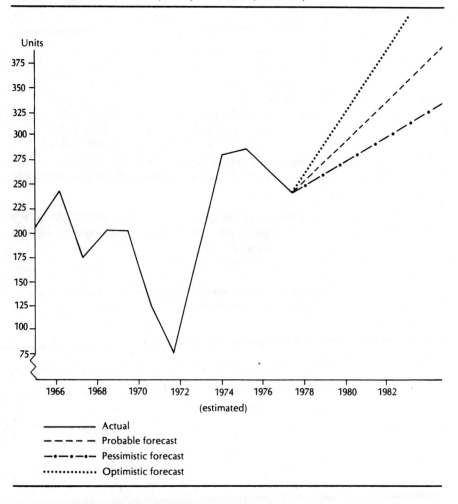

———————— Actual
— — — — — Probable forecast
—•—•—•— Pessimistic forecast
•••••••••••• Optimistic forecast

Ninety-seven percent of all scheduled-air-carrier passengers in the United States flew out of only 150 airports.

Flights were packed with tourists and other occasional travelers. This made it difficult to obtain reservations and impossible to work en route. The amount of executive time spent traveling was increasing and most of this travel time was being wasted.

Corporate planes provided the management of many companies with new flexibility and shortened reaction time in special situations.

Cost savings could be achieved; for example, Xerox flew 15,000 employees per year on a company-owned shuttle plane between its Stamford headquarters and its Rochester (N.Y.) plant, saving $410,000 annually over commercial air fares.

There was growing concern for the security and protection of top executives from the growing incidence of airplane hijackings.

Finally many organizations were trading up to newer or larger aircraft to replace outdated, older equipment. Essentially, technology permitted such improvements over the aircraft of 10 years earlier (for example in fuel economy) that the buyers could easily justify the update.

To cash in on the business jet bonanza, several manufacturers were planning to introduce new models. The following business jets would be on the market in some fashion by 1979:

Canadair's Challenger (large category).

Dassault-Breguet Falcon 50 (medium category).

Grumman Gulfstream III (large category).

Rockwell's Sabreliner 80A (medium category).

Cessna's Citation III (medium category).

Gates Learjet's 54/55/56 series (medium category).

Corporate Aircraft Categories

More than 100 different aircraft models were offered to the business flyer.[7] Hence, the selection of the right aircraft for an individual company was a complex task. John Pope, Secretary of the National Business Aircraft Association, emphasized this advice: "Any aircraft selected involves a compromise, because the worst error you can make is buying more aircraft than you need and underutilizing it."[8] The general categories in order of performance and price were: single-engine piston, multiengine piston, turboprop, turbojet, and turbofan.

> Single-engine piston aircraft, while not usually considered "corporate," did provide starting points for many smaller companies, as well as individuals who combined business and pleasure flying. . . . Multiengine piston aircraft were the next step up, offering the additional security and performance afforded by a second engine. . . . Piston-engine twins were considered excellent entry-level aircraft for smaller corporations, with a relatively high percentage owner-flown. . . . Turboprop aircraft were referred to by some as "turbojets with propellers attached.". . . Turboprops used significantly less fuel than pure jets but could easily cost more than $1 million.[9]

Turbojet and turbofan aircraft flew faster and, for the most part, farther than the other aircraft. A turbojet was not usually a first-time purchase for a smaller company. Prices in this category ranged from $1 million to $7.5 million. The turbofans offered greater low-altitude efficiency than the turbojets. The Challenger, JetStar II, Falcon 50, GII, and GIII were turbofans.

---

[7] "Corporate Aviation: The Competitive Edge," *Dun's Review*, January 1979, p. 89.

[8] Ibid.

[9] Ibid.

The following rules of thumb were often used to determine the suitability of different planes for different flying needs:

Average distance per flight	Appropriate type of aircraft for this distance
150– 200 miles	Single-engine piston
200– 500 miles	Multiengine piston and smaller turboprop
500– 750 miles	Turboprops and small turbojets
750–1,000 miles	Small turbojets
1,000–2,000 miles	Medium-size turbojets
2,000–4,000 miles	Large turbofans and large turbojets

Corporate Jet Competition

The Falcon 50, Gulfstream II and III, and JetStar II seemed to compete directly against the Challenger. Exhibit 4 summarizes sales by segment and model from 1965 to 1975. A schematic layout of each competitive plane is shown in Exhibits 5 and 6. Exhibit 7 compares the salient product differences for the Challenger and its competitors.

EXHIBIT 4 Worldwide corporate jet deliveries (units)

Model	1965	1966	1967	1968	1969	1970	1971	1972	1973	1974	1975	1976 prices (000s)
Small jet market												
Citation 1								52	81	85	69	$ 918
Falcon									1	21	26	1,905
Lear 23	80	18	1									—
Lear 24		24	26	28	33	20	10	16	21	22	18	—
Lear 25				18	25	18	10	23	45	40	14	1,315
Lear 35/36										4	47	1,679
Hansa			3	6	14	4	1	1	5			—
Sabre 40	26	31	5	5	1	6						—
Corvette										6	5	—
Westwind #1151/52/54	30	50	25	10	12	5	4	11	12	12	4	—
Total small jets	136	123	60	67	85	53	29	103	165	190	183	
Medium jet market												
Hawker Siddely 125	43	58	20	32	39	32	18	24	24	25	13	2,075
Sabre 60			11	20	14	6	9	4	4	20	9	2,200
Sabre 75								6	1	10	19	2,406
Falcon 20	14	43	63	38	25	18	7	24	46	17	29	3,005
Total medium jets	87	101	94	90	78	56	34	60	75	72	70	
Large jet market												
JetStar	18	22	18	18	11	2	4	10	6	1	0	5,035
Gulfstream			2	35	36	17	14	14	17	18	20	5,500
Total large jets	18	22	20	53	47	19	18	24	23	19	20	
Grand total	211	246	174	210	210	128	77	194	284	290	273	

EXHIBIT 5 Cabin floor outline

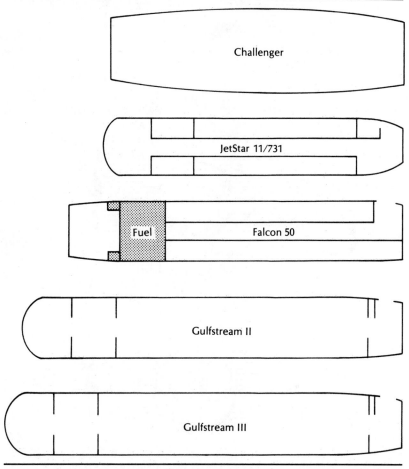

Note: Challenger data based on engineering statistical analysis. For performance guarantees see Technical Specification.

The new Dassault-Breguet Falcon 50, with its flight testing scheduled for completion by October 1978 and certification expected in December 1978, was slightly ahead of the Challenger program. The Challenger would probably not be certified until August 1979. Flight tests of the Falcon 50 had shown that its performance figures were better than expected in terms of landing strip required and rate of climb. The Falcon 50 was essentially a modification of the medium-sized Falcon 20, which had been introduced 14 years earlier.

The new Falcon 50 would be available for delivery by March 1979 and its performance in terms of projected operating cost per mile and range was second only to the Challenger. The print advertisement for the Falcon 50 claimed that it would be the fastest business jet in the world, although this statement was

EXHIBIT 6

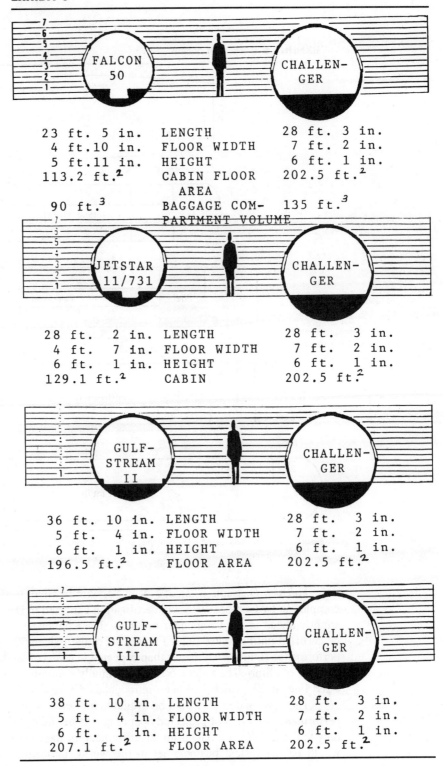

23 ft. 5 in.	LENGTH	28 ft. 3 in.
4 ft. 10 in.	FLOOR WIDTH	7 ft. 2 in.
5 ft. 11 in.	HEIGHT	6 ft. 1 in.
113.2 ft.^{2}	CABIN FLOOR AREA	202.5 ft.^{2}
90 ft.^{3}	BAGGAGE COMPARTMENT VOLUME	135 ft.^{3}

28 ft. 2 in.	LENGTH	28 ft. 3 in.
4 ft. 7 in.	FLOOR WIDTH	7 ft. 2 in.
6 ft. 1 in.	HEIGHT	6 ft. 1 in.
129.1 ft.^{2}	CABIN	202.5 ft.^{2}

36 ft. 10 in.	LENGTH	28 ft. 3 in.
5 ft. 4 in.	FLOOR WIDTH	7 ft. 2 in.
6 ft. 1 in.	HEIGHT	6 ft. 1 in.
196.5 ft.^{2}	FLOOR AREA	202.5 ft.^{2}

38 ft. 10 in.	LENGTH	28 ft. 3 in.
5 ft. 4 in.	FLOOR WIDTH	7 ft. 2 in.
6 ft. 1 in.	HEIGHT	6 ft. 1 in.
207.1 ft.^{2}	FLOOR AREA	202.5 ft.^{2}

EXHIBIT 7 Comparative specifications

| | Operating cost per nautical mile | Maximum range | Cruising speed | Fuel consumption 100 nm at cruise speed | Noise decibles* | | |
					Take-off	Sideline	Approach
Challenger†	$ .93	3,900 nm.	547 mph	4,160 lb.	78	87	90
JetStar II	$1.25	2,800 nm.	538 mph	7,250 lb.	n.a.	n.a.	n.a.
Gulfstream III	$1.16	3,600 nm.	534 mph	6,410 lb.	90	102	98
Gulfstream II	$1.26	3,187 nm.	541 mph	7,723 lb.	90	102	98
Falcon 50	$1.06	3,550 nm.	528 mph	6,200 lb.	87	94	97

* 1979 FAA 36 Regulation = Take-off: 89, Sideline: 94, and Approach: 98.

† Initial proposal for first 50 units.

Source: Canadair comparative advertising material (based on statistical analysis).

disputed by the calculations made by Canadair engineers. Messrs. Halton and Taylor believed that the Falcon 50 would be around for some time, although its fuel consumption would be a major competitive disadvantage.

Gulfstream II and III

The Gulfstream II first flew in October 1966 and represented the latest technology at the time of its certification. Its turbojet engines were powerful, but consumed considerably more fuel than used in the more recent high-bypass turbofans used by the Challenger. In addition, engine noise was high both inside and outside the cabin. Since 1966, 173 Gulfstream IIs had been sold around the world.

Grumman had accelerated developmental work on a new Gulfstream III to replace the Gulfstream II in response to new demands on the market and the news of the Challenger. The Gulfstream III would be an aerodynamically modified version of the Gulfstream II, but it would use the same engines. The first prototype of the Gulfstream III was scheduled for completion in August 1979 and the first production unit was scheduled for delivery in March 1980. A print advertisement showing the Gulfstream III is shown in Exhibit 8.

JetStar II

The JetStar II, available since January 1976, was a re-engineered version of the original JetStar which had been certificated in 1961. Although the new engines of the JetStar were turbofans, they were medium-bypass fans and not as efficient as high-bypass fans in minimizing fuel consumption. More than 112 JetStars had been sold since 1961.

According to a company spokesman, Lockheed-Georgia anticipated no new changes to its JetStar II in order to meet forthcoming competition from the Challenger, Falcon 50, and Gulfstream III. Lockheed was still attempting to determine its market share in the larger-cabin business fleet, with the performance and acceptance of the three new aircraft still unknown. JetStar IIs were being built at the rate of one per month and the earliest promised delivery date was June 1978.[10]

The Challenger Program

Early in 1976, much of Canadair's subcontract work was nearing completion, and Canadair was not selling enough of its own CL-25 water bombers to fill the gap. Canadair executives needed an ambitious project if they were to meet government demands for eventual self-sufficiency. Mr. Halton commented:

> We knew that we needed to do something in the general-aviation business and a market-research study indicated that business aviation would be a growth market.

---

[10] *Aviation Week and Space Technology*, September 11, 1978.

EXHIBIT 8 Gulfstream III ad

The faster the Gulfstream III flies, the farther behind it leaves every other executive jet.

If you drive any kind of vehicle, you know that speed impacts how far it's going to travel. Automobiles or airplanes, the law is the same: the higher the speed, the shorter the range.

For example, the long range cruise speed of the Gulfstream III is Mach .77, or about 510 mph. At that speed, the Gulfstream III has an NBAA IFR range of 4,205 statute miles.

That's more than enough range for the Gulfstream III to fly non-stop routinely between London and New York in about 8 hours with at least 8 passengers and baggage. (No other executive jet can do that.)

Boost the cruise speed of the Gulfstream III to its maximum—Mach .85, or over 560 mph—and its NBAA IFR range becomes 3,226 statute miles with the same payload.

That's still enough range to fly at least 8 people at *top speed* from Boston to London or between any two airports in the continental United States in less than 6 hours. (No other executive jet can do that, either. The fact is, the Gulfstream III can fly more people farther faster than any executive jet.)

But we're not advocating speed.

We're talking about *productivity*.

The Gulfstream III offers such unique flexibility in trade-offs between speed, range and payload that it can fly virtually any kind of mission—and do it with optimum productivity.

At a time when the world's businesses are placing increased emphasis on maximizing every investment, it is little wonder that the thoroughly proven Gulfstream III continues to dominate the market for long-range executive transports.

If you are planning for the acquisition of an aircraft that can help make your organization more effective and productive, now is the time to look into the Gulfstream III.

A full-scale demonstration of this remarkable airplane on one of your upcoming business trips at home or abroad could shape your thinking about business jets for years to come.

The man to talk to is Charles G. Vogeley, Senior Vice President of Gulfstream Marketing. Call him at (912) 964-3274; or write to him at Gulfstream American Corporation, P.O. Box 2206, Savannah, Georgia 31402 U.S.A.

He can show you why the Gulfstream III continues to leave its challengers farther and farther behind.

The Gulfstream III. The Ultimate.

Gulfstream American
Member GAMA

In November 1975, Fred Kearns talked with Bill Lear about his concept of an advanced business aircraft based on two known pieces of technology, the supercritical wing used on military aircraft and the high-bypass fanjet engine. In January 1976, I met with Bill Lear and by March 1976 we were negotiating options on the Lear design. Jim Taylor was hired in April 1976 to head up the marketing for the new aircraft and by May he had arranged a selling seminar to which he invited 200 chief pilots and senior corporate officers to Canadair's plant to unveil the Challenger concept.

Bill Lear, who built the first business jet in 1961, had developed the original concept of the Challenger around an 88-inch diameter fuselage. Representatives of the business market for the jet responded to the design encouragingly. However, Canadair decided to change the rear design drastically for a number of reasons, one of them a fuel-tankage problem. Also, at the original meeting with 200 chief pilots and executive officers, potential customers expressed demands for roominess. Consequently, Canadair engineers redesigned the jet with a 106-inch fuselage. As it happened, the extra width made the plane capable of seating four abreast. Lear disassociated himself from the Challenger program in response to this change and dubbed the Canadair design "Fat Albert." Canadair executives recognized the possibility of creating a "stretch" version of the Challenger that perhaps could carry up to 50 passengers.

It was clear at the beginning of 1976 that in order to finance the project, at least $70 million would have to be raised in addition to the company's own $70 million. Projects with this degree of leverage were not uncommon in the aerospace industry and the Canadian government agreed to *guarantee* a $70-million Eurobond for Canadair. A forecast schedule of investment outlays is shown in Exhibit 9.

The Challenger's most salient product benefits as conceived by Canadair's marketing and engineering staff were:

Large wide-body cabin: excellent size for executive, air taxi, third-level carriers, and cargo.

Fuel economy: lowest operating cost per nautical mile compared with direct competition.

Long range: long single-stage flight or numerous short-stage flights without refueling.

Competitive speeds: very competitive, high cruise speed in long-range configuration.

Low noise levels: most closely meets FAA standards for 1979.

Market forecast

Canadair was already building a test model for fatigue tests, a test model for static tests, and three preproduction models for the eventual production plan which would be as follows:

EXHIBIT 9

CL 600 CHALLENGER

Pro Forma* Cash Flow Profile as of June 1976

($000)

	Sept. 76–Dec. 79 not assignable	Dec. 77–Oct. 80 lot #1 aircraft 1–50	Apr. 79–Aug. 81 lot #2 aircraft 51–100	Feb. 80–Apr. 82 lot #3 aircraft 101–150	Oct. 80–Jan. 83 lot #4 aircraft 151–200	Jul. 81–Dec. 83 lot #5 aircraft 200–250	Total
Labor, overhead cost	$ 86,400	$ 72,460	$ 28,350	$ 26,350	$ 24,980	$ 25,315	$ 264,855
Material, equipment cost	20,925	81,148	94,970	107,450	113,045	126,100	543,638
Other costs (rentals, service)	21,600	17,550	925	713	760	750	42,298
Program support cost	6,075	18,936	10,440	11,100	12,784	14,475	73,810
Marketing		5,030	2,744	2,938	3,390	3,836	17,938
Finance		31,326	10,700				42,026
Total cost	$135,000	$226,450	$149,129	$148,551	$154,959	$170,476	$ 984,565
Revenue		$205,000	$225,500	$238,500	$253,000	$268,000	$1,190,000
Cumulative	$(135,000)	$(156,450)	$(80,079)	$ 9,870	$107,911	$205,435	$ 205,435
Date #1 aircraft ordered		Jul. 76					
Anticipated date last aircraft ordered		Nov. 76					
Delivery date #1 aircraft		Nov. 79	Apr. 78	Oct. 79	Apr. 81	Oct. 82	
Anticipated date last aircraft delivered		Sept. 80	Aug. 81	June 82	May 83	Apr. 84	
Assumed average price per aircraft		4,100	$4,510	$4,770	$5,060	$5,360	$4,750

* This data is presented for case study purposes only and does not purport to represent actual estimating data.

1979— 6 units
1980—50 units
1981—80 units

The first test unit was expected to fly by April 1978 and the preproduction models were to be available for delivery by the end of 1979. This production plan was adopted in response to an analysis of the market trends for this category. Table 2 traces the market history of jet sales in the medium and large categories.

TABLE 2 Market history (units): Sales of medium and large size jets (Gulfstream II, JetStar, Falcon 20, HS 125)

1966:	123	1971:	43
1967:	103	1972:	72
1968:	123	1973:	93
1969:	111	1974:	62
1970:	69	1975:	51

10-year total: 850 units

The United States was the major market for corporate aircraft. Table 3 summarizes the geographic distribution of corporate-aircraft sales during 1966–1975:

TABLE 3 Distribution of sales, 1966–1975 (all corporate planes)

	Units	Percent
North America	565	66.5
Europe	189	22.2
Central and South America	25	2.9
Asia	24	2.8
Africa	37	4.4
Oceania	10	1.2
	850	100.0

On the basis of this history, Canadair's marketing staff first calculated pessimistic, probable, and optimistic worldwide sales forecasts for the medium and large jet category from 1978 to 1988, judged to be the Challenger's sales life (Table 4).

Canadair executives then narrowed this down to a forecast for Challenger sales only (Table 5).

The most-probable-sales estimate for this period represented a 40 percent share of the probable world market during 1978–88. In the midterm, Canadair

TABLE 4 Worldwide business-jet sales forecast, 1978–1988
(Challenger category, executive configuration only)

	Pessimistic	Probable	Optimistic
North America	600	625	675
Europe	200	225	275
Central and South America	25	40	65
Asia	25	40	65
Africa	50	75	95
Oceania	10	15	20
	910	1,020	1,195

TABLE 5 Challenger sales forecast, 1978–1988 (executive
configuration only)

	Pessimistic	Probable	Optimistic
North America	150	250	300
Europe	55	80	105
Central and South America	15	20	25
Asia	15	25	35
Africa	20	30	50
Oceania	5	5	10
	260	410	525

executives could consider a stretched version of the Challenger for the commuter and freight market. Adding this version would raise the probable forecast to 560 units, the pessimistic to 333, and optimistic to 750 units. The average variable cost per unit for the first two hundred units was projected to be $4.1 million per jet but variable costs per unit were expected to show some improvement because of the experience curve effect after the first 200 jets. Exhibit 9 shows a pro forma cash flow for the first 250 Challengers that might be produced. No cost or investment data had been generated on the stretched Challenger model.

Pricing

The marketing staff had prepared several pricing options for the Challenger. It was necessary to finalize pricing for the first 50 orders and work out a *general* pricing plan for the rest of the projected sales. Exhibit 10 contains data on the existing competitive prices and the marketing staff's best estimate of future pricing moves by the competition.

One pricing option for the first 50 orders was to undercut the competition by $1.2 million, setting the price at $4.1 million per Challenger. To some executives, a $1.2 million discount seemed large for such a superior product, even though the Challenger had flown only "on paper." They pointed out that all new aircraft faced this issue of confidence and that most buyers understood the process of designing an all-new aircraft and the process of gearing up a volume

EXHIBIT 10 Expected pricing movement in the large-jet market ($000)

	1976 current price*	Expected BCA price†							
		1977	1978	1979	1980	1981	1982	1983	1984
Challenger‡	$4,100								
JetStar II	5,345	$5,195	$5,611	$6,057	$6,544	$7,068	$7,633	$8,244	$8,900
Gulfstream III	6,200	?	—	—	—	—	—	—	—
Gulfstream II	5,500	5,900	6,354	6,844	7,371	7,938	8,549	9,208	9,910
Falcon 50	5,750	5,750	5,750	5,750	6,153	6,583	7,044	7,537	8,060

* Average BCA equipped prices.
† Smith and Taylor were less certain of pricing activity after 1980.
‡ Initial proposal for first 50 units.
Source: Company records.

production system. Because the breakeven volume under the low-price option was larger than the probable-sales forecast, the price was expected to rise after the first 50 orders.

Alternatively, the Challenger could be priced at parity with the competition. In this case, the price would probably increase in step with inflation and the pricing of competitive products.

Some executives suggested that the Challenger's superior product characteristics required a premium price even in the short run. They believed that the Challenger could maintain a premium over competitive prices in the long run.

The purchase price for each Challenger would include training for captains, maintenance training for mechanics, programmed maintenance assistance from Montreal, and service and support from any of the three planned service facilities. Bill Lear, who had done the initial Challenger design, would receive 5 percent of the *sale* price of the first 50 units sold, 4 percent on the second 50, and 3 percent on all orders beyond the first hundred.

The following terms of purchase were proposed:

1. Each customer would be required to make a 5 percent deposit for each plane ordered. All deposits would be placed in escrow with accrued interest at the Canadian prime rate (10 percent in 1976).
2. One year before delivery, the customer would pay 30 percent of the purchase price.
3. Six months before delivery, the customer would pay 30 percent again.
4. The customer would pay the final 35 percent of the purchase price upon delivery.

Service

After-sale service was an important purchase criterion for the customer. Canadair executives tentatively had decided to build three factory-owned service centres which would service only Challengers. Their cost, $4.5 million each, was included in the planned $140 million investment. One centre would be located in Hartford, Connecticut, where Canadair's U.S. sales office was located, one in the southwestern United States, and one in Europe. The selection of these locations was based on the projection that these areas would provide the majority of Challenger sales. Only technical personnel would operate from these facilities.

The service facilities would have to be completed in time to service the first jets as they were sold at the end of 1979. Canadair would have to service early Challenger buyers very well to enhance its credibility and improve sales prospects. There was some concern at Canadair about whether factory-owned centres were the best way to provide service. Some corporate jet manufacturers such as Gulfstream and Hawker-Siddely utilized service distributors. Hence, the 200 Hawker-Siddely 125s in the United States were serviced by a distributor network of 14 outlets. This method of servicing, if chosen by Canadair, would eliminate the $4.5 million investment in each service facility, but because the Challenger was technically more advanced than its competition, special in-house expertise might offer certain advantages and would not require handing over technical information to distributors who serviced competitive aircraft.

Advertising and Promotion

The advertising and promotion budget for the Challenger program in 1976 was set at about $2.5 million. Because the Challenger was a new and unproven airplane, the marketing staff and its advertising agency had decided to mount a print advertising campaign in the leading technical and business magazines to support the sales force's personal selling activities. Domestic and international advertising campaigns were planned for journals such as *Professional Pilot, Business Week, Business and Commercial Aviation, Interavia,* and *The Wall Street Journal.* All of the Challenger's competitors advertised in these journals, trying to reach the executive in charge of purchasing a business jet and the pilot who would be flying the jet.

To achieve high readability scores for their advertising, Canadair executives were prepared to use a bold, confident, and "challenging" theme. Examples of the proposed advertisements are shown as Exhibits 11, 12 and 13. This copy differed markedly from what the competition typically employed. Of the total advertising and promotion budget, $625,000 was to be allocated to print advertising.

Studying the competition's advertising copy, Mr. Taylor sensed that the competition had already begun to react to the Challenger program. This was particularly evident in the Gulfstream II and JetStar II advertisements. Still, the Canadair marketing group was worried that its own bold campaign could backfire and damage the credibility of the Challenger by taking pot shots at the competition, especially when the Challenger had no flight tests to back it up. If their theme proved inappropriate, they could quickly develop other themes and

EXHIBIT 11

This business jet design is so advanced, it's making the competition airsick.

Enter the Canadair Challenger. Not just another business jet, but the first new concept in business jets in about 20 years.

And we're not just saying that with empty words. We're sending forth this solid challenge:

We challenge any business jet to fly as fast.

We challenge any business jet to offer as much range.

We challenge any business jet to fly as efficiently.

We challenge any business jet to match our wide-body comfort.

And now, we'd like to plunge into some specifics, demonstrating why our competition is feeling a bit queasy at the moment.

The Challenger challenges the JetStar II.

The Challenger is really much more of a star than the JetStar II. It will carry 17% less fuel, yet travel 1,400 statute miles further.

The Challenger will be faster, quieter, 40% less expensive to operate. As well as a sprawling 25 inches wider.

The Challenger challenges the Falcon 50.

Compared to the Challenger, the Falcon 50 is a bird of a different feather. The Challenger will fly up to 35 mph faster (New York to Los Angeles in 5 hours and 11 minutes).

The Challenger will also fly 1,000 miles further, be quieter, and burn 20% less fuel while doing so. And as for the inside story, the Challenger will have 42% more cabin volume than the Falcon 50, and 76% more baggage space.

The Challenger challenges the Gulfstream II.

The Challenger will carry 40% less fuel, yet travel 900 miles further.

The Challenger will be about ½ less expensive to operate.

And the Challenger will be easy to take in still another way. Noise. We'll be significantly quieter than the Gulfstream II. And because we'll be 10 inches wider, we'll even challenge their cabin for passenger comfort and room.

How we're meeting the challenge.

We're meeting the challenge of the Challenger by discarding the hand-me-down technology that the competition uses.

Our business jet will incorporate the most sophisticated and proven technology currently available.

That includes the Lycoming ALF-502 turbofan with a 5 to 1 high bypass ratio. Its power will provide us with the best thrust-to-weight relationship of any commercially obtainable plane.

We also bring you a new wing. An advanced, yet proven, airfoil concept that will delay the formation of shock waves.

So prepare yourself for this shock: we'll not be just faster than any business jet, we'll be faster than a DC-10.

The company that's behind all this is Canadair, makers of over 3,800 aircraft, 580 supersonic.

For more information on the Challenger, formerly known by the drawing board name LearStar, write to Jim Taylor at Canadair Inc., Dept. T, 274 Riverside Avenue, Westport, Conn. 06880. Or call him at (203) 226-1581.

You'll become convinced that the Challenger, the business jet that's making the competition airsick, can be a very healthy investment for your company.

canadair challenger
We challenge any business jet to match it.

*All performance figures in this advertisement for CHALLENGER are based upon wind tunnel tests and engineering statistical analysis with flight testing to begin in early 1978.

EXHIBIT 12

Our competition wastes a lot of energy. And they'll be wasting a lot more when they try to explain these figures.

On a 1,000 nautical mile trip, the *challenger* will burn:

- **36% less fuel than a JetStar II.**
- **45% less fuel than a Gulfstream II.**
- **20% less fuel than a Falcon 50.**
- **11% less fuel than a Falcon 20F.**

These are the numbers that add up to trouble for the competition.

The numbers that prove the Challenger will be the business jet that not only outperforms all the rest, but outconserves all the rest of the full-cabin business jets.

The environment will save. You will save. And with fuel costs taking off even faster than a Challenger, we don't have to tell you what the savings will be.

Our economy isn't a con.

The same engine that will let us go so fast (Montreal to London in 5 hours, 29 minutes) is also what will use up our fuel so slowly. It's the Lycoming ALF-502 turbofan with a 5 to 1 high bypass ratio. This design means exceptional fuel efficiency.

So does our new wing. An advanced configuration that will delay the formation of shock waves. So drag, which is such a drag, won't drag as much. And lift will be lifted. So the Challenger will fly faster, further, and more economically than any other business jet.*

Our economy will also apply to maintenance. The Challenger's engine is fully modular for on-airframe servicing. Meaning our engine is a snap to fix. You won't be paying $1,000 for labor to replace a $50 part.

Tomorrow's plane without yesterday's technology.

Scratch the twenty-year-old technology the competition embraces. The Challenger is being built from scratch.

Incorporating all the latest proven aspects of both design and technology.

Even our cabin is a big idea. The Challenger will be the first wide-body business jet. Almost a full foot wider than any other, and two spacious feet wider than most.

Now who's behind all this, you ask? Canadair. Canadair has built over 3,800 aircraft, 580 supersonic.

There's much more detailed information on the Challenger, formerly known by the drawing board name LearStar, and Jim Taylor has it. Write to him at Canadair, Dept. T, P.O. Box 6087, Montreal, Canada H3C3G9. Or call him at (514) 744-1511.

He'll spend all the time you need talking about the plane that will expend so little energy.

canadair challenger
We challenge any business jet to match it.

*All performance figures in this advertisement for CHALLENGER are based upon wind tunnel tests and engineering statistical analysis with flight testing to begin in early 1978.

EXHIBIT 13

Finally, the first new concept in business jets in twenty years. The Canadair Challenger. We hereby challenge any business jet to match it.

The Canadair Challenger is the class business jet that's in a class by itself.

Respectfully dismissing twenty-year-old technology, it's being built from scratch.

In fact, the engineering of this aircraft is so brilliantly eclectic that it lets us hurl forth the Canadair Challenger Challenge.

We challenge any business jet to fly as fast.*

We challenge them to offer as much range.*

We challenge them to fly as efficiently.

We challenge them to match our wide-body comfort.

And now we'd like to tell you just how we've engineered the best business jet yet.

We bring you a new wing.

Our newly designed wing is why the Challenger will outperform all the rest. This advanced configuration delays shock waves. So drag, which is such a drag, doesn't drag as much. And lift is lifted. What's more, the wing weighs less. The result:

The Challenger can fly from Montreal to London in 5 hours and 29 minutes. Faster than a 747!

*Guaranteed speed and range.

Room to move while you're moving.

Stretch your legs and stoop no more —the Challenger is the first wide-body business jet. Almost a full foot wider than all the rest. With six feet of headroom and a flat floor.

The Lycoming ALF. It's the best engine going.

The Challenger's engine is the Lycoming ALF 502 Turbofan with a 5 to 1 high bypass ratio. (These fans make the Challenger efficient.) On a 1,000 nautical-mile trip it will burn 54% less fuel than the JetStar I and 20% less than the Falcon 50.

After you take off, we don't take off.

Our service and support is as disciplined as our engineering. There'll be Company Owned and Operated Service Centers. There'll be other Authorized Service Stations. And a year of computerized maintenance comes free.

But let us not forget the company that's behind all this. Canadair. Canadair has built over 3,800 aircraft, 580 of them supersonic.

For more information on the Challenger, formerly known by the drawing board name LearStar, write to Jim Taylor at Canadair Inc., P.O. Box 6087, Montreal, Canada H3C3G9. Or call him at (514) 744-1511.

canadair challenger
We challenge any business jet to match it.

COPYRIGHT CANADAIR

advertisements. In any case, the advertising agency would be paid 10 percent of the expenditures for media space.

To reinforce the print advertising campaign, brochures and other sales literature were printed. An active direct mailing program could be used to solicit inquiries from potential prospects. The Challenger would also be promoted through press releases and press conferences, pilot seminars, photography, and newsletters, so that magazine articles would chronicle the progress of the Challenger engineering and marketing activities.

All competitors generally used this kind of promotion, but with varying degrees of intensity and success. The Falcon 50 marketers had used comparative advertising but had made no mention of the Challenger in their advertising. Canadair executives believed this obvious exclusion was an attempt by the Falcon 50 people to present the Challenger as unworthy of consideration. The JetStar II and Gulfstream II advertising did not use comparative approaches.

Exhibit 14 contains rate and reach data for full-page advertisements (the typical size in the large-jet business) in publications typically used by corporate-airplane advertisers. Media space could be purchased as early as the third week in July.

The Selling Task

President Kearns described the selling process this way:

> Each sale *is* different. It isn't like going to the military with a proposal and finding that you have just won a competition and the armed forces are going to buy 225 of your airplanes in the very first contract. It isn't like going to the airlines and selling batches of 10 or a dozen transports at once, all to the same specifications, with the same number of seats and the same colours inside and on the tail! It is, in fact, a matter of doing a complete presentation and proposal for every single prospect you approach. We start out with a prospect list made up of present business-aircraft operators plus other major corporations throughout the world who do not yet operate any aircraft. These organizations often have the need but we in the industry have yet to prove it to them. We gather data on the companies. We get an idea of their current needs by talking to their pilots, or we make some estimates if they have never operated an aircraft.
>
> We study the trips their people make, the points they routinely travel between, the longest and shortest flights, how many go on each trip, etc. Gradually a picture emerges to show us each prospect's specific requirement. And armed with that study, we approach the prospects with our sales proposals.

The first pitch was usually made to a firm's pilot. He generally had only veto power and not purchase power, but his acceptance was crucial. The salesman had to determine how much he would be able to use the pilot to make the sale. Mr. Taylor described three possibilities:

1. The pilot is strongly in your favour. He would act like an in-house salesman for you.

EXHIBIT 14 Print advertising rate data[1]

Publication	Edition	Circulation (000s)	Distribution	Full page (1 time)	Half page	Frequency discount 7 times	Frequency discount 13 times
The Wall Street Journal	Eastern	606	Daily	$14,101	$ 7,050		
	Midwest	458		11,366	5,683		
	West	289		7,958	3,534		
	Southwest	168		4,049	2,024		
	North America	1500		36,265	18,132		
Business Week	International	59	Weekly	$ 2,450			
	European	31		1,710			
	Northeast	218		6,180			
	Midwest	182		5,120		10%	5%
	Pacific Coast	131		3,640			
	Southwest	51		1,480			
	Southeast	66		1,900			
	North America	738		9,000			
Fortune	North America	600	Biweekly	$13,710			
	Eastern	201		7,000		8%	4%
	Midwestern	159		5,130			
	Southeastern	60		2,610			
	Southwestern	48		2,210			
	Western	115		3,820			
	International	70		4,020			
	European	46		3,070			
Forbes	North America	665	Monthly	$10,990		7%	4%

Publication	Edition	Circulation (000s)	Distribution	Full page (1 time)	3 times	5 times	7 times	13 times
Dun's Review	Eastern	90	Monthly	$3,405				
	Central	86		2,665	7%	6%	5%	
	Southern	32		1,515				
	Western	40		1,160				
	All	248		5,405				
Aviation Week and Space Technology	All North America	97	Weekly	$4,343	2.5%	1.8%		4%
Business and Commercial Aviation	All North America	50	Monthly	$2,850		11%		6%
Flight International*	All	47	Weekly	$1,670		6%		6%
Interavia*	All	3	Monthly	$ 390	14%	22%		

Notes: * International circulation.

[1] All rates are for black-and-white ads and are noncontract rates.

Source: Standard Rate and Data Service.

2. The pilot is unsure. The first task is to move him to neutral and then improve his and management's attitudes.
3. The pilot is against the product right off, clearly the least-preferred situation. The first task here is to cool him off and try to get to the chief executive officer and sell him first.

The salesman had to be very perceptive in assessing to what degree the influencers on the selling decision would be involved, and finding out who exactly would make the final decision.

Prospects were identified with the assistance of a *Business and Commercial Aviation*[11] study that measured the impact of company aircraft in the U.S. top 1000 industrials as compiled by *Fortune* magazine.

This summary of the business performance of the Fortune 1000 industrials showed that the aircraft operators, for whatever reason, were more efficient. The 514 aircraft-operating companies controlled 1,778 aircraft in 1975, an increase of 125 over 1974. This study concluded that:

> . . . nearly one half of the nation's biggest corporations are not operators even though their dollar volume of business indicates a cash flow that would support capital equipment such as an aircraft. In some cases, the nature of a firm's activities precludes the need for travel to locations not well served by public transportation; for others, the scheduling flexibility and effective utilization of personnel afforded by business aviation is not a strong incentive in the firm's type of business endeavors. But there are many corporations, we suspect, where the concept of business aircraft still is not appreciated or fully understood, and it is in this area that a greater knowledge of corporate aviation is needed.[12]

Hence, part of the selling task involved giving a potential customer an education in the advantages of corporate-owned aircraft in general before making a pitch for a particular model.

Another study identified companies owning the most expensive and largest fleets in the United States (Table 6).

TABLE 6 The most expensive corporate fleets

Company	Number of airplanes	Fleet value ($ millions)
Coca-Cola	5	$17.2
3M Co.	7	16.2
Rockwell International	21	15.6
Mobil	28	14.4
IBM	9	13.2
Atlantic Richfield	20	13.0
General Motors	14	12.8
United Technologies	14	12.3
Exxon	16	11.3
Tenneco	26	11.1
ITT	13	10.9
Shell	24	9.7

---

[11] Arnold Lewis, "Business Aviation and the Fortune 1,000," *Business and Commercial Aviation,* December 1978, pp. 1–4.

[12] Ibid.

TABLE 6 *(concluded)*

Company	Number of airplanes	Fleet value ($ millions)
Diamond Shamrock	3	9.0
Gannett	4	8.9
General Dynamics	5	8.8
U.S. Steel	4	8.8
Conoco	19	8.7
Texaco	8	8.3
Time	9	8.2
Johnson & Johnson	7	8.1
Marathon Oil	14	8.0

Data: Aviation Data Service Inc.

The People behind the Selling Task

Mr. James Taylor, 55, had been hired by Canadair in April 1976 to market the Challenger concept to the corporate market. Mr. Taylor's fascination with aircraft went back many years. His father had been a test pilot in both World War I and World War II. James Taylor had scored successes for the Cessna Aircraft Corp. and the French-based Dassault-Brequet Aircraft Corp. When Mr. Taylor joined Dassault in 1966, the "Fan Jet Falcon 20" soon became the industry sales leader in terms of both units and dollars. In 1966, Lear had sold 33 jets worldwide through 200 dealers, but in 1967, Mr. Taylor and his four salesmen sold 45 Falcon 20s in North America without the assistance of any dealers. Mr. Taylor believed in direct sales rather than a dealer network because, as he put it: "It is a narrowly defined market. When I sell direct, I have better control over hiring, training, the territory, and the price. I like to bring prospects in for seminars, take a mock-up to key cities, and make extensive use of direct mail."

Joining Cessna in March 1969, he became the architect behind the highly successful "Citation" marketing and product-support programs which transformed the aircraft into the world's most successful business jet in its initial four years of production.

Mr. Taylor brought three key people with him to Canadair. Mr. Bill Juvonen had been with Mr. Taylor on three previous marketing programs including the Falcon 20 and the Citation. He became the vice president of sales responsible for Canada and the United States west of the Mississippi. Mr. Dave Hurley had spent five years with Cessna and had worked with Mr. Taylor on two programs. He became the vice president of sales responsible for the eastern half of the United States. Barry Smith had been the director of corporate marketing services for Atlantic Aviation, a company that serviced and distributed such corporate jets as the Gulfstream II, the Hawker-Siddely 125 and the Westwind. He had later worked for James Taylor in the same capacity on the successful Cessna Citation program. Mr. Taylor immediately hired him as vice president, marketing services. Mr. Smith would be responsible for advertising, direct mail, and all the "inside" marketing services. These four men made up the marketing team that would have to sell 50 Challengers before September 30th, 1976.

Final Question

The Challenger's design was undergoing constant modification. Mr. Taylor described the chief engineer, Mr. Halton, as "the most open-minded engineer I've ever met. For example, one of our customers suggested an APU (auxiliary power unit) system to assure power to the cabin electricals in flight. Harry designed in the APU system. Similarly, traditional aircraft use DC electricals but there are customer advantages in using AC. Harry put in AC. When Harry cannot accommodate one of our design suggestions, he always has good reasons and he takes the time to tell us. Normally, a chief pilot would not want you talking to his boss, but with the Challenger, some pilots not only are talking to their bosses, they are relaying information to us and to them." However, it was time to finalize the design and move ahead on a production system that would produce 80 aircraft per year.

Although Mr. Taylor had been very successful using a direct sales approach, other companies made extensive use of dealer networks, particularly in foreign countries. The "five percenters" (agents) in foreign countries also raised the issue of controlling their selling practices, especially in countries where mordida[13] was almost a standard practice.

The pricing strategy and promotion strategy would have to provide fairly rapid market penetration. Advertising and service expenditures already comprised $16 million of the investment budget; changes in these expenditures would have to promise compensating paybacks. There had to be a high probability that the proposed marketing plan would deliver the sales forecast for the Challenger. Mr. Taylor smiled and commented wryly to his aides: "This is going to have to be the biggest selling job in history. I think we can count on working 6 days a week, 14 hours a day, from now until September 30."

Two manufacturers were rumoured to be looking at the Challenger statistics to see how best to compete with this wide-body turbofan. Messrs. Taylor, Halton, and Kearns sat down on the morning of July 4, 1976, to review the Challenger strategy for the next three months and the longer term.

---

[13] Mordida represents payments to government officials in return for favors.

Rogers, Nagel, Langhart (RNL PC), Architects and Planners*

It was August 1984. John B. Rogers, one of the founders and a principal stockholder in RNL, had just completed the University of Colorado's Executive MBA program. Throughout the program John had tried to relate the concepts and principles covered in his courses to the problems of managing a large architectural practice. In particular, he was concerned about the marketing efforts of his firm. As he put it, "Marketing is still a new, and sometimes distasteful, word to most architects. Nevertheless, the firms that survive and prosper in the future are going to be those which learn how to market as effectively as they design. At RNL we are still struggling with what it means to be a marketing organization, but we feel it's a critical question that must be answered if we're going to meet our projections of roughly doubling by 1989, and we're giving it lots of attention."

RNL

In 1984, with sales (design fees) of approximately $3,300,000, RNL was one of the largest local architectural firms in Denver and the Rocky Mountain region. The firm evolved from the individual practices of John B. Rogers, Jerome K. Nagel, and Victor D. Langhart. All started their architectural careers in Denver in the 1950s. The partnership of Rogers, Nagel, Langhart was formed from the three individual proprietorships in 1966, and became a professional corporation in 1970.

In 1984 the firm provided professional design services to commercial, corporate, and governmental clients, not only in Denver but throughout Colorado and, increasingly, throughout the western United States. In addition to basic architectural design services, three subsidiaries had recently been formed:

---

* This case was prepared by H. Michael Hayes, Professor of Marketing and Strategic Management, University of Colorado at Denver, as the basis for class discussion rather than to illustrate either effective or ineffective handling of an administrative situation. Copyright © 1985 by H. Michael Hayes.

Interplan, which provides pre-architectural services, programming, planning, budgeting, scheduling, and cost projections, utilized in corporate budgeting and governmental bond issues.

Denver Enterprises, formed to hold equity interests in selected projects designed by RNL and to take risk by furnishing design services early in a project and by participating in the capital requirements of a project:

Space Management Systems, Inc. (SMS), which provides larger corporations with the necessary services (heavily computer system supported) to facilitate control of their facilities with respect to space, furnishings, equipment, and the cost of change.

In 1984, the firm had 72 employees. John Rogers served as chairman, and Vic Langhart served as president. Nagel had retired in 1976. (See Exhibit 1 for an organization chart.) Development of broad-based management had been a priority since 1975. The firm had seven vice presidents. Two of these vice presidents, Phil Goedert and Rich von Luhrte, served on the Board of Directors, together with Rogers and Langhart.

Growth was financed through retained earnings. In addition, a plan to provide for more employee ownership, principally through profit sharing (ESOP in 1984), was initiated in 1973. Rogers and Langhart held 56 percent of RNL stock, and 66 percent was held by the four board members. The Colorado National Bank Profit Sharing Trust held 12 percent in its name. The remaining 22 percent was controlled by 23 other employees, either personally or through their individual profit sharing accounts. It was a goal of the firm to eventually vest stock ownership throughout the firm, in the interest of longevity and continuity.

The firm's principal assets were its human resources. Rogers and Langhart, however, had significant ownership in a limited partnership, which owned a 20,000-square-foot building in a prestigious location in downtown Denver. In 1984, RNL occupied 15,000 square feet. Use of the remaining 5,000 square feet could accommodate up to 30 percent growth in personnel. Through utilization of automation and computers, RNL felt it could double its 1984 volume of work without acquiring additional space.

Architectural Services

Architecture: the profession of designing buildings, open areas, communities, and other artificial constructions and environments, usually with some regard to aesthetic effect. The professional services of an architect often include design or selection of furnishings and decorations, supervision of construction work, and the examination, restoration, or remodeling of existing buildings.

Random House Dictionary

Demand for architectural services is closely tied to population growth and to the level of construction activity. The population in the Denver metropolitan area grew from 929,000 in 1960 to 1,620,000 in 1980, and it is estimated to grow to

EXHIBIT 1 Corporate organization

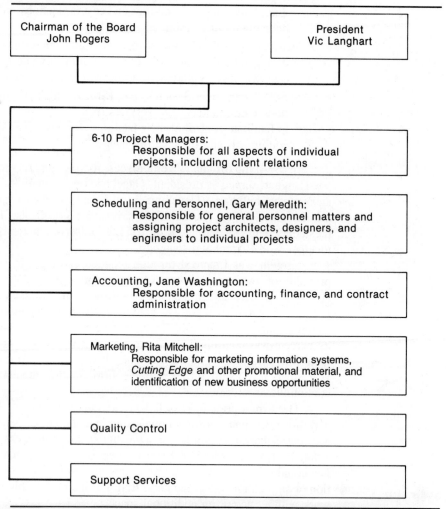

| Chairman of the Board
John Rogers | President
Vic Langhart |

6-10 Project Managers:
Responsible for all aspects of individual projects, including client relations

Scheduling and Personnel, Gary Meredith:
Responsible for general personnel matters and assigning project architects, designers, and engineers to individual projects

Accounting, Jane Washington:
Responsible for accounting, finance, and contract administration

Marketing, Rita Mitchell:
Responsible for marketing information systems, *Cutting Edge* and other promotional material, and identification of new business opportunities

Quality Control

Support Services

Note: RNL does not have a formal organization chart, as such. This exhibit was developed by the case writer to portray the general nature of work assignments and reporting relationships in the firm. As a general rule, project managers report to either John Rogers or Vic Langhart. Most administrative staff functions report to Vic Langhart. At the operational level, Interplan and SMS projects are handled similarly to RNL projects.

1,958,000 by 1990. Denver's annual population change of 3.4 percent in the decade 1970–80 ranked 10th for major American cities (Dallas and Phoenix ranked 1 and 2). The projected population growth for the Denver metropolitan area from 1978 to 1983 ranked third in the nation, and Colorado was predicted to be one of the 10 fastest-growing states during the 1980s.

Commercial construction permits grew from 340 in 1970, with an estimated value of $70,818,000, to 1,235 in 1980, with an estimated value of

$400,294,000. This growth was not steady, however. Year-to-year changes in dollar value of commercial construction varied from 0.2 percent to 91.6 percent, and the number of permits dropped from a high of 2,245 in 1978 to 1,235 in 1980. Similar patterns of growth and variation characterized industrial construction.

Translating construction growth into estimates of demand for architectural services is difficult. One rule of thumb holds that each additional person added to the population base requires 1,000 square feet of homes, schools, churches, offices, hospitals, manufacturing facilities, retail and shopping facilities, and transportation facilities. In the Denver metro area alone, this could mean 338 million square feet. At $50 average per square foot, total construction expenditure over the decade could reach $16.9 billion, involving as much as $845 million in design fees during the 1980s.

The past and projected growth in demand for architectural services was accompanied by a significant growth in the number of architects in Colorado. From 1979 to 1982, the number of state registrations of individual architects grew from 1,400 to 3,381, an increase of 141.5 percent. Over 100 architectural firms competed actively in the Denver market. (Over 500 architects are listed in the Yellow Pages of the Denver metro area phone directory.) In recent years, a number of national firms (e.g., Skidmore, Owens and Merrill) opened offices in Denver. Other major firms came to Colorado to do one job and then returned to their home offices (e.g., Yamasaki for the Colorado National Bank Office Tower, TAC for Mansville World Headquarters). Of the 26 major firms working on 38 selected jobs in Denver in 1983, 16, or 61.5 percent, were Denver based. Of the other 10, which have headquarters offices elsewhere, all but 2 had offices in Denver.

Major categories of customers for architectural services include:

Industrial.
Commercial.
   Owner.
   Developer.
Government.
   Federal.
   State.
   Municipal.
Residential (note: RNL did not compete in this market).

Within these categories, however, not all architectural work is available to independent firms, and not all architectural work on a project is awarded to one architect. A recent Denver survey, for example, indicated that of 49 commercial jobs under construction with a known architect, 11 were handled by an "inside" architect. Of the remaining 38 jobs, 20 included shell and space design whereas 18 involved space design only. In the 18 space designs, only 50 percent were actually done by architects.

The rapid growth in the construction market in Denver came to an abrupt halt in February 1982. Triggered by the broad realization that the oil boom was over, or had at least slowed significantly, project after project was put on hold. Construction of office space literally came to a halt. Of particular concern to RNL, which had just completed negotiations for a $1 million contract with Exxon, was the Exxon announcement of the closure of its Colorado Oil Shale activities at Parachute, Colorado.

It was against the backdrop of these changes that RNL felt the pressing need to review its marketing activities.

Marketing of Architectural Services

The basis of competing for architectural work has changed dramatically over the past several decades. As John Rogers recalled:

> At the beginning of my practice in 1956, you could establish an office, put a sign on your door, print calling cards, and have a "news" announcement with your picture in the *Daily Journal* that you had established a new practice of architecture. Beyond that, it was appropriate to suggest to friends and acquaintances that I was in business now and I hoped that they might recommend me to someone they knew. The Code of Ethics of the American Institute of Architects, like many other professions at the time, prohibited any kind of aggressive marketing or sales effort as practiced in recent times.
>
> In fact, after convincing one School Board member (an artist) in Jefferson County that design was important, and then being awarded a commission to design an elementary school, which led to another and another, it was not surprising to read in the *Daily Journal* that the School Board had met the previous evening and had elected me to design a new junior high school, one that I hadn't even known about. I called and said, "Thank you." Marketing expense was zero with the exception of an occasional lunch or courtesy call here and there.
>
> Today, the situation is vastly different. We have to compete for most jobs, against both local firms and, increasingly, large national firms. Clients are becoming more sophisticated regarding the purchase of architectural services [see Exhibit 2 for a brief description of buyer behavior]. Promotion, of some kind, and concepts such as segmentation have become a way of life.

During the 1960s, development of an architectural practice was a slow process, characterized by heavy reliance on word of mouth regarding professional experience and expertise. Overt communication about an architect's qualifications was limited to brochures. Personal acquaintances played a significant role in the development of new clients. Personal relations between principals and clients were an important part of continuing and new relations. This method of practice development tended to favor local firms, whose reputation could be checked out on a personal basis, and small firms, whose principals could provide personal management and design of client projects.

As Denver grew, the market changed. The advantage of being a successful, local architect and knowing the local business community diminished. Newcomers to Denver tended to rely on relationships with architects in other cities. For local architects there wasn't time to rely on traditional communica-

EXHIBIT 2   Buyer behavior

Purchase of architectural services is both complex and varied. Subject to many qualifications, however, there seems to be a number of steps that most buying situations have in common.

> Development of a list of potential architects.
>
> Identification of those architects from whom proposals will be solicited for a specific job (usually called the short list).
>
> Invitations to submit proposals.
>
> Evaluation of proposals and screening of final candidates.
>
> Selection of a finalist, based on proposal evaluation, or invitations to finalists to make oral presentations to an evaluation group.

From a marketing standpoint, the focus of interest is the process of getting on the short list and the process by which the final selection is made.

The Short List

Prospective clients find out about architects in a variety of ways. Those who are frequent users of architectural services will generally keep a file of architects, sometimes classified as to type or practice. Additions to the file can come from mailed brochures, personal calls, advertisements, press releases or, in fact, almost any form of communication. When a specific requirement develops, the file is reviewed for apparent fit. With many variations, a short list is developed and proposals are solicited.

Those who use architects infrequently tend to rely on various business of social networks to develop what is in essence their short list. In either case, a previously used architect is almost always on the short list, provided the past experience was satisfactory.

As the largest single customer for architectural services, agencies of the federal government follow a well-defined series of steps, including advertisement in the *Commerce Business Daily* and mail solicitation of local firms.

The Selection Process

The selection process is significantly influenced by the nature and scope of the work and its importance to the firm. Architect selection on major buildings is usually made at the highest level in the organization: by a principal or the president in a private organization or by various forms of boards in not-for-profit organizations such as churches. In some instances, the principal, president, or board are actively involved in all phases of the process. In others, the management of the process is delegated to others who develop recommendations to the decision makers. On smaller jobs, and those of an ongoing nature (e.g., space management), the decision is usually at lower levels and may involve a plant engineer or facilities manager of some kind.

Regardless of the level at which the selection process is made there seem to be two well-defined patterns to the process. The first, and predominant one, evaluates the firms on the short list, taking into prime consideration nonprice factors such as reputation, performance on previous jobs, and current workload. Based on this evaluation, one firm is selected and a final agreement is then negotiated as to the scope of the work, the nature of the working relationship, the project team, and specific details as to price. The second, and of limited but growing use, pattern attempts to specify the requirements so completely that a firm price can accompany the proposal. In some instances, the price and the proposal are submitted separately. Evaluation of the proposals includes a dollar differential, and these dollar differentials are applied to the price quotation to determine the low evaluated bidder.

Regardless of the process, there appear to be three main criteria on which firms are evaluated:

EXHIBIT 2 *(concluded)*

1. *The ability of the firm to perform the particular assignment.* For standard work this assessment is relatively easy and relies on the nature of past work, size of the organization, current backlogs, and so forth. For more creative work the assessment becomes more difficult. Much importance is put on past work, but the proposal starts to take on additional importance. Sketches, drawings, and, sometimes, extensive models may be requested with the proposal. In some instances, there may actually be a design competition. Much of this evaluation is, perforce, of a subjective nature.

2. *The comfort level with the project team that will be assigned to do the work.* For any but the most standard work there is recognition that there will be constant interaction between representatives of the client's organization and members of the architectural firm. Almost without exception, therefore, some kind of evaluation is made of the project team, or at least its leaders, in terms of the client's comfort level with the personalities involved.

3. *Finally, the matter of cost.* While direct price competition is not a factor in most transactions, the cost of architectural services is always a concern. This has two components. First, there is concern with the total cost of the project, over which the architect has great control. Second, there is growing concern with the size of the architect's fee, per se.

At least some assessment of the reputation of the architect with respect to controlling project costs is made in determining the short list. Once final selection is made, there is likely to be much discussion and negotiation as to the method of calculating the fee. The traditional method of simply charging a percentage of the construction price seems to be on the wane. Increasingly, clients for architectural services are attempting to establish a fixed fee for a well-defined project. The nature of architectural work, however, is such that changes are a fact of life and that many projects cannot be sufficiently defined in the initial stages to allow precise estimation of the design costs. Some basis for modifying a basic fee must, therefore, be established. Typically this is on some kind of direct cost basis plus an overhead adder. Direct costs for various classes of staff and overhead rates obviously become matters for negotiation. In the case of the federal government, the right is reserved to audit an architect's books to determine the appropriateness of charges for changes.

tion networks to establish relationships with these newcomers. The size of projects grew, requiring growth in the size of architectural staffs. Personal attention to every client by principals was no longer possible.

Concomitantly, there was a growing change in the attitude toward the marketing of professional services. New entrants in the fields of medicine and law, as well as architecture, were becoming impatient with the slowness of traditional methods of practice development. A Supreme Court decision significantly reduced the restrictions that state bar associations could impose on lawyers with respect to their pricing and advertising practices. In a similar vein, the American Institute of Architects signed a consent decree with the Justice Department, which prohibited the organization from publishing fee schedules for architectural services.

Perhaps of most significance for architects, however, was the start of the so-called proposal age. Investigations in Maryland and Kansas, among other states, had revealed improper involvement of architects and engineers with state officials. Financial kickbacks were proven on many state projects. Formal proposals, it was felt, would eliminate or reduce the likelihood of contract awards made on the basis of cronyism or kickbacks. Starting in the government sector, the requirement for proposals spread rapidly to all major clients. In 1984, for example, even a small church could receive as many as 20 detailed proposals on a modestly sized assignment.

Marketing at RNL

In 1984, RNL was engaged in a number of marketing activities. In addition to proposal preparation, major activities included:

> Professional involvement in the business community by principals, which provides contacts with potential clients. This included memberships in a wide variety of organizations such as the Downtown Denver Board, Chamber of Commerce, and Denver Art Museum.
>
> Participation in, and appearances at, conferences, both professional and business oriented.
>
> Daily review of *Commerce Business Daily* (a federal publication of all construction projects) along with other news services that indicate developing projects.
>
> Maintenance of past client contacts. (RNL found this difficult but assigned the activity to its project managers.)
>
> Development of relationships with potential clients, usually by giving a tour through the office plus lunch.
>
> VIP gourmet catered lunches for six invited guests, held once a month in the office. These involved a tour of the office and lively conversation, with some attempt at subsequent follow-up.
>
> Participation in appropriate local, regional, or national exhibits of architectural projects.
>
> Occasional publicity for a project or for a client.
>
> The *Cutting Edge*.[1]
>
> An assortment of brochures and information on finished projects.
>
> Special arrangements with architectural firms in other locations to provide the basis for a variety of desirable joint ventures.

RNL participated in a number of market segments, which it identified as follows, together with its view of the required approach.

---

[1] The *Cutting Edge* is an RNL publication designed to inform clients and prospects about new developments in architecture and planning and about significant RNL accomplishments (see Exhibit 3 for an example of an article on a typical issue).

EXHIBIT 3

The Cutting Edge

Planning for Parking

The recent boom in downtown Denver office building has resulted in tremendous increases in population density in Denver's core, bringing corresponding increases in the number of vehicles and their related problems as well.

Auto storage, or parking, is one of the major resulting problems. Most building zoning requires parking sufficient to serve the building's needs. Even building sites not requiring parking are now providing parking space to remain competitive in the marketplace.

RNL's design for this above-grade parking structure at 1700 Grant aided in facilitating lease of the office building.

Parking solutions can range from a simple asphalt lot to a large multi-floor parking structure; the decision is based on many factors including site access, required number of spaces, land costs, budget and user convenience.

For many suburban sites, where land costs are sufficiently low to allow on-grade parking, design entails mainly the problems of circulation and landscaping. Circulation includes issues of easy site access and optimal efficient use of the site. Landscaping, including landforming, can visually screen automobiles and break up ugly seas of asphalt common to poorly designed developments.

At the opposite end of the parking spectrum are downtown sites where high land costs necessitate careful integration of parking into the building concept. This is often accomplished by building parking underground, below the main structure. Parking design, in this case, becomes a problem of integrating the circulation and the structure of the building above. While building underground eliminates the need for

acceptable outer appearance, the costs of excavation, mechanical ventilation, fire sprinklering and waterproofing make this one of the most expensive parking solutions.

Between on-grade parking and the underground structure is the above-grade detached or semi-detached parking structure. This solution is very common in areas of moderate land cost where convenience is the overriding factor.

Site conditions do much to generate the design of an above-grade parking structure, but where possible the following features should ideally be included:

1. Parking is in double loaded corridors, i.e. cars park on both sides of the circulation corridor to provide the most efficient ratio of parking to circulation area;

2. Parking at 90 degrees to circulation corridors rather than at angles, once again the most efficient use of space;

3. Access to different garage levels provided by ramping the parking floors, efficiently combining vertical circulation and parking;

4. A precast prestressed concrete structure (this structure economically provides long spans needed to eliminate columns which would interfere with parking circulation and the fireproof concrete members have a low maintenance surface that can be left exposed).

5. Classification as an "open parking garage" under the building code, meaning that the structure has openings in the walls of the building providing natural ventilation and eliminating the need for expensive mechanical ventilation of exhaust fumes;

6. A building exterior in a precast concrete finish, allowing the designer to combine structure and exterior skin into one low cost element.

RNL recently completed work on the $20,000,000 1700 Grant Office Building for Wickliff & Company. The inclusion of a 415 car parking garage in the 1700 Grant project provided one of the amenities necessary for successful leasing in a very depressed leasing market.

A Publication of **RNL**/inerplan • by Richard T. Anderson • Vol. II No. I • 1576 Sherman Street Denver, Co. 80203 (303) 832-5599

Segment	Approach
Government	
City and county governments	Personal selling, political involvement.
School districts	Personal selling (professional educational knowledge required).
State government	Political involvement, written responses to RFPs (requests for proposals, from clients), personal selling.
Federal government	Personal selling, very detailed RFP response, no price competition in the proposal stage.
Private sector	Personal selling, social acquaintances, referrals, *Cutting Edge,* preliminary studies, price competition.
Semiprivate sector (includes utilities)	Personal selling, *Cutting Edge,* referrals, continuing relationships, some price competition.

Net fee income and allocation of marketing expenses by major segments is given in the following table. The general feeling at RNL was that there is a lapse of 6 to 18 months between the marketing effort itself and tangible results such as fee income.

	1982		1983		1984 (estimated)		1985 (estimated)	
	Net fee	Marketing expense	Net fee	Marketing expense	Net fee	Marketing expense	Net fee	Marketing expense
Government	$ 800	$104	$1,220	$101	$1,012	$150	$1,200	$140
Private	1,376	162	1,261	140	1,200	195	1,616	220
Semiprivate	88	11	118	24	100	25	140	30
Interiors	828	40	670	30	918	100	1,235	110
Urban design	95	20	31	10	170	30	220	40
Total	$3,187	$337	$3,300	$305	$3,400	$500	$4,411	$540

Note: All amounts are in $000s.

Salient aspects of budgeted marketing expense for 1985, by segment, were:

1. *Government.* Heavy emphasis on increased trips to Omaha (a key Corps of Engineers location), Washington, and other out-of-state, as well as in-state, locations plus considerable emphasis on participation in municipal conferences.
2. *Private.* Personal contact at local, state, and regional levels with corporations, banks, developers, and contractors plus local promotion through Chamber of Commerce, clubs, VIP lunches, *Cutting Edge,* promotion materials, and initiation of an advertising and public relations effort.
3. *Semiprivate.* Increased level of personal contact and promotional effort.
4. *Interiors.* Major allocation of salary and expenses of a new full-time

marketing person to improve direct sales locally plus other promotional support.

5. *Urban design.* Some early success indicates that land developers and urban renewal authorities are the most likely clients. Planned marketing expense is primarily for personal contact.

Additional marketing efforts being given serious consideration included:

A more structured marketing organization with more specific assignments.

Increased visibility for the firm through general media and trade journals; paid or other (e.g., public relations).

Appearances on special programs and offering special seminars.

Use of more sophisticated selling tools such as video tapes and automated slide presentations.

Increased training in client relations/selling for project managers and other staff.

Hiring a professionally trained marketing manager.

Determining how the national firms market (i.e., copy the competition).

Expansion of debriefing conferences with successful and unsuccessful clients.

Use of a focus group to develop effective sales points for RNL.

Training a marketing MBA in architecture versus training an architect in marketing.

RNL Clients

RNL described its clients as:

1. Having a long history of growing expectations with respect to detail, completeness, counseling, and cost control.
2. Mandating the minimization of construction problems, including changes, overruns, and delays.
3. Having an increased concern for peer approval at the completion of a project.
4. Having an increased desire to understand and be a part of the design process.

Extensive interviews of clients by independent market researchers showed very favorable impressions about RNL. Terms used to describe the firm included:

Best and largest architectural service in Denver.

Innovative yet practical.

Designs large projects for "who's who in Denver."

Long-term resident of the business community.

Lots of expertise.

Designs artistic yet functional buildings.

RNL's use of computer-aided design systems was seen as a definite competitive edge. Others mentioned RNL's extra services, such as interior systems, as a plus, although only 35 percent of those interviewed were aware that RNL offered this service. In general, most clients felt that RNL had a competitive edge with regard to timeliness, productivity, and cost consciousness.

Two major ways that new clients heard about RNL were identified. One was the contact RNL made on its own initiative when it heard of a possible project. The other was through personal references. All those interviewed felt advertising played a minor role, and, in fact, several indicated they had questions about an architectural firm that advertises.

Clients who selected RNL identified the following as playing a role in their decision:

Tours of RNL's facilities.

Monthly receipt of *Cutting Edge*.

Low-key selling style.

RNL's ability to focus on their needs.

Thoroughness in researching customer needs and overall proposal preparation and presentation.

RNL's overall reputation in the community.

Belief that RNL would produce good, solid (not flashy) results.

Clients who did not select RNL identified the following reasons for their decision:

RNL had less experience and specialization in their particular industry.

Decided to stay with the architectural firm used previously.

Decided to go with a firm that has more national status.

Other presentations had more "pizazz."

Overall, clients' perceptions of RNL were very positive. There was less than complete understanding of the scope of RNL services, but its current approach to clients received good marks.

Marketing Issues at RNL: Some Views of Middle Management

Richard von Luhrte joined RNL in 1979, following extensive experience with other firms in Chicago and Denver. In 1984, he led the firm's urban design effort on major projects, served as a project manager, and participated actively in marketing. He came to RNL because the firm "fits my image." He preferred larger firms that have extensive and complementary skills. He commented on marketing as follows:

RNL has a lot going for it. We have a higher overhead rate, but with most clients you can sell our competence and turn this into an advantage. I think RNL is perceived as a quality firm, but customers are also concerned that we will gold-plate a job. I'd like to be able to go gold-plate or inexpensive as the circumstances dictate. But it's hard to convince a customer that we can do this.

For many of our clients continuity is important and we need to convey that there will be continuity beyond the founders. RNL has done well as a provider of "all things for all people," and our diversification helps us ride through periods of economic downturn. On the other hand, we lose some jobs because we're not specialized. For instance, we haven't done well in the downtown developer market. We're starting to do more, but if we had targeted the shopping center business we could have had seven or eight jobs by now. One way to operate would be to jump on a trend and ride it until the downturn and then move into something else.

There's always the conflict between specialization and fun. We try to stay diversified, but we ought to be anticipating the next boom. At the same time, there's always the problem of overhead. In this business you can't carry very much, particularly in slow times.

I like the marketing part of the work, but there's a limit on how much of it I can, or should, do. Plus, I think it's important to try to match our people with our clients in terms of age and interests, which means we need to have lots of people involved in the marketing effort.

Oral presentations are an important part of marketing, and we make a lot of them. You have to make them interesting, and there has to be a sense of trying for the "close." On the other hand, I think that the presentation is not what wins the job, although a poor presentation can lose it for you. It's important that the presentation conveys a sense of enthusiasm and that we really want the job.

As comptroller, Jane Washington was involved extensively in the firm's discussions about its marketing efforts. As she described the situation:

There is little question in my mind that the people at the top are committed to developing a marketing orientation at RNL. But our objectives still aren't clear. For instance, we still haven't decided what would be a good mix of architecture, interiors, and planning. Interiors is a stepchild to some. On the other hand, it is a very profitable part of our business. But it's not easy to develop a nice neat set of objectives for a firm like this. Two years ago we had a seminar to develop a mission statement, but we still don't have one. This isn't a criticism. Rather, it's an indication of the difficulty of getting agreement on objectives in a firm of creative professionals.

One problem is that our approach to marketing has been reactive rather than proactive. Our biggest marketing expenditure is proposal preparation, and we have tended to respond to RFPs as they come in, without screening them for fit with targeted segments. From a budget standpoint we have not really allocated marketing dollars to particular people or segments, except in a pro forma kind of way. As a result, no one person is responsible for what is a very large total expenditure.

Another problem is that we don't have precise information about our marketing expenditures or the profitability of individual jobs. It would be impractical to track expenditures on the 500–1,000 proposals we make a year, but we could set up a system that tracks marketing expenditures in, say, 10 segments. This would at least let individuals see what kind of money we're spending for marketing, and where. We also could change from the present system, which basically measures performance in terms of variation from dollar budget, to one that reports on the profitability of individual jobs. I've done some studies on the profitability of our major product lines, but those don't tie to any one individual's performance.

Rita Mitchell, who has an MS in library science and information systems, joined RNL in 1981. Originally her assignment focused on organizing marketing records and various marketing information resources. In her new role as new business development coordinator she had a broader set of responsibilities. According to Rita:

We definitely need some policies about marketing, and these ought to spell out a marketing process. In my present job, I think I can help the board synthesize market information and so help to develop a marketing plan.

I do a lot of market research based on secondary data. For instance, we have access to Dialog and a number of other online databases, using our PC. Based on this research, and our own in-house competence, I think I can do some good market anticipation. The problem is what to do with this kind of information. If we move too fast, based on signals about a new market, there is obviously the risk of being wrong. On the other hand, if we wait until the signals are unmistakably clear, they will be clear to everyone else, and we will lose the opportunity to establish a preeminent position.

With respect to individual RFPs, our decision on which job to quote is still highly subjective. We try to estimate our chances of getting the job, and we talk about its fit with our other work, but we don't have much hard data or policy to guide us. We don't, for instance, have a good sense of other RFPs that are in the pipeline and how the mix of the jobs we're quoting and the resulting work fits with our present work in progress. The Marketing Committee [consisting of John Rogers, Vic Langhart, Phil Goedert. Rich Von Luhrte, Dick Shiffer, Rita Mitchell, and, occasionally, Bob Johnson] brings lots of experience and personal knowledge to bear on this, but it's not a precise process.

We have a number of sources of information about new construction projects: the *Commerce Business Daily* [a federal government publication], the *Daily Journal* [which reports on local government construction], the Western Press Clipping Bureau, Colorado trade journals, and so forth. Monitoring these is a major activity, and then we have the problem of deciding which projects fit RNL.

Bob Johnson, a project manager and member of the Marketing Committee, commented:

The way the system works now we have four board members and 12 project managers, most of whom can pursue new business. They bring these opportunities before the Marketing Committee, but it doesn't really have the clout to say no. As a result, people can really go off on their own. I'd like to see the committee flex its muscles a little more on what jobs we go after. But there's a problem with committing to just a few market segments. Right now we're involved in something like 30 segments. If we're wrong on one it's not a big deal. But if we were committed to just a few then a mistake could have really serious consequences.

For many of us, however, the major problem is managing the transfer of ownership and control to a broader set of individuals. Currently the prospective owners don't really have a forum for what they'd like the company to be. My personal preference would be to go after corporate headquarters, high-tech firms, speculative office buildings, and high-quality interiors. But there probably isn't agreement on this.

Marketing Issues: The Views of the Founders

Vic Langhart started his practice of architecture in 1954 and has taught design in the Architecture Department of the University of Colorado. He was instrumental in developing new services at RNL, including Interplan and SMS, Inc., and was heavily involved in training of the next level of management. In 1984, he supervised day-to-day operations and also served as president of Interplan and SMS, Inc. Looking to the future, Vic observed:

Our toughest issue is dealing with the rate of change in the profession today. It's probably fair to say there are too many architects today. But this is a profession of highly idealistic people, many of whom feel their contribution to a better world is more important than dollars of income and so will stay in the field at "starvation wages." We wrestle with the question of "profession or business?" but competition is now a fact of life for us. The oil boom of the 1970s in Denver triggered an inrush of national firms. Many have stayed on, and we now have a situation where one of the largest national firms is competing for a small job in Durango. We're also starting to see more direct price competition. Digital Equipment recently prequalified eight firms, selected five to submit proposals that demonstrated understanding of the assignment, and asked for a separate envelope containing the price.

Our tradition at RNL has been one of quality. I think we're the "Mercedes" of the business, and in the long haul an RNL customer will be better off economically. A lot of things contribute to this—our Interplan concept, for instance—but the key differentiation factor is our on-site-planning approach.

In 1966–68, we were almost 100 percent in education. Then I heard that they were closing some maternity wards, and we decided to diversify. Today we have a good list of products, ranging from commercial buildings to labs and vehicle maintenance facilities. In most areas, the only people who can beat us are the superspecialists, and even then there's a question. Our diversification has kept our minds free to come up with creative approaches. At Beaver Creek, for example, I think we came up with a better approach to condominium design than the specialists. Plus, we can call in special expertise, if it's necessary.

Over the past several years we've had a number of offers to merge into national, or other, firms. We decided, however, to become employee owned. Our basic notion was that RNL should be an organization that provides its employees a long-time career opportunity. This is not easy in an industry that is characterized by high turnover. Less than 10 percent of architectural firms have figured out how to do it. But we're now at 35 percent employee ownership.

I'm personally enthusiastic about Interplan. It has tremendous potential to impact our customers. In Seattle, for instance, a bank came to us for a simple expansion. Our Interplan approach, however, led to a totally different set of concepts.

We've had some discussion about expansion. Colorado Springs is a possibility, for instance. But there would be problems of keeping RNL concepts and our culture. We work hard to develop and disseminate an RNL culture. For example, we have lots of meetings, although John and I sometimes disagree about how much time should be spent in meetings. A third of our business comes from interiors, and there is as much difference between interior designers and architects as there is between architects and mechanical engineers.

In somewhat similar vein, John Rogers commented:

In the 1960s, RNL was primarily in the business of designing schools. We were really experts in that market. But then the boom in school construction came to an end, and we moved into other areas. First into banks and commercial buildings. We got started with Mountain Bell, an important relationship for us that continues today. We did assignments for mining companies and laboratories. In the late 1960s, no one knew how to use computers to manage office space problems, and we moved in that direction, which led to the formation of Interplan. We moved into local and state design work. One of our showcase assignments is the Colorado State Judicial/Heritage Center.

In the 1980s, we started to move into federal and military work, and this now represents a significant portion of our business.

We have done some developer work, but this is a tough market. It has a strong "bottom line orientation," and developers want sharp focus and expertise.

As we grow larger we find it difficult to maintain a close client relationship. The client wants to know who will work on the assignment, but some of our staff members are not good at the people side of the business.

Currently we're still doing lots of "one of a kind" work. Our assignment for the expansion of the *Rocky Mountain News* building, our design of a condominium lodge at Beaver Creek, and our design of a developer building at the Denver Tech Center are all in this category. A common theme, however, is our "on-site" design process. This is a process by which we make sure that the client is involved in the design from the start and that we are really tuned in to his requirements. I see this as one of our real competitive advantages. But I'm still concerned that we may be trying to spread ourselves too thin. Plus, there's no question that there is an increased tendency to specialization: "shopping center architects," for example.

We need to become better marketers, but we have to make sure that we don't lose sight of what has made us the leading architectural firm in Denver: service and client orientation.

Case Index